ART

A History of Painting · Sculpture · Architecture

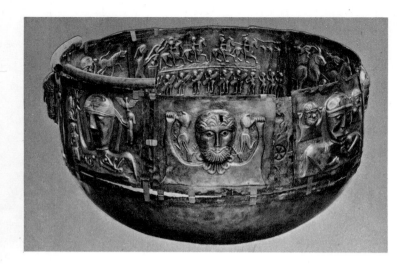

FREDERICK HARTT
Paul Goodloe McIntire Professor of the History of Art · University of Virginia

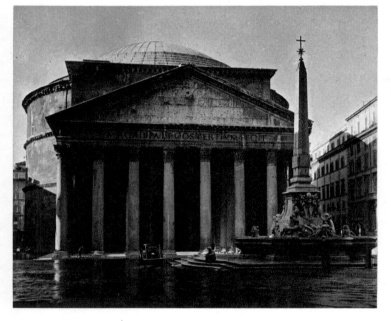

A History of

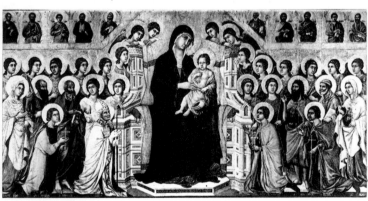

Volume I

ART

Painting · Sculpture · Architecture

PREHISTORY · ANCIENT WORLD · MIDDLE AGES

Thames and Hudson · London

John P. O'Neill, *Editor*

First published in the UK in 1976 by
Thames and Hudson Ltd, London

Printed and bound in Japan

TO

MEYER SCHAPIRO

Scholar, teacher, counselor, friend

Contents

PART THREE

The Middle Ages
PAGE 243

PHOTOGRAPHIC CREDITS

COLORPLATES

Colorplates 1–16 follow page 128 • Colorplates 17–33 follow page 208 • Colorplates 34–52 follow page 336 • Colorplates 53–71 follow page 416 •

MAPS

1. Europe and the Near East–Page 24 • 2. Southwestern France–Page 29 • 3. West Africa–Page 40 • 4. South Pacific–Page 44 • 5. Ancient Egypt–Page 55 • 6. Mesopotamia and Persia–Page 76 • 7. Peloponnesos and Crete–Page 92 • 8. Southern Italy, Greece, and Western Asia Minor–Page 102 • 9. The Acropolis, Athens–Page 128 • 10. Etruria–Page 171 • 11. Central America and Northwestern South America–Page 233 • 12. Europe–Page 248 • 13. Near East, Middle East, and Asia–Page 274 • 14. Mesopotamia–Page 282 • 15. Romanesque Western Europe–Page 310 • 16. Burgundy–Page 311 • 17. Southern France–Page 317 • 18. Italy–Page 323 • 19. Western and Central Europe–Page 369 • 20. France–Page 374 • 21. Southern England–Page 394 • 22. Romanesque and Gothic Italy–Page 403 •

ART

A History of Painting · Sculpture · Architecture

Foreword

This book is primarily intended to be used in courses in the general history of art in colleges and universities. I believe that the nonacademic reading public interested in art also will find it useful.

No one-year introduction to the history of art can possibly utilize all the material and all the illustrations offered in these two volumes. I have deliberately erred on the side of overinclusiveness in order to provide individual teachers with a wide possibility of choice, according to their own judgments of what should be presented to the beginning student. After much painful deliberation, the publishers and I decided to omit consideration of the art of the Far East. To do justice to the arts of China, Japan, India, and Southeast Asia in anything like their due proportion to Western art would have meant expanding these volumes beyond the limits of what is economically practicable, or else reducing the arts of East and West alike to a skeletal state. Also, to the best of our knowledge, most introductory courses do not take up Far Eastern art, but leave it for another course.

It has always seemed to me that the first thing a student wants from a book of this sort is a gateway to a new and unfamiliar world. I have tried to keep this primary purpose of the book in mind in writing every page.

At this juncture I look back on my increasingly remote youth with a nostalgia colored by warm gratitude to the great scholars who taught me about many of the works I describe in the following pages, and above all to Meyer Schapiro, my first teacher in the history of art. Not only did he introduce me to the fields of medieval and modern art, in which his knowledge is vast, but also he opened my eyes to the meaning of art-historical studies and to methods of art-historical thought and investigation. Here and there throughout the book Meyer Schapiro's name is mentioned, but to acknowledge my full indebtedness to

his intellect, his erudition, and his imagination it should appear on every page.

In my special field of Italian art, I shall always be grateful to the teaching and example of Millard Meiss in the study of Italian painting, and of Richard Krautheimer in that of Italian architecture. In innumerable ways I am grateful to other magnificent teachers now no longer living, especially to Walter W. S. Cook, Walter Friedlaender, Karl Lehmann, Richard Offner, Erwin Panofsky, George Rowley, and Rudolf Wittkower. The faith, advice, and inspiration of Bernard Berenson stood me in good stead in many a difficult moment. I am not likely to forget what I owe to the knowledge, generosity, and courage of Katherine S. Dreier, who opened to me in 1935 her pioneer collection of modern art. At this moment I think also of all my classes since I began teaching in 1939 and the host of students who have accompanied me in the exploration of the world of art.

My colleagues at the University of Virginia—Malcolm Bell III for ancient art, John J. Yiannias for Byzantine and early medieval, Marion Roberts Sargent for late medieval and Northern Renaissance, Keith P. F. Moxey for Baroque, and David Winter for the eighteenth and nineteenth centuries—read the sections of the manuscript that pertain to their special fields, gave me the benefit of their learning and insight, caught errors of fact and interpretation, and made many crucial suggestions.

I am deeply appreciative of the confidence of Harry N. Abrams for having entrusted me with the task of writing this book, and grateful to the unforgettable Milton S. Fox for starting me off on it, and to the patient Paul Anbinder for having put up with the innumerable delays in completing it. My thanks also go to Margaret Kaplan and to John P. O'Neill, who has an eagle eye in the pursuit of an error, for their invaluable editorial assistance, and to Barbara Lyons, who—with infinite labor—assembled all the illustrative materials.

My final debt is to Janice F. Gurley, for four years the faithful secretary of the Art Department at the University of Virginia, who typed every word of the manuscript in her spare time.

Frederick Hartt
Old Ordinary
Charlottesville, Virginia

May 25, 1975

The news of Professor Meiss' tragic death has reached me only after this manuscript went to press. Now I must add to my acknowledgment of lifelong indebtedness to Professor Meiss this halting expression of deep personal grief at his loss.

Frederick Hartt
Bergen, Norway

July 6, 1975

Editor's Note: In the preparation of Volume I for publication, the editor wishes to acknowledge the assistance of Stephanie M. O'Neill, Ann Luce (captions); Thomas W. Hut (time lines); Grace Sowerwine (glossary); Neil D. Thompson (bibliography); and Nora Beesor (index). In the preparation of Volume II for publication, the editor wishes to acknowledge the assistance of Thomas W. Hut, Maryan Schachter (captions); Thomas W Hut (time lines); Grace Sowerwine (glossary); Neil D. Thompson (bibliography); and Ellen Grand and Susan Bradford (index). The maps for both volumes were created by Rafael D. Palacios.

Volume I was designed by Michael Perpich, and Volume II was designed by Nai Chang. Preparation and production were by Patrick Cunningham, Ashton Newton, Julie Bergen, and Robin Fox.

John P. O'Neill, Editor

The author wishes to thank Professors Miles Chappell, Kenneth J. Conant, and Martin S. Stanford for calling his attention to several errors of interpretation in the first edition.

Frederick Hartt
Old Ordinary
Charlottesville, Virginia

March 30, 1976

INTRODUCTION

The Nature Of Art

What is art? That question would have been answered differently in almost every epoch of human history. The word *art* comes from the Latin *ars*, meaning skill, way, or method. It could in ancient times be applied to professional occupations, such as *artes ingenuae* (honorable professions), as distinguished from *artes sordidae* (the occupations of slaves). It could mean the rules or theory of an occupation, such as *ars poetica* (the laws of poetry), the products of the various arts, or even the conduct or character of a person. In the Middle Ages the word meant almost exclusively activities or professions. There were the liberal arts, consisting of the trivium, concerned with words: grammar, logic, and rhetoric; and the quadrivium, dealing with numbers: arithmetic, geometry, music, and astronomy. The mechanical arts, which required from the beginning the use of the hand, could include any number of pursuits, not excepting painting, sculpture, and architecture. In medieval Italy the *arti* were the guilds—associations of tradesmen, manufacturers, and craftsmen—on which the political structure of the republics was based.

Many of the ancient and medieval meanings of the word *art* are still in force. We speak of the art of cooking, without implying that its practitioners are to be ranked with Michelangelo or Monet; of the art of medicine, without ascribing to that essential profession any "artistic" qualities. We can even call a person's behavior "artful," without implying a compliment, or a woman's appearance as determined less by nature than by art, without suggesting inspiration. We have the current term "performing arts," which has come in the second half of the twentieth century to mean any artistic activity that takes place during a period of time before an audience. The expression "liberal arts" still persists, and in modern education has come to include every subject from algebra to zoology, as long as it does not specifically prepare a student to embark on a moneymaking activity, in contradistinction to "professional education" and "vocational training," which do.

In the course of time, however, at least since the sixteenth century, the term *art* has taken on in most modern societies the implication of aesthetic appreciation, that is, of enjoyment through what are considered the nobler senses of sight and hearing. It does not matter whether such enjoyment is the primary purpose of a work of art, as long as it is a major factor in determining character, appearance, or style. That consideration is crucial in regard to architecture, which exists first of all to provide shelter. A great building is a work of art by general agreement quite as much as a great statue or a great painting, regardless of its purpose, if it provides enjoyment. But great speeches, on the other hand, no matter how moving they were when originally delivered, or in such cases as Lincoln's Gettysburg Address still are, experience difficulty in being admitted to the category of art, since their skill is directed not to pleasing the listener but to convincing him. And works of philosophy, no matter how magnificently written, are not generally considered art since their absorbing purpose is the consideration of abstract ideas, in the course of which their beauty of phrase is incidental.

Music, the dance, and every form of literature are arts in the modern sense of the word, since the energies of the writer, composer, or performer are dedicated to an enjoyable experience. It should be noted, however, that intense enjoyment can and often does consist in the appreciation of the artist's skill and understanding in the presentation—of anything whatsoever, even an object or person generally considered ugly, or a situation, which, if it occurred to the spectator in real life, or to anyone else before his eyes, or even to distant persons in a newspaper account or on a television screen, would be experienced as acutely painful or distasteful—as long as the observer is convinced that that situation has been conveyed with a full realization of the human values involved.

Finally, when we refer to art today we generally mean activities that appeal to sight alone and do not require temporal performance, the so-called visual arts. When we speak of an artist, we think first of all of a painter or a sculptor, and secondly—perhaps—of an architect, even though a great architect *is* a great artist and in many regions and periods, such as ancient Greece and Rome and the Middle Ages in Europe, architecture was the leading art. Art schools, or schools of fine arts, may or may not include music or drama, never include professional writing, but never exclude painting and sculpture. Often, due to its special technical nature, architecture requires a separate school. In England, where architecture was a respectable profession for a gentleman when painting and sculpture were still viewed with some distrust, the titles of books can include the phrase "art and architecture," although in the United States the term art is all-inclusive.

That the purpose of a work of art is to be enjoyed means, of course, that the experience of works of art can greatly enrich our lives, not only while we are actually looking at them but also in retrospect. The comparison of works of art with each other, and the analysis of their style and character, can be a rewarding intellectual occupation, from which we emerge with sharpened perceptions and enlarged mental horizons. The experience of the vision of artists from many periods can also draw our attention to aspects of our surroundings that we had previously overlooked, and can greatly enhance our awareness of beauty (and ugliness) in daily life, everywhere.

But there is a bridge that must be crossed before we can readily understand works of art, and that bridge is experience. It is difficult to enjoy something that seems strange and, therefore, uncomfortable. (On the other hand, it is difficult to enjoy something we have seen or heard too often; Beethoven's Ninth Sympony is a sublime work of music, but after the Beethoven Bicentennial of 1970 some listeners would willingly give it a rest.) Few great works of art seem great the first time we see them unless we can establish some connection between them and our own lives. But the more works of art we see, and the wider their variety and the contrast among them, the more our artistic experience deepens and strengthens. It is thus much easier for people who have seen and analyzed a great many works of art over a period of years to understand something new, as long as such observers do not come to new experiences with their minds already made up.

I clearly remember periods in my youth when works of archaic, medieval, or contemporary art seemed remote, strange, and even repulsive. It is easy for me to put myself in the place of today's student, who may at first experience many of the same reactions. Even after many years of looking at contemporary art, I found it difficult to accept immediately the work of Jackson Pollock; conversely, after ten years of enjoyment of Pollock and the other Abstract Expressionists, the shaped canvases of Frank Stella seemed completely unacceptable. The only cure for hostile reactions is constant exposure, study, and

analysis. Interestingly enough, however, works of art without real quality or depth, such as most advertising art, let us say, or the mass-produced pseudolandscapes sold in department stores, will not get better no matter how long one looks at them. Analysis discloses only their utter emptiness. Conversely, to observers with long experience of works of art strangeness and newness may seem virtues, and the new may be automatically accepted as good just because it is new. Again, time tends to bring to the surface any errors implicit in such hasty judgments.

One highly successful course at an American university starts the student with what is easiest for him to understand and like, and that is French Impressionism of the nineteenth century, which in these days of beautiful colorslides packs more students into classrooms than any other style or period. This is not surprising, as enjoyment of sunlight and the out-of-doors is a vivid aspect of the experience of late twentieth-century youth. From Impressionism, with its dazzling views of sunlight translated into spots of colored paint, the course works backward to other less familiar periods, which bring out other aspects of human life, and finally moves forward to those innovations of contemporary art that are less easy to accept at first.

If our appreciation of art is subject to alterations brought about by time and experience, what then is quality? What makes a work of art good? Are there standards of artistic value? These essential questions, perpetually asked anew by each person contemplating the nature and meaning of art, elude satisfactory answer on a verbal plane. One can only give examples, and even these are sure to be confusing and contradictory. The nineteenth-century American poet Emily Dickinson was once asked how she knew when a piece of verse was really poetry. "When it takes the top of your head off," she replied. But what if a work of art that ought to take the top of your head off obstinately refuses to do so? Demonstrably, the same work that deeply moves some viewers is totally unrewarding to others. And, as we have seen, time and experience can change the attitude of even a relatively experienced person.

Often a dynamic new period in the history of art will find the works of the preceding period so distasteful as to invite destruction, and countless works of art, many doubtless of very high quality, have perished simply because the next generation did not like them. (As we shall presently see, there are other motives for destruction as well.) Interestingly enough, even observers of long experience—in art there really are no "experts"—can disagree in matters of quality. The author recalls a recent discussion between two equally sensitive and learned colleagues in the field of nineteenth-century painting over the relative merits of Manet and Monet, contemporaries in the evolution of French nineteenth-century Impressionism. To one scholar Manet was a genius and

Monet a relatively weak painter, while to the other Monet was one of the great innovators of history and Manet a sharply limited artistic personality.

The twentieth century, blessed by methods of reproduction of works of art never before available, has given readers an unprecedented possibility of access to works of art of the widest variety of styles, periods, and national origins. Incidentally, André Malraux in his book, *The Museum Without Walls*, has pointed out the dangers of this very opportunity in reducing works of art of every size and character to approximately the same dimensions and texture. There is, of course, no substitute for the direct experience of the real work of art, sometimes overwhelming in its intensity no matter how many times the student has seen reproductions in books and on the lecture screen. One cannot truly understand a painting until one can see in person the quality of its actual surface, nor a work of sculpture until one can walk around it. Most of all, the space and scale of architecture can simply not be reproduced on a flat surface and on the scale of a book illustration. Even the best of slides can give the observer little idea of how it feels to be enveloped by the space, forms, and colors of a Gothic cathedral. But at least modern methods can afford the reader the possibility of comparison between artists, periods, and styles seldom easily available for experience in the same museum, no matter how large and comprehensive.

The ideal of the twentieth century is to like every good work of art. There is an obvious advantage in such an attitude—one gains that many more wonderful experiences. But total catholicity of taste is probably impossible. There are inborn differences between people that no amount of experience can change. Some will always prefer classical, balanced works of art, others romantic and dynamic ones. Some will enjoy the most refined and sophisticated periods in the history of art, others the most direct and primitive. If after reading many books and seeing many works of art the student admits to ineradicable personal preferences and even blind spots, he should by no means be ashamed of them. Barriers of temperament are natural and should be expected. But—and this is all-important—such admissions should come *after*, not before, a wholehearted attempt to accept the most disparate works of art on their own grounds; one must not merely condemn them because they are unfamiliar. The world of art is wide and rich, and there is room in it for every person who wants to learn, to experience, above all to *see*.

THE PURPOSES OF ART

Why do people make works of art? In modern life the question is not hard to answer. People make works of art because they want to, because they enjoy the excitement of creation and the feeling of achievement, not to speak of the triumph of translating their sensory impressions of the visible world into a personal language of lines, forms, and colors. We must remember, however, that such enjoyments, stronger in some than in others—in fact, at times so strong that for their sake an individual will willingly renounce the relative security of a niche in commerce or industry for the unpredictable life of an artist—relate to our contemporary, predominantly secular Western society, in which everyone has had some chance, no matter how elementary, to draw, paint, or model in grade school, and in which individual talents and preferences are usually discovered quite early.

This was not always so. Even in the relatively recent past artistic activity of any sort played no part whatever in education in any country, yet art flourished nonetheless. Today the artist is, with the exception of the architect, characteristically on his own. He generally works to please himself, and seldom on commission. Often he complains that a commission hampers him in the development of his individual style, or in the "expression" of himself. This, too, was not always so. Throughout most of history, with the exception of a relatively late period in the development of Greek culture, and up to the seventeenth century in certain European countries—even later in others—the artist worked characteristically on commission, and never thought of undertaking a major work without the support of a patron and the security of a legal contract and a substantial advance payment. In most periods of history the artist in any field had a clear and definable place in society, and his creations thus inevitably tended to reflect the desires of his patrons and the forces in his human environment.

Today the desires that prompt patrons, whether private or corporate, to buy works of art are, on the surface at least, aesthetic. Collectors and buyers for museums and business corporations do really like certain kinds of painting, sculpture, and architecture, and experience a deep pleasure in surrounding themselves with beautiful things. But there are other purposes, even today, often as strong as the aesthetic sense and sometimes stronger. Patrons want to have the best, or the latest, which is often equated with the best, in order to acquire or retain social status, sometimes without really seeing or understanding what they buy. An artist who, by whatever means—and these are not always praiseworthy —has "made it" with any well-known New York gallery is relatively certain of selling his works. Without the gallery label, as without the couturier's label, these works will attract only the most independent and discerning collectors who are willing to risk their money. Inevitably, the thought of eventual salability can, and often does, play a formative role in determining aspects of an artist's style. It takes a courageous artist to go on turning out works of art that will not sell.

In earlier periods in history these dominant modern factors of aesthetic enjoyment and social prestige were also important. A great monarch or pope enjoyed hiring talented artists not only to build a palace or a cathedral, but also to paint pictures by no means restricted to portraits of the patron and his family, to carve statues, to illustrate rich manuscripts, or to make splendid jewels—even to complete a magnificent tomb during the patron's lifetime—partly because he enjoyed the beautiful forms and colors, the richness of marble, and the radiance of colored paint or glass, or the glitter of gold and precious stones, but partly also to increase his apparent power and prestige not only in the eyes of his contemporaries but also in the eyes of posterity.

But there were other extremely important factors involved in the production of works of art in past societies; if these factors operate at all in the twentieth century (and they probably do), they are much harder to locate and define now than in previous epochs. These factors may be considered under the heading of social demands on art, and they are by no means chiefly aesthetic. Such demands could, in theory, be satisfied with works of art of a wide variety of styles, as long as the subjects are rendered according to the patron's wishes. In almost every society, up to and probably including the present, what we call today *iconography* (from two Greek words meaning *image* and *write*), that is, the subject matter of art, is of primary importance. Even today, amusingly enough, a painting of an attractive young person will sell more easily and at a higher price than a work of equal quality by the same artist representing an old person, because in contemporary Western society few enjoy contemplating the results of the aging process. And even with the phenomenon of what is known as "aesthetic distance"—the barrier placed by the canvas or the stage, the very idea of representation, between the viewer and reality—there are pictures of violence that few would enjoy in their dining room or bedroom.

In the past iconography was generally related predominantly to religion or politics or both, and was therefore likely to be systematic. In a religious building the subjects of wall paintings, stained-glass windows, or sculpture were usually worked out by the patron, often with the help of a learned adviser, so as to narrate in the proper order scenes from the lives of sacred beings, or to present important doctrines in visible form through an array of images in which degree of sanctity, not aesthetic preference, determined order and placing, and even color might have been theologically prescribed. The artist was usually presented with such a program and required to execute it. Sometimes, as in the wall paintings in the interior of Byzantine churches, the subjects, the ways of representing them, and the places in which they could be painted were codified down to the smallest detail. Such matters were keyed delicately to the Liturgy, and no variation could be permitted without doing violence to the very reason why such a church was built.

In such cases, before passing aesthetic judgment on what is known as a cycle of religious works of art, which may often assume the character of a clear-cut visual pattern, we have to consider the ritual and the theology on which the order of the scenes was founded. Such knowledge does not merely help us to understand certain aspects of order and pattern, it quite literally explains them. Even in those periods in history in which powerful artistic personalities were consulted on the order of scenes and on the manner of representation, and worked in sometimes sympathetic, sometimes controversial relationship with the patron and his advisers, the artist was still not free to choose any subjects his fancy might suggest.

Obviously, in regard to secular subjects as well, when the patron wished to commemorate in form and color his historic deeds, those of his ancestors and allies, the quality of his government, and the defeats of his enemies, he was certain to direct the artist as to how these should be represented. Only an extremely learned artist, in certain relatively late periods of historic development, might occasionally be in a position to make crucial decisions regarding secular iconography on his own, and even then only with the general approval of the patron. Often in regard to both religious and secular subjects the artist worked with the aid of iconographic handbooks compiled for the purpose.

Often the patron, religious or secular, dictated some of the principal colors to be used, such as gold or blue, and in what proportion. Also, although we have little documentary evidence, the desires of the secular or religious patron for an effect aiming at such qualities as grandeur, magnificence, austerity, or delicacy were perforce taken into consideration by the artist, and therefore determined the prevailing mood of a work of art. We know of many instances in which religious or secular works of art were refused as being unsuitable to the purpose for which they had been commissioned, or in which the artist was required to change certain crucial aspects that offended the patron. A sensitive and discerning study of the subjects of contemporary art—in those cases in which subjects are still recognizable—might well suggest patterns of social preference that have influenced the artist without his being fully aware of them.

In a somewhat less precise manner patronage, in exercising an influence on iconography, may also affect style. For example, Christianity held the representation of the nude human body in horror, save in such specific instances as when the soul appears naked before God for judgment or when a saint is stripped (shamed) before martyrdom. It is not likely, therefore, that art thoroughly dominated by rigorous forms of Christianity, as in certain periods during the Middle Ages, could show much comprehension of or interest in the movement of the clothed human figure, which can only be understood through careful study of the human body, its structure and possibilities, in an uncovered state. Similarly, a culture that placed a high evaluation on the total human being, including his physical enjoyment and athletic prowess, such as that of ancient Greece with its divinely protected Olympic Games, and displayed images of the nude human body in places of great prominence is likely to place certain instinctive restrictions on the use of colors and ornaments that would surpass the body in brilliance, and render it insignificant in an artistic whole.

The study of iconography can also assist us in the understanding of what one might call the magical aspects of works of art. For the process of representation has always seemed to have something magical about it. Totems and symbols in early societies warded off evil spirits and propitiated favorable ones. Even today certain still primitive peoples will defend themselves by force against the taking of photographs, which might drain off some of their strength. In many societies the injury of an image of a hated person is deemed to aid in bringing about his illness or death. Enemies are still burned in effigy, and a national flag, an object devoid of any inherent material powers, is so potent a symbol as to be able to excite enormous emotional reactions; laws are made to govern its care and use, and to protect it from disrespect.

In ancient times, when a Greek or Roman city-state was defeated in battle, the conquerors often made a point of destroying or carrying off the statues from the enemy's temples, because in so doing they deprived the enemy of his gods and, therefore, of his power—even though the defeated inhabitants might profess to believe their deities resided in some aspect of nature, such as the sky or the sea. The instances of miracle-working images in the history of Christianity are innumerable, and still occur from time to time. In Serbian medieval frescoes few saints within reach of the worshiper retain both eyes; one has usually been gouged out and ground to powder, which was popularly believed to have a curative effect on eye diseases. During World War II in Tuscany, by no means an uneducated region of Italy, rural populations who seldom or never looked at their religious images, sometimes locked up in unused churches, refused to allow them to be removed for urgently needed restoration for fear of losing their magical protection.

Many today feel a power emanating from a great work of art so strong that it cannot be explained on material grounds. A picture may be said to "fill a room" in which it occupies only a small fragment of wall surface, or a building to "dominate a town" when in reality it constitutes a negligible fraction of the total volume of the place, simply because of the supernatural power we still instinctively tend to attribute to man-made images or forms. There are actions we hesitate to perform or words we refrain from saying in the presence of certain kinds of images or symbols, or in certain interiors, although no words of ours, nor even actions short of physical contact, can have the slightest effect on these inanimate objects or environments.

Finally, the very existence or nonexistence of works of art has been until relatively recent times due first of all to their subjects. The patron wanted a statue or a picture of a god, a saint, an event, or a person, not primarily because of its beauty—although this has always been an exceedingly important factor—but for a specific iconographic purpose. Even in seventeenth-century Holland, in the early days of the open market for works of art, the artist often painted certain kinds of subjects rather than others because he thought they would readily find buyers.

The converse is often true. The Second Commandment, when taken literally, severely limited if it did not indeed rule out entirely the creation of religious images by the Hebrews, the Muslims, and the Calvinists. Even more unhappily, strict interpretation of this and other religious prohibitions has resulted in the mutilation or total destruction of countless works of art, often of the highest quality, and sometimes in the presence of their creators. Many of the tragic losses of Greek, Roman, early Byzantine, medieval English, and Netherlandish art have been due to what we might term destruction for anti-iconographic purposes, even when the very groups carrying out the destruction nonetheless encouraged the production of secular images or decorations, such as plant and animal ornament, portraiture, landscapes, or still lifes. Even in the primarily utilitarian art of architecture the deterioration or demolition of historic churches and country houses in twentieth-century England is often traceable to their being no longer needed as symbols of a church that is losing its adherents or a ruling class that has been prevented by economic means from continuing to rule. Often these very structures could conceivably have been utilized for other purposes, but perish because they are felt to be unsuitable.

It is the iconographic purpose of art, especially in the representation of events or ideas but also in the depiction of people and of nature, that has given the work of art its occasionally quite strong affinity with religion. An artist can be so deeply moved by religious meditation, or by the contemplation of human beauty or human suffering, or by communion with nature that he can create compelling works of art that offer a strong parallel to religious experience. The present century began with a meticulous, dispassionate, and impersonal study, *The Varieties of Religious Experience*, by William James in 1902, and has offered few celebrated examples of individual religious experience that could compare to those that abound in past ages. In the twentieth century, then, at least in the great urban centers of Western civilization, the religious art of the past generally offers the most persuasive access to religious ideas. So effective can be religious art that many scholars who profess agnosticism find themselves unconsciously dealing with religious images with the same reverence as if they were confirmed believers; some, indeed, are converted by prolonged contact with religious art, music, or literature.

The links between art and religion are observed at their strongest in the creative act itself, which mystifies even the artist. However carefully the process of creation can be documented in preparatory sketches and models for the finished work of art, or in the twentieth century by photographs of successive stages in the evolution of a single canvas, or even filmed while the artist is actually at work, it still eludes our understanding. We know it exists, it commands our awe, but we cannot hope to define, analyze, or explain it. In the Judeo-Christian-Islamic tradition, and in many other religions as well, God (or the gods) plays the role of an artist. God is the creator of the universe and of all living beings, chiefly man. Even those who profess disbelief in a personal god nonetheless often speak of creative power or creative energy as inherent in the natural world, although they are at a loss to explain such a concept.

In medieval art God is often represented as an artist, sometimes specifically as an architect, tracing with a gigantic compass a system and an order upon the earth, which was previously "without form, and void." Conversely, in certain periods artists themselves have been considered to be endowed with divine or quasi-divine powers. Certain artists (alas, all too few) have been considered saints. Soon after his death Raphael was called "divine." Michelangelo was often so addressed during his lifetime, in his presence or on paper. The intense emotion art lovers sometimes feel in the presence of overpowering works of art is clearly akin to religious experience. An individual can become carried away and unable to move in the presence of the stained-glass windows of Chartres Cathedral, let us say, or of the *David* by Michelangelo.

This is not to say that those who do not react so strongly, or even those works of art that were not made to inspire such feelings, do not deserve their own important place in the world of art. Many works of art in the past, and many more today, were made for purposes that have a merely peripheral iconographic intent. We enjoy a well-painted realistic picture of a pleasant landscape partly because it *is* a pleasant landscape, with no purpose in any iconographic system, and partly because it possesses in itself agreeable shapes and colors. Furthermore, a jewel, an arch or column, a passage of nonrepresentational ornament, or a work of abstract art may be felt as beautiful entirely in and for itself. In every country and period there have been visual configurations that are difficult or even impossible to trace to any overt symbolic purpose, yet people have ordered them, made them, bought them, or imitated them just because they are felt to have strong aesthetic properties in themselves.

In most societies, however, such configurations have been limited to decoration, sometimes to personal embellishment. Only when such nonrepresentational images as those in Christian art (the Cross, the Alpha and Omega, the initial letters in illuminated manuscripts) are endowed with strong symbolic significance have they been raised to a considerably higher level, and permitted to assume prominent positions (except, of course, in architecture, where certain basic forms exist primarily of constructional necessity and often symbolize nothing). Only in the twentieth century have people created works

of painting, sculpture, or graphics with no recognizable subjects, the so-called abstractions.

Abstractions often do suggest some external object or event, but such suggestions generally tell us more about the observer's psychological makeup, on the analogy of a Rorschach test, than about the artist's intention. Generally, abstractions have been made to stand or fall on their own merits as beautiful—or otherwise impressive—objects without reference to a subject. Abstractions, too, can excite strong emotion (negative, if we are not attuned to looking at them). But they can please quite independently of the change of taste and fashion. Abstractions depend on the operation of form, line, color, mass, space, rhythm, and other aesthetic properties on the human consciousness. "Laws" have been designed to explain or even supposedly to limit such effects, but these laws seem to have been honored as much in the breach as in the observance.

Abstract art is frequently paralleled with music, which, at least since the Middle Ages, very often symbolizes or represents absolutely nothing, and has its own laws, formulated as harmony, counterpoint, and so forth. Historically, all artistic laws exist to be broken. Contemporary music disobeys all the time-honored rules of Western tradition, sometimes at its peril, but often with great success. The variety of forms and images produced by the new abstract art is no less rich than that of past works of representational art, and places the same strain on our catholicity of taste.

THE DEVELOPMENT OF STYLES

Why do styles in art change? Since the impressions of man and nature transmitted by light to the retina follow the same principles with any healthy pair of eyes in any era, why are the accounts of visual experience given by artists so strikingly different from one period to the next? Are there laws that govern and, therefore, if discovered can explain to our satisfaction the transformation between the style of one period in the history of art, such as Gothic, Renaissance, or Baroque, and the next? Or the change from one phase of style to the next in any given period, or within the work of a single artist? Questions such as these would seem to be basic for our understanding of the history of art. Yet, although the literature on the history of art is colossal and ever-growing, and comprises countless studies on almost every aspect of the art of every period and every region, these basic questions do not seem to have been often asked in modern times. Generally, however, we can deduce an art historian's underlying assumptions about the principles of historic change from the way his account proceeds from the analysis of one stylistic phase to the next.

The earliest explanations of stylistic development we know anything about can be classified as *evolutionary in a technical sense*. We possess no complete ancient account of the theory of artistic development, but references to lost Greek writings, especially those of the Hellenistic sculptor Xenokrates, have been preserved in the *Natural History* of the Roman writer Pliny the Elder (A.D. 23–79). The Greeks appear to have assumed a steady progression from easy to constantly more difficult stages of technical achievement, such as that from pure outline drawing to the use of a single color, then of two colors, then of a number of colors, and in a culminating stage of technical perfection to the total harmony of all the colors, exemplified in the art of the perfect painter of the fourth century B.C., Apelles (none of whose works survive). This kind of thinking, which parallels progress in representation with that in the acquisition of any other kind of technical skill, is easy enough to understand, but tends to depreciate the importance of early stages in any evolutionary sequence. Implicit also in such thinking is the idea of a summit of perfection beyond which no artist can ascend, and from which the way leads only downward, unless every now and then a later artist can recapture the lost glories of a Golden Age.

The Middle Ages, for which history was already fixed in all its major outlines by the drama of the Fall and Salvation of man, had little notion of history in the modern sense of the word, and gave us only chronologies of events. Artists were seldom named, since they were considered mere mechanical executants of the commissions of great patrons, such as princes or bishops. But since the beginning of the revival of interest in Classical antiquity in Italy in the fourteenth century, a revival of ancient artistic style has always been possible. The conviction that such a revival was taking place was clearly expressed by a number of writers and artists, such as the poet Petrarch in the fourteenth century and the sculptor Ghiberti in the fifteenth.

A new pattern of art-historical thinking, which can be characterized as *evolutionary in a biographical sense*, is stated in the writings of the sixteenth-century Italian architect, painter, and decorator Giorgio Vasari, who has often been called the first art historian. Vasari undertook an ambitious series of lives of the artists, first published in 1550 and then revised and enlarged in 1568; his account began with Cimabue and arrived at Vasari's own time. He was the first to compare the development of art to the life of a human being, saying that the arts, "like human bodies, have their birth, their growing up, their growing old and their dying." For him Cimabue and Giotto (see fig. 513, colorplate 70) represented the birth (or more properly the rebirth) of art, after its eclipse during the Middle Ages, the fifteenth century its youth, the High Renaissance—especially Michelangelo—its maturity, and his own period, during Michelangelo's last years and after his death, its old age.

Vasari refrained from making uncomfortable predictions about the death of art after his time, but his successors were not so wise. Much of the theoretical and historical writing on art during the seventeenth century looks backward nostalgically to the lost glories of the High Renaissance. In such works only those contemporary artists are praised who attempted to revive High Renaissance principles, and little sympathy is shown with the vital artistic currents of the Baroque, then going on in force on every side of the writers. This Vasarian pattern of thought underlies a surprising amount of writing about art well into the eighteenth century, during which the three main phases of Greek art—archaic, Classical, and fourth-century—were paralleled with the three principal stages in the development of Renaissance art. Roman art became at best an attempt to revive the Golden Age of fifth-century Greece, at worst the decadent precursor of the "barbaric" Middle Ages. Every now and then one can still read contemporary accounts of the death of art, invariably, to borrow Mark Twain's famous remark about his own reported demise, "greatly exaggerated."

Meanwhile, many adventurous persons in the mid-eighteenth century had already begun to devote considerable interest and study to medieval art, and the problem of art-historical development took on a new dimension, which gradually superseded the biographical-evolutionary premise. In the formerly despised art of the Middle Ages, sensitive observers began to discover considerable aesthetic charm, which had little or nothing to do with ancient Greek principles. No attempt was at first made to impose on this newly evaluated art any system of development; the facts had first to be ascertained. Then in the late eighteenth and early nineteenth centuries followed an awakening of interest in the art of the Near and Far East and in the twentieth a fascination with "primitive" art as having an aesthetic as well as a merely ethnological attraction.

Imperceptibly, the ideas of Charles Darwin (1809–82) began to affect the thought of art historians, and a third tendency, seldom clearly expressed but often implicit in the methods and evaluations of late nineteenth- and early twentieth-century writers, began to make itself felt, tending to explain stylistic change according to an inherent process that we might call *evolutionary in a biological sense*. Ambitious histories were written setting forth the art of entire nations or civilizations, and monographs analyzing the careers of individual artists, in an orderly manner proceeding from early to late works as if from elementary to more advanced stages. The biological-evolutionary pattern may recall that of the Greek technical theory of evolution, save that it presupposes an underlying affinity with the evolutionary process in nature rather than being derived from the acquisition of increasing technical competence, and was never to recognize any stage of ultimate perfection.

The biological-evolutionary tendency underlies much art-historical writing and thinking even today, and is evident in the frequent use of the word *evolution*, generally in a Darwinian sense. Clear evolutionary patterns can be persuasively demonstrated in the arts of certain countries, such as ancient Greece, for example, or in the architecture of French cathedrals during the Gothic period. The German art historian Heinrich Wölfflin (1864–1945) published several important studies culminating in 1915 in a highly influential work called *Basic Concepts of Art History* (now translated as *Principles of Art History*), in which he developed a set of five carefully contrasted categories to demonstrate the change from Renaissance to Baroque as a model for the evolution of style in general.

As we examine the art of many eras, however, it becomes apparent that artistic evolution does not always proceed in an orderly fashion. In ancient Egypt, for example, after an initial phase lasting for about two centuries, a complete system of conventions for representing the human figure in painting and sculpture was devised shortly after the beginning of the third millennium B.C. (see fig. 55) and changed very little—with the exception of a revolutionary period during the reign of a single monarch—for nearly three thousand years thereafter. Certainly, one cannot speak of evolution from simple to complex, or indeed of any evolution at all. Even more difficult to explain in terms of any evolutionary theory is the sudden decline in interest in the naturalistic representation of the human figure and the surrounding world in late Roman art (see fig. 281), as compared to the subtle, complex, and complete Greek and early Roman systems of representation, which had just preceded this problematic period. It looks, on the surface at least, as if the evolutionary clock had been turned backward and now moved from the complex to the simple.

There are other cases of striking *devolutions* closer to our own time. Jacques Louis David (1748–1825), a painter brought up in the highly developed tradition of Rococo art, with its soft figures, fluid colors, and easy movement of forms in space (see Vol. 2, fig. 330), understandable according to Wölfflin's theory as the ultimate phase of the Baroque, suddenly reverted to a strict Classicism of form and design based partly, at least, on the Renaissance (see Vol. 2, fig. 366). And artists of the twentieth century have deserted the "late" phases of the developmental cycle en masse, often taking as their models the arts of extremely early phases in man's development (or so they thought)—especially those of Africa and the South Seas (see fig. 35). Obviously, there must be some other explanation of such striking reversals of the evolutionary process.

A fourth major tendency of art-historical interpretation, which might be described as *evolutionary in a sociological sense*, has emerged during the twentieth century. Many historians have written about separate periods or events in the history of art along sociological lines, but the most ambitious and comprehensive attempt has been the *Social History of Art* (1951), strongly colored by Marxist theory, by the Hungarian-born art historian Arnold Hauser. Both Hauser and others have been able to demonstrate what appear to be strong interconnections between forms and methods of representation in art and the demands of the societies for which these works were produced.

Often, however, sociological explanations fail to hold up when examined minutely in an attempt to demonstrate specific examples. How does one explain, for example, the simultaneous coexistence of two or more quite different—even mutually antagonistic—styles, representative examples of which were bought or commissioned by persons of the same social class or even by the selfsame person? Or how can one detect any sociological reason for the frequently abrupt reversal in styles that characterizes the twentieth century, when a whole school of art, formerly accepted as the latest and best, can suddenly find itself out on a limb, the victim of a new and completely unforeseen stylistic innovation?

In these volumes no single theory is consistently followed. Stylistic tendencies or preferences are regarded as individual instances, often explicable by widely differing interpretations (the notion of cause and effect in the history of art is always dangerous), sometimes not responsive to any clear-cut explanation. Three of the four theories discussed above are still useful in different ways and at different moments. The second of the four, the biographical premise beloved by Vasari, his Renaissance contemporaries, and his seventeenth-century followers, is generally renounced as suffering from a fallacious kind of reasoning by analogy. Vasari's premise was probably abandoned as an indirect consequence of the reevaluation of the Middle Ages, which he had consigned to outer darkness.

There is, however, something inherently valuable about the Greek theory of technical evolution. This can be shown to correspond, for example, to the learning history of a given individual, who builds new experiences into patterns created by earlier ones, and may be said to evolve from stage to stage of always greater relative difficulty. The stopping point in such a cycle might correspond to the gradual weakening of the ability to learn, and varies widely among individuals. Certain artists never cease developing, others reach their peak at a certain moment and repeat themselves endlessly thereafter. From the achievements of one artist, the next takes over, and the developmental process continues. The element of competition also plays its part, as in the Gothic period when cathedral builders were trying to outdo each other in height and lightness of structure (see fig. 476), or the Impressionist period, when painters worked side by side attempting to seize the most fugitive aspects of sunlight and color (see Vol. 2, fig. 421). Such an orderly development of refinements on the original idea motivating a school of artists can also be made to correspond to the biological-evolutionary theory, showing (as it seems) a certain inherent momentum. So, in point of fact, the Greek theory perhaps stands up a little better than the pseudo-Darwinian one, which like the notions of Vasari suffers somewhat from the effects of reasoning by analogy. At least the Greek account corresponds to the observable circumstances of life in a studio or a workshop, or for that matter a scientific laboratory.

But what of the sudden about-faces, like that of David, whose art might be considered to fit the biological-evolutionary notion of a mutation, a sharp change that produces, unpredictably, an entirely new species? Such mutations have often been explained on sociological and historical grounds, and in certain instances they may well be susceptible to such interpretations. David, however, has been the most striking example because during the French Revolution he was artistic dictator of France and responsible for all artistic standards. His first thoroughly Neoclassic picture, the *Oath of the Horatii* (see Vol. 2, fig. 366), would seem at first glance to be sternly republican in subject as well as revolutionary in form. This probability is clouded by the fact that the work was painted in 1784–85, after David had been living in Rome for years, far from the French political scene; that it glorified an incident that was supposed to have taken place under the Roman *kingdom*; and that it was com-missioned by King Louis XVI, at that time in little danger of losing either his throne or his head.

Changes of style may result from sheer boredom. When a given style has been around to the point of saturation, artists and public alike may thirst for something new. Or mutations may even occur from time to time through purely accidental discoveries, a factor that has yet to be thoroughly explored. On investigation, apparent artistic accidents may turn out to be in reality the result of subconscious tendencies that had long been brewing in an artist's mind, and that almost any striking external event could bring into full play. The only certainty in art-historical studies is that as we try to penetrate deeply into the work of art, to understand it fully, and to conjecture why and how it came to be as it is we must examine carefully in each individual instance all the factors that might have been brought to bear on the act of creation, and regard with healthy skepticism any theory that might tend to place a limitation on the still largely mysterious and totally unpredictable forces of human creativity.

PART ONE

Art Before Writing

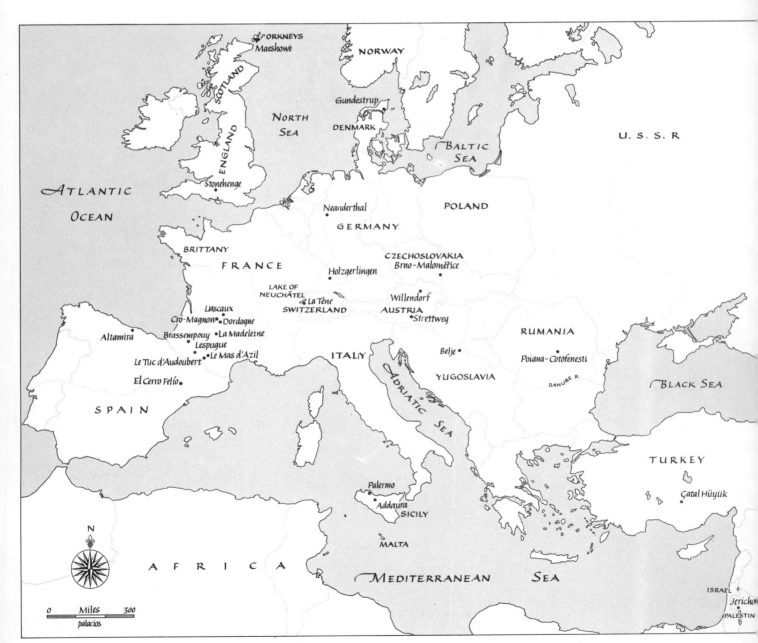

MAP 1. *Europe and the Near East*

The words *primitive* and *prehistoric* are often used to denote early phases in the artistic production of mankind. Both adjectives can be misleading. Primitive suggests crudeness and lack of knowledge, yet some of the oldest works of art we know, such as the ivory carvings and cave paintings of the first true men in western Europe, show great refinement in their treatment of polished surfaces and considerable knowledge of methods of representation, while much later works, presumably by their descendants, sometimes betray loss of skill in both respects. The highly formalized objects made by African and North American Indian cultures close to our own time have been valued by some twentieth-century European artists because of their supposed primitivism; nonetheless, the few really ancient works as yet discovered from these same cultures are strikingly naturalistic. Prehistoric implies the absence of both a feeling for the past and a desire to record it, but we know from African societies that history was carefully preserved in an oral tradition whose accuracy can at times be corroborated when checked against the written records of invading cultures. Nordic and Celtic epics, orally transmitted and not set down in writing for many centuries, and the equally unwritten legends of the Eskimo and North American Indians may well have had a basis in historic fact.

The first section of this book brings together the arts of certain societies that lacked the ability to compile permanent records. But that is by no means all these arts have in common. One extremely important trait is the identification of representation with magical or religious power, so that the object of art itself comes into existence as the embodiment of an attempt to control or to propitiate, through ritual, natural beings or natural forces. A second universal trait is the total lack of concern for space. Animals, birds, fish, to a lesser extent human beings, are widely represented, usually in conformity with transmitted stereotypes; plants appear only quite late, and then are ornamentalized. Landscape elements (save for the volcano of Çatal Hüyük, see fig. 18) never demand representation, and the immense spaces surrounding mankind, which must have appeared mysterious and challenging, are not even suggested. Some of the arts described in this section precede chronologically the more developed phases of civilization; others persist side by side with them right up to the present time. Oddly enough, the twentieth century, which has conquered physical space to such an extraordinary degree, and which has transcended representation by photography, the cinema, and television, and writing by means of electronic communication and records, is the first to find the art of early people artistically appealing.

1
Paleolithic Art
(Old Stone Age),
30,000 to 19,000 B.C.

We do not know when or how human beings took the significant step of making objects for their own interest and enjoyment rather than for pure utility; probably, we shall never know. But we do have extensive evidence, almost all of it discovered within the past hundred years, regarding human artistic production at a very early stage. Such subhuman groups as Neanderthal man did not make works of art. The first artists were the ancestors of modern European man, the Cro-Magnon people, who roamed over Europe, equipped with stone tools and weapons, during the last glacial period, when the Alpine region, northeastern Europe, and most of the British Isles were covered deep in glacial ice. So much of the world's water was frozen in polar ice caps and continental glaciers that coastlines were very different from their present shape, and the southern portions of the British Isles were connected with each other and the Continent. Vegetation was subarctic; most of western Europe was a tundra, and forests were limited to the Mediterranean region. In this inhospitable environment early man, vastly outnumbered by the animals on which he depended for food, lived in caves or in temporary settlements of shelters made from mud and branches.

There seem to be no early stages in the evolution of Paleolithic art; the earliest examples are of an astonishingly high quality that, coupled with the great period of time covered by the finds, suggests the existence of a strong tradition in the hands of trained artists, transmitting their knowledge and skill from generation to generation. While these early works of art have been found all the way from southern Spain and Sicily to southern Siberia, most of the discoveries have come to light in south-central France, northern Spain, and the Danube region. The approximate dates given here are based on analysis of organic material at the sites, according to the known rate of disintegration of radioactive carbon 14, absorbed by all living organisms, into nonradioactive nitrogen 14 after death. Even more sur-

prising than the immense age of the earliest finds is the extraordinary duration of the cave culture, some twenty thousand years, or nearly twice as long as the entire period that has elapsed since.

Sculpture

The tiny female statuette jocularly known as Venus (fig. 1), found near Willendorf in Lower Austria, is datable between 30,000 and 25,000 B.C. It is one of the earliest known representations. Grotesque as it may at first appear, the *"Venus" of Willendorf* is a superb work of art. The lack of any delineation of the face, the rudimentary arms crossed on the enormous bosom, and the almost equally enlarged belly and genitals indicate that the statuette was not intended as a naturalistic representation but as a fertility symbol; as such, it is compelling. From the modern point of view, the statue harmonizes spherical and spheroid volumes with such power and poise that it has influenced twentieth-century abstract sculpture, particularly the art of Brancusi (see Vol. 2, fig. 474). A similar but larger statuette, from Lespugue in southwestern France, is tentatively dated much later, about 20,000–18,000 B.C. (fig. 2). In this work, carved in ivory, the swelling, organic forms of the *"Venus" of Willendorf* are conventionalized and become almost ornamental. Across the back of the figure (colorplate 1) runs a sort of skirt, imitating cloth, which dates weaving back to a remarkably early moment. One of the finest of these tiny sculptures is the delicate ivory head of a woman from the cave called Grotte du Pape at Brassempouy in southwestern France (fig. 3). As in the *"Venus" of Willendorf*, the hair is carved into a grid suggesting an elaborate coiffure, which hangs down on the sides to flank a slender neck. The pointed face is divided only by nose and eyebrows; the mouth and eyes may originally have been painted on.

As compared to these stylized images of human beings,

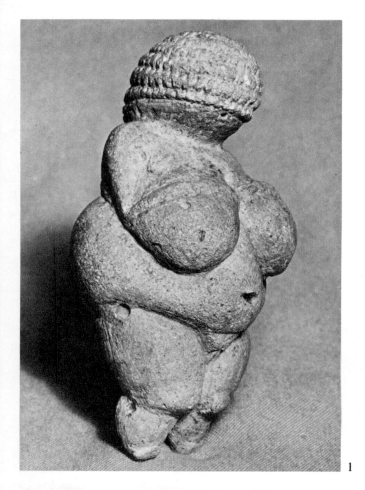

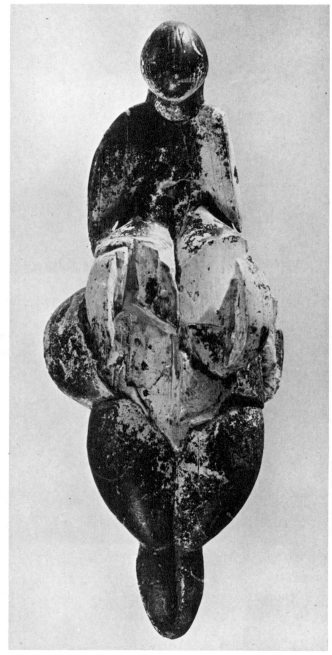

1

2

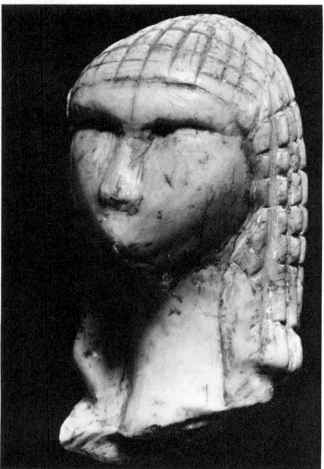

1. *"Venus" of Willendorf.* c. 30,000–25,000 B.C. Limestone, height 4⅜". Naturhistorisches Museum, Vienna

2. *"Venus" of Lespugue.* c. 20,000–18,000 B.C. Ivory, height 5¾". Musée de l'Homme, Paris. See Colorplate 1

3. Woman's Head, from Grotte du Pape, Brassempouy, France. c. 22,000 B.C. Ivory. Musée des Antiquités Nationales, St.-Germain-en-Laye, France

3

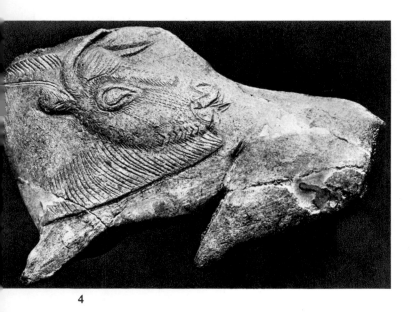

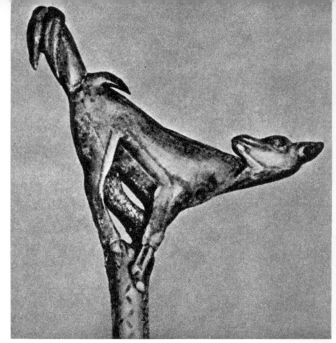

4

5

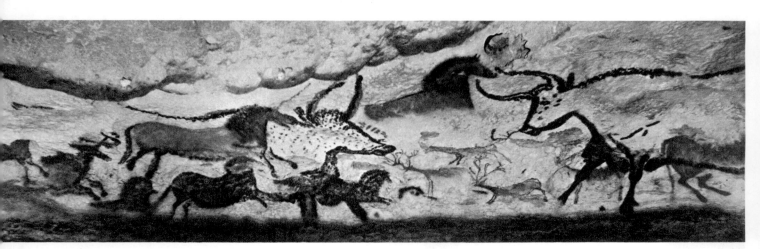

6

4. *Bison,* from La Madeleine (Tarn), France. c. 12,000
   B.C. Antler, length 4″. Musée des Antiquités
   Nationales, St.-Germain-en-Laye, France

5. *Chamois,* from Le Mas d'Azil (Ariège), France. Antler,
   length 11⅝″. Collection Péquart, St.-Brieuc, France

6. *Hall of Bulls.* Cave painting. c. 15,000–10,000 B.C.
   Lascaux (Dordogne), France

7. Wounded Bison Attacking a Man. Cave painting.
   c. 15,000–10,000 B.C. Length of bison 43″. Lascaux
   (Dordogne), France

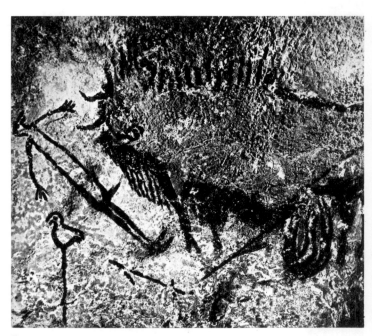

7

the earliest represented animals are strikingly naturalistic. A little bison (fig. 4) carved about 12,000 B.C. from a piece of antler was found at La Madeleine in south-central France. The legs are only partially preserved, but the head, turned to look backward, is convincingly alive, with its open mouth, wide eye, mane, and furry ruff indicated by firm, sure incisions. The projections are so slight that the relief approaches the nature of drawing. Another brilliant example of animal art is the little spearthrower from Le Mas d'Azil in southwestern France (fig. 5), representing a chamois in a similar pose of alarm, its head turned backward and its feet brought almost together in a precarious perch on the end of the implement.

Cave Art

The most impressive creations of Paleolithic man are the large-scale paintings, almost exclusively representing animals, which decorate the walls and ceilings of limestone caves in southwestern France and northern Spain (see colorplate 2; figs. 6, 7). Their purpose is still obscure. By analogy with the experience of surviving tribal cultures, it has been suggested that these paintings are an attempt to gain magical control, by means of representation, of the animals early man hunted for food. Recent investigation has shown this explanation to be untenable. Judging from the bones found in the inhabited caves, the principal food of the cave dwellers was reindeer meat. But the chief animals represented, in order of frequency, were the horse, the bison, the mammoth, the ibex, the aurochs, and at long last several species of deer. Most of the paintings are found at a distance from the portions of the caves, near the entrances, where early man lived, worked, cooked, and ate. Often, the painted chambers are accessible only by crawling through long, tortuous passages or by crossing underground streams. This placing, together with the enormous size and compelling grandeur of some of these paintings, suggests that the remote chambers were sanctuaries for magical or religious rituals to which we have as yet no clue. Evidence indicates that the chambers were used continuously for thousands of years, and microscopic analysis by the American scholar Alexander Marshack has shown that the paintings were repainted periodically, many times in fact, in layer after layer. Abstract signs and symbols, which may be the ancestors of writing, appear consistently throughout all the painted caves and also on many of the bone implements found in them. One day these symbols may yield to interpretation; possibly, they will provide the answer to the mysterious questions of the meaning and purpose of these magnificent paintings.

In the absence of natural light, the paintings could only have been done, with the aid of stone lamps filled with animal fat, with wicks of woven moss fibers or hair. The colors were derived from easily found minerals, and include red, yellow, black, brown, and violet, but no green or blue. The vehicle could not have been fat, which would

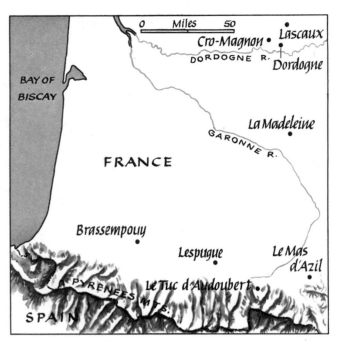

MAP 2.   *Southwestern France*

not penetrate into the chronically damp, porous walls; a water vehicle could amalgamate with the moisture and carry the color into the structure of the limestone. No brushes have been found, so in all probability the broad black outlines were applied by means of mats of moss or hair. The surfaces appear to have been covered by paint blown from a tube; color-stained tubes of bone have been found in the caves.

The paintings have always been described as "lifelike," and so they are, but they are also in some respects standardized. The animals were invariably represented from the side, and generally as standing in an alert position, the legs tense and apart, the off legs convincingly more distant from the observer, the tail partially extended. Rarer running poses show front and rear legs extended in pairs, like the legs of rocking horses. No vegetation appears, nor even a groundline. The animals float as if by magic on the rock surface. Their liveliness is achieved by the energy of the broad, rhythmic outline, set down with full arm movements so that it pulsates around the sprayed areas of soft color.

The cave of Altamira in Spain was the first to be discovered, a century ago, but was not at once accepted as authentic. Today it is considered the finest. The famous bison on the ceiling of Altamira, vividly alert (colorplate 2), are as powerful as the representation of animals can be. Although artists of periods later in human history analyzed both surface and anatomical structure more extensively, the majesty of the Altamira animals has never been surpassed. The cave of Lascaux in France, dating from about 15,000 B.C. and discovered in 1940, is a close

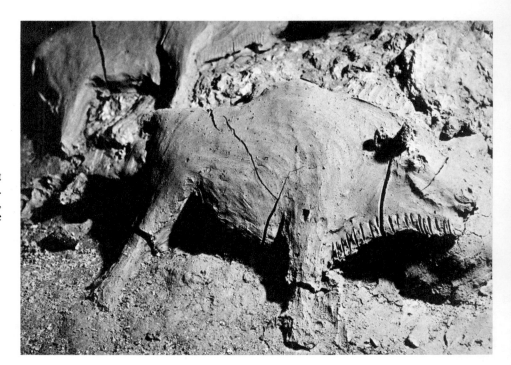

8. *Two Bison*, from the cave at Le Tuc d'Audoubert, France. Low relief. c. 15,000 B.C. Clay, length 24″ each. Ariège, France

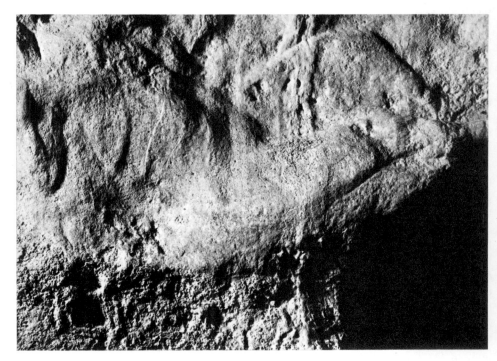

9. Reclining Woman, from the cave at La Madeleine (Tarn), France. Low relief

competitor to Altamira. It is one of a large number of painted caves in the Dordogne region. The low ceiling of the so-called Hall of Bulls at Lascaux (fig. 6) is covered with bulls and horses, often partly superimposed, painted with such vitality that they fairly thunder off the rock surfaces at us. In another chamber is the tragic painting of a bison pierced by a spear (fig. 7), dragging his intestines as he turns to gore a man who is represented only schematically as compared to the naturalistic treatment of animals.

Some images are in low relief, such as the tense, still throbbing bison modeled in clay (fig. 8) about 15,000 B.C.

on the sloping ground of a cave at Le Tuc d'Audoubert in France; some have been carved into the rock, as are the far-from-schematic, half-reclining nude women occasionally found, always without heads. The easy pose of the relief at La Madeleine (fig. 9) is in sharp contrast with the stylization of the *"Venus" of Willendorf*.

MESOLITHIC ART

The disappearance of the great glaciers and the consequent rise in temperature brought early man out of the caves and fostered a gradual transition to the farming

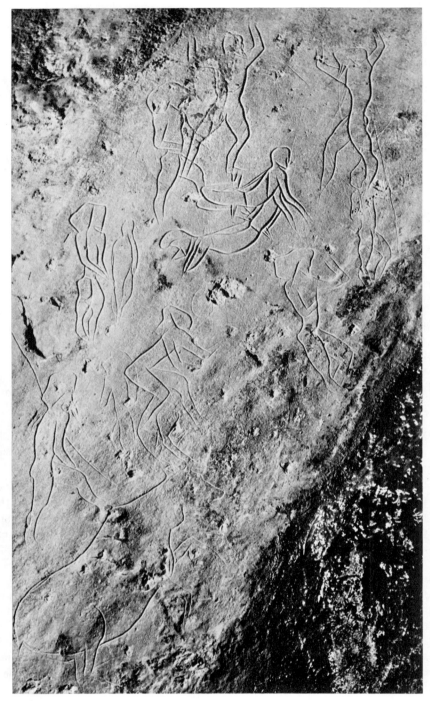

11. *Ritual Dance*, from the cave
at Addaura, Sicily. Drawing.
c. 15,000–10,000 B.C. Height
of figures 10"

10. Hunting Scene, from El
Cerro Felio (near Alacon),
Spain. Watercolor copy of a
cave painting

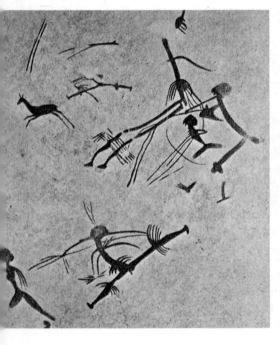

society of the Neolithic period (New Stone Age). This intermediate stage, known as the Mesolithic (Middle Stone
Age), is far less rewarding artistically than the
Paleolithic. Paintings were made on the walls of open
shelters on rocky cliff faces. More than sixty sites have
been located in eastern Spain, but the small-scale paintings of animals lack not only the size but also the vigor of
the cave paintings, and were usually done in a single tone
of red. An example from El Cerro Felio (fig. 10) shows a
group of male and female hunters, greatly schematized
but nonetheless pursuing at remarkable speed an
antelope that seems to have eluded their spears and

arrows. Mesolithic rock paintings of a somewhat similar
style are scattered from Scandinavia to South Africa. By
all means the most striking works of art from the
Mesolithic period are the brilliant series of outline
drawings of human figures and animals discovered in
1952 on the walls of a small cave at Addaura, just outside
Palermo, Sicily (fig. 11). The figures, depicted in a variety of attitudes, may be engaged in a ritual dance,
perhaps including acts of torture; the vigor and freedom
of their movements remind one of certain twentieth-
century works, notably those of Henri Matisse (see Vol.
2, fig. 448).

2

Neolithic Art

(New Stone Age),

8000 to 3000 B.C.

With the recession of the last glaciers, the climate grew irregularly but inexorably warmer, and man, all the way from the British Isles to the Indus Valley, was able to set up a new existence free from the limitations of the caves. Wild grains and legumes now flourished throughout a wide area and were eventually domesticated; so, one by one, were various species of animals. Although stone remained the principal material for weapons and tools, here and there man discovered how to smelt certain metals. Pottery, often richly decorated, began to replace utensils of wood or stone, and weaving became highly developed. Objects made of materials from far away indicate the existence of travel and commerce. Although man was still a hunter, he was no longer utterly dependent on wild animals, and representations of them consequently lost the intimate naturalism so impressive in Paleolithic art. More lasting settlements grew up, some of a considerable size, and the beginnings of architecture made their appearance, these early examples generally constructed of perishable materials but sometimes of stone. From the evidence available, what may have been Paleolithic religious life is scarcely distinguishable from magic, but in the Neolithic period structures appear that can only be described as sanctuaries, implying the existence of an organized religion, with a priestly class making new demands on art.

Jericho

Recent partial excavations have brought to light the remains of a considerable town at Jericho in southern Palestine. Around 8000 B.C. the settlement was composed of oval mud-brick houses on stone foundations. By about 7500 B.C. it was surrounded by a rough stone wall whose preserved portions reach a height of twelve feet and was further defended by a moat cut in the rock and by at least one stone tower thirty feet high (fig. 12), the earliest known fortifications in stone. Even more impressive are the human skulls found here (fig. 13). Their features were reconstructed in modeled plaster, with shells inserted for eyes. These skulls belonged to bodies buried beneath the plaster floors of the houses, and were doubtless intended to serve as homes for ancestral spirits, to be propitiated by the living. The soft modeling is very delicately observed, and, when painted, these heads must have been alarmingly vivid.

Çatal Hüyük

From 1961 to 1963, excavations in the mound of Çatal Hüyük on the plain of Anatolia, in central Turkey, disclosed a small portion of a city that, according to carbon 14 dating, enjoyed a life of some eight hundred years, from 6500 to 5700 B.C. The city was destroyed and rebuilt twelve times, the successive layers of mud brick revealing a high level of Neolithic culture, whose artifacts included woven rugs with bold decorative patterns (not preserved, but simulated in wall paintings) and polished mirrors made from obsidian, a hard volcanic stone. Oddly enough, the inhabitants had not yet discovered pottery, and made their receptacles from stone or wood, and from wicker. The houses (fig. 14) were clustered together without streets in a manner not unlike that of the pueblos of the American Southwest (see fig. 43), with a common outer wall for defense, and they could be entered only by means of ladders. The furniture was built in; it consisted of low plastered couches under which the bones of the dead were buried after having been exposed to vultures to remove the flesh. A remarkable series of religious artifacts has been found, including statues of a mother goddess (fig. 15) whose immense breasts and belly recall the "Venus" of Willendorf. The head of a child, possibly a deity, appearing between her knees clearly symbolizes childbirth.

Alongside the rooms intended for lay habitation, shrines are occasionally found with couches doubtless

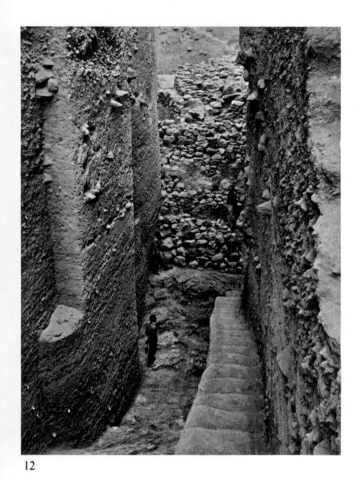

12

12. Fortifications. c. 7500 B.C. Jericho, Jordan

13. *Plastered Skull.* c. 7000–6000 B.C. Jericho, Jordan

14. Houses at Çatal Hüyük, Turkey. 6500–5700 B.C. (Architectural reconstruction after J. Mellaart)

15. *Goddess Giving Birth,* from Çatal Hüyük, Turkey. c. 6500–5700 B.C. Archaeological Museum, Ankara, Turkey

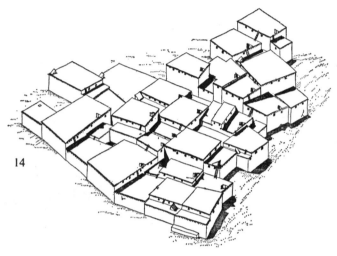

14

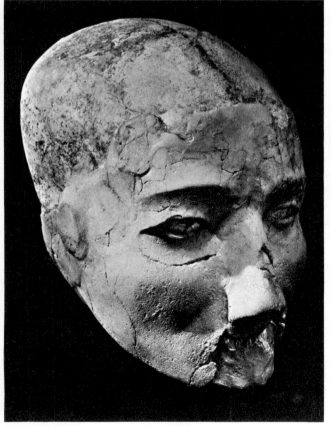

13

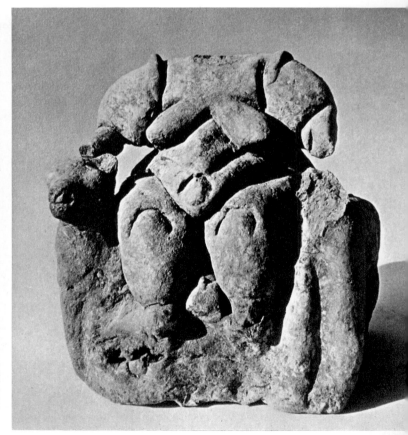

15

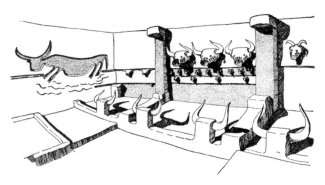

16. Shrine at Çatal Hüyük, Turkey, with bull horn and skull decoration. 6500–5700 B.C. (Architectural reconstruction after J. Mellaart)

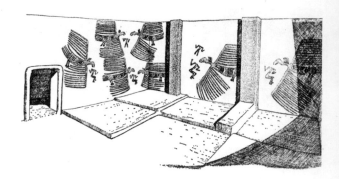

17. Shrine at Çatal Hüyük, Turkey, with wall paintings of vultures. 6500–5700 B.C. (Architectural reconstruction after J. Mellaart)

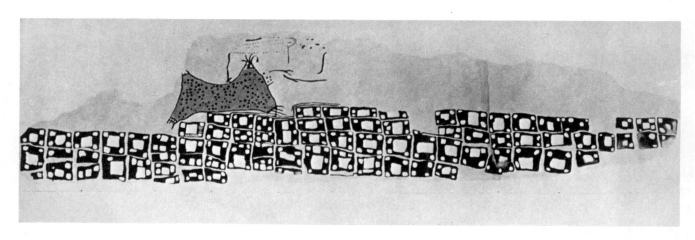

18. *Landscape Painting* (copy). Çatal Hüyük, Turkey

meant for the priesthood. These shrines enclose symbols of magical potency and—even in reconstruction—of awesome grandeur. Some shrines were adorned by rows of paired wild bull horns mounted on the floor, facing entire bull skulls fixed to the walls above (fig. 16). These were probably male symbols. A stylized but very aggressive silhouette painting of a bull appears on a flanking wall. Other shrines (fig. 17) were apparently dedicated to death, symbolized by wall paintings of huge vultures devouring tiny, headless humans depicted in the poses in which corpses were buried. Schematized and flattened though they are, these birds, whose wings spread diagonally across whole walls as if wheeling through the air, must have struck terror in the hearts of the inhabitants. On one wall was found the earliest known landscape painting (fig. 18), showing Çatal Hüyük itself, represented as a series of rough squares surmounted by an erupting volcano.

Megalithic Architecture

A number of sites, generally on islands or near the seacoast, preserve impressive remains of monuments made partially or wholly of giant stones (megaliths). The accepted dating of these buildings has been revised in the light of the discovery that the carbon 14 method consistently underestimated by as much as eight hundred years the age of California bristlecone pine trees, in some of whose cross sections more than eight thousand rings have been counted, one for each year of life. The ancient civilization on the Mediterranean island of Malta, for example, which lasted about eight hundred years, has now been dated before 3000 B.C. A hard limestone was used for the exterior walls of the temples and for the trilithon (three-stone) portals (fig. 19). A double vinescroll ornament of unexpected rhythmic grace, the earliest known appearance of this motive that later became universal in Classical decoration, is carved in low relief on the entrance slab of one of the temples at Tarxien (fig. 20). The interiors of tombs and temples generally follow a trefoil plan; the stones are corbeled (projected one beyond the other) to form a sloping wall that probably supported a wooden roof. An actual corbel vault, the earliest known, roofs a tomb chamber in the center of a mound at Maeshowe, on a remote island of the Orkneys, north of Scotland. It is datable about 2800 B.C. (fig. 21).

Long famous are the megaliths of Brittany, giant

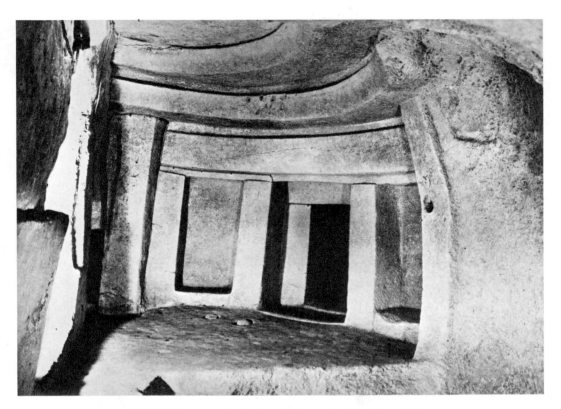

19. Trilithon portals. Before 3000 B.C. Hal Saflieni, Malta

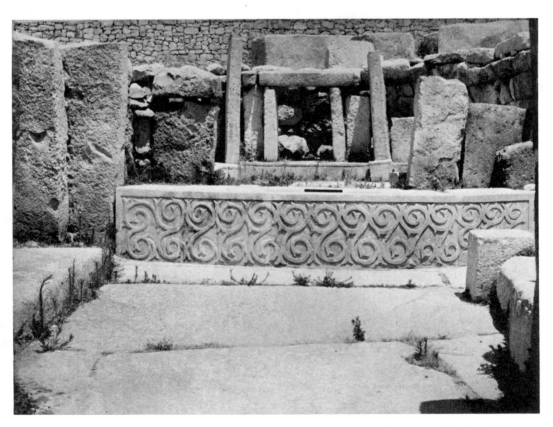

20. Entrance slab of Temple. Low relief. Late 3rd millennium B.C. Limestone. Tarxien, Malta

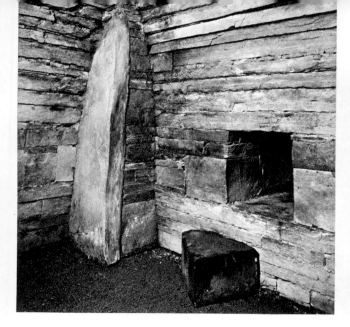

21. Tomb chamber. c. 2800 B.C. Maeshowe, Orkney Islands, Scotland

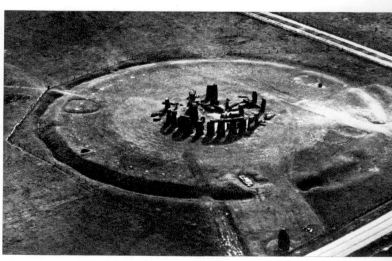

22. Aerial view of Stonehenge. c. 2000 B.C. Salisbury Plain, England

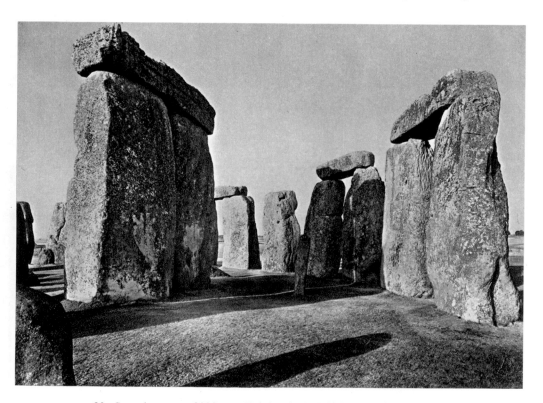

23. Stonehenge. c. 2000 B.C. Height 13'6". Salisbury Plain, England

single stones known as menhirs, which march across the countryside for miles, and the dolmens or trilithons, probably intended as graves to be surrounded by mounds. A number of cromlechs, ritual stone circles, are preserved in England, the grandest of which is Stonehenge on the Salisbury Plain (figs. 22, 23), now datable about 2000 B.C. This is the third and most ambitious circle built on the site. Claims of extraordinary astronomical competence on behalf of these Stone Age builders, surpassing even that of the later Greeks, have been strongly challenged, but it is clear that the stones were arranged to coincide at least roughly with sunrise at the summer solstice. The impression of rude majesty they impart is tempered somewhat by the observation of considerable subtleties: these stones, weighing as much as fifty tons, were dragged for twenty-four miles by hundreds of men, dressed (trimmed) to taper upward, and even endowed with a slight swelling known later to the Greeks as *entasis*; the lintels were curved according to their places in the circle.

3

The Bronze and Iron Ages,

3000 to First Century B.C.

When first discovered, metals were valued chiefly for their beauty. Gradually, man learned to mine ore and smelt it in kilns. Then, probably by accident, he hit upon alloys. Bronze replaced stone for tools and weapons, casting was invented, and eventually iron and steel were adopted. Pottery became universal, the wheel was devised, and large towns were built. Hundreds of sites of ancient settlements have now been excavated, and the thousands of artifacts unearthed often show the highest degree of technical skill in the handling of metal. The surviving paintings possess little of the quality of the cave murals, but the metal objects, generally intended for personal adornment or for ritual use, are extremely imaginative in their exploitation of geometrical forms and rhythmic relationships. Elements of this new metal art were eventually inherited by Europeans in the early Middle Ages, and came to be endowed with Christian content (see figs. 382, 403). Entire populations migrated across eastern, central, and northern Europe, bringing with them their artifacts and their technical knowledge, and carrying on commerce and war with each other, with indigenous populations, and with the great contemporary civilizations of the Mediterranean world (see Part Three, page 272).

A magnificent example of Bronze Age metalwork is a gold bracelet (fig. 24), probably dating from the second millennium B.C., found at Belje in Yugoslavia. The triple gold armband is ornamented on the inner flanges by an incised scallop pattern; on the outer the scallop becomes tendrils similar to the vinescrolls at Tarxien (see fig. 20). The back flares into broad scrolls suggesting the volutes of a Greek Ionic capital many centuries later (see fig. 153), also ornamented by tendrils. The finest example of Bronze Age figurative art is the small bronze wagon found at Strettweg in Austria (fig. 25), from the so-called Hallstatt culture, probably of the seventh century B.C. A

tall goddess dressed only in a belt supports a bronze bowl in the center of the wagon; she is preceded and followed by pairs of warriors on horseback and on foot, and by pairs of male figures flanking stags, doubtless perpetuating some now unknown religious ritual. Although there

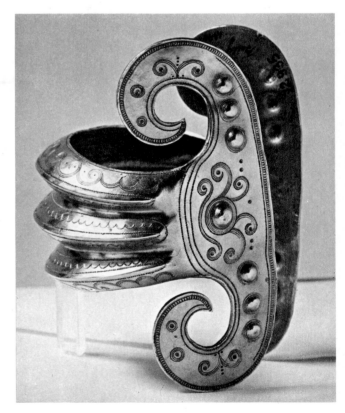

24. Bracelet, from Belje, Yugoslavia. c. 2nd millennium B.C. Gold. Naturhistorisches Museum, Vienna

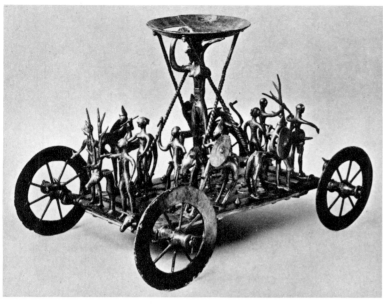

25

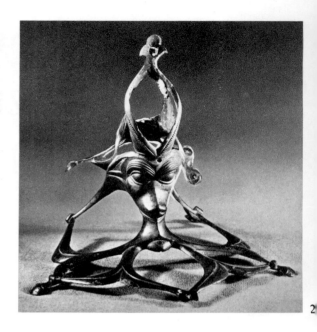

2

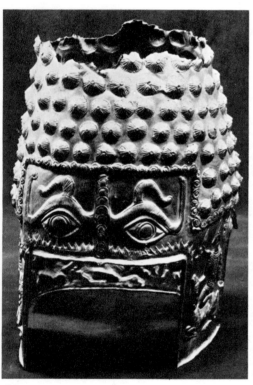

26

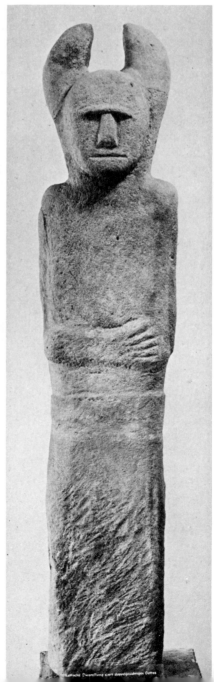

28

25. Cult wagon, from Strettweg,
Austria. c. 7th century B.C.
Bronze, height of goddess 8¾".
Landesmuseum Joanneum,
Graz, Austria

26. Tiara, from Poiana-Coțofenești,
Rumania. c. 4th century B.C.
Gold, height 9½". Museum of
History of the Socialist Republic
of Rumania, Bucharest

27. Openwork ornament, from
Brno-Maloměřice,
Czechoslovakia. c. 3rd century
B.C. Bronze, 4¾ x 5¾".
Moravian Museum, Brno,
Czechoslovakia

28. Figure, from Holzgerlingen,
Germany. c. 2nd century B.C.
Stone, height 79⅞".
Württembergisches Landesmuseu
Stuttgart, Germany

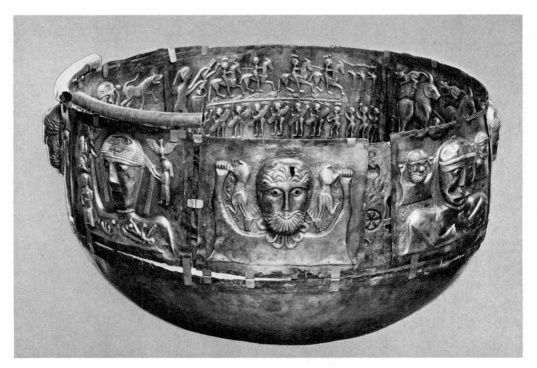

29. Caldron, from Gundestrup, Denmark. 2nd century B.C.–5th or 6th century A.D. Silver. Nationalmuseet, Copenhagen

seem to be similarities to the art of the Geometric period in Greece (see fig. 141), the lively arrangement of figures is entirely original. A very different and disturbingly barbaric object is the great gold tiara (fig. 26), perhaps dating from the fourth century B.C., found at Poiana-Coṭofeneṣti in Rumania. It is adorned with staring eyes of great intensity and eyebrows that flare into horns. Horses and riders appear on the back.

The La Tène culture, named after a site on Lake Neuchâtel in Switzerland, was produced by Celtic peoples who reveled in geometric forms, generally with biomorphic suggestions and often enfolding recognizable animal or human heads. A superb example is the three-dimensional bronze ornament from Brno-Maloměřice in Czechoslovakia, whose organic shapes well outward and upward, enclosing large segments of open space (fig. 27). Some stone sculpture survives, generally very rude in comparison with the metalwork, yet harshly expressive. The figure from Holzgerlingen in Germany (fig. 28), from about the second century B.C., is two-headed like the Roman god Janus, looking forward and backward, and very powerful in its shaftlike simplicity. The most spectacular and mysterious object of Iron Age art is the great silver caldron from Gundestrup in Denmark (fig. 29), which has been variously dated from the second century B.C. to the fifth or sixth century A.D. Its raised relief seems to contain an entire mythology in its staring heads and warriors on horseback or marching on foot.

4

Black African Art

Below the Sahara Desert stretches a vast region of Africa, including uplands, open steppes, and tropical rain forests, the home even today of an incredible number and variety of artistically productive black tribal cultures that in certain respects resemble those of early man. European contacts with the arts of black Africa have undergone at least five distinct phases. At first, artifacts were brought home as curiosities by early explorers, traders, and colonists. To this activity we often owe the continued existence of wooden objects, doomed to a short life in central African heat and humidity. Then, with the growth of anthropological studies in the nineteenth century, the objects were exhibited as specimens in museums of natural history. Next, in the opening years of the twentieth century, the aesthetic properties of African art were discovered as a powerful source of inspiration by German Expressionists (see Vol. 2, figs. 453, 454) and by artists working in Paris, especially Picasso (see Vol. 2, fig. 464). Since then, archaeological investigation, still all too rare and limited, has discovered works of courtly art of

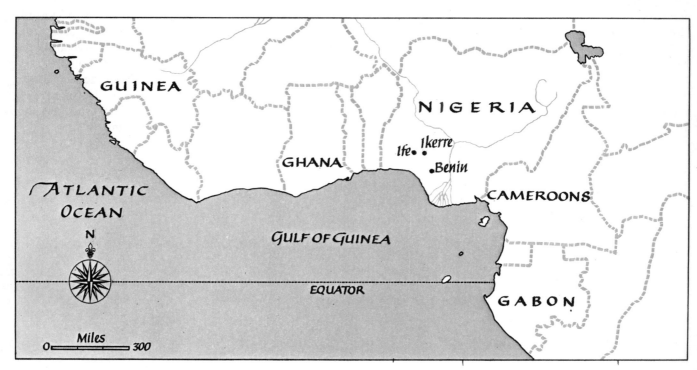

MAP 3. *West Africa*

astonishing beauty and great antiquity, antedating any contacts with Europeans. Finally, in our own time, quantities of cheaply produced imitations of tribal artifacts —so-called airport art—have flooded the market, while young African artists have turned to art schools, studios, and exhibitions, like artists anywhere else in the modern world.

The discovery in 1938 of a superb series of naturalistic heads and busts in clay and in bronze at Ife in Nigeria in central West Africa came as a total surprise. Ife artists had been thoroughly familiar with the lost-wax process of casting, in which a work is built up on a fireproof core with a thin layer of wax, and then covered with a fireproof mold usually based on clay. When the mold has hardened, it is heated, the wax runs out, and molten metal, which assumes the shape of the original wax layer, is poured in. Invented by Bronze Age man, this method was known throughout the Mediterranean world in antiquity. No contacts have been traced between the Ife civilization, which flourished between the eleventh and fifteenth centuries A.D., and the Mediterranean; it is quite possible that the Ife artists discovered the lost-wax method independently. The royal heads, such as the one believed to represent the early queen Olokun (fig. 30), are of striking nobility and beauty. The broad, smooth surfaces of the skin are striated with parallel grooves representing ritual scars and are perforated around the mouth with holes possibly intended for the insertion of jewels. Probably, these heads were made to surmount wooden bodies.

Sixteenth-century Portuguese explorers were the first Europeans to visit the nearby Nigerian kingdom of Benin. Its art, however, was not widely known until the city of Benin was destroyed in 1897 and a large number of splendid bronze objects from the palace were taken to England. Among them was the elegant and serene head of a girl, dating from the fourteenth, fifteenth, or sixteenth century, known as the "Princess" (fig. 31). She wears a high, beaded collar and a beautiful horn-shaped woven headdress. The refined workmanship of the very thin bronze casting is derived, according to oral tradition, from the older Ife culture, but a certain stylization has softened the overwhelming sense of reality of the Ife heads. Handsome leopards of ivory studded with brass disks, symbols of royal power (fig. 32), and many grand bronze reliefs from the palace, like the one (fig. 33) representing a king symmetrically enthroned between smaller attendants, show other possibilities of the Benin style, which is very dense in its opposition of cylindrical volumes to surfaces enriched by parallel grooves, striations, and incised ornament.

A very few examples must suffice to indicate some of the superb artistic and expressive qualities of more recent tribal art, which doubtless perpetuates the forms of older and now lost works. Rich figural reliefs, such as the carved-wood doors from the Yoruba culture at Ikerre in Nigeria (fig. 34), which illustrate scenes from tribal life

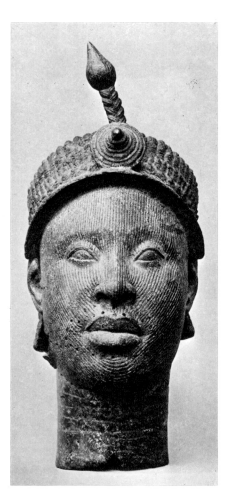

30. *Head of Queen Olokun,* from Ife, Nigeria. c. 11th–15th century A.D. Clay and bronze, height to top of ornament c. 36". British Museum, London

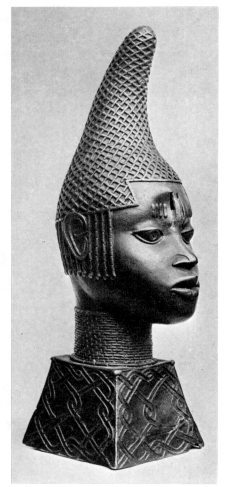

31. *"Princess,"* from Benin, Nigeria. c. 14th–16th century A.D. Bronze, life-size. British Museum, London

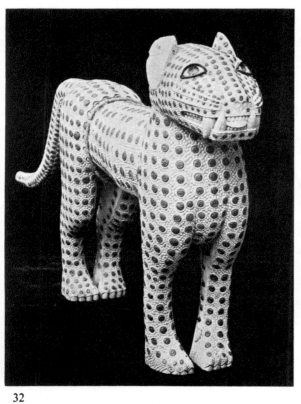

32

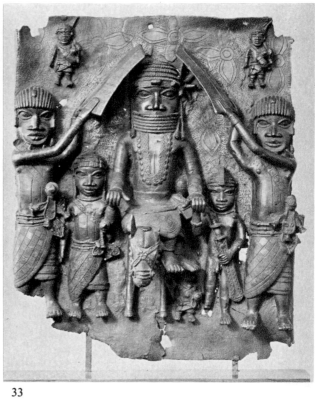

33

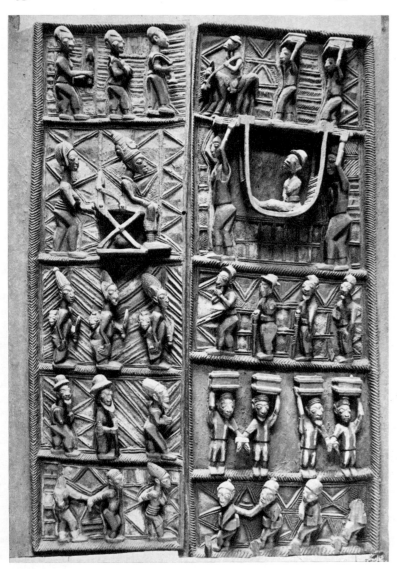

34

32. Leopard, from Benin, Nigeria. c. 16th–17th century A.D. Ivory with brass inlay. British Museum, London

33. *Mounted King with Attendants*, from Benin, Nigeria. Relief plaque. c. 1550–1680 A.D. Bronze, height 19½″. Museum of Primitive Art, New York

34. Yoruba door, from Ikerre, Nigeria. Wood. British Museum, London

35. Bakota guardian figure, from Gabon, West Africa. Wood covered with sheet brass, height 21¼″. L. van Bussel Collection, The Hague, The Netherlands

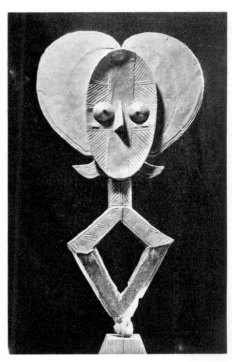

35

36. Yoruba helmet mask, from Nigeria. Height 30¾".
Koninklijk Museum voor Midden-Afrika, Tervuren,
Belgium

37. Simo mask of the goddess Nimba with carrying yoke,
from the Guinea Coast. Wood, height 52". Private
collection, New York

36

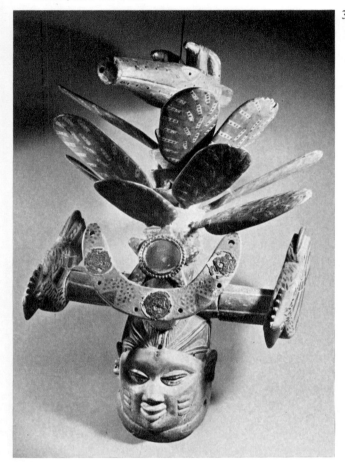

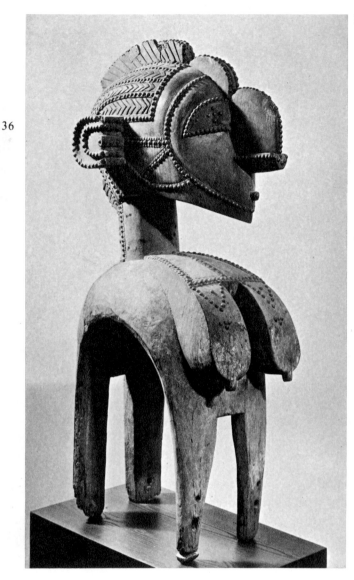

and ritual, continue some aspects of the ornamentalized Benin tradition. Much more familiar are the guardian figures of wood covered with sheet brass (fig. 35) from the Bakota tribe of Gabon in West Africa, which were originally set over urns containing ancestral skulls to ward off evil spirits. The clear-cut, tense geometric forms and strong magical content of these figures aided greatly in the development of abstract art in Europe (see Vol. 2, figs. 480, 489). Yoruba ceremonial masks from Nigeria were often far more complex. The one in fig. 36, for instance, culminates in a veritable explosion of cactus forms, crouching birds, and an animal head. One should imagine the effect of such masks moving in complex and sometimes bloody religious rituals, with a grass fringe concealing the wearer. An even more frightening example is the mask of the goddess Nimba (fig. 37) from the Simo culture of the Guinea coast. On either side of a monstrous arc-shaped nose the eyes of the goddess stare from above pendulous breasts; all forms are emphasized by rows of raised dots like nailheads. No twentieth-century white sculpture has ever surpassed the grandeur or severity of these almost architectural forms.

5
Oceanic Art

A strikingly different but equally wide range of aesthetic and emotional value was exploited by the mixed Mongoloid and melanotic (dark-skinned) peoples from Asia, who as early as the second millennium B.C. settled the innumerable islands that dot the western Pacific Ocean, aided by the lower water level that then, as in Europe, left much of the continental shelf uncovered. The separate tribes that flourished in the rain forests of the coastal areas, the river valleys, and the mountainous uplands were often headhunters, sometimes ritual cannibals. Usually carved in wood and painted, and

therefore of quite recent date, their splendid artifacts were designed to satisfy practical and ceremonial necessities. Human and animal figures of compelling physical presence coexist with shapes that, at first sight, appear entirely abstract. But the dizzying effect on the modern observer, and presumably on the enemy, of the swirling curves and floating ovoids that decorate a war shield from the Sepik River region of northern New Guinea (fig. 38) is stabilized by the realization that the shield is in fact a gigantic mask, with nose, eyes, and ornamentalized teeth, bearing on its brow a smaller and

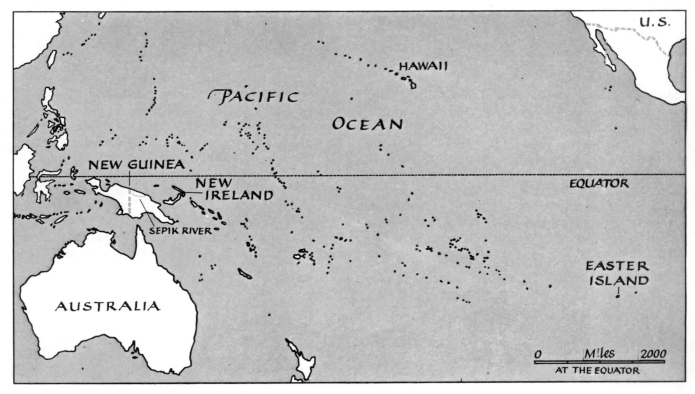

MAP 4.   *South Pacific*

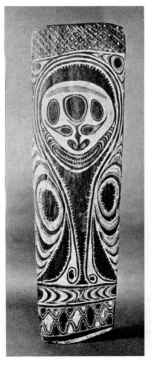

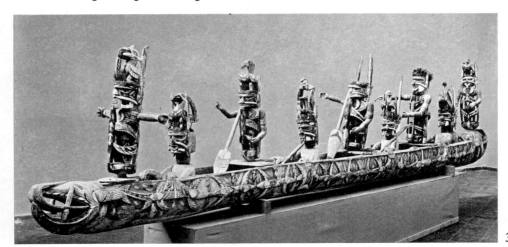

38. War shield, from the Sepik River region of New Guinea. Height 61⅜″. University Museum of Archaeology and Ethnology. Cambridge, England

39. "Soul boat," from New Ireland, New Guinea. Length 19′. Linden-Museum. Stuttgart, Germany

40. Stone images. Height 30′; weight c. 16 tons each. Easter Island, South Pacific

38

39

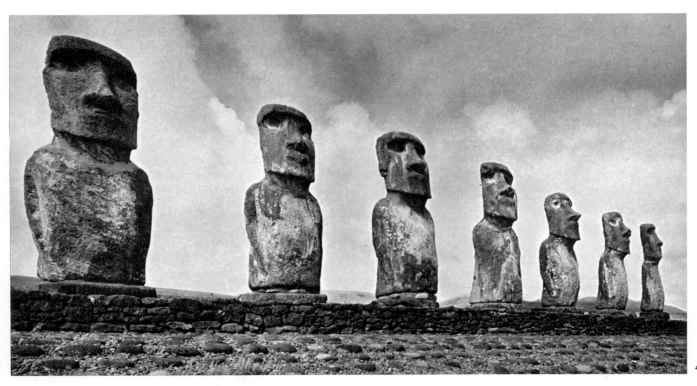

40

even more frightening face. Such objects were, of course, never intended to be seen apart from the context of tribal life, some of whose intensity engulfs us in the huge "soul boat" from New Ireland (fig. 39) commemorating a dead chieftain sent to sea in a canoe with the bodies of his enemies. The fierce and jagged shapes of the figures, the bird heads that crown them and the wings that enfold them, and the great boat itself with its fins and its open, toothy mouth and lashing tongue reenact the mysteries of an ancient rite.

Still unexplained are the colossal stone figures that stand in long rows, suggesting the menhirs of Brittany, and lead to volcanic craters on isolated Easter Island (fig. 40). They were carved from lava in quarries that still exist, but as early as the seventeenth century the first European explorers noted that the inhabitants had lost track of the meaning of the statues and had pushed many of them into the sea. The backs of the heads are entirely absent, the bodies barely suggested, so that the images are really a succession of staring masks, overpowering largely because of their gigantic scale, which unites them with the desolate landscape.

6

North American Indian Art

The first Europeans in North America may have been closer to the truth than we recognize when they called the inhabitants "Indians"; these peoples had in fact wandered from Asia, by way of a land bridge formed about 10,000 B.C. by what are now the Aleutian Islands, and they may even have brought Asiatic traditions with them. Many of these nomadic tribes of hunters were still in the Old or perhaps the Middle Stone Age, and some have remained so, in spite of enforced mass migrations, until the present century. Among the enormous variety of artifacts they produced—painted tepees and shields, carved figures, pottery, baskets, beaded clothing —perhaps the most impressive are the superb blankets

(fig. 41) whose lively, flickering designs, produced by the complex interaction of basic geometric shapes, have much in common with the abstract paintings of the twentieth century.

We tend to underrate the importance of ancient, sedentary Neolithic civilizations, such as that of the Mound Builders of the central United States or the Cliff Dwellers of the Southwest. The midwestern mounds, some as high as a hundred feet, were often grave tumuli surmounting burial chambers built of logs and containing a wealth of stone and sometimes metal ornaments; some were platforms for temples and palaces, of which only fragments survive. Others traced the forms of gigantic serpents, or

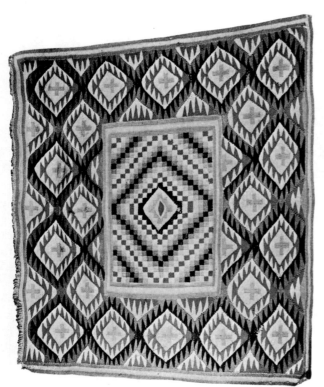

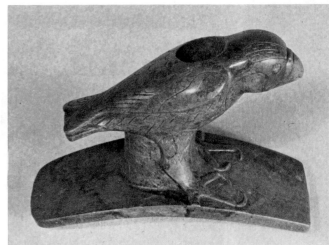

41. Nobility blanket woven by the Salish tribes. Peabody Museum, Harvard University, Cambridge, Massachusetts

42

42. Hopewell pipe in the form of a hawk, from Tremper Mound, Ohio. c. 200 B.C.–300 A.D. Gray pipestone, height 3"; length 3½". Ohio Historical Society, Columbus

41

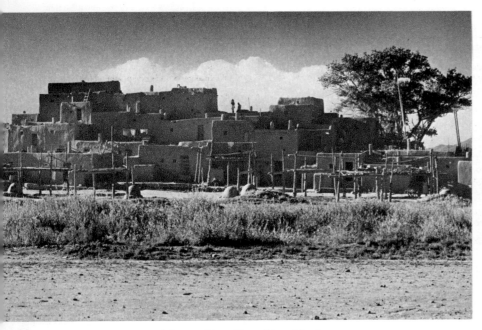

43. Adobe pueblos. Taos, New Mexico

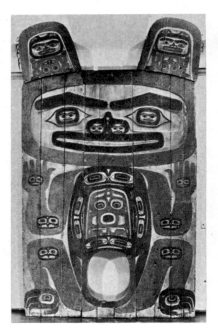

44. Tlingit bear screen. 1840. Carved and painted wood, 15 x 9'. The Denver Art Museum, Colorado

birds with wings spread, reminding us forcibly of the wall paintings of Çatal Hüyük. Such objects as the stone pipe in the form of a hawk (fig. 42) from the Hopewell culture (named after the family on whose Ohio farm the original discoveries were made), datable from 200 B.C. to A.D. 300, show a high degree of formal mastery and technical finish, suggesting the art of the Old Kingdom in Egypt. The Indians of the Southwest built superb walled towns of stone in the shelter of cliffs as far back as the twelfth century. The adobe pueblos of New Mexico (fig. 43), their descendants, look much like the reconstructed view of Çatal Hüyük (see fig. 14).

Perhaps the most powerful of more recent Indian works are the ceremonial animal sculptures of the Pacific Northwest. An effect of great mass is obtained by surrounding broad areas with incised rectangular contours with slightly rounded corners. The larger animals surprisingly disclose smaller ones—in their ears, their body joints, or even in their eyes and mouths—like the Scythian panther from southern Russia (see fig. 344). A Haida bear mask of painted wood is provided with turquoise eyes and teeth, suggesting that we are looking past and through the staring animal into distant sky (colorplate 3). Even more majestic are the towering wood sculptures of the Tlingit—doorjambs, totem poles, gables, house partitions—of which one of the grandest is a colossal bear screen (fig. 44). While commercialized versions of the great Indian objects are being made in ever-growing numbers for the tourist trade, talented Indian artists are becoming increasingly assimilated into the general currents of the dominant white culture.

From the earliest artistic productions of mankind down to works of art made by preliterate societies close to our own time, and throughout the widest variety of climatic environments and cultural systems, it is clear that in art created before writing fantasy and magic generally operate outside the control of reason. Measure, the basis of order in art as in life, can exist only with writing, and measure is conspicuously absent from all preliterate art forms save only those which, like weaving, are by their very nature dependent on a considerable number of material elements of approximately identical size, subject to distribution and repetition. Without the rational overlay governing the art of most subsequent periods, basic human impulses find expression in rhythmic form. In a magical art the motion of the hand holding the tool takes on the quality of a dance, and visual patterns that of choreography. No wonder that works of art produced for magical purposes and based on antirational principles should have been considered "barbaric" by historic societies whose culture was based on writing, or codified as evolutionary stages in human development by the encyclopedic science of the later nineteenth century. Only the twentieth, which has discovered the irrational basis of much of man's inner life through the researches of psychology, has found preliterate art emotionally accessible. From time to time, throughout the history of art in literate cultures, it will become apparent that the irrational and impulsive nature of man lies fairly close to the surface, and at moments of intense individual or collective experience can again determine essential aspects of the work of art.

TIME LINE

The numbers in italics refer to illustrations in the text.

	CLIMATE / GEOGRAPHY	CULTURES	REGIONS	PERIODS	MATERIAL CULTURE / TECHNOLOGY
30,000 B.C.	L Alternate cold and mild phases.	*Homo Sapiens* totally replaces Neanderthal hominids in Eurasia; Cro-Magnon man		U	"Blade" cultures develop throughout Eurasia and Africa
	A Franco-Cantabrian region is western boundary of Eurasian ice sheet			P	
	S	CHÂTELPERRONIAN		P	Toolmaking becomes commonplace
	T			E	Increased specialization of tools; invention of bow and arrow, spear-thrower, and chisel (burin)
	G	A U R I G N A C I A N	G R A V E T T I A N	R	
	L			P	
	A			A	
	C			L	
	I		EURASIA	E	
	A			O	
20,000	T	S O L U T R I A N		L	
	I			I	
	O			T	
	N	M A G D A L E N I A N		H	
16,000			Mongoloid migrations from East Asia into North and South America begin	I C	
14,000			Increased expansion of Paleolithic man into Northern Europe and Asia as European ice sheet withdraws	M	
			Hunting-fishing-fowling cultures prevail	E	
10,000	Postglacial period; continual (though intermittent) withdrawal of glacial sheets. Light birch forests and parkland appear in Northern Europe and parts of Asia	AZILIAN	Southwest and Central Europe	S O	Increase in tool repertory and characteristic use of multiple hafted tools of microlithic flint
		TARDENOISIAN	Spanish levant	L	Development of bone harpoons, fish traps, and heavy adzes and axes
			Hunters in North America continue to migrate south and east	I	
			Lakeshore settlements develop in Central Europe, transformation of older Paleothic cultures and seminal Mesolithic cultures	T H I	Domestication of the dog
8000		NATUFIAN (Palestine)		C	
	B Steady rise of average temperatures Increased foresting of land	JERICHO	Southwest Asia: first Neolithic cultures appear; Jericho, Jarmo develop agriculture and herding along with older Mesolithic hunting practices Diffusion of practice of farming and stockraising in settled hamlets from Southwest Asia by sea to Crete, Sicily, and South Italy	N E	Techniques of irrigation, plant cultivation, and animal husbandry gain prominence and sophistication
	O Rise of sea levels; increase of lakeshore frontage	JARMO			Pottery
	R	ÇATAL HÜYÜK		O	Ground and polished tools
	E			L	Beginning of mining and quarrying
	A	SAMARRA		I	
	L	EL FAIYÙM (Egypt)		T	(Increased diversity of local cultures)
5000	A Progressive desiccation of Egypt and other former temperate zones			H	
4000	T L			I	
3000	A N CLIMATIC OPTIMUM (c. 4000–2000): T Worldwide warm spell I C	MALTA (fl.)	Tigris-Euphrates civilizations flourish	C	
2000		CRETE (fl.)		B R	Metallurgic knowledge spreads from Near East to Egypt and then to Mediterranean coast, Anatolia, and Troy
1000	Stabilization of climatic conditions	TROY (fl.)	Mongoloid and melanotic settlements in Oceania	O	
700		HALSTATT		N I	
400		LA TÈNE		Z R	
200				E O	
				N	
				A	
				G A	
				E G	
				E	

PAINTING	SCULPTURE	ARCHITECTURE	
	"Venus" of Willendorf (1) Head of a woman from Grotte du Pape *(3)*		30,000 B.C.
	"Venus" of Lespugue (2, colorplate 1)		20,000
Painted caves at Lascaux *(6,7)* Bison at Altamira *(colorplate 2)* Drawings of human figures and animals at Addaura *(11)*	Relief of bison at Le Tuc d'Audoubert *(8)* Bison from La Madeleine *(4)* Chamois spear-thrower from Le Mas d'Azil *(5)* Reclining woman at La Madeleine *(9)*		16,000
			14,000
			10,000
Hunting Scene at El Cerro Felío *(10)* Wall paintings in shrine at Çatal Hüyük *(17,18)*	Plastered skulls from Jericho *(13)* Statues of mother goddess from Çatal Hüyük *(15)*	Stone fortifications, Jericho *(12)* Çatal Hüyük *(14)*	8000
			5000
	Relief of vinescroll ornament at Tarxien *(20)*	Trilithon portals, Malta *(19)*	4000
			3000
		Corbel vault from tomb chamber, Maeshowe *(21)*	
	Gold bracelet from Belje *(24)*	Stonehenge *(22, 23)*	2000
			1000
			700
	Bronze wagon from Strettweg *(25)*		
	Gold tiara from Poiana-Coţofeneşti *(26)* Bronze openwork ornament from Brno-Maloměřice *(27)*		400
			200
	Figure from Holzgerlingen *(28)* Silver caldron from Gundestrup *(29)* Hopewell pipe from Ohio *(42)*		

49

TIME LINE

The numbers in italics refer to illustrations in the text.

	PAINTING	SCULPTURE	ARCHITECTURE
1000 A.D.		Head of Queen Olokun from Ife *(30)*	Walled Indian towns, North America
1300		*"Princess"* from Benin *(31)*	
		Ivory leopards and bronze reliefs from Benin *(32, 33)*	
		Stone figures on Easter Island *(40)*	
		Yoruba carved-wood doors from Ikerre *(34)*	
		Bakota guardian figures from Gabon *(35)*	
		Yoruba helmet masks from Nigeria *(36)*	
		Simo mask of the goddess Nimba from Guinea Coast *(37)*	
		War shield from Sepik River region of New Guinea *(38)*	
		"Soul boat" from New Ireland *(39)*	
		Haida bear mask from Pacific Northwest *(colorplate 3)*	
		Tlingit bear screen from Pacific Northwest *(44)*	

PART TWO

The Ancient World

For many thousands of years, Neolithic man was able to produce and preserve food and thus develop permanent settlements, yet he depended entirely on his memory for records, communications, and the preservation of history, religion, and literature. No matter how highly developed, memory is notoriously fickle. No large-scale systematic enterprise, whether political, economic, or religious, was possible in the absence of reliable and enduring records. How man first hit on the idea of setting down information in visible form, thus arriving at a system of writing, we do not know, but this essential change seems to have taken place a little more than five thousand years ago, in Mesopotamia and Egypt, on both sides of the land bridge connecting Asia and Africa. In both of these civilizations the earliest writing was pictographic, but soon the little images became codified and developed connections with syllables and words independent of their original derivation. Egypt, which possessed both quantities of hard stone and swamps from whose reeds a paper-like material called papyrus was fabricated, long retained the pictorial shapes the Greeks named hieroglyphs (sacred writing, because its use was a prerogative of the priesthood). Mesopotamia, however, relied on soft clay as a writing surface, and there the pictographs were rapidly codified into groups of impressions made with the wedge-shaped end of a reed stylus—a form of writing we call cuneiform (from the Latin word for *wedge*).

Records and communications facilitated commerce and systematic agriculture, as well as the development of governmental authority. Cities grew to considerable size. Monarchies arose and extended their sway to ever wider regions by the subjugation of neighboring states. By the middle of the second millennium B.C., three powerful and prosperous empires had developed: in Egypt, in Mesopotamia, and in the islands of the Aegean Sea. The end of the second millennium, however, was a time of great upheaval for the ancient world, and none of the major powers escaped unscathed. From the ensuing chaos arose the glorious, if partial and short-lived, democratic experiment of the Greek city-states. But despite the enormous influence of Greek culture on the future, the separate Greek political systems, weakened by Macedon, could not resist the march to power of Rome. By the end of the first millennium B.C., all the states of the Mediterranean world and many of the still tribal polities of northern, central, and eastern Europe were either absorbed or on the road to absorption by the Roman Empire. Political unification prepared the ancient world for religious unification as well, and the religions surviving from the ancient states proved no match for the universal claims of Christianity or, a few centuries later, of Islam.

Along with writing and the new attitudes and systems it made possible, there arose entirely new modes of intellectual activity based on writing and aimed at the intellectual and physical control of the environment and of man himself. History and epic and religious poetry were put in writing in Egypt and Mesopotamia. The sciences of zoology, botany, anatomy, and medicine made remarkable progress. Numbers, considered apart from enumerated objects, became transferable to any object, or became subject to abstract analysis. Arithmetic and geometry were discovered, including principles still valid and methods still taught. Optics, perspective, and astronomy made remarkable beginnings, and scientific calendars were devised. Speculation and abstract reasoning followed observation, and under the Greeks and Romans the major branches of philosophy were established. New scientific attitudes began to replace mythological systems with a cosmology based on scientific method.

The adoption by the Greeks of the Phoenician alphabet

about 750 B.C. facilitated the codification of language and the establishment of regular grammar and syntax. Recorded literature included not only the heritage of preliterate Greek oral poetry, which could at last be set down, but newly composed dramas, lyrics, and epics, and a systematic attempt at history. Ancient music, now almost entirely lost, was based on scales and mathematical principles still in use; it apparently reached great heights. But along with the earliest steps in the evolution of science, and before any presently known achievements of philosophy, literature, and music, the mental attitudes born of writing made possible entirely new purposes, standards, and practices for the visual arts. For the first time, in Egypt and Mesopotamia, emphasis in figural art was transferred from animals to humans, individually or in groups, described with accuracy and analyzed with understanding, and set upon a continuous groundline or within an increasingly complex spatial environment. Compositions could be measured and controlled. Empirical Neolithic building methods gave way to a rational architecture composed of regular and regularly recurring modular units and spaces, often mathematically interrelated, and constructed with so accurate an understanding of physical stresses that, if they had been kept in repair, most ancient masonry structures would be standing today.

In all fields of human endeavor, reason is the triumphant discovery of the ancient world. The best works of ancient art, founded upon reason, are of a quality that has seldom since been equaled and never surpassed. The social upheavals following the dissolution of ancient empires were responsible for the destruction of most of mankind's early artistic achievements. What remains is often mutilated, sometimes as fast as it comes to light from beneath the soil, in order to satisfy modern greed. But in spite of violence and cupidity, what is left of ancient art, no matter how scarred and battered, no matter how brutally torn from its original setting, remains as a supreme intellectual and spiritual heritage—and inspiration—for us today.

1
Egyptian Art

THE ARCHAIC PERIOD AND THE OLD KINGDOM, c. 3200–2185 B.C.

The antiquity and continuity of Egyptian civilization were legendary, even to the Greeks and Romans. In fact, the period of roughly three thousand years during which Egyptian culture and Egyptian art persisted, unchanged in many essential respects, is longer by half than the entire time that has elapsed since the identity of Egypt was submerged in the larger unity of the Roman Empire. Although the rival cultures of the Near East, especially Mesopotamia, had a somewhat earlier start, and even influenced to a limited extent some of the early manifestations of Egyptian art, the Mesopotamian region did not enjoy natural barriers like those that protected Egypt. Consequently, group after group of invaders overwhelmed, destroyed, or absorbed preceding invaders throughout Mesopotamia's stormy history. Moreover, with few observable outside influences, the Egyptians rapidly developed their own highly original forms of architecture, sculpture, and painting earlier than any comparable phenomena in Mesopotamia, and it is Egyptian rather than Mesopotamian art that provided norms for the entire ancient world. It seems preferable, therefore, to commence our story with Egypt.

The dominating reality of Egyptian life has always been the gigantic vitality of the Nile River. For nearly a quarter of its four thousand miles, it flows through Egyptian territory. The Nile Valley, nowhere more than twelve and a half miles wide, forms a winding green ribbon between the barren rocky or sandy wastes of the Libyan Desert to the west and the Arabian Desert to the east. During the fourth millennium B.C., the valley was inhabited by a long-headed, brownskinned ethnic group, apparently of African origin, while the Nile delta to the north was the home of a round-skulled people originally from Asia. Abundant remains of Neolithic cultures have been found in both regions, including a rich variety of decorated ceramics.

The chronology of Egyptian history is still far from clear, and most dates are approximate and disputed. But, according to an account set down by a Hellenized Egyptian called Manetho in the second century B.C., the separate kingdoms of Upper (southern) and Lower (northern) Egypt were united by a powerful Upper Egyptian monarch called Menes, founder of the first of those dynasties into which Manetho divided Egyptian history. Menes has been identified by modern scholars as Narmer, the king depicted on the slate tablet in fig. 47. His tremendous achievement—establishing the first large-scale, unified state known to history—took place either shortly before or shortly after 3000 B.C.

The Egyptian king, or pharaoh as he is known in the Old Testament (from an Egyptian word originally meaning *great house*), was considered divine. He participated, therefore, in the rule of universal law that governed the natural life of the entire valley. The sun rose over the eastern cliffs in the morning and set over the western cliffs in the evening. All day the sun sent down its vivifying rays until it was devoured by the night, but one could be perfectly sure that next morning it would be resurrected. In the same way the Egyptian faced death with the certainty that, like the sun, he would live again. Every autumn the river overflowed, spreading over the land the fertile silt brought from central Africa. Even in the almost total absence of rainfall, abundant crops could be produced. The unchanging order of the natural world was personified by a complex and often changing pantheon of nature deities engaged in a continuous mythological drama rhythmically repeated according to the cycles of nature. By these deities the pharaoh was believed to have been generated, and to them he would return after a life spent maintaining in the state an order similar to that

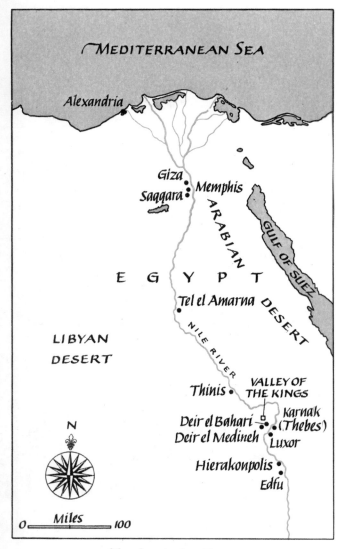

MAP 5. *Ancient Egypt*

A striking illustration of the difference between preliterate, predynastic Egypt and the subsequent tightly organized civilization that was to prove so amazingly durable can be seen by comparing the earliest known example of an Egyptian mural painting, made shortly before 3000 B.C. (fig. 45), with almost any subsequent works of Egyptian figurative art. The painting comes from the plaster wall of a tomb chamber at Hierakonpolis, a city in Upper Egypt about fifty miles south of Thebes. Not essentially different from Neolithic rock paintings found in the Spanish Levant, the random composition shows three Nile boats, possibly carrying coffins, attended by tiny figures with raised arms who may represent mourning women. Antelope and other animals are scattered about, and men fight animals and each other.

The Stone Palettes

Within a relatively short time after this improvised mural with its diagrammatic figures—perhaps as little as a century or two—Egyptian art had changed totally, reflecting the character of the monarchy, which had impressed itself on all aspects of Egyptian life. A fragment of a slate tablet (fig. 46) datable about 3000 B.C. shows a mighty bull that has overthrown and is about to gore and to mount a helpless man. Interpreted according to later references, the fearsome animal symbolizes the king of Upper Egypt triumphing over his defeated Lower Egyptian foes. The horizontal shapes below, some headed by hawks, some by lions, are the standards of royal troops, which have hands grasping a rope attached to another enemy, whose head can still be seen above the broken edge. The parallelism of the standards shows a new sense of order; so indeed does the artist's analysis of both the bull and the humans. He is aware of the difference between muscles, bones, and veins, although he has simplified and formalized these elements. The bull's hoof presses sharply into the soft muscle of his enemy's calf, immobilizing him. The features are carved with sufficient naturalism to indicate, by means of curly hair and beard, that they belong to Asiatic northerners.

The tablet is a fragment of a stone palette apparently used, in early Egypt, to mix the paint applied to the eyes of divine images in order to provide the gods with sight. The finest of these palettes is that of King Narmer (fig. 47), whose capital was at Thinis in Upper Egypt. In this work a sense of total order prevails. The king appears in his own right, standing firmly on a definite groundline, adorned with the bull's tail, wearing the crown of Upper Egypt, and grasping his enemy by the forelock with his left hand while his uplifted right hand brandishes a mace. On both faces of the palette, cow heads (sign of the goddess Hathor) representing the four corners of the heavens flank an abbreviated representation of a palace within which appears the king's name. Below, behind the king walks a servant bearing his sandals, as if to indicate

which they had ordained for the Nile Valley—beyond which, at the start of Egyptian civilization at least, little was known and nothing mattered.

The Egyptians built their houses, their cities, and even their palaces of simple materials such as palm trunks, papyrus bundles, Nile mud, and sun-dried bricks. Little is left of the palaces beyond an occasional foundation or fragments of a floor or painted ceiling, and almost nothing of the dwellings of ordinary men. But tombs and temples were soon to be constructed of stone, of which there was an abundance in the desert—sandstone, limestone, granite, conglomerate, and diorite, to name only a few. The Egyptians devoted their major artistic efforts to the gods and to the afterlife, not only in architecture but also in sculpture—both of which were often of colossal dimensions, meant to rival the immensity of the landscape and the sky—and in those delightful decorative reliefs and paintings from which we derive most of our knowledge of Egyptian life.

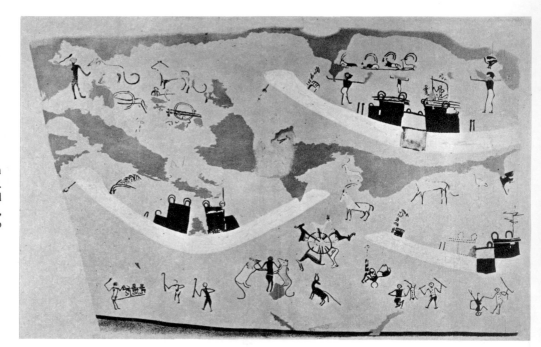

45. Tomb painting, from Hierakonpolis, Egypt. Before 3000 B.C. Painted plaster. Egyptian Museum, Cairo

the sanctity of the moment (as later with Moses on Mount Sinai). A hawk, symbol of the sky god Horus, protector of the pharaohs, holds a rope attached to a head growing from the same soil as the papyrus plants of Lower Egypt. Below the king's feet his foes flee in terror.

On the other side of the palette (fig. 48), which is divided into three registers, the king, now wearing the crown of Lower Egypt, strides forth, followed by the sandal bearer and preceded by warriors carrying standards, in order to inspect ten decapitated bodies, their heads placed between their legs. In the central register two panthers, perhaps representing the eastern and western heavens, led by divinities from barbaric regions to the east and west of Egypt, entwine their fantastically prolonged necks to embrace the sun disk, hollowed out to form a cup for the paint. (The meanings of these early images are often far from certain; the panthers can also be interpreted as symbols of Upper and Lower Egypt.) Below, as in the earlier fragment, a bull gores a prostrate enemy before his captured citadel, its walls and towers represented in plan—the earliest architectural plan known. The naturalism and sense of order that appear for the first time in these reliefs are no more striking than the introduction of a set of conventions that controlled Egyptian representations of the figure for the next three thousand years. Apparently in order to provide the observer with complete information, the eyes and shoulders are shown frontally while the head, legs, and hips are represented in profile. The weight is evenly divided between both legs, with the far leg advanced. Exceptions are made only when both hands are engaged in the same action, as in the agricultural occupations depicted in wall paintings; then the near shoulder is folded around so that it, too, appears in profile.

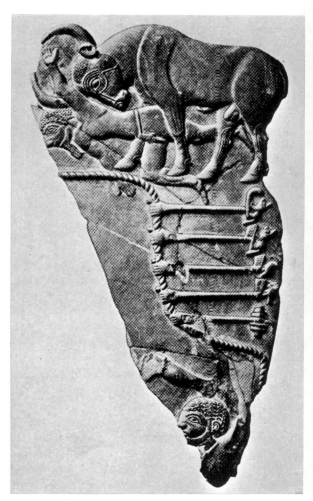

46. Cosmetic Palette (fragment), probably from Abydos. c. 3000 B.C. Slate, height 10¼". The Louvre, Paris

The Tomb and the Afterlife

The Old Kingdom began in earnest with the Third Dynasty and the removal of the capital to Memphis, in Lower Egypt. Now appear for the first time in monumental form those amazing manifestations of the belief in existence beyond death that dominated Egyptian life and thought. Each human had a mysterious double, the *ka* or life force, that survived his death but still required a body; hence the development of the art of mummification. In case the mummy were to disintegrate, the *ka* could still find a home in the statue of the deceased, which sat or stood within the tomb in a special chamber provided with a false door to the other world and with a peephole through which incense from the funeral rites could penetrate to its nostrils. The deceased was surrounded with all the delights of this world to ensure that he could enjoy them in the next: the tomb was filled with food, furniture, household implements, a considerable treasure, and sometimes even with mummified dogs and cats. The coffin, in the shape of the mummy, could be made of wood and merely painted with ornamental in-

scriptions and with the face of the deceased, or, in the case of the pharaoh, made of solid gold. The walls of the tomb were adorned with paintings or painted reliefs depicting in exhaustive detail the deceased's life on earth, as well as the funeral banquet at which he was represented alive and enjoying the viands. Once the ceremonies were over and the tomb sealed, all this beauty was, of course, doomed to eternal darkness and oblivion. But not quite all, because the royal tombs were systematically plundered even during the Old Kingdom, perhaps by the very hands that had placed the precious objects in their chambers—an odd commentary on the discrepancy between belief and practice.

The characteristic external form of the Egyptian tomb, doubtless descended from the burial mounds common to many early cultures, is called by the name *mastaba* (Arabic for *bench*), a solid, rectangular mass of masonry and mud brick with sloping sides, on one of which was the entrance to a shaft leading diagonally to interconnected tomb chambers excavated from the rocky ground of the western desert (fig. 49). The location was important: the tombs had to be placed out of reach of the

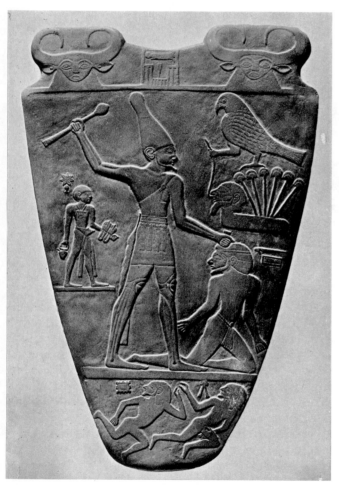

47. *Palette of King Narmer* (front view). c. 3200–2980 B.C. Stone, height 25″. Egyptian Museum, Cairo

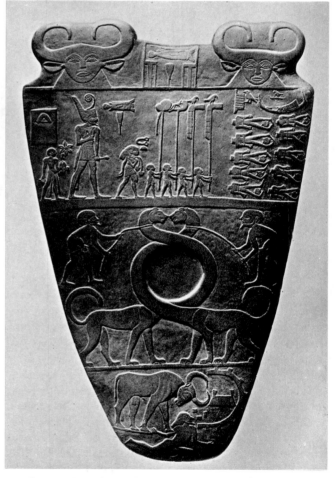

48. *Palette of King Narmer* (back view)

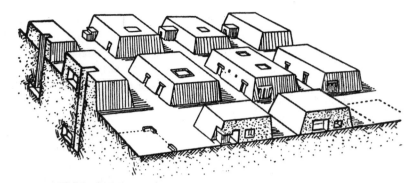

49. Group of Mastabas. (Architectural reconstruction after A. Badawy)

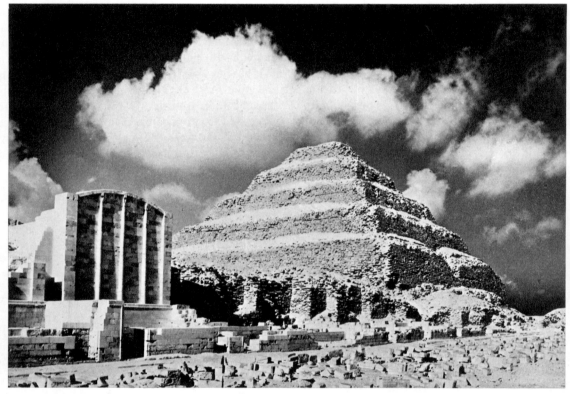

50. Iмнотер. Funerary Complex of King Zoser with step pyramid. c. 2750 B.C. Limestone. Saqqara, Egypt

annual floods that inundated the entire Nile Valley, and to the west, where the sun sank nightly into the desert, was the direction from which the deceased began his journey into the other world. The earliest colossal stone structure we know, the step pyramid of King Zoser at Saqqara, to the west of Memphis (figs. 50, 51), was originally planned about 2750 B.C. as such a mastaba. However, it occurred to the royal architect Imhotep, the first artist whose name has come down to us, to set five mastabas of constant height but diminishing area one upon the other to form a majestic staircase ascending to the heavens. His creation, rising from the desert, is still a work of overwhelming grandeur, and Imhotep was revered by posterity as a god. The funerary temple was far more impressive when its complex series of surrounding courtyards and temples was intact (fig. 52). All

of Imhotep's forms were derived from wooden palace architecture, which he imitated with the utmost elegance in clear golden-white limestone. The surrounding walls, now partly reconstructed, were divided into projecting and recessed members, each paneled. The processional entrance hall, recently partly rebuilt largely from its original stones (fig. 53), had a ceiling made of cylindrical stones in imitation of palm logs, supported by slender columns reflecting in their channeled surfaces the forms of plants, probably palm branches lashed together since the capitals appear to be formalized palm leaves (fig. 54). These are the earliest known columns, and apparently Imhotep did not entirely trust them to bear so great a weight, because he attached them to projecting walls that do most of the work. But the essentials of the Classical column—shaft, capital, and base—are already here.

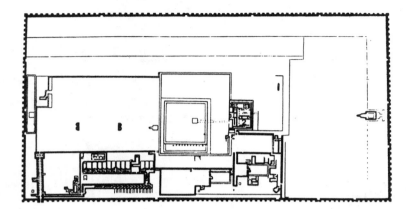

51. Plan of the Funerary Complex of King Zoser, Saqqara

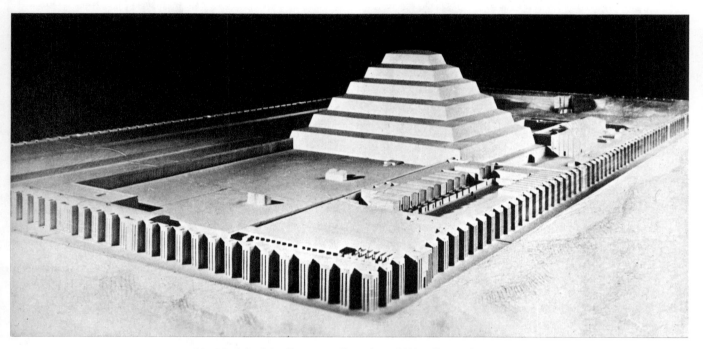

52. Model of the Funerary Complex of King Zoser, Saqqara

Similar plant forms of the greatest elegance appear throughout the architecture of the courtyards, in which stood statues of the king and his family, including a colossus, the earliest known, of which only fragments survive. But one splendid seated lifesize statue of Zoser in limestone, still another first (the earliest known royal portrait) among the achievements of this extraordinary reign, has survived relatively intact. In its majestic pose we have the prototype of all subsequent seated statues for the rest of Egyptian history. It bears the name of Imhotep on its base (fig. 55). The statue was originally placed in the *serdab*, or sealed statue chamber, built against the center of the north wall of the step pyramid, with two peepholes through which the king could look forth to the sky. The statue's appearance must have been less solemn when the rock crystal eyes, gouged out by tomb robbers, and the original surface paint were intact. The king wears the "divine" false beard, and his massive wig is partly concealed by the royal linen covering. He is swathed in a long mantle descending almost to his feet. The statue is absolutely frontal, utterly immobile, and perfectly calm. Obviously, it was drawn upon three faces of the block of stone and carved inward till the three sides of the figure merged into one another; its nobility of form arises from the perfect discipline of this procedure, recommended for sculptors as late as the Italian Renaissance by the artist and writer Vasari, who derived the idea from Michelangelo.

Later stages of the carving process are illustrated in a Sixth Dynasty relief from Saqqara (fig. 56) in which we see two sculptors finishing a statue with mallet and bronze chisel, then polishing it with stone tools.

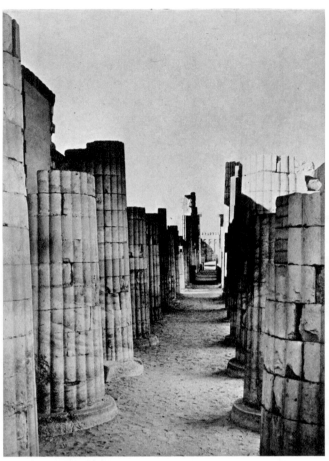

53. Entrance Hall of the Funerary Complex of King Zoser, Saqqara. (Partly rebuilt)

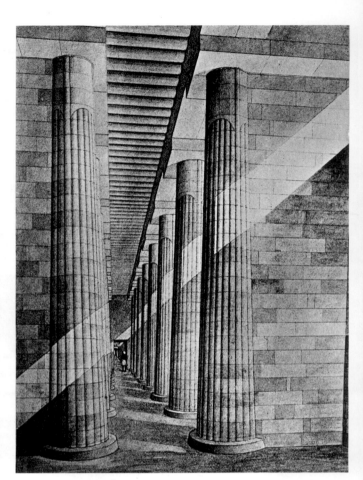

54. Entrance Hall and Colonnade of the Funerary Complex of King Zoser. Saqqara. (Reconstruction drawing by Jean Philippe Lauer)

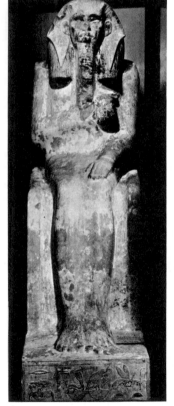

55. *King Zoser*. c. 2750 B.C. Limestone with traces of paint. height 55". Egyptian Museum, Cairo

Interestingly enough, while the sculptors are represented with shoulders frontal or folded round according to the necessities of the action, the statue does not conform to the conventions governing living figures, and remains in profile throughout. Immense dignity, if not the majesty of the divine monarch, is shared by court officials such as Hesira (fig. 57), holding symbols of his authority as well as writing instruments, in a wooden relief from his tomb at Saqqara. Although slenderer than King Narmer, he stands before us in the same manner, with weight evenly distributed on both feet. Convention also invariably and inexplicably gives relief figures two left hands, except when the right hand is holding something, and two left feet (or two right, in the rare instances when they move from right to left). This convention continues in force save for a brief period in the Eighteenth Dynasty when the feet, but not the hands, are shown as in nature (see colorplate 7); immediately thereafter the old convention returns. The present impression of beautifully controlled surfaces of wood given by the Hesira relief would be sharply different if it still retained its original bright paint, but it must always have shown the grace, authority, and firm handling of shapes characteristic of Old Kingdom art.

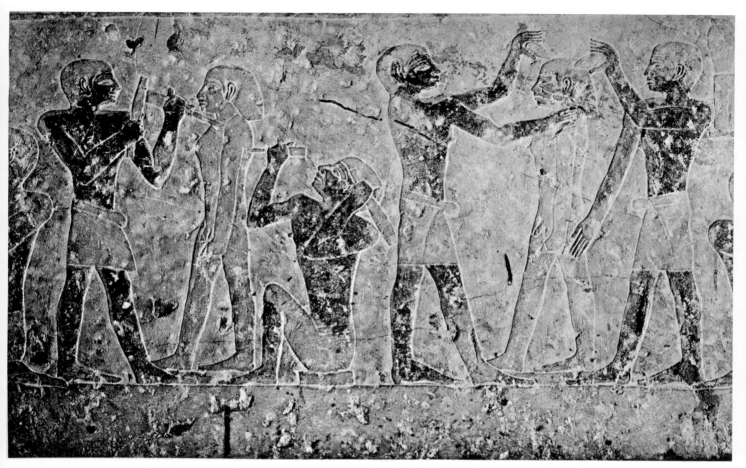

56. *Sculptors at Work*, from Saqqara. Relief. c. 2340–2170 B.C. Egyptian Museum, Cairo

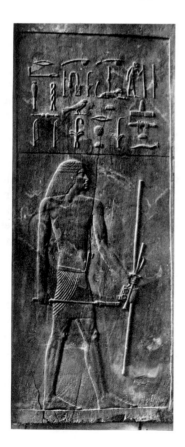

57. *Hesira*, from Saqqara. c. 2750 B.C. Wood relief, height 45″. Egyptian Museum, Cairo

The Pyramids of Giza

The grandest monuments of the Old Kingdom, and the universal wonder of mankind ever since, are the great pyramids of Giza (fig. 58), a few miles to the north of Saqqara. They were built by three kings of the Fourth Dynasty who are generally known by their Greek names: Cheops, Chephren, and Mycerinus (Egyptian: Khufu, Khafre, and Menkure). It is still unclear whether the perfect shape, with its four isosceles-triangular sides (fig. 59), evolved from the step pyramids at Saqqara and elsewhere, or whether it had special religious significance. The earliest of the Giza pyramids, that of Cheops, is also the largest, originally 480 feet high, more than twice the height of the step pyramid of Zoser. Whether seen from modern Cairo some eight miles distant or across the rocky ledges and sands of the desert or towering close at hand, these amazing structures convey an impression of unimaginable size and mass. Originally, they also had the characteristic Old Kingdom perfection of form, but this, alas, has vanished since the smooth, finely dressed limestone surface was stripped from the underlying blocks for use in the buildings of Cairo. Only a small portion at the top of Chephren's pyramid

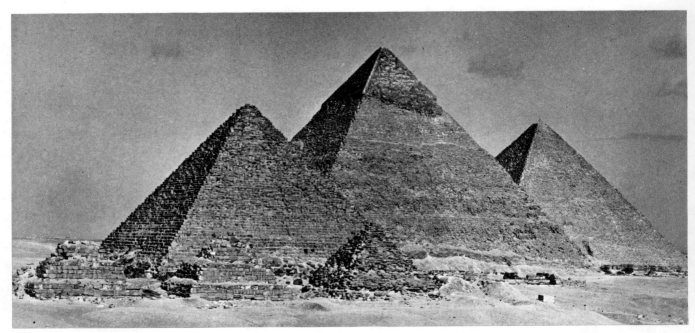

58. Pyramids of Mycerinus (c. 2500 B.C.), Chephren (c. 2530 B.C.), and Cheops (c. 2570 B.C.). Limestone, height of Cheops pyramid c. 480'. Giza

remains. No elaborate courtyards were ever contemplated. Each pyramid had a small temple directly before it, united by a causeway with a second or valley temple at the edge of cultivation (fig. 60); the valley temple was accessible from the Nile by canal or, during the floods, directly by boat. Flanking the great pyramids were extensive and carefully planned groups of smaller pyramids for members of the royal family and mastabas for court officials. The great pyramids were oriented directly north and south, and the pyramids of Cheops and Chephren were constructed along a common diagonal axis.

The accounts by Greek and Roman writers of forced labor used to build the pyramids are probably legendary. The concept of large firms of contractors and paid labor is more consistent with what we know of Egyptian society, and remains have been found of a considerable settlement that grew up at the edge of the valley to house workers, supervisors, and planners. Brick ramps, later dismantled, were built up; on these the limestone blocks, transported by boat from quarries on the other side of the Nile, could be dragged, probably on timber rollers (the wheel was as yet unknown).

Only the valley temple of Chephren can now be seen (fig. 61); in contrast to Imhotep's architecture at Saqqara, all its forms derive their beauty from the very nature of stone. The walls are built of pink granite blocks, the shafts and lintels are granite monoliths, and the floor is paved with irregularly shaped slabs of alabaster. All the masonry is fitted together without mortar and with perfect accuracy, creating an impression of austere harmony. Alongside the valley temple rises the Great Sphinx (fig. 62), carved from the living sandstone;

it is not only the earliest colossus to be preserved but also by far the largest to survive. In spite of later damage by Muslims, which has almost destroyed the face, this immense lion with the head of Chephren is possibly the most imposing symbol of royal power ever created.

Old Kingdom Statues

A statue of Chephren (colorplate 4), which once stood in his valley temple, is luckily almost undamaged. Immobile, grand, unchanging, the pose of the figure derives from that of Zoser. Seated on a lion throne, the king is clad only in a richly pleated kilt and a linen covering, horizontally pleated over the shoulders, that completely conceals the customary wig. The lines of this massive headdress are perfectly aligned with the wings of the hawk-god Horus, spread in protection behind the king's head. The broad, simple treatment of the shapes, the grand proportioning of the elements, and the smooth movement of the unbroken surfaces of diorite all culminate in the noble features of the king, whose serene expression bespeaks calm, total, unchallengeable control. In lesser works the systematic method of the Egyptian artists sometimes results in uniformity and mediocrity, but in the hands of the finest Old Kingdom sculptors the method itself exemplifies Egyptian beliefs regarding the divinity of the king and is the visual counterpart of the unalterable law governing earth and sky, life and death. By common consent, the statue of Chephren is not only one of the supreme examples of ancient sculpture but also one of the great works of art of all time.

59. North-South section of the Pyramid of Cheops. Giza. (Drawing after L. Borchardt)

60. Plan of the Pyramid of Chephren and Valley Temples. Giza

61. Valley Temple of Chephren. c. 2530 B.C. Granite and alabaster. Giza

62. *The Great Sphinx.* c. 2530 B.C. Sandstone, 65 x c. 240'. Giza

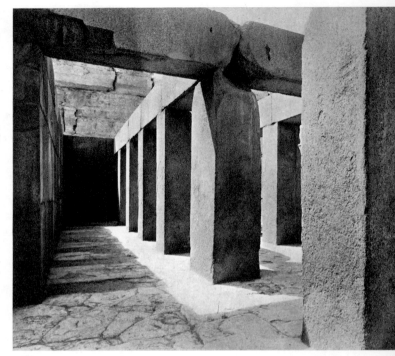
61

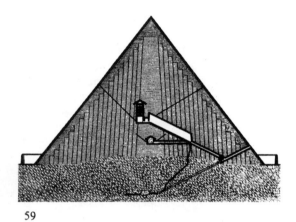
59

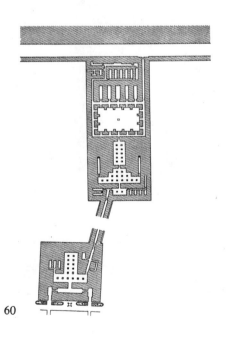
60

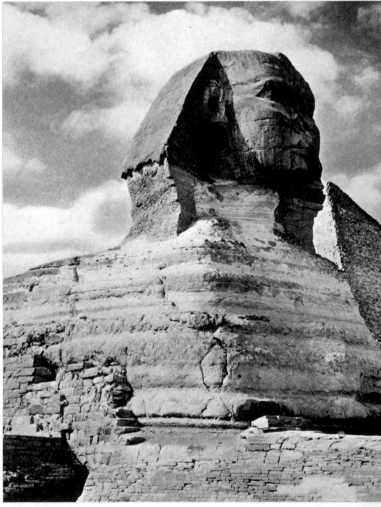
62

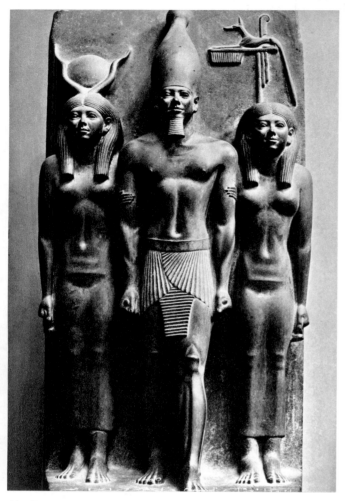

63. *King Mycerinus Between Two Goddesses,* from the Valley Temple of Mycerinus, Giza. c. 2570 B.C. Gray-green schist, height 37⅜". Egyptian Museum, Cairo

Somewhat less impersonal than the *Chephren* is the superb group statue showing King Mycerinus, wearing a kilt and the crown of Upper Egypt, flanked by the cow-goddess Hathor and a local deity (fig. 63). Each of the goddesses has an arm around Mycerinus as if to demonstrate his habitual intimacy with divinities. The work is carved from gray-green schist, and although the sculptor has not maintained quite the exalted dignity so impressive in the *Chephren,* he has delightfully contrasted the broad-shouldered, athletic figure of the king with the trim, youthful, sensuously beautiful forms of the female divinities, fully revealed by their clinging garments. Interestingly enough, while the king stands with legs apart, weight evenly distributed on both feet as in the Hesira relief, Hathor takes only a timid step forward and the local goddess keeps her feet together as if rooted to the spot.

While the royal statues are obviously individualized portraits, Old Kingdom naturalism is held in check by the need to emphasize the majesty and divinity of the pharaoh. But even in the more vividly lifelike statues of princes and officials, the dignity, simplicity, and balance characteristic of the Old Kingdom are consistently maintained. *Prince Rahotep and His Wife Nofret* (fig. 64) is carved from limestone, softer and easier to work than

diorite or schist. The pair retain most of their original coating of paint. Rahotep is brown, his wife yellow ocher—the colors used by the Egyptians to distinguish male from female, probably to show that men braved the fierce sun from which delicate female skin was protected. The coloring, combined with the inlaid eyes of rock crystal, Rahotep's little mustache, and Nofret's plump cheeks, gives the pair an uncanny air of actuality that, to modern eyes, contrasts strangely with their ceremonial poses. On a far higher plane is the painted limestone bust of *Prince Ankhhaf* (fig. 65), son-in-law of Cheops. The aging forms of body and face are clearly indicated, but the whole is pervaded with a mood of pensive melancholy that provokes in the observer unanswerable speculation as to its origin. This wonderful psychological portrait is unique in its subtlety among the more forthright Old Kingdom figures.

The Fifth Dynasty wooden statue of Kaaper (fig. 66), originally painted, betrays a lower-class allegiance; its uncompromising realism, not sparing the fat belly and smug expression of the subject, has earned the statue the modern nickname of *Sheikh el Beled* (Arabic for *headman of the village*), but the artist has not sacrificed any of the firmness and control typical of the best Old Kingdom work. Another brilliant Fifth Dynasty portrait is the painted limestone *Seated Scribe* (fig. 67), doubtless portraying a bureaucrat, alert and ready to write on his papyrus scroll.

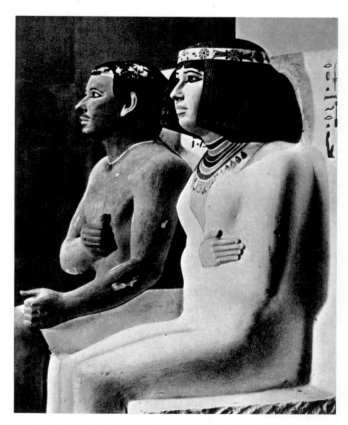

64. *Prince Rahotep and His Wife Nofret.* c. 2610 B.C. Painted limestone, height 47¼". Egyptian Museum, Cairo

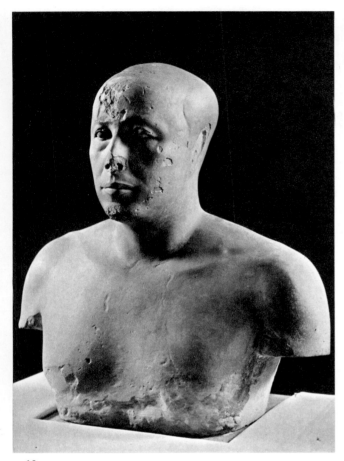

65

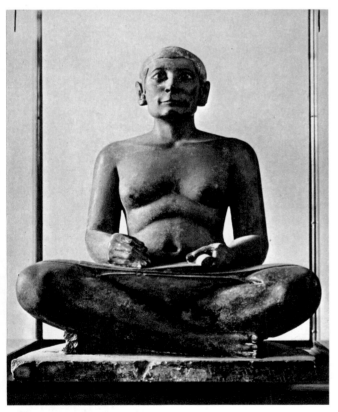

67

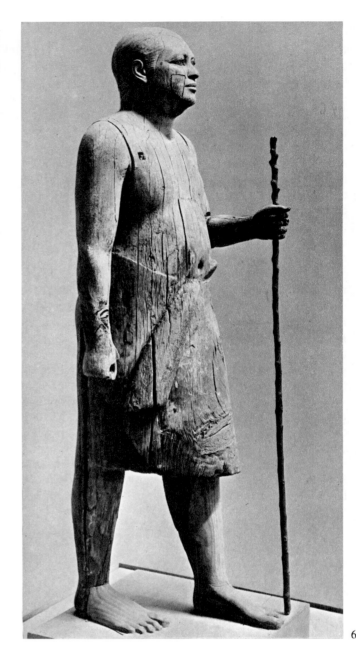

66

65. *Bust of Prince Ankhhaf*, from Giza. c. 2550 B.C. Painted limestone, height 22⅛″. Museum of Fine Arts, Boston

66. *Kaaper* (Sheikh el Beled), from Saqqara. c. 2400 B.C. Wood, height 43″. Egyptian Museum, Cairo

67. *Seated Scribe*, from Saqqara. c. 2400 B.C. Painted limestone, height 21″. The Louvre, Paris

Relief Sculpture and Painting

Our understanding of life in Old Kingdom Egypt is illustrated with a completeness beyond any expectations by the innumerable scenes—carved in low relief on the limestone blocks of tomb chambers and then painted, or painted directly without underlying relief—that describe in exhaustive detail the existence the deceased enjoyed in this world and that he hoped would be perpetuated in the next. Only such generic scenes are represented; the paintings are not biographical. Within the conventional structure of Egyptian style, these scenes describe in encyclopedic fashion all the elements of what we know to be taking place, not just the incident as we might see it from one vantage point. Usually the walls are divided into registers, each with a firm and continuous groundline and no indication of distant space. For example, in a relief representing a high official, *Ti Watching a Hippopotamus Hunt* (colorplate 5), the owner of the tomb is represented at least twice the size of the subordinate figures, and he merely contemplates, but does not participate in, the events of daily existence. Yet, since the scenes line the walls of the tomb chambers on all sides, they provide us with the illusion of an enveloping space in which we walk among the humans, animals, birds, and plants of 4,500 years ago. In this case the background consists of vertical grooves to indicate the stems of a papyrus swamp. Ti stands in his boat, posed according to the principles of relief representation we have already seen, holding his staff of office, while men in a neighboring boat spear the hippopotamuses. Toward the top of the relief are scattered papyrus flowers, among which

wild animals lurk and birds fly or nest in an amazing variety of beautifully rendered poses. There is none of the random waywardness of the Hierakonpolis mural (see fig. 45); an exact sense of order prevails—even the spears of the huntsmen are drawn parallel to one line of the triangle formed by Ti's kilt. Among the innumerable incidents that line the tomb is a touching scene (fig. 68) in which cattle are being led across a river and a terrified calf, too small to ford the stream, turns its head as it is carried over and cries to its anxious mother. The water is convincingly suggested by parallel vertical zigzags, over which the legs of humans and animals are painted, not carved.

The celebrated *Geese of Medum* (colorplate 6), actually a strip from a continuous series of wall paintings, shows the extent to which the Old Kingdom could carry both its naturalism and its strong sense of form, so fused that the formalization characteristic of almost all Egyptian art seems to be derived effortlessly from the actual motion of these delightful birds, rather than being imposed from outside, as is so often the case with representations of human beings.

Luckily, a few unfinished tomb designs are preserved, left in that state because the deceased, for some unknown reason, had to be buried in haste. An unfinished passage from the later tomb of the pharaoh Horemheb (colorplate 7), in the Eighteenth Dynasty, shows us how the reliefs were made. First, as we see in the left-hand figure, the painter did his preparatory drawing on the stone, according to a fixed system of proportions represented by ruled lines. But the artist was clearly very sensitive to nuances of contour, and changed his outline two or three times before he was satisfied. Then, either he or a specialized stone carver cut out the shallow relief according to the drawing, down to a uniform background level. Finally, the painter returned to color the figures and objects. Even more revealing is a scene from the tomb of Neferirkara (fig. 69), from the Fifth Dynasty, in which only the preliminary drawing was ever done. Presumably the finished birds would have been drawn and painted with the same precision as the *Geese of Medum*, but the present airy grace of the descending pigeons comes not only from the astonishing variety of their poses but from the lightness of the brush drawing as well.

Although it was in Old Kingdom Egypt that man first learned to be fully human, our ideas of Old Kingdom art and life are entirely formed on the funerary art through which the Egyptian faced eternity. His houses, palaces, and temples have mostly vanished, leaving hardly a clue. In the very nature of things, the beautiful system that sustained and gave meaning to the life of the Old Kingdom could not last forever. Perhaps the cost of the great funerary temples and pyramids was too heavy to bear. A king who is also a god must be able to act the part. At any rate, the weak kings of the Seventh and Eighth dynasties could not meet these demands, and their

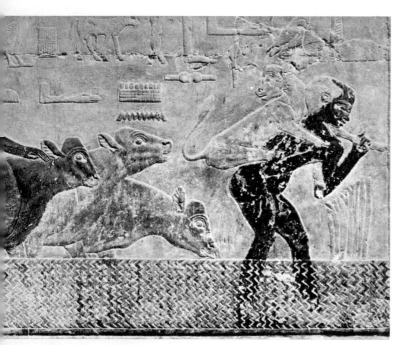

68. *Cattle Fording a River* (portion of a relief from the Tomb of Ti). c. 2400 B.C. Painted limestone. Saqqara. See Colorplate 5

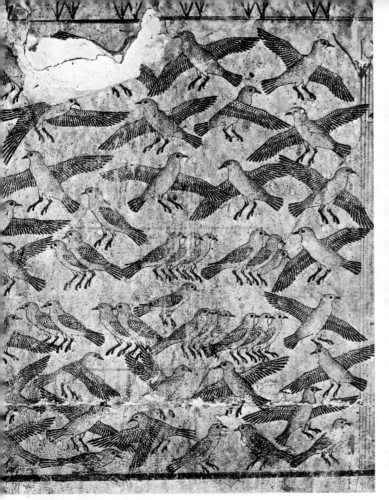

 70

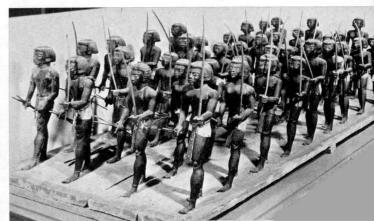

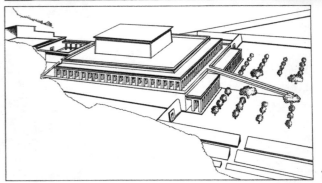

71

9

69. *Birds in Flight,* from the Tomb of Neferirkara (preparatory drawing). c. 2480–2340 B.C. Limestone. Saqqara

70. Model of a troop of Nubian mercenaries, from a tomb at Assiut. Painted wood, height 15¾″. Egyptian Museum, Cairo

71. Funerary Temple of Mentuhotep III, Deir el Bahari. (Architectural reconstruction after Dieter Arnold)

reigns were followed by a period of great social disorder during which the real power passed into the hands of provincial rulers and little art worthy of notice was created.

THE MIDDLE KINGDOM, c. 2040–1650 B.C., AND THE EMPIRE, c. 1550–1070 B.C.

Middle Kingdom Architecture

In a prolonged struggle, the kings of the Eleventh Dynasty regained power from provincial rulers and reunited the country, whose capital oscillated between Memphis in Lower Egypt and Thebes in Upper Egypt. Power no longer depended upon the divine authority of the pharaoh but on military force. Tombs often contained remarkable miniature groups in wood, representing every kind of daily activity, including the all-important military ones. A company of forty Nubian mercenaries (fig. 70) advancing toward us is a brutal indication of the changed conditions of the Middle Kingdom. Some small stone-faced brick pyramids were built, and numerous tombs whose chambers and columned halls were cut directly into the rock; but the most impressive architectural work we know from this period is the funerary temple of Men-

tuhotep III at Deir el Bahari, across the Nile from Thebes. From what remains of the building, alongside which Queen Hatshepsut was later to build her even more ambitious temple (see fig. 74), we can reconstruct its original appearance (fig. 71). From a grove of geometrically aligned trees a long ramp led to a terrace supported by a row of square piers; from there one entered a second colonnade through a canted doorway and moved into a courtyard from the center of which rose a massive block with canted sides like a huge mastaba outlined against the immense cliffs of the western mountain. The scale, as compared to Old Kingdom tombs, is almost human.

Middle Kingdom Sculpture

Some royal portraits reveal with devastating frankness the chronic anxiety in which, according to literary accounts, Middle Kingdom monarchs lived, tormented by the military struggles needed to maintain their rule. Especially intense are the brooding portraits of Sesostris III (fig. 72), whose careworn face shows none of the serene confidence of the Old Kingdom. Against such a background, the exquisite seated statue of *Princess Sen-*

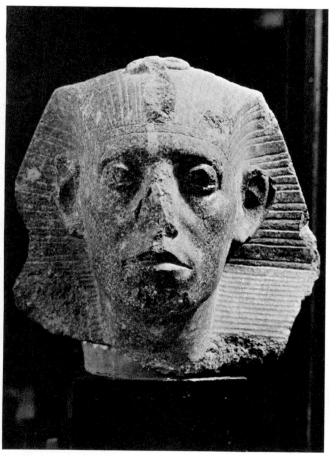

72. *King Sesostris III*, from Medamud. c. 1878–1843 B.C.
Granite. Egyptian Museum, Cairo

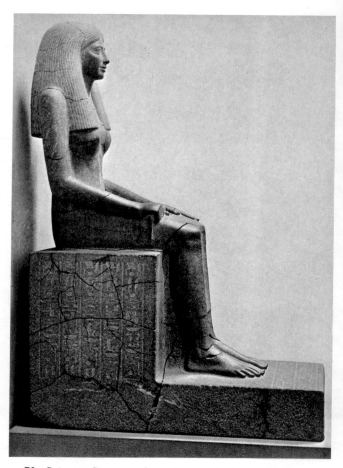

73. *Princess Sennuwy*, from Kerma, Sudan. c. 1950 B.C.
Granite, height 67½″. Museum of Fine Arts, Boston

nuwy (fig. 73) comes as a delightful surprise. Posed like a pharaoh, this masterpiece in polished granite shows in its slender forms and softly flowing surfaces a style as sensuous as that of the best Old Kingdom female figures, but endowed with a wholly new elegance and grace.

At the close of the Twelfth Dynasty ensued a new period of political chaos, during which Lower Egypt was invaded by Asiatic rulers known as the Hyksos, or shepherd kings. These conquerors imported two commodities soon to be triumphantly adopted by the Egyptians—the horse and the wheel. After a century of foreign rule, pharaohs from Upper Egypt for the third time regained power, and the Eighteenth Dynasty saw not only the expulsion of the Hyksos and the reunification of the country, with its capital at Thebes, but also the extension of Egyptian power over neighboring lands as well—Syria, Palestine, Libya, Nubia, an area more than 2,000 miles in length.

Architecture of the Empire

The next five centuries constitute a period of unprecedented imperial power and wealth, celebrated by enormous architectural projects, largely in the surroundings of the Theban metropolis—at modern Karnak and Luxor on the east bank of the Nile and Deir el Bahari on the west. Amen, the local deity of Thebes, was promoted to the ruling position among the gods in recognition of his services to the Empire, and identified with Ra, the sun god, thus becoming Amen-Ra. The new temples were often decorated with statues, reliefs, and paintings representing the imperial power and historic exploits of the pharaohs. Among the earliest large-scale undertakings of the Empire was the funerary temple of Queen Hatshepsut (fig. 74), who governed as pharaoh and was the first great female ruler of whom we have any record. Its three rising colonnaded terraces are connected by ramps. The colonnades of the two lower terraces employ simple square pillars. Two open halls of the middle terrace (fig. 75) contain painted reliefs of great coloristic brilliance that illustrate incidents from Hatshepsut's reign and include a number of portraits of her architect, Senmut, who may have been her lover. A worthy successor to Imhotep of the Old Kingdom, Senmut planned the uppermost courtyard to abut the mass of the cliff into which the sanctuary chamber is carved. Thus

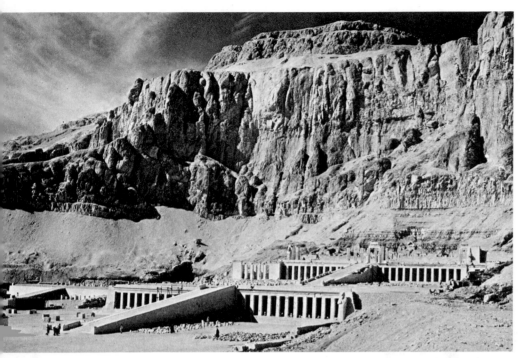

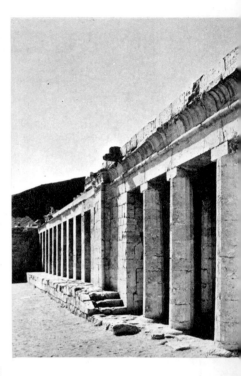

74. SENMUT. Funerary Temple of Queen Hatshepsut. c. 1480 B.C. Deir el Bahari

75. Portico of the Anubis Sanctuary, Funerary Temple of Queen Hatshepsut. c. 1480 B.C. Deir el Bahari

the living rock of the western mountain substitutes for a man-made pyramid.

A powerful priesthood in Thebes administered the royal temples of Amen, his wife Mut, and their son Khonsu at Luxor and at Karnak. These were originally connected by an avenue of sphinxes more than a mile in length, of which hundreds are still in place. Egyptian temples, unlike those of the later Greeks, offered no unified outer view. They were built to enclose a succession of spaces of increasing sanctity and exclusiveness along a central axis, starting with the entrance gateway, which was flanked by slanting stone masses called pylons. Our illustration is drawn from the much later Temple of Horus at Edfu, which closely followed the principles and shapes established in the Empire (fig. 76). Through the gateway the worshiper was admitted to a colonnaded court; then came a lofty hall whose stone roof was sup-

ported by immense columns; and finally there were the smaller and more secret sanctuaries containing cult statues, spaces reserved for the priesthood and their rituals. A second hall and courtyard were added in front of the Temple of Amen-Mut-Khonsu at Luxor (fig. 77) by Ramses II, who had to deflect the axis to avoid the nearby Nile. The immensity of the columns of the original courtyard built by Amenhotep III, some thirty feet high, is far removed from the elegance and purity of Imhotep's architectural forms, but the problems themselves required new solutions (fig. 78). The unknown architect at Luxor built massive freestanding columns of local sandstone rather than of the fine limestone available at Saqqara, and he shaped them according to the conventionalized forms of bundles of papyrus reeds, traditional supports for the more ephemeral architecture of the vanished Egyptian houses and palaces. The

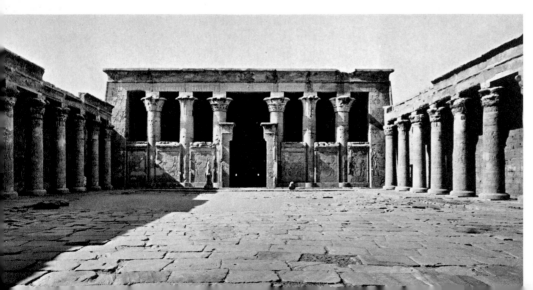

76. Temple of Horus.
3rd–1st century B.C. Edfu

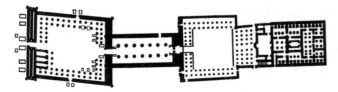

77. Plan of the Temple of Amen-Mut-Khonsu. Luxor (after N. de Garis Davies)

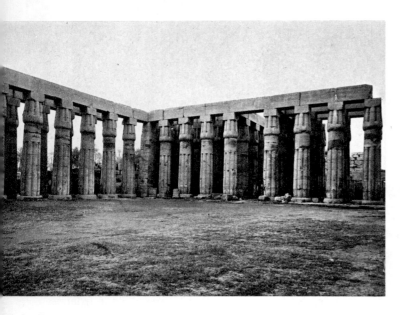

78. Court of Amenhotep III and Entrance Hall to the Temple of Amen-Mut-Khonsu. c. 1375 B.C. Luxor

79. Hypostyle Hall of the Temple at Karnak (begun by Seti I and completed by Ramses II; portion). c. 1290 B.C. Sandstone

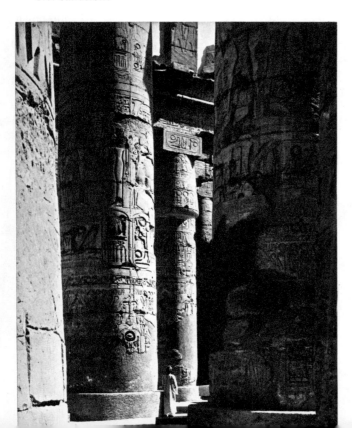

columns sustain huge undecorated sandstone lintels that surround the courtyard and continue in the columned hall, where they supported a now-fallen roof of stone slabs. Light came from the sides over low walls, so that the center of the hall must have remained mysteriously dim. The grand proportions of the columns, which seem to continue in all directions, create an effect of majestic solemnity.

The even larger and far more complex temple at Karnak was one of the most extensive sanctuaries of the ancient world, with a perimeter wall about a mile and a half in circumference. The partially ruined temple was constructed piecemeal by so many pharaohs that the overall effect is confusing, yet many of the surviving portions are very beautiful. The great hall built by Seti I and Ramses II in the Nineteenth Dynasty was filled with columns so massive that diagonal views are impossible from the central axis (fig. 79). Wherever one looks, the vista is blocked by these immense shapes, decorated by bands of incised hieroglyphics and painted reliefs.

Tomb Decorations

Scores of tombs survive from the period of the Empire. Pharaohs and aristocracy alike gave up building monumental tombs, which could not be defended against robbers. The dead were buried deep in rock-cut chambers in mountain valleys, and the entrances carefully hidden. Even the royal tombs in the Valley of the Kings, west of Thebes, were invariably discovered and plundered, but the wall decorations remain. In the splendid Eighteenth Dynasty painted tomb of Nebamun at Thebes (colorplate 8), the deceased is shown fowling. Accompanied by his hunting cat, he plays havoc among the brilliantly drawn and painted birds of a papyrus swamp. A fragment from this same tomb (fig. 80) shows an entrancing banquet scene, at which both the revelers and the musicians wear cones of perfumed unguents on their heads. Delightful female dancers, clad only in jeweled collars and tiny golden belts, clap their hands as they move with exquisite lightness and grace. While most of the figures are shown from the side, two of the crouching musicians unexpectedly face directly outward, and all the crouching figures point the soles of their feet toward us. In the subtle, delicate style of the Eighteenth Dynasty there can also be great pathos, as in the relief of the *Blind Harper* (fig. 81) from the tomb of Patenemhab at Saqqara, in which the harper gently strums his octave of strings. His song is inscribed on the wall beside him:

Pass the day happily, O priest.
. . . have music and singing before you,
Cast all ill behind you and think only of joy,
Until the day comes when you moor your boat in the
land that loves silence.

Characteristic of the arrangement of scenes in superimposed strips is the tomb of Sen-nedjem at Deir el Medineh, from the Nineteenth Dynasty (fig. 82). At the end of the chamber the deceased crosses to the other world in the boat of the dead to be received by the gods, and below are shown the harvest of his grainfields and the rows of his fruit trees. On the right the gods themselves are aligned above his funeral feast. As in the tomb of Ti, scenes like these in registers continuing around the chamber create a special kind of space that, once one accepts the conventions of Egyptian art, becomes surprisingly real.

Akhenaten

Just when everything about Egyptian life and art seemed to be safely settled for an indefinite period, an unexpected reformer appeared who tried his best to unravel the entire fabric, and indeed succeeded for a limited time. During the reign of Amenhotep III in the Eighteenth Dynasty, there arose at the imperial court a new cult that worshiped the disk of the sun, called the Aten. Amenhotep's son, first his coruler and then his successor, changed his name from Amenhotep IV to Akhenaten in honor of the new solar god, of whom he declared himself to be the sole earthly representative. This extraordinary religion, a kind of early monotheism, required the closing of the temples of Amen-Ra and the disinheriting of the priesthood, which had become the true ruling class of Egyptian society. Although Akhenaten built a new Temple of Aten at Karnak, he moved the capital from Thebes to an entirely new site, dedicated to Aten, at a spot now called Tell el Amarna. The insubstantial secular buildings of the Egyptians usually vanished, like those of Çatal Hüyük, under new structures, leaving few traces, but when Akhenaten died his successors were so anxious to wipe out the memory of the heretic that they destroyed the new city of Akhenaten immediately. The plans and even painted floors from the palace and from the houses of state officials have, however, been excavated, and the entire contents of a sculptor's studio were discovered, including casts from life, models for sculpture, and unfinished works.

Something of the character of this royal visionary who neglected the military necessities of empire to promulgate his new religion can be seen from strange statues and reliefs of him and others, which have been found in considerable numbers because they were used as building blocks by later pharaohs. One colossal pillar statue from the Temple of Aten at Karnak (fig. 83) shows his slack-jawed, heavy-lipped features and dreamy gaze and, instead of the athletic male ideal of the earlier pharaohs, an exaggeratedly feminine body with swelling breasts—as if the king in his new messianic role were to embody both paternal and maternal principles. An incised relief (this method, which freed the sculptor from

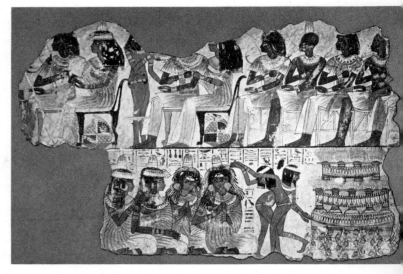

80. *Banquet Scene* (fragment), from the Tomb of Nebamun, Thebes. c. 1400 B.C. British Museum, London. See Colorplate 8

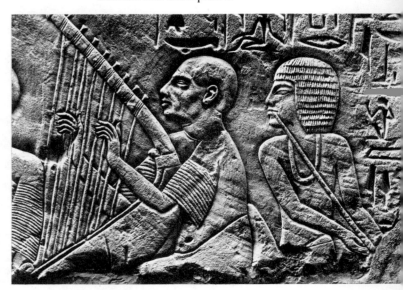

81. *Blind Harper*, from the Tomb of Patenemhab, Saqqara. Relief. c. 1552–1306 B.C. National Museum of Antiquities, Leiden, The Netherlands

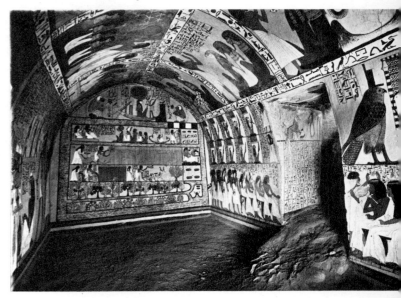

82. Tomb of Sen-nedjem. Wall paintings. c. 1150 B.C. Deir el Medineh (Thebes)

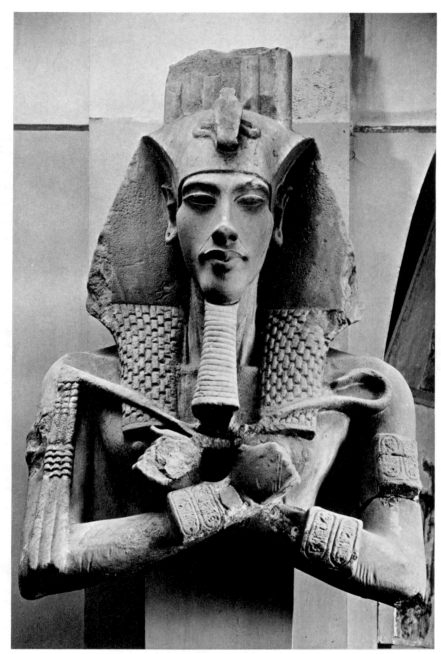

83. *King Akhenaten*, from the Temple of Aten, Karnak.
c. 1360 B.C. Sandstone. Egyptian Museum, Cairo

the necessity of reducing the entire background, was characteristic of large-scale Empire reliefs) shows the king sacrificing to Aten (fig. 84), whose rays terminate in hands that bestow life to the earth, represented by papyrus plants. He is followed by the queen, Nefertiti, whose figure is shaped just like his, though in smaller scale, and by a still smaller daughter. The famous painted limestone bust of Nefertiti (colorplate 9), which is a model found in the sculptor's studio, shows the queen at the height of her beauty. The slender, long-necked ideal of elegance and grace is irresistible to twentieth-century eyes.

Tutankhamen

Through a happy accident of history, even more is preserved to show the brief life and activities of Akhenaten's successor, known to us by the name Tutankhamen, who died between eighteen and twenty years of age. The young king may have been Akhenaten's younger half brother; his name was forced upon him by the revived priesthood of Amen. His is the only royal tomb that has been found intact; it had been obscured and protected by debris from a later tomb. When discovered in 1922, the chambers contained a dazzling array of beautiful objects, displaying the taste of the imperial court for delicacy and grace. The king's many coffins, one inside the other, were found intact. The innermost, of solid gold, weighs 2,448 pounds! The cover of the coffin (colorplate 10) has a breathtaking portrait of the boy king in solid gold, with the ceremonial beard, the eyebrows, and lashes all inlaid in lapis lazuli. To the effect of splendor produced by the intrinsic value of the materials is added an impression of the greatest poetic sensitivity and beauty. No other work of art from antiquity brings us so close to the personality of a deceased monarch. Among the thousands of objects from the tomb, one of the most beautiful is the carved wood throne, covered with gold and inlaid with faience, glass paste, semiprecious stones, and silver. The charming relief on the back (fig. 85) still shows the disk of Aten shining on the young king, who is seated on a delicately carved chair while his queen, Ankhesenamen, lightly

touches his shoulder as she presents him with a beautiful bowl.

Later Pharaohs

Succeeding monarchs, particularly the Ramesside pharaohs, were anxious to reestablish symbols of imperial might along with the neglected cult of Amen. Ramses II had himself portrayed in immense statues, characteristic of the megalomania of his dynasty, such as those placed between the columns of his new forecourt for the temple at Luxor (fig. 86).

Even under the Greek rulers of Egypt in the last centuries B.C., the principles of Egyptian architecture, sculpture, and painting continued virtually unchanged. If some of the conviction may have gone out of Egyptian art, the late works, such as the Temple of Horus at Edfu, south of Luxor (see fig. 76), are often impressive. This is

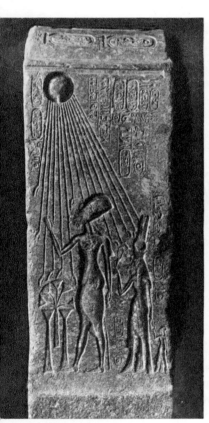

84. *King Akhenaten and His Family Sacrificing to Aten*, from Tell el Amarna. Relief. c. 1360 B.C. Limestone. Egyptian Museum, Cairo

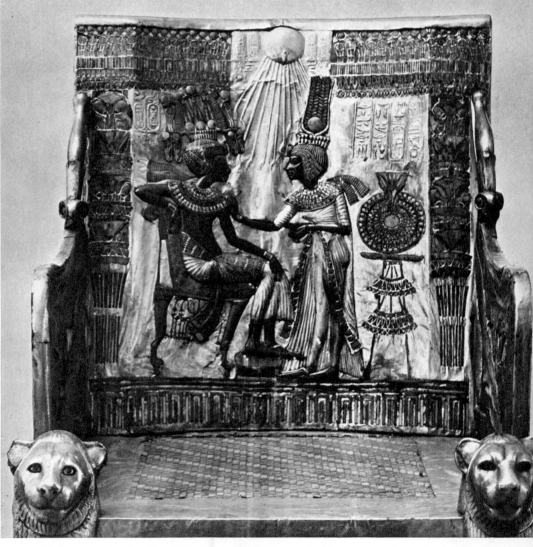

85. Throne of King Tutankhamen and His Queen Ankhesenamen (rear view), from the Tomb of Tutankhamen, Valley of the Kings. c. 1355–1342 B.C. Carved wood covered with gold and inlaid with faience, glass paste, semiprecious stones, and silver, height of throne 41″. Egyptian Museum, Cairo

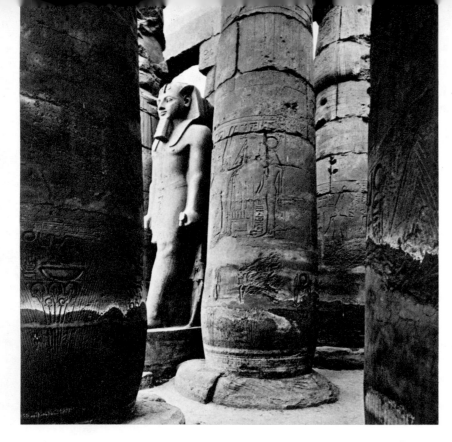

86. *Ramses II.* c. 1290 B.C.
Stone. Luxor

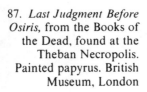

87. *Last Judgment Before
Osiris,* from the Books of
the Dead, found at the
Theban Necropolis.
Painted papyrus. British
Museum, London

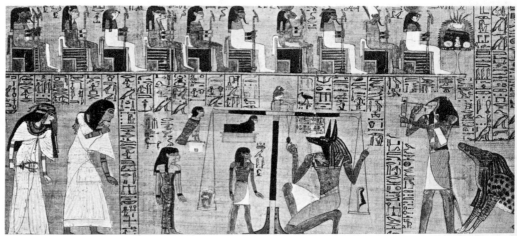

the best preserved of all major Egyptian temples, still retaining the stone roof over its great hall. Its traditional pylons, terminated by simple, crisp moldings, are punctuated by recessed shafts for flagpoles and decorated with beautifully incised reliefs showing the (Greek!) pharaoh before Horus.

We cannot leave the Egyptians without a word about another of their inventions, the illuminated manuscript. These illustrated books were written and painted on rolls of papyrus, a surface made from the thin-shaved pith of the papyrus plant, glued together to form a continuous sheet. The most important of these are the so-called Books of the Dead, collections of prayers for the protection of the deceased during his perilous adventures in the other world. The best-known scene in every Book of the

Dead is the dramatic moment (fig. 87) when, below a formidable lineup of enthroned gods, the heart of the dead man (who is the little human-headed hawk just above the heart toward the left) is weighed against a feather. Luckily, it has just balanced, or he would have been thrown to the crocodile-hyena-hippopotamus hungrily awaiting him at the right.

While the great architectural and figurative achievements of the Egyptians are often considered preparations for those of the Greeks, the Books of the Dead prefigure the illuminated manuscripts that form such an important part of medieval culture, and the weighing of the dead man's heart is a forerunner of the Christian Last Judgment. But we would do better to enjoy the beauties of Egyptian art for themselves.

2

Mesopotamian Art

Roughly parallel with the civilization of Egypt, another, in some ways equally great, historic culture was developing in the region of the Near East known as Mesopotamia, from the Greek word meaning *land between the rivers*. Traversed by the almost parallel courses of the Tigris to the northeast and the Euphrates to the southwest, this fertile valley was as attractive to ancient peoples as that of the Nile. But unity, stability, and permanence, the three foundation stones of Egyptian culture, were denied by nature to Mesopotamia. The narrow ribbon of the Nile Valley was protected from all but the best-organized invaders by the natural barriers of the Libyan and Arabian deserts, and the placid Nile itself formed a splendid means of communication between all parts of the realm, facilitating unified control. The broad valley of the two turbulent rivers, on the contrary, was open to invasion from all directions and had no easy means of internal communication. Consequently, the natural shape for human communities to assume was that of a city-state in the middle of supporting territory rather than a unified nation. Mesopotamian cities were under frequent and repeated siege from their neighbors or from foreign invaders, and had to be heavily fortified. Nevertheless, Mesopotamian texts tell us of the continual destruction of these cities and of the removal of their power to other centers.

The climate itself, as compared to the rainless warmth that favored Egypt, watered only by its friendly river, was often hostile. Mesopotamia is subject to sharp contrasts of heat and cold, flood and drought, as well as to violent storms that parallel in the realm of nature the endemic conflicts between human communities. Not surprisingly, little attention seems to have been paid by Mesopotamian cultures to the afterlife, so important to the Egyptians. Security in this life, which except for the intermediate periods of disorder was taken for granted throughout Egypt's long history, could be achieved in Mesopotamia only by strenuous and concerted efforts, and was at best unpredictable. Propitiation of the deities who personified the mysterious and often menacing forces of nature was essential. At the opening of recorded history, the city-state was organized around the service of a local deity, who could intervene for its protection in the councils of heaven. The central temple controlled much economic activity, and shops and offices were grouped around it. Writing, laboriously taught in the earliest recorded schools, was accomplished by means of pressing the sharpened end of a reed into clay tablets to make cuneiform (wedge-shaped) marks. Originally pictographs, these soon became ideographs, paralleling the hieroglyphs of Egypt. The tablets, which have been found by the thousands in Mesopotamian excavations, permit the reconstruction of economic and social life in the early theocracies down to the minutest details.

Elected rulers (the Sumerian word *Lugal* means merely *great man*) rapidly assumed authority in their own right as kings and aspired to the control of neighboring states and eventually of the entire region, even of those outlying areas that produced the raw materials required by the economy of the state. Mesopotamian history is, in consequence, a bewilderingly complex succession of conquests and defeats, of rises and falls, of city-states and eventually of hastily conquered empires with universal pretensions, which melted away after a century or so of power, sometimes after only a few decades. Any attempt, therefore, to give an orderly account of the welter of conflicting societies in the Mesopotamian world is sure to be an oversimplification. As in Egypt, the basic ethnic structure of Mesopotamian civilization was not unified. One people, the Sumerians, apparently entered the region from the mountains to the north, but their exact origin is as mysterious as their language, which is not inflected and bears no relation to any other. The Sumerians in turn were conquered by the Akkadians, Semitic invaders from the west, but eventually Sumerian culture was adopted by the conquerors. Regardless of the ethnic origin of any Mesopotamian peoples, however, certain essentials characterize Mesopotamian cities for about three thousand years.

First, the central temple was invariably raised on a platform above the level of the surrounding town. Generally, the temple consisted of a series of superimposed solid structures forming a broadly based tower or artificial mountain known as a ziggurat, on the summit of which propitiatory ceremonies to the gods of nature took place. These ziggurats, the one best known to us being, of course, the Tower of Babel (Babylon), represented an immense communal effort and were visible for great distances across the Mesopotamian plain. They clearly symbolized man's attempt to reach the celestial deities and, during heavy weather with low-hanging clouds, may often have appeared to succeed. One should recall that according to the Greeks the gods dwelt on Mount Olympus, and that Moses went to the top of Mount Sinai for his conversations with the Almighty. Even in the later period of empires, the royal palace in Mesopotamia always contained a ziggurat.

Second, there were no local supplies of stone, so architecture in the manner of the Egyptian pyramids, tombs, and temples was out of the question. Mud brick, sometimes reinforced by timber, was the basic material for all Mesopotamian buildings, as it had been for the ephemeral dwellings of the Egyptians (see page 55). Although fired brick was sometimes used as a facing for Mesopotamian structures, most of them survive only in ground plan or in foundations, when these could be built of imported stone. Even sculpture, forced to rely on materials brought from a distance, was limited to modest dimensions, save for the ambitious palace decorations of the Assyrians, who lived in a northern region closer to a supply of stone. Under such circumstances neither architecture nor sculpture could be expected to function on the exalted level of Egyptian art, with its endless sources of material and its continuous artistic tradition,

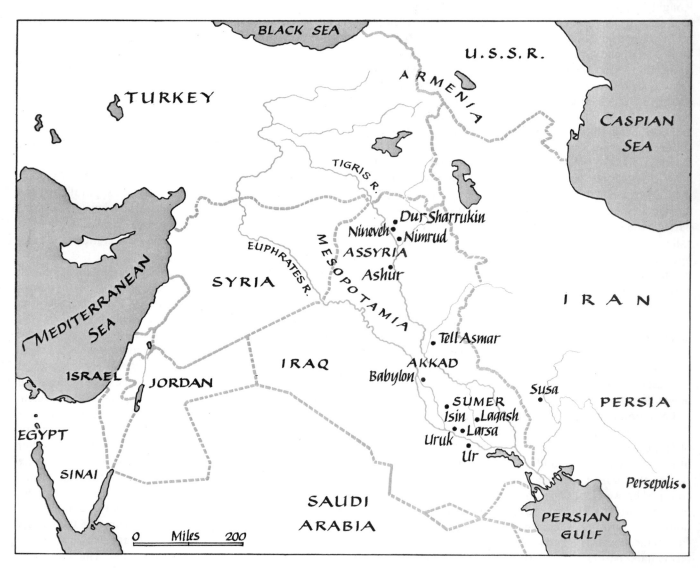

MAP 6. *Mesopotamia and Persia*

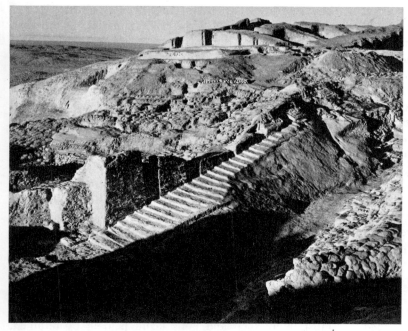

88. The White Temple on its Ziggurat. c. 3500–3000 B.C.
Uruk (present-day Warka, Iraq)

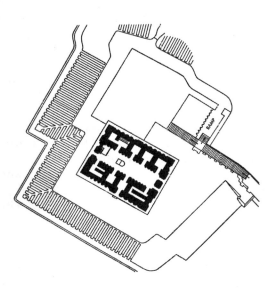

89. Plan of the White Temple on its
Ziggurat (after H. Frankfort)

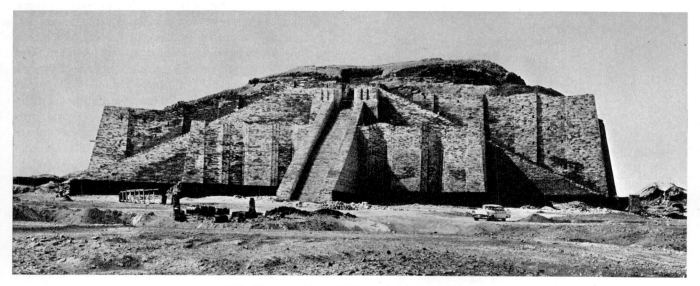

90. Ziggurat, Ur. c. 2100 B.C. Brickwork. Iraq

but Mesopotamia did achieve some brilliant creations of its own.

Third, and this is truly surprising, paintings, even traces of paintings, are extremely rare in Mesopotamian culture before Assyria. This deficiency cannot be easily explained, since the materials were at hand and the immense wall surfaces would seem to have invited pictorial imagery.

SUMER

The earliest of the ziggurats to survive was built in the land of Sumer at Uruk (biblical Erech, modern Warka) on the banks of the Euphrates in southern Mesopotamia between 3500 and 3000 B.C., and dedicated to the sky god Anu (figs. 88, 89). It is older than any known Egyptian monument. The building owes its partial preservation to having been enclosed in a far later Hellenistic sanctuary. The mound was so oriented as to direct the corners toward the four points of the compass, and was sheathed by sloping brick walls so as to form a gigantic oblong platform, standing some forty feet above the level of the surrounding plain. On this terrace stood a small whitewashed brick temple (nicknamed the White Temple), only the lower portions of which remain. Curiously enough, the entrances do not face the steep stairway ascending the mound, and the altar is tucked into a corner of the interior, possibly for protection from wind. The buttressed walls were reinforced by timber, but it is not known just how the building was roofed. Since the Sumerian name for such temples means *waiting room*, the enclosure may well have provided a setting in which the worshipers could await the descent of the deity.

The better preserved and considerably larger ziggurat at Ur (fig. 90), near the confluence of the Tigris and the Euphrates, was built much later, during the so-called Neo-Sumerian period, when the Sumerians temporarily regained power after the collapse of the Akkadian Empire, about 2100 B.C. Three stairways, each of a hundred steps, converge at the top of the first platform; others ascended a second and then a third level, on which stood the temple. The remaining masses of brickwork, recently somewhat restored, dominate the plain for many miles. The original monument, perhaps planted with trees and other vegetation, must have made a majestic setting for religious ceremonials.

Two pieces of sculpture from Uruk, dating from the period of the White Temple, give us some insight into the character of these ceremonies. A superb alabaster vase (fig. 91) some three feet in height was probably intended to hold libations in honor of E-anna, the goddess of fertility and love. The cylindrical surface of the vase, only slightly swelling toward the top, is divided into four

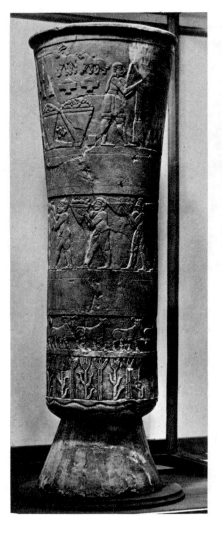

91. Sculptured vase, from Uruk. c. 3500–3000 B.C. Alabaster, height 36". Iraq Museum, Baghdad

bands of low relief celebrating her cult. In the lowest, date palms alternate with stalks of barley; in the next, ewes with rams; the third tier shows naked worshipers bringing baskets of fruit and other offerings; and the fourth the crowned goddess receiving a worshiper whose basket is brimming with fruit. (Nakedness survives in the Christian tradition that all will be naked before God at the Last Judgment; see fig. 396; Vol. 2, fig. 181.) Some of the strength of the composition derives from the alternation, from one level to the next, of the directions in which the bands of figures are moving; some derives from the sturdy proportions and simple carving of the stocky figures. Their representation is governed by conventions not unlike those of Egyptian art; the entire torso is seen in three-quarter view even though the legs and heads are in profile.

E-anna herself may be the subject of the beautiful *Female Head* (fig. 92) carved from white marble. It was probably intended to surmount a wooden statue. Originally, the eyes were filled with colored material, most likely shell and lapis lazuli held in by bitumen, which would have made the magical stare even more intense. The eyebrows were probably inlaid with bitumen and the hair plated with gold. Even in its present stripped condition, the contrast between the enormous eyes and the sensitively modeled surfaces of the delicate mouth and chin renders the head unforgettable. A much later assemblage of small marble statues (fig. 93) from the sanctuary of Abu, god of vegetation, at Tell Asmar shows the hypnotic effect of these great, staring eyes in Sumerian religious sculpture when the shell and lapis lazuli inlays (in this case, shell and black limestone) are still preserved. Grouped before the altar, the statues seem to be solemnly awaiting the divine presence. It is thought that the largest figures represent the god, whose emblem is inscribed on its base, and his spouse, but more probably they are meant to be the king and queen, since their hands are folded in prayer like those of the smaller figures. Their cylindrical shape, characteristic of Mesopotamian figures, is far removed from the cubic mass of Egyptian statues, which preserve the shape of the original block of stone.

Some of the splendor of a Sumerian court can be imagined from the gorgeous harp found in the tomb of Pu-abi, queen of Ur (colorplate 11). The strings and wooden portions have been restored, but the gold-covered posts and the bull's head, with its human beard of lapis lazuli, are original; so are the four narrative scenes on the sound box, inlaid in gold, lapis lazuli, and shell (fig. 94). The bearded bull is a royal symbol throughout Mesopotamian art (also, recall the bull on the early Egyptian palette in fig. 46). Intensely real, the animal with its wide-open eyes and alert ears seems to be listening to the music. The uppermost scene on the sound box, showing a naked man wrestling two bearded bulls, all of whom stare out at us vacantly, and the lowest, a scorpion-man

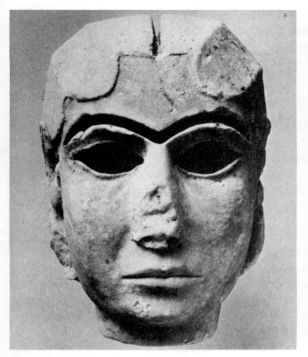

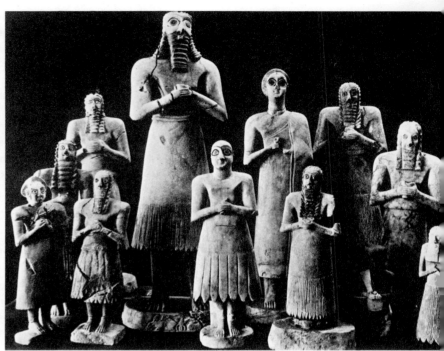

92. *Female Head*, from Uruk. c. 3500–3000 B.C. White marble, height c. 8″. Iraq Museum, Baghdad

93. Statues from the Abu Temple, Tell Asmar. c. 2700–2500 B.C. Marble with shell and black limestone inlay, height of tallest figure c. 30″. Iraq Museum, Baghdad, and The Oriental Institute, University of Chicago

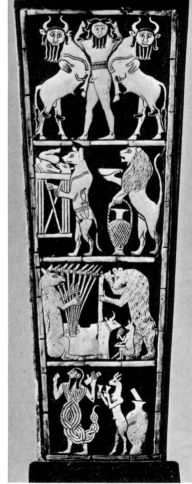

attended by a goat bearing libation cups, come from the epic of Gilgamesh, the half-historical, half-legendary hero. But the two incidents between are, alas, not so easy to trace. In one a table heaped with a boar's head and a sheep's head and leg is carried by a solicitous wolf with a carving knife tucked into its belt, followed by a lion bearing a wine jug and cup; in the other a donkey plays a bull-harp while a bear beats time and a jackal brandishes a rattle and beats a drum. Possibly these human-handed beasts come from some Sumerian legend yet unknown, but they suggest with perhaps illusory ease the tradition of animal fables known to us in every era from the days of Aesop to those of *Peter Rabbit*.

That such representations may contain a far deeper meaning than we tend to give them is suggested by the splendid goat, made of wood overlaid with gold and lapis lazuli, also found in the royal graves at Ur (fig. 95). We know from contemporary representations on the stone seals used to imprint clay tablets that this is the kind of offering stand customarily set before the male fertility god Tammuz. The he-goat, proverbial symbol of masculinity, stands proudly erect before a gold tree, forelegs bent, eyes glaring outward with great intensity. The artist has executed every lock and every leaf with crispness and elegance. Descendants of such symbolic animals persist in heraldry even into modern times and are still endowed with allegorical significance.

A grim reminder of the impermanence of Mesopotamian society is given by the *Stele of King Eannatum* (fig. 96), found at Lagash, the modern Tello. This boundary stone is also called the *Stele of the Vultures*. In the upper

94. Sound box of the Royal Harp, from the Tomb of Queen Puabi, Ur. c. 2685 B.C. Wood with inlaid gold, lapis lazuli, and shell. University Museum, University of Pennsylvania, Philadelphia. See Colorplate 11

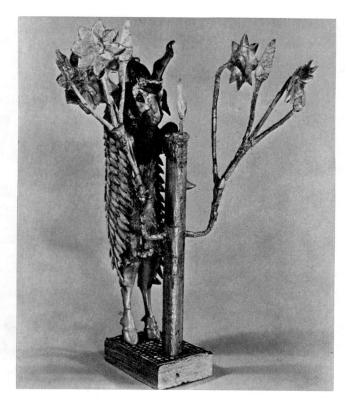

95. He-Goat, from Ur. c. 2600 B.C. Wood overlaid with gold and lapis lazuli, height 20″. University Museum, University of Pennsylvania, Philadelphia

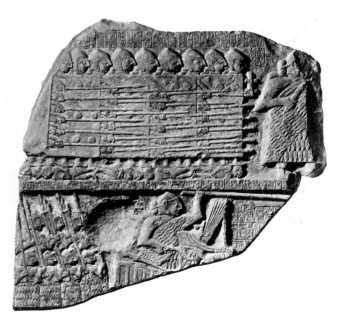

96. *Stele of King Eannatum (Stele of the Vultures),* from Lagash (present-day Tello). c. 2560 B.C. Limestone, height 71″. The Louvre, Paris

register the king, conqueror of both Ur and Uruk, leads a phalanx into battle. He is clad in goatskins and carries a mace. The battalion is represented symbolically by a solid block of four shields originally surmounted by nine identical helmeted heads. From each shield protrude six spears, one above the other, each held by a pair of hands; below the shields a steady row of feet tramples a shapeless mass of prone naked bodies. In the broken lower register the king in his chariot, his cuiver bristling with arrows, leads light infantry into battle. To modern eyes accustomed to mechanized warfare, this relentless and inhuman attack is all too familiar.

AKKAD (c. 2340–2180 B.C.)

Such endemic warfare was to be followed by something far worse, the virtual collapse of the Sumerian social order under the weight of entirely new conceptions of divine monarchy, like that of Old Kingdom Egypt but maintained wholly by force of arms. A Semitic ruler, Sargon I, usurped the throne of Kish and then ruled for fifty-six years from neighboring Akkad, whose site has not yet been discovered. Sargon founded a dynasty of five kings who aspired to world conquest and in fact controlled the Middle East from the Mediterranean Sea to the Persian Gulf. The magnificent bronze *Head of an Akkadian Ruler* (fig. 97) is so great a work of art that it makes us regret that so little survives from the days of these Akkadian monarchs save the literary texts in which their power and majesty were extolled. Even in the absence of the eyes, gouged out long ago, the head is overwhelming. The hair, braided and bound to form a kind of diadem, is gathered in a chignon on the neck. The face is half hidden in a beard whose two superimposed tiers of curls, each made up of spirals moving in the opposite direction to those in the tier below, exert an almost dizzying effect on the beholder by their blend of formal grandeur and linear delicacy. The great, flaring eyebrows plunge in convergence upon an aquiline nose below which the sensual lips are held quietly in a superb double curve of arrogant power not to be approached again until the greatest of Greek and Roman sculpture. The identity of this monarch is unknown, but it is hard to believe that the great Sargon looked much different.

The only other work of art of first importance remaining from Akkadian rule also exudes an emotional violence that makes Sumerian art look bland in contrast. The sandstone *Stele of King Naram Sin* (fig. 98), Sargon's grandson, shows him protected by the luminaries of heaven and about to dispatch the last of his enemies. The king stands proudly beside the sacred mountain, mace in hand. One crumpled enemy attempts in agony to pluck the spear from his throat, another pleads for his life, two others hang over the edge of a cliff down which still another falls headlong. Meanwhile, up the ascending levels of the landscape stride the victorious soldiers of the king. The tremendous drama of this relief,

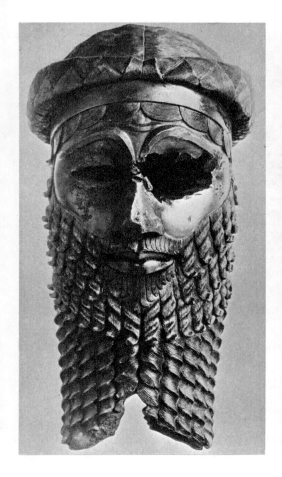

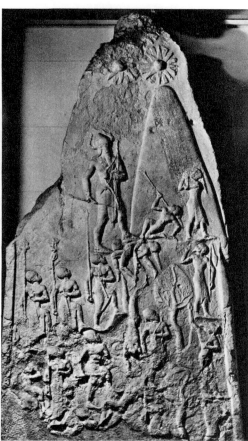

97. *Head of an Akkadian Ruler,*
from Nineveh. c. 2300–2200 B.C.
Bronze, height 14⅜". Iraq
Museum, Baghdad

98. *Stele of King Naram Sin,*
from Susa, Iran.
c. 2300–2200 B.C.
Sandstone, height 78".
The Louvre, Paris

the strength of the projection of the sculptural figures, and the freedom with which they move at various heights within the landscape space give the stele a unique position in Mesopotamian art.

Akkad, which lived by the sword, perished by it as well. A powerful people called the Guti invaded Mesopotamia from the mountainous regions to the northeast, conquered the Akkadian Empire, and utterly destroyed its capital, only to pass into history without positive achievements. Ironically, the proud *Stele of King Naram Sin* was carried off as booty.

NEO-SUMER AND BABYLON (c. 2125–1750 B.C.)

Only the city-state of Lagash mysteriously escaped the general devastation wrought by the Guti, and its ruler, Gudea, interpreted this deliverance as a sign of divine favor. In gratitude he dedicated a number of votive statues of himself, all carved either from diorite or from dolerite, imported stones of great hardness, as gifts to temples in his small realm. All the Gudea statues radiate a sense of calm, even of wisdom. Holding a plan of a building on his lap, Gudea sits quietly with hands folded (fig. 99). Only the tension of the toes and the arm muscles betrays his inner feelings kept in check by control of the will. The surviving heads (fig. 100), often crowned with what appears to be a lambskin cap, show this same

beautiful composure, expressed artistically in the broad curves of the brows and the smooth volumes of the cheeks and chin, handled with firmness and accuracy. While less dramatic than the *Akkadian Ruler,* the modest Gudea portraits achieve real nobility of form and content.

Remarkably enough, Gudea was able to win control by peaceful means over a considerable region of the former Akkadian Empire. In 211, Urnammu, governor of Ur, usurped the monarchy of Sumer and Akkad and built the great ziggurat at Ur (see fig. 90). Little else of artistic merit survives from his reign, after which Mesopotamia reverted to its former chaotic pattern of conflicting city-states. From the brief Isin-Larsa period (2025–1763 B.C.), so called from the ascendancy of the cities bearing these names, dates a terra-cotta relief of extraordinary power and beauty, the first voluptuous female nude known from antiquity (fig. 101). This creature, at once alluring and frightening, represents the goddess of death, the baleful Lilith, possibly the screech owl of Isa. 34: 14. Adorned only with gigantic earrings and the characteristic four-tiered headdress of a deity, she smilingly upholds a looped cord that passes behind her head—either the symbol of human life or the instrument with which she brings it to an end. Her great wings are partially spread behind her full-breasted, round-hipped body. Instead of feet she has terrible feathered talons; flanked by staring owls, she

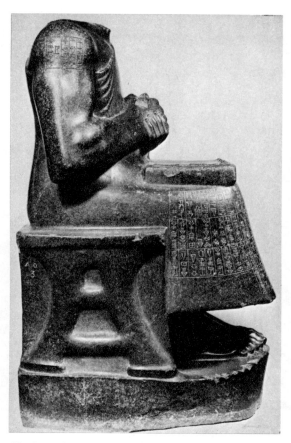

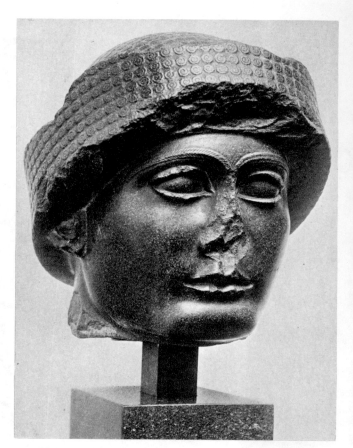

99. Seated statue of Gudea with architectural plan, from Lagash. c. 2150 B.C. Diorite, height 29". The Louvre, Paris

100. *Head of Gudea*, from Lagash. c. 2150 B.C. Diorite, height 9". Museum of Fine Arts, Boston

perches upon the rumps of two lions back to back. Originally, her body was painted red, one owl black and the other red, and the manes of the lions black. The setting is established by the pattern of scales along the base, a conventionalization of the sacred mountain.

The great king Hammurabi (1792–1750 B.C.) briefly brought all of Mesopotamia under the rule of Babylon and reduced its various and often conflicting legal systems to a unified code; this code is inscribed on a tall stele of black basalt at whose summit Hammurabi, in a simple and noble relief (fig. 102), stands before the throne of the god Shamash, again on a sacred mountain indicated by the customary scale pattern. Wearing the same four-tiered headdress as Lilith and with triple flames emerging from his shoulders, this magnificent being extends his symbols of power, a rod and a ring. At first sight prosaic, this elemental colloquy between man and god becomes grander as one watches; like Moses on Mount Sinai, the king talks familiarly with the deity who sanctifies his laws. The cylindrical figures typical of early Mesopotamian art are conventionalized in pose, as indeed they are throughout pre-Greek art, so that the torso is shown frontally while the hips and legs, insofar as they can be seen within the enveloping drapery, are depicted in profile. For the first time, however, the eyes are not frontal; the gaze between man and god is direct and unswerving.

About 1595 B.C., the Babylonian kingdom was conquered by the Hittites, a people from Anatolia. The sturdy, virile art of the Hittites is seldom of a quality to compete with the best of Mesopotamian art, but the rude and massive lions (c. 1400 B.C.) that flank the entrance to the gigantic stone walls of the Hittite citadel near modern Boğazköy (fig. 103) are the ancestors of the winged beasts that guard the portals of the palaces of the Assyrian kings. It is interesting that after the death of Tutankhamen, the Hittites were so powerful in the Middle East that Ankhesenamen, the distraught widow of the young pharaoh, besought the Hittite king Suppiluliuma I for the hand of one of his sons in marriage as protection.

ASSYRIA (c. 1000–612 B.C.)

In the welter of warring peoples—including the Elamites, Kassites, and Mitannians—who disputed with each other for the succession to Babylonian and Hittite power, a single warlike nation called the Assyrians, after their original home at Ashur on the Tigris River in northern Mesopotamia, was both skillful and ruthless enough to gain eventual ascendancy over the entire region. In fact, for a considerable period their power extended to the west over Syria, the Sinai Peninsula, and into Lower Egypt, where they destroyed Memphis, and to the north into the mountains of Armenia. The Assyrians gloried in

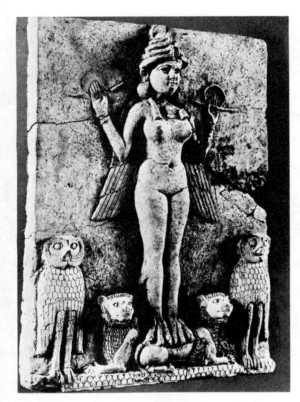

101. *The Goddess Lilith.* c. 2025–1763 B.C. Terra-cotta relief, height 19⅝". Collection Colonel Norman Colville, United Kingdom

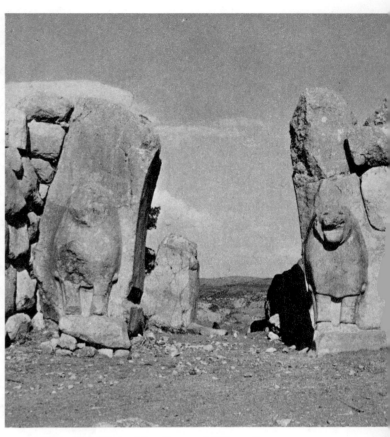

103. *The Hittite Lion Gate.* c. 1400 B.C. Stone. Bogazköy, Turkey

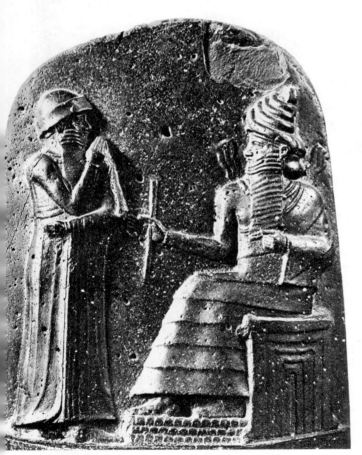

102. Stele with the Code of Hammurabi (upper portion). c. 1792–1750 B.C. Basalt, height of relief 28"; height of stele 84". The Louvre, Paris

what from their voluminous historical records and their art seems to have been very nearly continuous warfare, mercilessly destroying conquered populations along with their cities before they in turn were vanquished and their own cities razed to the ground.

Only one of the great Assyrian royal residences is known in some detail, the eighth-century palace of King Sargon II at Dur Sharrukin, the modern Khorsabad, which has been systematically excavated (fig. 104). This massive structure was built into the perimeter of a citadel some five hundred feet square, which was in turn incorporated into the city wall. The entire complex was laid out as symmetrically as possible in the absence of material on which to draw precise plans (fig. 105). Above a network of courtyards on either side surrounded by administrative buildings, barracks, and warehouses rose a platform the height of the city wall. On this eminence stood the palace proper, protruding from the wall into the surrounding plain, so that the king and the court could survey the countryside from its ramparts. It was defended by its own towers. The entire complex was dominated by a lofty ziggurat, descendant of those at Uruk and at Ur (see figs. 88, 90) and doubtless intended for a similar purpose. It was, however, much more carefully formalized. Its successive stages—there may have been seven of these, each painted a different color—were not separate platforms; the structure was

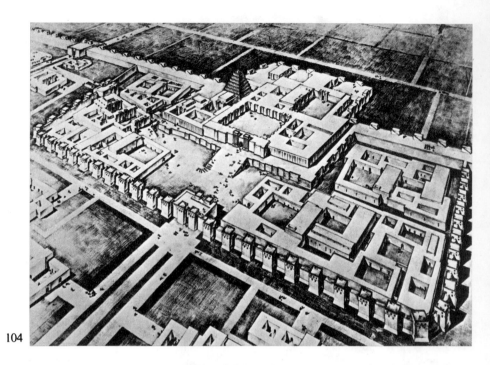

104. Citadel of King Sargon II, Dur Sharrukin (present-day Khorsabad, Iraq). c. 742–706 B.C. (Architectural reconstruction by Charles Altman)

105. Plan of the Citadel of King Sargon II

106. Gate of the Citadel of King Sargon II (during excavation). Limestone

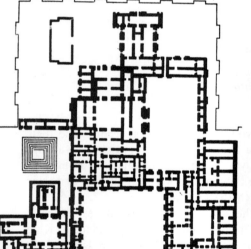

105

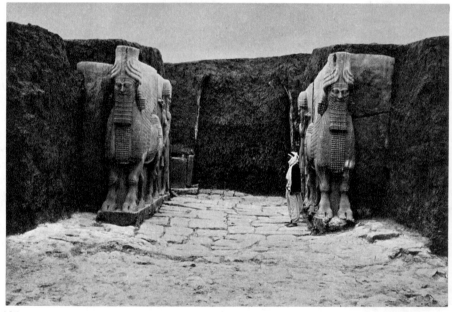

106

ascended counterclockwise by a continuous ramp, a square spiral as it were, so that the worshiper always had the paneled wall on his left while on his right he looked out over ever-widening views of the plain.

Like all Mesopotamian buildings, the palace of Sargon II was mostly built of mud brick (although certain crucial portions were faced by baked and glazed brick), which accounts for the ease of its demolition by the next wave of invaders. Considerable use seems to have been made of arches and barrel vaults. Luckily, the Assyrians had access to stone for sculpture, and they were able to flank the entrances to the brightly painted throne room with colossal limestone guardians, in the tradition of the Hittite lions (see fig. 103). Two of these majestic creatures are shown still in place (fig. 106). They were monstrous beings with the bodies of bulls (one recalls the royal bulls of archaic Egyptian palettes, figs. 46, 48), grand, diagonally elevated wings, and human heads with long curly beards and many-tiered divine headdresses (compare figs. 97, 107), doubtless symbols of the supernatural powers of the king. Built into the gates and visible only from two sides, they were really a kind of relief sculpture rather than statues in the round. So that the viewer might see four legs from any point of view, the sculptors generously provided these creatures with five.

Sargon II himself can be seen in a superb limestone relief (fig. 107) from the Dur Sharrukin palace, possibly intended to recall the bronze *Head of an Akkadian Ruler* (see fig. 97) but lacking its calm majesty. There is an almost hysterical intensity about the flare of the eyelids and eyebrows and the cruel set of the narrow lips, increased by the ornamental curves of the sharply separated forms characteristic of the stylization of Assyrian relief sculpture throughout its brief history.

Emissaries of friendly or tributary rulers could attain the presence of the monarch only through a succession of halls whose walls were lined with continuous reliefs intended to overawe the visitors not only with the king's intimacy with the gods but also with his military exploits and personal courage. These historical reliefs are ancestors of the lengthy political narratives of Roman imperial sculpture (see figs. 277, 278). In continuous strips, often superimposed in the manner of Egyptian tomb reliefs, the Assyrians can be seen fighting battles that they always win and cheerfully burning cities, dismantling the fortifications, and slaughtering the inhabitants. The reliefs were drawn on the surface of alabaster slabs and the background was then cut away to give just a slight projection, as in Egyptian relief. Yet the contours are so bold and so strongly ornamentalized and the proportions are so chunky that they convey an impression of massive volume instead of Egyptian delicacy and elegance. The innumerable scenes of unrelieved mayhem can become monotonous, especially because the quality of the reliefs, which were apparently turned out at some speed, is not uniformly high. But there were great sculptors in the group who could find in their narrative subjects inspiration for an epic breadth of vision entirely new in art. Sometimes the scenes have an unconscious humor, as in *Elamite Fugitives Crossing a River* (fig. 108), from the palace of Ashurnasirpal II at Nimrud. Two Assyrian bowmen shoot from the bank at two fully clothed Elamites who cling to inflated goatskins and at a third who has to rely entirely on his own strength to stay afloat as they swim toward the walls of their little city, defended by Elamite warriors on the tops of the towers.

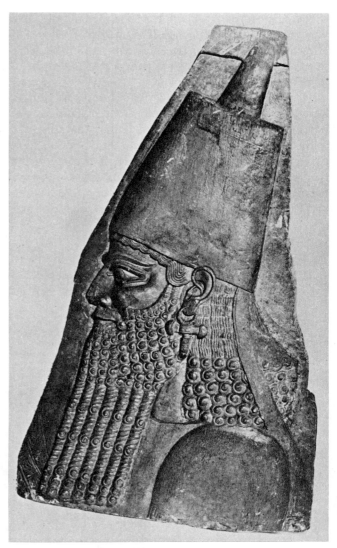

107. Portrait of King Sargon II, from Dur Sharrukin. Limestone relief, height 35″. Museo Egizio, Turin, Italy

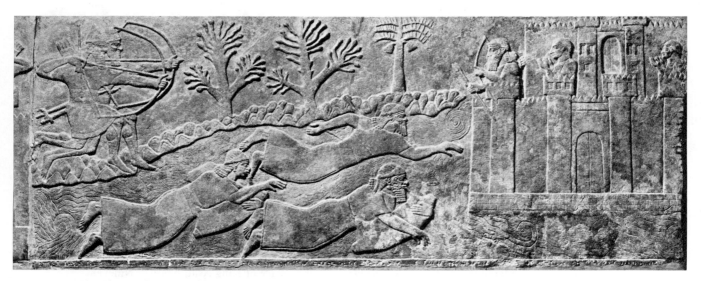

108. *Elamite Fugitives Crossing a River,* from the Palace of King Ashurnasirpal II, Nimrud. c. 883–859 B.C. Alabaster relief. British Museum, London

In the manner of Egyptian reliefs and paintings, the swimmers have two left hands. The undulating shapes of the swimmers and the ornamentalized trees on the bank create the strong and effective pattern characteristic of the best Assyrian relief.

Strangely enough, while human expressions remain impassive under any conditions, those of animals are represented with a depth of understanding that turns the conflicts between men and beasts into the grandest action scenes in Mesopotamian art—in fact, into some of the most powerful in the entire history of art. Lions were released from their cages, after having been goaded into fury, so that the king could display his strength and courage by shooting down the maddened beasts from his chariot. The best sculptors seem to have been employed for these heroic reliefs, which unleash an astonishing explosion of forces—the swift flight of the horses, the resolute power of the monarch, the snarling rage of the tormented beasts. Not since archaic Egypt (see fig. 46) have the muscles of humans and animals been shown swelling with such tremendous tension as in the relief depicting Ashurnasirpal engaged in his cruel sport (fig. 109). Almost unbearable in its tragic intensity is the detail of the *Dying Lioness* from the palace of Ashurbanipal at Nineveh (fig. 110). Pierced by three arrows, bleeding profusely, and howling in impotent defeat, the

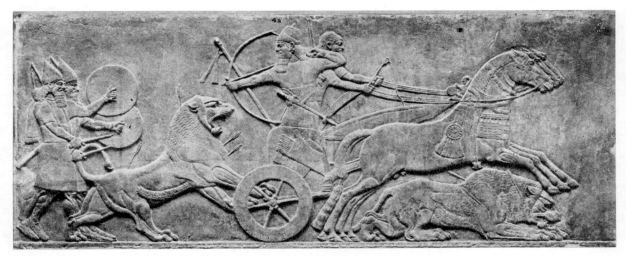

109. *King Ashurnasirpal II Killing Lions*, from the Palace, Nimrud. c. 883–859 B.C. Alabaster relief, 39 x 100". British Museum, London

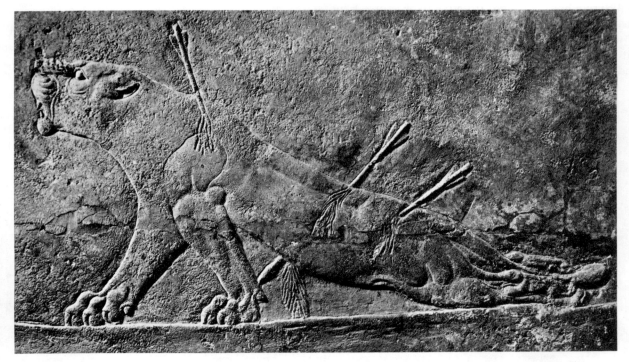

110. *Dying Lioness* (detail of *The Great Lion Hunt*), from the Palace of King Ashurbanipal, Nineveh. c. 668–627 B.C. Alabaster relief. British Museum, London

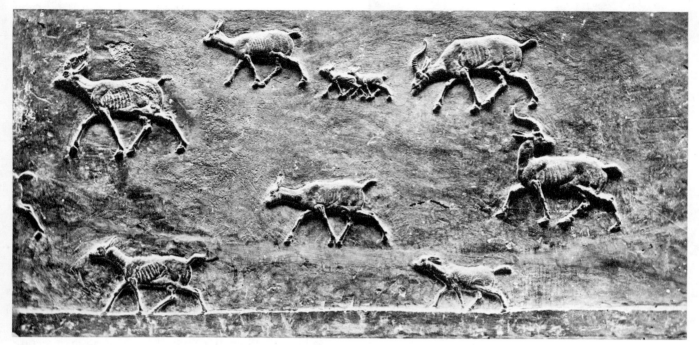

111. *Herd of Fleeing Gazelles* (portion of relief), from the Palace of King Ashurbanipal, Nineveh. c. 668–627 B.C. Alabaster, height 20⅞". British Museum, London

poor beast drags her paralyzed hindquarters desperately along. After these horrors the relief of a flock of gazelles from the same palace (fig. 111) is totally unexpected in its airy grace. One turns his head in fear, the others plod along, the little ones struggling to keep up, as they flee their archenemy, man. Equally surprising is the device of scattering the animals lightly about the surface of the slab to suggest open space.

NEO-BABYLONIA (605–539 B.C.)

The collapse of Assyria in 612 B.C. was brought about by invasions of Scythians from the east and Medes from the north. Order was restored by Nebuchadnezzar II, ruling from Babylon in the south, which had never lost its cultural importance even under Assyrian domination. In the scanty remains of Neo-Babylonian stone sculpture an attempt can be discerned to emulate the style of Sargon I, some eleven hundred years earlier, but the brief revival of Babylonian glory is best known for its architectural remains. For two hundred years or so Babylon had possessed the Hanging Gardens, one of the wonders of the ancient world, a series of four brick terraces rising above the Euphrates, whose waters were piped up to irrigate a splendid profusion of flowering trees, shrubs, and herbs. Nebuchadnezzar added a splendid palace with a ziggurat, which was the biblical Tower of Babel, and built eight monumental arched gates in the fortified city walls. One gate, connected with the inner city by a processional way and dedicated to the goddess Ishtar, was faced with glazed brick (fig. 112). Excavated early in this century, it is installed, with missing portions liberally supplied, in East Berlin, the only place in the world where one can gain any idea of the scale and brilliance of the ephemeral brick architecture of ancient Mesopotamia.

The clear, bright blue of the background glaze sets off the geometric ornament in white and gold and the widely spaced, stylized bulls and dragons in raised relief. They are composed of many separately molded and glazed bricks, and form a happy postlude to the interminable slaughters of the bloodthirsty Assyrians. Nebuchadnezzar's gorgeous Babylon must have deserved the boastful title he gave it—"navel of the world."

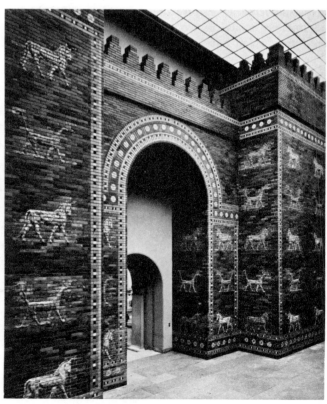

112. The Ishtar Gate (restored), from Babylon. c. 575 B.C. Glazed brick, height 47'. Staatliche Museen, Berlin

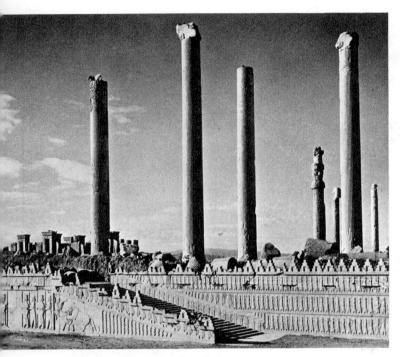

113. Audience Hall of Darius and Xerxes. c. 500 B.C.
Persepolis, Iran

PERSIA (539-331 B.C.)

We obtain a one-sided account of the Persian Empire from the history of the Greeks, to whom the Persians appeared as a juggernaut threatening to crush the cherished independence of the Greek city-states. The tidy administration of the Persians may in fact have come as a relief to the weary peoples of the Near East. Out of the mountainous regions of what is today Iran, northeast of Mesopotamia, came the nomadic Persians under Cyrus the Great; under his successors Darius I and Xerxes I they conquered an empire that was centered on Mesopotamia but included also Syria, Asia Minor, and Egypt on one side and parts of India on the other. Although they set themselves up as kings of Babylon they styled

themselves, and quite rightly, kings of the world. Only the Greeks prevented them from extending their rule into Europe, and the Greeks, under Alexander the Great, eventually brought about their downfall. Their orderly and decent government made cruelties like those of the Assyrians unnecessary. The Persian Empire, more than twice as extensive as any of its predecessors, was divided into provinces called satrapies, administered by governors, or satraps, responsible directly to the king. The capital moved about, but the great palace of the kings was at Persepolis, near the edge of the mountains above the Persian Gulf, to the east of Mesopotamia.

There Darius commenced his residence, continued and completed by his son Xerxes about 500 B.C.; it was an orderly and systematic complex of buildings and courts surrounded by the inevitable, and now vanished, mud-brick wall. Persian art, perhaps not as imaginative as some that preceded it, included many elements borrowed from the subject peoples; in fact, many of the artisans were Babylonians, and others were Greeks from Asia Minor. The Persians worshiped the god of light, Ahura-mazda, at outdoor fire altars for which no architecture was needed, so there were no ziggurats. But the palace was built like that of Sargon II on a huge platform, this time of stone, quite well preserved (fig. 113). The king had no need to terrify his visitors, so the relief sculpture showed interminable superimposed rows of neatly uniformed bodyguards mounting the steps, as in reality they did, and the great king himself giving audience (fig. 114). For the first time, relief in the Near East was not just surface drawing with the background cut away, but was so carved as to give the impression that actual figures, having cylindrical volume, move on a shallow stage. This idea was derived from Greek art, and the sculptors may have been Ionian Greeks. The statue-like figures are shown in true profile, although the eyes are still frontal. The prim rows of curls in hair and beard are obviously

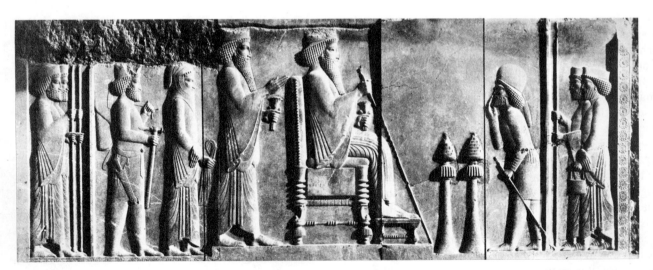

114. *Darius and Xerxes Giving Audience.* c. 490 B.C. Limestone relief, height 100″. Persepolis, Iran

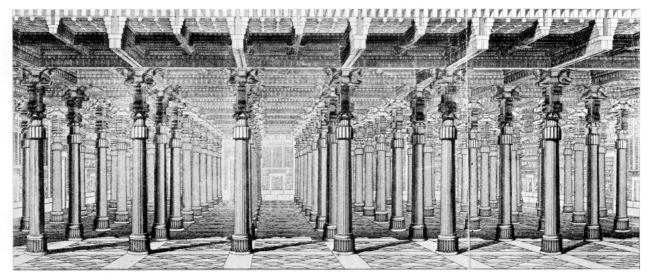

115. Xerxes' Hall of 100 Columns, Persepolis. (Architectural reconstruction by C. Chipiez)

derived from Akkadian and Assyrian forebears, but the drapery folds now have edges that ripple in long, descending cataracts as in archaic Greek sculpture (cf. fig. 149), and the garments clearly show underlying limbs, as in Old Kingdom Egyptian sculpture (fig. 63). In a civilization like that of the Persians, individualization was not encouraged, but there is a crisp, fresh elegance of drawing and carving that gives Persian decorative sculpture great distinction. It was doubtless even more striking with its original brilliant colors and gilding.

Persian rooms were characteristically square, and the great hall of Xerxes must have been one of the most impressive in the ancient world (fig. 115). Its hundred stone columns, each forty feet high (several are still standing) and brightly painted, were delicately fluted and terminated in paired bulls that acted as brackets and helped to support the gigantic beams of imported wood, also painted. No such interior had, of course, existed in the Mesopotamian world, where columns were unknown.

Quite possibly the Persians drew their idea partly from the columned porticoes of Ionian Greek temples, partly from the columned temple halls of the Egyptians. The notion of a forest of columns, with no dominant axis in any direction, may have been the origin of the typical plan of many Islamic mosques several centuries later (see colorplate 46; fig. 354). The gold and silver rhytons or libation vessels (fig. 116), with their hybrid animal forms, show the Persian love of elegance, grace, and rational organization of elements. The linear rhythms of the animals themselves still suggest those of prehistoric pottery from Susa, not far from Persepolis, three millennia earlier (fig. 117), not to speak of many characteristic elements of later Mesopotamian cultures, but the alternating palmette and floral ornament on the upper border is already characteristically Greek. Sadly enough, it is upon the Greeks that the responsibility rests for the destruction of the palace, burned by Alexander after a long and violent banquet.

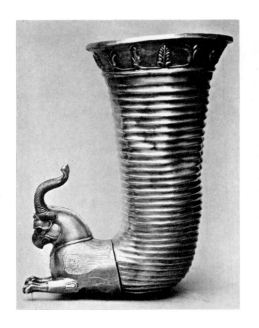

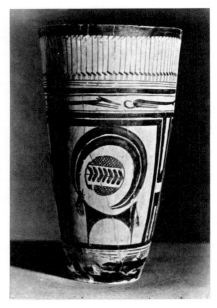

116. Rhyton, from the Oxus Treasury, Armenia. Silver, height 10″. British Museum, London

117. Painted beaker, from Susa, Iran. c. 5000–4000 B.C. Height 11¼″. The Louvre, Paris

3

Aegean Art

Somewhat later than the first manifestations of the splendid cultures that flourished in the Nile Valley and in Mesopotamia, a third artistically productive civilization arose in the islands and rocky peninsulas of the Aegean Sea. The rediscovery of this vanished civilization, like that of the cave paintings and of Sumer and Akkad, has been an achievement of the past hundred years or so. Nineteenth-century scholarship had taken it for granted that the cities and events described in the poems of Homer were largely if not entirely mythical, but the excavations of the German amateur archaeologist Heinrich Schliemann, beginning at the site of Troy in 1870 and continuing later at Mycenae and other centers on the Greek mainland, made clear that the Homeric stories must have had a basis in fact and that the cities mentioned in the poems had indeed existed. Subsequent excavations, beginning with those initiated by the British scholar Sir Arthur Evans in 1900, brought to light a completely unsuspected group of buildings on the island of Crete, containing works of art of surprising originality and freshness of imagination. It has now become clear that there were two distinct cultures. One was centered on Crete and has been called Minoan, after Minos, the legendary Cretan king; the other is known as Helladic, after Hellas, the Greek mainland. The final phase of Helladic culture, and its most interesting artistically, is known as Mycenaean, from its principal center at Mycenae.

CYCLADIC ART

But even before the rise of the Minoan and Helladic civilizations, there had been still another artistically creative culture in the Aegean world. Called Cycladic, from the circle of islands where its remains are found, this late Neolithic culture flourished in the third millennium B.C. and has left no trace of writing.

The Cycladic tombs have yielded many stone sculptures, ranging from statuettes to images about half-lifesize. The meaning of these figures is not known, but the female ones with their folded arms (fig. 118) seem to be descendants of Neolithic mother goddesses elsewhere (see fig. 15). Interestingly enough, however, their whole character has changed; they are no longer abundantly maternal but touchingly slight and virginal, with delicate proportions, gently swelling and subsiding shapes, and subtle contours. The simplicity and understatement of these Cycladic figures has made them particularly attractive to contemporary artists. It should be borne in mind, however, that the flattened faces originally displayed other features than the sharply projecting noses that are all that now remains. Traces of pigment make clear that eyes and mouths, as well as other details, were originally painted on. Of equal interest are the less frequently found male musicians, such as the *Lyre Player* (fig. 119), perhaps intended to commemorate a funerary celebration or even intended as an evocation of music in the afterlife. The musicians are almost tubular in their stylization, and the forms of body, lyre, and chair enclose beautifully shaped open spaces that prefigure those of some twentieth-century sculpture (see Vol. 2, figs. 478, 481).

MINOAN ART

Minoan civilization is almost as much of a mystery as that of preliterate man. The Minoan and Helladic peoples spoke different tongues, and Minoan scripts are still undecipherable. Their language, apparently non–Indo-European, is completely unknown. However, a late form of Aegean writing, found both in Crete and on the mainland, was first interpreted in 1953 and turned out to be a pre-Homeric form of Greek. The now legible documents, of a purely practical nature and without

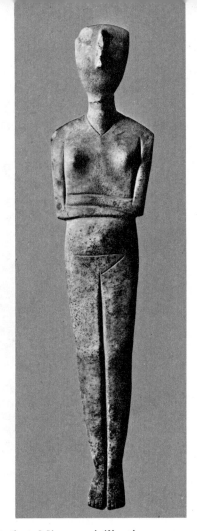

118. Cycladic idol,
from Amorgos.
2500–1100 B.C.
Marble, height 30".
Ashmolean Museum,
Oxford, England

on the dump heap. Yet clay fragments are virtually indestructible, and the lowest layers of potsherds in any heap are naturally the earliest, the next later, and so on. Because the shapes and methods of manufacture of these pots and the style of their decoration changed from one period to the next, sometimes quite rapidly, it has been possible for archaeologists to establish a relative chronology for the development of style by recording the potsherds according to the layers in which they were found. Often the Minoan and, later, the Greek pots are supremely beautiful as works of art, in both shape and decoration, and their style is strongly related to that of wall painting and other arts. Thus their chronology is applicable to other works of art as well. Sometimes, also, the circumstances of a find link a dated group of pots to the building in or near which it was discovered.

Since we know so little of their writing, we cannot yet say whether the Minoans themselves accurately recorded dates and specific events. But luckily they were great seafarers and traders. Their pots have turned up in Egyptian sites whose dates can be determined by numerous inscriptions, and the chronology based on the potsherds can thus often be anchored to firm historical knowledge. Approximate dates have, therefore, been assigned to the early, middle, and late periods into which Minoan art has been divided.

Not until the Middle Minoan period, about the nineteenth century B.C., does the art of the potter achieve truly great artistic stature, but objects of the quality of the beaked Kamares jug from Phaistos (fig. 120) would

literary interest, suggest that Minoan civilization eventually succumbed to Mycenaean overlords. Thus our slight knowledge of Aegean history, social structure, and religious beliefs must be gleaned largely from the study of Aegean buildings and other works of art and from the mythology of the later Greeks—however much distorted by the later poetic tradition that culminated in Homer —which seems to have been woven, in part at least, from surviving memories of the Aegean world. Even *Minos* may only be a generic Cretan name for *king*.

Approximate dates for Minoan art have been ascertained largely by the systematic excavation of pottery. Minoan and Helladic artifacts have now been traced as far back as 3000 B.C., and some even earlier, but the great artistic periods of both civilizations belong to the second millennium B.C., roughly between the years 1900 and 1200—a period contemporary with the Empire in Egypt and with the Babylonian period in Mesopotamia. Around 1400 B.C. Minoan civilization perished in a catastrophe of unknown nature and origin, and Mycenaean culture survived only another three centuries before succumbing to the combined effects of internal dissent and attacks by other Greek invaders.

Pottery

Baked clay pots, produced in abundance by almost all Mesopotamian and Mediterranean peoples for household use, were worthless after breakage and were tossed

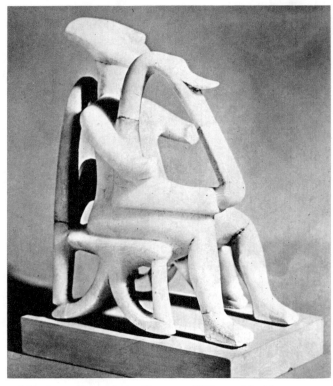

119. *Lyre Player,* from Keros. c. 2000 B.C. Marble,
height 9". National Archaeological Museum, Athens

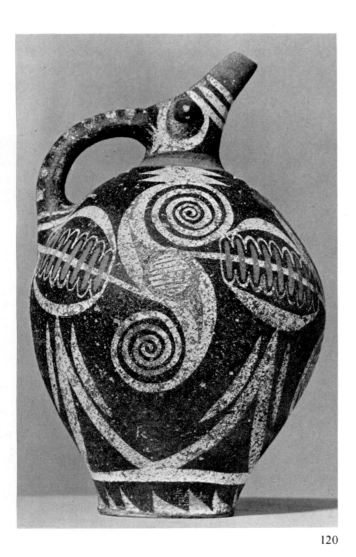

120

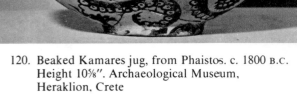

12

120. Beaked Kamares jug, from Phaistos. c. 1800 B.C.
Height 10⅝″. Archaeological Museum,
Heraklion, Crete

121. Octopus vase, from Palaikastro, Crete. c. 1500
B.C. Height 11″. Archaeological Museum,
Heraklion, Crete

be welcomed as masterpieces in any period. The curvilinear shapes have an extraordinary vitality and are different in style from anything we have previously seen, save perhaps for the ornamental motives of La Tène art (see fig. 27) or the carved decorations of the temple at Tarxien (see fig. 20). Palmlike shapes in soft white quiver against a black ground among curling and uncurling spirals and counterspirals, all beautifully related to the shape of the vessel itself. In Late Minoan, about 1500 B.C., the swirling shapes take on naturalistic forms. The entire front of a vase from Palaikastro (fig. 121), for example, is embraced by the tentacles of an octopus, writhing in splendid and menacing profusion. The abstract shapes on the first vase have now become naturalistic, but the principle of dynamic curvilinear decoration is the same and reappears in the wall paintings as well.

The Palaces

In Middle Minoan times, after about 2000 B.C., the inhabitants of Crete, previously at a rather modest stage of Neolithic development as compared to their contemporaries in Egypt and Mesopotamia, adopted metals and

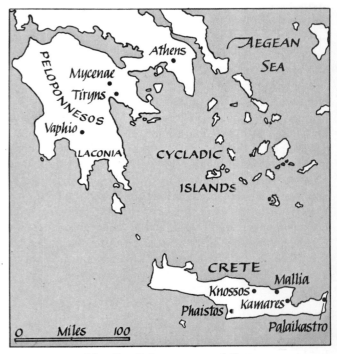

MAP 7. *Peloponnesos and Crete*

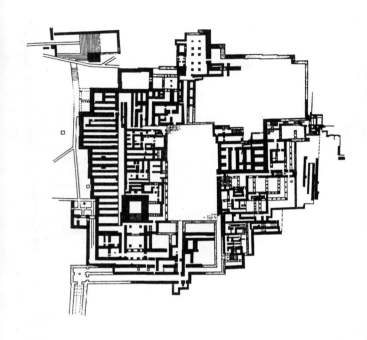

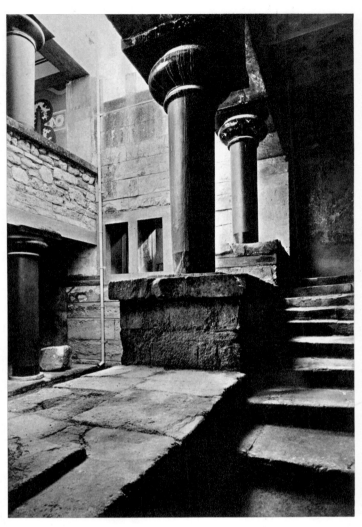

122. Plan of the Palace at Knossos, Crete. c. 1600–1400 B.C. (after Pendlebury)

123. Lower section of the main staircase and light well, east wing, Palace at Knossos (reconstruction). c. 1600–1400 B.C.

a system of writing, and rapidly developed an urban, mercantile civilization. Interestingly enough, the Minoans seem to have depended for protection entirely on their command of the sea; not a trace of fortification has ever been found. This reliance may well have proved their undoing. Immense palaces were built at Knossos and Mallia on the north coast of the island, at Phaistos on the south, and elsewhere. Devastated about 1700 B.C., these first palaces were soon repaired or rebuilt. The most extensive and artistically important is the vast palace at Knossos, about which we know more than about any other palace before Persepolis. Although Knossos was again laid waste between 1450 and 1400 B.C., it has been largely—perhaps even excessively—reconstructed from the ruins. A stroll through it affords an insight into the delightful existence of these mysterious people, who seem to have concerned themselves little with religion and not at all with the hereafter (they left no temples, only tiny shrines, and few monumental tombs), but entirely with the pleasures of the here and now. From the plan (fig. 122) and from the surviving and reconstructed portions, it is clear that the palace could never have presented the imposing, symmetrical, and ordered appearance of Mesopotamian royal residences.

Built around a not perfectly oblong central courtyard (fig. 123), the hundreds of rooms and connecting corridors climb gently up the slopes of the hill in such a haphazard manner as to give color to the Greek legend of the Cretan labyrinth, at the center of which King Minos was supposed to have stabled the dreaded Minotaur, half man, half bull.

Clearly, the Minoan monarchs felt no need to impress visitors with royal might and cruelty. Entrances are unobtrusive; the apartments sprout terraces, open galleries, and vistas at random; even the decorated rooms intended for the royal family are small, with low ceilings and a general air of bright and happy intimacy. The walls are of massive stone masonry; some supports are square piers recalling those in the valley temple of Chephren (see fig. 61), but wooden columns were frequently used. These are now lost, but their form can be reconstructed through representations in wall paintings, from their bases, which are square stone slabs with a socket for the column, and from their cushion-shaped stone capitals, distant ancestors of the Doric capitals of the Greeks (see figs. 152, 154). Strangely enough, the columns tapered downward, which further increased the feeling of lowness and intimacy in the rooms.

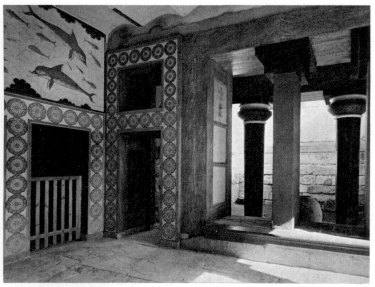

124

125

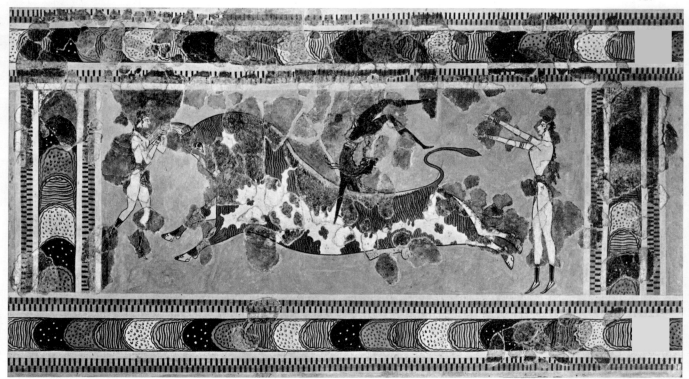

Painting

The mural decorations, painted on wet plaster like the frescoes of Renaissance Italy (see page 407), have survived only in tiny fragments, which have been pieced together; large gaps are filled by modern restorations. The painted interiors must have been joyous. A room at Knossos known as the Queen's Megaron (fig. 124; *megaron* means *great hall*) is illuminated softly by a light well. The doorways are ornamented with formalized floral designs, the columns and capitals are painted red and blue. On one wall we look straight into the sea, as if through the plate glass of an aquarium; between rocks in-

dicated by typical Minoan free curves, fish swim freely before us around two huge and contented dolphins.

In murals as in ceramics, unfettered rhythmic contours are the chief delight of Minoan painting, astonishing when compared to the stratified compositions typical of Egypt and Mesopotamia. In the still enigmatic *Bull Dance* from Knossos (fig. 125), these pulsating contours are extremely effective. Unlike the murderous bulls in Egyptian and Mesopotamian art, this resilient creature seems almost to have been trained for his role. He and his attendants are engaged not in mutual slaughter but in some kind of ritual dance. One almost nude girl dancer (painted yellow as in Egyptian art) grasps with impunity

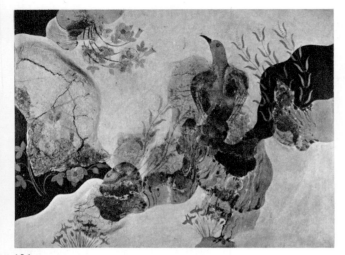

126

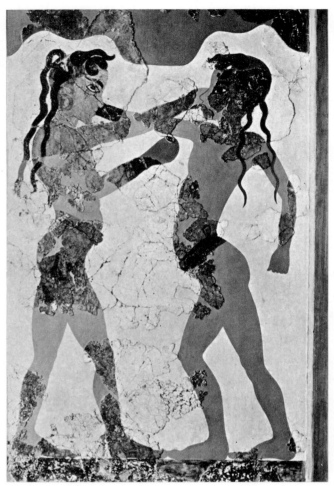

127

the bull's horns; a second waves from the sidelines; and the boy (red-brown) vaults over the bull with the agility of an acrobat. The forward lunge of the bull and the arching movement of the boy are enhanced by the sideward and upward thrust of the conventionalized rocks of the borders. It is believed that the bull ritual of this fresco actually took place in the great court of the palace itself, suitably barricaded and sealed off.

The naturalism of Minoan frescoes, such as the fragment from Knossos showing a bird in a landscape (fig. 126), recalls Egyptian paintings, which Minoan merchants must have seen on their visits to the Nile Valley. But the spirit of Minoan art is quite different. Birds fly, animals scamper, plants grow, the very hills seem to dance with a rocking rhythm as if the waves or the sea wind were carrying them along. Some of the most brilliant Minoan paintings have only recently come to light on the island of Thera, part of which sank into the sea in a violent volcanic explosion about 1500 B.C., the rest being buried under volcanic ash. A marvelous room has now been pieced together, with red, violet, and ocher hills and precipices undulating about all four walls like live things, asphodel growing from their crests and saddles in dizzying spirals, and swallows fluttering from plant to plant or conversing in midair (colorplate 12). This earliest known European landscape painting is the ancestor of the landscape frescoes of Roman art (see colorplate 28; fig. 273) and eventually of such panoramas as those in fourteenth-century Sienese painting (see colorplate 71; fig. 523) and even of Monet's *Water Lilies* (see Vol. 2, fig. 418), little though he could have known it. Among the most delightful of the Thera finds is the fresco representing two small boys boxing (fig. 127) with a single pair of gloves between them. Despite the determined expressions in their large, soft eyes, the strongest movement in the fresco is not that of their rather gentle blows but the characteristic pulsation of their fluid contours.

Sculpture

Monumental sculpture can hardly be expected from a civilization that built no temples and revered no divine monarchs. What little Minoan sculpture survives is small in scale and often uncertain in purpose. Faience statuettes have been found (fig. 128), representing a youthful female figure with bared breasts, a tight bodice, and richly flounced skirt. This impressive personage, who brandishes a snake in either hand, is often called a priestess but is more probably a goddess of the still unknown Minoan religion. In the elegance of her contours and in the softness of her movement, she betrays the same sensibility that distinguishes the wall paintings.

Surprising and thus far unique is the upper portion of a small black steatite vase known as the *Harvester Vase* (fig. 129), on which is carved in low relief a crowd of young men, nude to the waist, marching as if in ritual procession but overlapping freely—in contrast to the regimented movement of Egyptian or Mesopotamian figural groups. The harvesters carry long-handled implements, including a pitchfork, and one shakes a sistrum (rattle) with such force that his ribs and rib muscles swell within the skin of his torso; some have their mouths open

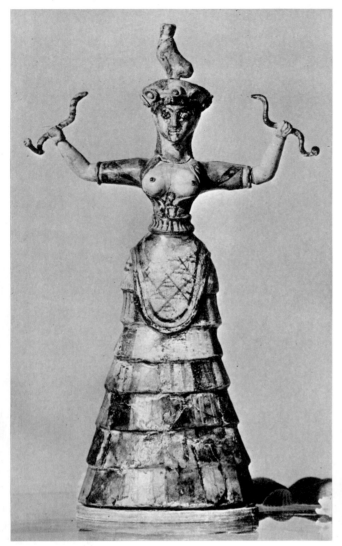

as if singing in exultation. Never up until this moment have we encountered such freedom of emotional expression in ancient art. The bull, dear to ancient civilizations and possibly sacred to the Minoans, reappears in a splendid black steatite rhyton (fig. 130), with horns and eyes inlaid with shell and rock crystal. The powerful curves of the flaring horns contrast with the delicate, meandering motion of the incised lines indicating locks of hair.

MYCENAEAN ART

The Greek mainland was inhabited by the Achaeans, an early Greek ethnic group whose commercial and political relations with the Minoans have yet to be thoroughly explored. They were soldiers, and their palaces were citadels utilizing the massive outcroppings of rock that tower above the narrow Greek valleys as natural defenses. The outer walls of such citadels were "cyclopean," built of irregular stone blocks so huge that the

128. *Snake Goddess*, from the Palace at Knossos. c. 1600 B.C. Faience, height 13½". Archaeological Museum, Heraklion, Crete

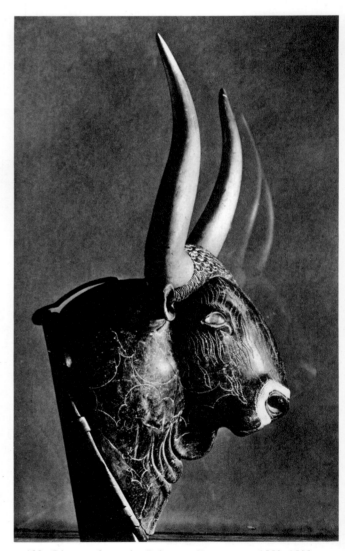

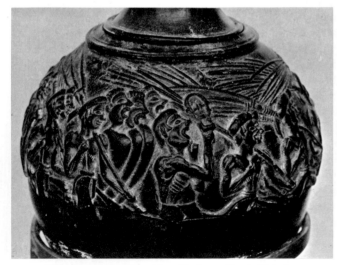

129. *Harvester Vase* (detail), from Hagia Triada. c. 1550–1500 B.C. Steatite, width 4½". Archaeological Museum, Heraklion, Crete

130. Rhyton, from the Palace at Knossos. c. 1550–1500 B.C. Steatite with inlaid shell and rock crystal. Archaeological Museum, Heraklion, Crete

later Greeks thought them the work of the Cyclopes, a race of one-eyed giants. Within the wall, however, the palaces were built of sun-dried brick as in Egypt and Mesopotamia. We gain entrance to the palace proper in the thirteenth-century-B.C. citadel of Tiryns (fig. 131) through a columned gateway. Before us rises the columned facade of the royal audience hall, or megaron, whose roof was supported within by four columns around a circular hearth. Traces of rich painted decoration have been found on the plastered floor, and there were numerous wall paintings. The relative positions of gateway and megaron foretell those of the Athenian Propylaia, or entrance gate to the Acropolis (see fig. 196), and the Parthenon in Classical times.

The formidable walls of the citadel at Mycenae, also built of cyclopean masonry, were entered through a trilithon gate that reminds one of the megalithic architecture of the Late Stone Age. The triangle framed by the lintel and the progressively projecting blocks above is occupied by one of the few pieces of monumental sculpture surviving from Aegean times, a massive high relief showing two muscular lions (alas, now headless) placing their front paws upon the base of a typical Minoan tapering column (fig. 132). Clearly the column had a religious significance that required it to be flanked and protected by the royal beasts.

By far the most accomplished and ambitious of these cyclopean constructions is the so-called Treasury of Atreus at Mycenae (fig. 133), actually a thirteenth-century royal tomb, some 43 feet in height and 47½ in diameter. Although all the rich decoration (possibly in precious metals) that once enlivened the interior and the entrance has been plundered, the effect of the simple masonry vault is majestic in the extreme. It is a corbel vault, with superimposed courses of masonry projecting one beyond the other as at Maeshowe in the Orkneys (see fig. 21). The blocks are trimmed off inside to form a colossal beehive shape of remarkable precision and accuracy. This is the largest unobstructed interior space known to us before that of the Pantheon in imperial Rome (see fig. 285).

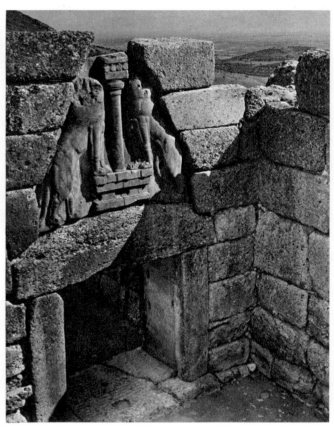

132. The Lion Gate. c. 1250 B.C. Limestone high relief. height c. 9'6". Mycenae

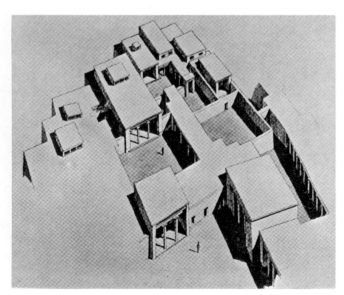

131. Citadel of Tiryns. 13th century B.C. (Architectural reconstruction after G. Karo)

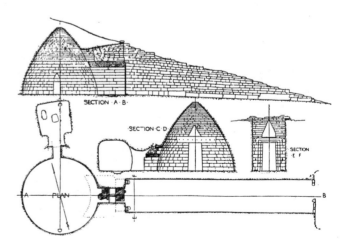

133. Plan of the Treasury of Atreus. 13th century B.C. Mycenae (after A. W. Lawrence)

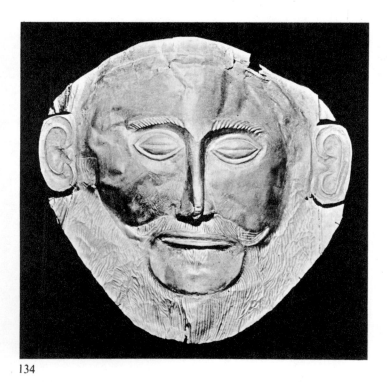

134

134. Funeral mask, from the royal tombs, Mycenae. c. 1500 B.C. Beaten gold, height c. 12". National Archaeological Museum, Athens

135. Dagger, from the Citadel of Mycenae. c. 1570–1550 B.C. Bronze inlaid with gold and electrum, length c. 9½". National Archaeological Museum, Athens

136. *The Vaphio Cups*, from Laconia. c. 500 B.C. Gold, height c. 3½". National Archaeological Museum, Athens

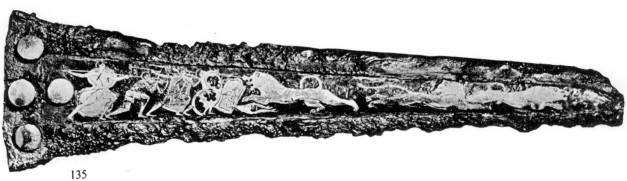

135

136

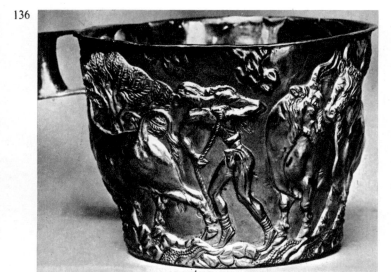

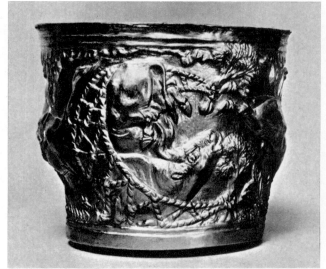

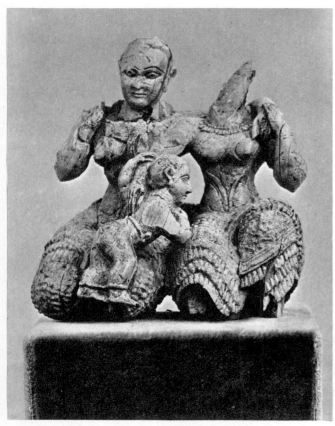

137. *Three Deities*, from Mycenae. c. 1500–1400 B.C. Ivory, height 3″. National Archaeological Museum, Athens

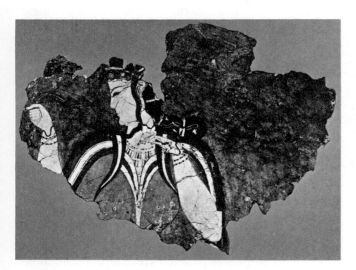

138. Female head (fragment), from Mycenae. Fresco

Schliemann's excavations of the royal graves at Mycenae in 1876 yielded a dazzling array of objects in gold, silver, and other metals, some ceremonial, some intended for daily use. A number of masks in beaten gold (fig. 134) were probably intended to cover the faces of deceased kings. Although hardly to be compared with the refinement of the gold mask of Tutankhamen (see colorplate 10), their solemn honesty is nonetheless impressive.

The Mycenaean warrior kings attached great importance to their weapons, and superb examples have been found. A bronze dagger blade inlaid with gold and electrum, a natural alloy of silver and gold (fig. 135), shows a spirited battle of men against lions, surpassing anything we have thus far seen in swiftness of movement. One lion assaults lunging warriors protected by huge shields while two other lions turn tail and flee with inglorious speed, toward the point of the dagger.

Even more beautiful are two golden cups (fig. 136) found at Vaphio in Laconia and datable to about 1500 B.C. These works, to be ranked among the masterpieces of ancient art, are covered with continuous reliefs of extraordinary vivacity and power, showing the capture of bulls. While the style is clearly Minoan, recalling the movement and expressive intensity of the *Harvester Vase*, these violent bulls are far removed from the graceful creature in the Knossos fresco. Various methods of entrapment are shown, ranging from lassoing by a rope around the ankle, held by a characteristically wasp-waisted, muscular young man, to capture by nets, and enticement by a friendly cow. The cups pulsate with the movement of the powerful bodies and flying hooves; the motion subsides only in the romantic tête-à-tête of the bull and the cow.

A little ivory group of unknown purpose has recently been found near a sanctuary at Mycenae (fig. 137). It shows three deities, possibly Demeter, the earth-goddess, her daughter Persephone, and the young god Iakchos, although this is pure conjecture. The affectionate grouping of the figures, with arms over shoulders and free and playful poses, combined with the fluid movement of the full skirts, renders this one of the most poetic works of Aegean art.

Little by little, paintings of high quality come to light, including a superb female head under strong Minoan influence (fig. 138). Under the attacks of another group of Greek invaders from the north, the Dorians, the rich and powerful Mycenaean civilization was overwhelmed and destroyed about 1100 B.C., to be succeeded by a period often known as the Dark Ages.

4

Greek Art

Of the three great historic arts we have considered up to this point, that of Egypt alone left a measurable influence on later periods, and even Egyptian influence was only occasionally fruitful or decisive. Splendid though they were, the arts of Mesopotamia and of the pre-Hellenic Aegean world vanished almost entirely from the sight and memory of man until very nearly our own times. When we turn to ancient Greece, however, we are dealing for the first time with an art that has never been entirely forgotten. Greek art, like Greek culture in general, influenced in one way or another the art of every subsequent period of Western civilization, including the present, sometimes to an overwhelming degree. Even when later cultures felt they must revolt against Greek influence, each revolt in itself was a tribute to the greatness of Greek achievement. The only other culture that has left a comparable impression on later periods is that of Rome, and this is in large part because Rome was the transmitter, by commerce and by conquest, of the artistic heritage of Greece.

If we attempt to account for the great depth and the astounding durability of Greek influence, we will probably come to the conclusion that they are both due to the primacy of Greek civilization and Greek art in developing rational norms for every aspect of the arts, as distinguished from the rigid conventions imposed by Egyptian society upon Egyptian art. The Greeks derived these norms from the nature and behavior of man himself, accessible to Greek thinkers, writers, and artists through their unprecedented powers of observation, inquiry, and analysis. "Man is the measure of all things," said the Greek philosopher Protagoras in the fifth century B.C., and while Protagoras' own subjectivity aroused considerable controversy in his own day, his celebrated remark may still be taken as typical of the Greek attitude toward life and toward art. The dignity and beauty of the individual human being and the rich texture of physical and psychological interplay among human beings constitute at once the subject, the goal, and the final determinant of Greek artistic and literary creation.

Both land and climate stimulated the unprecedented concentration of Greek culture on the quality of human life and on physical and intellectual activity. Greece is a land of mountainous peninsulas and islands, separated by narrow, fjordlike straits and bays, with scanty arable land. It is subject to strong contrasts of winter cold and summer heat and to fierce and unpredictable sea winds. Horizons are limited by mountains and rocky islands. Under a sunlight whose intensity is credible only to those who have experienced it, the land takes on a golden color against a sea and sky of piercing blue. Day gives way to night almost without intervening twilight. Against such a background and in such light, forms and relationships are clear and sharp.

In such an environment it was neither easy nor necessary to establish cooperative relationships between one community and the next, separated by mountain walls or by arms of the sea. A living had to be wrested by force and by intelligence from rocky land and treacherous water. The beautiful but often hostile Greek surroundings fostered an athletic and inquiring attitude toward existence that contrasts strongly with Egyptian passivity and that precluded submission to universal systems of government. Farming was not easy in the rocky soil; grain crops required great expenditure of effort, and the olive tree and the vine needed careful tending. In addition to the limited agricultural class, a trading class eventually arose, and finally a manufacturing class engaged in the production of such characteristic Greek artifacts as pottery and metalwork, which were exported to the entire Mediterranean world. Like the Minoans before them, the Greeks were excellent sailors; like the Mycenaeans, they were valiant soldiers. Greek systems of government were experimental and constantly changing. It is no accident that so many English words for governmental forms derive from Greek—democracy, autocracy, tyranny, aristocracy, oligarchy, and monarchy, to name only a few. Even the word *politics* comes from the Greek *polis*, meaning the independent city-state with its surrounding territory, which was the basic unit of Greek society. All six of the forms of government just mentioned were practiced at one time or another by the Greek city-states on the mainland, the islands, Asia Minor, Sicily, and southern Italy, often in rapid succession or alternation. But even when popular liberties were sacrificed for a period to a tyrant or to an oligarchic group, the Greek ideal was always that of self-government. The tragedy of Greek history lies in the inability of the Greek city-states to subordinate individual sovereignty to any ideal of a permanent federation that could embrace the whole Greek world and put a stop to the endemic warfare that sapped the energies of the separate states and eventually brought about their subjugation. Until the time of Alexander the Great, who borrowed the idea from the Near Eastern cultures he conquered, the notion of a god-king on the Egyptian or Mesopotamian model was wholly absent from Greek history. We can find a special significance in the fact that, while the Egyptians and Mesopotamians recounted their history in terms of royal reigns or of dynasties, the Greeks measured time in Olympiads, the four-year span between the Olympic Games, an athletic festival celebrated throughout ancient Greek history.

The Greeks peopled their world with gods who, like themselves, lived in a state of constant rivalry and even conflict, often possessed ungovernable appetites on a glorified human scale, took sides in human wars, and even coupled with human beings to produce a race of demigods known as heroes. Only in their greater power and knowledge and in their immortality did the gods differ essentially from humans. Just as no single mortal ruled the Greek world, so no Greek god was truly omnipotent, not even Zeus, the king of the gods.

The Greeks were strongly aware of their achievements, and not least of their history, as a record of individual human actions rather than merely of events. Their art is the first to *have* a real history in our familiar sense of an internal development. Egyptian art seems to spring into existence fully formed and can hardly be said to have developed after its initial splendid creations. In fact, many critics hold that the earliest works of Old Kingdom Egypt were never again approached by the Egyptians in point of sheer quality. And certain basic forms and ideas run throughout Mesopotamian art from the Sumerians to the Persians. But Greek art shows a steady evolution from simple to always more complex phases, some of which are for convenience labeled Archaic, Classical, and Hellenistic. Although this development was not steady, nor uniform at all geographic points, it is strikingly visible and has often been compared with that of European art from the late Middle Ages through the Renaissance

and the Baroque periods. From start to finish, the entire evolution of Greek art took only about seven centuries, or less than one-quarter of the long period during which Egyptian art continued relatively unchanged. The Age of Pericles, often considered the peak of Greek artistic achievement, lasted only a few decades.

Despite the anthropocentric nature of Greek culture, the Greeks were under no illusions about the limitations or indeed the inevitable downfall of human ambitions. One of their favorite literary forms, which they indeed invented and in whose composition they rose to unrivaled heights of dramatic intensity and poetic grandeur, was tragedy (the very word is Greek). In Greek tragedy, human wills pitted against each other bring forth the highest pitch of activity of which men and women are capable; yet these activities lead to disaster through inevitable human shortcomings. In all of Greek art there are no colossal statues of monarchs like those of the Egyptian pharaohs. Only gods were represented on a colossal scale, and although none of these immense statues survive, the literary accounts indicate that in spite of their superhuman size they were entirely human and beautiful. In contradistinction to the hybrid deities of the Egyptians and the Mesopotamians, in ancient Greece only monsters were part human and part animal. These hybrids were invariably dangerous (satyrs, centaurs, and sirens), often totally evil (the Minotaur).

But while Greek rationality gave rise to arithmetic, geometry, philosophy, and the beginnings of astronomy, zoology, and botany (again the words are Greek), and at times a vision of the good life and the perfect state, in actuality Greek communal life was seldom able to achieve a lasting order. Even in the Classical period the Greek polis permitted both chattel slavery and the disenfranchisement of subject states. In spite of the rationality of Greek philosophers, at no point in Greek history was there any serious or widespread threat to belief in a host of anthropomorphic deities. Yet one of the great charms of the Greeks is the fact that, side by side with the development of the intellect, the life of the passions continued with undiminished intensity, endowing the coldest creatures of reason with an irrational but poetic beauty.

What remains to us of Greek art is of such high quality that it is painful to contemplate the extent of our losses. The survivals constitute, in fact, only a small and irregularly distributed proportion of Greek artistic production. We possess some ancient written accounts of what were considered the greatest works of Greek art, notably those of the first-century Roman encyclopedic naturalist Pliny the Elder and the Greek traveler Pausanias of the second century A.D. From these sources we know of many celebrated Greek buildings that have totally vanished; the few that remain standing are all in more or less ruinous condition. Only two statues survive that can be attributed to the most famous Greek sculp-

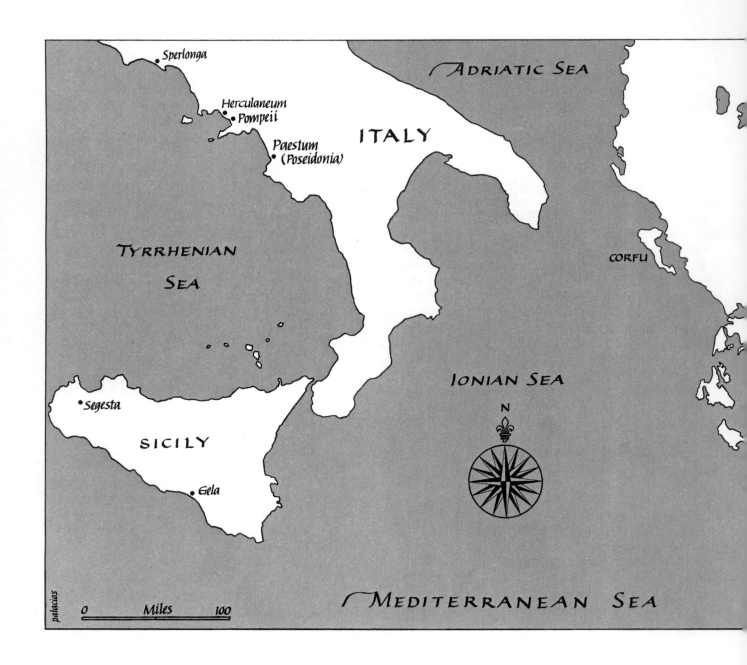

tors: one, the *Victory* of Paionios (see fig. 202), is in fragments, and the other, *Hermes* (see fig. 215), is not universally accepted as the work of Praxiteles. The other preserved Greek original sculptures are either the work of unidentified masters or quite late signed works of secondary importance, such as *Laocoön* (see fig. 234) and *Polyphemos Blinded by Odysseus* (see fig. 235), both by the same trio of sculptors from Rhodes. Many Roman copies of Greek statues were made with a mechanical aid, the pointing machine, which transferred adjustable points on a metal frame from the original to the copy, enabling the copyist to reproduce sizes, poses, proportions, and details with some fidelity. Roman copies, therefore, give us a fairly clear idea, however diluted in quality, of the appearance of many lost masterpieces. The general reli-

ability of Roman copies is, of course, susceptible to demonstration when several copies of the same original are checked against each other. But thousands of statues must still lie underground, and a lucky find can always turn up an original of high quality, as has happened even in excavations for buildings or highways.

Monumental painting, to which the Greeks attached the highest importance, is totally and irrevocably lost. Not the smallest piece of any famous Greek painting has ever been recovered, nor, in the nature of things, is any likely to be, for the very buildings on whose walls most of them were painted have long since vanished. Only literary descriptions survive, and occasional "copies," which may not be copies in our sense at all. The local Italian artists who reproduced renowned Greek paintings

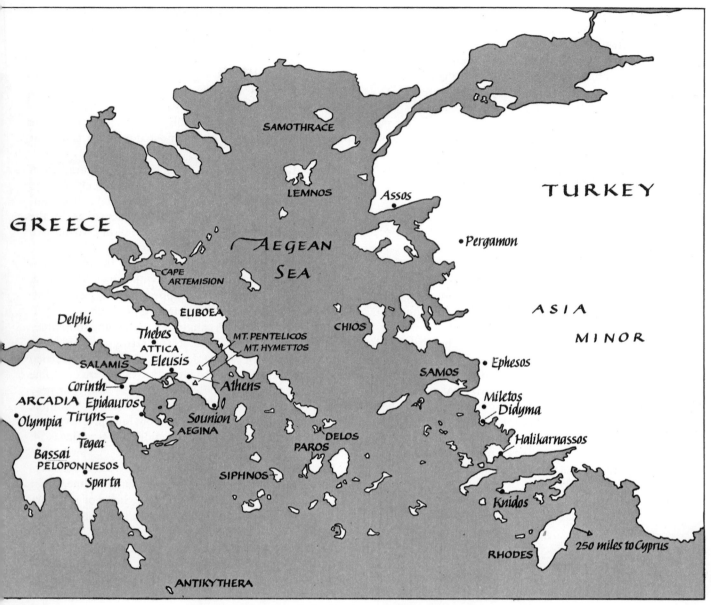

MAP 8. *Southern Italy, Greece and Western Asia Minor*

may never have seen the original works in distant Greece or Asia Minor, but only portable sketches or replicas brought home by travelers. We have, therefore, only the most general idea of what the style of the great Greek painters must have been like, and only now and then are we able to reconstruct the order of figures in one of their compositions.

Another serious loss is that of color. Under the influence of marble statues and capitals from which the original coloring leached out centuries ago, we tend to think of Greek art—and Greek costumes, too—as white. Nothing could be further from the truth. In early periods the coloring applied to the statues was quite bright, even garish, judging from traces of the original paint still remaining here and there. In the Classical period and in

the fourth century, coloring was undoubtedly more restrained but was certainly used to suggest actual life, especially in eyes, lips, and hair. Garments were colored, and certain details were added in gold or other metals in all periods. Limestone or sandstone temples were coated with fine plaster tinted to resemble marble. In all temples, including the marble ones, capitals and other architectural details were brightly painted. Wall decorations from the Hellenistic era survive to indicate that the interiors of prosperous homes were also ornamented in color (see colorplate 21). If the well-known Greek sense of harmony and of the fitness of things gives us any basis for speculation, then Greek color must have been harmoniously adjusted and must have formed an essential part of the total effect of works of architecture and sculpture. We must attempt to restore this effect in our imaginations if we are to understand the work of art as the artist intended it. Only the pots, which as we have seen (page 91) are unlikely ever to be totally destroyed, survive in vast numbers and with their coloring intact. In Greek ceramics the color is generally limited to red terra-cotta; black and white slip, baked on; and an occasional touch of violet. But even the pots, made for practical, everyday purposes, were intended to be seen not, as now too often, in superimposed rows in museum cases, but as small, movable accents in richly colored interiors.

GEOMETRIC AND ORIENTALIZING STYLES
(800–600 B.C.)

The three centuries from about 1100 B.C. to about 800 B.C. are still an era of mystery and confusion, often called—by analogy with the later one following the breakup of the Roman Empire—the Dark Ages. The title is intended to suggest not only the dimness of our present knowledge of this era but also the fact that what little has been unearthed about it indicates a fairly low stage of cultural development—indeed, a sharp decline from the splendor of Mycenaean art and civilization. At the beginning of this period tribes from the north, probably the Danube basin, moved south into the areas formerly ruled by Mycenaeans, settling largely in the Peloponnesos, the cluster of peninsulas that makes up southern Greece. Later Greeks called these people Dorians; Sparta, always

the most conservative and warlike of the Greek city-states, prided itself on its Dorian origin. Some of the older peoples of Mycenaean derivation fled to the islands of the Aegean and to Asia Minor, where they founded such important centers as Ephesos and Miletos. These tribes, known as Ionians, were, however, not wholly driven out of Greece by the invaders. Some were able to preserve their identity, notably the inhabitants of the peninsula of Attica, with its most important center at Athens.

Understandably enough, architectural remains from this earliest period of Greek art are extremely scanty, although some foundations of temples have been uncovered. But we possess precious evidence as to the modest external appearance of such buildings from two small terra-cotta models and fragments of another, which can be dated about the middle of the eighth century B.C. by comparison with contemporary pottery (fig. 139). Basically, these temples appear to be direct descendants of the Mycenaean megaron type, such as that at Tiryns (see fig. 131). A single oblong room, sometimes square-ended, sometimes terminating in an apse (semicircular end), was roofed with a gable and preceded by a columned portico. Probably the walls were of rubble or mud brick and the columns of wood; the roof may even have been woven from thatch. These are humble buildings indeed, yet they are the obvious prototypes of the Greek temples of a more splendid era (see figs. 154, 159, 187).

The finest remains of eighth-century Greek art are certainly the pots, covered with the abundant ornament that gives the period its name, Geometric. Some of them are truly majestic, especially the huge *amphora* (jar for oil or wine, fig. 140) from the Dipylon Cemetery in Athens, of a type which was placed over graves and perforated at the bottom so that offerings of oil or wine could seep through. The shape, with powerful body and lofty neck, slender handles, and slightly flaring lip is of the greatest elegance. The surface is divided into almost innumerable bands of constantly varying width, ornamented with slender black lines describing against the terra-cotta background geometric figures—dots, diamonds, lozenges, and three different versions of the meander or "Greek fret" motive so common in later Greek decoration, some bands apparently moving from right to left, some from left to right, some readable either way. A single band on the neck shows simplified and very graceful antelope grazing, moving from left to right. At the level of the handles, the frets seem to be parted, as it were, and forced to run vertically to make way for a funerary scene. The deceased, represented schematically and frontally on his bier, is flanked by identical wasp-waisted mourners with their arms elevated, looking like abstract versions of Aegean figures. Across the grand volume of the jar the slender lines of geometric ornament seem to shimmer in contrast to the strong black of the expanding and contracting figures.

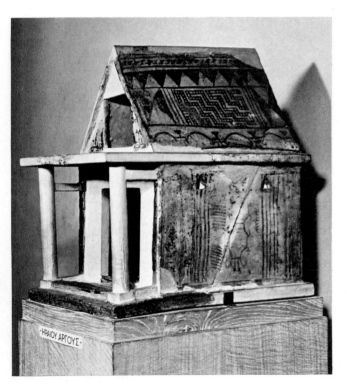

139. Model of a Temple, from the Heraion near Argos.
c. Middle 8th century B.C. Terra-cotta, length
c. 14½". National Archaeological Museum, Athens

A large number of statuettes in terra-cotta and in bronze remain from the Geometric period. A delightful example is the tiny bronze *Deer Nursing a Fawn* (fig. 141), hardly more naturalistic than the figures on the *Dipylon Vase* but just as intense in pattern and feeling. From none of the works of visual art, however, could we possibly guess that during this same crucial eighth century were written the two great Homeric epics, the *Iliad* and the *Odyssey*, which seem to us in retrospect the very foundation stones of European literature. The discrepancy between these elaborate narratives, which display in a highly developed phase every facet of the epic poet's skill, and the stylized images of Geometric painting and sculpture does not, however, constitute a unique instance as we follow the relations between the arts throughout history. It is perhaps significant that words and meanings in ancient Greece developed earlier and more rapidly than visual images.

But these did not remain long behind. Seventh-century vases show a considerable loosening of the tight Geometric style. A massive amphora at Eleusis (fig. 142), almost as tall as the *Dipylon Vase*, is a striking example of the Proto-Attic style, so called because it precedes the full development of vase painting in Athens in the sixth and fifth centuries. The relatively inert Geometric ornament of the eighth century, which only suggested motion, has now "come alive" and depicts motion. The very shape of the vase has changed. The bottom is narrower, so that the body seems to swell, and the neck flares more sharply. The handles have grown enormously and are composed of cutout shapes, largely crosses and palmettes. The greatly reduced ornament, consisting largely of intertwined black and white bands, is extremely active. The main fields of the vase are now taken over by figures. Visible on this side of the body are two of the fierce, snake-haired Gorgon sisters, confronted by Athena (whose figure is only partially preserved); in the panel above is a fight between a lion and a boar. The most terrible scene is enacted on the neck, where Odysseus and two companions force a burning stake into the one eye of the Cyclops Polyphemos. The action of the figures seems reinforced by the centralized floral ornaments scattered freely throughout the background. These derive from Near Eastern sources and have given rise to the term Orientalizing for this second phase of Greek art. How energetic the style can be in other areas of Greece as well as in Attica is shown by the contemporary Proto-Corinthian oenochoe (wine pitcher) known as the *Chigi Vase* (fig. 143).

Although made at Corinth in the Peloponnesos, the *Chigi Vase* was found at an Etruscan site in central Italy and thus attests to the widespread commercial activity of the Greeks. The upper register, painted in black, white, and two tones of brown against the creamy terra-cotta background, shows foot soldiers equipped with helmets, shields, and spears hurrying into battle with a vigor and freedom that surpass even contemporary Assyrian sculp-

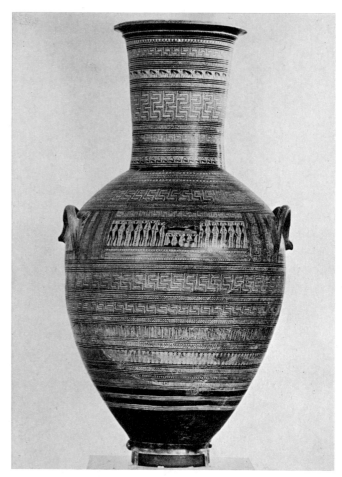

140. *Dipylon Amphora* (Geometric Style), from the Dipylon Cemetery, Athens. c. 750 B.C. Height 61". National Archaeological Museum, Athens

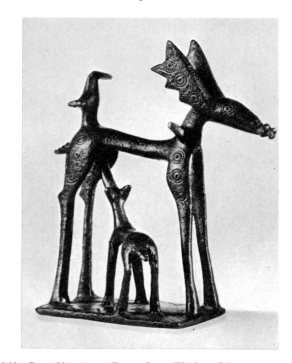

141. *Deer Nursing a Fawn,* from Thebes. 8th century B.C. Bronze, height 2⅞". Museum of Fine Arts, Boston

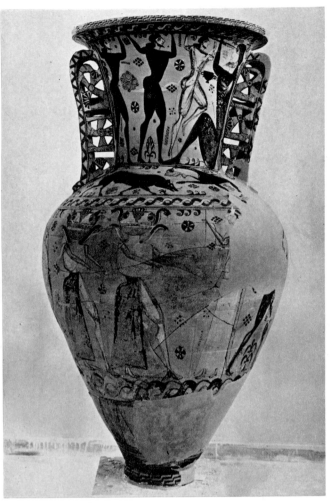

142. Amphora with *Odysseus Blinding Polyphemos* (Pro-Attic Style). Middle 7th century B.C. Height 56". Archaeological Museum, Eleusis, Greece

ture (see fig. 109). In the central zone horses and riders move easily along, and below are lively hunters. The Macmillan Painter, as the artist who decorated this vase is called, was able to suggest depth in a new and original way by the overlapping of the limbs of humans and animals. The *Chigi Vase* is just over ten inches high; compared to the almost five feet of the Eleusis amphora it seems a masterpiece in miniature.

Some sculpture in stone survives. Although less than lifesize, the limestone *Lady of Auxerre* (fig. 144), so called because she once stood in a museum in that French city, is impressive in her combination of linear precision and a rude massiveness that suggests at all points the original contour of the block. Her tight costume forms a pillowy shaft that conceals her legs, and it is decorated with a delicately incised meander pattern. About her bosom the costume tightens to reveal firm and abundant breasts. Her huge head is surmounted by a wiglike mass of hair, falling in four great locks on either side and so bound at intervals that they appear to be separated into little cushions. Her remaining eye and her mouth, with its delicate smile, are executed with a sensitivity that renders the relative clumsiness of hands and feet the more surprising. Although this statue offers only a slight challenge to the then already two-thousand-year-old Egyptian tradition of figure sculpture, it is, nevertheless, a powerful work.

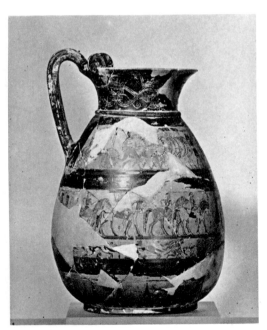

143. THE MACMILLAN PAINTER. *Chigi Vase* (Proto-Corinthian Style), from Corinth. Middle 7th century B.C. Terra-cotta, height 10¼". Museo Nazionale di Villa Giulia, Rome

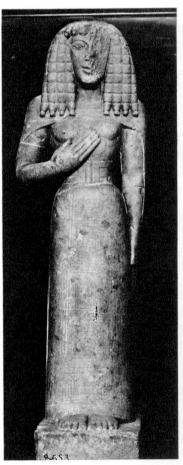

144. *Lady of Auxerre.* c. 650 B.C. Limestone, height 24½". The Louvre, Paris

THE ARCHAIC PERIOD (600–480 B.C.)

The term *Archaic*, from a Greek word meaning *early*, is applied to the unexpectedly vigorous and inventive period in which the main lines of the arts in Greece were rapidly established. Enormous developments were made in a very brief span of time. Although it is a matter of personal taste, many prefer the incisive strength and brilliance of Archaic art, perhaps even because of its stylizations, to the richer, fuller, and more harmonious Classical phase that succeeded it. What is undeniable is that the sixth century B.C. is one of the great creative periods in world art. Beginning modestly, temple building achieved structures of the greatest originality and on an increasingly grand scale. Architecture was adorned with sculpture at many crucial points, sometimes almost enveloped by it. Painting, as we know from countless thousands of painted vases, kept abreast of the other arts and perhaps—although we shall never know, since the wall paintings are forever lost—outstripped them. Since we have chosen Protagoras' famous saying, "Man is the measure of all things," as a text for our consideration of Greek art, it is perhaps best to start with the evolution of the human figure in Greek sculpture and then to consider how the figure was used as a measure for the other arts.

Freestanding Sculpture

Greece is a land dominated by stone, and fortunately much of it is usable for sculpture. The Greek islands, notably Paros, and Mount Hymettos and Mount Pentelicos near Athens yielded marble of superb luminosity and clarity, far more beautiful than Egyptian limestone. Greek marble was not only easier to carve but more appropriate to the representation of human flesh than either the speckled granite or the dark diorite utilized by the Egyptians for monumental statues. And the Greeks' possession of iron gave them tools more effective than the softer bronze implements relied upon by the Egyptians. Iron points, claw chisels, and drills made it possible for the sculptor to bring out all the expressive beauty of the marble, which he could then smooth by the time-honored methods of abrasion and finally wax in order to carry the surface to the highest degree of perfection.

An impressive series of standing marble figures remains from the sixth century. For want of more precise terms the male statue is generally called *kouros* (youth), the female *kore* (maiden). Some statues were signed by their sculptors, others inscribed with the name of a donor. Some were dedicated to various deities; some were placed over graves. Votive and commemorative statues they certainly were, but not portraits in the sense of likenesses. Apparently, we should regard these statues as idealizations.

Strangely enough to modern eyes, the male figures are always totally nude, the female always fully clothed, but the conventions of male nudity and female modesty correspond to the fact that, while nude male athletes were seen daily in the palaestra, women never appeared unclothed. Moreover, men were completely free to go where they wished, while women were generally restricted to the house, which they seldom left.

The largest and grandest, and one of the earliest, of the kouros figures—a statue almost ten feet high—was found at Sounion near Athens and is datable about 600 B.C. (fig. 145). It shows undeniable Egyptian influence in the rigid stance of the figure, with the arms close to the sides and the left leg advanced. Given Greek commercial relations with Egypt, such influence is easier to account for than the as yet unexplained suddenness of its appearance. We still do not know why the Greeks began carving large-scale figures at the end of the seventh century B.C. At first sight the figure, for all its grandeur, seems nowhere near as advanced from the point of view of naturalism as Old Kingdom statues dating from two thousand years earlier. But there are telltale differences that suggest the enormous development soon to take place. First, although the Egyptian sculptor thought of his stone figures as freestanding (see the drawings of sculptors at work, fig. 56), in practice he invariably left a smooth wall of uncut stone between the legs and arms and the body (see fig. 63). Apparently, he was trying to avoid fracture in carving with soft bronze tools, on which enormous pressure had to be exerted. Such inert passages of stone must have been intolerable to the Greek artist as restrictions on the mobility and freedom of his figure, and he reduced them to the smallest possible bridges of stone between hand and flank. Second, while the weight of an Egyptian figure rests largely on the right (rear) leg, that of the kouros statue is always evenly distributed, so that the figure seems to be striding rather than standing. Finally, the total calm of the Egyptian figure, which never seems to have known the meaning of strain, gives way to an alert look and, where possible, to a strong suggestion of tension, as in the muscles around the kneecap and especially in the torso, whose abdominal muscle is cut into channels as yet neither clearly understood nor accurately counted. The preternaturally large and magnificent head of the *Kouros of Sounion* (see fig. 145), while divided into stylized parts in conformity with a lingering Geometric taste, shows the characteristic Greek tension in every line.

In the *Anavyssos Kouros* (fig. 146), done only some sixty to eighty years later and placed over the grave of a fallen warrior called Kroisos, the stylistic revolution hinted at in the *Sounion Kouros* has been largely achieved. At every point the muscles seem to swell with actual life. Although the full curves of breast, arm, and thigh muscles may as yet be imperfectly controlled, the pride of the figure in its youthful masculine strength is unprecedented. The sharp divisions between the muscles have relaxed; forms and surfaces now flow easily into each other. Even the lines of the still stylized locks are no longer absolutely straight but flow in recognition of the fact that hair is soft.

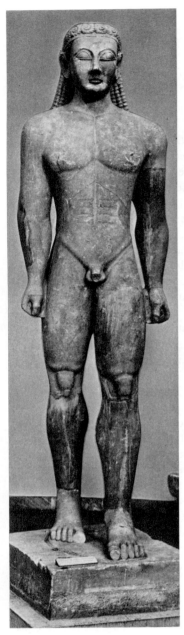

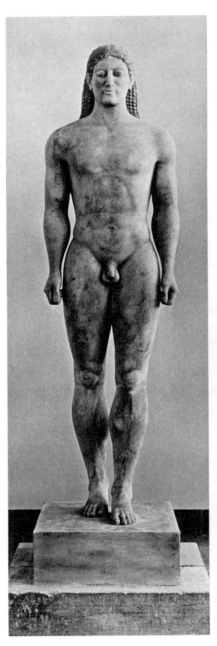

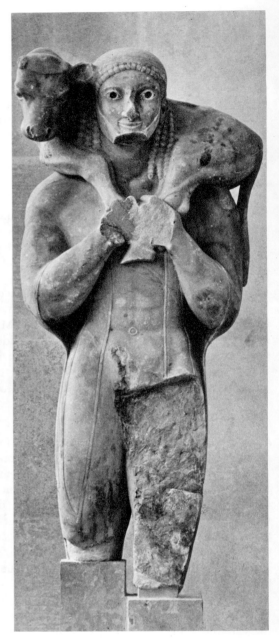

145. *Kouros of Sounion.* c. 600
B.C. Marble, height c. 10′.
National Archaeological
Museum, Athens

146. *Anavyssos Kouros.*
c. 525 B.C. Marble,
height 76″. National
Archaeological
Museum, Athens

147. *Calf Bearer,* from the
Acropolis, Athens. c. 570
B.C. Marble, height 66″.
Acropolis Museum

A somewhat more mature, bearded figure, the *Calf Bearer* (fig. 147), of about 570 B.C., shows the transition between the two phases. The sharp divisions of the muscles have softened, and the channels in the abdominal muscle are correctly placed and counted. The now largely destroyed legs originally had the characteristic kouros pose. The meaning of the famous "Archaic smile" that lifts the corners of the mouth still eludes us, but this smile is characteristic of Archaic art throughout the sixth century, whenafter it soon disappears. While still proclaiming the original surface of the block, the head of the calf the man bears as an offering is modeled with great sensitivity.

A superb funerary stele carved as an idealized portrait of the Athenian warrior Aristion (fig. 148) shows the rich possibilities opened up by Archaic artists. The sculptor Aristokles, who signed this work, was able to control gradations of low relief with great delicacy so as to suggest the varying distance of the left and right legs and arms from the viewer's eye and the fullness of the torso inside its armor. Aristokles' attention to visual effects freed the warrior completely from the Egyptian convention of two left hands and two left feet, and he seems to have delighted in contrasting the smoothly flowing surfaces of the body, neck, and limbs with the delicate folds and rippling edges of the *chiton* (garment worn next to

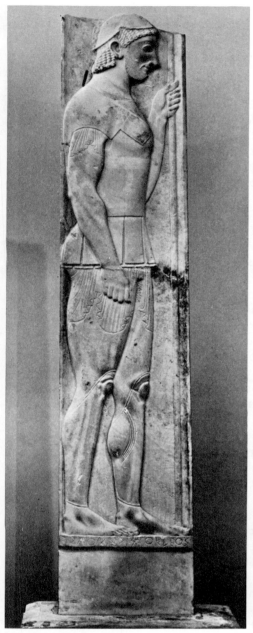

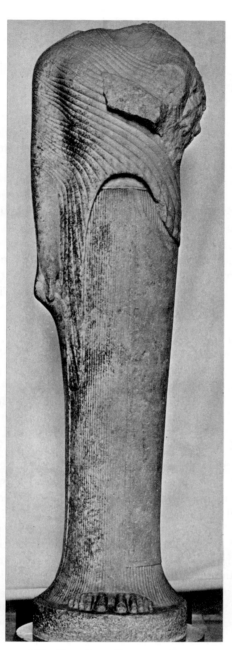

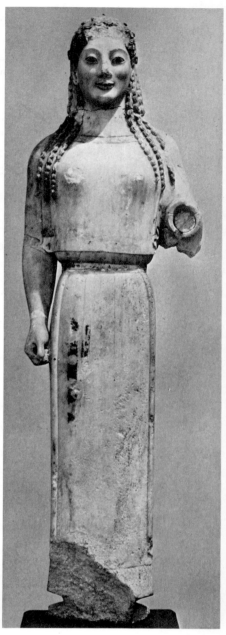

148. ARISTOKLES. *Stele of Aristion.* c. 525 B.C. National Archaeological Museum, Athens

149. *Hera,* from Samos. c. 565 B.C. Marble, height 76". The Louvre, Paris

150. *Peplos Kore,* from Athens. c. 530 B.C. Marble, height 48". Acropolis Museum, Athens

the skin), which escape from beneath the armor and cling gently to the upper arm and the strong thigh.

One of the earliest of the kore figures was found in the Temple of Hera on the island of Samos (fig. 149) and is majestic enough to have been a statue of a goddess. About contemporary with the *Calf Bearer,* the figure shows a striking change from the *Lady of Auxerre* (see fig. 144); the block, as is customary in Samian work, has here become a cylinder. When the missing head was intact, the hair fell over the back. The missing left hand probably held a gift. The *himation* (cloak), looped at the waist, is thrown around the torso and gathered lightly with the fingers of the right hand, enveloping the right

arm extended down the hip. The forms of the bosom are at once concealed and revealed by the streaming spiral folds, which contrast strongly with the tiny vertical pleats of the chiton. The profile of the figure, often compared to a column in its verticality, has much in common with the elastic silhouette of an early amphora (see figs. 140, 142), expanding and contracting, elegant and restrained.

Another sixth-century masterpiece is the *Peplos Kore* from Athens (fig. 150), so named because the figure wears the *peplos,* a simple woolen garment. The statue is somewhat blocky in its general mass and beautifully reticent in its details. The severe peplos falls simply over the noble bosom and hangs lightly just above the narrow girdle about the waist. The left arm was originally extended, thus freed entirely from the mass of the body with a daring we have never before witnessed in stone sculpture. In fact, it had to be made of a separate piece of marble and inserted into a socket, where a piece of it may still be seen. The right arm hangs along the body, the contours beautifully played off against the subtle curve of the hip and thigh, which the heel of the hand barely touches, eliminating the necessity for a connecting bridge. The broad face is unexpectedly happy, almost whimsical in its expression, and the soft red locks, three on each side, flow gently over the shoulders, setting off the full forms of the body. The *Peplos Kore* is dated about 530 B.C. The climax of the Archaic style can be seen in the enchanting kore nicknamed *La Delicata* (colorplate 13), of just a few years later. The corners of the large and heavy-lidded eyes are lifted slightly, and the smile has begun to fade; indeed, the face looks almost sad. The folds and rippling edges of the rich Ionian himation, together with the three locks on either side, almost drown the basic forms of the figure in the exuberance of their ornamental rhythms. Much of the original coloring is preserved, which adds to the delight of one of the richest of all the kore figures. The next steps in the evolution of both male and female figures belong to another era.

Architecture and Architectural Sculpture

Great as were the new developments in Greek sculpture in the sixth century, they were at least equaled, perhaps even surpassed, by the achievements of Greek architects. These were not in the realm of private building, for houses remained modest until Hellenistic times. Neither kings nor tyrants, nor least of all, of course, democratic magistrates, built palaces like those of Mesopotamia, which incorporated temples into their far-flung complexes. The principal public building of the Greeks was the temple (fig. 151). Generally in a sanctuary dedicated to one or several deities, some temples were in lowland sites, others set upon a commanding height, like the Acropolis at Athens. Oddly enough, the Greek temple was not intended for public worship, which took place before altars in the open air. Its primary purposes were to house the image of the god and to preserve the offerings brought by the faithful. The shrine, at first of modest dimensions and never of a size remotely comparable to that of Egyptian temples, was impressive only in its exterior. Its appearance was dominated by the colonnaded portico, or *peristyle*, which surrounded all larger temples and existed in the form of porches even in very small ones. In a Greek polis a portico provided shelter from sun or rain and a freely accessible public place in which to discuss political or philosophical principles, conduct business, or just stroll. In fact, in Hellenistic times independent porticoes known as stoas were built for just these purposes. They were walled on three sides and open on the fourth, and were sometimes hundreds of feet long. The walls of early colonnaded temples were built of mud brick and the columns of wood. In the course of time stone was substituted for these perishable materials, but the shapes of wooden columns and wooden beams continued to be followed in their stone successors, just as the architecture of Imhotep at Saqqara (see fig. 50) perpetuated palm-trunk and reed-bundle construction.

Clearly differentiated systems known as orders governed all the forms of any Greek temple. The orders may be thought of as languages, each with its own vocabulary and rules of grammar and syntax, or as scales in music. At first there were only two orders, named for the two major ethnic divisions of the Greeks, the Doric and the Ionic. In the fifth century the Corinthian appeared; this order was seldom used by the Greeks but became a favorite among the Romans, who added two orders of their own, the Tuscan and the Composite. In Hellenistic times individual variants of the Greek orders appeared here and there, but these are occasional exceptions that prove the universal rule.

The column and the entablature, the basic components of the Greek orders (fig. 152), are simply more elaborate versions of post-and-lintel construction. The column was divided into shaft, capital, and base (Greek Doric columns had no base; one was added in the Roman version), the entablature into architrave, frieze, and cornice. The capital (from the Latin word for *head*) was intended to transfer the weight of the entablature onto the shaft. The Doric capital consisted of a square slab known as the *abacus* above a smooth, round, cushion-shaped member called the *echinus*. The Ionic capital, more elaborate (fig. 153), had a richly ornamented abacus and echinus separated by a double-scroll-shaped member, the *volute*. The Doric architrave was a single unmolded stone beam, and the frieze was divided between *triglyphs* and *metopes*. The triglyph (from a Greek word meaning *three grooves*) was a block with two complete vertical grooves in the center and a half groove at each side. The triglyphs derived from the beam-ends of wooden buildings; the metopes were the slabs between the beams. The Ionic architrave was divided into three flat strips called *fasciae*, each projecting slightly beyond the one below. The Ionic frieze had no special architectural character but could be ornamented or sculptured. The temple was usually roofed by a low gable whose open triangular ends, backed by slabs of stone, were called *pediments*.

Ancient writers considered the Doric order masculine and robust, the Ionic feminine and elegant. In every Doric or Ionic temple the basic elements were the same. The columns were made of cylindrical blocks, called *drums*, turned on a lathe. These were held together by metal dowels and fluted in place after erection, that is, channeled by shallow vertical grooves. The earliest Doric columns had twenty-four flutes, which increased their apparent verticality and slenderness. Doric flutes met in a sharp edge; Ionic flutes were separated by a narrow strip of stone. Whatever may have been their purpose, the

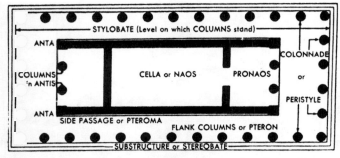

151. Plan of a typical Greek Temple (after Grinnell)

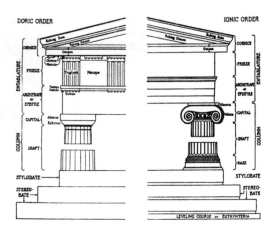

152. The Doric and Ionic Orders (after Grinnell)

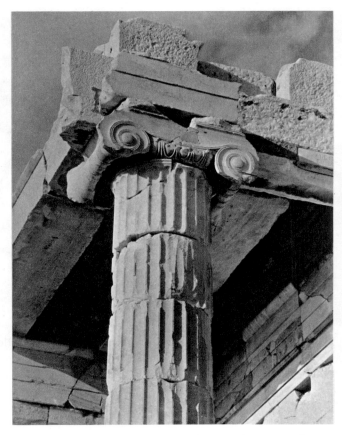

153. Ionic capital on column in central passage of Propylaia. The Acropolis, Athens

flutes have the effect of increasing the clarity of progression from light to shade in easily distinguishable stages around a shaft. The flutes may possibly be related to the polygonal columns occasionally used in Egypt (see fig. 75).

Unlike Egyptian polygonal and convexly fluted columns, which were always straight, and Aegean columns, which tapered downward, Greek columns tapered noticeably toward the capital. Egyptian cylindrical columns, generally based on plant forms, showed a considerable bulge near the bottom (see fig. 78); Greek columns, instead, had a slight swell, known as the *entasis*, suggesting the tonus of a muscle. They were, moreover, governed by the proportions of contemporary human sculptured figures. As the Greek figure grew slenderer and the head proportionately smaller, so the column diminished in bulk and its capital in size. On occasion the column could even be substituted by a human figure carrying the architrave (see figs. 157, 201).

Like the parts of the orders, the shapes of the temples were controlled by rules as stringent as those of grammar and music. Small temples often consisted only of a *cella* (the central rectangular structure housing the image of the deity), whose side walls were prolonged forward to

carry the entablature and pediment directly and to frame two columns; such a temple was called *in antis* (see fig. 154). If the portico ran across its entire front, the temple was *prostyle*; if it had front and rear porticoes, it was *amphiprostyle* (see fig. 198); if the colonnade, known as a *peristyle*, ran around all four sides, the temple was *peripteral* (see colorplate 17); if the portico was two columns deep, the temple was *dipteral* (see fig. 188).

Yet just as sonnets written in the same language or fugues composed according to the same rules will vary infinitely according to the ideas and talents of the poet or the musician, there are a surprising number of individual variations within what appear to be the stern limitations of Greek architectural orders and types. As we have already seen, there was a rapid change in the proportion of the columns corresponding to those of contemporary sculptured figures. The tapering and entasis also changed. The earliest examples show a sharp taper and a very muscular bulge, with sharply projecting capitals, suggesting physical strain in carrying the weight of the entablature. In later columns, along with the increase in height, both taper and entasis rapidly decrease and the projection of the capital sharply diminishes, until the lofty columns of the Parthenon in the middle of the fifth

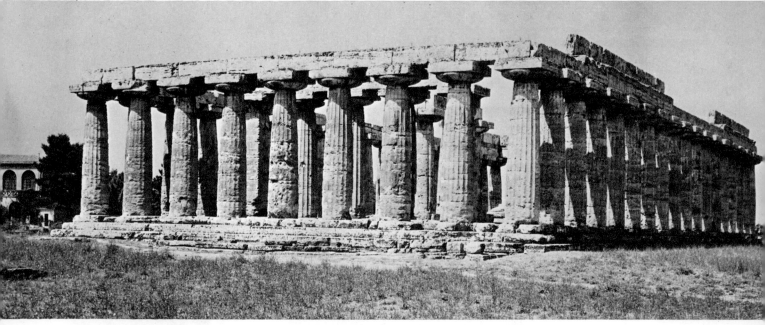

154. "Basilica" (Temple of Hera I). Middle 6th century B.C. Paestum, Italy

century appear to carry their load effortlessly. The changes in style and taste from temple to temple, subtle though they may at first appear, are distinct enough to enable one to recognize individual temples of either Doric or Ionic order at a glance.

The corner columns invariably caused difficulties. Since there was always one triglyph above each Doric column and another above each *intercolumniation* (space between two columns), either half a metope would be left over at the corner of the building or the corner triglyph would not be over a column. This discrepancy was solved by delicate adjustments of distances, so that a two-faced triglyph always appeared at the corner, with adjacent metopes slightly extended, and the corner column was brought a little closer to its neighbors. In the Ionic order, since the capitals had two scrolled and two flat sides, the problem was again how to turn the corner. This was solved by giving the corner capital two adjacent flat sides, with a volute coming out on an angle for both, and two inner scrolled sides (see fig. 218).

But these adjustments were by no means all. Architects also toyed with the effects of varying proportions. Early temples were nearly three times as long as their width, while the Classical formula of the fifth century provided that the number of columns on the long side of a temple should be twice the number of those at either end plus one. The relatively simple interiors were lighted only by the large door. Numerous methods of supporting the roof beams were experimented with in early temples, including projecting spur walls like those at Saqqara (see fig. 54), and even a row of columns down the center, which had the disadvantage of obscuring the statue of the deity. The sixth- and fifth-century solution was generally two rows of superimposed orders of small columns, each

repeating in miniature the proportions of the external peristyle (see fig. 179). Roof beams in early temples were still of wood and tiles of terra-cotta; in the sixth and fifth centuries marble was often used for roof tiles.

Sculpture could be placed almost anywhere in Egyptian temples; huge statues could sit or stand before or inside the temples; walls, columns, and pylons were alive with rows of figures carved in the shallowest relief, mingled with hieroglyphics, and painted. From the very start the Greeks made a clear-cut distinction between those sections of a temple that could be ornamented with sculpture and those that could not. Walls and columns were inviolable, save in the rare instances when a sculptured figure could become a bearing member. But into the empty spaces of a Greek temple sculpture could logically be inserted. Triglyphs were blocks of some size; the intervening metopes made splendid places for relief sculpture. Naturally, the reliefs had to be of a certain depth in order to compete with the surrounding architectural elements, and there had to be some continuity in content among the metopes running round a large building. An Ionic frieze was also an obvious place for a continuous strip of relief sculpture. The corners of the pediments afforded the possibility of silhouetting sculptures (*acroteria*) against the sky. And above all the empty pediments, which needed nothing but flat, vertical slabs to exclude wind and rain, provided spaces that could be filled with sculptured figures of a certain depth, preferably statues in the round. In those regions of Greece that enjoyed good stone for carving, and in those temples that could afford sculptural work, an unprecedented new art of architectural sculpture arose, never surpassed or even equaled until the Gothic cathedrals of the twelfth and thirteenth centuries were built (see Part

Three, Chapter 9). In ancient Greece, for the first time in human history, the architectural creations of man were in perfect balance with the figure of man himself.

The earliest well-preserved Greek temple is not in Greece itself but in the Greek colony of Poseidonia, now called Paestum, on the western coast of Italy about fifty miles southeast of Naples. This limestone building, erroneously called the "Basilica" in the eighteenth century but more probably dedicated to Hera, queen of the gods, has lost its cella walls but still retains its complete peristyle (fig. 154). The temple is unusual in having nine columns across the ends; most others show an even number. The bulky, closely spaced columns with their strong entases and widespread capitals appear to labor to support the massive entablature. Although the temple has no sculpture, it gives us an idea of how the slightly earlier Temple of Artemis on the Greek island of Corfu must originally have looked (reconstruction in fig. 155).

Considerable fragments of one of the limestone pediments remain (fig. 156). This pediment was carved in high relief, approaching sculpture in the round. The central figure, so huge that she must kneel on her right knee in order to fit, is the Gorgon, Medusa, grinning hideously and sticking out her tongue. She was probably placed there to ward off evil spirits, and is aided in her task by the two symmetrical leopards that crouch on either side (one thinks of the heraldic lions of Mycenae; see fig. 132). On her left, as an odd anachronism and in smaller scale, appear the head and torso of the boy Chrysaor, who sprang from her neck when Perseus struck off her head; to her right was Pegasus, the winged horse, born in the same way and at the same moment. The modeling strongly suggests that of the *Calf Bearer* (see fig. 147). In the empty corners of the pediment were placed smaller, battling figures of gods and giants. So symmetrical a grouping, with fillers at the corners, looks tentative when

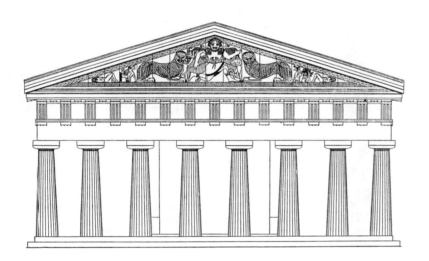

155. West façade, Temple of Artemis, Corfu. Early 6th century B.C. (Reconstruction drawing after G. Rodenwaldt)

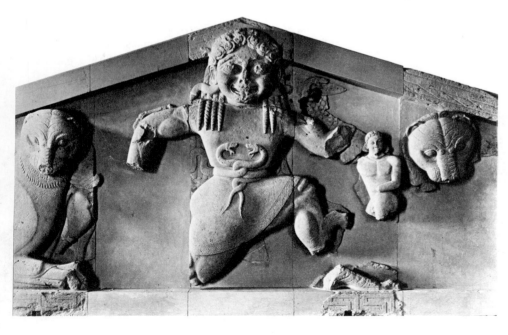

156. *Medusa,* from the west pediment of the Temple of Artemis, Corfu. c. 600–580 B.C. Limestone high relief, height 9′2″. Archaeological Museum, Corfu

we compare it to the more unified pediments that were created later. Nonetheless, the contrast between large and small masses of smooth stone is delightful, and so is the writing movement of Medusa's belt, formed of live, intertwined, and very angry snakes.

A more refined and elegant, as well as more active and complex, use of sculpture appears in the little marble treasury built at the sanctuary of Apollo at Delphi around 530 B.C. by the inhabitants of the Greek island of Siphnos to hold their gifts. The Treasury of the Siphnians has been partially reconstructed from fragments (fig. 157). Here columns are replaced by two graceful kore figures, strongly resembling *La Delicata* (see colorplate 13), on whose heads capitals are balanced to carry effortlessly the weight of entablature and pediment. The frieze is a continuous relief, largely depicting battle scenes. The *Battle of Gods and Giants* (fig. 158) shows that the sculptor had a completely new conception of space. No longer does he have to place one figure above another to indicate distance. All stand or move on the same ground level and overlap in depth. Although none of the figures are in the round—they are all more or less flattened, in keeping with the character of a relief—those in the foreground are sharply undercut. The projection diminishes so that the figures farthest from the eye are only slightly raised from the background. This relief, for the first time in the history of art as far as we know, strives to achieve the optical illusion of space receding horizontally inward from the foreground. This recession is limited to a maximum of three figures (or four horses), but it is revolutionary nonetheless. The pediment contains, again for the first time, actual groups of almost freestanding statues, carved in more or less the same scale, in poses progressively adjusted to the downward slope of the pediment. The intense activity of the reliefs is kept in check only by the severity of the unrelieved wall surfaces below.

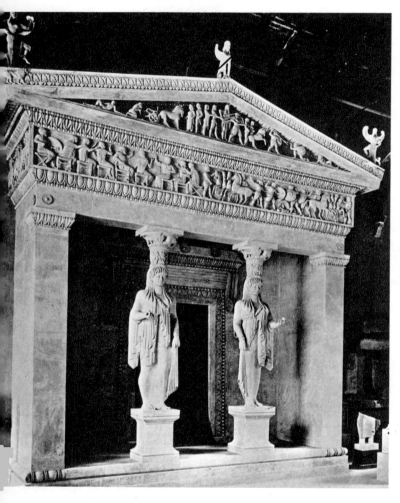

157. Façade, Treasury of the Siphnians, Sanctuary of Apollo, Delphi (partial reconstruction). c. 530 B.C. Marble. Archaeological Museum, Delphi

158. *Battle of Gods and Giants* (fragment), from the north frieze of the Treasury of the Siphnians, Delphi. c. 530 B.C. Marble, height 26″. Archaeological Museum, Delphi

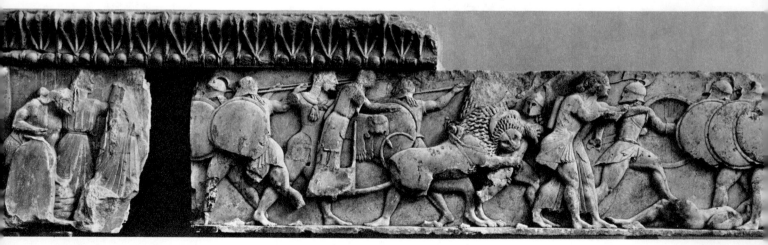

The climax of Archaic architecture and sculpture, at the threshold of the Classical period, is the temple of the local goddess Aphaia on the island of Aegina in the Gulf of Athens. The building was constructed about 500 B.C. of limestone stuccoed to resemble marble. Portions of the temple still stand (fig. 159). A plan of its original appearance (fig. 160) shows the outer Doric peristyle, with six columns at each end and twelve on each side. These columns are slenderer, taller, and more widely spaced than those at Corfu or in the Temple of Hera I at Paestum (see figs. 155, 154). For the first time the architect achieved what later became the standard solution of two superimposed interior colonnades. The marble pedimental statues were excessively restored in the nineteenth century, but these restorations have recently been removed (see figs. 161, 162, 163). These statues are

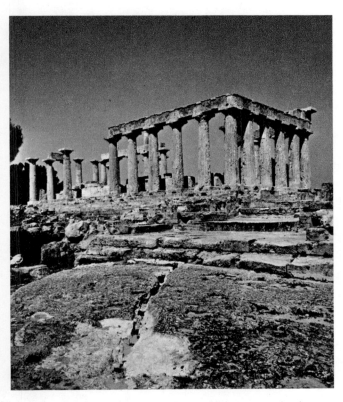

159. Temple of Aphaia. c. 500 B.C. Limestone. Aegina

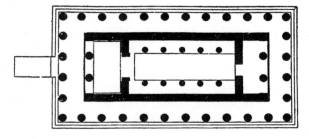

160. Plan of the Temple of Aphaia

superb, full of the same vitality visible in the reliefs from the Treasury of the Siphnians (see figs. 157, 158) yet simpler and more successfully balanced. It is interesting to compare the *Oriental Archer* (so called because of his Phrygian cap) from the western pediment, carved about 510 B.C., with the *Archer* carved some fifteen or twenty years later (figs. 161, 162). Nobly poised though the earlier statue is, it is somewhat schematic; one does not really feel the play of muscles. The masses of the later figure are held in position entirely by its beautifully understood muscular movement and tension, which must have been even more effective when the missing bronze bow was intact. The *Dying Warrior* (fig. 163) embodies at long last the heroic grandeur of the Homeric epics in the simple, clear-cut masses of the figure and in its celebration of the nobility of self-possession and calm even at the moment of violent death. The latest statues at Aegina have, in fact, brought us to the beginning of the Classical period in content and in style.

Vase Painting

Painting was always considered one of the greatest of the arts by Greek writers, and a splendid tradition of painting on walls and on movable panels surely flourished during the late Archaic period. Yet so little survives that we cannot even form a clear idea of what we have lost. Nonetheless, a few echoes of this vanished art persist in far-off Etruscan tomb paintings (see colorplate 25). Given their clear-cut, continuous outlines and flat areas of color, not unlike those of Egyptian painting, and considering also the strict limitations of Archaic sculptures with their smooth surfaces and strong, active contours, we can arrive at some notion of what the style of Archaic monumental painting must have been. Its quality, however, can only be guessed at; in this we are assisted by the beauty of the vast numbers of sixth-century painted vases still preserved.

The Archaic period saw the climax of Greek vase painting, which reached a high level of artistic perfection, rivaling sculpture and architecture. Even more than contemporary sculpture, Archaic vase painting shows the flexibility of the new art, whose brilliant design is based on action and movement. How highly the Greeks themselves valued their vases is shown by the fact that so many of them were signed by the painter. Some were also signed by the potter. Through comparison with signed vases, unsigned pieces can be attributed to individual artists on account of similarities in style. In this way the development of personal styles can sometimes be followed for decades. This is the first moment in the history of art when such distinctions can be made and such evolutions traced. It is a very important consideration, because the art we are analyzing is, after all, one whose very principles of design are based on the interaction of individual human beings—in contrast to the mere alignment of standardized types so common in Egyptian and Mesopotamian art.

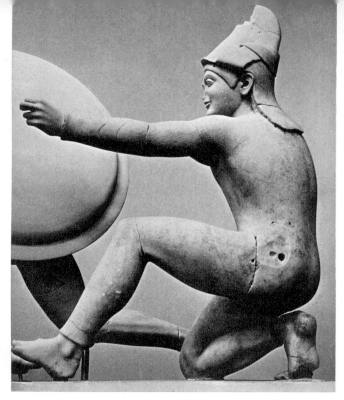

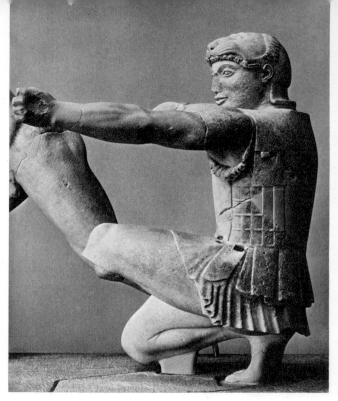

161. *Oriental Archer,* from the west pediment of the Temple of Aphaia, Aegina. c. 510 B.C. Marble, height 41". Staatliche Antikensammlungen und Glyptothek, Munich

162. *Archer,* from the east pediment of the Temple of Aphaia, Aegina. c. 490 B.C. Marble, height 31". Staatliche Antikensammlungen und Glyptothek, Munich

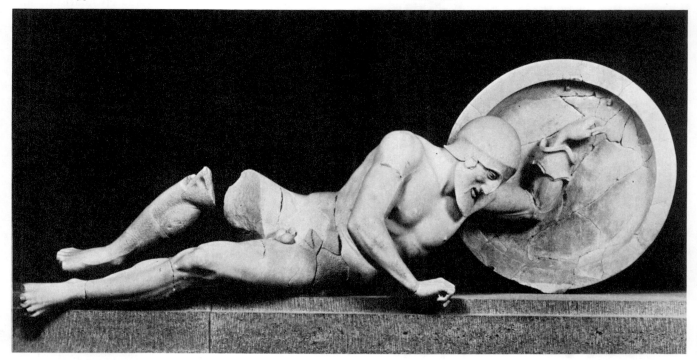

163. *Dying Warrior,* from the east pediment of the Temple of Aphaia, Aegina. c. 490 B.C. Marble, 24 x 72". Staatliche Antikensammlungen und Glyptothek, Munich

Vases were made for both local use and export in several Greek cities, especially Corinth and Athens. In the seventh century Corinthian vases, made of pale, yellowish clay, were most popular, but in the early Archaic period the orange-red pots of Athens took the lead. The miniature style of the Corinthian painters could no longer compete with the strength, grace, and intellectual clarity of the Athenians.

Many of the finest Greek vases are preserved because they found their way to Etruria, whose inhabitants prized them highly and buried them in the tombs of the dead. The best Athenian vases are masterpieces of drawing and design, operating within a very restricted range of colors. The natural color of the clay was sometimes heightened by a brighter clay slip painted on for the background. The most important tone was black, used for figures and for the body of the vase. Gone is the cluttered decoration of the earlier periods. Within the contours of the black figures, details were drawn in lines incised by a metal tool. The glossy black was also a clay slip, its color achieved by controlling the air intake during the delicate and complex firing process.

One of the most ambitious sixth-century vases, known as the *François Vase* (fig. 164), of about 570 B.C., was found in an Etruscan tomb at Chiusi in central Italy. It is a *krater*, a type of vase intended for mixing water and wine, the customary Greek beverage, and was proudly signed by the painter Kleitias and the potter Ergotimos. The grand, volute-shaped handles grow like plants out of the body of the vase before curling over to rest upon its lip. The vase is still divided into registers like the *Dipylon Vase* (see fig. 140), but Geometric ornament has been reduced to a single row of sharp rays above its foot; the handles are decorated with palmettes. The other registers are devoted to a lively narration of incidents from the stories of the heroes Theseus and Achilles. The figures still show the tiny waists, knees, and ankles and the full calves, buttocks, and chests that were standard in the Geometric style, but they now move with a vigor similar to that of the sculptures on the Corfu pediment (see fig. 156), and both men and animals have begun to overlap in depth in a manner foreshadowing the deployment of figures in the frieze of the Treasury of the Siphnians (see fig. 158).

A splendid example of Archaic design based on organic movement is the *Oriental Between Two Horses* (fig. 165) by the painter Psiax, dating from about 520–10 B.C. The Oriental, who seems to be a horse trainer, moves rapidly forward with knees sharply bent, in the style of the Medusa at Corfu (see fig. 156), and turns his head to look backward over his right shoulder. The forcefulness of the movement and the angularity of the bent limbs recall the almost contemporary *Oriental Archer* (see fig. 161) from Aegina. On either side horses rear in a heraldic grouping, their slender legs overlapping the archer's body, their bodies seeming to swell with the expansion of the amphora itself. The incised lines, at once delicate and firm, are left in the red of the background.

One of the most delightful of all Archaic vase paintings is on the interior of a *kylix*, or wine cup, painted by Exekias about 540 B.C. (fig. 166); Dionysos, god of wine, reclines in a ship from whose mast he had caused a grape-laden vine to spring in order to terrify some pirates who had captured him and whom he then transformed into dolphins. The almost dizzying effect of the free, circular composition, appropriately enough, is not unusual in decorations for the insides of wine cups. In this case the feeling of movement is heightened by the bellying sail (originally all white) and by the seven dolphins circling hopelessly about the vessel. The entire scene, with all its suggestions of wind and sea, is carried off without the actual depiction of even a single wave.

Toward the end of the sixth century, vase painters discovered that their compositions would be more effective and their figures more lifelike if left in the red color of the terra-cotta, with the black transferred to the background, just as in pediments or friezes the figures shone in white or softly colored marble against a darker background of red or blue. At first the change was tentative; some vases even show red figures on one side, black on the other. But once it was generally accepted, the change was lasting. One of the earliest red-figure vases, and certainly one of the finest Greek vases in existence, is a calyx-krater by Euphronios (colorplate 14), datable about 515 B.C. The

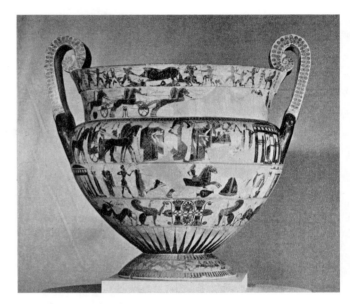

164. KLEITIAS and ERGOTIMOS. *François Vase* (krater), found at Chiusi, Italy. c. 570 B.C. Height c. 26″. Museo Archeologico, Florence

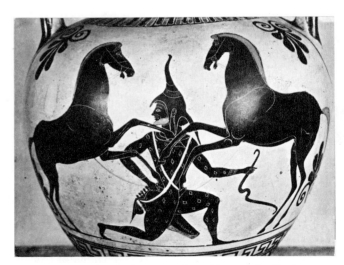

165. PSIAX. *Oriental Between Two Horses* (detail of an amphora found at Vulci, Italy). c. 520–510 B.C. Height of amphora 14½″. British Museum, London

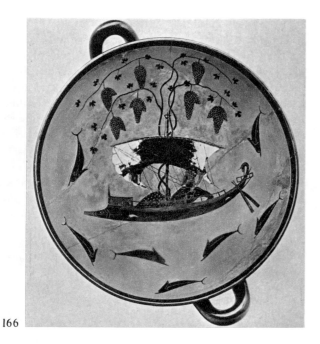

166

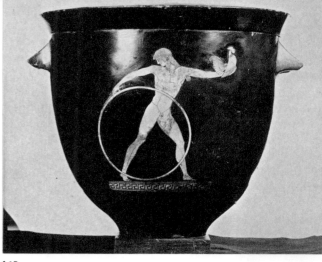

168

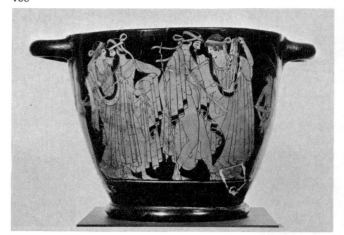

169

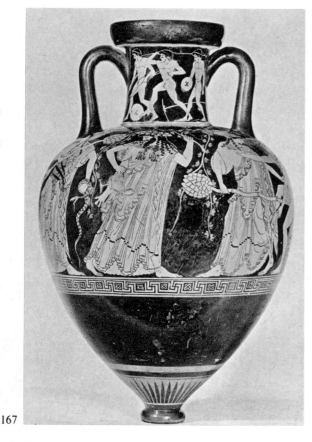

167

166. Exekias. *Dionysos in a Ship* (interior of a kylix found at Vulci, Italy). c. 540 b.c. Diameter 12". Staatliche Antikensammlungen und Glyptothek. Munich

167. The Kleophrades Painter. *Dionysos Between Maenads* (detail of the pointed amphora found at Vulci, Italy). c. 500–490 b.c. Height 22". Staatliche Antikensammlungen und Glyptothek, Munich. See Colorplate 15

168. The Berlin Painter. *Ganymede*, from a bell-shaped krater found in Etruria. Early 5th century b.c. Height c. 13". The Louvre. Paris

169. The Brygos Painter. *Revelling*, from a skyphos. c. 490 b.c. Height c. 8". The Louvre. Paris

principal scene depicts a rarely illustrated passage from the *Iliad*, narrating how the body of the Trojan warrior Sarpedon, son of Zeus, was removed from the field of battle by the twin brothers Hypnos and Thanatos (Sleep and Death) under the supervision of Hermes, to be washed in preparation for a hero's grave. The extraordinary combination of great sculptural force, equaling that of the actual statues at Aegina, with extreme tenderness of feeling is completely unexpected. The blend is achieved by a line that surpasses almost anything in Greek vase painting in its tensile strength and descriptive delicacy. From the beautiful analysis of the muscular body of Sarpedon to the knife-sharp wing feathers of Hypnos and Thanatos, even to the slight curl at the tips of the fingers and toes, the movement is carried out with perfect consistency and control. The very inscriptions, usually naming adjacent figures, are not allowed to float freely against the black, but move in such a way as to carry out the inner forces of the composition. *Thanatos*, for example, is written backward so as to lead the eye toward the crucial central figure of Hermes.

But vase painting did not always remain on the plane of high tragedy; the very fact that so many vases were destined to hold wine tended to promote a certain freedom in both subject and treatment. Among the followers of the great Euphronios, two sensitive masters have been distinguished—one called the Kleophrades Painter because his work is so often found on vases signed by the potter of that name, the other called the Berlin Painter. The body of a pointed amphora from an Etruscan site at Vulci (fig. 167) shows Dionysos between maenads (the wine-god's ecstatic female followers), and athletes in smaller scale gambol about the neck. Especially brilliant is the treatment of a rapt, blonde maenad, with lips slightly parted (colorplate 15). The deft, sure linear contours contrast sharply with the sketchy quality of the hair, painted in a different thickness of slip so that it would fire to a soft, light color, and with the garland about the head, even more rapidly brushed in soft violet. A bell-shaped krater by the Berlin Painter (fig. 168) shows Ganymede, the favorite of Zeus, holding a rooster in one hand and glancing coyly over his shoulder as he rolls a hoop—a triumph of rhythmic grace and poise. The Brygos Painter, another master named for the potter on whose vases his paintings appear, treats an amatory subject with restrained excitement (fig. 169). Two nude men, past their first youth, have begun to embrace two young women who are clothed (but not for long). The eye slips happily from nude forms to drapery masses swinging in a controlled abundance of linear movement.

THE CLASSICAL PERIOD—THE SEVERE STYLE (480–450 B.C.) AND ITS CONSEQUENCES

In the early decades of the fifth century B.C., the individualism of the Greek city-states was put to its severest test in a protracted struggle against Mesopotamian autocracy in the form of the Persian Empire, first under Darius I and then under his son Xerxes I. Persia had succeeded in subjugating all the Greek cities of Asia Minor and then insisted on extending her domination to European Greece. The resistance to the Persian threat brought about one of the rare instances of near-unity among the rival Greek states. In 480 B.C. Xerxes conquered Attica, occupied Athens (which had been evacuated by its citizens), and laid waste the city. Yet in this selfsame year the Greeks managed to trap and destroy the Persian fleet at Salamis, and after another defeat on land in 479, Xerxes was forced to retire. Although the struggle continued sporadically in northern Greece, the Greek states were temporarily safe. Athens, which had led the resistance, embarked on a period of unprecedented prosperity and power.

The new development of the Classical style in the years immediately following Salamis shows above all an increased awareness of the role of individual character in determining human destiny, and it incorporates the ideal of ennobled humanity in a bodily structure of previously unimagined strength, resilience, and harmony. This development was no accident, any more than it was an accident that the Classical belief in the autonomy of the individual was revived in the early Renaissance in fifteenth-century Florence under remarkably similar circumstances (see Part Four, Chapter 1). We need only set the new images of heroic, self-controlled, and complete individuals that followed (especially figs. 173, 174) against the standardized soldiers of Persian autocracy in order to realize the extent of the revolution that came to fulfillment in Greek art of the Classical period.

Freestanding and Relief Sculpture

The brief and significant generation between the close of the Archaic period and the height of Classical art in the Age of Pericles shows a remarkable transformation not only in style but also in general tone. The term Severe Style suggests the moral ideals of dignity and self-control that characterize the art of the time and mirror the short-lived Greek resolve to repel the Persian invader. We may well commence our consideration of this period with the earliest of the rare Greek lifesize bronzes to come down to us, the superb *Charioteer of Delphi* (fig. 170), dedicated by Polyzalos, tyrant of the Greek city-state of Gela in Sicily, to celebrate his victory in the chariot race at the Delphic Games just before 470 B.C. Originally the charioteer stood in a bronze chariot and controlled four bronze horses with their bridles; only fragments of the horses survive. The dignity and calm of the figure remind us that the metaphor of a charioteer was later used by Plato to symbolize man's control of the contrary forces in his soul. The bronze, originally polished, is relieved in the face by inlaid copper lips and eyelashes and by eyes made of glass paste. We should mentally restore these features wherever they are missing in Greek and Roman bronzes. The figure stands with a resiliency new to Greek sculpture; the folds of the long chiton worn by charioteers drape easily across the chest and fall from the high belt in full, tubular shapes as cloth actually does, rather than in the ornamentalized folds of the Archaic period. Most important of all, the pointed features and sprightly linearity of the Archaic period have vanished along with the Archaic smile. The face is constructed of square and round forms; the square, broad nose joins the brows in a single plane; the mouth is short, the lips full, the eyes wide open, the chin and jaw rounded and firm.

A slightly earlier statue (fig. 171), called the *Kritios Boy* because it embodies what is thought to have been the style of the sculptor Kritios, should be compared with the Archaic kouros figures (see figs. 145, 146) to bring out the scope of the transformation in Greek sculpture.

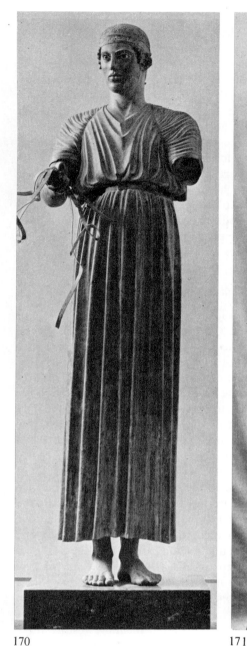

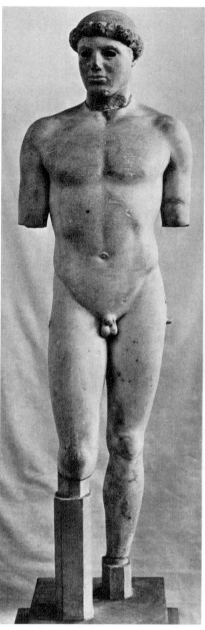

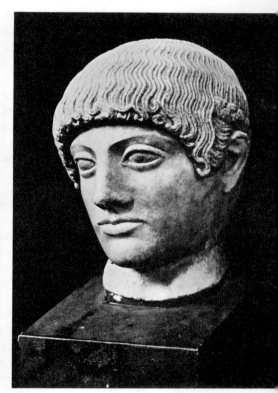

172

170. *Charioteer of Delphi*, from the Sanctuary of Apollo, Delphi. c. 470 B.C. Bronze, height 71". Archaeological Museum, Delph*

171. *Kritios Boy*, from the Acropolis, Athens. c. 480 B.C. Marble, height 33". Acropolis Museum

172. *Blond Youth*, from the Acropolis, Athens. c. 480 B.C. Marble, height 9⅝". Acropolis Museum

170   171

Although the kouros figures are also standing, they appear frozen in a pose derived from walking, with the weight evenly distributed on both legs. In the *Kritios Boy*, the figure stands *at rest*, as people actually do, with the weight placed on one leg while the other remains free. In consequence the left hip, on which the weight rests, is slightly higher than the right. In recompense, the right shoulder should be higher than the left, but the sculptor does not seem to have noticed this. He has discovered that in a resting figure the masses respond to stresses just as in a moving one, and that rest in a living being is not equivalent to inertia, as in Egyptian sculpture, or to the unreal symmetry of the Archaic, but to a balanced composure of stresses. The fullness, richness, and warmth of

the human body, hinted at for the first time in the *Anavyssos Kouros* (see fig. 146), are now fully realized, the forms blending effortlessly into each other. The firm beauty of the features and facial proportions preferred by the Severe Style is seen at its grandest in the *Blond Youth* (fig. 172), also dating from about 480 B.C., so called because traces of blond coloring could once be seen in the hair. The irises of the characteristically heavy-lidded eyes still retain considerable color, and the typical pensive, serene expression of the Severe Style is beautifully realized. The hair, it should be noted, is still ornamentalized and worn almost like a cap, although occasionally a lock breaks free.

Fortunately, a single original bronze action statue of

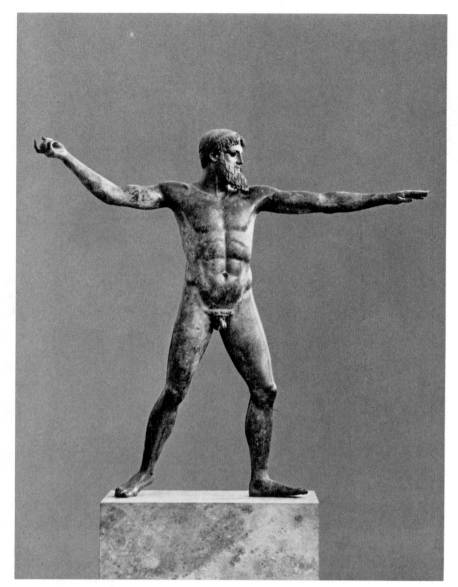

173. *Zeus*, found in the sea off Cape Artemision. c. 460 B.C. Bronze, height 82".
National Archaeological Museum, Athens

the Severe Style has come to light, a splendid, over-lifesize figure of the nude Zeus, found in the sea off Cape Artemision (fig. 173). The subject is often considered to be Poseidon, god of the sea, but if the trident (three-tined spear) wielded by Poseidon were to be placed in the figure's right hand it would obscure the face; more likely the figure represents Zeus hurling a thunderbolt. In no other remaining example can we see the magnificence of the Greek athletic ideal in the very person of the ruler of the gods. While the hair, bound in by a braid, and the beard and eyebrows are still stylized, the muscles of the body and the limbs vibrate with a new intensity.

The leading sculptors of the period immediately following, especially Myron and Polykleitos, were trained in the Severe Style, of which their work is an immediate outgrowth. Both were chiefly concerned with athletic subjects, which enabled them to exemplify the Classical principles of rhythmic organization derived from the poses of powerful nude male figures. In his bronze *Diskobolos (Discus Thrower)*, of about 450 B.C., which we know only through Roman copies in marble (fig. 174), Myron chose the moment when the athlete bent forward, in a pose of great tension and compression, before turning to hurl his discus. The composition, operating in one plane like the *Zeus of Artemision*, is built on the transitory equipoise of two intersecting arcs formed by the arms and the torso. Like all Classical figural groupings, this one dissolves the moment the action is over; its beauty lies in the lasting grandeur of a geometrical composition abstracted from a fleeting moment of action. The new dynamics of the Severe Style have been concentrated into a single image of extraordinary power.

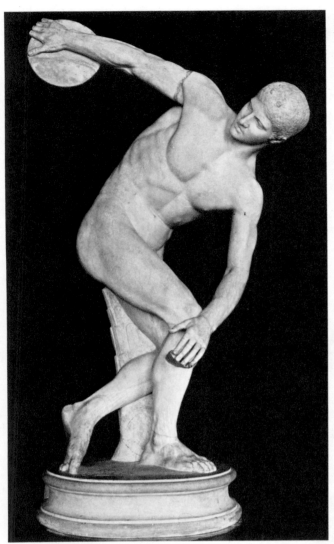

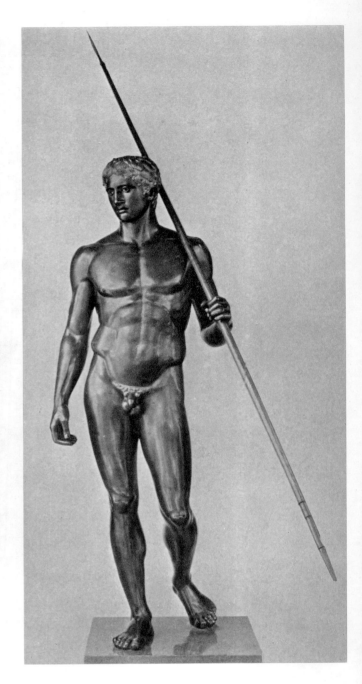

174. MYRON. *Diskobolos (Discus Thrower)*. c. 450 B.C.
Roman marble copy of bronze original, life-size.
Museo delle Terme, Rome

175. POLYKLEITOS. *Doryphoros (Spear-Bearer)*.
c. 450–440 B.C. Bronze reconstruction.
Universität, Munich

The ultimate development of the kouros type can be seen in the *Doryphoros (Spear-Bearer)* by Polykleitos, executed probably between 450 and 440 B.C. Again the lost bronze original is accessible only through a number of Roman copies and ancient literary descriptions. A remarkably successful attempt was made in 1935 to reconstruct in bronze the probable appearance of Polykleitos' masterpiece (fig. 175). The problem of the standing figure, posed in the *Kritios Boy* (see fig. 171), has now been completely solved. The right leg bears the full weight of the body, so that the hip is thrust outward; the left leg is free; the tilt of the pelvis is answered by a tilt of the shoulders in the opposite direction; and the whole body rises effortlessly in a single long S-curve from the feet to the head, culminating in the glance directed slightly to the figure's right. Regardless of the fact that the figure is at rest—as never before—the dynamism of the pose transforms it into an easy walk and is expressed in the musculature by means of the differentiation of flexed and relaxed shapes, producing a rich interplay of changing curves throughout the powerful masses of torso and limbs. A fragmentary Roman copy in black basalt (fig. 176) shows what must have been the effect in dark bronze of the superb muscular structure of the torso, with its characteristically prominent external oblique muscles and sharply defined, U-shaped pelvic groove. Polykleitos wrote a treatise to explain his meticulous system of proportions as exemplified by this statue, but the book is

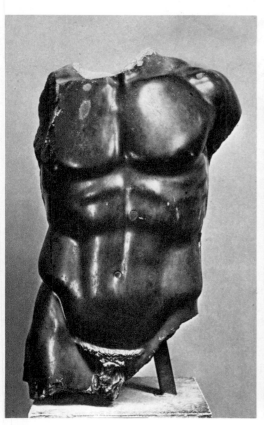

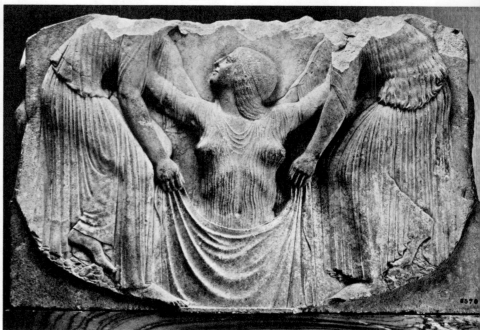

176. POLYKLEITOS. *Doryphoros* (fragment). c. 450–440 B.C. Roman copy in black basalt of original bronze. Galleria degli Uffizi, Florence

177. *Birth of Aphrodite*, from the *Ludovisi Throne* (low reliefs). Early 5th century B.C. Marble, width 56". Museo Nazionale Romano, Rome

lost and his system still imperfectly understood. Polykleitos called both the *Doryphoros* and the book his "Canon" (measuring rod or standard).

An exquisite example of the treatment of the female figure in the Severe Style is the group of low reliefs known as the *Ludovisi Throne*; more probably, these reliefs once formed an altar. Perhaps made in a Greek city in southern Italy, the reliefs nonetheless show early fifth-century sculpture at the height of its perfection. A relief that probably represents the *Birth of Aphrodite* (fig. 177) delineates full and graceful female figures seen through clinging garments that seem almost transparent. As Aphrodite was born from the sea, the device of sheer garments (often known as "wet drapery") seems appropriate; in any case it was used consistently in fifth-century sculpture to reveal the beauty of female forms even when fully clothed.

Architecture and Architectural Sculpture

The greatest architectural and sculptural project of the first half of the fifth century was the Doric Temple of Zeus at Olympia, whose construction and decoration may be dated 470–56 B.C. The temple was the principal building of the sanctuary at Olympia, center of the quadrennial games that provided one of the few unifying threads in the chaotic life of the endemically warring Greek city-states. The temple, which has disappeared save for the stylobate and the lowest drums of the columns, has been carefully excavated, and its appearance can be reconstructed with accuracy. It was built of local limestone, coated with a plaster made of marble dust, but the sculpture and roof tiles were of Parian marble. The architect, Libon of Elis, designed a peristyle six columns wide and thirteen long. Something of the grandeur of its original appearance may be felt in the probably contemporary and somewhat smaller Temple of Hera II at Paestum (fig. 178), despite its more massive proportions and closer spacing of columns due to local taste. Libon's columns are slenderer and more elegant than any we have seen so far, and both their entasis and the projection of their capitals slighter and subtler (fig. 179). Both interiors utilized the double row of superimposed columns we saw at Aegina.

The sculpture, much of which is preserved, ranks among the noblest Greek architectural sculpture. Neither the name of the sculptor nor the city of his origin are known, but a single leading master and a host of assistants must have been at work to produce so rich a cycle of sculpture in so short a time. The mythological subjects were chosen to symbolize the civilizing effect of the Olympic Games, held under divine protection. The two pedimental groups are fairly well preserved, but since the exact order and location of the statues is not clear, several conflicting attempts at reconstruction have been made. The west pediment deals with the *Battle of Lapiths and Centaurs*, a frequent subject in Greek art (fig. 180). The centaurs, half man and half horse, descend on the

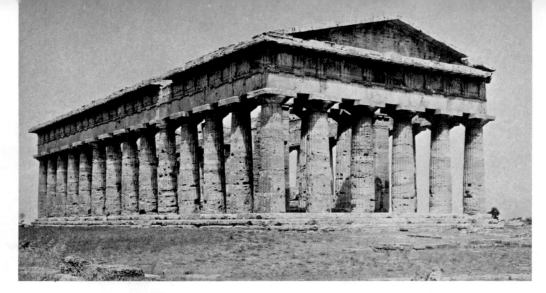

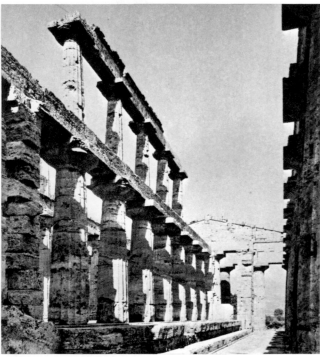

179. Interior, Temple of Hera II

woman, her pose may be mentally reconstructed. She struggles in the embrace of a centaur's forelegs, pushing him off with her hands. While the stern Apollo figure shows—naturally enough, given his commanding role in the action—none of the relaxation of the *Doryphoros* (see fig. 175), the structure and definition of the musculature are in keeping with the principles of the Severe Style. So indeed is the beautiful face, with its nose descending in a straight line from the forehead, its full jaw and rounded chin, and the caplike mass of ornamentalized hair. Despite their freedom of movement, the drapery folds are proportioned to harmonize with the fluting of the columns below.

The metopes of the outer peristyle were left blank, but as the observer ascended the ramp before the temple he could see between the outer columns the frieze above the two columns of the inner portico in antis at either end of the cella, each end having six metopes representing the Labors of Herakles. The high reliefs, almost statues in the round, were kept austerely simple, their broad, full masses contrasting with the flat slab behind. One of the finest (fig. 182) shows Atlas bringing back to Herakles (who has temporarily relieved him in his task of supporting the heavens) the Golden Apples of the Hesperides. The goddess Athena gently assists the hero. Garbed in her simple Doric peplos, she is one of the grandest female figures of the century, and Herakles is sculptured with a reticence and dignity typical of the Severe Style. Some of the breadth of treatment of the Aegina sculptures remains here, but with a new roundness of shape and smoothness of transition from one form to the next.

Painting

Vase painting continued throughout the Classical period, but a sharp decline in quality is notable, as if the painters had lost interest, perhaps due to the sudden increase in scope offered by the great commissions for wall paintings. One of the leading vase painters of the Severe Style is known as the Niobid Painter, after a vase depicting the slaughter of the children of Niobe by Apollo. He is less

wedding feast of the Lapith king Peirithoös, where they taste wine for the first time. Under its influence they attempt to carry off the Lapith women, whom Peirithoös and his friend Theseus strive to rescue. Apollo, god of light and, therefore, of order and reason, presides over the subjugation of the centaurs, possibly an allegory of the effect of the Olympian sanctuary in subduing the struggles between Greek states, all consideration of which had to be laid aside before contestants could enter its sacred gates.

However the statues were arranged, the poses were carefully calculated for the raking cornices, and the pedimental composition was more closely unified than any of its predecessors. The stupendous figure of Apollo, standing erect and with his right arm outstretched, commands the centaurs to desist in their depredations (fig. 181). In spite of heavy damage to the statue of a Lapith

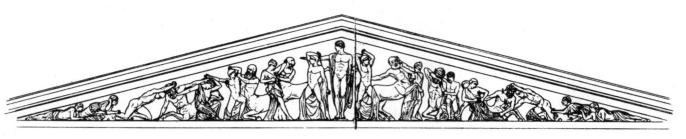

180. *Battle of Lapiths and Centaurs*, from the west pediment of the Temple of Zeus, Olympia. c. 470–456 B.C. (Architectural reconstruction after G. Treu)

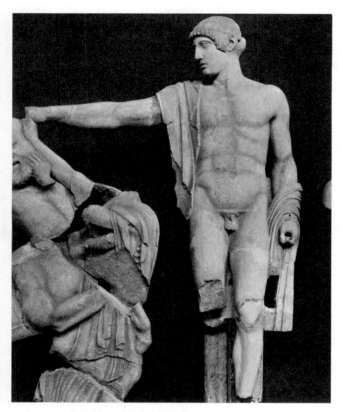

181. *Apollo with a Centaur and a Lapith Woman* (fragment), from the west pediment of the Temple of Zeus, Olympia. c. 470–456 B.C. Marble, height of Apollo c. 10'2". Archaeological Museum, Olympia

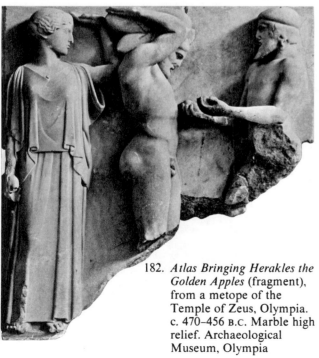

182. *Atlas Bringing Herakles the Golden Apples* (fragment), from a metope of the Temple of Zeus, Olympia. c. 470–456 B.C. Marble high relief. Archaeological Museum, Olympia

important in his own right than because his paintings may tell us something about the vanished works of mural art, particularly those of Polygnotos, the most celebrated painter of the age and, in many ways, a pictorial counterpart of Polykleitos. According to ancient literary descriptions, Polygnotos gave his figures the nobility we have found in the sculpture of the Severe Style and of Polykleitos, as well as a new quality of emotional expression. He was also able to paint transparent or translucent draperies, through which could be seen the forms of the body (like those in the *Ludovisi Throne*; see fig. 177). While he did not use shading, and was thus constrained to rely on line to indicate form, Polygnotos was in one respect a great innovator: he scattered his figures at various points in space, freeing them for the first time from the groundline to which they had previously been confined. He also indicated such landscape elements as rocks and trees. One of the finest works by the Niobid Painter, a calyx-krater found at Orvieto in central Italy and dating from about 455–50 B.C., shows on one side a still unidentified subject that includes both Herakles and Athena and possibly Theseus (fig. 183). The noble, relaxed figures remind us of the sculpture of the Severe Style, and they correspond to the descriptions of Polygnotos' art. Even more striking is the free placing of figures at various points to indicate depth. Each is standing on a separate patch of ground, and all are united by a single wavy line running from one to the next. Another indication of the new interest in actual visual experience, freeing the painter from age-old conventions, is that, for the first time in the history of art, the eyes of profile figures are drawn in profile rather than in full face.

There the story would have stopped had it not been for the extraordinary discovery in 1968 of a painted Greek tomb, datable to about 470 B.C., in a cemetery outside the city of Paestum. The boxlike tomb was formed of six slabs of stone—for the ends, sides, top, and bottom—and all but the bottom slab were painted in fresco, that is, pigment on wet plaster. A layer of coarse plaster was first spread over the slab, and preparatory drawings were made on that. Then smooth plaster was laid on, which had to be painted rapidly so that the colors would amalgamate with the plaster before it dried. This technique was later used widely throughout Etruscan and Roman wall painting, and was revived in the later Middle Ages and the Italian Renaissance.

On the four side slabs of the Paestum tomb were painted figures playing and listening to music and drink-

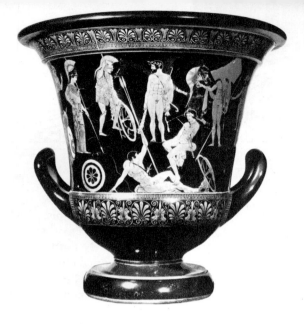

183. THE NIOBID PAINTER. Calyx-krater, found at Orvieto, Italy. c. 455–450 B.C. Height 21¼"; diameter of the mouth 21⅝". The Louvre, Paris

ing wine (fig. 184), while on the lid appeared an unexampled scene—a nude figure in early manhood diving from a kind of springboard into the sea (colorplate 16). This may represent a scene from real life, or perhaps its significance is allegorical—the soul plunging into the waters of the Beyond, in which it is purified of the corruption of the body. There are neither texts nor images to support either interpretation, but an allegory of the future life would seem probable for an image on the *inside* of a closed coffin, visible only to the deceased. Whatever their significance, all the figures show a new suppleness of line, used to describe the fullness of muscular forms as well as a wide range of expressions; between the contours the solid areas of brown flesh tones contain no hint of shading. The eye is shown, as in the work of the Niobid Painter, in profile rather than full face. Schematic landscape elements appear, also for the

first time in Greek painting; a tree is represented, as well as the waves of the sea. All this is in keeping with what we read about Polygnotos' paintings.

If a provincial painter, decorating the tomb of an unknown youth with images destined for eternal darkness, could draw and paint like this, what must have been the lost masterpieces of Athens?

THE CLASSICAL PERIOD—THE AGE OF PERICLES (450–400 B.C.)

The culmination of the Classical period in architecture and sculpture in Athens coincided with the greatest extent of Athenian military and political power, and with the peak of Athenian prosperity—also, unexpectedly, with the height of democratic participation in the affairs of the Athenian polis. This was no accident; the vision and vitality of a single statesman, Pericles, brought Athens to her new political hegemony, and it was Pericles who commissioned the monuments for which Athens is eternally renowned. And with the inevitability of an Athenian tragedy, it was the long and disastrous war begun by Pericles that brought about the defeat of Athens in 404 B.C. and the end of her political power. Had Pericles not died in 429 the end might well have been different. Nevertheless, in some twenty dizzying years Pericles and the great architects and sculptors who worked under his direction created a series of monuments that have been the envy of the civilized world ever since, perhaps because they first proclaimed the new ideal of a transfigured humanity, raised to a plane of superhuman dignity and freedom. The sublime style of the Age of Pericles, as this transitory period should properly be called, was in many respects never equaled; it can be paralleled only by the even briefer period of the early sixteenth century in central Italy, the High Renaissance, also dominated and inspired by a single political genius, Pope Julius II (see Part Four, Chapter 3). It is instructive

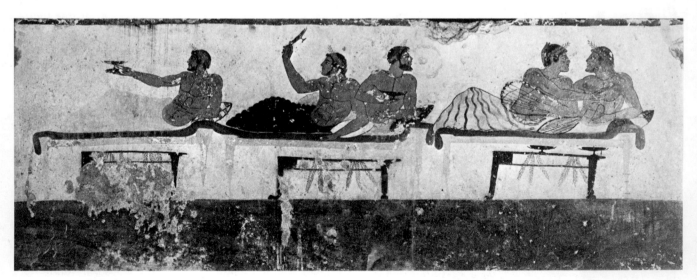

184. *Banqueting Scene*, from a Greek tomb at Paestum, Italy. Fresco. c. 470 B.C. Museo Archeologico Nazionale, Paestum. See Colorplate 16

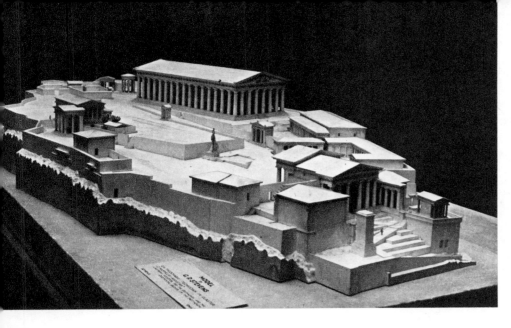

185. Model of the Acropolis, Athens (by G. P. Stevens)

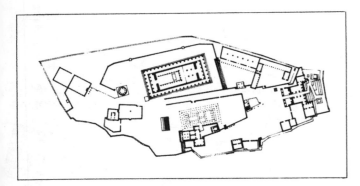

186. Plan of the Acropolis

to remember that with Egypt and Sumeria we thought in millennia and with Archaic Greece in centuries, while with Classical Greece we must think in decades.

The Acropolis at Athens and Its Monuments

The massive limestone rock dominating Athens had been in Mycenaean times the site of the royal palace, and in the Archaic period it contained the principal sanctuaries of the city. When the Persians attacked in 480 B.C., they succeeded in capturing the fortress and in setting fire to the scaffolding around a great new temple to Athena, patron deity of Athens, which was then rising on the highest point of the Acropolis. When the Athenians returned to their city the following year, they vowed to leave the Acropolis in its devastated condition as a memorial to barbarian sacrilege. Nonetheless, they utilized marble fragments, including unfluted drums from the first Parthenon and many Archaic statues, as materials for new fortifications. By 449 B.C. the Athenians seem to have repented of their vow, for in that year they embarked on one of the most ambitious building programs in history. Money was, apparently, no object. But it could not be provided by the rudimentary system of taxation then in effect. Pericles' solution was

simple. After the victories of 480–79 B.C., Athens had led an alliance of Ionic states (known as the Delian League because its meeting place and treasury were on the island of Delos) against the Persian invaders. For years Athens had kept the smaller states in line, and imperceptibly and inevitably the Delian League had been transformed into a veritable Athenian Empire. States that attempted to secede were treated as rebels and severely punished. Ostensibly for greater security, the treasury was moved to Athens in 454 B.C. Before many years had passed, its contents were being used to finance the rebuilding of the Acropolis and its monuments, not to speak of other splendid buildings in Athens. Pericles was sharply criticized, but the work went on with astonishing rapidity.

Given the Greek ideals of harmony and order, one might have expected the newly rebuilt center of Athenian civic pride and state religion to have been organized on rational principles at least as highly developed as those that were so successful in Egyptian temples and in Mesopotamian palaces. Nothing could be further from the truth. Only an imperial autocracy, apparently, could impose a sense of order on all the disparate elements of such a traditional center. In fact, no Greek sanctuary before the Hellenistic period was organized along symmetrical lines, or for that matter along any rational principles save those of ready accessibility. The greatest of all Greek sanctuaries, that of Zeus at Olympia, was at any moment in its history a jumble of temples large and small, shrines, altars, colonnades, and throngs of statues, each erected without the slightest consideration for its neighbors. The Temple of Zeus itself was not even centrally placed.

When Pericles rebuilt the Acropolis (figs. 185, 186), he erected the temples on ancient, sacred sites, and where he could he utilized foundations remaining from older buildings, with the result that the Parthenon, the principal structure on the Acropolis and by general acclaim the supreme monument of Greek architecture, could

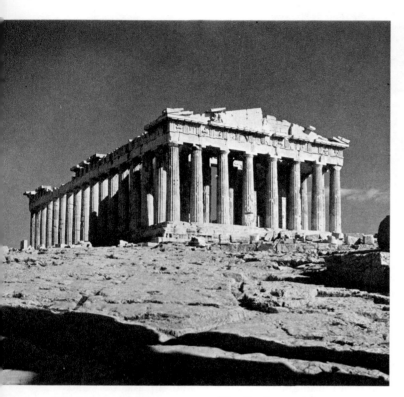

187. IKTINOS and KALLIKRATES. The Parthenon (view from the west and north). c. 447–432 B.C. The Acropolis, Athens

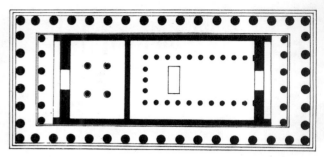

188. Plan of the Parthenon on the Acropolis

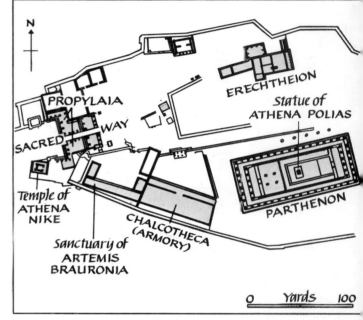

MAP 9. *The Acropolis, Athens*

never have been seen in ancient times from what we would today call a satisfactory, uninterrupted view, much less in any reasonable relationship to other buildings. The view of the Parthenon from the west, as one ascends the Sacred Way, today as in antiquity the main approach, would have been partially cut off to the right by the Chalcotheca (armory) and by the sanctuary of Artemis Brauronia. The center of the façade would have been largely blocked from view by a small temple in antis, and the view of the north colonnade interrupted by Phidias' colossal bronze statue of Athena Polias. The south colonnade was too close to the rampart to afford proper visibility. Only the east front, directly overlooking the city, could be seen in its entirety. This was reasonable enough since the east front was the principal entrance. But it could be reached only by walking along the long northern side of the building, and the available area before it (the small round temple visible in fig. 185 is a Roman addition) was too small to afford what we would consider today a good view of the east front. Clearly, the ancient Greeks were able to conceive to their complete satisfaction a mental image of a building in its entirety from the most interrupted and fragmentary of views. But the crystalline architectural shapes of the Periclean buildings, even in their present ruinous condition, tower in unexampled majesty above the city and the narrow plain, and vie with the surrounding mountains, without in any way giving in to nature, unless compelled to by irregularities of terrain. These structures are absolutes,

conceived without relation to any environment, as if set down on the great rock by a divine hand.

Most of the smaller structures of the Acropolis are known today only through excavations, and the statues that once adorned it are lost without a trace. But the Parthenon was preserved for centuries as a religious building. It was converted successively into a Byzantine church, a Catholic church, and a mosque, in which latter phase it sported a minaret. Although the interior had been repeatedly remodeled, the exterior remained intact with all its sculptures in place until 1687. The Turks, at that time at war with the Venetians, were using the temple as a powder magazine. A Venetian mortar shell struck the building, and the resultant explosion blew out its center. The Venetians carried the destruction a step further in an ill-fated attempt to plunder some of the pedimental statues, which fell to the rocky ground in the

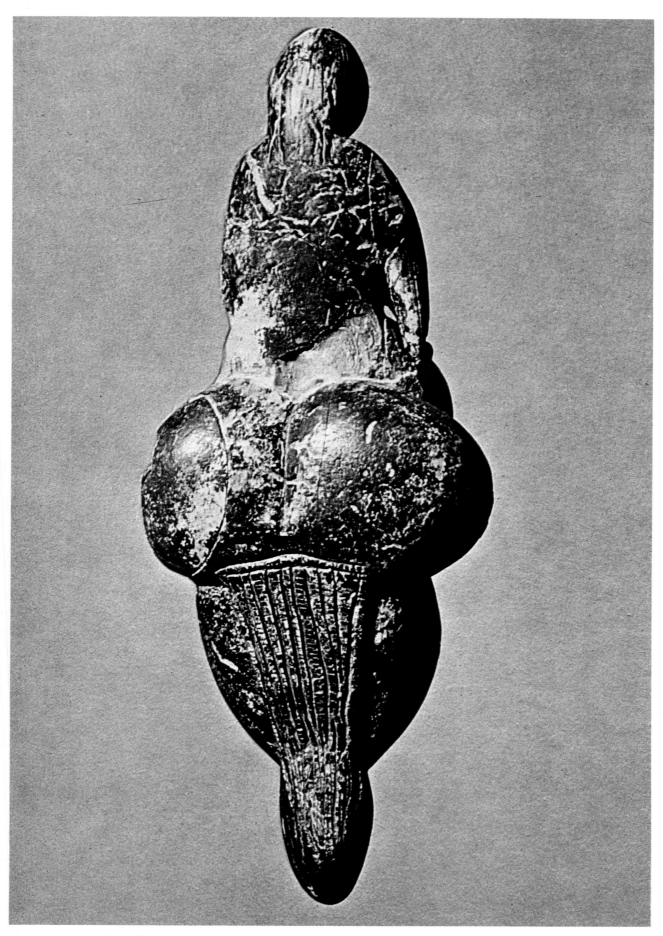

Colorplate 1. Paleolithic. *"Venus" of Lespugue.* c. 20,000–18,000 B.C. Ivory, height 5¾". Musée de l'Homme, Paris

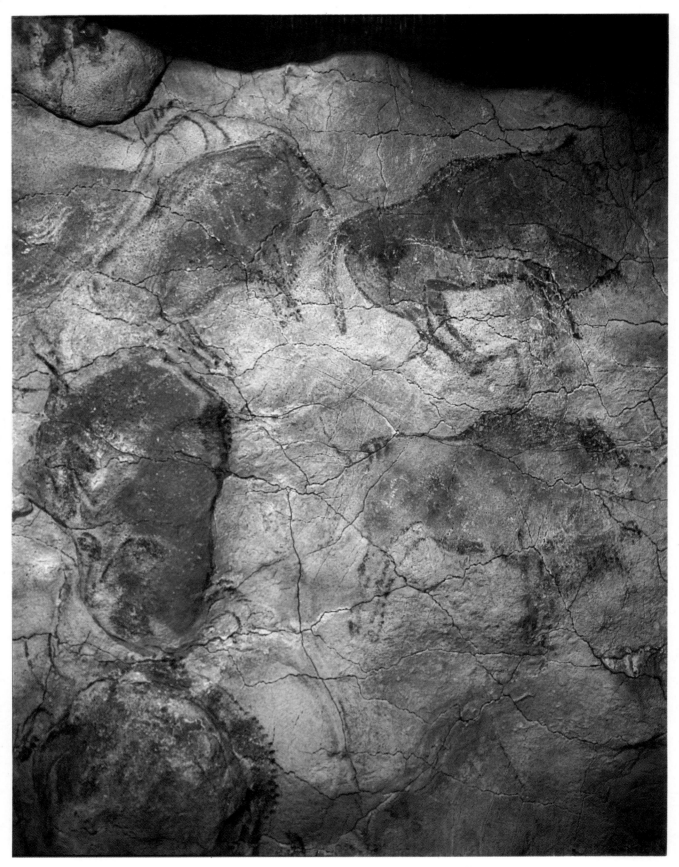

COLORPLATE 2. Paleolithic. *Bison.* Cave painting. c. 15,000–10,000 B.C. Altamira, Spain

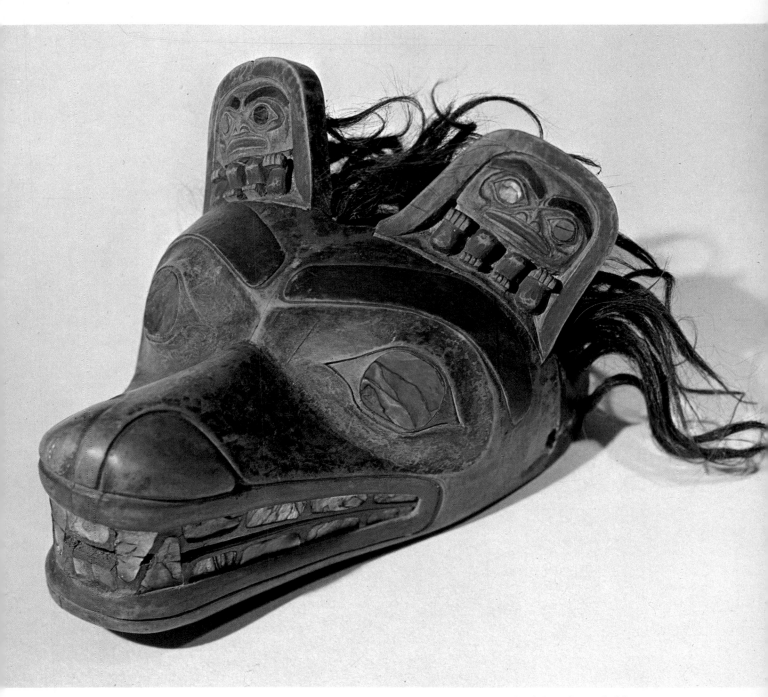

COLORPLATE 3.   North American Indian. Haida Bear Mask. Painted wood with turquoise inlay. Carnegie Museum, Anthropological Center, Meridian, Pennsylvania

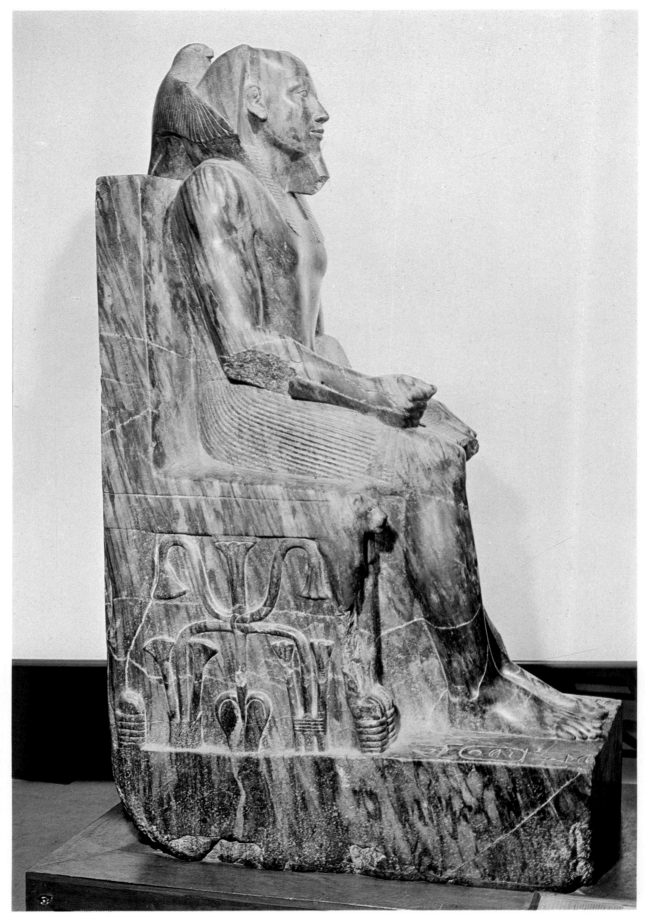

COLORPLATE 4. Egyptian. *King Chephren*, from Giza. c. 2530 B.C. Diorite, height 66⅛". Egyptian Museum, Cairo

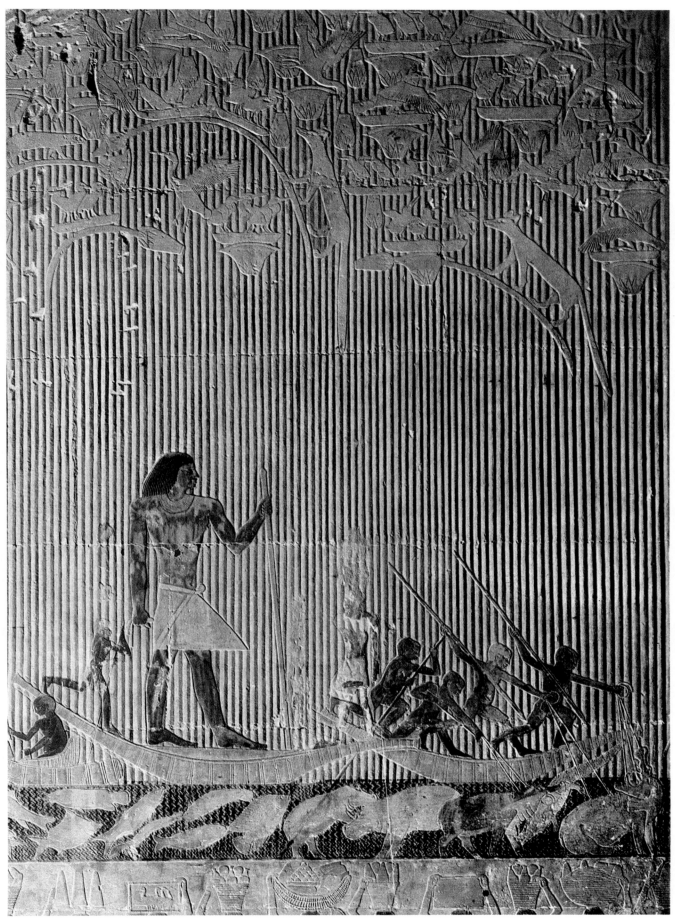

COLORPLATE 5. Egyptian. *Ti Watching a Hippopotamus Hunt*. Relief from the Tomb of Ti. c. 2400 B.C. Painted limestone. Saqqara, Egypt

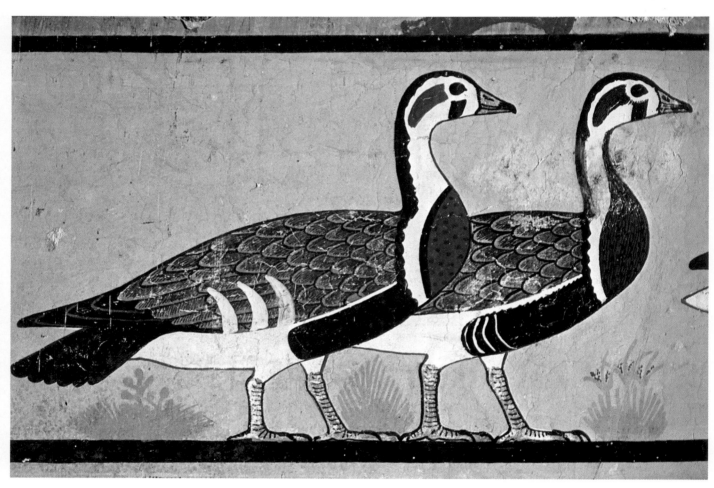

COLORPLATE 6. Egyptian. *Geese of Medum* (portion of fresco). c. 2600 B.C. Egyptian Museum, Cairo

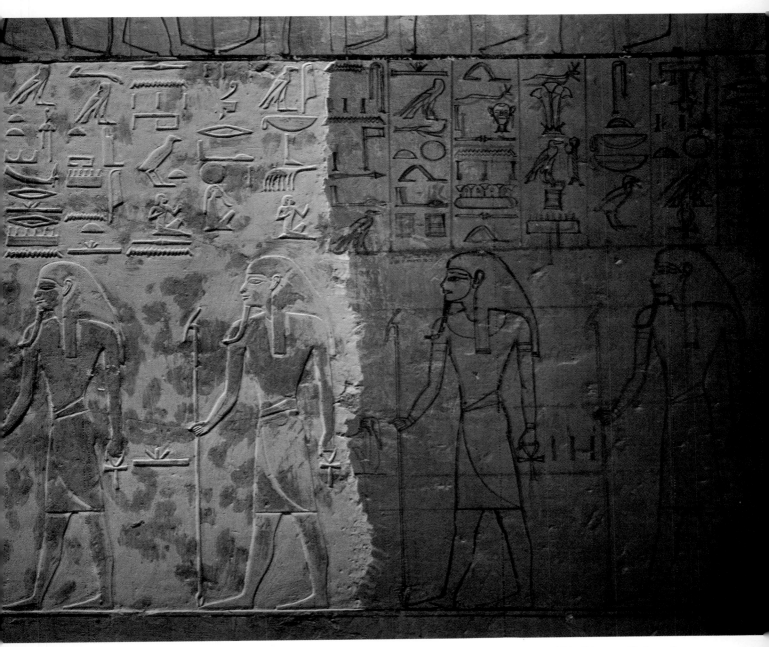

COLORPLATE 7.   Egyptian. Preparatory drawing and relief from the Tomb of Horemheb. c. 1334–1306 B.C. Valley of
the Kings (west of Thebes), Egypt

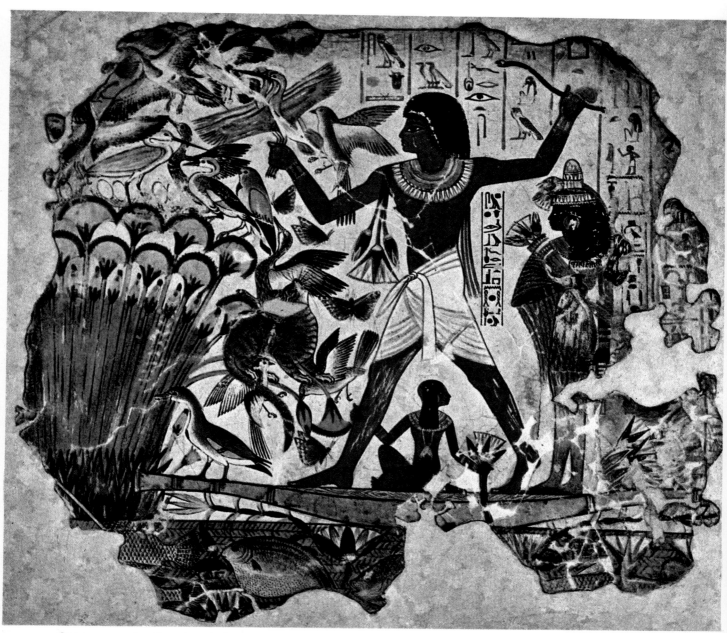

COLORPLATE 8. Egyptian. *Nebamun Hunting Birds.* Fragment from the Tomb of Nebamun at Thebes. c. 1400 B.C.
Painted stucco. 32⅝ x 38″. British Museum, London

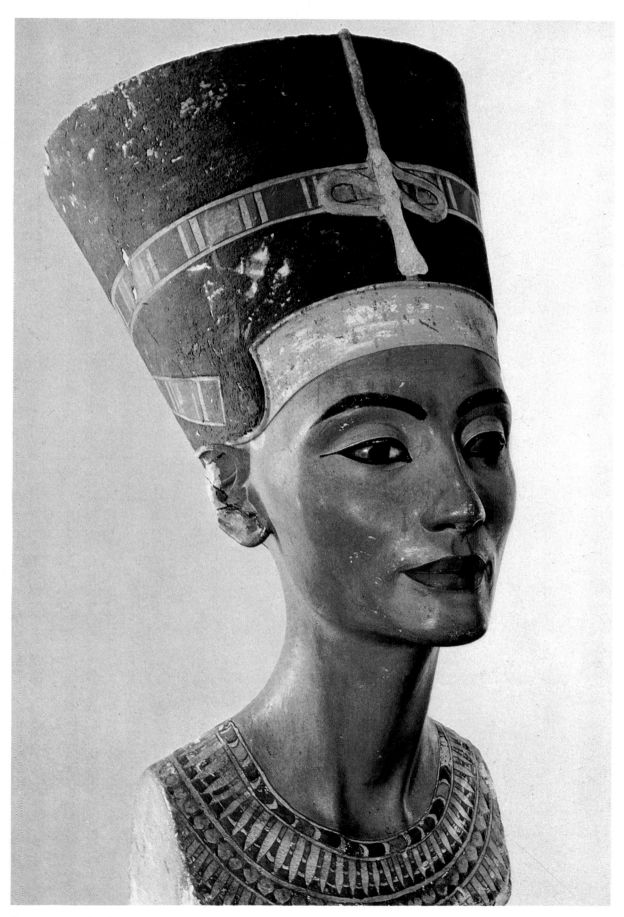

COLORPLATE 9. Egyptian. *Nefertiti.* c. 1365 B.C. Painted limestone, height 19⅝″. Staatliche Museen, Berlin

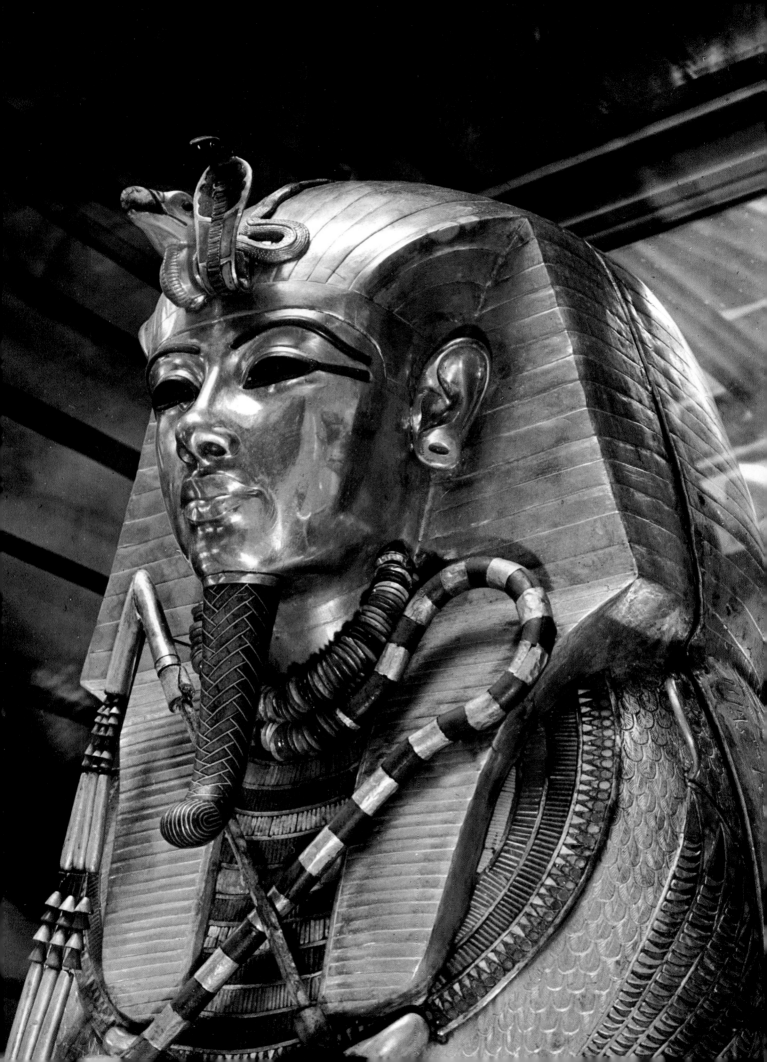

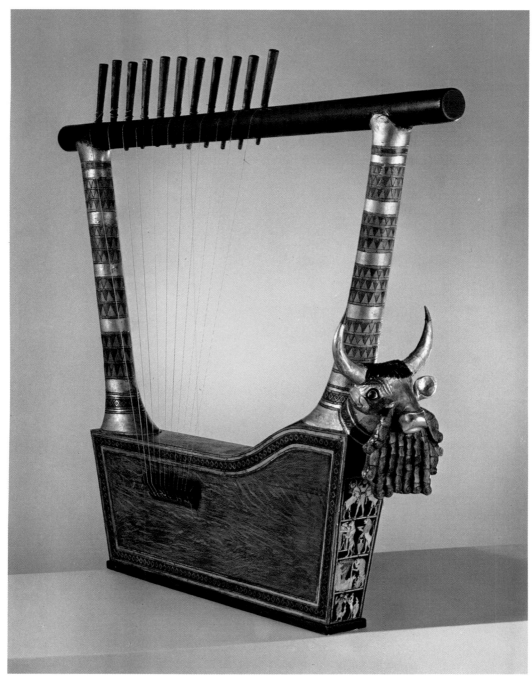

COLORPLATE 11.   Mesopotamian. Royal Harp from the Tomb of Queen Puabi, Ur. c. 2685 B.C.
Wood with inlaid gold, lapis lazuli, and shell. University Museum, University
of Pennsylvania, Philadelphia

◄ COLORPLATE 10.   Egyptian. Coffin of King Tuthankhamen
(portion of lid). c. 1360 B.C. Gold with inlaid lapis lazuli
and semiprecious stones, height 72⅞″.
Egyptian Museum, Cairo

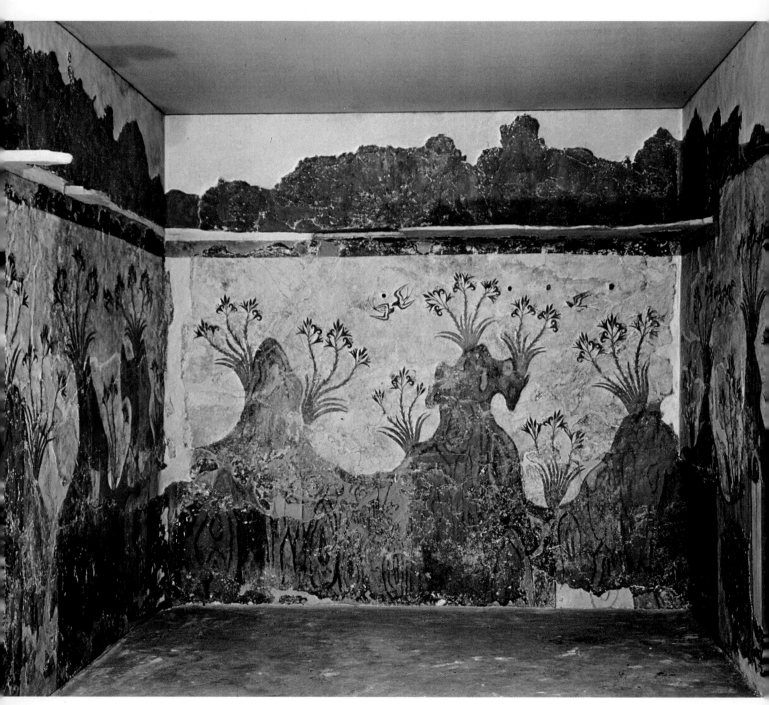

COLORPLATE 12.   Minoan. Room with landscape frescoes from Thera. Before 1500 B.C.
National Archaeological Museum, Athens

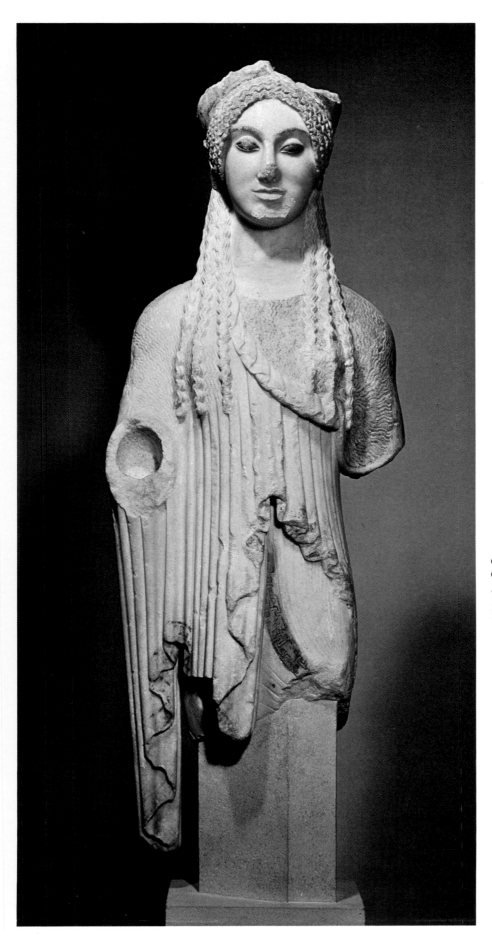

COLORPLATE 13.
Greek. *La Delicata*, from the
Acropolis, Athens. c. 525 B.C.
Marble, height 36″. Acropolis
Museum

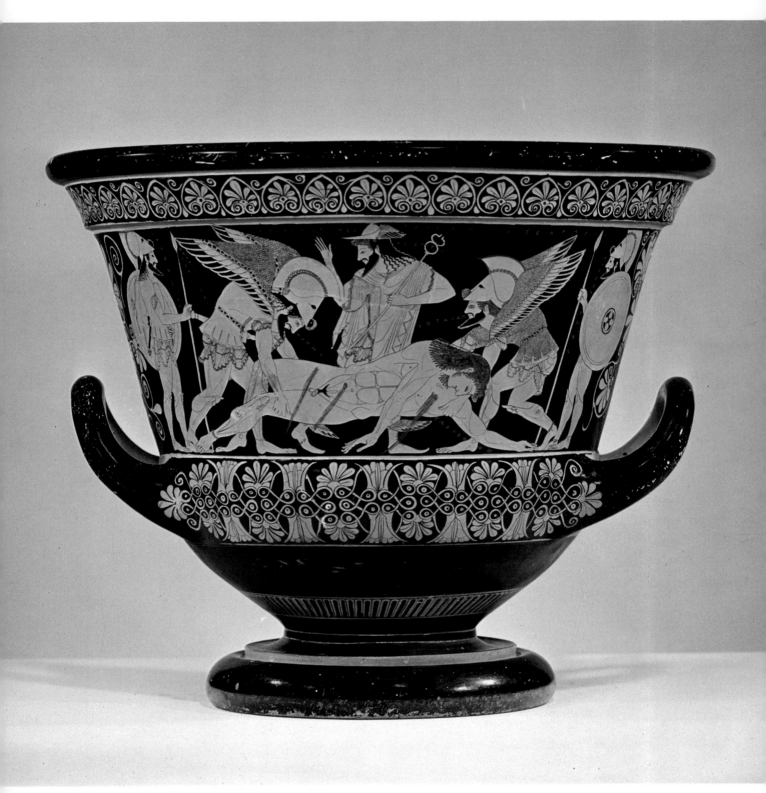

COLORPLATE 14. Greek. EUPHRONIOS. *Sarpedon Carried Off the Battlefield* (portion of calyx-krater). c. 515 B.C. Height, 18¼″. The Metropolitan Museum of Art, New York. Bequest of Joseph H. Durkee. Gift of Darius Ogden Mills and C. Ruxton Love, by exchange, 1972

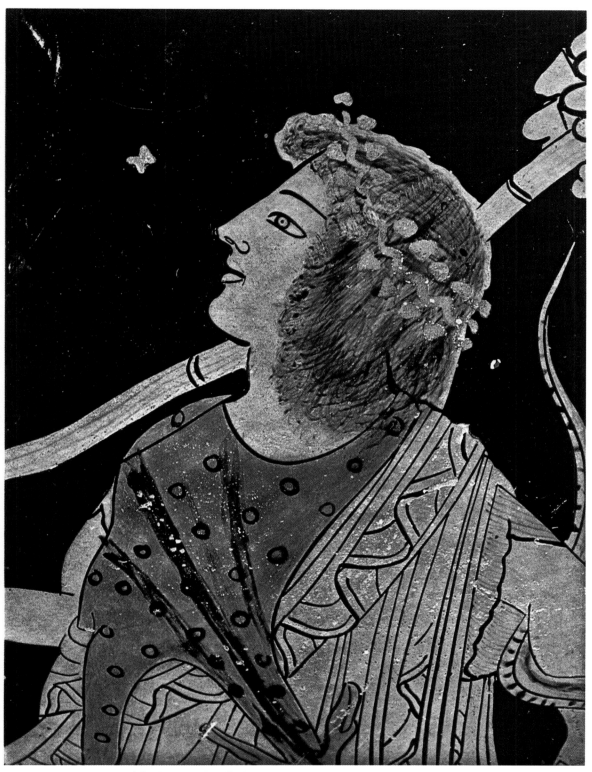

COLORPLATE 15.   Greek. The KLEOPHRADES PAINTER. *Rapt Maenad* (detail of the pointed amphora found at Vulci, Italy). c. 500–490 B.C. Staatliche Antikensammlungen und Glyptothek, Munich

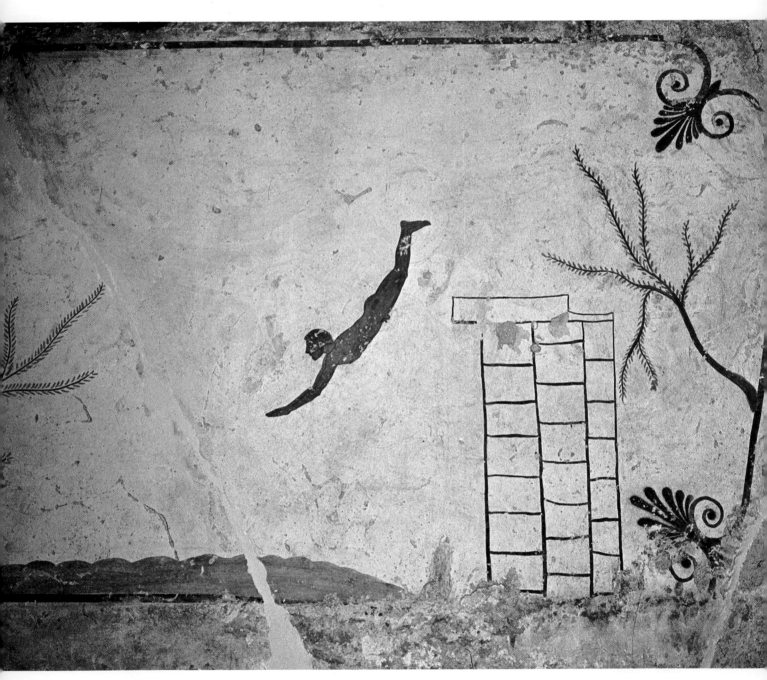

COLORPLATE 16. Greek. *The Diver.* Fresco from a Greek tomb at Paestum, Italy. c. 470 B.C. Museo Archeologico
Nazionale, Paestum

process of removal and were dashed to pieces. In 1801–3 Thomas Bruce, Lord Elgin, a British diplomat, saved most of what remained of the sculptures from possible destruction in the disordered conditions then prevailing in Athens by removing many statues and reliefs to London. In the present century the north colonnade has been carefully set up again, almost entirely with the original drums, and work has begun on the south colonnade.

Pericles is believed to have placed the Athenian sculptor Phidias in general charge of all of his artistic undertakings. It is noteworthy that he did not choose either of the great sculptors of the single athletic figure, Myron and Polykleitos, who were in their prime. The principal designer of the Parthenon appears to have been the architect Iktinos, working in a still imperfectly understood partnership with Kallikrates. Construction began in 447 B.C. and was finished in the extraordinarily brief time of nine years, save for the sculpture, which was all in place by 432 B.C. Iktinos utilized and extended the foundations of the older temple of Athena for his new structure, which was not called the Parthenon (*parthenos*, meaning *virgin*, referred to Athena) until much later; originally, the title was applied only to the treasury. While the dimensions of the "great temple," as the inscriptions call it, are not much larger than those of the Temple of Zeus at Olympia, it must have looked far larger. It is a regular Doric temple (figs. 187, 188), but differs from most of its predecessors in having eight rather than six columns across the front, and seventeen rather than thirteen along each side. The columns are far higher in proportion to their thickness than earlier Doric columns, and this greater slenderness is matched by a decrease in entasis and in the projection of the capitals, as well as in the mass and weight of the entablature. A glance at the Temple of Hera I (see fig. 154) at Paestum shows how greatly Greek architecture evolved in little more than a century. The wonderful sense of unity, harmony, and organic grace experienced by visitors to the Parthenon derives largely from the infinite number of refinements in the traditional elements of the Doric order. For example, the stylobate is curved upward several inches in the center to avoid the appearance of sagging, the columns lean progressively inward as we approach the corners, and the intercolumniations are progressively narrower toward the ends. Few of these refinements are immediately visible, but a great many have been measured, and even the most minute ones play their part in the total effect of the building. The whole structure, even the roof tiles, was built of Pentelic marble.

The decoration of the Parthenon was by far the most ambitious sculptural program ever undertaken by the ancient Greeks. The east and west pediments were filled with over-lifesize statues; the ninety-two metopes were sculptured in high relief; and a continuous frieze in the Ionic manner, uninterrupted by triglyphs, ran right round the building along the top of the cella wall for a total length of 550 feet. The backgrounds of the pediments were painted bright blue, those of the metopes and friezes red. Many ornaments were added in metal. Hair and eyes were also painted, and the capitals were decorated with ornament in bright colors. The whole building must have shone with color.

The interior of the cella, entered only from the east (the direction of the city), was intended to house the colossal statue of Athena by Phidias. We do not know what the ceiling was like, but it was certainly supported by two superimposed Doric colonnades like those still in place in the Temple of Aphaia at Aegina and the Temple of Hera II at Paestum (see figs. 159, 178). No access existed between the cella and the treasury, which was entered from the west and was apparently the principal treasury of the city. Its ceiling was supported by four Ionic columns, the first to be used in any Athenian temple.

The magnificent array of sculptures for the Parthenon was produced in only twelve years. The belief that they were all executed under the general supervision of Phidias, and at the least show aspects of his style and artistic intention, is supported by a remarkable unity of taste and feeling that runs through the entire series. But the scope of the undertaking and the speed of its execution must have required an army of artists; some of these were clearly sculptors of great power, others were stonecutters, presumably executing ideas sketched out by the major masters in clay models or perhaps working from drawings on papyrus. That all of these preparatory studies could have been made by Phidias himself, who was then busily occupied in work on his statue of Athena, is unlikely. The surviving statues for the two pediments, in spite of the heavy damage they have sustained, are among the most majestic in the whole history of art. The east pediment represented the *Birth of Athena*, the west the *Contest Between Athena and Poseidon*. From the individual statues, as well as from sketches made by a French traveler when they were still in place, it is clear that the compositions were not symmetrically organized on either side of a static central figure in the manner of the Olympia pediments (see figs. 180, 181), but were at every point based on action, which came to its climax toward the center.

Some of this movement runs through the *Three Goddesses* (fig. 189)—probably Hestia, Dione, and Aphrodite—who recline nobly in a group that sloped along with the downward movement of the raking cornice of the east pediment. Aphrodite rests her elbow and shoulders against her mother, Dione, while Hestia turns toward the center of the composition. The intricate drapery folds cling to the figures and reveal rather than conceal the splendid masses of the bodies and limbs. As may be expected, the folds no longer show a trace of the ornamental drapery forms of the Archaic, but neither does the drapery fall into the simple, naturalistic folds of the Severe Style. It seems to be endowed with an energy of its own, and to rush around the figures in loops and even in spirals, as if communicating to the very corner of

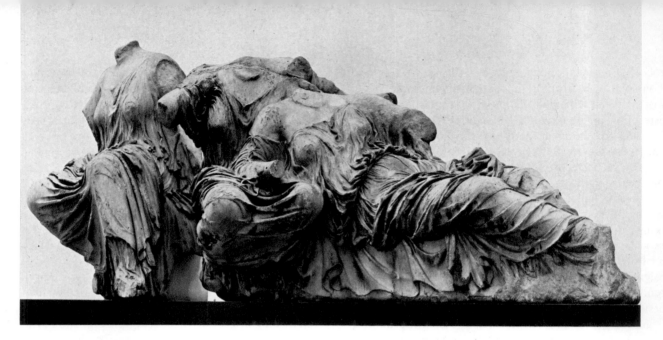

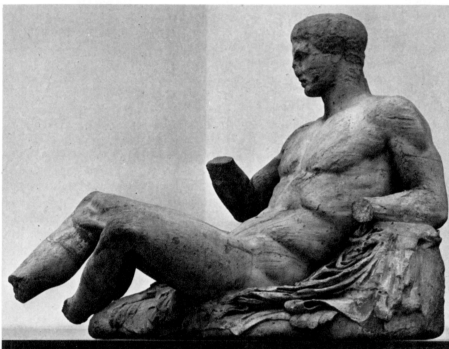

189. *Three Goddesses,* from the east pediment of the Parthenon. c. 438–432 B.C. Marble, over life-size. British Museum, London

190. Male figure (perhaps Herakles), from the east pediment of the Parthenon. c. 438–432 B.C. Marble, over life-size. British Museum, London

the pediment the high excitement of the central miracle, the birth of Athena from the head of Zeus. From this moment onward drapery movement becomes a vehicle for the expression of emotion, not only in Greek art but also in that of most subsequent civilizations.

A splendid male figure, perhaps Herakles (fig. 190), leans back on one elbow in lordly ease in the opposite corner of the pediment (most of the intervening figures are lost). He is as powerful as any of the nudes of the Severe Style, if less ostentatiously athletic. New and unexpected is the beautiful relaxation of the abdominal muscles below the rib cage, which seems almost to expand with an intake of breath. In consequence of the restful pose, new and smoother transitions carry the eye from one muscular or bony form to the next. No nobler embodiment of the Greek ideal of physical perfection and

emotional control can be imagined. The figure seems so prophetic of what Michelangelo was striving for in the High Renaissance (see Vol. 2, figs. 153, 154) that it is hard to believe what we know to be true—that he never saw the Parthenon sculptures and that neither he nor any of his Italian contemporaries was even aware of their existence.

The metopes all depicted battle scenes—Greeks against Trojans, Greeks against Amazons, gods against giants, Lapiths against centaurs. In the interests of legibility from the ground more than forty feet below, and in order to fit into the ninety-two restricted spaces, the narratives were mostly broken into pairs of figures in hand-to-hand combat, which "our side" does not invariably win. Incredible richness of invention characterizes the many variations on this single theme. One of the

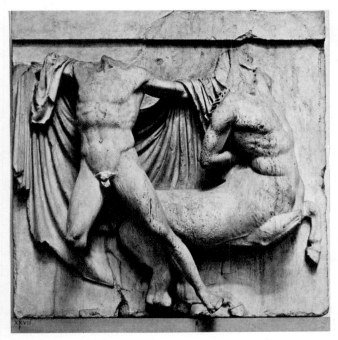

191. *Lapith Fighting a Centaur* (fragment), from a metope on the south side of the Parthenon. c. 438–432 B.C. Marble, height 56″. British Museum, London

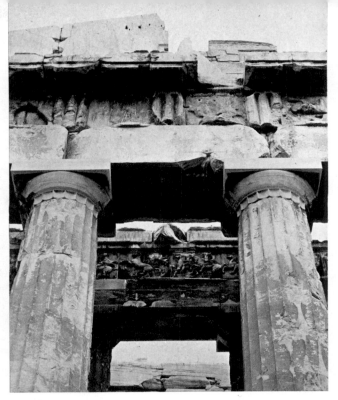

192. The west entrance of the cella of the Parthenon, showing a portion of the *Panathenaic Procession.* Frieze completed 432 B.C. The Acropolis, Athens

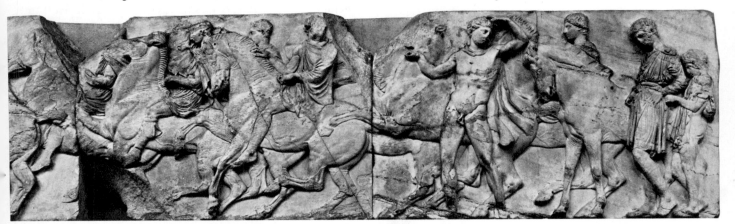

193. *Mounted Procession Followed by Men on Foot* (detail of the *Panathenaic Procession*), from the north frieze of the Parthenon. Frieze completed 432 B.C. Marble, height 41¾″. British Museum, London

finest (fig. 191), in spite of the destruction of the heads, shows a Lapith in a proud action pose, charging toward his right, with his head turned over his left shoulder, as he drags a centaur backward by the hair. The tension of the composition, in which the figures are pulled together by the force of their own opposite movements, is expressed in curves of the greatest beauty; these are amplified by the broad sweep of the cloak over the Lapith's arms, which falls into crescent-shaped folds decreasing steadily in curvature as they move upward.

The frieze around the top of the cella wall (fig. 192) represented the Panathenaic Procession—an annual festival in which the youth of Athens marched to the Acropolis to pay homage to the city's patron deity and in which, every fourth year, a new peplos was brought to clothe her ancient wooden image in the nearby Erechtheion. The procession, of necessity, was not represented as if taking place at one moment but as a cumulative experience, because the observer moving around the building could only see one section at a time. Some of the most impressive parts of this long composition are those representing riders on horses and youths leading horses in a splendid flow of striding youths and galloping steeds, overlapping to suggest greater depth (fig. 193). In order to maintain uniformity of scale throughout the frieze, the sculptors adopted a convention, followed throughout Greek relief sculpture, of reducing the size of the horses as compared with the riders. Very beautiful is the passage originally over the east doorway to the cella, where the procession converges from both sides of the building. The standing figures show all the new ease and grace of posture, clothed in

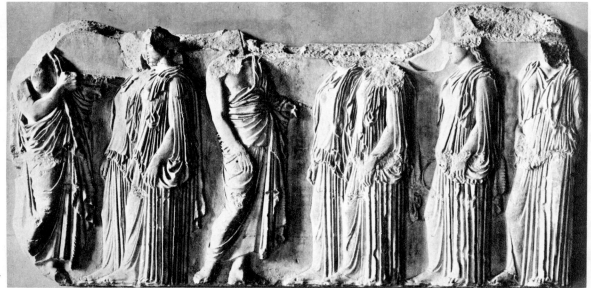

194

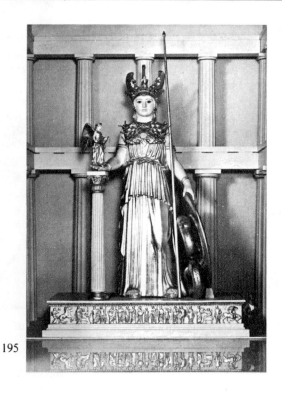

195

194. *Maidens and Stewards* (fragment of the *Panathenaic Procession*), from the east frieze of the Parthenon. Frieze completed 432 B.C. Marble, height c. 43″. The Louvre, Paris

195. PHIDIAS. *Athena* (reconstruction), from the east cella of the Parthenon. c. 438–432 B.C. Wood covered with gold and ivory plating, height c. 4′. The Royal Ontario Museum, Toronto

196. MNESIKLES. The Propylaia (view from the south). c. 337–332 B.C. The Acropolis, Athens

197. The Propylaia (view from the east)

drapery that flows with all the new rhythmic beauty (fig. 194). Admittedly the frieze, in the only location permitted by the rules of the Greek orders, was not placed in the best position for perfect visibility, some thirty feet above the stylobate and under the shadow of the peristyle ceiling. Nonetheless, it was far from being as difficult to view as some writers maintain. At most moments of the day, the strong Greek sunlight, reflected upward from the marble stylobate and (on the south side) from the cella wall, must have cast a soft, diffused light into the shadow under the marble ceiling beams and slabs. Moreover, the heads and shoulders of the figures were carved in a higher projection than the lower portions; and, finally, the red background set off all the figures with considerable sharpness.

Once inside the cella the observer stood in the awesome presence of Phidias' forty-foot-high statue of Athena, dimly illuminated, since the only light in the windowless temple came from the east door and was, of course, at its strongest in the morning. From literary accounts of the statue and from tiny, ancient replicas, a remarkable small-scale model has been made (fig. 195). With this as a basis, and with a good deal of poetic imagination, one can form some idea of what must have been the grandeur of the original. Thin plates of ivory and sheets of gold attached to plates of wood were arranged on a framework of great complexity so that it looked as though all the flesh portions were solid ivory and all the drapery solid gold. A shallow basin of water in the floor before the statue served as a humidifier to protect the ivory in the dry climate of Athens and also, doubtless, as a pool to mirror the majestic goddess and as a source of reflected light to play upward on her features. Athena's left hand sustained a shield above the folds of the sacred serpent, and on her extended right hand stood a golden statue of Victory six feet tall. So enormous was the *Athena Parthenos* that splendid reliefs by Phidias decorated both sides of the shield, the pedestal, and even

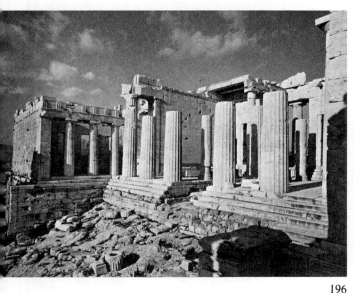

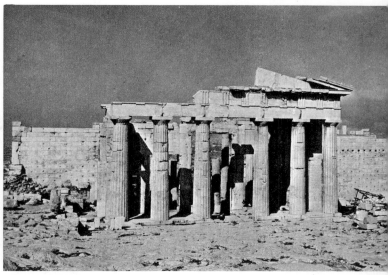

196   197

the thickness of the soles of the goddess' sandals. According to ancient literary sources, Phidias also executed an even finer gold-and-ivory statue of the enthroned Zeus for the Temple of Zeus at Olympia. It was so tall that if Zeus had risen to his feet his head would have burst through the temple roof.

Although we possess not a scrap of sculpture that we can with certainty attribute to Phidias' own hand, the work done under his direction and possibly from his models on the Parthenon is consistent with the architecture of the building and with the literary accounts of Phidias' style. He invented new ways of combining figures on foot and on horseback into free action groups; he was responsible for a new majesty of proportions and harmony of movement; he was the first to use drapery in order to reveal the masses of the figure, increase the impression of movement, and express the drama of the subject; he was responsible for a new dynamic harmony between figural compositions and architecture. Clearly, we are confronted by a universal genius, the first in history, the only one in the ancient world, and probably one of the greatest who ever lived. It is sad to record that Phidias, like so many of the great men of Athens (one recalls Themistocles, who was exiled; Socrates, who was forced to drink poison), met an ignominious end, imprisoned (or perhaps exiled) on trumped-up charges of impiety by jealous citizens of the very city to whose lasting glory his artistic achievements had contributed so much.

The Acropolis was entered through a monumental gateway called the Propylaia, constructed—doubtless under Phidias' supervision—by the architect Mnesikles from 337–32 B.C., while the sculptures of the Parthenon were being completed. The problems posed for the erection of a suitable gateway were not easy. One could approach the site only by means of the Sacred Way, a pathway zigzagging steeply up the rock. A formal entranceway was clearly needed. The solution was a central pedimented Doric portico of six columns facing west, flanked by two smaller and lower Doric porticoes at right angles (figs. 196, 197). Pedestrians could climb steps on either side, but a ramp was required for horses and sacrificial animals, and to accommodate this the central intercolumniation was widened by one triglyph and one metope—not an ideal solution, perhaps, but the only one consistent with the strict principles and limited vocabulary of the Doric order. Inside the building the roadway was lined with Ionic columns, three on each side, and the inner gateway was again a pedimented Doric portico. This inner gateway was to have been flanked by two halls, whose prospective use is not known; construction was halted by the outbreak of the Peloponnesian War, and the halls were never built. Whether seen from below as one toils up the ramps, or from the higher ground within the Acropolis, the exterior of the Propylaia is noble and graceful; the columns are similar in their lofty proportions and elegance of contour to those of the Parthenon. The small flanking structure to the north (on the south only the portico was built) was a picture gallery, the earliest one on record, erected to accommodate paintings on wood to be set around the marble walls below the windows.

About 425 B.C., four years after the death of Pericles, the tiny Temple of Athena Nike (Victory) was constructed, presumably by Kallikrates, coarchitect of the Parthenon, on the bastion flanking the Propylaia to the south in celebration of the victories of Alcibiades, which brought about a temporary lull in the catastrophic Peloponnesian War. The amphiprostyle temple has four Ionic columns on each portico (fig. 198). The proportions are unusually stocky, possibly so as not to contrast too strongly with the Doric columns of the Propylaia. The little structure was dismantled by the Turks and its stones used for fortifications; it was reassembled only in the nineteenth century. The finest sculptures carved for this temple originally decorated the parapet, and showed per-

198. KALLIKRATES. Temple of Athena Nike. c. 425 B.C.
The Acropolis, Athens

199. *Victory Untying Her Sandal,* from the parapet of the
Temple of Athena Nike, Athens. c. 410 B.C. Marble,
height 42″. Acropolis Museum, Athens

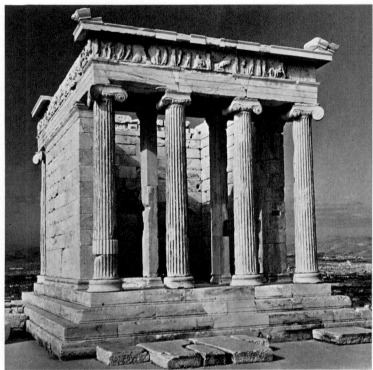

198

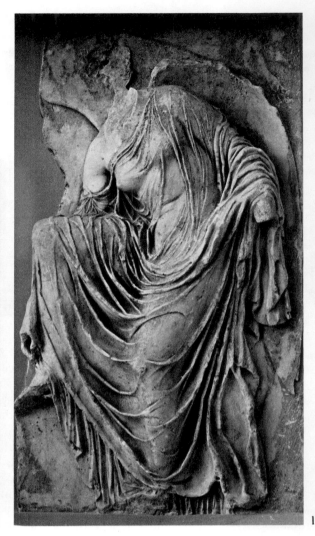

199

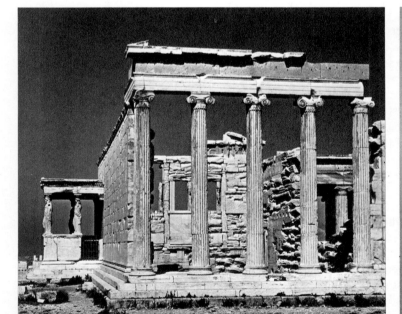

200

200. The Erechtheion (view from the east). c. 421–405 B.C. The
Acropolis, Athens

201. Porch of the Maidens, the Erechtheion

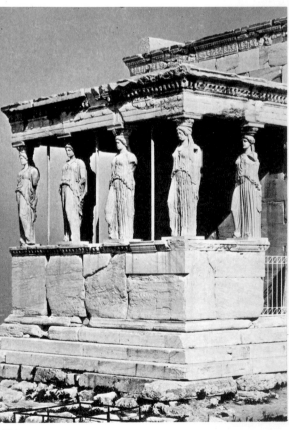

201

sonifications of Victory either separately or before Athena. These reliefs were apparently carved by masters trained initially under Phidias in the sculpture of the Parthenon. The loveliest is the exquisite *Victory Untying Her Sandal* (fig. 199), in which the transparent drapery of the Phidian style is transformed into a veritable cascade of folds bathing the graceful forms of the Victory. It has been suggested that the taste of the sculptor Kallimachos, credited with the invention of the Corinthian capital, is responsible for this refined, late phase of fifth-century style, which, however ingratiating its melodies may be, has certainly lost the grand cadences of Phidias.

The final fifth-century building on the Acropolis, the Erechtheion, built from 421–405 B.C., was named after Erechtheus, a legendary king of Athens; it contained the ancient wooden image of Athena, and possibly sheltered the spot where the sacred olive tree sprang forth at Athena's command. Rarely for a Greek temple, and presumably because of the now not entirely understood requirements of the religious rites for which it was designed, the Erechtheion is strikingly irregular. The four rooms culminate in three porches of sharply different sizes facing in three separate directions (fig. 200). Yet from any view the proportions are so calculated that the effect is unexpectedly harmonious. Two porticoes are Ionic, with extremely tall, slender columns and elaborate capitals; the taller portico had four columns across, the smaller six (see fig. 200; one column is lost). On the third portico (fig. 201), instead of columns, six korai upheld modified Doric capitals and an Ionic entablature, in the manner of those in the Treasury of the Siphnians at Delphi (see fig. 157). Despite disfiguring damage, the figures stand so calmly that the masses of marble above them seem almost to float. Anyone who has ever watched Mediterranean women carry heavy loads on their heads without the slightest apparent effort will recognize the pose.

Epilogue for the Phidian Style

Perhaps the most spectacular outgrowth of the Phidian style was the *Victory* (fig. 202) by Paionios, a marble statue set up at Olympia about 420 B.C., on a tall shaft, triangular in cross section, with its apex presented to the spectator so that in most lights it would almost disappear, leaving the Victory, with arms and wings (now lost) extended, tunic pressed by the breeze against her full body, and her drapery billowing behind in the wind, looking as if she were really flying. Although the experiment was daring, one misses the grandeur of the Phidian style, whose absence from this work makes it seem almost meretricious.

The deeper aspects of Phidian style seem to have been better understood by modest artisans, such as the sculptors of the grave stelai carved in great numbers in Athens, often for export, and of uniformly high quality.

An especially touching example is the *Stele of Hegeso* (fig. 203), which shows the deceased seated in a chair holding a piece of jewelry (painted, not carved) and accompanied by a standing girl, perhaps a daughter. The gentle melancholy of the group is not achieved by expressions—the faces are almost blank—but rather by the rhythm of their poses, especially the bowed heads suggesting resignation. The sculptor, who may well have been among the host of stonecutters trained on the Parthenon, has an unusual command of space. He has placed his two figures so that the back of the standing woman and the chair of Hegeso overlap the frame, causing them to emerge into our space. Yet the veil over Hegeso's head is so slightly projected from the marble background as to indicate an airy space within the frame.

Although the principles of the Doric and Ionic orders as applied to temples were by now firmly established, experimentation was still possible. One of the most striking variants, dating from around 420 B.C., the Temple of Apollo at Bassai in the wilds of Arcadia, has been attributed to Iktinos himself. The peripteral exterior is not exceptional (colorplate 17); in fact, it shows fewer refinements than the Parthenon. The dramatic effect of the interior, however, is utterly new (fig. 204). The cella was lined with Ionic columns, engaged to the walls by projecting piers, supporting capitals with three equal faces. At the west end stood at least one, perhaps three, Corinthian columns, the earliest known. The abacus of a Corinthian capital (see fig. 208) resembles that of the Ionic, but the volutes are rudimentary; the distinguish-

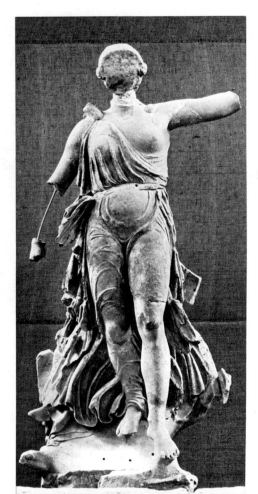

202. PAIONIOS. *Victory*, from Olympia. c. 420 B.C. Marble, height including base 85". Archaeological Museum, Olympia

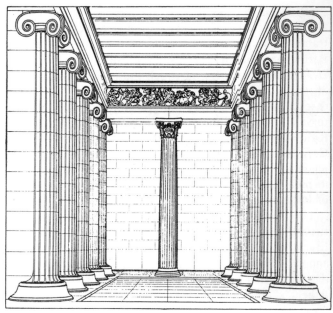

204

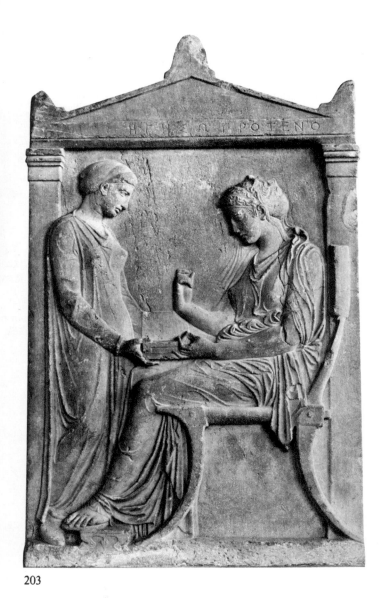

203

203. *Stele of Hegeso,* from Athens. c. 410–400 B.C. Marble, height 59″. National Archaeological Museum, Athens

204. IKTINOS. Interior, Temple of Apollo, Bassai, Greece. c. 420 B.C. (Architectural reconstruction after F. Krischen). See Colorplate 17

205. *Amazonomachy* (portion of a frieze), from the cella of the Temple of Apollo, Bassai, Greece. Marble high relief, height 25¼″. c. 420 B.C. British Museum, London. See Colorplate 17

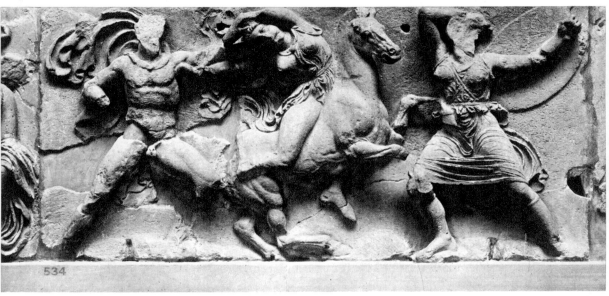

205

ing feature is the profusion of carved acanthus leaves (the acanthus is a Mediterranean plant of the thistle family) that envelop it, at first one row, later two, giving a rich and splendid appearance. The frieze above the columns made the cella interior even more exciting. It was carved in high relief with the typical subjects of battles between Lapiths and centaurs, Greeks and Amazons (fig. 205), but with unusually energetic poses and sharp exaggerations of movement and gesture—still in the Phidian tradition, but with a touch of wildness hardly to be expected after the controlled equilibrium of the Parthenon metopes.

Another large Doric temple at Segesta (fig. 206), in Sicily, commenced possibly by Attic builders for a local community in the process of Hellenization, was abandoned for unknown reasons in an unfinished condition; the cella was, in fact, not even started. We have, therefore, the privilege of seeing the columns already set up, preparatory to being fluted in place, and the stones of the stylobate retain the bosses left to provide holds for the tackle used in transporting them to this wild and lonely spot.

Ancient literary accounts have much to say about the advances made by painters in the second half of the fifth century, especially a new realism in depicting everyday life and a new ability in rendering the expression of in-

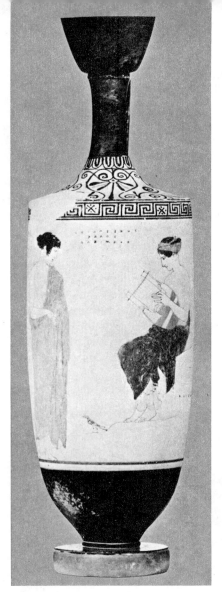

207. THE ACHILLES PAINTER. *Muse on Mount Helikon,* from a lekythos. c. 440–430 B.C. Height c. 14½". Staatliche Antikensammlungen und Glyptothek, Munich

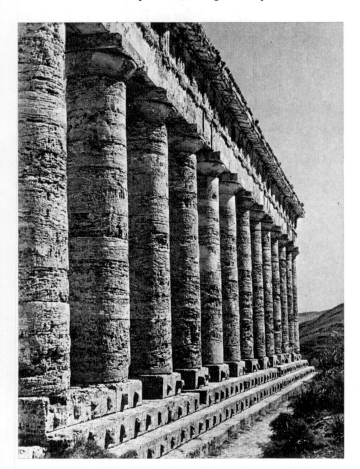

206. Unfinished Temple. c. 416 B.C. Segesta, Sicily

tense emotion. Even more important, the masters of the period are credited with having invented the means of painting light and shade in order to give form its full roundness and set it into depth. No Classical paintings showing these new achievements have yet come to light. Their effect on vase painting seems to have been to weaken even more the firm linearity and the attachment of flat design to the vase surface, which had been the delights of Archaic vase painting, and to lure the best masters away from that limited art to more exciting new fields. Only faint hints of the new pictorial freedom can be detected in the white-ground *lekythoi* (vases made to contain oil or perfume). In these, a painted white background could be used because they were intended as funeral gifts and would never be washed. In the enchanting *Muse on Mount Helikon* (fig. 207) by the Achilles Painter, we can see a new softness of form and a wavering, sketchy line which suggests space and light.

Looking back at the meteoric development of Greek art in the fifth century, it is sobering to reflect that a person born toward the end of the Archaic period could have watched during a long lifetime the entire evolution of the Classical style.

THE CLASSICAL PERIOD—
THE FOURTH CENTURY

Toward the end of the fifth century B.C. a succession of military disasters stripped Athens of her imperial role and left the city a prey to severe social disorders. First Sparta, then Thebes exercised leadership among the Greek city-states in the first half of the fourth century, except for the Ionian cities of Asia Minor, which submitted to Persian rule. By the middle of the century the final threat to Greek independence had appeared. Philip II, King of Macedon, ruler of a land just to the north of Greece which had previously been considered outside the sphere of Hellenic civilization, established Macedonian primacy over the Greek mainland. His son, Alexander III (the Great), in a series of lightning military ventures absorbed and then attempted to Hellenize the entire Persian Empire, carrying his domination even into India. Alexander adopted Persian dress and court customs, claimed Zeus as his father, and had himself worshiped as a god in the manner of Mesopotamian and Egyptian monarchs. Despite her diminished political power, Athens remained the center of Greek intellectual life. The foundations of Western philosophy were laid in this period in the work of Plato and Aristotle, who first submitted traditional standards to the questioning test of reason.

Clearly, the fourth century was not to be a period of ambitious building programs in mainland Greece, but some splendid new structures did make their appearance. One of the handsomest must have been the *tholos* (circular building) at Epidauros, dating from about 360 B.C. The tholos plan, derived from the round huts and tombs of Helladic times, could be devoted to a variety of purposes. For example, a fifth-century tholos in Athens served as a dining hall for the city administration. The Tholos of Epidauros, designed by Polykleitos the Younger as a place for sacrifices, consisted of a cylindrical wall surrounded by an outer Doric peristyle supporting a conical roof. The inner colonnade was composed of Corinthian columns—the first such colonnade we know. Sections of this tholos have been recomposed (fig. 208), showing ex-

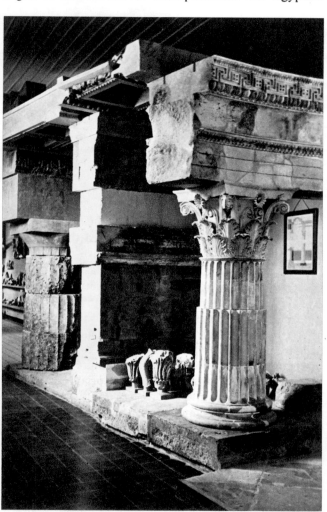

208. POLYKLEITOS THE YOUNGER. Tholos of Epidauros (reconstructed section). c. 360 B.C.

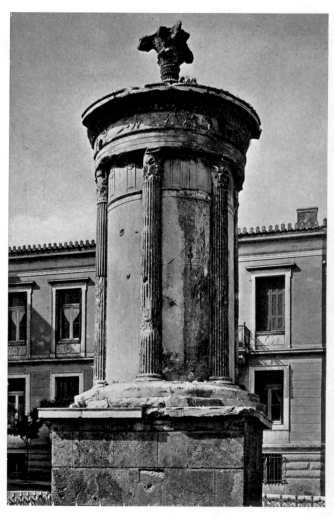

209. Monument of Lysikrates. c. 334 B.C. Athens

treme elegance and refinement of carving. The Corinthian capital already appears in very much the form later adopted by the Romans and revived in the Italian Renaissance, with two superimposed, staggered rows of acanthus leaves. The volutes are undercut, and so is each leaf, curving over at the tip with a jagged contour of great brilliance and technical virtuosity. The earliest example we know of a Corinthian peristyle on the exterior of a building is the Monument of Lysikrates at Athens (fig. 209), a charming little structure intended to support the tripod Lysikrates won in 334 B.C. when he provided a chorus for the theater at Athens. The Corinthian columns are in reality only half columns, engaged to the central cylinder, which although hollow has no entrance; the conical roof, a single block of marble, supports an acanthus pedestal resembling a somewhat overblown Corinthian capital.

A new type of building that appeared in the fourth century is the monumental outdoor theater. The largest and finest of these—so considered even in antiquity—is the well-preserved theater at Epidauros, designed, like the Tholos, by Polykleitos the Younger (colorplate 18). During the great age of Greek drama in the fifth century, theaters had consisted of mere rows of wooden benches on a hillside, grouped roughly around the *orchestra* (meaning dancing place), a circular area where the chorus and the actors—never more than three at a time—sang and spoke. This idea is monumentalized at Epidauros in the form of a half cone of some fifty rows of marble benches separated by radiating aisles, still built around slightly more than half the orchestra circle. Originally, the theater had no stage; the building behind the orchestra circle supported temporary scenery. For all its simplicity, the harmony and grandeur of the space are as impressive as its acoustics. A word uttered in the orchestra circle can be clearly heard in the farthest reaches of the vast space.

The traditional elements of Greek architecture were forced to perform new functions in buildings erected outside of Greece. The most spectacular of these was the Mausoleum at Halikarnassos; the familiar name derives from its function as the tomb of Mausolus, prince of Caria in Asia Minor, who died in 353. Work began during his lifetime and continued after his death. The tomb, some 150 feet in height, was demolished by the Knights of Saint John in the Middle Ages, and only fragments have been recovered. Ancient literary descriptions, unfortunately, were incorrectly copied, so that it is now impossible to tell exactly what the building looked like (fig. 210 is one of several possible reconstructions). We do know that the mausoleum had a lofty pedestal supporting a peristyle of thirty-six Ionic columns, each forty feet high, either in a single or a double row, surrounding the burial chamber. The whole was surmounted by a pyramid, in imitation of the Egyptians, culminating in a great marble chariot with four horses driven by Mausolus himself. At several still uncertain locations on the tomb, perhaps in the customary and inconvenient position at the top of the base, ran friezes representing the customary battle subjects, carved by four of the most prominent Greek sculptors of the age.

We do not know for certain the name of the master who executed the grand statue of Mausolus (fig. 211)—it may have been Bryaxis—but clearly it is animated by the new dramatic spirit of the time. While this realistic portrait, one of the earliest known, lacks the sense of majestic control visible in all Athenian sculpture of the fifth century, the movement of the drapery, the depth of the carving, and the intensity of the expression produce a great sense of excitement. It is instructive to compare this swaying, windblown charioteer with the serene *Charioteer of Delphi* (see fig. 170) executed little more than a century earlier.

The most eminent of the Halikarnassos sculptors was Skopas, born on the island of Paros but trained in Athens, known in antiquity for his ability to render movement and to convey drama. He may have been responsible for the *Battle of Greeks and Amazons* (fig. 212), in which the free movement of the figures in space is carried even beyond the stage of the frieze at Bassai (see fig. 205). In the section illustrated two Greek warriors are about to slay an Amazon who has fallen to her knees and cries for mercy, while a third Greek pulls an Amazon from her horse. The impression of speed is produced largely by the wide spacing of the figures, which leaves considerable areas of blank background to be traversed. Despite their mutilation, fragmentary heads from the Temple of Athena Alea at Tegea (fig. 213) show how Skopas revealed new depths of passion by means of an exceptionally deep eye cavity, thus producing a powerful shadow around the eye and intensifying the expression of wildness. Even the surging rhythms of the ornaments on the helmet are used to heighten the excitement of the moment.

A complete contrast to Skopas is furnished by the Athenian Praxiteles, whose fame was based on the grace and softness of his style. His most celebrated work in antiquity was the marble statue of Aphrodite in her sanctuary at the city of Knidos in Asia Minor, which we know only from Roman copies (fig. 214). This is the first nude statue of the goddess, and one of the earliest Greek statues of a female nude. Compared to the partially nude female figures of the fifth century, and in spite of faulty restorations (the head comes from another statue, and the hands and feet are new), the copy shows a greater fullness of forms and an almost imperceptible transition from one form to the next. The result is a wholly new sense of warmth and life.

In recent years the beautiful *Hermes with the Infant Dionysos* (fig. 215) at Olympia has been dismissed as a Hellenistic or even Roman copy of a lost original by Praxiteles, but the quality of this statue is so much higher than that of any ancient copy known to us that this judgment is hard to accept. The least that can be said of the

Hermes is that no other surviving ancient work approaches its consistent pitch of refinement in the treatment of surface. Apparently, Praxiteles was one of the first to become fully aware of the crystalline and translucent nature of marble, and to discover a way of exploiting its special quality by softening and veiling all transitions, abrading and polishing them until sharp edges could no longer be seen. Eyelids, for example, and the edges of lips are deliberately blurred, as is the transition from muscle to muscle in the soft and glowing torso and limbs of the god. Shadows play gently over the fluid surfaces, and light is reflected from within the crystalline structure of the marble. Even the curly locks of the god's hair are softly sketched in the marble, particularly when compared to the still clear-cut definition of hair in the fifth century. The subject itself, far from the majestic themes of the fifth century, has a quality of gentle, aesthetic dalliance. Hermes dangles a bunch of grapes to tease the infant Dionysos; a dreamy half smile plays about his luminous features. In many ways this kind of attitude and treatment seem to have more in common with the nature of painting than with sculpture, and is thus often called "pictorial." Soon such pictorial ideals were to be pursued in a spectacular manner by Hellenistic and Roman sculptors, and later they were revived briefly in the Florentine Renaissance (see Vol. 2, fig. 70) and triumphantly in the Italian Baroque (see Vol. 2, fig. 236).

The third great sculptor of the fourth century, Lysippos, took up again, but from a new point of view, the athletic themes of Myron and Polykleitos. If one judges from the surviving Roman copies, his lost bronze *Apoxyomenos* (fig. 216) showed a subject visible wherever athletes gathered—a young man scraping dust and sweat from his body with an S-shaped terra-cotta instrument called the strigil. Again according to the Roman copies, Lysippos employed a new system of proportion in keeping with the increased slenderness, height, and grace of Greek columns after the middle of the fifth century. The head is smaller, the torso and limbs longer and lither, the divisions between the muscles less strongly marked (in common with Praxiteles) as compared with fifth-century sculpture in general. More important, the arms are raised in such a way as to make use of the space in front of the body, thereby finally breaking through the invisible fron-

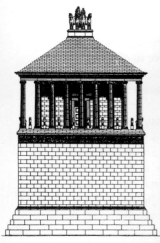

210. Mausoleum, Halikarnassos. c. 353 B.C. (Architectural reconstruction after F. Krischen)

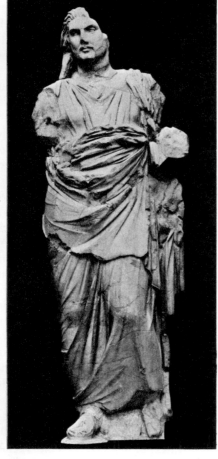

211. *Mausolus*, from Halikarnassos. c. 353 B.C. Marble, height 9′10″. British Museum, London

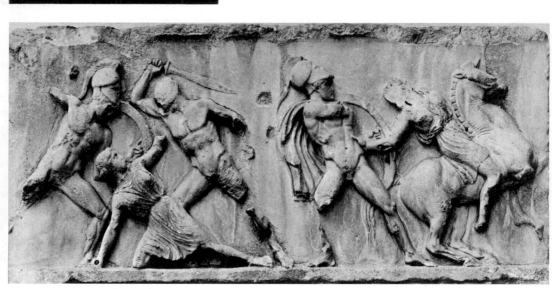

212. *Battle of Greeks and Amazons* (portion of a frieze), from the Mausoleum, Halikarnassos. Middle 4th century B.C. Marble, height 35″. British Museum, London

tal plane to which even such vigorous action figures as the *Diskobolos* (see fig. 174) and the *Zeus of Artemision* (see fig. 173) had been restricted. How a Lysippan bronze statue would have looked may perhaps better be seen in the wonderful figure of a youth (colorplate 19) found in the sea off Antikythera, in the wreck of a Roman vessel presumably laden with works of Greek art. Originally, the bronze did not have the greenish patina we now admire, but must have been polished to a luminous brown to suggest the deep tan of a Mediterranean youth who constantly exercised in strong sunlight. The inlaid eyes and copper lips are, luckily, still preserved. The brilliant naturalism of the work takes us across the centuries straight into a Greek palaestra.

For no moment in the history of art, perhaps, do we mourn the disappearance of painting so keenly as for the fourth century. According to voluminous and graphic literary accounts, painters had made almost incredible strides since the not-too-distant days when Polygnotos was content to define form with line and to fill in the areas between contours with flat color. The names of many painters are known, and their styles were described in great detail. The leading master was apparently Apelles, whose studio was visited by Alexander himself. Artists no longer chiefly painted monumental murals on commission. Instead they specialized in panel paintings done on easels in the studio, working to satisfy themselves and hoping for sales to the wealthy and powerful. Painters employed either *encaustic*, using colors dissolved in hot wax and painting while the wax was still soft, or *tempera*, utilizing colors mixed with egg yolk. Both techniques were fairly laborious, but the effects the artists achieved were totally new. First of all, they had discovered the full meaning of light for the first time in the long story of the art of painting. They were able to indicate the source of light and follow its effects in diffusion, transparency, reflection, and cast shadow. So many of these light effects turn up as common practice in the Roman paintings done at Pompeii and Herculaneum (see figs. 253, 254, colorplate 21) by anonymous provincial artists three centuries later that the literary accounts are more than believable. Furthermore, these effects correspond to those that the sculptors were seeking to achieve in marble and in bronze. The painters were also able to indicate depth, especially by means of foreshortening objects placed at an angle to the picture plane; and finally they were greatly interested in human character and emotion. Many portraits are described, and many dramatic scenes in which passion was represented with great success. Accounts of the lost pictures were, of course, read in the Italian Renaissance, and Botticelli attempted to recreate Apelles' glowing masterpiece showing Aphrodite born from the sea in his delicate *Birth of Venus* (see Vol. 2, colorplate 12). One extremely important device discovered by fourth-century masters was glazing, or covering the surface of a painting with a quick-drying, transparent coating (which could be a var-

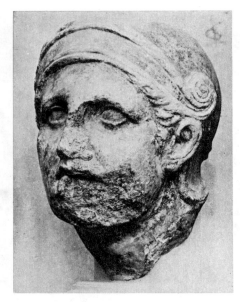

213. SKOPAS. *Head*, from the Temple of Athena Alea, Tegea. c. 350–340 B.C. Marble. National Archaeological Museum, Athens

nish) in which small amounts of color had been dissolved. This gave otherwise very brilliant tones an effect of greater depth and resonance, much like the soft colors transmitted by sunlight at certain times of day.

We do at least possess occasional attempts, however halting, to reconstruct fourth-century paintings. One is a mosaic (a technique of building up a pictorial image by combining small pieces of hard, colored material: in Classical times stone was used) found at Pompeii. This mosaic appears to be a late Hellenistic copy of the *Victory of Alexander over Darius II* (colorplate 20), painted about 300 B.C. by Philoxenos for King Cassander of Macedon. Despite the difficulty of translating a painting into such a picture-puzzle technique, and the heavy damage that has destroyed most of the left side of the mosaic copy, we can still experience the grandeur of a very noble composition. The artist has not tried to show the whole battle, but to sum up its central action in a selected grouping of figures and accessories. He has represented very effectively the impact of Alexander's cavalry on the routed army of Darius, who turns in his chariot with a gesture of intense compassion for his fallen bodyguard, run through by the Macedonian king. Tides of battle surge through what is clearly deep space within the picture, even though the background is a flat white. The horses turn and twist in depth, some foreshortened from the front, others from the back; still others are seen diagonally. A sheaf of long Greek spears shows that Darius is almost surrounded, but the spears also serve as a compositional device pointing to Alexander, who can be seen over the damaged area, reining in his rearing horse. The ground is littered with weapons. Light, as we have never seen it represented before, gleams on Alexander's armor, on the tree, the shields, and the glossy bodies of the horses, and casts strong shadows on the ground. A fallen Persian is reflected in the polished surface of his shield. Anguish contorts the faces and dilates

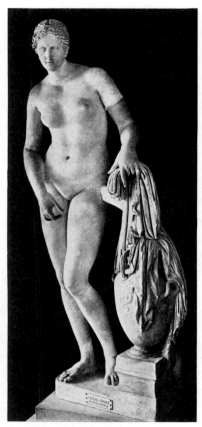

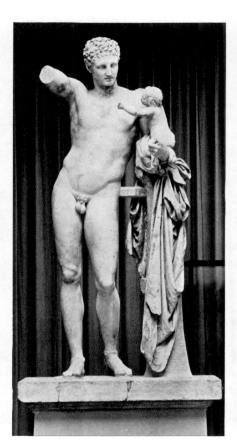

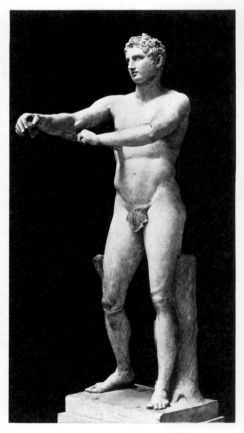

214. PRAXITELES. *Aphrodite of Knidos.* c. 350 B.C. Roman marble copy of marble original, height 80″. Vatican Museums, Rome

215. PRAXITELES. *Hermes with the Infant Dionysos,* from Olympia. c. 330–320 B.C. Marble, height 85″. Archaeological Museum. Olympia

216. LYSIPPOS. *Apoxyomenos (Scraper).* c. 330 B.C. Roman marble copy of bronze original, height 81″. Vatican Museums, Rome

the eyes of the defeated. Certainly the great fourth-century discoveries—light, space, and emotion—appear to an extraordinary degree in this picture, which opens artistic vistas leading to modern times.

THE HELLENISTIC PERIOD (323–150 B.C.)

During the Archaic and Classical periods Greek culture had spread, through a steady process of colonization, as far west as the Mediterranean coast of Spain. The conquests of Alexander produced almost overnight a veritable explosion of Hellenism throughout the entire eastern Mediterranean region as well, including Egypt, and throughout all of western Asia extending to the Indus River. Ironically enough, the propelling energy for this new burst of Hellenism came from the ruler of Macedon, a country previously considered to lie on the fringe of the Greek world; yet so durable were the effects of Alexander's conquests that Greek remained the principal language spoken in Lower Egypt and in the eastern Mediterranean region, even under the Roman Empire. Throughout the conquered countries Alexander founded

new Greek cities, some of which grew rapidly to enormous size; meanwhile, the older Ionian centers in Asia Minor, freed from Persian domination, enjoyed a new period of great prosperity. After Alexander's death in Babylon in 323 B.C., at only thirty-three years of age, his generals divided his empire between them and ruled as kings. Among the major divisions were Macedon itself under the Diadochi, the kingdom of the Seleucids in Asia Minor with its capital at Antioch in Syria, and the kingdom of the Ptolemies who ruled Egypt as pharaohs from the new Greek capital at Alexandria. Antioch and Alexandria eventually became the first cities of the ancient world with populations of a million or more.

The riches of the eastern kingdoms contrasted sadly with the poverty and relative impotence of the Greek city-states, left with only a semblance of their former autonomy, to carry on their usual fratricidal warfare except when interrupted by one or another of the Hellenistic kingdoms. Athens was respected for her distinguished history and cultural achievements, but she had slight commercial or political importance. As the city-states declined so did their old cults; religious feeling

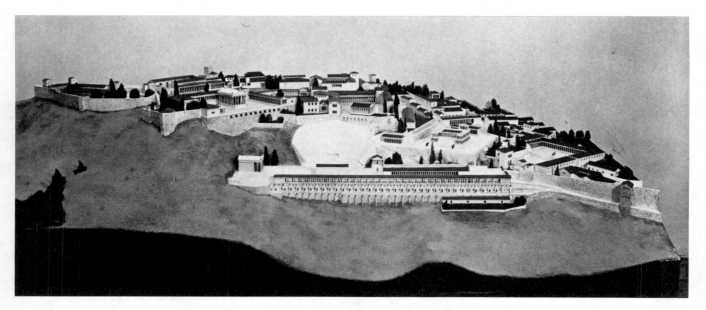

217. Model of the City of Pergamon, Asia Minor. Staatliche Museen, Berlin

became intensely personal, and the individual sought direct and often ecstatic contact with the gods in such Oriental religions as the worship of Cybele, the mother-goddess, or the cult of Isis, imported from Egypt. Learning flourished, not only in Athens but also in the great new cities, especially Alexandria, with its Mouseion, or gathering place of philosophers, scientists, and scholars, and its library, the largest in the ancient world.

No longer could sanctuaries and civic centers grow up higgledy-piggledy, as often in the older cities of Greece. The new royal capitals and princely cities required planning on a grand scale. Straight streets intersecting at right angles, open spaces, and public buildings to house all the varied activities of metropolitan life characterize the Hellenistic age. Town plans were designed to be as regular as possible, even when, as at Pergamon in Asia Minor, the rocky slopes of the terrain made planning extremely difficult. A restored model shows some of the principal buildings of this splendid city (fig. 217). The large temple in the center of a square at the upper left is Roman and should be disregarded in this context. In the center is the theater, higher and narrower than that at Epidauros, because it was not built around an orchestra circle; in fact, only a semicircle was planned, and the action took place on a stage dominated by a high building for the support of scenery. Above the theater every attempt was made—in contrast to the free arrangements of the Classical period—to impose the appearance of regularity on a very irregular terrain. At the extreme right of the model is the Agora, an open square surrounded by that most typical of Hellenistic buildings, the *stoa*, essentially a continuous colonnade, closed by a wall behind, intended for the transaction of business or just for strolling, and generally connected with shops and markets. To the left of the Agora, at a higher level but not in exact alignment, is an enormous square in the

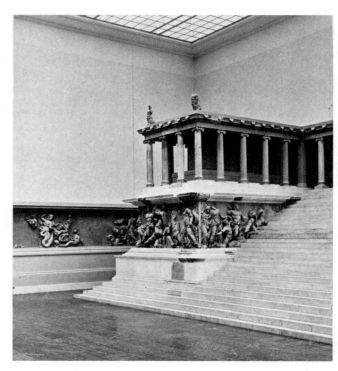

218. Altar of Zeus (northern projection), from Pergamon. c. 181–159 B.C. Pergamonmuseum, East Berlin

center of which rises the Altar of Zeus (fig. 218), a monumental structure in itself. Higher up and just behind the theater, at right angles to one of its aisles, is the Temple of Athena; it is isolated and clearly visible from all sides in a plaza, formed by a two-story stoa, not in exact alignment but handled as if it were. The second story of the stoa, towering above the exact center of the theater, gave access to the royal library, second only in importance to that of Alexandria.

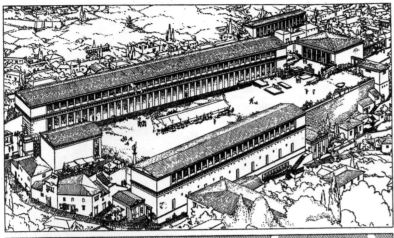

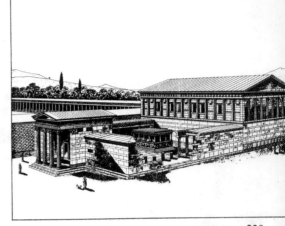

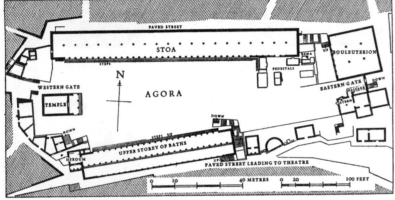

219

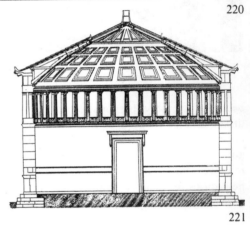

220

221

219. The Agora, Assos, Asia Minor. (Architectural reconstruction after A. W. Lawrence)

220. The Bouleuterion (Council House), Miletos. c. 170 B.C. (Architectural reconstruction after A. W. Lawrence)

221. The Arsinoeon (with roof in section), Samothrace. (Architectural reconstruction after A. W. Lawrence)

An agora of the Pergamene type at Assos in Asia Minor (reconstruction in fig. 219) had handsome stoas along both sides, divergent but treated as if parallel, a temple at one end, and at the other the *bouleuterion* (council hall). With their long, straight colonnades such complexes must have made magnificent spatial impressions. The traditional orders were still used, although Doric columns are often as tall and slender as Ionic, and Doric entablatures are correspondingly light. Generally, in two-story buildings the lower story is Doric, the upper Ionic. A superb bouleuterion of about 170 B.C. (reconstruction in fig. 220) at Miletos was preceded by an enclosure, entered through a Corinthian portico resembling a small temple. The courtyard was surrounded on three sides by a Doric colonnade, in the center of which was an open-air altar. The fourth side was formed by the lower story of one long side of the council hall itself, whose upper story was an engaged Doric colonnade, with

a pediment at either end. The Doric columns are more widely spaced than in the Classical period, with three rather than two triglyphs per column. Windows admitted light to the interior.

Large Hellenistic public buildings posed new problems for which the Greeks, thinking always in terms of post-and-lintel construction, had no organic structural solutions. Generally, interiors were roofed with wood, with sloping beams upheld in a stoa by a central row of taller columns, or sometimes in a bouleuterion by four interior columns so placed as least to obstruct the view. An ingenious device was employed at Samothrace, in a tholos called the Arsinoeon (reconstruction in fig. 221), whose cylindrical wall was surmounted outside by an engaged peristyle of Doric pilasters, inside by engaged Corinthian columns, supporting a wooden roof with a conical inner ceiling of wood, elegantly coffered (divided into recessed panels). Here is an early approach to the problem of the centralized interior without inner supports, which was solved later by the Romans through new and more imaginative constructional methods (see figs. 283, 285), and taken up again in the great domes of the Byzantine (see figs. 339, 340) and Renaissance (see Vol. 2, fig. 184) periods.

Hellenistic temples, when compared with those of the Archaic and Classical periods, represent a strong departure from what archaeologists have liked to consider "good taste." Nonetheless, if we are willing to forget for a moment preferences based on Classical style, and see these buildings in the context of the splendid municipal spaces of the Hellenistic cities, we must agree that they were very dramatic structures. A completely original example was the so-called Didymaion, the Temple of Apollo at Didyma, near Miletos, begun about 300 B.C. (figs. 222, 223). Like a number of earlier temples in this region, the Didymaion was dipteral (with two peristyles, one inside the other). The structure was gigantic—358 feet long by 167 feet wide, with 110 columns. These were the tallest of all Greek columns, sixty-four feet in height, and there were ten across each end and twenty-one along

each side; the entrance porch was five columns deep. The central doorway, raised to make it inaccessible to the public, was used only for the promulgation of oracles. By means of a dark, barrel-vaulted passageway the worshiper emerged not into the expected dim interior, but into a giant courtyard blazing with Apollo's sunlight, and lined with pilasters, whose capitals carved with griffins correspond to no conventional order. At the end of the court stood the sanctuary proper, an elegant Ionic temple approached by a flight of steps. Not only the dimensions and the enormous number of columns but also the stages in approach to the sanctuary and the general air of mystery remind us of the great temples at Luxor and Karnak (see figs. 78, 79). Temple architecture intended to produce a similar overwhelming emotional experience appeared in the second century in Athens itself, the center from which the intellectual style of the Classical period had emanated. The Temple of the Olympian Zeus (fig. 224), begun in 174 B.C. by the architect Cossutius (a Roman citizen working in Greek style) and commissioned by Antiochos IV, king of Syria, belongs to the same dipteral type as the Didymaion, which it almost

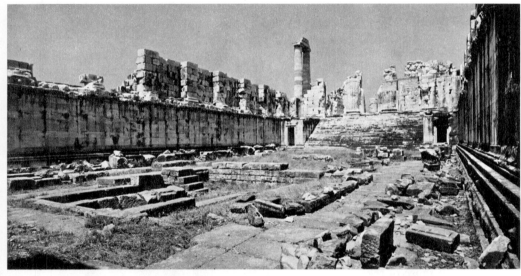

222. Temple of Apollo (view toward the east). c. 330 B.C. Didyma

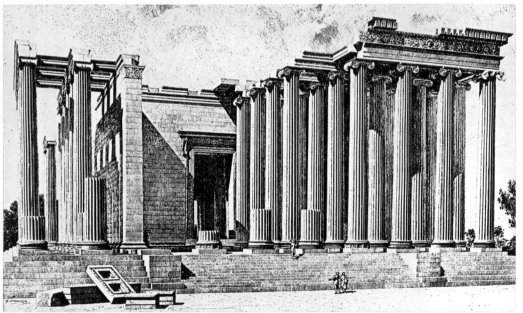

223. Temple of Apollo, Didyma. (Architectural reconstruction by H. Knackfuss)

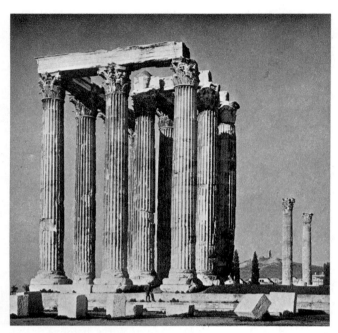

224. COSSUTIUS. Temple of the Olympian Zeus (view from the east). c. 174 B.C.–2nd century A.D. Athens

equaled in scale. It is the first major Corinthian temple, and was so elaborate that it was not finished until the second century A.D. under the Roman emperor Hadrian. The small sections still extant, with their towering columns and rich capitals, hint at what must have been the majesty of the entire building, especially when it was surrounded by its original immense walled precinct.

The sculptors of the Hellenistic age must have been almost embarrassed by the richness of their Classical heritage. Through the teaching of the innumerable followers of the great fourth-century masters—Skopas, Lysippos, and Praxiteles—Hellenistic sculptors were enabled to master the entire repertory of Classical virtuosity; they could represent anything in marble or bronze, from the vibrant warmth of nude flesh in the sunlight to the soft fluffiness of youthful hair. There are, in fact, works in which Hellenistic sculptors strove consciously to emulate their predecessors, even those of the sixth and fifth centuries, and since the great artistic conquests had already been made, it is not possible to follow in Hellenistic sculpture the steady evolution so clearly visible in earlier periods of art. Consequently, unless we have inscriptions or external evidence, Hellenistic sculpture is extremely difficult to date. Strikingly new in Hellenistic sculpture are an increased interest in naturalism, and a new dimension given to drama, which violates at times all previous boundaries and standards, in keeping with the new frontiers of the dramatic period itself, and with the new spaces and light of Hellenistic architecture.

Distinct schools grew up at Athens, at Alexandria, on the island of Rhodes, and at Pergamon in Asia Minor, to name four of the most important. It is appropriate to begin with a second-century portrait of Alexander

himself (fig. 225), who was the motive force behind the new era and its art. The head was found at Pergamon, and it once formed part of a now lost, larger-than-lifesize statue of the brilliant young monarch. Although done long after his death, it is a convincing portrait of the strange hero—part visionary, part military genius—driven by the wildest ambition, stranger to no physical or emotional excess, restrained by no moral standards (he ordered his own nephew executed and murdered his closest friend in a wild debauch). The rolling eyes, the shaggy hair, the furrowed brow, the already fleshy and sagging contours of cheeks and neck, all betray the character of this astounding man. As in all sculptures of the Pergamene school, the master—certainly one of the most gifted sculptors of his time (see below, page 165)—has maintained a carefully controlled system of exaggerated incisions and depressions in eyes, mouth, and hair in order to increase light-and-dark contrasts and to achieve a heightened emotional effect.

A different kind of portraiture—more searching perhaps and less dramatic, but equally influential on the later art of Rome—must have characterized the lost original bronze of the archenemy of Macedon, the Athenian orator Demosthenes. This work is known from several Roman copies (fig. 226; the hands and forearms are an accurate modern restoration). The sculptor has embodied with great success the quiet intensity of the pensive, aging statesman, enveloped in his worn cloak; no realistic detail is spared. Hellenistic sculptors, in fact, shrank from no representations of decay or even deformi-

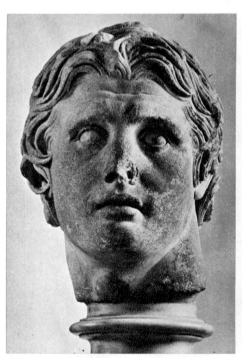

225. *Portrait of Alexander*, from Pergamon. 1st half of 2nd century B.C. Marble, height 16⅛". Archaeological Museum, Istanbul

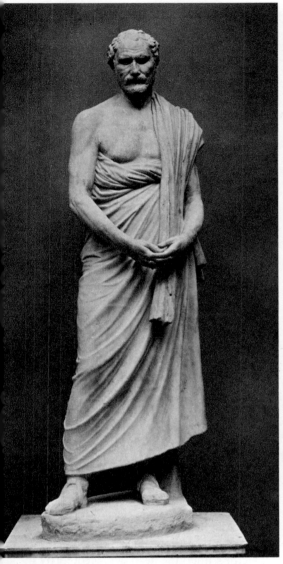

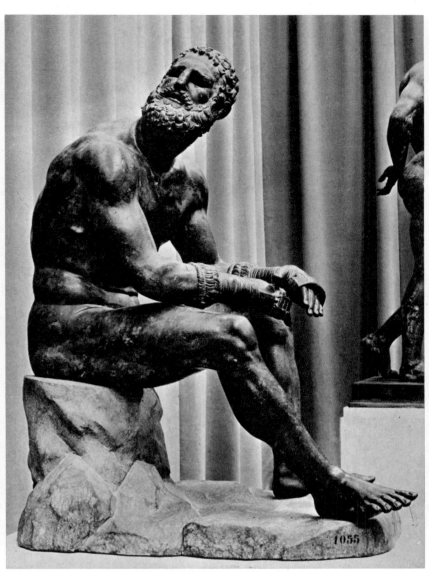

26. *Demosthenes.* c. 280 B.C. Roman marble copy of bronze original, height 79½″. Nationalmuseet, Copenhagen

227. *Seated Boxer.* Middle 1st century B.C. Bronze, height 50″. Museo delle Terme, Rome

ty in their attempt to present an intense and convincing picture of human life. A tragic example of human degradation is shown in the bronze *Seated Boxer* (fig. 227), probably dating from about the middle of the first century B.C., about a hundred years after Athens had lost its independence to Rome. The sculptor controlled the entire repertory of anatomical knowledge and bronze technique known to Polykleitos and Lysippos, but instead of a graceful athlete in serene command of his own destiny, he preferred to show us a muscle-bound, knotty boxer, with broken nose, cauliflower ears, and swollen cheeks. Blood oozes from still open wounds on his face. What is left of a human soul seems almost to ask for release in the expression of the stunned face, possibly even more harrowing when the inlaid eyes were preserved.

Mythology itself was seen from the point of view of the new naturalism; the satyr, a happy and irresponsible denizen of the glades in Archaic and Classical art, is shown heavy with wine (fig. 228) in an excellent Roman copy of a lost Hellenistic original from about the middle of the third century B.C. The bestially sensual anatomy and the brutal face disturbed by dreams in its drunken stupor radiate the same sense of tragic imprisonment so impressive in the *Seated Boxer.* The dreamy, languorous naturalism of Praxiteles lingers on throughout the Hellenistic period, even in representations of divinities, who never radiate the impersonal grandeur of the fifth century. The *Aphrodite of Cyrene* (fig. 229), found in a bath in that North African Greek city, is an exquisite work of the early first century B.C. The curving surfaces and soft, warm flesh of the goddess, who has just risen from the sea (in emulation of the *Aphrodite of Knidos* of

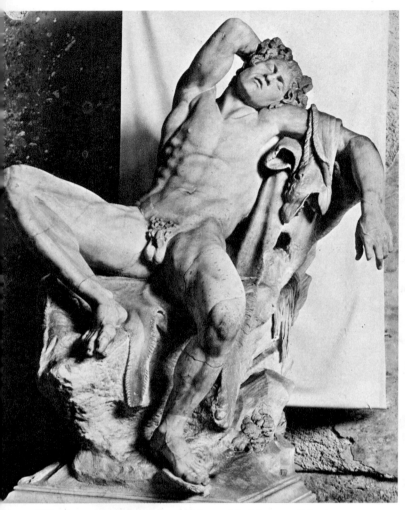

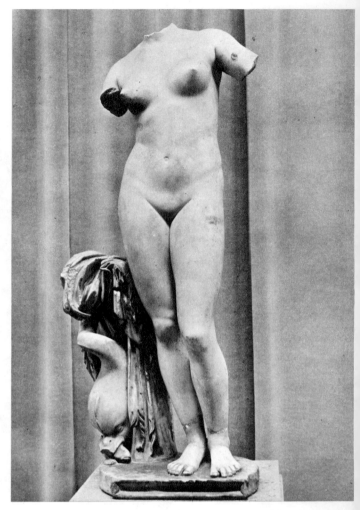

228. *Satyr* (Roman copy). c. 220 B.C. Marble, over life-size. Staatliche Antikensammlungen und Glyptothek, Munich

229. *Aphrodite of Cyrene,* from Cyrene, North Africa. Early 1st century B.C. Marble. Museo Nazionale Romano, Rome

Praxiteles, see fig. 214), contrast with the beautiful curves of the dolphin and with the delicate folds of the garment beside her. In the *Head of a Girl* (fig. 230), probably of the third century, from the island of Chios, Praxitelean style is carried to its furthest extreme. The marble head was doubtless inserted in a statue made of another kind of marble, part of which was carved into drapery covering the girl's head. The upper lids melt into the brows, so soft has definition become, and the lower lids are hardly represented at all. The face is a masterpiece of pure suggestion, through luminous surfaces of marble and tremulous shadow.

In the magnificent *Nike of Samothrace* (fig. 231), we have an echo of Paionios' famous statue at Olympia (see fig. 202), but this time the unknown Hellenistic sculptor has won; his statue is far more dramatic than its Classical prototype. It was originally erected in the Sanctuary of the Great Gods at Samothrace by the Rhodians in gratitude for their naval victory over Antiochos III of Syria about 190 B.C., and it stood upon a lofty pedestal representing in marble the prow of a ship. The right hand, discovered in 1950, shows that the fingers original-

ly held a metal victor's fillet; the head is turned partly to the left. The sea winds whip the drapery into splendid masses, producing a rich variation of light and shade. The contrast between the tempestuous movement and the power of the outstretched wings renders this one of the grandest of ancient statues.

The most dramatic of all the Hellenistic schools of sculpture flourished at Pergamon, which in the third century B.C. was attacked by tribes of Gauls from the north. The victory of King Attalos I over the invaders was celebrated in a series of bronze statues and groups, known through Roman copies. One of the most naturalistic of these, the *Dying Trumpeter* (fig. 232), is obviously a descendant of such works as the *Dying Warrior* of Aegina (see fig. 163), but the beautiful reticence and geometric clarity of Late Archaic sculpture should not blind us to the accomplishments of Pergamene art in rendering the collapse of the barbarian from a wound in his side streaming blood, represented with a deep and unexpected sympathy of the victor for the vanquished.

The triumph of the Pergamenes is celebrated allegorically in the huge Altar of Zeus (see fig. 218), erected between 181 and 159 B.C. and partially reconstructed in Berlin. It stood on a raised platform, in the manner of a ziggurat, in the center of a court, and was accessible by a steep flight of steps. Around the altar were two peristyles, the outer one of widely spaced Ionic columns, with wings projecting on either side of the staircase. Around the entire base ran a frieze more than seven feet high, representing the *Battle of Gods and Giants* (symbolizing, of course, the triumph of the Pergamenes over the barbarian hordes), second only to the Parthenon frieze as the largest sculptural undertaking of antiquity. But the great artist who designed the frieze changed the customary place for such a decoration from the top of a high wall or entablature (Treasury of the Siphnians, Parthenon, Temple of Apollo at Bassai, and possibly the Mausoleum at Halikarnassos), where it could be read only with difficulty, to a position only just above eye-level, where the larger-than-lifesize figures, almost entirely in the round, seem to erupt from the building toward the spectator; some have even fallen out of the frieze so that they are forced to support themselves on hands and knees up the very steps that the worshiper also climbs (see fig. 218). No pains were spared to achieve an effect of overwhelming power and drastic immediacy. The fragile architec-

ture is borne aloft, as it were, on the tide of battle. So dense is the crowding of intertwined, struggling figures as at times to obscure the background entirely. Figures of unparalleled musculature lunge, reel, or collapse in writhing agony. To our left Zeus has felled a giant with a thunderbolt aimed at his leg (fig. 233), and he bursts into flames; to our right a giant with serpents for legs beats against the thundering wings of Zeus' eagle. Projections and hollows, large and small, were systematically exaggerated so as to increase both the expressive power of the work and the contrasts of light and dark as the sun moved around the monument. Compared to this wild surge of violence, the battle reliefs of the fifth and fourth centuries look restrained, governed by laws of balance and measure which here are swept aside. The reliefs bear several sculptors' signatures; unfortunately, we do not know the name of the master who designed the entire work and who also may well have carved the giant head of *Alexander* (see fig. 225), which has so much in common with this relief.

By analogy with the art of the seventeenth century A.D., especially that by such masters as Bernini and Rubens (see Vol. 2, Part Five, Chapters 1 and 4), the style of the Altar of Zeus has often been called the "Pergamene Baroque." It continued throughout Hellenistic times, and was revived repeatedly in the art of the Roman Empire. One of the most extraordinary examples is the group representing *Laocoön and His Two Sons* (fig. 234). The priest Laocoön was assailed by sea serpents sent by Poseidon, and was strangled before the walls of Troy. The group is the work of three sculptors from Rhodes —Hagesandros, Polydoros, and Athenodoros—but we do not know when it was created. Its customary dating to the second century B.C. has recently been upset by an extraordinary find at Sperlonga on the coast of Italy, northwest of Naples, of fragments of four huge sculptural groups in a cave that had been turned into a pleasure grotto. One of these groups, repeating the old Homeric theme of *Odysseus Blinding Polyphemos*, was signed by the same three Rhodian sculptors. It has recently been suggested that both the *Laocoön* and the *Odysseus* may have been done as late as the first century A.D. for a Roman patron, possibly the emperor Tiberius. The head of Odysseus (fig. 235) shows strong similarities to that of Laocoön—the same cutting of the marble, the same wildly rolling eyes, and the same treatment of hair and beard. Although the expert rendering of muscular strain in the *Laocoön* may seem forced to us, in comparison to the Altar of Zeus, it was a revelation to the Italian Renaissance, above all to Michelangelo, when the group was unearthed near Rome in 1506.

Unfortunately, we possess no more original paintings from the Hellenistic period than we do fourth-century ones, but many of the finest Roman paintings preserved at Pompeii and Herculaneum are believed to reflect lost Hellenistic pictures. A fresco of *Herakles and the Infant Telephos* from Herculaneum (colorplate 21) even repeats

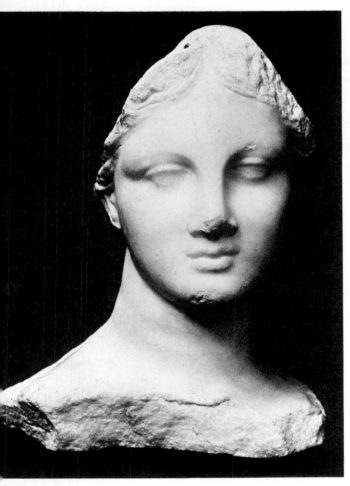

230. *Head of a Girl,* from Chios. c. 3rd century B.C. Marble. height 14⅛". Museum of Fine Arts. Boston

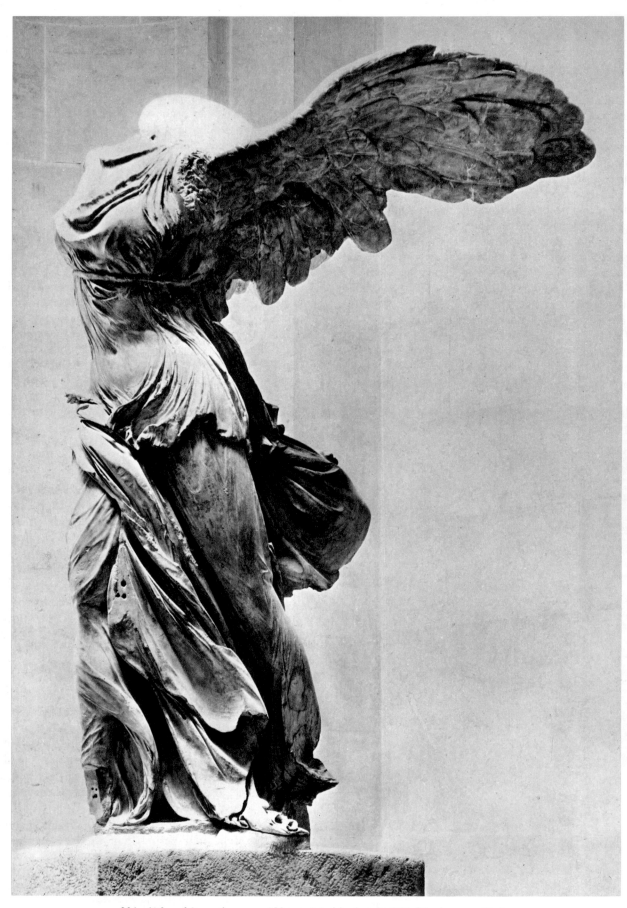

231. *Nike of Samothrace.* c. 190 B.C. Marble, height 96″. The Louvre, Paris

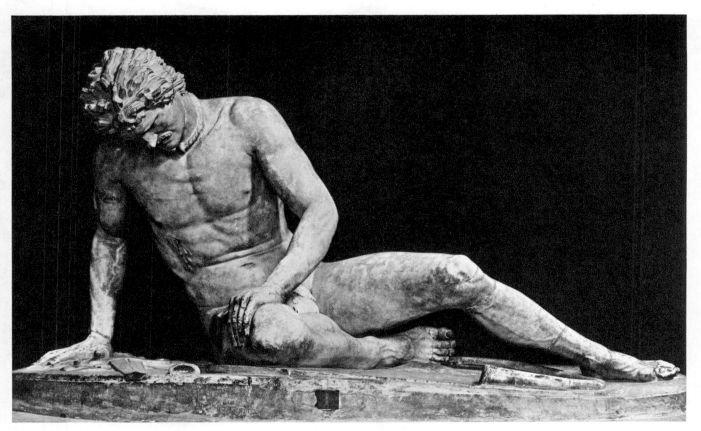

232. *Dying Trumpeter,* from Pergamon. c. 230–220 B.C. Roman marble copy of bronze original, life-size. Museo Capitolino, Rome

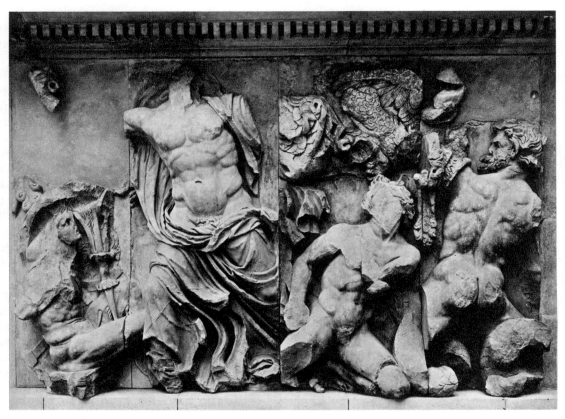

233. *Zeus Fighting Three Giants,* from the Altar of Zeus, Pergamon. c. 181–159 B.C. Marble. Pergamonmuseum, East Berlin

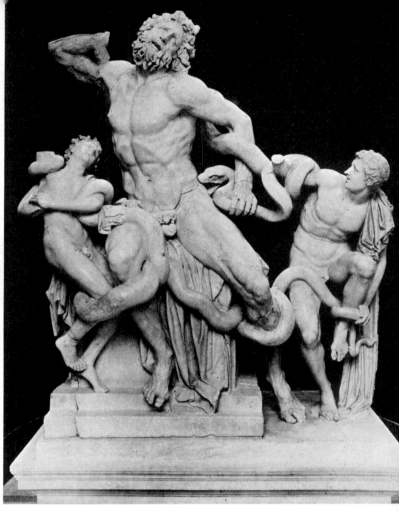

234. HAGESANDROS, POLYDOROS, and ATHENODOROS.
Laocoön and His Two Sons. 1st century A.D. Marble,
height 96″. Vatican Museums, Rome

235. HAGESANDROS, POLYDOROS, and ATHENODOROS.
Head of Odysseus, part of
Odysseus Blinding Polyphemos, from Sperlonga,
Italy. 1st century A.D. Marble, life-size. Museo
Archeologico Nazionale, Sperlonga

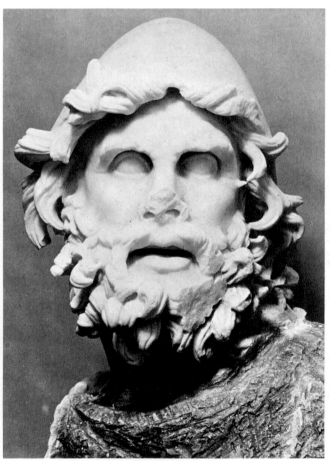

a composition carved in the interior of the Altar at Pergamon. The sensuous richness of the style appears at its·height in the painting of Herakles' deeply tanned body, in the shadows on his fierce lion, and in the range of light and shade on the doe suckling Herakles' infant son Telephos. Hellenistic pictorial style can be clearly seen in a number of pebble mosaics used for floors, especially the beautiful third-century series unearthed at Pella in Macedon, the birthplace of Alexander. Even through the difficult medium of colored pebbles, the artist has been able to show the movement of light and shadow across the nude bodies and flying cloaks of two youths engaged in a *Stag Hunt* (colorplate 22), each pebble treated as if it were a separate brushstroke. The blue-gray background accentuates the play of light, and the motion is enhanced by the rhythmic surge of the vinescrolls framing the scene, and played off against the wave pattern in the border.

A final word should be said about Hellenistic houses lavish enough to have such floors. Throughout Greek history up to this moment the private residence had been meanly simple—rough stone or mud-brick walls, supporting a tiled roof around a central court whose pillars were mere wooden posts. Demosthenes writes that in his time, the end of the fourth century, houses in Athens were becoming larger and richer, and during the wealthy Hellenistic period every city could boast entire streets of luxurious residences. These houses were invariably blank

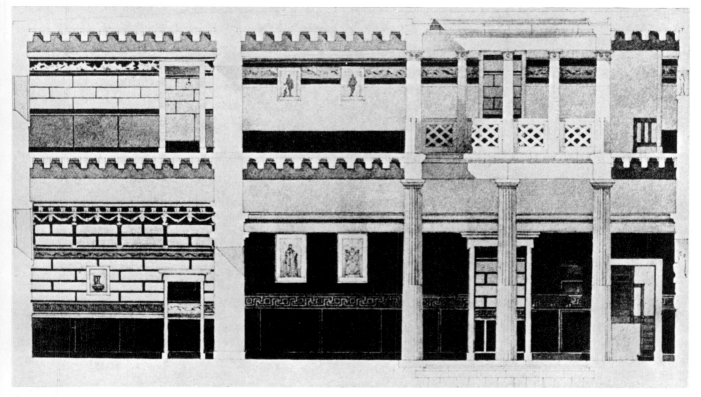

236. Section of a house at Delos showing mural decoration. c. 2nd century B.C. (Architectural reconstruction after A. W. Lawrence)

on the exterior and flush with the street, but once the visitor entered the interior through a hallway (L-shaped to keep out prying eyes), he found himself in a handsome courtyard graced at least on the north side, and sometimes on all four, by a peristyle, and giving access to a splendid dining room (fig. 236). Other rooms opened off the court, and the houses were often two stories high. The walls were decorated with an elaborate system of panels painted to resemble marble slabs (the so-called incrustation style taken up later by the Romans). Figural paintings appeared here and there, as if hanging on the wall.

Hellenistic palaces, temples, and prosperous private houses must have been sumptuously furnished with objects making lavish use of luxurious materials and precious metals. We are aided in forming a mental picture of such vanished splendors by a treasure comprising eight wine vessels of pure gold, dating from about 300 B.C., which was discovered by accident at Panagyurishte, near Plovdiv, Bulgaria. Probably intended for ritual use, these wine vessels seem to have been produced in the Greek East, since measurements are indicated on them according to both Greek and Persian systems. The central object of the group is a superb amphora (colorplate

23). Drinking spouts around the base are formed by Negro heads, and the handles—produced as if by chance—are formed by sprightly, youthful centaurs whose forehoofs overlap the rim and whose arms are uplifted in delight at the sight of the wine within. Traditional ornament is restricted to four bands widely scattered so as not to compete with the refulgence of the smooth, gold surfaces in the neck of the vessel and in the human and animal figures. The body of the amphora is covered with a vigorous relief, whose nude male and clothed female figures possibly narrate the tale of Achilles at Skyros. Terrified that her son might join the Greek armies marshaling for war against Troy, Thetis, Achilles' mother, clothed him as a woman and hid him among the daughters of the king of Skyros. The moment shown is that of the sudden revelation of Achilles' masculinity after the wily Odysseus, disguised as a peddler, set up arms before Achilles' quarters in order to tempt him to handle them and, thereby, betray his identity. Ignoring the female trinkets, Achilles seizes and fondly wields a sword; in so doing he sheds his garments and displays his muscular figure. formed in flashing gold with all the vitality we have seen in monumental Hellenistic sculpture.

5

Etruscan Art

Beyond the borders of the coastal Greek city-states of southern Italy, the hinterland was inhabited by less developed, indigenous peoples. To the north, in the region between the Tiber and the Arno rivers, flourished an extraordinary and still mysterious culture, that of the Etruscans. Herodotos, the Greek Classical historian, reported that the Etruscans came from Lydia in Asia Minor, and there is a good deal of evidence to support his contention. Another ancient tradition, however, causes some modern scholars to believe that the Etruscans inhabited Italy from prehistoric times. This view is difficult to reconcile with the fact that the Etruscans spoke a non-Indo-European language which, as ancient authors noted, had nothing in common with the other tongues current in ancient Italy, not even with their roots. On account of this linguistic discrepancy the Etruscans were, in fact, sharply isolated from their neighbors. The discovery on the Aegean island of Lemnos of an inscription in a language resembling Etruscan adds weight to the arguments for an Eastern origin.

Regardless of how the debate may eventually be settled, the fact remains that for about four hundred years this energetic people controlled much of central Italy, the region of Etruria, which has retained the name of Tuscany (from the Latin *Tuscii* for *Etruscans*) until the present day. They never formed a unified nation, but rather a loose confederation of city-states, each under the rule of its own king. Many of these cities are still inhabited, among them Veii, Tarquinii (Tarquinia), Caere (Cerveteri), Perusia (Perugia), Faesulae (Fiesole), Volaterrae (Volterra), Arretium (Arezzo), and Clusium (Chiusi). Although populated centers are generally impossible to excavate, others, since abandoned, such as Populonia and Vetulonia, have been systematically uncovered. We often know more about Etruscan cemeteries, which have been excavated, than about Etruscan towns.

During the sixth and fifth centuries B.C, the Etruscan states colonized an ever-expanding domain in central Italy, including Rome itself, which was ruled by a succession of Etruscan kings until the founding of the Roman Republic at the end of the sixth century. In fact, Etruscan rule spread into Campania in the south, and into the plain of the Po River to the north, as far as the foothills of the Alps. Etruscan commerce in the Mediterranean vied with that of the Greeks and the Phoenicians, both of whom had reason to dread Etruscan pirates. From the fifth century onward, the expanding military power of Rome doomed the Etruscan hegemony, and eventually even Etruscan independence. During the fourth century, constant warfare against the Romans attacking from the south and the Gauls from the north forced the Etruscans to develop the urban fortifications for which they were renowned. During the third century, Roman domination destroyed Etruscan power forever, and in the early first century B.C. the Etruscan cities were definitively absorbed into the Roman Republic.

Etruscan literature is lost; we know of no Etruscan philosophy or science, nor can it be claimed that the Etruscans developed an art whose originality and quality could enable it to compete with the great artistic achievements of the Egyptians, the Mesopotamians, or above all the Greeks. In many respects Etruscan art follows, about a generation behind, the progress of the Greeks, whose vases the Etruscans avidly collected. Yet many works of Etruscan sculpture and especially Etruscan painting are very attractive in their rustic vigor, and every now and then in museums of Etruscan art we encounter a real masterpiece.

Little Etruscan architecture is standing, even in fragmentary condition. A detailed prescription for an Etruscan temple based on examples visible in his day is given by Vitruvius, a Roman architect and theoretical writer of the first century B.C. If we judge from Vitruvius,

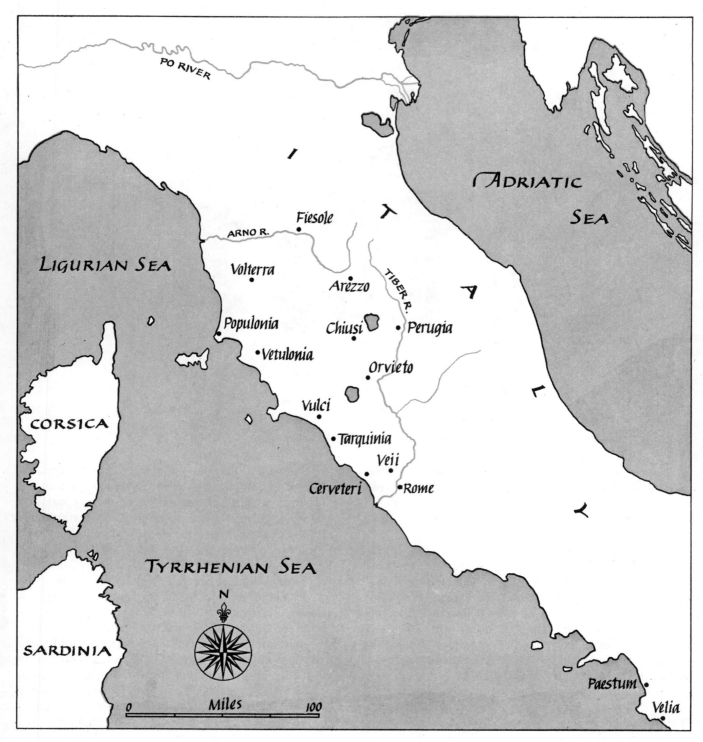

MAP 10. *Etruria*

a typical Etruscan temple was roughly square in plan (fig. 237), and placed upon a high podium of stone blocks, often tufa (a volcanic stone which was handy and easy to cut). Access was provided by a flight of steps in the front, unlike the continuous, four-sided platform of the Greek temple. The mud-brick cella occupied only the rear half of the podium; the rest was covered by an open portico; the low-pitched wooden roof had widely overhanging eaves to protect the mud-brick walls. Early columns were

of wood, with stone capitals and bases; later examples were of stone throughout. Vitruvius thought that all Etruscan columns were unfluted, with molded bases and capitals close to those of the Doric order, including both echinus and abacus; he therefore postulated a fourth or Tuscan order. However, surviving examples show that the Etruscans did on occasion flute their columns, and did imitate, however roughly, both Ionic and Corinthian capitals. The heavy roof beams and protecting tiles left

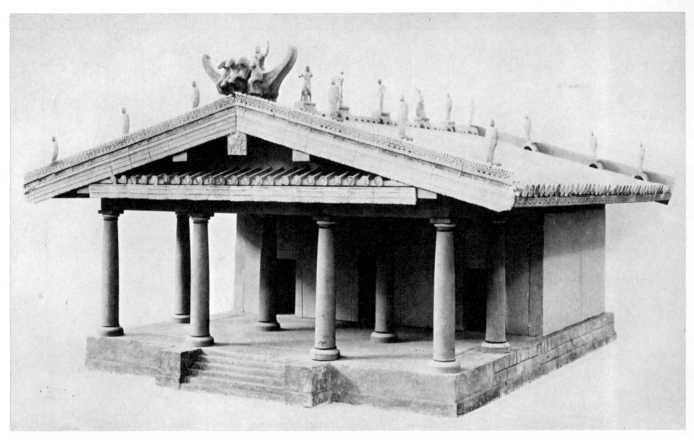

237. Reconstruction of a typical Etruscan Temple as described by Vitruvius

little room for pedimental sculpture. But the Etruscans were extremely adept at terra-cotta work, having learned the technique from the Greeks to the south, and their roof lines and ridgepoles often bristled with a sizable terra-cotta population.

The appearance of an Etruscan temple, with its squat proportions and crowded roof, could scarcely compete with the elegance and harmony of Hellenic proportions, but the Etruscan examples were, nonetheless, the basis for the Roman experience of a temple. Several existed in Rome itself, and a very large one, 175 feet by 204 feet, with a triple cella and columns continuing along the sides, was dedicated in 509 B.C. on the Capitoline. Although this great temple burned down in 83 B.C., it was rebuilt in 69 B.C. with lofty marble columns on the Greek model. This very circumstance tells us much about the double derivation of Roman architecture, with Greek elements grafted, so to speak, onto Etruscan trunks.

The Greeks knew the arch but used it very rarely, mostly in substructions. One of the few Greek arches above ground is in the city wall of Velia, a Greek town south of Paestum. Borrowing the idea from their Greek neighbors, the Etruscans embellished and elaborated it. Like the Babylonians, they displayed the arch proudly, at the major entrances to their cities—places which had special religious meaning. The gates of Perugia—for example, the Porta Marzia (fig. 238; originally open; the brick filling is later)—are true arches, composed of trapezoidal stones called archivolts, each of which

presses against its neighbors so that the structure is essentially self-sustaining. The arch proper is flanked by pilasters of two different sizes, in rather clumsy imitation of Greek originals; nonetheless, these are important early examples of the combination of the arch with the Greek orders, a combination that later typified Roman architectural thinking.

Etruscan sculpture, most of which we know from funerary examples, shows from the beginning the typical Etruscan facility in terra-cotta. Many terra-cotta statuettes of the deceased have been found; small terra-cotta urns, made to hold incinerated remains, were widely used. A seventh-century urn of hammered bronze from Chiusi (fig. 239) is surmounted by a staring terra-cotta head of great expressive power, the whole set upon a bronze model of a chair. The Etruscans developed a new kind of funerary sculpture in painted terra-cotta that shows the deceased, singly or in couples, relaxing happily on the left elbow on a couch, in the pose of banqueters. The finest of these is from Cerveteri (fig. 240). These delightful images, whose smooth bodies, braided hair, and Archaic smiles remind us of Greek sculpture, seem to show a very happy view of the future life, in keeping with the festive paintings (see below, page 175) that decorate the interiors of the tomb chambers. But the most imposing Etruscan terra-cotta works were such rooftop statues as the famous *Apollo of Veii*, which still retains some of its original coloring (colorplate 24). This figure was part of a group showing Herakles carrying off

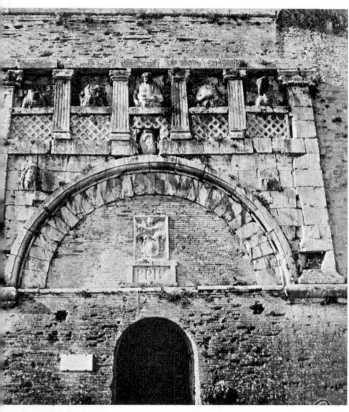

238. Porta Marzia. 3rd or 2nd century B.C. Perugia, Italy

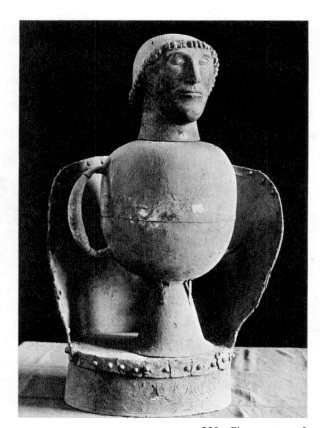

239. Cinerary urn, from Chiusi,
Italy. 7th century B.C.
Hammered bronze with
terra-cotta head,
height c. 33″.
Museo Etrusco, Chiusi

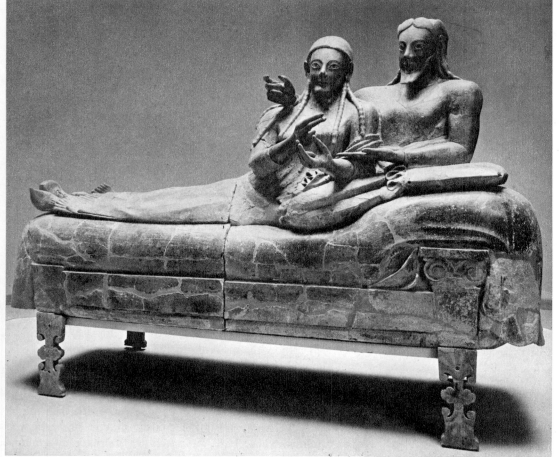

240. Sarcophagus, from Cerveteri
Italy. c. 520 B.C.
Painted terra-cotta,
length 79″.
Museo Nazionale
de Villa Giulia, Rome

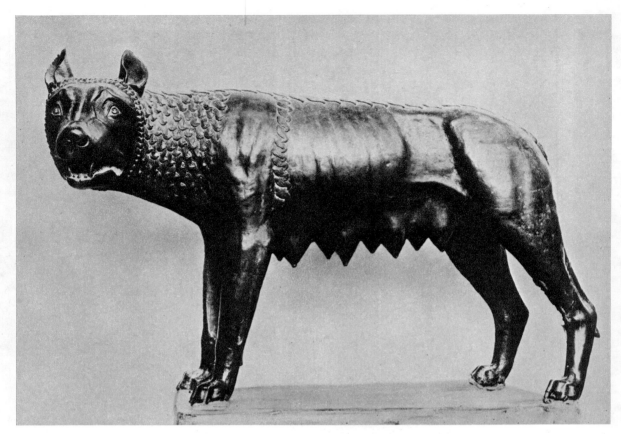

241. *She-Wolf.* c. 500 B.C. Bronze, height 33½". Museo Capitolino, Rome

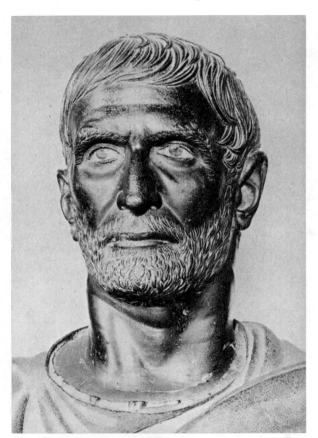

242. *Bearded Man (Lucius Junius Brutus).* Head,
3rd century B.C. Bronze, height 12⅝".
Palazzo dei Conservatori, Rome

the sacred hind, with Apollo in hot pursuit. Provincial though it may appear in comparison with such contemporary Archaic Greek works as the earliest sculpture at Aegina (see figs. 161, 162, 163), the athletic god, with his grand stride and swinging drapery, shows a freedom of motion which in Archaic Greek sculpture is generally restricted to reliefs; the borrowed Archaic smile and stylized folds seem almost anachronistic. This statue helps us form an idea of the terra-cotta statue of Zeus once in the Etruscan temple on the Capitoline (see above, page 172), whose sculptor also came from Veii, a town eight miles north of Rome.

The fierce, bronze *She-Wolf*, a symbol of the origins of Rome because a she-wolf suckled Romulus and Remus, the legendary founders of Rome, is an Etruscan work of about 500 B.C. (fig. 241). Its crisp and brilliant detail was incised in the bronze after casting. A similar precision of detail and intensity of expression are still seen in the powerful portrait of a *Bearded Man* (fig. 242), dating from the third century, whose air of strong resolution has given it the nickname of Lucius Junius Brutus, the leader of the Roman revolt against the last Etruscan king.

We know the most about the Etruscans from their innumerable tombs, of which hundreds have been explored and thousands more still lie unexcavated, a prey to tombrobbers. Most of the Greek pottery so far recovered has been found in these tombs. Typically, the Etruscan tomb was covered by a simple conical mound of earth, or tumulus, whose base was often held in place by a plain circle of masonry. Some tomb chambers were also circular, with corbel vaults like that of the so-called Treasury of Atreus at Mycenae (see fig. 133). More often they were rectangular, rock-cut rooms, which at Tarquinia and other cities contain some of the richest treasures of ancient wall painting we know. Early fifth-century tombs, such as the *Tomb of the Triclinium* at Tarquinia (fig. 243), were painted with scenes of daily life; sometimes the funeral feast was shown, somewhat as in Egyptian tombs, and sometimes incidents from daily life were depicted. In the absence of firm knowledge of Etruscan religion, it is impossible to say whether these wall paintings were meant to comfort the deceased or to indicate the existence he would enter in the afterlife. Their energetic contours and flat surfaces betray the influence of Greek painting, but with a typically Etruscan vigor of movement. The most spectacular of these paintings, representing hunting and fishing (colorplate 25), derives from such Greek originals as the *Diver* from Paestum (see colorplate 16). Interestingly enough, both the dolphin and the red and blue birds joyously elude capture, taking refuge in the billowing sea or the endless air.

Later tombs, such as the burial chamber in the *Tomb of the Reliefs* at Cerveteri (fig. 244), take a more gloomy view of the other world. The rock-cut pillars, whose capitals are derived from Greek sources, are supplied with stucco reliefs of household instruments, weapons, and even a small dog, all for the use of the deceased, but a demon of death appears at the end of the chamber, with snaky legs like those of the giants at Pergamon (see fig. 233), and he is accompanied by Cerberus, the three-headed dog who guarded Hades. The tomb has become an image of the underworld, and the joyous vitality of the earlier tombs has been forgotten.

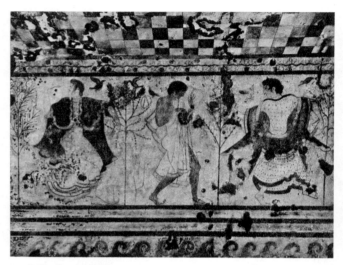

243. *Dancing Woman and Lyre Player,* from the *Tomb of the Triclinium.* Wall painting. 5th century B.C. Tarquinia, Italy

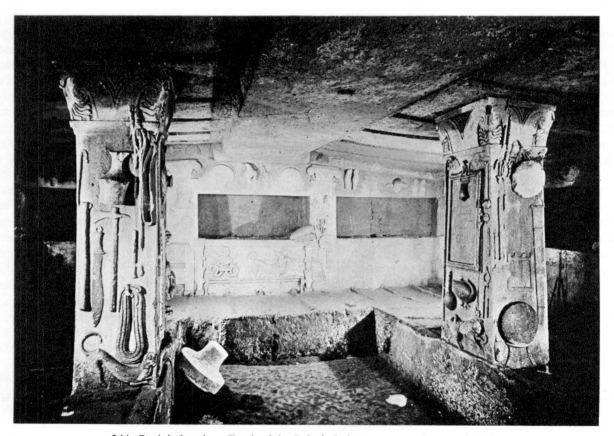

244. Burial chamber, *Tomb of the Reliefs.* 3rd century B.C. Cerveteri, Italy

6
Roman Art

The culminating phenomenon of ancient history was the rise of a single austere central Italian city-state from total obscurity to imperial rule over most of the then known world. Far-reaching as were the effects of Alexander's rocketlike trajectory, they can scarcely be compared to the steady, inexorable expansion of Rome. At the start the Romans were chiefly concerned with maintaining their autonomy against their aggressive neighbors. In 510 B.C. they threw off the Etruscan yoke, yet in 386 B.C. the invading Gauls were strong enough to sack and burn Rome itself. Then the tides reversed; in the third century B.C. Rome, in constant warfare with her African rival Carthage, first dominated, then absorbed all of Italy, Sicily, and most of Spain. In the course of the second century B.C., she conquered the Balkan peninsula including Macedon and Greece, destroyed Carthage and annexed its territory, and expanded into Asia Minor and southern Gaul (modern France). In the first century B.C., the rest of Gaul, Syria, and Egypt fell into Roman hands; in the first century A.D., she conquered Britain and much of Germany; in the second, Dacia (modern Romania), Armenia, and Mesopotamia.

At the death of the emperor Trajan in A.D. 117, the Roman Empire extended from the Tigris River in Mesopotamia to the site of the Roman wall built by his successor Hadrian across Britain, close to the present Scottish border, and from the banks of the Elbe to the cataracts of the Nile. This incredible expansion, which not even the Romans could have foreseen, was partly forced upon them by their enemies, especially the Gauls and the Carthaginians, and partly engineered by well-disciplined armies and ambitious generals operating at great distances from any political control. Wherever the Romans went, they took with them their laws, their religion, their customs, and their extraordinary ability to organize. Moreover, on these lands they also imposed the Latin language, with its rigorous grammatical structure and its capacity to express complex ideas. This process of Romanization did not extend to Greece or to the Hellenized East, whose peoples continued to speak Greek and to preserve many elements of Greek culture. Given the universal extent of Roman power, the history of Roman art is really the history of Mediterranean and European art for half a millennium—so rich, so complex, and so many-sided that only a few of the principal types and historical phases can be treated carefully in a general account.

Quite early in the expansionist career of Rome, two developments became manifest which were destined to have profound artistic consequences. First, the almost continuous process of imperial growth led to a rapid increase in the population of Rome itself and of most of the cities under her control; this growth of population was accompanied by such inevitable problems as mass unemployment and poverty. As a result, not only the prosperous productive classes but also a numerous, idle proletariat required food, water, housing—and entertainment. New types of public buildings—especially vast interior spaces—were needed on an unprecedented scale, and the traditional emphasis of Mediterranean architecture and decoration was thus transformed. Second, the conquest of the Hellenic world—and to a more limited extent that of Egypt and Mesopotamia as well—opened Rome to the influence of cultures that far surpassed her own in their antiquity, intellectuality, and aesthetic achievement. Parallels to the Roman gods were found in Greek religion and mythology, so that Zeus became Jupiter, Hera Juno, Athena Minerva, and so on. Borrowed artistic elements were superimposed on the practical inventions of the Romans, and foreign artists, especially Greek, were often employed to carry out typically Roman projects. Thus, also, Rome found herself in the odd historical position of becoming the vehicle through which forms and ideas of Greek origin were conveyed to western and northern lands that had previously had little or no contact with Hellenism.

THE REPUBLIC (509–27 B.C.)

If we judge from Roman literary accounts, we must conclude that the Romans of the early Republic were a resolutely anti-aesthetic people. Scornful of what they considered the luxurious ease of their chief competitors in Italy, the Etruscans and the Greeks, the early Romans prided themselves on their austere virtues, frugal life, and military valor. Oddly enough, at first they do not even seem to have paid much attention to town planning—in spite of the example of the Greek cities in southern Italy and Sicily, which were laid out on regular plans, and the planned Etruscan towns in the plain of the Po River. Rome itself was the last Roman city to receive a plan. After its destruction by the Gauls in 390 B.C., the town was rebuilt along the same disorderly lines. During the Republic and the first years of the Empire, Rome was a pell-mell collection of structures, often rebuilt to the height of several stories, with the most slipshod methods, in order to accommodate its ever-increasing population. Contemporary descriptions record vividly the discomforts and hazards of life in the metropolis. Public buildings, such as the great temple on the Capitoline Hill (see above, page 172), were rebuilt from time to time, however, according to new and imported Greek principles of style. The rectilinear layout of Roman military camps, on which the Romans prided themselves and which they later adapted for their colonial cities, was borrowed from the Etruscans. From them, in fact, the Romans appear to have received their first lessons in building fortifications, bridges, aqueducts, and sewers, in which practical undertakings they took a great deal of pleasure and found—and were able to communicate—a special kind of austere beauty.

Sculpture

Significantly enough, the most impressive witnesses to the formative period of Roman Republican art that have come down to us are the portraits of these sturdy Romans themselves. We have already seen the bronze Etruscan portrait from the third century, whose subject may be a Roman (see fig. 242). Another splendid example in bronze, the so-called *Arringatore* (*Orator*), dates from the first century B.C. (colorplate 26). Found at Sanguineto near Lake Trasimeno in southern Etruscan territory, the statue bears an Etruscan inscription which includes the Roman name Aulus Metellus, probably the subject of the portrait. Whether the sculptor himself was Roman or Etruscan is almost beside the point, since the work was done at a period when the territory had already been Romanized; Aulus Metellus may have been a Roman official. The directness and force of the representation show a new and characteristically Roman attitude toward portraiture. The simple stance, with some weight on the free leg and the hand thrust forward in an oratorical gesture, has nothing to do with the tradition of organic grace that runs through even the most naturalis-

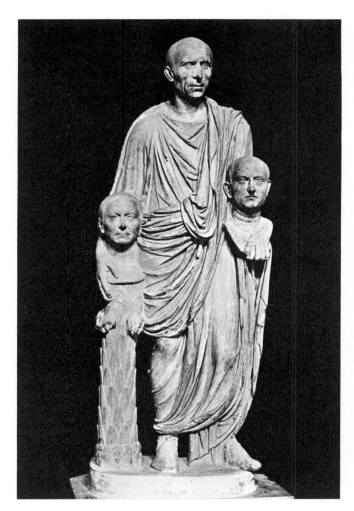

245. *Patrician Carrying Two Portrait Heads.* c. 50 B.C.–15 A.D. Marble, life-size. Museo Capitolino, Rome

tic poses of the Hellenistic period. The subject himself, with close-cropped hair, wrinkled forehead, and tight lips, is represented with an uncompromising directness that makes no concessions to Hellenic beauty.

The Greeks never accepted the idea of the separate portrait head or bust because to them a separate portrait bust made the head appear to have been decapitated. But as we have seen, such heads were in the Etruscan tradition (see fig. 242). In Roman Republican times, exact portrait masks of the deceased were made of wax, and were preserved in a wooden cabinet in the home, to be carried by relatives at later funeral ceremonies. This custom reflects a kind of ancestor worship, by means of which the old patrician families preserved their identity. The artistic result was uncompromising realism. A statue of a *Patrician Carrying Two Portrait Heads* (fig. 245) embodies this atavistic tradition with a brutal directness that would have horrified the Greeks and, incidentally, illustrates several stages in the early development of Roman portraiture. The heads, which show a strong family resemblance, represent wax images—that in the

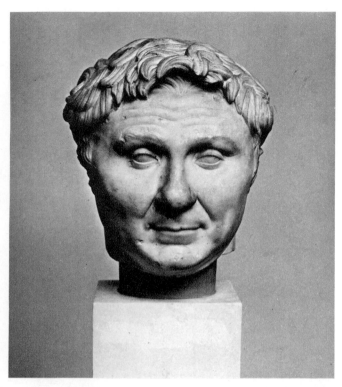

246. *Head of Pompey*. c. 100 B.C. Marble, height 9⅞". Ny Carlsberg Glyptothek, Copenhagen

Romans only objects of adornment. In the homes of wealthy Roman patricians, extensive collections of Greek art were rapidly built up by plunder or by purchase. When no more originals were available, copies were manufactured by the thousands, often in Athens and in other Greek centers as well as in Rome, to satisfy the voracious market.

Architecture

It is significant that, although Roman literature gives us admiring accounts of Greek art and artists, doubly precious to us in the absence of the original Greek works, the Romans had little to say about their own art; they seldom recorded the names and never discussed the styles of the many artists—some of them great—who carried out ambitious Roman projects. The profession of painter or sculptor had little social standing, and the necessity of making numerous quasi-mechanical copies must have lowered the artists' own self-esteem. In consequence, no distinct artistic personalities comparable to those known to us from Greek art emerge from the thousands of preserved Roman works. In its anonymity and in its collective character, Roman art can be more easily paralleled with that of Egypt or Mesopotamia. Only in the field of architecture—in the writings of the first-century-B.C. architect Vitruvius—do we find much interest in theory, and even here it is largely applied to the codification of an already accepted body of architectural knowledge, for much of which Vitruvius was obliged to resort to Greek terminology.

In the absence of extensive knowledge about the magnificent Temple of Jupiter Optimus Maximus, rebuilt on the Capitoline Hill in 69 B.C. (see page 172), with lofty marble columns imitated from Greek models and bronze roof tiles covered lavishly with gold leaf, we have to rely on comparatively modest examples for an idea of Republican architecture. One of these is the well-preserved second-century building known as the Temple of Fortuna Virilis (fig. 247; a misnomer—the building was probably dedicated to Portunus, the god of harbors), near the Tiber in Rome. Elements of Etruscan derivation are immediately visible—the podium, the flight of steps at the front, and the deep portico. But equally obvious is the attempt to Hellenize the building. The slender proportions were derived from Greece, as was the Ionic order (see figs. 153, 198). A compromise is apparent in the way in which the peristyle was carried around the sides and back of the temple only in engaged columns rather than in the freestanding columns generally preferred by the Greeks. Also, when compared to Hellenic architecture, there is something cold and grim about this little building; the capitals, in particular, lack the organic fluidity of Greek models.

Even more illuminating for the future of Roman architecture was the circular so-called Temple of the Sibyl (fig. 248) at nearby Tivoli. Although this Corinthian structure may derive ultimately from Roman

right hand an original of about 50–40 B.C., that in the left done around 20–15 B.C. Both show stern, bleak Romans, but the statue itself, with its elaborately draped toga, can be dated in the early years of the Empire, about A.D. 15. By an irony of fate, the statue's original head is missing, and was replaced in recent times with an unrelated one dating from about 40 B.C.

The typical Roman Republican portrait strove to render the subject with a map-maker's fidelity to the topography of his features, in keeping with the air of simplicity stoutly maintained by even the most prosperous citizen. An unexpectedly subtle Republican portrait, the *Head of Pompey* (fig. 246), was almost certainly carved by a Greek sculptor. This master had at his fingertips all the traditional devices of Hellenistic art for the differentiation of the textures of the full cheeks, the wrinkled forehead, the bulbous nose, the sharp eyelids, and the short, crisply curling locks of hair, and for the manipulation of the play of light over marble surfaces. Yet if we compare this head to the *Portrait of Alexander* (see fig. 225), we can see that the Roman subject is treated with a psychological reserve respected by men who placed ultimate value on decisive action.

But the influence of Greek art on Roman culture was by no means limited to the importation of Greek artists; beginning with the sack of Syracuse in 212 B.C., actual works of Greek art—sculpture, painting, and minor artifacts of all sorts—arrived in Rome in great numbers. Stripped from their original settings, these works, often intended for religious or political purposes, became to the

circular huts, some of which were religiously preserved on the Palatine Hill into imperial times, it owes its immediate formulation to the Greek tholos type (see fig. 133). The round temple at Tivoli has one remarkable feature. Instead of the coursed masonry characteristic of almost all Greek historic architecture, the cella is built of concrete. Roman concrete was not the semiliquid substance in use today, but a rougher mixture of pebbles and stone fragments with mortar, poured into wooden frames or molds. While the concrete was being formed, wedge-shaped stones (and later flat bricks) were worked into its sides, thus forming an outer skin that both protected the concrete and served to decorate the surface when it was exposed. This technique, used occasionally for fortifications in Asia Minor, was adopted by the Romans for architecture on a grand scale. They were thus freed from the limitations of the post and the lintel—which had governed architecture since the days of the Egyptians—and were able to enclose huge areas without inner columnar supports. They could for the first time sculpture space itself, so to speak. Rapidly in Roman architecture the column became residual, an element of decoration to be applied to the rough concrete walls, like the marble paneling or stucco with which the concrete was often veneered. Most Roman ruins, stripped of their gorgeous coverings, look grim; to gain a true idea of their original effect, we must resupply them in imagination with their missing decoration.

As early as the second century B.C., the Romans appear to have discovered how to exploit the new opportunities given to them by concrete by establishing an architecture based not on straight colonnades but on open spaces of constantly changing size and shape, and how to combine their new discoveries with a dramatic conquest of landscape itself. In this respect the great civic centers built by the Hellenistic monarchs in Asia Minor were pioneers. However, Hellenistic spaces were limited by the convention of the straight colonnade, and irregular terrain could prove embarrassing, forcing an unwanted asymmetry on the architects. The flexibility of concrete construction gave Roman architects new freedom of action, and they pressed home their advantage with imaginative boldness.

A striking early example of such planning is the sanctuary of the goddess Fortuna at Praeneste—the modern Palestrina—long thought to be a work of the early first century B.C. But the date has been pushed back well into the second century by newly discovered evidence. The city on the plain was connected with the temple of the goddess some three hundred feet above by an elaborate system exploiting to the maximum the dramatic possibilities of the steep slope. A destructive air raid in World War II stripped from the Roman ruins the medieval buildings that had covered them for centuries, and made visible the underlying concrete constructions (fig. 249). A model of the sanctuary as it originally appeared (fig. 250) shows that worshipers entered by means of two covered ramps, which converged on either side of a central land-

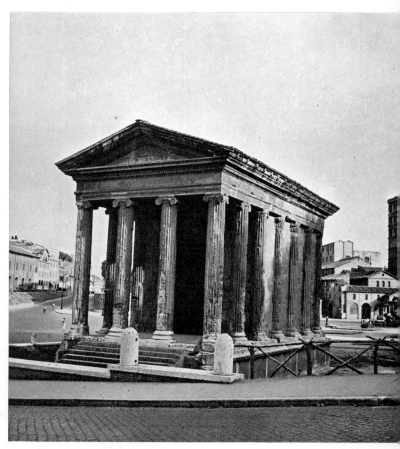

247. Temple of Fortuna Virilis (Temple of Portunus). Late 2nd century B.C. Rome

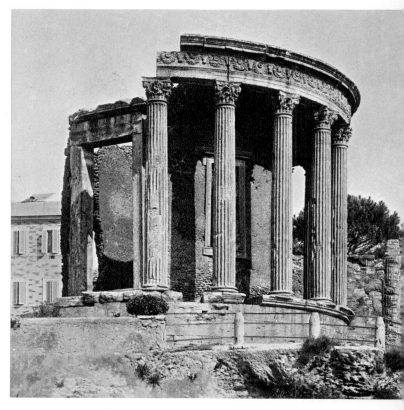

248. Temple of the Sibyl. Early 1st century B.C. Tivoli, Italy

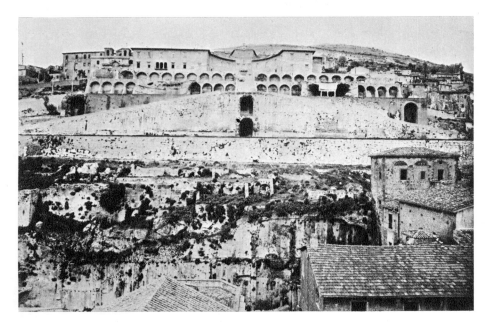

249. Sanctuary of Fortuna. 2nd century B.C. Praeneste (present-day Palestrina). Italy

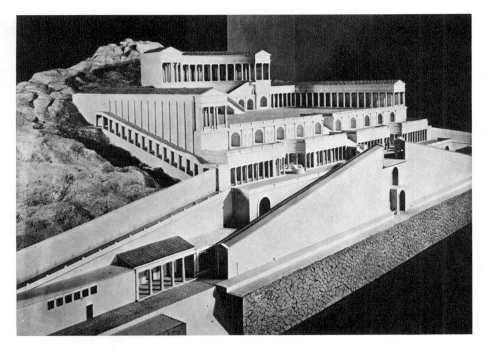

250. Sanctuary of Fortuna (architectural reconstruction). Museo Archeologico Nazionale, Palestrina, Italy

ing, affording an immense view of the new city, the surrounding plain, and the distant sea. From this landing a steep staircase led upward to four terraces of different sizes and shapes. On the first a remarkable vaulted colonnade, punctuated by two semicircular recesses called *exedrae*, protected a continuous row of barrel-vaulted rooms (now clearly visible; see fig. 249). On the second similar rooms were enclosed by an engaged colonnade—one of the earliest appearances of the arch embraced by columns and entablature, a motive that became standard in Roman imperial architecture and was revived enthusiastically in the Renaissance. The third terrace was a vast, open square, surrounded on two sides and part of a third by L-shaped colonnades reminiscent of Hellenistic stoas, terminating in pediments. Finally

came a theaterlike structure, apparently intended for religious festivals, surmounted by a lofty colonnaded exedra, also terminated by pediments. Almost hidden behind the exedra was the circular Temple of Fortuna. This series of ascending and interlocking masses and spaces of constantly changing character shows a new kind of architectural thinking, made possible only by the sculptural freedom afforded by concrete. Such thinking later found its grandest expression in the succession of forums (open civic centers) which were the chief architectural glory of imperial Rome.

A vast number of Roman town houses are known, many from recent excavations in all parts of the Roman Empire but the majority from the southern Italian cities of Pompeii and Herculaneum, which were buried by the eruption of Vesuvius in A.D. 79. The excavation of these two cities, begun in the middle of the eighteenth century, disclosed not only the houses themselves but furniture, implements, and even food in a sufficiently good state of preservation to enable a detailed reconstruction of the daily life of their inhabitants. In fact, by pouring plaster into holes in the hard-packed ash, it has been possible to rediscover the long-dissolved forms of humans and animals in their death agony. Pompeii and Herculaneum were designed according to a grid plan imitated from their Greek neighbors. Both cities were inhabited by a mixture of Italians and Greeks, among whom the Samnites, an indigenous people related to the Romans, were predominant. Both cities were brought under Roman rule by the dictator Sulla in 80 B.C. The basic plan of the house, called by the Romans the *domus* (from which the English word *domestic* is derived), seems to have been common to the Etruscans, the Samnites, the Romans, and other Italic peoples.

As often in Italian town houses even today, the street entrance was flanked by shops. A corridor led to a central space called the *atrium*, bordered by smaller, generally windowless rooms. The atrium roof sloped toward a central opening which let rainwater into a basin in the floor, at first of tufa or terra-cotta, later of marble, whence it drained into a cistern. At the far side of the atrium was the *tablinum*, a shrinelike room for the storage of family documents and wax portraits. By the second century B.C. every fine domus was also provided with a peristyle court, entered through the tablinum, remarkably similar to the contemporary Hellenistic examples at Delos (see fig. 236). In the center of the court might be a garden with fountains and statues. The family living and sleeping rooms were entered from the peristyle. The House of the Silver Wedding at Pompeii (fig. 251) is one of many such residences, more luxurious than the palaces of the kings at Pergamon. The corners of the atrium were sustained by stately Corinthian columns of marble; the open tablinum provided a delightful view of the garden in the peristyle court. Plaster casts of the holes left by roots in the earth have made it possible to identify the original flowering plants, and these have been replaced today.

The earliest known Roman apartment houses were also discovered at Pompeii. Careful examination has determined that these were formed in the later decades of the Republic, probably by real-estate operators who bought up numbers of domus houses, joined them together, and built second or even third stories on top—not to speak of rooms on balconies jutting into the street—all erected sloppily enough to justify the bitterest complaints of ancient writers regarding similar dwellings in Rome.

Painting

Late Republican houses glowed with color. The interior walls were often decorated, as in contemporary second-century houses at Delos (see fig. 236), with painted and

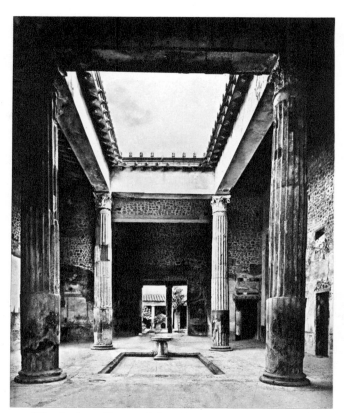

251. Atrium, House of the Silver Wedding. Early 1st century A.D. Pompeii, Italy

modeled stucco panels imitating marble incrustation. The stucco was mixed with marble dust, like that used for the exteriors of Greek temples (see page 123), and smoothed to give the appearance of marble. Panels of rich red, tan, and green were enclosed by white frames modeled in stucco. This method has been called the First Pompeiian Style, although late examples date from just before the eruption of Vesuvius. The Second Pompeiian Style, which appears to be contemporary with Julius Caesar (100–44 B.C.), is far more imaginative; instead of paneling, the wall was transformed into an architectural illusion by paintings, often of amazing skill. In a delightful little room from a villa of the late first century B.C., found at Boscoreale near Naples (colorplate 27), the walls have been simply painted away. Rich red porphyry columns, entwined with golden vinescrolls and surmounted by gilded Corinthian capitals, appear to support the architrave, to which is attached a superbly painted mask. Through this illusionistic portico we look into a sunlit garden, then out over a gilt-bronze gate framed by a marble-encrusted doorway into a view of rooftops and balconies rising in the soft, bluish air that culminates in a grand colonnade, somewhat on the principle of the view up the hillside to the sanctuary at Praeneste (see fig. 250). For all the apparent naturalism of the painting, which shows such details as a balcony room accessible only by a ladder, it is evident that the painter felt no responsibility to depict the entire scene as it would appear from a single viewpoint at a single moment in time. Disconcertingly,

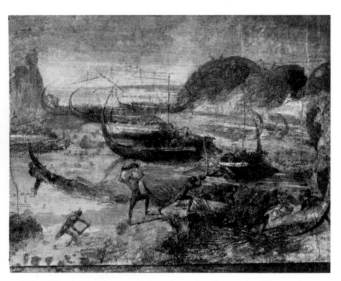

252. *The Laestrygonians Hurling Rocks at the Fleet of Odysseus*, from a villa on the Esquiline Hill. Wall painting. Middle 1st century B.C. Vatican Museums, Rome

world of the past, as in the landscapes with scenes from the *Odyssey* discovered in the nineteenth century in a villa on the Esquiline Hill, and datable about the middle of the first century B.C. (fig. 252). Although the painters may not have been Greek (there are errors in the occasional Greek inscriptions), it is now believed they were working on the basis of Greek originals of the second century B.C., possibly Alexandrian or southern Italian. The square piers, bright red with gilded Corinthian capitals, form a shadowed portico through which one looks happily, as from a tower, into a far-off land of sunny rocks and blue-green sea, toward which Odysseus and his companions escape in their ships from the attacks of the fierce Laestrygonians. The landscapes were painted with ease and speed in a fluid style contrasting deliberately with the uncanny precision of the architecture.

A grand room still in place in the Villa of the Mysteries at Pompeii (fig. 253) shows another aspect of Second Style illusionism. The actual walls have been transformed by painted architectural elements into a sort of stage on which gods and mortals sit, move, converse, even turn their backs to us, their attitudes ranging from quiet, classical serenity to occasional and startling terror. Apparently, the subject—still not entirely understood—was drawn from the rites attending the worship of the Greek god Dionysos, one of several competing mystery cults brought to Rome from various parts of the Empire. The nobility of the broadly painted, sculptural figures, almost lifesize, is heightened by contrast with the brilliance of the red background panels, green borders and stage, vertical black dividing strips, and richly veined marble attic.

some buildings are seen from below, some from head on, and some from above. Both artist and patron were apparently content with an arrangement that stimulated without ever quite satisfying a desire to explore distant space. To our eyes the evident contradictions contribute a dreamlike quality of unreality, which is enhanced by the absence of even a single person in this magical city.

The Second Pompeiian Style could also utilize the illusion of a portico as a springboard into a mythological

253. *Dionysiac Mystery Cult*, from the Villa of the Mysteries. Wall painting. 1st century B.C. Pompeii, Italy

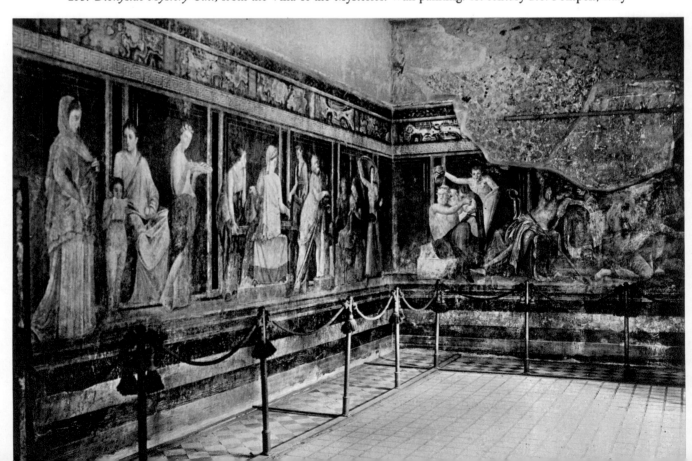

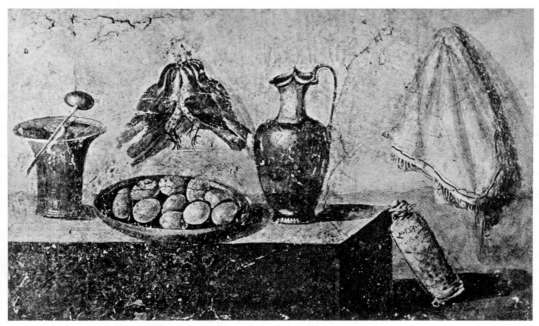

254. *Still Life*, from the House of Julia Felix, Pompeii, Italy. Wall painting. 1st century B.C.–early 1st century A.D. Museo Archeologico Nazionale, Naples

Often the illusionistic skill of the Second Style painters, doubtless deriving from Hellenistic tradition, could be dazzling, as in the frequent still lifes painted on the walls of Roman houses. An example from the House of Julia Felix in Pompeii (fig. 254) shows a corner in a kitchen, with dead birds, a plate of eggs, metal household instruments, and a towel, all arranged in a strong light from a single source, which not only reveals forms and casts shadows, but conveys beautifully reflections in the polished metal. An even more spectacular illusionistic work, in fact unparalleled in all of ancient art, is the garden room from a villa at Prima Porta which once belonged to Livia, the third wife of the emperor Augustus, possibly before their marriage (colorplate 28). All four walls disappear, in a manner attempted more modestly long before in the Minoan landscape room at Thera (see colorplate 12). A fence and a low wall are all that separate us from an exquisite garden, half natural, half wild, in which no earthbound creature can be seen; only fruit trees and flowering shrubs compete for the attention of the songbirds which perch here and there or float through the hazy air. Our vision roams freely around this enchanted refuge which, however, encloses us so entirely as to exclude all but the blue sky. The poetic delicacy of the conception and the consummate skill of the rapid brushwork make this a masterpiece among the world's landscape paintings.

THE EARLY EMPIRE (27 B.C.–A.D. 96)

For more than a century, it had been apparent that the traditional political machinery of the Roman city-state—the popular assemblies, the patrician senate, and the two consuls chosen annually—was inadequate to cope with the problems posed by a vast and expanding empire and a set of freewheeling armies, often separated by weeks or even months of travel from any decree that might be issued in the capital. In several periods of bloody civil warfare, the armies competed with each other for power. Only briefly, under the dictatorships of Sulla (82–79 B.C.) and Julius Caesar (49–44 B.C.), could any form of stability be maintained. In 31 B.C. Octavian, Caesar's great-nephew and adopted son and heir, defeated Antony and Cleopatra in the Battle of Ac   ., an event that sealed the fate of both the Roman Re   .ic and the Hellenistic world. Cleopatra was the   .n-dependent Hellenistic monarch; after her defe   gypt became Roman. Four years later, in 27 B.C., t'   .nan senate voted Octavian the title of *Augustι̦ · .d he became in effect the first legitimate Roman emperor.

Augustus ruled as emperor for forty-one years, a period of unprecedented peace and prosperity. The façade of republican government was piously maintained, but power was in fact exercised by Augustus and his successors, who controlled all military forces and appointed governors for the important provinces. The title *Imperator* meant army commander; nonetheless, the emperors, who rarely held office in the obsolete but well-nigh indestructible framework of the Republic, in truth governed as monarchs. Augustus' hybrid compromise survived for more than four centuries. With predictable immediacy the emperors were deified after death; Augustus erected a temple to Julius Caesar, and some of his successors demanded worship as gods while still alive, in the manner of Egyptian and Mesopotamian divine monarchs.

Sculpture

Now that the Romans had had time to digest their avidly devoured diet of Greek culture, they were able to profit by it and to bring forth a new art of their own. It was to be expected that its Etruscan and Greek sources would at first be plainly visible. Equally predictable was that the new art would deal less with religion and mythology, the primary concerns of the Greeks, than with transforming the often brutal facts of Roman military and political life into partly mythologized images for public consumption. In the celebrated statue of Augustus from the imperial villa at Prima Porta (fig. 255), the new ruler is seen as *Imperator*, in a grand pose easily recognizable as a blend of the *Doryphoros* (see fig. 175) and the *Arringatore* (see colorplate 26) in equal proportions. The statue was probably carved immediately after Augustus' death (otherwise, he would have been shown wearing military boots, which, as a god, he did not need), but the emperor is represented as a young man. The head is a portrait, belonging to an official type known in all parts of the Empire through its appearance on coins. Yet the features have been given a distinct Hellenic cast, idealized and ennobled. The figure stands easily, as if the oratorical gesture of the right arm grew from the very stone below the left foot. The cloak seems to have fallen accidentally in coldly Phidian folds from the shoulders to drape itself around the waist and over the arm, thus revealing a relief sculptured on the armor, retelling in mythological terms the story of the emperor's rise to power.

A deliberate contrast is offered by the statue of *Augustus as Pontifex Maximus* (the *pontifex maximus* was the Roman high priest; fig. 256), in which the emperor is shown about to perform a sacrificial rite, his head veiled in a fold of his *toga* (the outer garment worn in public by male citizens). Unbelievably, the statue must have been made when the emperor was more than seventy years old; all signs of advancing age have been blurred by an almost Praxitelean softness in the handling of the marble. The still recognizable face radiates a deliberately godlike wisdom and benignity.

In a detailed account of the achievements of his reign, Augustus boasted that he "found Rome of brick and left it of marble." Although this could scarcely be said to apply to the multistory tenements inhabited by the populace, Augustus energetically continued the building program initiated by Julius Caesar, and constructed innumerable public buildings on his own. He desired first of all to celebrate the *Pax Augusta* (Augustan peace) with buildings in which the new imperial power was to be dignified by the cadences of an imitated Attic style.

Chief among these monuments was the Ara Pacis (Altar of Peace; fig. 257), commissioned by the senate in 13 B.C. and finished in 9 B.C. Although the monument suggests in form the Altar of Zeus at Pergamon (see fig. 218), it is on a far more intimate scale, and is in every respect less dramatic. The altar itself is surrounded by a marble screen-wall, visible as a square block divided by

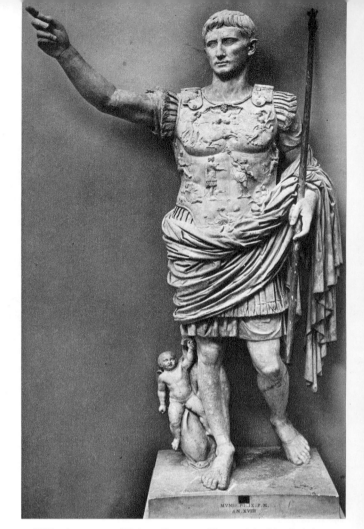

255. *Augustus of Prima Porta.* c. 20 B.C. Marble, height 80″. Vatican Museums, Rome

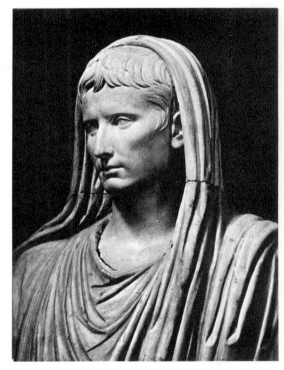

256. *Augustus as Pontifex Maximus.* c. 20 B.C. Marble, height 81½″. Museo delle Terme, Rome

delicate pilasters. These and the lower half of the wall are covered with a tracery of vinescrolls of the utmost delicacy and elegance. Above a meander pattern are a series of reliefs, some illustrating events from Roman history and religion, some showing contemporary events. The emperor himself, his head veiled for sacrifice, leads the numerous and recognizable members of the imperial family (fig. 258). In the rhythmic movement of the drapery, the frieze recalls that of the Parthenon (see fig. 194) and was doubtless intended to. But there are instructive differences; first, the Panathenaic Procession was represented on the Parthenon as a timeless institution, while the scene on the Ara Pacis shows a specific historic event, probably that of 13 B.C., when the altar was begun; second, the figures on the Ara Pacis are far more closely massed, as undoubtedly they would have been in reality; finally, the background slab of the frieze seems to have moved away from us, allowing room for figures behind figures, with progressively reduced projections. One of the reliefs flanking the east doorway shows Mother Earth with a personification of Tellus (Earth) accompanied by Air and Sea (fig. 259); all are portrayed as gracious, very Hellenic-looking goddesses, seated respectively on a rock, on a swan, and on a sea monster. The delicately observed landscape elements come from Hellenistic sources, and the same type of billowing, parachutelike veils over the heads of Air and Water turn up again and again in later Roman and in Byzantine art to characterize personifications.

In a marvelous cameo, the *Gemma Augustea* (colorplate 29), probably cut for Augustus' son-in-law and successor Tiberius, the seminude emperor shares a benchlike throne with the goddess Roma, made to resemble a Greek Athena; he is attended by relatives and by allegorical figures, one of whom is about to place a laurel wreath on his head. Above Augustus is his zodiacal sign, Capricorn. In the lower zone two barbarians, male and female, crouch disconsolately while Roman soldiers erect a trophy, a pole carrying armor stripped from the barbarian; two other barbarians are pulled in by the hair. With consummate skill and grace, the artist has worked the intractable semiprecious stone into a delicate relief, constantly suggesting space in the foreshortening of the human figures, the chariot, and the horse. In its allegorical version of history and in its exquisite refinement, this work sums up the ideals of the early Empire.

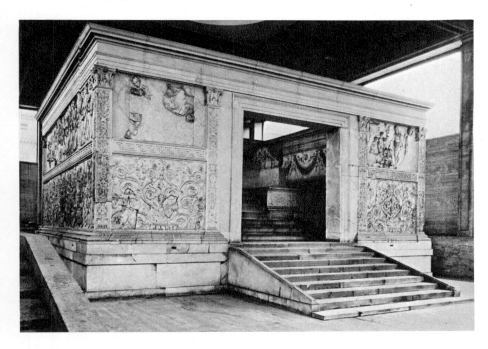

257. *Ara Pacis.* c. 13–9 B.C. Marble, width of altar c. 35'. Museum of the Ara Pacis, Rome

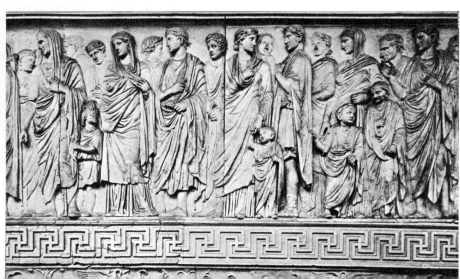

258. *Imperial Procession*, from the *Ara Pacis* frieze. Marble relief

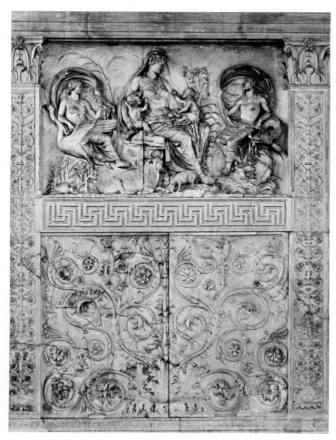

259. *Earth, Air, and Sea Personified,* and *Vinescroll Ornament,* from the *Ara Pacis* frieze. Marble reliefs

Architecture

Unfortunately, no Augustan temple survives in Rome in sufficiently good condition to enable us to appreciate the qualities of style the emperor desired. Luckily, this gap can be partly filled by an Augustan temple at Nîmes in southern France; nicknamed the Maison Carrée (fig. 260), it was begun about 19 B.C. This little structure can claim to be the best preserved of all Roman buildings. We recognize the familiar podium, front steps with flanking postaments, deep porch, and shallow cella of the Etrusco-Roman tradition. The temple, moreover, revives the Republican system of ornamenting the cella wall with an engaged pseudoperistyle. But the Corinthian order, henceforward the favorite in Roman buildings, is far richer than the austere Ionic of the Temple of Fortuna Virilis (see fig. 247), and its frieze, no longer blank, is enriched by the kind of delicately carved vinescroll we have seen in the Ara Pacis.

It is with all these aspects of Augustan art in mind that we should attempt to reconstruct mentally the vanished magnificence of the ruined Forum of Augustus, which met the Forum of Julius Caesar at right angles (plan, fig. 261). The Temple of Mars Ultor (Mars the Avenger; fig. 262), of which four side columns remain standing, stood at the end of the Forum of Augustus on the usual podium. Its back abutted an enclosing wall 115 feet high,

which described an exedra on either side of the temple, cut off the view of surrounding buildings (including a slum), and protected the forum from the danger of fire. The eight lofty Corinthian columns across the front formed part of a freestanding peristyle that continued on both sides as well, but ended at the enclosing wall. In front of the exedrae and along either side of the rectangular plaza in front of the temple ran a row of smaller Corinthian columns, upholding an attic story which was ornamented with a row of caryatid figures, mechanical copies of the famous maidens of the Erechtheion porch (see fig. 201). The white marble columns shone against back walls paneled in richly colored marbles, producing on a grand scale an effect as brilliant as that of the *Gemma Augustea.*

Not all of Augustus' successors shared his concern with maintaining the public-spirited "image" he desired for the Julian-Claudian dynasty (the family relationships were often tenuous). Nero, last of the line, was known for the most extravagant abode of antiquity, the famous Golden House, of which only fragments remain. This residence was, in effect, a country villa in the heart of Rome, stretching from the Palatine to the Esquiline, with gardens that enclosed a huge artificial lake. The delights of the villa included a banqueting-room ceiling that showered perfumes upon the guests, a statue of Nero more than one hundred feet high, and a dome that revolved so guests could follow the motions of the heavenly bodies.

The caprices of Nero should not blind us to the fact that, after the well-nigh inevitable fire of A.D. 64 (for which he has often been unjustly blamed), he promulgated a building code designed to prevent recurrences of

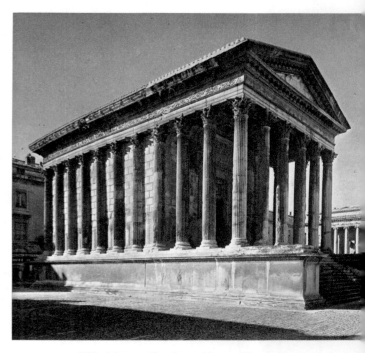

260. Maison Carrée. c. 19 B.C. Nîmes, France

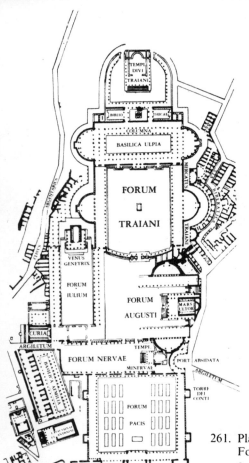

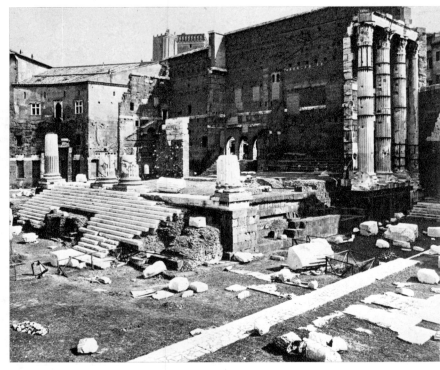

261. Plan of the Imperial
Forums, Rome.
c. 46 B.C.–117.A.D.

262. Temple of Mars Ultor, Forum of Augustus. Late
1st century B.C. Rome

such a disaster. Streets were widened, excrescences limited, building materials controlled, and structures rebuilt in stronger form and along more rational lines. The outgrowth of Nero's code was the block-shaped apartment house known as the *insula* (island), strikingly similar to those built in Italy almost up to our own times. These insulae were massive buildings (fig. 263), four or five stories in height and made of brick or stuccoed concrete. Many are partially preserved at Ostia, the port of Rome. The ground floor usually contained shops, including perhaps a tavern, and common latrines. Staircases led from a central court to the apartments. Exterior balconies were provided for some of the lower suites, which were the most desirable. Every effort was made to give these insulae a monumental character and to avoid uniformity.

An extraordinary witness to Roman ability to deal with utilitarian structures in monumental terms is provided by the aqueducts erected by the Romans. These aqueducts were essential to the growing cities of the Empire; some still extend for miles in partially ruined state across the rolling plains outside Rome. One of the most daring is the Augustan aqueduct called the Pont du Gard (fig. 264) in southern France, constructed in the late first century B.C. by Augustus' lieutenant Agrippa to carry the water for Nimes across a river gorge. The arches were built from unadorned, giant blocks of masonry, beautifully proportioned, in three stories; four smaller arches of the third story correspond to each single arch of the lower

two. The majestic effect is, if anything, enhanced by the frankness with which the architect left blocks of stone protruding here and there as supports for scaffolding to be erected when repairs were necessary. Once an aqueduct reached a city, however, a richer treatment was appropriate, as can be seen in the Porta Maggiore at Rome (fig. 265), a double archway of travertine erected by Claudius, the fourth emperor of the Julian-Claudian dynasty, to carry water across two major Roman streets. The piers supporting the arches are adorned by Corinthian *aediculae* (small shrines) with pediments, but interestingly enough all the stones save those of the capitals, bases, and pediments were left untrimmed, as if to indicate the basically utilitarian nature of the enterprise and to convey a sense of rude power. This treatment, known as *rustication*, was revived extensively in the Italian Renaissance (see Vol. 2, fig. 28).

Following the suicide of Nero in A.D. 68 and the disastrous year A.D. 69, in which three emperors rapidly succeeded each other, the rough soldier and farmer Vespasian founded the Flavian dynasty, which set about to erase the memory of the self-indulgent Nero and to reestablish Augustus' imperial system. On the site of the artificial lake of Nero's Golden House, Vespasian commenced the largest arena ever built before the enormous stadiums of the twentieth century. The Colosseum (fig. 266), as this building is generally known, was dedicated in A.D. 80 by Vespasian's son and successor Titus. It belongs to a new type of structure invented by the

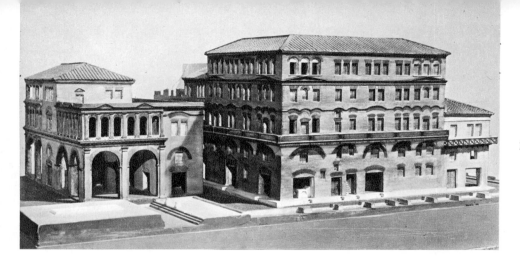

263. Reconstruction of an
Insula. Ostia, Italy

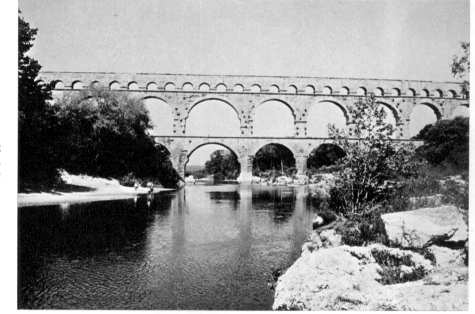

264. Pont du Gard. Late 1st
century B.C. Near Nîmes,
France

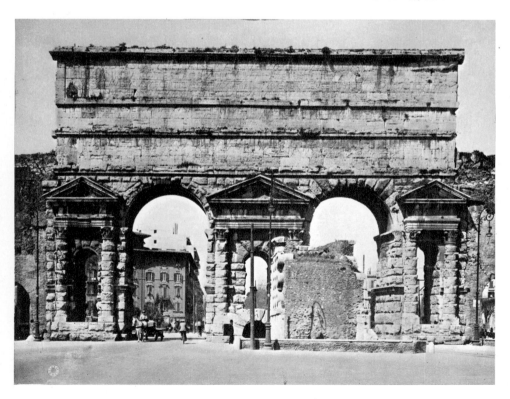

265. Porta Maggiore. c. 50
A.D. Travertine. Rome

Romans and built throughout the Empire in order to house the spectacles with which vast audiences, including the jobless proletariat, were amused. These buildings were known as *amphitheaters* (double theaters) because, in order to bring the greatest number of spectators as close as possible to the arena, two theaters were, in effect, placed face to face. The resultant shape is always elliptical, and the Colosseum is, in fact, the first elliptical building known. While the kind of spectacle in which Roman audiences delighted—gladiatorial combats, mock naval battles, fights between wild beasts, and contests between animals and humans—hardly bears contemplation, the remains of the Colosseum enable us to see that it was one of the grandest of ancient structures. The now-vanished marble seats were supported on multilevel corridors of concrete and masonry, providing for rapid handling of as many as fifty thousand spectators, each of whom entered by a ticket numbered to correspond to a specific gate. The exterior is composed of blocks of travertine, the somewhat porous, warm tan stone preferred also by Renaissance and Baroque architects for Roman church and palace façades. (Unhappily, these architects used the Colosseum as a quarry for their buildings.)

The arcades were decorated by columns that no longer served any structural function but acted only as a means of dividing the surface harmoniously and as a bridge between the otherwise bleak arches and the spectator. Three major orders stood one above another: Tuscan (probably used in place of Doric because the triglyphs would have been aesthetically troublesome), Ionic, and Corinthian. Above the uppermost order was a lofty wall, articulated by Corinthian pilasters; sockets at its summit were used for the insertion of masts, from which gigantic awnings were stretched across the arena to protect spectators from the sun. Windows in this fourth story alternated with applied shields of gilded bronze.

The corridors were covered with concrete, both in the familiar barrel vault and the groin vault (fig. 267), the latter formed by two barrel vaults intersecting at right angles, thus directing all weight to the four corners. The groin vault, like the barrel vault, was known to the Greeks, but they never used it for monumental buildings. Eventually (see page 207), the groin vault became extremely useful to the Romans as a means for covering vast spaces. The vaults of the Colosseum, now bare, were originally enriched with an elaborate surface decoration of stucco.

The Flavian emperors pulled down much of the Golden House of Nero, erecting on part of the site the now-vanished Baths of Titus, one of the earliest examples in Rome of a type of monumental building extensively built by later emperors throughout the city and the Empire (see below, pages 206–207, and see fig. 298) as a means of providing useful public services for growing populations. Having thus converted to public use much of the land Nero had enclosed for his private pleasures, the Flavians incorporated part of the remnant of the Golden House into an extensive imperial residence on the Palatine. Now visible only in stripped condition, from which little idea of its original magnificence can be gained, the Flavian Palace contained grand-scale vaulted audience halls in which the emperor could be seen in fitting splendor, and it was thus in a sense a public building; the Flavian Palace remained the official imperial residence until the late Empire.

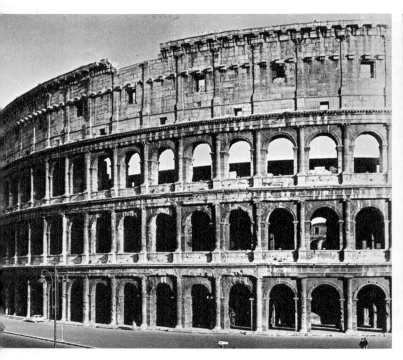

266. The Colosseum. c. 72–80 A.D. Rome

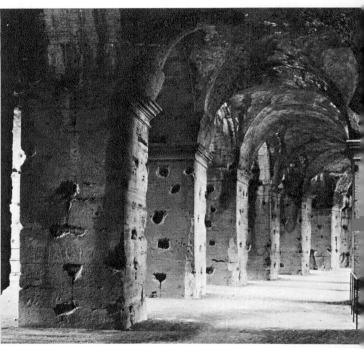

267. Interior (second floor), Colosseum

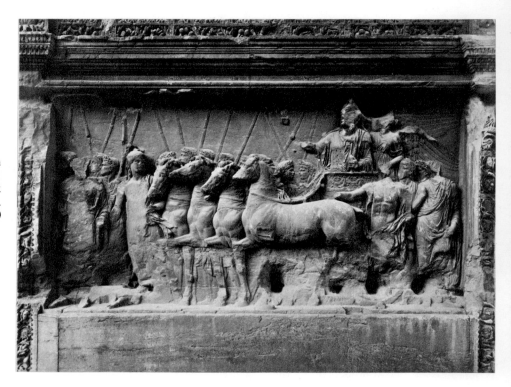

268. *Triumph of Titus,* from the Arch of Titus. c. 81 A.D. Marble relief, height of relief 79". Rome. See Colorplate 30

To commemorate his brother Titus' capture of Jerusalem in A.D. 70 and destruction of the Temple, the emperor Domitian dedicated eleven years later a white marble triumphal arch at the summit of the Sacred Way, the street which connected the imperial forums with the Colosseum. The Arch of Titus (colorplate 30) was a permanent version of the kind of temporary arch customarily built by Roman commanders to celebrate their triumphal return to the capital at the head of armies bearing the spoils of war and leading fettered prisoners. By the end of the Roman Empire, some sixty-four marble triumphal arches adorned Rome, and others were scattered throughout the Empire. The Arch of Titus, built of Pentelic marble around a concrete core, is a relatively simple structure (for a more elaborate version, see the later Arch of Trajan at Benevento; fig. 280). A single arch between square piers is crowned with an attic story, undoubtedly once supporting a bronze, four-horse chariot driven by the emperor. The applied decorative (or "screen") architecture is formed of paired columns upholding an entablature with a sculptured frieze. Two special innovations are apparent: first, the capitals are no longer strictly Corinthian, but Composite, an even richer fifth order mentioned by Vitruvius and distinguished from the Corinthian in that the volutes have been enlarged to the scale of those in the Ionic; second, the entablature is no longer continuous, but broken so that it projects over the lateral columns, recedes close to the massive piers, and projects again over the central columns and the connecting arch. Thus screen architecture is now being molded with the same liberty as the underlying architecture of concrete, in the interests of freedom of shape and the movement of light and dark. The last shackles of the post-and-lintel system, with its endless, straight horizontals, have been thrown off.

Flavian Sculpture

The spectator passing along the Sacred Way in Rome was addressed by two reliefs in the inner surfaces of the piers of the Arch of Titus, one depicting the *Triumph of Titus* (fig. 268) and the other the *Spoils from the Temple at Jerusalem* (fig. 269), in which Roman legionaries are seen carrying off the trumpets, the seven-branched candlestick, and the golden table. These reliefs were, if anything, more revolutionary than the architecture. For the first time Roman historical relief came into its own. Memories of the Ara Pacis still linger, but the Attic stateliness of Augustan relief has been swept away by a new dynamism in keeping with that of the architecture. We are reminded less of the Parthenon than of Hellenistic Baroque—although these relatively small reliefs lack the grandiloquence of the Altar of Zeus at Pergamon (see fig. 233). The relief space is much deeper than that of the Ara Pacis, and several devices have been utilized to increase its apparent depth. At the right, an archway has been placed at an angle to the spectator so that it dissolves into the background. Even with the loss of much of the relief, it is clear that the figures exploit their newly gained space, moving freely at various levels in depth as if passing before us on a stage. Some are so sharply projected that they are almost freestanding—and for that reason have suffered the most damage—while others, deeper in space, are represented in very slight projection. As in the varying levels in depth of the sur-

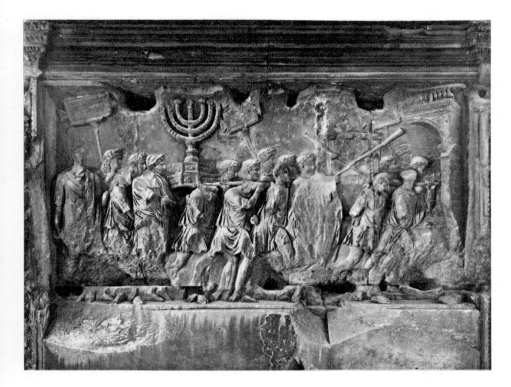

269. *Spoils from the Temple at Jerusalem,* from the Arch of Titus. c. 81 A.D. Marble relief, height of relief 94". Rome. See Colorplate 30

rounding architecture, light and shade have been thus utilized to enrich the drama.

In Flavian portraiture this new dynamism of form and new interest in light and shade were richly explored. A superb *Portrait of Vespasian* (fig. 270) shows that lessons from Praxitelean and Hellenistic sculpture have been applied to bring out in marble the full play of light and dark across the weather-beaten face of the old general. The eyeballs are no longer fully carved; they are actually slightly recessed so that the shadow of the eyelids can give the impression of the colored iris. The folds of flesh are rendered with the same pride in ugliness we found in Republican portraiture (see fig. 246), and the subject seems to be caught in a transitory moment between reflection and speech. A brilliant example of a standard type of Flavian female portraiture is a beautifully poised young matron (fig. 271), whose elegant and sensitive features are almost overpowered by a lofty Flavian coiffure of curls. The contrast of the rich shadows in the headdress with the translucency of the features suggests the actual coloration of hair and flesh, and again a slight depression hints at the color of the eyes. The Flavian portrait style is often characterized as coloristic, which is a very expressive term for the range of tonal values embodied in each head.

Painting

In the late Augustan period, the illusionistic achievements of the Second Style were overlapped and eventually succeeded by paintings in the Third Style that show an unexpected combination of pure architectural fantasy

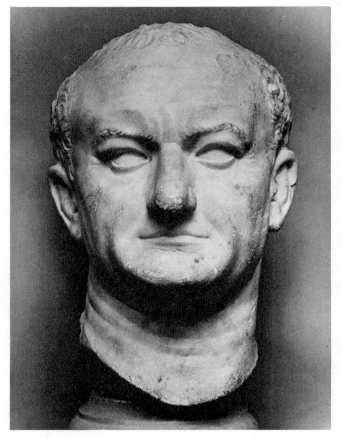

270. *Portrait of Vespasian.* c. 75 A.D. Marble, life-size. Museo delle Terme, Rome

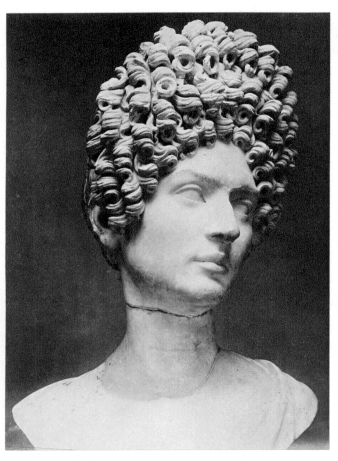

271. *Portrait of a Lady.* c. 90 A.D. Marble, life-size. Museo Capitolino, Rome

with prim refinement, such as in a painted wall from the house of M. Lucretius Fronto at Pompeii (fig. 272). The lower two-thirds of the wall, painted glossy black or red, is divided by columns prolonged into spindles; against the side panels stand equally attenuated lamps, on which appear to be suspended tiny panel paintings showing views of villas by the sea, and a mythological painting is "hung" against the center panel. Above the wall one looks out into an array of fantastic structures, reduced to toylike slenderness—columns like reeds, open pergolas—all in a perspective that takes us deep into unreal space, but is exactly repeated in reverse on the opposite side. Undeniably, this style shows some of the mannered elegance and grace of official Augustan art.

Most fantastic of all Pompeiian art is the Fourth Style, which flourished after the earthquake of A.D. 63 and was terminated at Pompeii and Herculaneum only by the eruption of Vesuvius in A.D. 79, a period corresponding to the last years of the reign of Nero and the first decade of the Flavian dynasty. A new and wildly imaginative manner appeared, with architectural vistas even more fantastic and far more convincingly lighted and painted in an astonishing array of rich colors (colorplate 31 shows a fine example from Herculaneum). Curtains, masks, broken pediments, and simulated bronze statues are irradiated with a sunlight as warm as that which charmed us in the Second Style.

Especially beautiful are the Fourth Style landscapes (fig. 273). In these views of an imagined nature, the art-

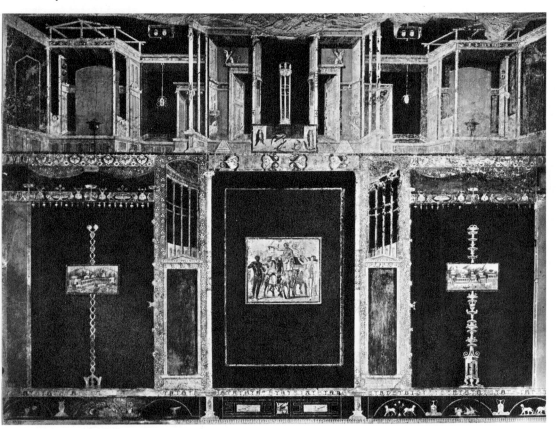

272. Architectural View and "Panel Paintings" from the house of M. Lucretius Fronto. Wall painting. First half 1st century A.D. Pompeii, Italy

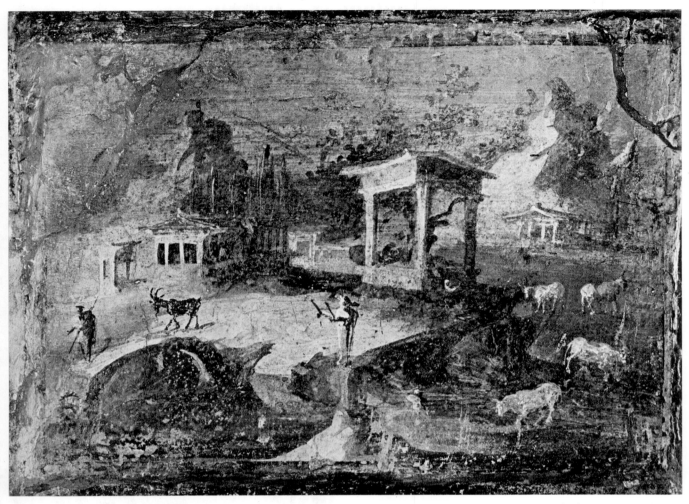

273. *Sacred Landscape*, from Pompeii, Italy. Wall painting. c. 63–79 A.D. Museo Archeologico Nazionale, Naples

ists exploited every device then known in order to render sunlight and atmosphere. Rapid brushstrokes sketched in a delightful dream world of mountains and glades, shrines, Etruscan-looking temples, cattle, and lakes and bridges, all dissolved in light and air in a manner that has often been compared with nineteenth-century Impressionism. Actually, the comparison is misleading, because the Impressionists (see Part Six, Chapter 4) derived their effects of light and air from the direct analysis of the real country or city views before their eyes. The imaginary landscapes of the Fourth Style might better be compared with the equally fantastic natural backgrounds of Watteau and Fragonard in the eighteenth century (Part Five, Chapter 7). Interestingly enough, the whole subject matter of Roman landscape painting could be modeled in stucco, with remarkably convincing effect and without any color whatever, in the reliefs often appearing on Roman ceilings. Stucco dries rapidly, and requires a working speed comparable to that of the sketchy paintings so impressive in the Second, Third, and Fourth styles. A typical example, from an Augustan house near the Farnesina Palace in Rome (fig. 274), shows the usual shrines, trees, little figures, animals, and rocks so arranged and so treated as to suggest distance, light, and air.

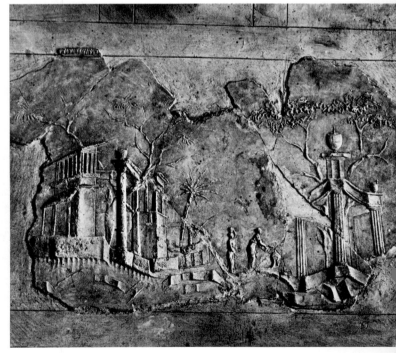

274. *Landscape with Figures*, from an Augustan house near the Farnesina Palace, Rome. Stucco relief. Museo Nazionale Romano, Rome

Trajan

The assassination in A.D. 98 of the tyrannical Domitian, last of the Flavian dynasty, resulted in the rule of a new and stable succession of six emperors, the first five of whom have become known—in contrast to their immediate predecessor and several of their appalling successors—as the "good emperors." The first, the aged Nerva, lived only two years before he was succeeded by his adopted son, the brilliant general Trajan, born in Spain—the first non-Italian emperor. Under Trajan the Roman Empire reached its greatest expansion, and his achievements were fittingly commemorated by the dedication in A.D. 113 of the grandest of all the imperial forums (fig. 275). The Forum of Trajan, in fact, covered more ground than those of Julius Caesar, Augustus, and Nerva together. To design this project Trajan called on a Greek architect from Syria, Apollodorus of Damascus, whose imagination was equal to the grandiose ideas of his imperial patron. Apollodorus combined elements from Roman tradition with others derived from the bygone architecture of Egypt. The axial plan of the forum, in certain aspects, recalls strikingly the general layout of Egyptian temples. A vast colonnaded plaza, similar to the Egyptian peristyle court, contained a bronze statue of the emperor on horseback; beyond was the Basilica Ulpia, corresponding to the Egyptian columned hall, which the visitor must traverse before arriving at the Temple of the Divine Trajan, erected by his successor Hadrian. We do not know what kind of structure was originally destined for this position. The plaza and the basilica were each flanked by semicircular spaces; exedrae, like those of the Forum of Augustus, rose behind the colonnades at either side of the plaza; apses closed off either end of the basilica; in the center of a single huge exedra stood the temple. As was by now the universal custom, the exedrae were built of concrete and faced with brick, but details were made of travertine; the east exedra of the columned plaza still stands, with its two stories of barrel-vaulted shops.

The Basilica Ulpia, named after Trajan's family, was the largest of Roman basilicas, some four hundred feet in length. The origin of the basilica type remains obscure, but the basilica is certainly related to Hellenistic stoas and served a similar purpose. An early example at Pompeii dates from the second century B.C., and two earlier basilicas stood near the Basilica Ulpia in the great complex of Republican and imperial forums. Generally, a basilica was built with a long, narrow central space, or *nave* (from the Latin word for ship), supported by colonnades, which separated the nave from the side aisles and

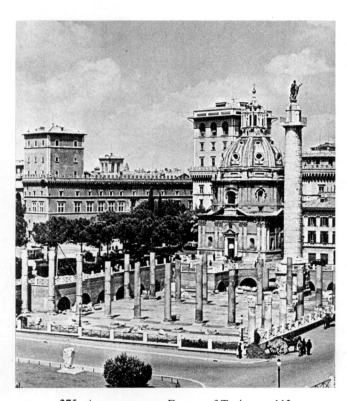

275. APOLLODORUS. Forum of Trajan. c. 113 A.D. Rome

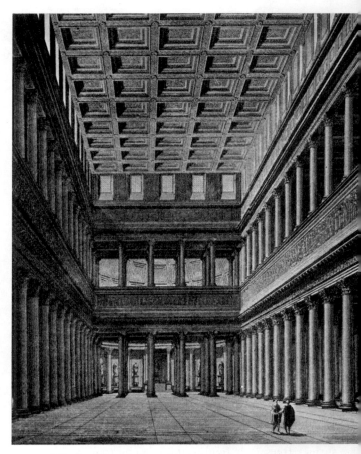

276. Basilica Ulpia. c. 98–117 A.D. Rome.
(Architectural reconstruction after Canina)

which were generally carried across both ends as well, forming a division before the apses, where judges held court. The side aisles often supported colonnaded galleries. Light came through the windows in the galleries and from a *clerestory* of windows in the walls above the galleries, which were roofed separately from the nave. Until the fourth century, basilicas were always roofed with timber, protected by tiles. The nave, side aisles, and galleries should be imagined as crowded with groups of businessmen, clients, and scribes, the apses with plaintiffs, defendants, and attorneys.

The Basilica Ulpia (fig. 276) seems to have differed from its predecessors only in size and magnificence. Two aisles on each side of the nave were supported by a forest of monolithic columns carved of gray Egyptian granite. The roof was concealed by a coffered ceiling, covered with plates of gilded bronze.

On leaving the Basilica Ulpia, the visitor found himself in a small court between Trajan's Greek and Latin libraries. Through the columns he could look out to the final exedra with its temple, if his attention could be distracted from the extraordinary monument in the center of the court (fig. 277), a marble column that, together with its podium, rose to a height of 125 feet and was topped by a statue of Trajan in gilded bronze (destroyed in the Middle Ages and replaced in the sixteenth century

by a statue of Peter). The podium was decorated with captured weapons carved in low relief; a golden urn containing the ashes of the emperor was placed within it after his death in A.D. 117. The column base was carved into a giant laurel wreath. In a spiral around the column winds a relief some six hundred and fifty feet long, on which are narrated events from Trajan's two successive Dacian campaigns.

No precedent for this extraordinary idea has ever been found, but it is noteworthy that the column was placed between two libraries. Ancient books did not have pages; they were *rotuli* (scrolls), wound between two spindles (see Part Three, Chapter 1). The reader saw a column of text at a time—sometimes with an accompanying illustration—then wound it away to read the next column. Just under the Doric capital of the Column of Trajan, a glimpse of fluting appears above the scroll-like relief. It has been suggested that the idea of the historiated column was derived from rotuli with endless narrative illustrations, but the only such rotuli known are much later (see fig. 427) and were influenced by the Column of Trajan and other monuments imitating it, rather than the reverse. The originality of the idea—and we do not know whether to attribute it to Apollodorus or to an artist working under his supervision or even to the emperor himself—lies in the idea of the continuous narrative, un-

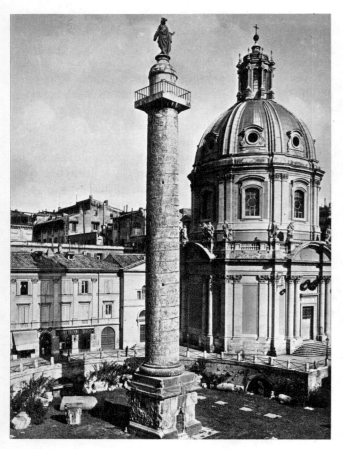

277. Column of Trajan. c. 106–13 A.D. Marble, height 125′; length of spiral low relief 650′. Rome

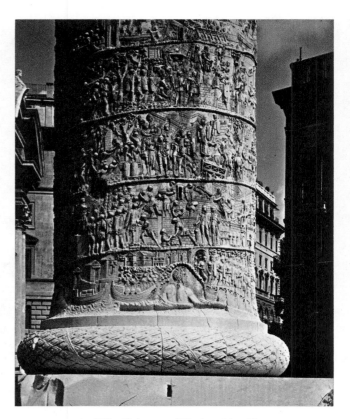

278. Column of Trajan (detail)

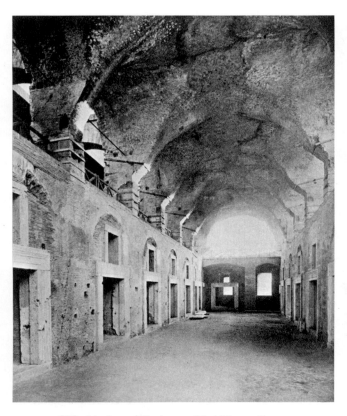

279. Market of Trajan. c. 98–117 A.D. Rome

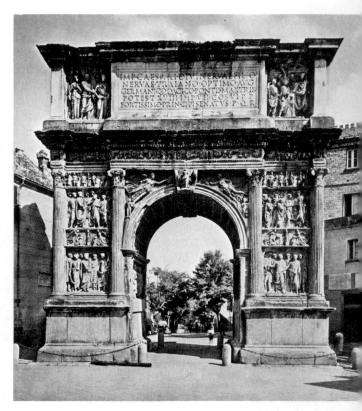

280. Arch of Trajan. c. 114–17 A.D. Marble. Beneventum (present-day Benevento). Italy

folding with cinematic power in more than one hundred and fifty incidents. Through camps, sacrifices, harangues, embassies, sieges, river crossings, pitched battles, routs, tortures, suicides, and mass slaughters, the story of the campaigns is told. In contrast to the battle reliefs of Assyria, which spring constantly to mind, the objectivity of the Trajanic narrative is impressive. Nowhere is the enemy underrated, and the Romans must put up a good fight for their victories. In the reliefs of the Column of Trajan, Roman sculpture at last came into its own; these creations owe no debt to any previous period. Doubtless the work, like that of the sculptures adorning the Parthenon, was executed by many different assistants. But the breadth and dignity of the narration—which has been compared with Julius Caesar's literary account of his Gallic wars—the power of the individual scenes, and the overall uniformity of accents and design show the conception of a single great master, whose name, unfortunately, is not known to us.

In figure 278, several incidents can be read. At the bottom, a personification of the Danube River, represented as a bearded giant, rises from the waves in amazement as the Roman legions issue forth from a city gate onto a bridge of boats to cross the river. In the second level, Roman soldiers carry blocks of stone to reinforce a fortification. In the third, Roman cavalry emerges from the gate of a walled camp to cross a wooden bridge over a moat as they embark on a patrol. In the fourth, the emperor stands upon a high podium to address his troops. As in almost all Classical reliefs, the sculptures

on the Column of Trajan were painted in order to bring out the figures and the details of the narrative with greater clarity.

Four major differences, however, separate this continuous narrative from the illusionistic reliefs on the Arch of Titus (see figs. 268, 269). First, because deep carving such as that on the Arch of Titus would have destroyed the integrity of the column and created ragged contours, the work on the Column of Trajan was carried out in low relief. Second, concern with narrative legibility caused its sculptors to give every figure an almost uniform degree of accentuation. Third, the figures are displayed as if on a steeply mounting terrain, providing a panoramic view, rather than overlapping in depth. Finally, just as in the Parthenon frieze (see fig. 193), a different scale was adopted for the horses from that of the figures; buildings are also shown relatively small, while city walls are the same height as people. Since these principles were by no means uniformly followed in other Trajanic reliefs, it must be assumed that they were adopted here because of necessity. The difficulty of reading the upper episodes was overcome to some extent by increasing the scale slightly as the spiral mounted. Legibility would have been enhanced, in all probability, by viewing the upper portions from the terraces above the libraries and from the roofs of the Basilica Ulpia and the connecting colonnade. Even so the topmost levels must have been very difficult to distinguish.

Nothing of the Temple of the Divine Trajan is now aboveground, but we know that it had a portico even higher than that of the Temple of Mars Ultor, with a peristyle of monolithic columns in the same gray Egyptian granite that was used for the Basilica Ulpia. A handsome utilitarian structure connected with the Trajanic complex still stands on the slope of the Quirinal Hill—a two-story market (fig. 279), whose concrete, groin-vaulted central nave is flanked by barrel-vaulted shops, built of concrete faced with brick; each travertine opening, serving as entrance and shopwindow, was surmounted by a window to provide ventilation for the mezzanine story, where the shopkeeper or his clerk resided. Traditional wooden centering was supplemented in the construction of the groin vault by forms molded in terracotta.

Entrance to the entire Trajanic complex was afforded by a triumphal arch, which has disappeared. However, a noble marble arch built by Trajan in A.D. 114–17 at Beneventum (modern Benevento) in southern Italy, to celebrate the opening of a highway, still stands in remarkably good condition (fig. 280). The general shape of the relatively modest Arch of Titus is here enriched by a series of panels sculptured in high relief, which fill every surface not occupied by the commemorative inscription. Large, rectangular panels alternate with narrower strips. The public deeds of the emperor are shown here, rather than his military exploits; the folds of the togas are obviously scaled to harmonize with the fluting of the Composite columns. The relation between architecture and sculpture here can only be characterized as symphonic, in the bewildering variety of accents and cross-accents grandly sustained by the columns, bases, and entablature. This arch is beyond comparison the finest example of balance between architecture and sculpture remaining to us from the Roman world.

Hadrian

Trajan was succeeded by his nephew Hadrian, an excellent administrator who had little interest in military conquests—he, in fact, let some unruly border provinces slip from Roman grasp. Hadrian was, however, deeply concerned with cultural activities and artistic monuments, especially those of the Hellenic world, with which he felt a strong kinship. He undertook several long tours of his vast empire, embellishing provincial centers with new buildings and doing his utmost to support the continuing intellectual life of Athens. Hadrian seems to have had little interest in the epic themes of Trajanic sculpture, and sculpture surviving from Hadrian's reign reflects the emperor's Hellenism. Several medallions made for a Hadrianic monument but later incorporated into a new triumphal arch in the fourth century by the emperor Constantine, who had the imperial heads recarved to portray himself, vibrate with echoes of Classical and Hellenistic sculpture (fig. 281). In the muscular horses and the free drapery rhythms of the *Wild Boar Hunt*, memories of the Parthenon frieze and the Temple of

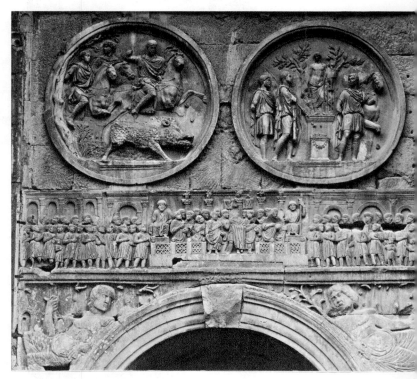

281. *Wild Boar Hunt*, and *Sacrifice to Apollo* (details of the Arch of Constantine). Medallions c. 117–38 A.D.; frieze c. 312–15 A.D. Rome

Apollo at Bassai (see figs. 192, 205) are very clear; in the soft treatment of the nude and in the gentle drapery folds of the *Sacrifice to Apollo*, the graceful tradition of Praxiteles and Lysippos is quoted. Interestingly enough, although the horse in the *Sacrifice* emerges from a space clearly indicated as behind that of the attendant, the horses and riders of the *Hunt*, to show that they are behind the wild boar, appear above it. Illusionism is at an end, and the artist's devices are directed toward informing the observer rather than describing a visual situation.

Perhaps the most Hellenic of all Hadrianic sculptures is the *Portrait of Antinoüs* that Hadrian gave to the sanctuary of Apollo at Delphi (fig. 282). The emperor had showered statues of his favorite throughout the Empire; these works are recognizable by the portrayed youth's slightly aquiline nose, full lips, and deep chest. Most of these statues show a figure at least partly draped, but this example is connected with an older Roman tradition in which realistic portrait heads were superimposed on idealized nude bodies copied from Greek statues. Generally, the results were grotesque. In the Antinoüs of Delphi, however, a Greek sculptor working for Hadrian was able to treat this unlikely combination with convincing unity. Revivalist though it is, the statue achieves an extraordinary success in its contemporary adaptation of a Classical Greek concept.

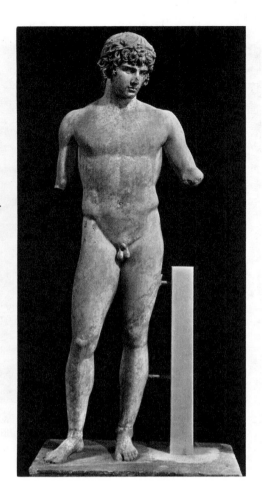

282. *Portrait of Antinoüs (Antinoüs of Delphi).* c. 117–38 A.D. Marble. Archaeological Museum. Delphi

Interestingly enough, Hadrianic architecture in Italy owes little to Hellenic tradition, but in fact sums up authoritatively the most progressive spatial tendencies of Roman building. The grandest of all Hadrianic monuments is the rebuilt Pantheon in Rome (figs. 283, 284), which owes its extraordinary state of preservation to its rededication as a church in the early history of Roman Catholicism. The Pantheon has exercised an incalculable influence on all the architecture of the Middle Ages, the Renaissance, the Baroque period, and modern times. The building must be imagined in its original state, approached by parallel colonnades flanking a central plaza, and elevated on a podium now concealed by the sharp rise in the level of the surrounding terrain. Viewed from below, the circular cella (derived, of course, from the tholos tradition), which is the extraordinary innovation of the building, would have been sensed rather than seen. The Corinthian columns of the portico are monoliths of polished granite; the cella is built of formed concrete, faced with fine brickwork. The roof was covered with gilded tiles.

Once one enters the Pantheon its revolutionary character becomes apparent—in one of the few truly overwhelming spatial experiences in architecture, so grand in fact that it cannot be represented convincingly by photographic means. We must have recourse to a painting done in the eighteenth century (fig. 285). The crowning dome is an exact hemisphere of concrete 143

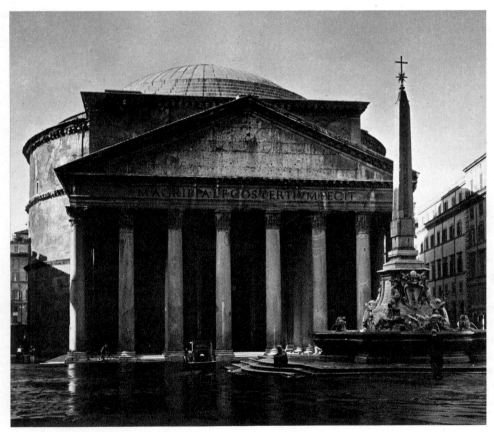

283. The Pantheon. c. 118–25 A.D. Rome

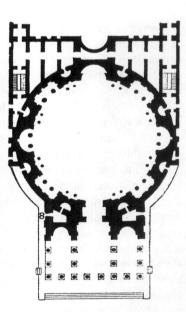

284. Plan of the Pantheon

feet in diameter, formed at the top of lightweight materials and very slight in thickness. Farther down, the shell becomes both thicker and heavier, and it is supported not only by the walls of the cylindrical drum but by relieving arches within the walls, invisible from the interior. The height of the drum is equal to its radius, which is identical to that of the dome.

The interior of the Pantheon conveys the effect of a colossal sphere, whose perfect beauty is untroubled by excrescences. The continuous entablature is upheld by paired, fluted Corinthian columns of softly colored marble in front of eight recesses, alternating with eight flat wall surfaces encrusted with colored marble, from which project aediculae, once containing statues of the gods, framed by unfluted columns of polished granite. The now-bare concrete coffering of the dome was originally painted blue; each coffer contained a rosette of gilded bronze. A single great circular opening at the apex is the sole and abundant source of light, and it allows the eye to move freely out into the sky above. The effect of this vast, spherical space, whose enclosing wall is softened by the fluid colors of the marble, can only be described as sublime. No interior before or after the Pantheon has achieved quite this impression. A long tradition in ancient times associated architectural domes with the Dome of Heaven, the sky itself, a tradition also appropriate for a building dedicated to the worship of all the gods as was the Pantheon. The breathtaking interior space of this great building arouses in the observer a sense of liberation analogous to what we feel when we gaze into the open sky.

The most imaginative architectural achievement of Hadrian's reign was the villa he constructed near Tivoli, which to modern eyes suggests nothing so much as the pleasure dome of Kubla Khan as described in Coleridge's poem (fig. 286). Several square miles of gently rolling countryside were adorned with a rich array of buildings and gardens. In contrast to the rigorous axial planning of the imperial forums, the constructions and spaces of Hadrian's Villa were freely scattered in groups in order to take advantage of varied levels, exposures, and vistas. Within each group, however, the buildings were arranged with close attention to harmonious and generally symmetrical relationships. The individual spaces were seldom large but almost infinitely complex, exploiting all the freedom of shape offered by Roman concrete architecture. Some interiors contained not a single straight line, only alternating convex and concave forms.

The villa had several elaborate *nymphaea* (fountain buildings), Greek and Latin libraries, a theater, baths both large and small, courtyards, plazas, and temples. A circular colonnaded pool was adorned with a central island, attainable by bridges on wheels, on which stood a tiny, self-contained abode. Many reproductions—more symbolic than accurate—of sights that Hadrian had seen on his travels throughout the Empire were constructed at the villa. These included the Grove of Academe and the Stoa Poikile (painted porch), both of Athens, and the

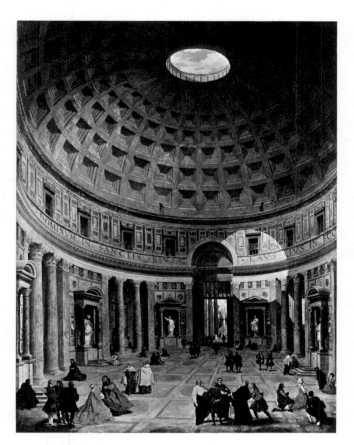

285. GIOVANNI PAOLO PANNINI. *Interior of the Pantheon.* c. 1750. Oil on canvas, 50½ x 39". National Gallery of Art, Washington, D.C. Samuel H. Kress Collection

Canopus of Alexandria (fig. 287), a long canal culminating in a temple to the Egyptian god Serapis. This temple was also a nymphaeum, and it was ornamented with Egyptian sculptures preserved today in the Vatican Museums. The end opposite the temple was colonnaded, and the entablature seems to have been bent into arches as if made of clay. When intact, Hadrian's Villa offered an unimaginable richness of forms, spaces, and colors to excite the senses and to enshrine the intellectual life of the imperial hedonist, who unfortunately died before its completion.

The Antonines

The uneventful reign of Hadrian's successor, Antoninus Pius, was appropriately memorialized by an undecorated column of pink marble, erected after the emperor's death in A.D. 161. The cubic base, which is all that remains, is a powerful work of art in itself. On the front face is shown the flight of the emperor and the empress to heaven; on either side is represented the ceremonial circular gallop of the cavalry around groups of armored infantrymen holding standards at the imperial funeral (fig. 288). Surprisingly, the hard-won illusionistic space of the Hellenistic tradition, already compromised by the devices of

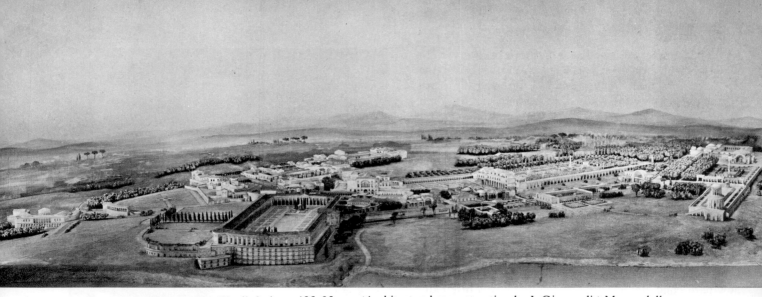

286. Hadrian's villa, Tivoli, Italy, c. 125–35 A.D. (Architectural reconstruction by I. Gismondi.) Museo della Civiltà Romana, Rome

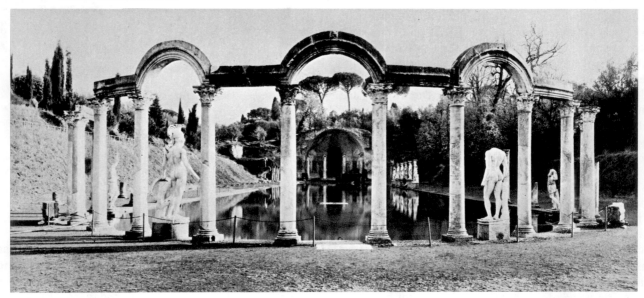

287. The Canopus of Alexandria, Hadrian's villa (reconstruction). c. 125–35 A.D. Tivoli, Italy

Trajanic narrative style, has been completely dismissed. Although the distinction has been preserved between near figures in high relief and those farther from us in low relief, all that remains of the traditional setting is a few patches of ground under the feet of men and horses. The figures seem to float in a free space, unregulated and un-enclosed, in front of the neutral marble background. What is behind is now represented as above, as if in rever-sion to the far-off days of Polygnotos.

The new abstract conception of space and the new carving techniques were employed in the relief sculpture on the column of Antoninus' successor, Marcus Aurelius. As an emperor, Marcus Aurelius was an extraordinary blend of an efficient general, on the model of Julius Caesar and Trajan, with a Stoic philosopher. Marcus Aurelius loathed war, and he fought only defensive ac-tions aimed at preserving the Empire from incursions of Germanic tribes, particularly in the Balkans. For him duty was man's highest goal and only reward; his own

duty was to administer the Empire as a brotherhood of man under the rule of an all-pervasive God, which in-volved the sacrifice of his own well-being in favor of the unity of the state.

One of the most memorable works of art from Marcus Aurelius' reign is his noble equestrian statue in bronze (fig. 289), originally in front of the Lateran Palace in Rome, in which the emperor was born, but transferred to the Capitoline unwillingly by Michelangelo in 1536 at papal command. The statue owes its preservation to the mistaken belief that it represented Constantine, the first imperial protector of Christianity, and is the only well-preserved ancient equestrian statue to come down to us; needless to say, it has been imitated countless times from the Renaissance almost to our own day. The statue shows the emperor unarmed, his right arm outstretched in the characteristic Roman oratorical gesture (see colorplate 26, fig. 262) and his left guiding the now-vanished reins of his spirited horse. As we have seen in relief sculpture, the rider here is also represented in a larger scale than the horse. The bearded emperor (the beard was a Hadrianic innovation, in imitation of the Greeks) looks out calmly on the world; the rich curls of his hair and beard, in contrast to the smooth parts of his face, show a revival of Flavian colorism, which precludes the traditional device of inserting eyes made of glass paste. The horse is superbly modeled, revealing extensive knowledge of the proper position and function of bones, muscles, tendons, and veins.

One of the most significant and lasting of all Roman achievements was the foundation of hundreds of towns and cities throughout the Empire, many of which are still inhabited. Where possible, the typical Roman town had the foursquare plan of the Roman camp, straight streets intersecting at right angles, a central capitol, a forum, walls with monumental gateways, temples to Roman and indigenous deities, a theater, an amphitheater, a basilica, and a bath. But these architectural undertakings were by no means uniform in style at any one moment in all parts of the Empire. For example, urban complexes and country villas in Britain, Gaul, and Germany were far less sumptuous than those designed for provinces that still cherished a Hellenistic tradition of architecture and decoration. The most dazzling provincial centers were perhaps those in Syria, such as Baalbek and Palmyra, and in North Africa, especially Leptis Magna, Sbeitla, and Timgad, large portions of which are still standing. A vista (fig. 290) down the central colonnaded street of Timgad toward a late second-century gateway erroneously known as the Arch of Trajan gives some inkling of the splendor of these North African and eastern Mediterranean cities in the time of Marcus Aurelius. The great central arch for horse-drawn traffic is flanked by two smaller ones for foot passengers, embraced by columns designed to culminate the colonnaded walkways rather than to relate to the central arch. These columns are united at the top by a new invention, an arched pediment, whose lower cornice is broken.

This kind of pictorial freedom in architecture can be seen at its extreme in a number of splendid eastern Mediterranean and North African gateways, façades, fountains, libraries, and above all theaters, such as that at Sabratha dating from the late second century A.D. (fig. 291). The relatively simple Greek and Hellenistic structures are far behind us. In the Roman theaters a high stage, here with a front composed of alternating square and semicircular recesses ornamented with carved reliefs, is dominated by a towering structure designed only for pictorial richness. With the greatest imaginative freedom three stories of Corinthian columns, now smooth, now fluted, are superimposed; some are single, some paired, some grouped in fours, some receding, some projecting for a maximum pictorial effect which bids fair to capture in stone the fantasies imagined in paint by the Pompeiian decorators of the Fourth Style.

The reigns of the five "good emperors" were followed in A.D. 180 by that of Marcus Aurelius' unworthy son and successor Commodus, who took part in gladiatorial combats, experimented with imported mystery cults, and went about dressed as Hercules, complete with lion skin and club. A celebrated bust (fig. 292) shows Commodus in the role of Hercules, extending nervously the Golden Apples of Hesperides, although his unsparingly rendered effete expression and slight physique are completely incongruous. As throughout Antonine sculpture, the locks of hair and beard, roughened and deeply undercut to suggest their color, are contrasted with the transparent pallor of the face. The eyes too are now rendered coloristically, the irises and pupils actually carved, a device that

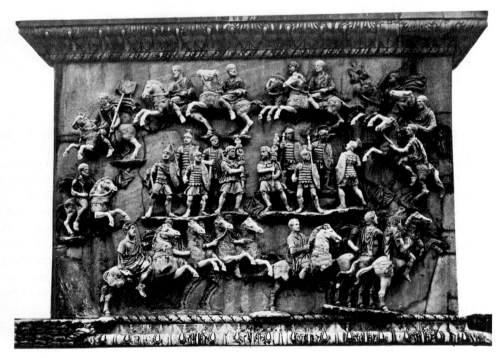

288. *Ceremonial Circular Gallop of the Cavalry,* from the base of the Column of Antoninus Pius. Marble relief. c. 161 A.D. Vatican Museums, Rome

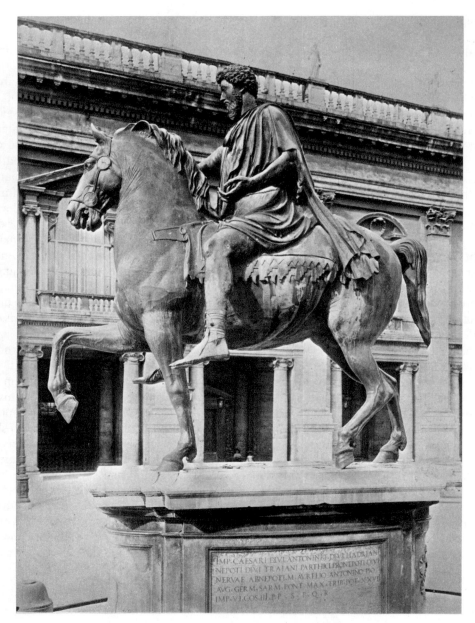

289. *Equestrian Statue of Marcus Aurelius.* c. 161–80 A.D. Bronze,
over life-size. Piazza del Campidoglio, Rome

frees sculpture entirely from applied pigment and allows it to function pictorially in its own right. The serpentine complexity of the shapes, as disturbing as the portrait itself, reminds one of the nervous forms and patterns used in the sixteenth century in an Italian style known as Mannerism (see Vol. 2, Part Four, Chapter 6). In A.D. 192, members of Commodus' household conspired to have him strangled by a wrestler inappropriately named Narcissus. So ended the Antonine line, in a manner that prepared the way for the near chaos of the third century.

Little second-century painting remains, except a numerous series of portraits discovered at El Faiyûm in the Nile Valley. These images of the deceased were substituted for the traditional masks in mummies, which the Egyptians continued to make. They are the only ancient paintings in the encaustic, or hot wax, technique that have been discovered. Many are strikingly expressive, rendering with great vividness the members of the multiracial society of the Roman world. A Graeco-Roman Egyptian (colorplate 32) looks at us with utter candor from superbly painted brown eyes, showing that in the rendering of light on flesh and hair the painters of the second century A.D. still retained the knowledge gained from half a millennium of Hellenic tradition. These paintings also admit us to the very presence of people of great sensitivity and grace, in whom are summed up the traditions of more than three thousand years of continuous civilization.

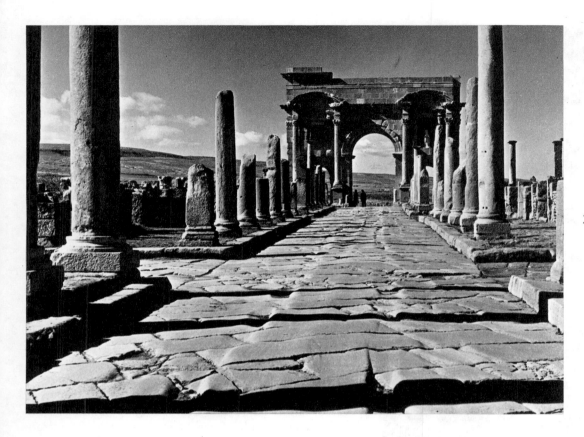

290. Colonnaded street
with arched gateway.
Late 2nd century A.D.
Timgad, Algeria

291. Theater
(reconstruction).
Late 2nd century A.D.
Sabratha, Libya

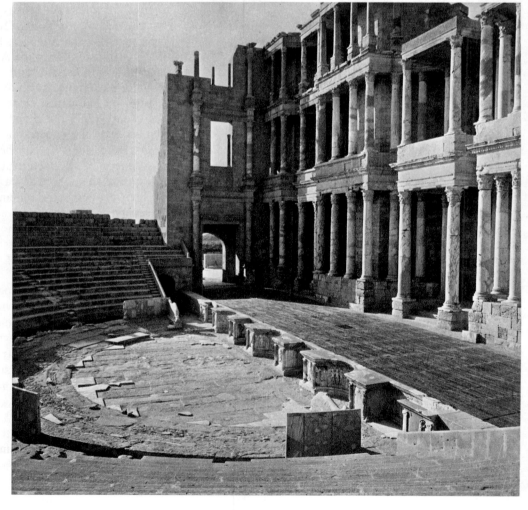

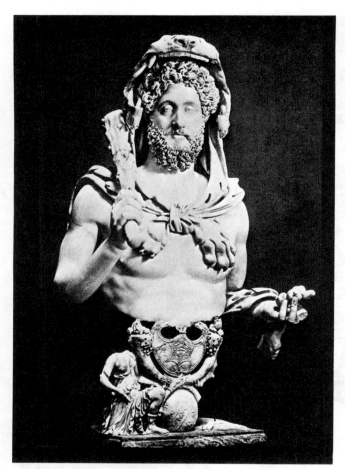

292. *Commodus as Hercules.* c. 180–83 A.D. Marble,
height 42½". Palazzo dei Conservatori, Rome

THE THIRD CENTURY (192–284)

The assassination of Commodus inaugurated a period of almost unbelievable deterioration in Roman life and, consequently, in that of the entire Mediterranean and European world, culminating in a loss of Roman and even Italian preeminence and power in the Empire at large. For the next ninety-two years one brief imperial reign followed another, except for those of Septimius Severus (ruled 193–211) and Claudius II surnamed Gothicus (ruled 268–70), terminated by violence, usually assassination by troops or by the Praetorian Guard. This bodyguard of the emperor was the single agency in the Empire still strong enough to make and unmake emperors. With provincial and uneducated soldiers serving as emperors, the vast structure of the international and intercontinental imperial state tottered virtually leaderless; only the administrative bureaucracy maintained a semblance of order. Coinage was rapidly and alarmingly debased; inflation followed; agriculture and trade stagnated. The sole uniting factor was the all-pervasive fear of invasion by Germanic tribes to the north and by Parthians to the east.

In imperial portraiture the devastating frankness of the portraits of Commodus had already opened up new and unpleasant psychic vistas. Three third-century imperial portraits lead us even further into this hitherto unexplored realm. Caracalla (ruled 211–17), the brutal son and successor of the energetic Septimius Severus, appears so frighteningly his true self (fig. 293) that we hardly need to be told that he caused the murder of many persons, including his own brother Geta. The features, the skin, and above all the hair and eyes are still rendered with a sense of the Hellenistic heritage of colorism, handed down from Flavian and Antonine art. But the cruelty concentrated in the intense gaze and fixed frown is new and terrible.

The insecurity of the third-century emperors could scarcely be more graphically rendered than by a detail (fig. 294) from a carved marble sarcophagus. These stone coffins had already in the second century replaced funerary urns as incineration gave way to burial. The boy shown to the left is generally taken to be the pathetic Gordianus III (ruled 238–44), who was made sole emperor by the senate at the age of thirteen after his grandfather and father, Gordianus I and Gordianus II, had both been murdered in the same year. The Genius of the Senate is shown as a bearded figure pointing to the unfortunate youth, whose countenance looks terror-struck. Under the anxious faces, the traditional curving folds of the voluminous togas still play about the figures, but there is a world of difference between these exaggerated, often meaningless lines and the firm structure of the Classical folds in the Ara Pacis (see fig. 258). The hand of a bald-headed man who looks over Gordianus' shoulder is stretched forth as if in protection—a useless gesture, for the young emperor was murdered when he was twenty years old by an Arab officer called Philip, who assumed the imperial power. The face of *Philip the Arab* (ruled 244–49) has been preserved for us in a masterpiece of characterization (fig. 295) even more devastating than the Caracalla portrait. The eyes peer out furtively above the endemic frown of the period; the expression is wretched and without intelligence; behind the brutish features the remnants of a debased mind cringe in fear of inevitable assassination. One recalls with nostalgia the far-off days of the godlike Augustus portrait (see fig. 255).

To delineate such psychological factors, a new and unsparing technique came into being; the features were constructed in broad, harsh planes; short, quick strokes of the chisel rendered the close-cropped hair and beard. The last remnants of Hellenic structure and Hellenic vision have vanished from images such as this portrait, just as the last echoes of Hellenic humanity seem to have deserted a society whose hero was the gladiator instead of the athlete.

Sarcophagus sculpture of the third century reflects the inner disorder of the period in a transformed relief style. The *Ludovisi Battle Sarcophagus* (fig. 296) is one of the most powerful examples. In comparison with the historical reliefs of the Arch of Titus and the Column of Trajan (see figs. 268, 269, 278), through which the Romans move in evident command of their own destiny and triumph through their own valor, here both Romans and barbarians seem trapped in a perpetual conflict for which even victory offers no solution. The Romans conquer by sheer weight, pressing down on a shapeless tangle of anguished barbarian faces and tormented torsos and limbs. Space, mastered through centuries of Greek and Roman effort, has been swallowed up. Neither depth nor background is represented; the wall of bodies is piled in the foreground plane like the heap of weapons on the base of the Column of Trajan (see fig. 277). And along with space the integrity of the human body has disappeared; not a single figure in this strange composition retains the capability of motion.

The new emotional style of third-century relief sculpture required still other methods than those we noted had been employed in the bust of Philip the Arab; a direct and extensive use of the drill, for example, was necessary to reinforce with dark holes the shadows in eyes and mouths and between the writhing locks of hair. Third-century art has been described as expressionistic; the word is as inex-

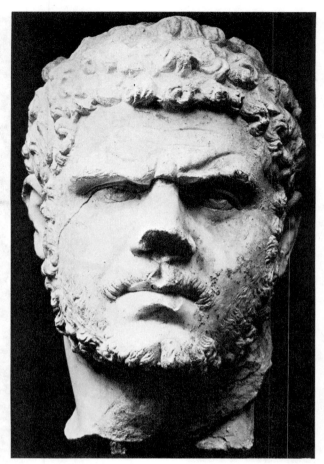

293. Portrait of Caracalla. c. 211–17 A.D. Marble, life-size. Vatican Museums, Rome

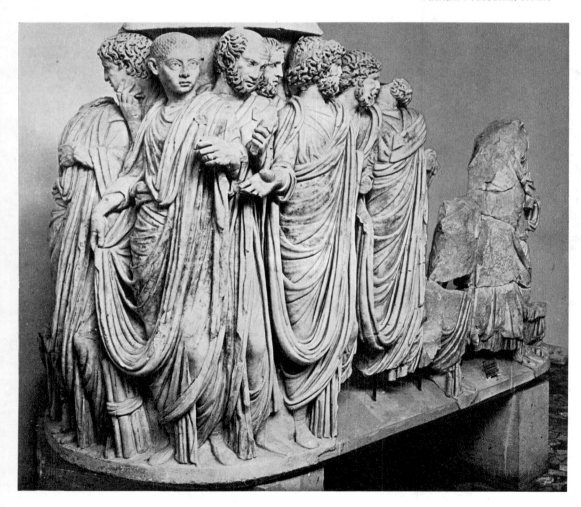

294. *The Genius of the Senate Pointing to Gordianus III* (detail of a sarcophagus from Acilia). c. 238–44 A.D. Marble. Museo delle Terme, Rome

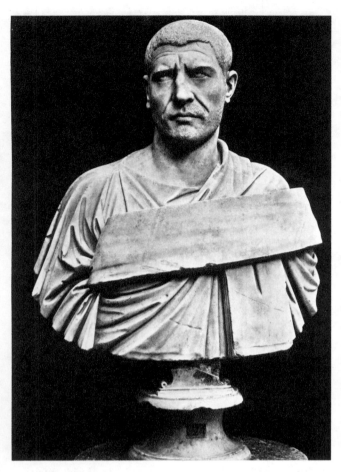

295. *Philip the Arab.* c. 244–49 A.D. Marble, life-size.
Vatican Museums, Rome

act as is impressionistic for first-century landscape painting, but at least it underscores the new emphasis on raw emotion to the detriment of structure and tradition.

We turn almost with relief from the atmosphere of chaos and terror suggested by such sculptures to the tiny portraits on gold leaf between panels of glass, which are among the rare treasures of third-century painting. The people shown in the *Family of Vunnerius Keramus* (fig. 297) may not have been Christian, yet they project an image of the dignity and self-possession we ideally assign to early Christians. Their special cast of countenance and the size and depth of their eyes seem to point to a Near Eastern origin for this gentle family, far from uncommon in Italy under the later Empire. Their name is Greek and written in Greek letters, but in an odd hybrid of Greek and Latin grammar. The painter still retains the ability to project features in depth—note the beautifully foreshortened ears—and to render with great precision the play of diffused light on features, costumes, and jewelry. But it is above all the calm composure of the figures that affords us a glimpse into a counterculture that retained human dignity inviolate in a hostile world.

During the early part of the third century, under Septimius Severus and his immediate successors and before the crisis of imperial power had really set in, extensive building projects were undertaken in the constantly growing capital. The most ambitious of these was the Baths of Caracalla (fig. 298), built well to the south of the older

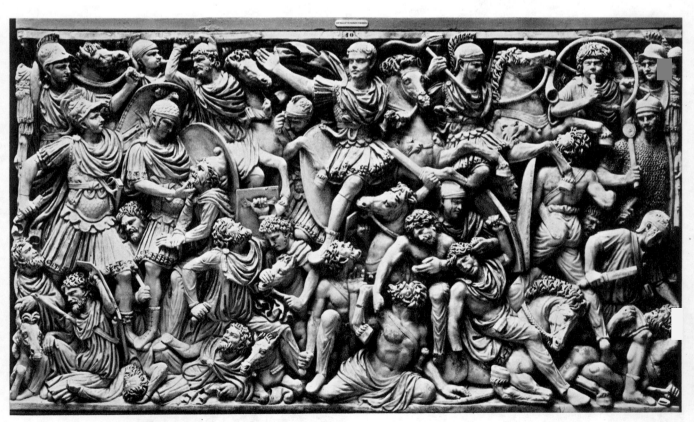

296. *Battle Between Romans and Barbarians*, (detail of the *Ludovisi Battle Sarcophagus*). 3rd century A.D.
Museo delle Terme, Rome

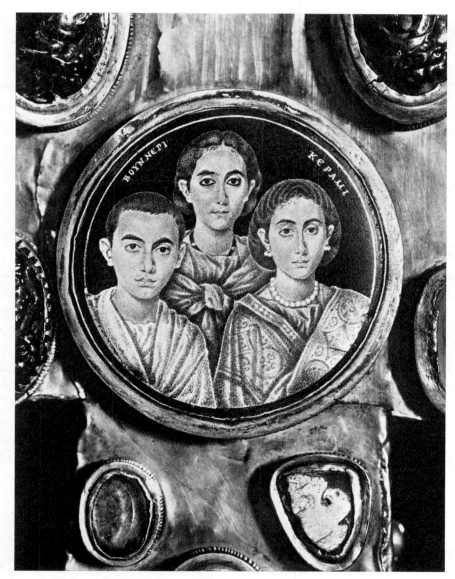

297. *Family of Vunnerius Keramus.* Painting on gold leaf c. 250 A.D.,
sealed between glass, diameter 2⅜″; set into a cross, 7th century
A.D. Civico Museo dell'Età Cristiana, Brescia, Italy

city center. Now stripped of their marble paneling, the
vast concrete ruins presently form a grandiose historical
setting for opera performances. Baths, ever more luxurious, were typical constructions of the Empire; there
were 952 baths in operation in Rome in the middle of the
fourth century. Caracalla clearly desired to outdo in
magnificence the largest baths before his time, the
second-century Baths of Trajan. The compact, carefully
planned central structure, more than seven hundred feet
in length, was divided into interconnecting halls for hot,
cold, and tepid baths (*caldarium*, *frigidarium*, and *tepidarium*); a swimming pool on one side; and at each end a
palaestra for exercise. In the thickness of the masses of
masonry were rooms for services, including the heating
of the air and of the water which arrived in its own

aqueduct and was piped to the appropriate baths in terra-
cotta conduits. The caldarium, whose foundations are
visible in the foreground of the aerial view, was a circular, domed structure (only slightly smaller than the
Pantheon), illuminated by a row of windows under the
dome. Openings between the halls must have provided
magnificent architectural vistas.

A reconstruction of the central tepidarium (fig. 299)
shows a hall about two hundred feet long, roofed by groin
vaults apparently supported by eight colossal Composite
columns, each having its intervening block of entablature, but actually resting more heavily on the piers concealed behind the columns. Under galleries on either side
were four small cold bathing pools. Light came from
clerestory windows grouped in threes under the arches of

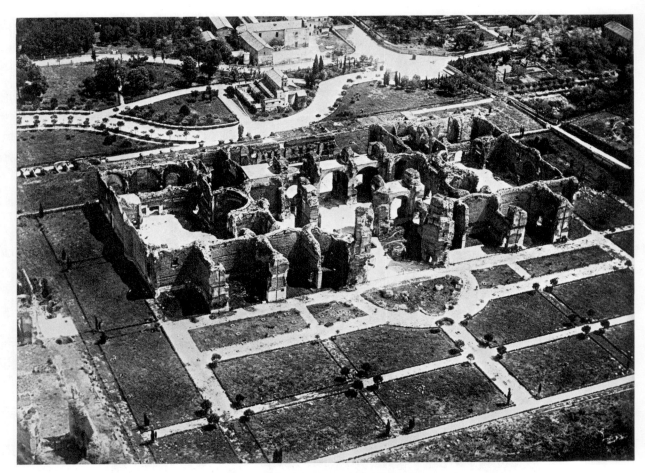

298. Baths of Caracalla. c. 211–17 A.D. Rome

the groin vaults, which were coffered, stuccoed, painted, and gilded; the walls, floors, and columns were sheathed in colored marbles. The interior must have made an impression not only of great spatial openness but also of constantly changing light and color.

The most extraordinary structure of the third century is the little Temple of Venus, which was added to the vast second-century Roman sanctuary of the Syrian deity Baal at Baalbek (now in Lebanon; fig. 300). The portico is conventional enough, but the cella behind it is circular. The peristyle is carried around it, supported on free-standing Corinthian columns. Here the architect had his most brilliant idea, making the podium and entablature curve inward from each column to touch the cella, and then outward again to the next column, producing a scalloped shape. This flow of outer concavities against inner convexity produces a free architectural fantasy as astonishing as some of the painted examples in the Fourth Pompeiian Style. The Temple of Venus at Baalbek has often been proclaimed an ancestor of the highly imaginative architectural inventions of the Italian Baroque (see Vol. 2, Part Five, Chapter 1). At this moment, it is almost more useful to regard it as one of the last examples of such fantasy before it was terminated by the rigidity of the later Empire.

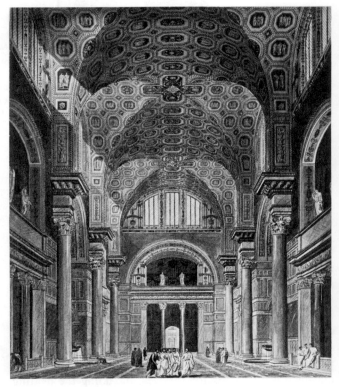

299. *Tepidarium*, Baths of Caracalla. (Restoration drawing by G. Abel Blonet)

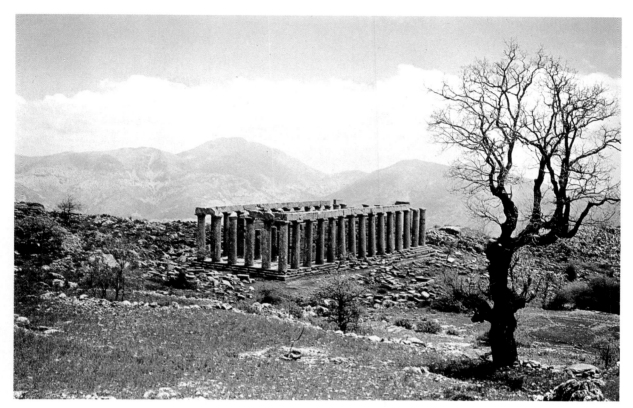

COLORPLATE 17.   Greek. IKTINOS. Temple of Apollo. c. 420 B.C. Bassai, Greece

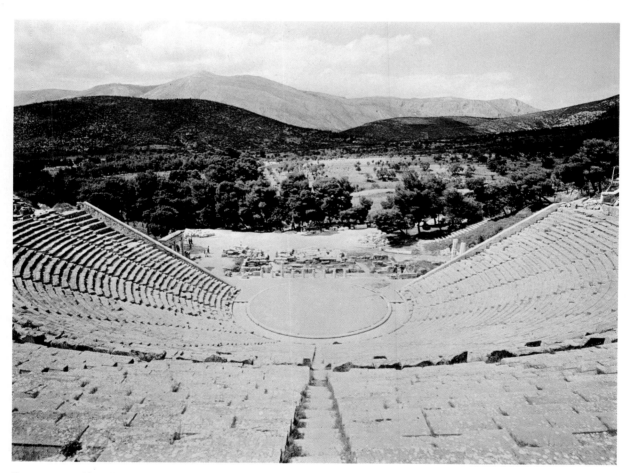

COLORPLATE 18.   Greek. POLYKLEITOS THE YOUNGER. The Theater. c. 350 B.C. Epidauros, Greece

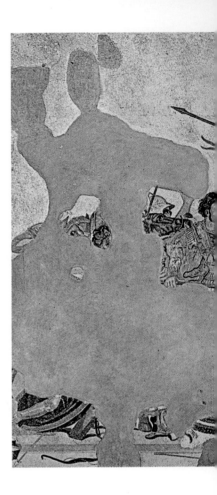

COLORPLATE 19.   Greek. Youth, found in the sea off Antikythera. c. 340 B.C. Bronze, height 77″. National Archaeological Museum, Athens

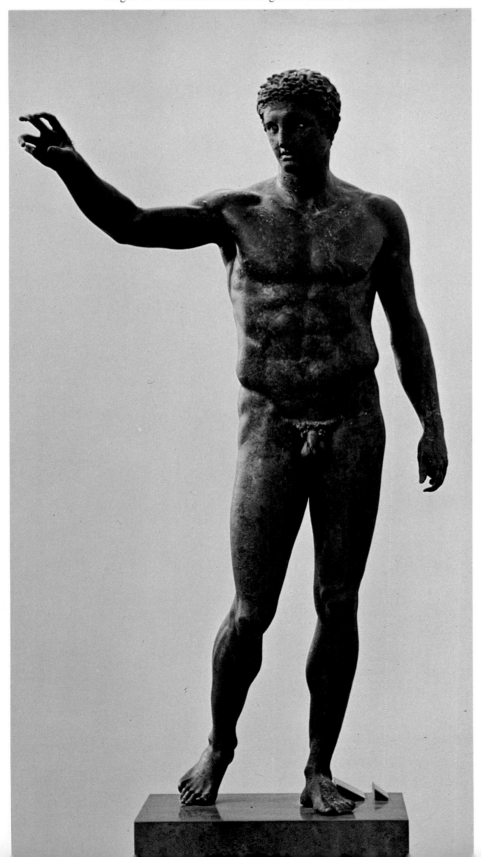

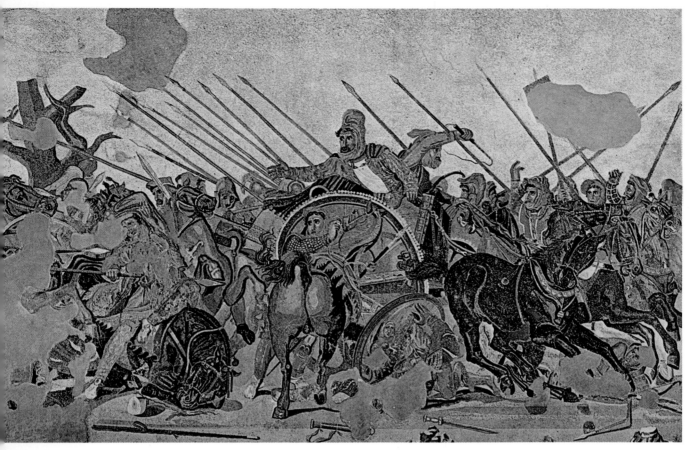

COLORPLATE 20.   Greek. *Victory of Alexander over Darius II.* Hellenistic mosaic copy of the painting by Philoxenos.
c. 300 B.C. Height 10'3¼". Museo Archeologico Nazionale, Naples

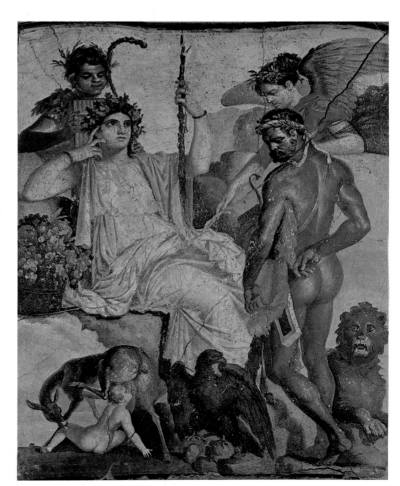

COLORPLATE 21.
Greek. *Herakles and the Infant
Telephos.* Roman copy of the fresco
from Herculaneum. 2nd century B.C.
Height 67½". Museo Archeologico
Nazionale, Naples

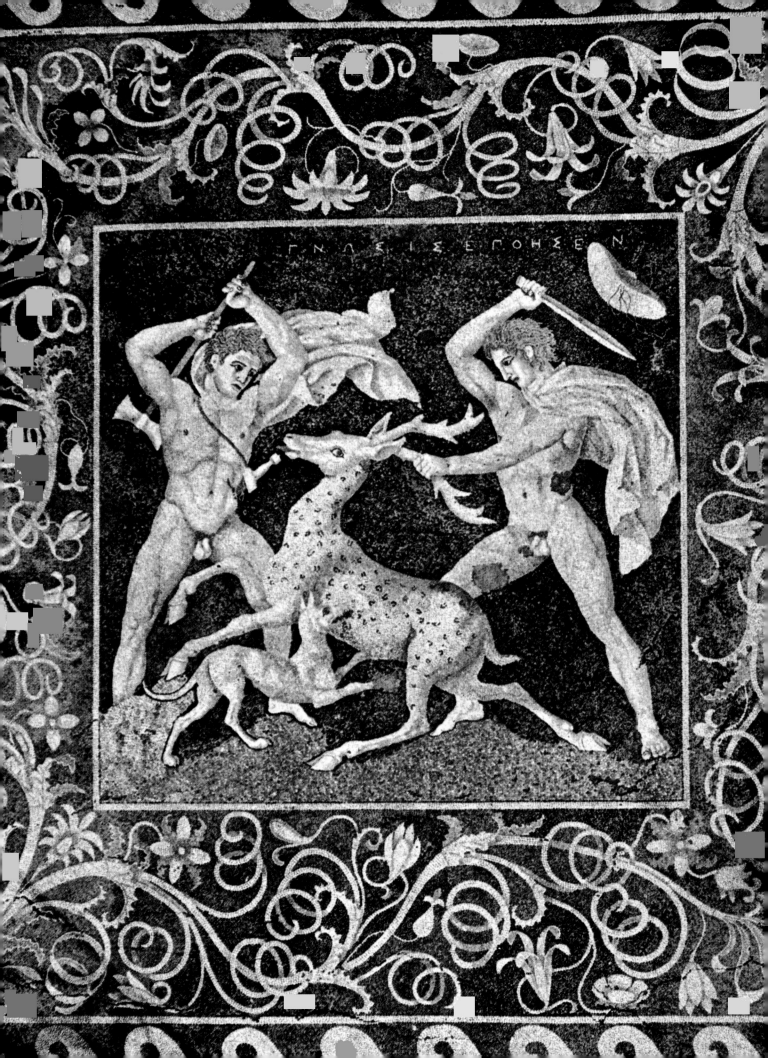

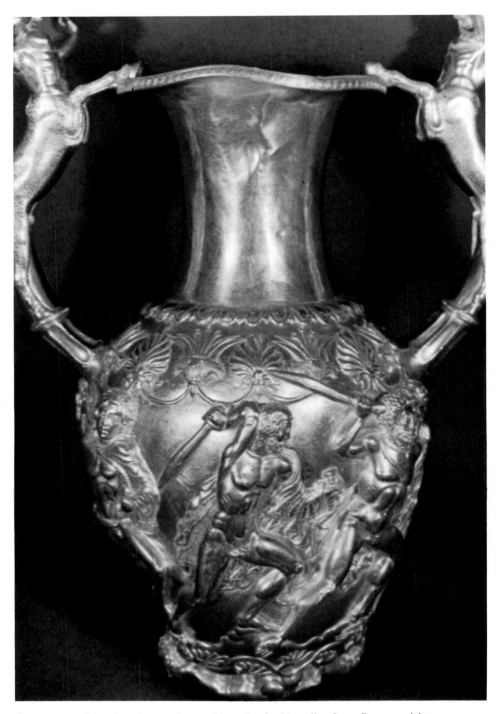

COLORPLATE 23. Greek. Amphora with sculptured handles from Panagyurishte, Bulgaria. c. 300 B.C. Gold, height c. 10″. National Archaeological Museum, Plovdiv, Bulgaria

◄ COLORPLATE 22. Greek. *Stag Hunt*, from Pella, Greece. Pebble mosaic. 3rd century B.C. Archaeological Museum, Pella

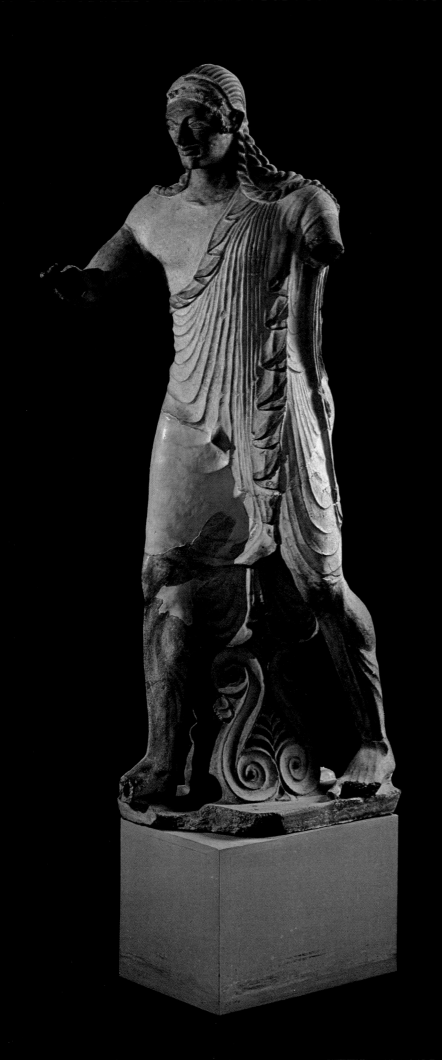

COLORPLATE 24
Etruscan. *Apollo of Veii.* c. 510 B.C.
Painted terra-cotta, height c. 70″.
Museo Nazionale di Villa Giulia,
Rome

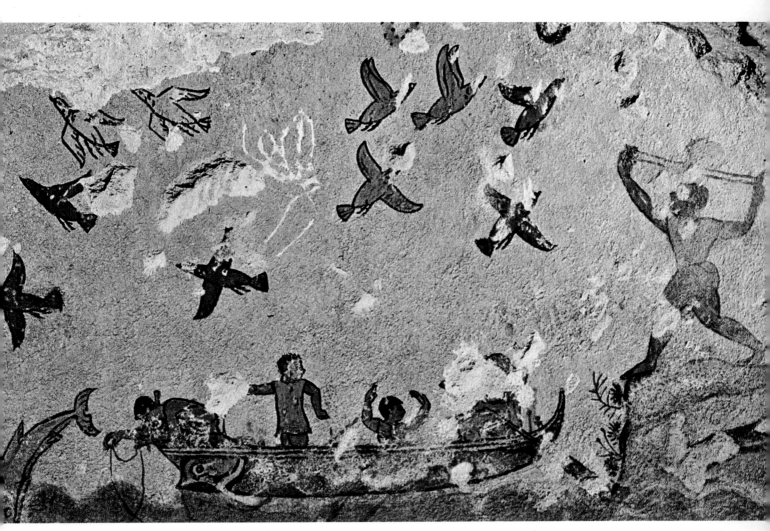

COLORPLATE 25. Etruscan. *Hunting and Fishing.* Wall painting from the Tomb of Hunting and Fishing. c. 500 B.C. Tarquinia, Italy

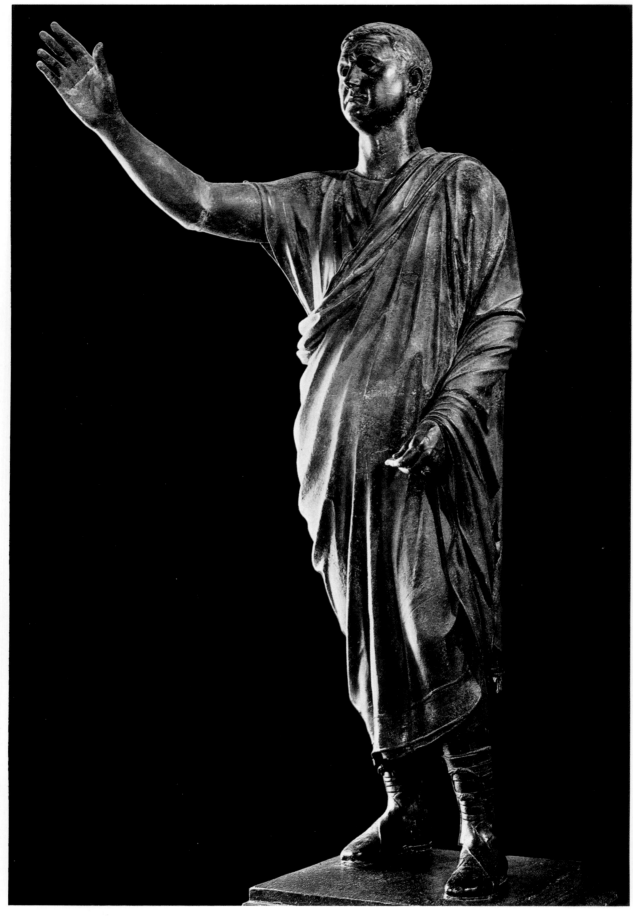

COLORPLATE 26.   Roman. *Arringatore*, from Sanguineto near Lake Trasimeno. 1st century B.C. Bronze, height 71″.
Museo Archeologico, Florence

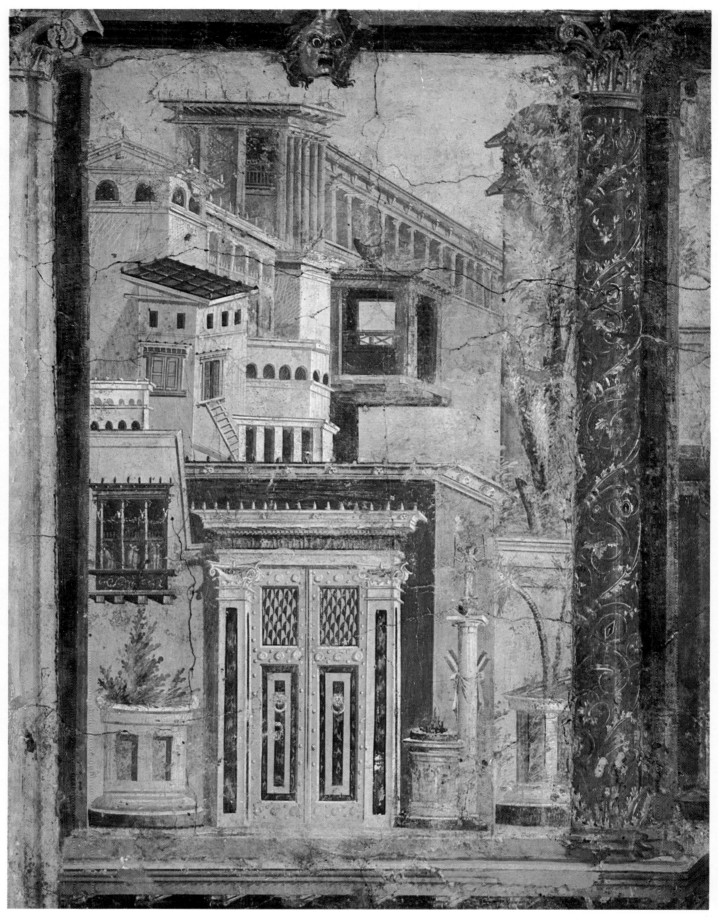

COLORPLATE 27. Roman. *Architectural View.* Wall painting from a villa at Boscoreale, near Naples. Late 1st century B.C. Height 96″. The Metropolitan Museum of Art, New York. Rogers Fund, 1903

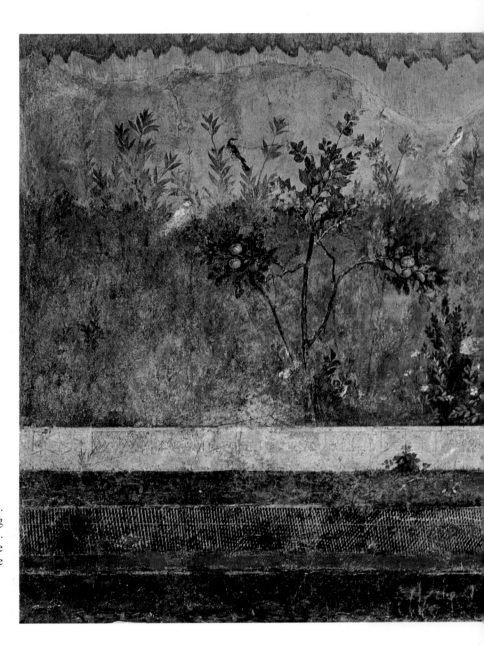

COLORPLATE 28.
Roman. *Garden Room.* Wall painting
from the Villa of Livia at Prima Porta.
Late 1st century B.C. Museo delle
Terme, Rome

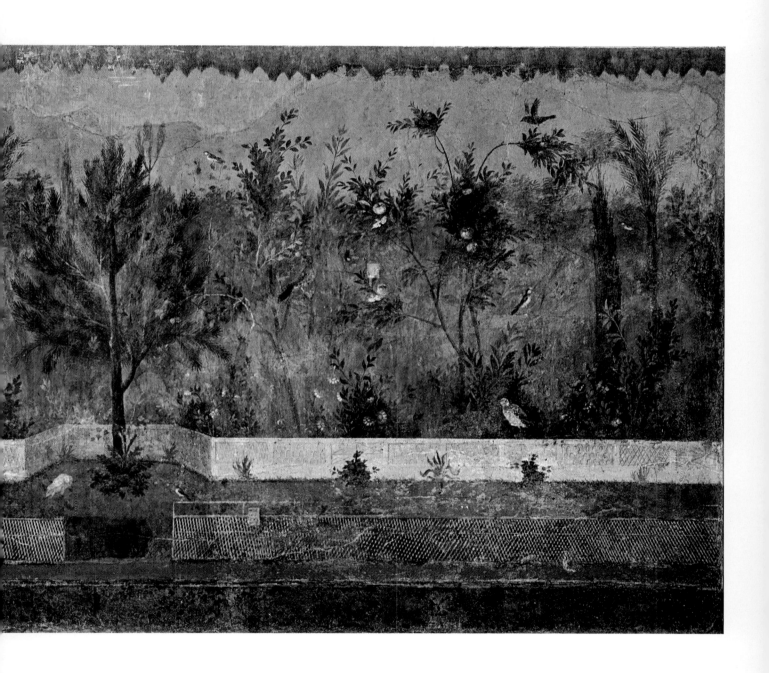

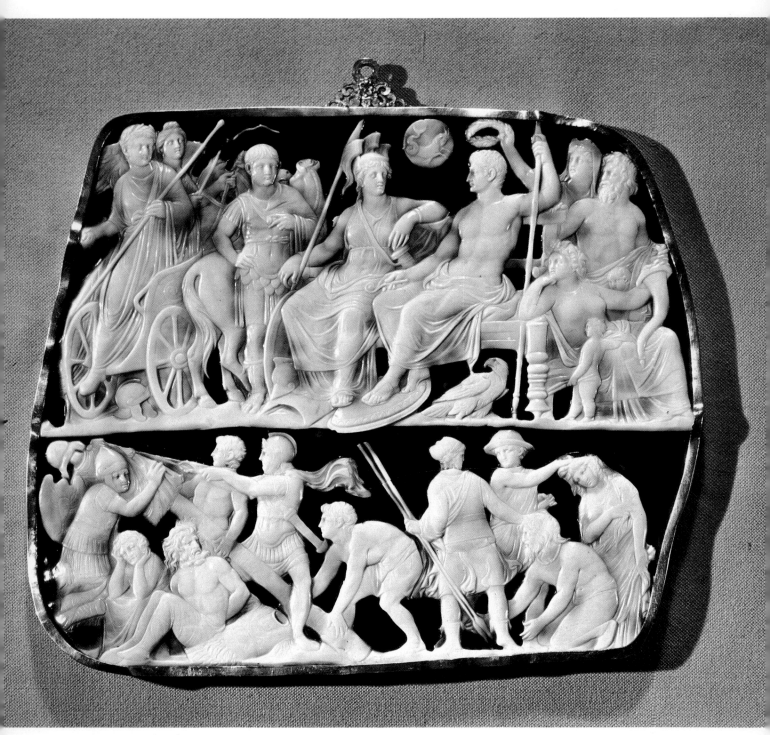

COLORPLATE 29. Roman. *Gemma Augustea.* Cameo. Early 1st century A.D. Onyx, 7½ x 9″. Kunsthistorisches Museum, Vienna

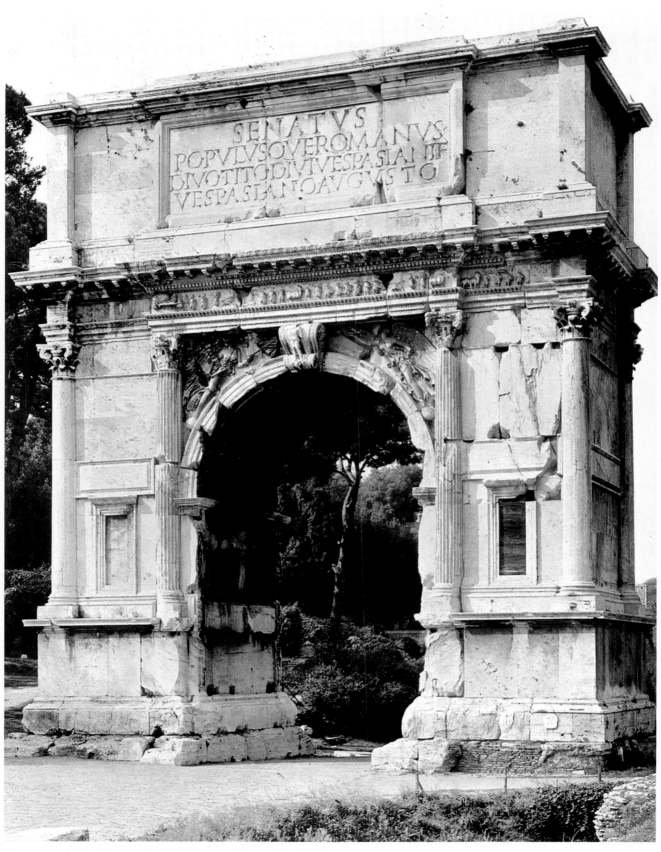

COLORPLATE 30. Roman. Arch of Titus. c. 81 A.D. Marble. Rome

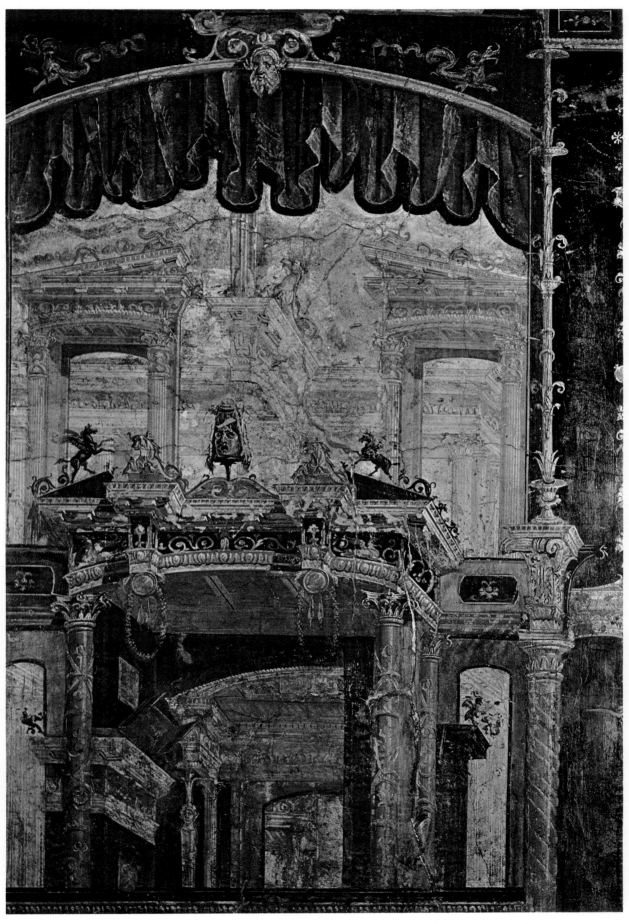

COLORPLATE 31. *Architectural View.* Wall painting from Herculaneum, near Naples. c. 63–79 A.D. Museo Archeologico Nazionale, Naples

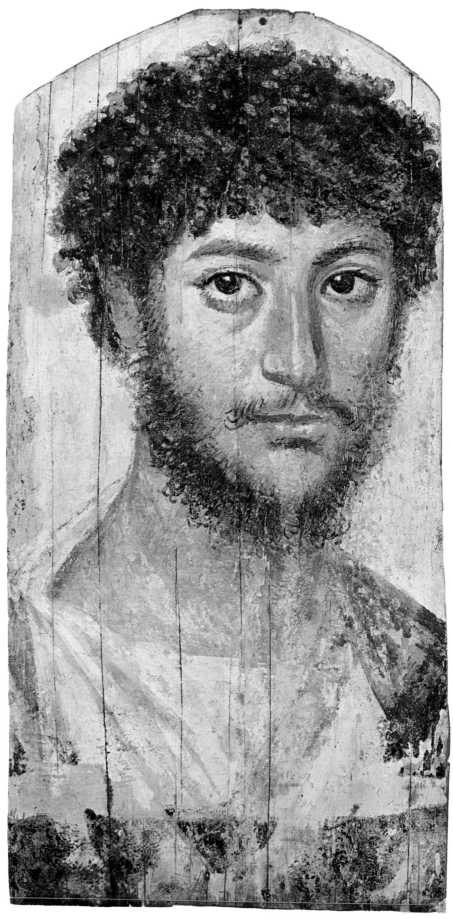

COLORPLATE 32. Roman. Portrait of a Graeco-Roman Egyptian from a mummy case found at El Faiyûm, in the Nile Valley. 2nd century A.D. Encaustic on panel, 17⅞ x 9″. Staatliche Museen, Berlin

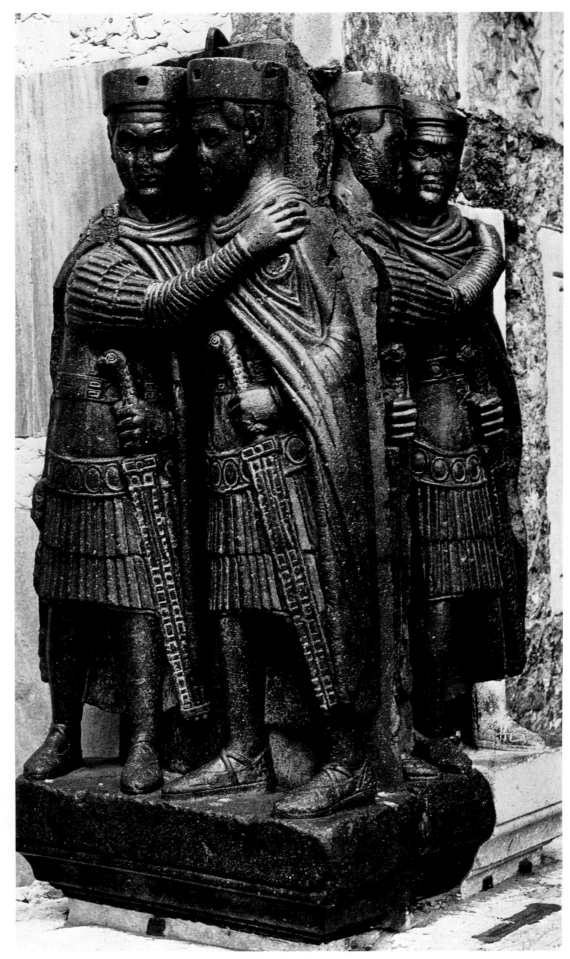

COLORPLATE 33.   Roman. The Tetrarchs. c. 305 A.D. Porphyry, height c. 51″. Façade of
S. Marco, Venice

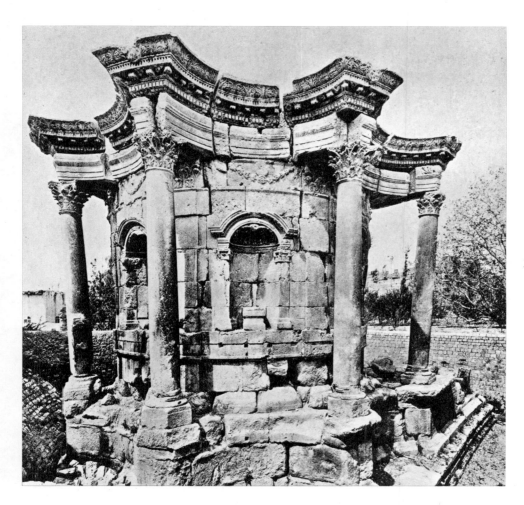

THE END OF THE PAGAN EMPIRE (284–323)

Under the "barracks emperors" of the third century, the government of the Empire degenerated into a situation bordering on anarchy and was frequently rent by civil war among rival claimants to imperial power. A rugged general of peasant stock from Illyria (modern Yugoslavia), the emperor Diocletian (ruled 284–305), attempted to put an end to disorder and in so doing imposed upon the Roman world a system which can only be compared with the despotism of Mesopotamian rulers. Even the shadowy authority still cherished by the senate was set aside; personal rule was directly exercised by the emperor through an elaborate system of administrative levels, military and governmental, which functioned better in theory than in fact. Since the days of Septimius Severus, the imperial person had been considered sacred, a notion that contrasts bitterly with the ease with which individual emperors were murdered. Debasement and consequent collapse of coinage had led to economic breakdown and reversion to barter. A wealthy landowning class, precursors of the medieval nobility, had arisen throughout the Empire. Agricultural workers were increasingly attached to the land and workmen to their trades. Communications throughout the Empire had deteriorated.

The rigidity of Diocletian's system was a formal expression of an economic and political paralysis which was beyond any then-known cure. Because of the difficulty of governing the entire imperial territory from a single center—and Rome had largely given way to Milan as the seat of administration in Italy—Diocletian divided power between two theoretically coequal emperors, each known as Augustus, one ruling in the West, the other in the East. Each Augustus took on a deputy and successor with the title of Caesar. This short-lived experiment was known as the tetrarchy (government of four rulers), and it heralded the inevitable breakup of the Empire, whose numerous political subdivisions were already infiltrated with barbarians. Under emperors as different as Nero and Marcus Aurelius, Christianity had long been recognized as a danger to the state, in that the Christians refused to burn incense before imperial statues and to render military service. Sporadic persecutions of Christians became intense; the last was ordered by Diocletian in 303. Two years later he abdicated and retired to a palace he had built at Split, near his birthplace.

A rapid succession of tetrarchies only perpetuated the anarchic situation that had existed before Diocletian. After a six-year struggle one tetrarch, Constantine the Great (ruled 306–37), seized sole imperial power after defeating his rival Maxentius at the Milvian Bridge over

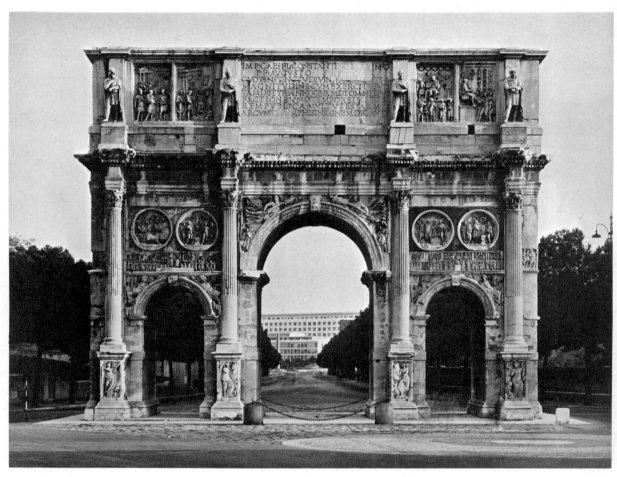

301. Arch of Constantine. c. 312–15 A.D. Rome

the Tiber River in 312, reportedly after a dream in which an angel appeared to him bearing the Cross, and saying, "In this sign thou shalt conquer." In the Edict of Milan in 313, Constantine proclaimed toleration of Christianity, which had become the single most powerful spiritual and intellectual force in the Empire; in the same year Diocletian died in retirement. In 325 Constantine called and participated in the Council of Nicaea, which considered questions essential to the new religion. But Helleno-Roman polytheism did not rapidly die out; it was necessary in 345 to decree the death penalty for adherence to pagan cults. A short-lived attempt was made to restore paganism under Julian the Apostate (ruled 361–63), but at his death Christianity rapidly triumphed. In point of fact, however, the ancient gods were never entirely forgotten, but lived a subterranean existence in folklore as well as in the literary heritage. They were to surface at unexpected moments in the Middle Ages, and on occasion they triumphed in the Renaissance.

An astonishing, in fact, rather touching red porphyry group, about half-lifesize (colorplate 33) and formerly attached to a column, represents four tetrarchs—we are not sure which ones, but probably Diocletian and his colleagues. Each Augustus embraces a Caesar with his right arm, and each figure firmly grasps the hilt of a sword.

The style would have impressed Gudea of Lagash as archaic (see fig. 99). Nothing remains of the naturalistic tradition in the representation of the human body, which had evolved in Egypt, Mesopotamia, and the Hellenic world throughout more than three thousand years. The figures have been reduced to cylinders, their legs and arms to tubes, their proportions to those of dolls, and their faces to staring masks. But if freedom and beauty of face and body have been sacrificed, anxiety has not. The figures clutch each other like lost children, and an art that no longer cares to analyze features cannot forget frowns. In fact, only the individuality of their frowns differentiates these figures.

The grand triumphal arch that Constantine erected in Rome from 312–15 to celebrate his assumption of sole imperial power owes much of its splendor to its predecessors (fig. 301). The three-arched shape was used earlier in the Arch of Septimius Severus in the Roman Forum, and most of the sculpture was lifted bodily from monuments built by Trajan, Hadrian, and Marcus Aurelius, whose heads were recarved into portraits of Constantine and his generals. The sculpture contributed by Constantine's artisans (see fig. 281) is startling. Tiny figures with huge heads, stiffly posed, are aligned on either side of the emperor as he addresses the people from

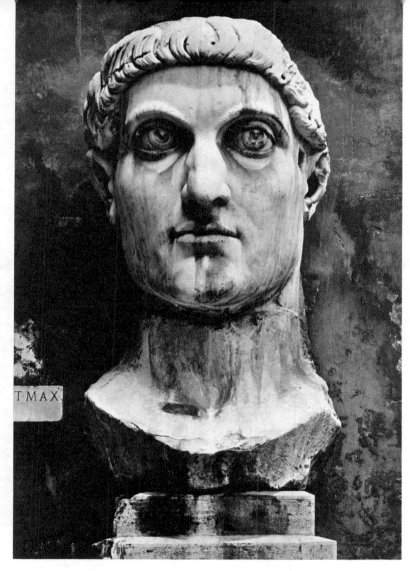

302. *Constantine the Great.*
c. 330 A.D. Marble. height 8′.
Palazzo dei Conservatori.
Rome

the rostrum in the Roman Forum, whose buildings have been reduced to toys in the background. A few channels made by the drill suffice to indicate what had been the glory of Roman ceremonial sculpture, the melodic cadences created by the folds of the togas. Only here and there in faces and gestures can one distinguish a trace of the Hellenic tradition. Figures and architecture have been locked into an embracing structure of pattern that allows for no possibility of independent movement.

Technical inadequacy may account for part of the change; no official relief sculpture had been made in Rome for eighty years, and only artisans were available to Constantine. But the renunciation of the Classical tradition seems to have been deliberate. A new and impressive Constantinian style was rapidly formed, to be carried out by better-trained artists. One gigantic remnant is the marble head of a colossal statue of the emperor (fig. 302), which once was enthroned in the apse of his basilica. Head, arms, and legs were of marble, and the drapery probably of bronze plates over a masonry core. It is hard to keep from thinking of an august predecessor—the Zeus of Phidias at Olympia. No accusation of technical decline can be leveled at this magnificent head. The features and the neck muscles are superbly modeled, showing a full understanding of

Hellenistic tradition—with one significant and disturbing exception: the eyes are enlarged beyond all verisimilitude. Carved with all the colorism of Antonine sculpture, even to the extent of a tiny fleck of marble having been left in each eye to represent the reflection of light in the transparent cornea, they stare above and beyond us as if we could never reach their owner—as if his godlike gaze were fixed upon eternity. This enormous enlargement of the eyes as an indication of sanctity or of inspiration became a convention in Early Christian and Byzantine art.

Two structures of great size and importance from this brief transitional period between the ancient world and the early Middle Ages still remain partially standing. One is the gigantic palace which Diocletian began to build in 293 for his retirement near his birthplace at Salona. Much of the present-day city of Split is built inside the palace walls, but its original appearance has been reconstructed in a model (fig. 303). The plan (fig. 304) and appearance of the palace reflect the changed conditions of the Empire. A free arrangement of structures like Hadrian's Villa at Tivoli (see fig. 286) was no longer possible. The complex had to be defended, and it was thus laid out on the plan of a Roman camp, with the main streets intersecting in the exact center. The palace was

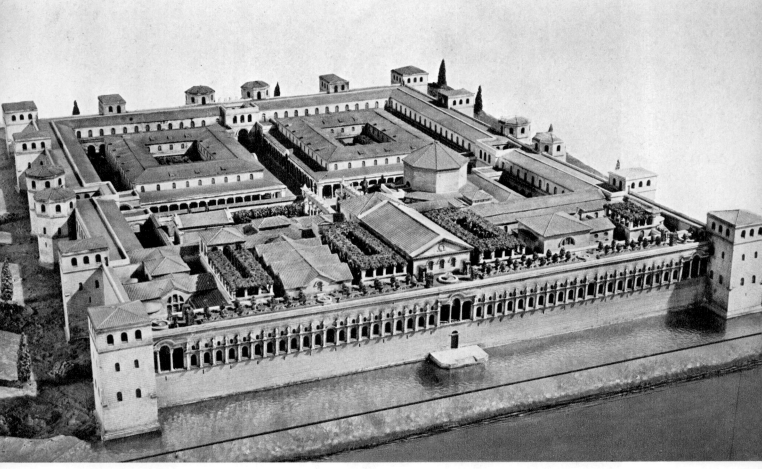

303. Palace of Diocletian, Split, Yugoslavia. c. 293 A.D.
(Architectural reconstruction by E. Hebrard.)
Museo della Civiltà Romana, Rome

surrounded by walls and towers except on the south side, which overhung the sea and could be approached only by boat; the imperial apartments ran along this side, with arched windows embraced by an engaged colonnade. An octagonal structure visible toward the right side of the model was designed as the emperor's mausoleum; it is in good condition, and is now in use as a cathedral. A peristyle court, now forming the principal square of Split (fig. 305), gave access to the mausoleum on the left and the imperial apartments at the end through a sort of triumphal arch once crowned with the customary bronze group of a four-horse chariot driven by the emperor. The most remarkable feature of this court is the complete change in the customary relationship of column and arch since the first century B.C. Under the central pediment the entablature is bent upward to form an arch, as we have previously seen at Hadrian's Villa (see fig. 287). But the monolithic Corinthian columns in gray granite along both sides of the court no longer *embrace* arches; for the first time in Roman architecture, the columns *support* the arches directly. This decisive step prepares us for the structural innovations of Early Christian architecture in the mid- and late fourth century.

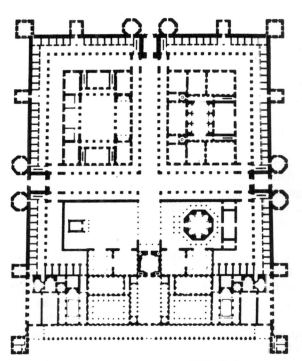

304. Plan of the Palace of Diocletian

The other great pagan structure of the early fourth century is the basilica started by Maxentius in 306 and terminated under Constantine in 313, a massive section of which still dominates the imperial forums in Rome (figs. 306, 307). Curiously enough, the architect decided to relinquish the traditional basilican plan as we have seen it in the Basilica Ulpia (see fig. 276), with its long nave, side aisles, twin apses, and timber roof, in favor of the groin-vaulted form of hall used in the tepidaria of Roman baths, such as that of Caracalla (see fig. 299). The downward thrust of the heavy groin vaults upon the eight colossal Corinthian columns and the piers behind them must have been to a certain extent abutted by the six massive, octagonally coffered barrel vaults running at right angles to the nave; these replaced the usual side aisles of a basilica. The grandeur, simplicity, and openness of the interior seem to us so easily adaptable for religious use that it is hard at first sight to realize why the building was not adopted as a model for Early Christian churches. The answer (see Part Three, Chapter 1) tells us much about the nature of early Christianity. Equally important is the fact that this mighty ruin was universally believed in the Renaissance to have been a temple; Alberti used it, in part, for the design of the Church of Sant' Andrea in Mantua (see Vol. 2, fig. 35), and the architects of the Counter-Reformation in the later sixteenth century derived some of the ideas for their church interiors from this noble space (see Vol. 2, figs. 188, 235).

In a final glance at the dying pagan tradition, we might note its survival, well into the fourth century, in floor mosaics in North Africa and in Syria, where these decorations have been discovered in great numbers. But the most spectacular find of all has been the villa at Piazza Armerina in Sicily, excavated since World War II. In striking contrast to the fortified palace of Diocletian, this country residence, which may have been designed for the

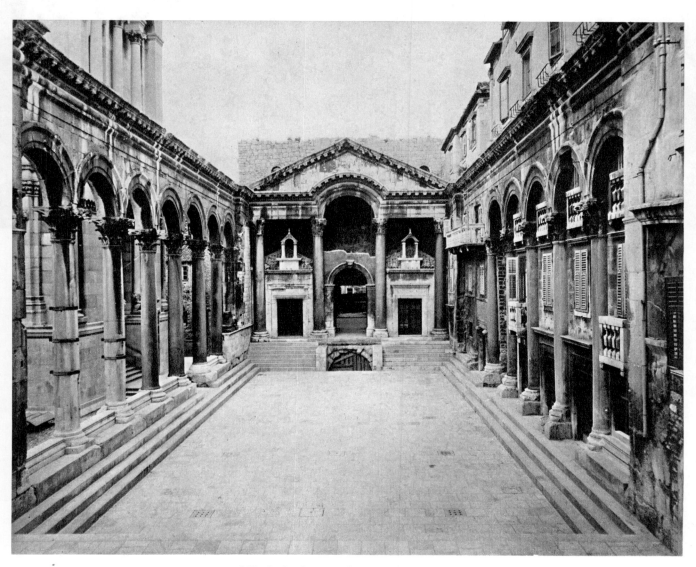

305. Peristyle court, Palace of Diocletian

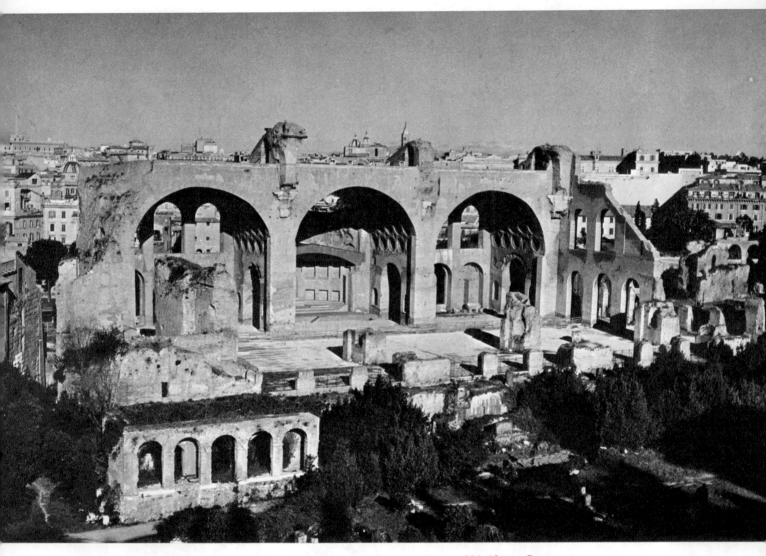

306. Basilica of Maxentius and Constantine. c. 306–13 A.D. Rome

contemporaneous ˙retirement of Diocletian's colleague Maximian, is freely arranged on the slope of a hill. The complete series of late imperial mosaics that enliven the pavements of all the interiors of the villa at Piazza Armerina must have been done by a workshop from North Africa over a considerable span of time. Among the most striking is the group representing *Exploits of Hercules*, seen as separate episodes scattered over a white background. A nude warrior, sprawled over his dead horse and with one leg in the air (colorplate 34), plunges his sword into his breast. The powerful masses of his muscular body recall the Pergamene style of half a millennium earlier (see figs. 232, 233), and the rich changes of light, shade, and color which play over his tanned skin and establish the volumes of his body and limbs in depth show that even at this late date Hellenistic colorism was very much alive. In the next Part of this book, we shall see this colorism employed not in the rendition of violence and bloodshed but in the depiction of hitherto unsuspected aspects of spiritual experience.

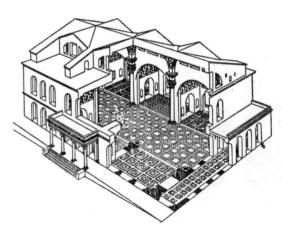

307. Basilica of Maxentius and Constantine. (Architectural reconstruction after Huelsen)

7

Pre-Columbian Art

Among the civilizations of the ancient world should certainly be counted those that flourished in Central America and northern South America before the arrival of the Europeans in the sixteenth century. The small bands of Spanish adventurers who, with the aid of gunpowder defeated and subjugated with ease the Aztec and Inca empires and the Mayan states, were astonished at the high level of urban culture they found. Where not precluded by mountainous terrain, cities had been laid out on a grid plan with wide, straight streets. Before the Spaniards tore it down, house by house, in the protracted battle of 1520–21, Montezuma's capital, the lake-city of Tenochtitlán, boasted a luxurious palace and fine residences united by a network of canals. Both the Maya and the later Aztecs possessed a complex system of hieroglyphic writing, as yet only partially deciphered, and each had a calendar so precise that both Mayan and Aztec inscriptions can be dated down to the day according to our system. While their massive temples were intended mostly for exterior use, the Maya and the Aztecs knew and employed the post-and-lintel system, the corbel arch, and the corbel vault. The Spaniards admired the craftsmanship of Aztec sculpture and minor arts, but they saw in them little artistic merit and melted down most of the gold and silver objects. They also systematically destroyed almost all Aztec manuscripts, which were written on a kind of paper made from the bark of the fig tree; only a very few illuminated examples survive. Montezuma showed the Spaniards with pride his botanical garden, which had a specimen of every identifiable plant that grew in his Empire. Arithmetic and astronomy were among the great interests of both Aztecs and Maya. The Aztecs had even developed a system of universal education. Astonishingly enough, none of these original Americans knew the use of the wheel, and they had no draft animals. In most respects it can be said that the Maya and the Aztecs, at least, had reached a stage of development analogous to that of the ancient Sumerians, and that the Incas, at the very least, had arrived at about the level of predynastic Egypt.

One of the most remarkable aspects of these vanished cultures to us is the lack of any certain evidence of contact between them and the rest of the world; the Incas and their predecessors in the Andes even developed in total isolation from the Aztecs in Mexico and the Maya in Yucatán. We can speculate that all the early Americans, including the North American Indians, arrived from Asia by way of a land bridge formed by the Aleutian chain during the last glacial period and cut off when the glaciers receded and the water level rose. After settling in Central and South America, these peoples must have independently recapitulated much of what Asiatic, North African, and European peoples were inventing. Until about 3000 B.C. the early Americans remained in the Old Stone Age. The first mature pottery and clay statuettes can be dated about 1500 B.C. Metals and the techniques of working them were discovered fairly late, around A.D. 1000; many of the finest works of architecture and sculpture were executed with tools made of stone or bone.

The Aztecs were aware that they were relative latecomers to the Mexican highland and that they had had predecessors there in a happier era before human sacrifice, on which the entire religious life of the Aztec was founded, became "necessary." These earlier peoples built cities, the most impressive of which was Teotihuacán, whose main avenue of temples, dating from well before A.D. 600, has been excavated (fig. 308). The rites of early American nature worship required hilltops, and when these were unavailable, mounds were built. By the beginning of the Christian era, the mounds had reached the form of carefully constructed step-pyramids, ascended by a central flight of stairs. The parallel in form and purpose with Mesopotamian ziggurats (see figs. 88, 90) is

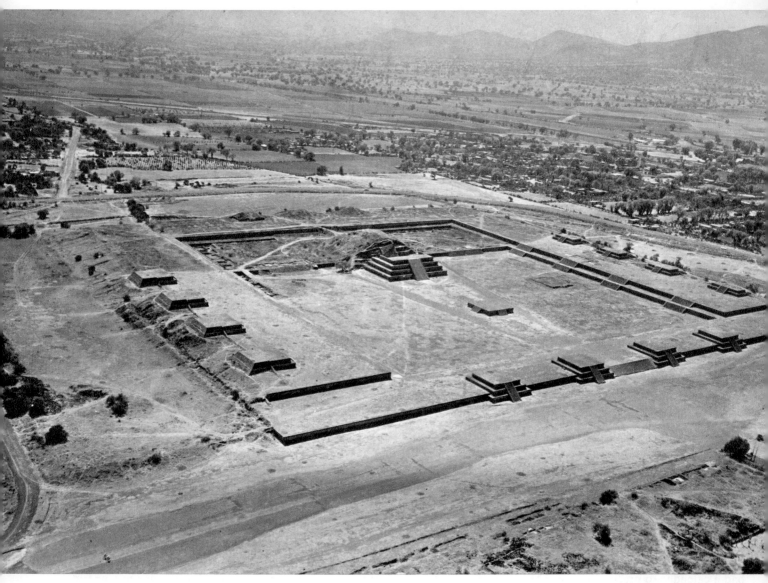

308. Ciudadela court (view from the west). Before 600 A.D. Teotihuacán. Mexico

compelling. The American structures were, however, not built of mud brick but according to an elaborate system of inner stone piers and fin walls, filled in with earth and rubble, and faced with well-cut stone masonry. Not only in sheer craftsmanship but also in the feeling for mass and proportion, and in the disposition of spaces, these pyramids of Teotihuacán are majestic works of architecture. With a single exception, the various levels are ornamented only with simple paneling, which accentuates their cubic grandeur.

The still-mysterious Olmec culture, which flourished along the Gulf Coast of Mexico from about 800 B.C. to about A.D. 600, produced a surprisingly naturalistic sculpture in the round, including a series of colossal heads of unknown purpose. An example from San Lorenzo Tenochtitlán (fig. 309) has been provided with a close-fitting helmet, under which the brows are knitted in a

frown; the prominent lips are partly open, and the large eyes stare. The mass of basalt has thus been transformed into the appearance of living flesh with astonishing power and intensity.

The type of pyramid with central staircase, established at Teotihuacán, was recapitulated in countless variations of size, shape, and proportion throughout central Mexico and Yucatán, becoming sharply steeper and higher in the Mayan civilization. The Maya had their own religious rites, one of which was a ball game in which the rubber ball passing back and forth overhead symbolized the course of the sun through the heavens. The reconstruction of a ball court at Copán, representing it as it appeared about A.D. 600 (fig. 310), shows the Mayan genius for the deployment of architectural masses, often unrelieved, crowned here with a windowless story richly ornamented with the relief sculpture at which the Maya

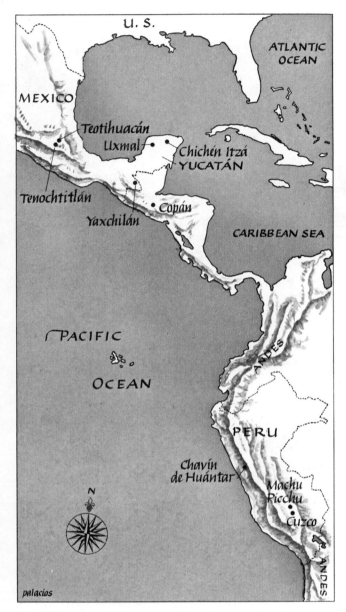

MAP 11. *Central America and Northwestern South America*

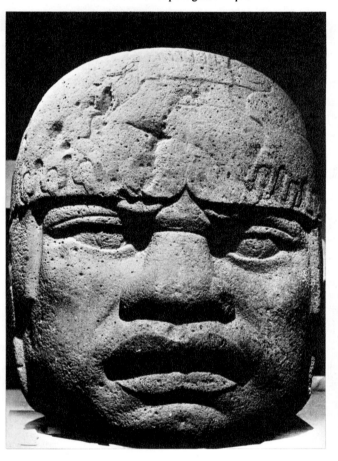

309. Colossal Olmec head, from San Lorenzo Tenochtitlán. c. 800 B.C.–c. 600 A.D. Basalt, height 70⅞″. Museo de Antropología, Jalapa, Mexico

excelled. In the so-called Nunnery of the tenth century at Uxmal (fig. 311; its actual purpose is unknown), the customary cubic masonry of the lower story is contrasted with an upper zone or ornament in which lattice shapes alternate with carved masks. This horizontality of accent produces an effect unlike that of any Old World architecture. Even when the Maya were under the domination of the Toltec, who seem to have introduced human sacrifice, the originality of Mayan architecture was maintained. The Mayan-Toltecan center of Chichén Itzá is filled with structures whose massive grandeur and delicate relief carving create an impression of the greatest variety and richness. The Caracol (observatory) is one of the most impressive—a cylindrical building on a lofty platform (fig. 312). Over the doorway grins a fierce mask strikingly suggestive of the Haida bear masks (see colorplate 3) of the Pacific Northwest. The interior is formed by two concentric circular corridors, roofed by pointed corbel vaults.

During the "classic" Mayan period (to use the designation employed by archaeologists), which corresponds to about the first millennium of our era, sculpture in the round was rare and generally limited to ceramics and stucco. Painting, while extensive and of high quality, was executed on walls in narrow spaces, and is extremely difficult to reproduce today except in copies in which all idea of the style of the original is lost. Sculpture in low relief was abundant, and beautiful both in its characteristic contrast of blank and enriched areas and its spontaneous transformation of inert to live masses, of blocks to cubes. A very fine relief from the lintel of a house at Yaxchilán (fig. 313), datable from 692–726, shows a possibly ceremonial, possibly visionary subject, difficult to interpret exactly in the present state of our knowledge

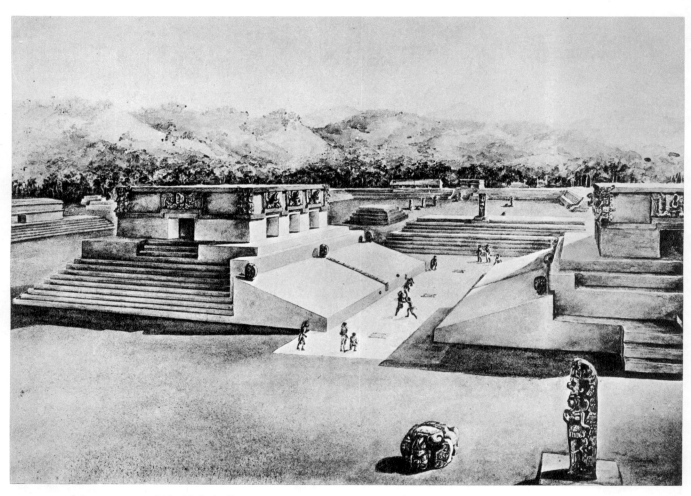

310. Main ball court (reconstruction). c. 600 A.D. Copán. West Honduras

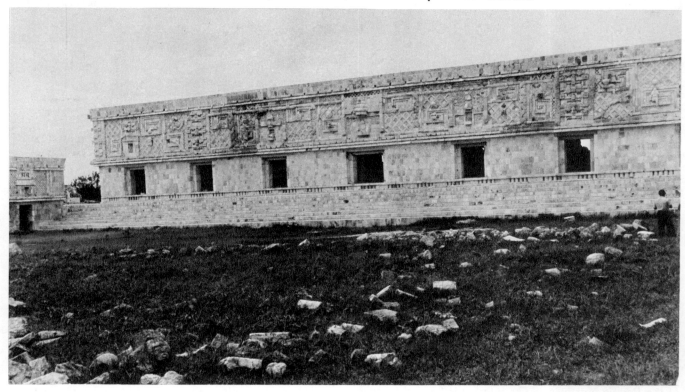

311. Nunnery Quadrangle (west building). 10th century A.D. Uxmal. Yucatán. Mexico

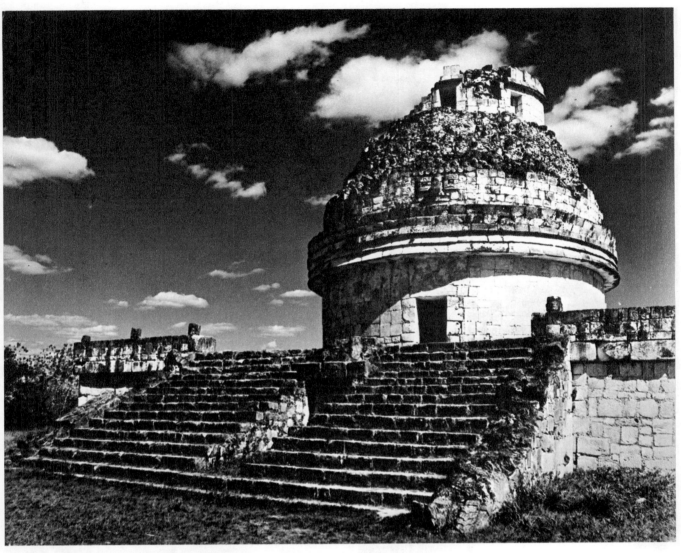

312. The Caracol (observatory). 11th
century A.D. Chichén Itzá, Yucatán,
Mexico

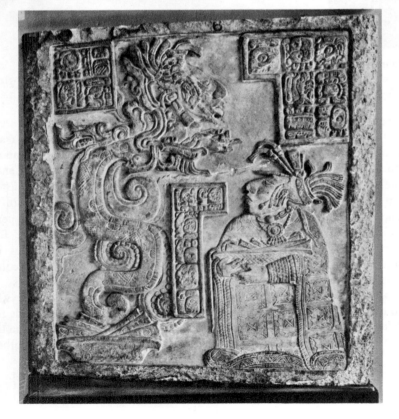

313. Lintel relief, from a Mayan house,
Yaxchilán, Mexico. c. 692–726 A.D.
Stone. British Museum, London.
Maudslay Collection

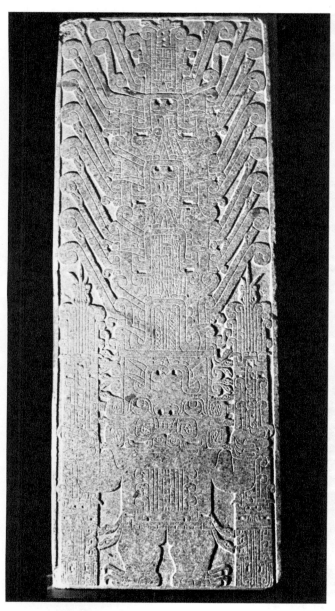

314. *Raimondi Monolith*, from Chavín de Huántar, Peru. c. 500 A.D. Stone, height 72″. Museo Nacional de Antropología y Arqueología, Lima

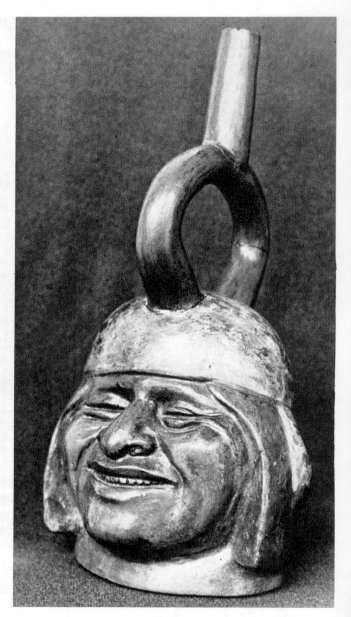

315. *Laughing Man* (Mochica vessel). c. 500 A.D. Museo Nacional de Antropología y Arqueología, Lima

of Mayan hieroglyphs. These appear in the upper corners of the relief and in an upside-down, L-shaped area in the center. On the left a strange design of scrolls and scales resolves itself into a fantastic serpent or dragon, above a delicately drawn bowl, seen slightly from below, containing instruments of unknown purpose. On the right kneels a richly robed and crowned figure, apparently a priest, whose sensitively observed features have the typical Mayan cast. He holds a basket of instruments, and looks up in wonder at the apparition of a crowned head and hand from the serpent's mouth. The extreme delicacy and suppleness of the draftsmanship, and the manner in which ornament suddenly comes to life, make this and other Mayan reliefs works of art of fascinating and compelling beauty.

The Andean region formed a totally distinct area of pre-Columbian culture, whose origins cannot be traced. The Spaniards arriving in Peru in 1536 found an even more recent empire than that of the Aztecs of Tenochtitlán. The Incas had no writing, and their vast Empire was held together by an extraordinary system of oral communication, messages being delivered by runners in short and frequent relays, making it possible for a message to travel one hundred and fifty miles in a day—as compared to the twelve to fifteen days required by the later Spanish system of post-horses. The Spaniards were astonished to find themselves everywhere expected. In the absence of writing, the Incas made relief models of areas of their mountainous Empire to aid them in moving subject peoples from one region to another in order to forestall revolt. In Andean architecture we find many of the familiar features we have encountered in Mexico—platforms, step-pyramids, gridiron cities. Mining was extensively practiced, and the smelting, casting, beating, and chasing of metals done with the utmost skill. It cannot be claimed, however, that Andean art often reached the level of Mayan art at its best.

Andean carvings were generally incised on stone in patterns of great complexity, but not further carved save for reduction of the background. One of the most fascinating Andean reliefs is the *Raimondi Monolith* (fig. 314) from Chavín de Huántar in northern Peru, datable to about 500. This was probably a ceiling decoration, intended to be read in either direction. At first sight one distinguishes a chunky personage, with claws on his feet, in the lower third of the relief; his short arms and massive hands extend to hold two richly carved scepters. His face is a mask, displaying a grinning mouth, full of square teeth, and saucer-shaped depressions for nostrils and eyes. The upper two-thirds of the relief appears to be filled with a towering headdress from which feathers sprout on either side until one turns the picture around. Then the upper sections become a series of masks, each hanging from the jaws of the one above. The magical intensity of the complex pattern renders it extremely attractive to modern eyes.

At the opposite pole from this very nearly abstract art, with its probable religious significance and ritual purpose, the same region of northern Peru, at roughly the same period, produced strikingly naturalistic pottery intended for daily use, in which the entire pot was turned into an image of a human head. The Mochica potters experimented with different types of facial expressions until they were able to produce natural, spontaneous, and infectious ones, an example of which is shown in the *Laughing Man* (fig. 315), whose features are irradiated with a wide and happy grin, and whose eyes are almost closed in laughter.

The grandest productions of the short-lived Inca Empire, which governed an enormous Andean area from its capital at Cuzco in southern Peru, were its cities, built of masonry that has been sculptured to fit, stone against stone, so that literally (as is almost too widely known) the blade of a knife cannot be inserted between them. The city of Machu Picchu, most of whose buildings are datable to about 1500, is probably the most fantastic of all early American cities known to us (fig. 316). Its extensive ruins stand on a crag that towers among other crags about two thousand feet above a misty valley.

The culture of the Spanish Renaissance, however, jumping the Middle Ages, ended the indigenous styles of the American civilizations in the sixteenth century.

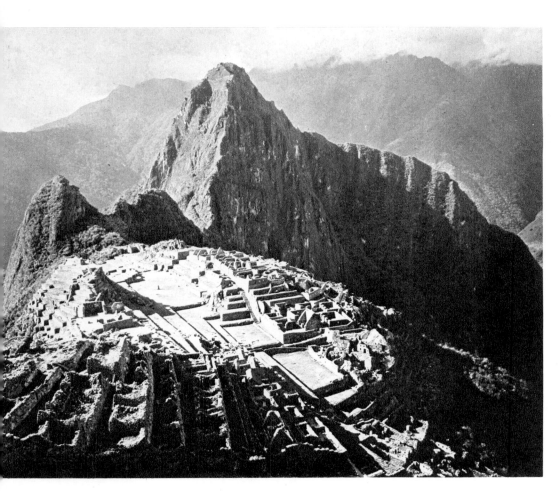

316. Machu Picchu (aerial view). c. 1500 A.D. Peru

TIME LINE

The numbers in italics refer to illustrations in the text.

	POLITICAL HISTORY	RELIGION, LITERATURE	SCIENCE, TECHNOLOGY
5000 B.C.			
4000	Sumerians settle in lower Mesopotamia Archaic (Thinite) period, Egypt: Narmer-Menes unites Upper and Lower Egypt (c. 3100); founds Memphis	Pictographic writing, Sumer (c. 3500)	Wheeled carts, Sumer (c. 3500–3000) Sailboats in Egypt (after c. 3500) Use of potter's wheel, Sumer (c. 3250)

3000	Protodynastic period, Sumer (c. 3000–2340)
	Dynasties I-II, Egypt (2955–2665)
	Old Kingdom, Egypt: Dynasties III-VI (2665–2155)
	III Dynasty, Egypt (2665–2570): Zoser
	IV Dynasty, Egypt (2570–2450): Cheops (r. 2545–
	  2520), Chephren (r. 2510–2485), Mycerinus
	  (r. 2485–2457)
	Akkadian period (c. 2340–2180); Sumerian city-states
	  united under dynasty of Sargon I of Akkad
	VI Dynasty, Egypt (2290–2155)
	Collapse of Akkadian Empire (c. 2230); invasion by
	  Guti
	First intermediary period, Egypt: Dynasties VII-X
	  (2155–2040)
	Neo-Sumerian period (2125–2025); Gudea of Lagash
	  wins control of much of former Akkadian Empire
	III Dynasty of Ur; Urnammu usurps monarchy (2111)
	Middle Kingdom, Egypt: Dynasties XI-XII
	  (c. 2040–1785)
	Fall of Ur; Isin-Larsa period (2025–1763)
		Hieroglyphic writing, Egypt (c. 3000)
		Cuneiform writing, Sumer (c. 2900)
		Divine kingship of the pharaoh
		Theocratic socialism in Sumer
			First bronze tools and weapons, Sumer
			Plows drawn by oxen

2000	Mentuhotep I, Mentuhotep III, Sesostris I
	  (r. 1971–1929)
	Cycladic colonies develop
	Elamite kingdom subdued by Babylonia (c. 1800)
	Hammurabi (r. 1792–1750) brings all of Mesopotamia
	  under Babylonian rule
	Hyksos invasions at close of XII Dynasty, Egypt;
	  Hyksos dominate Egypt during Second intermediary
	  period: Dynasties XIII–XVII (1786–1554)
		Code of Hammurabi (c. 1760)	Bronze tools and weapons in Egypt
			Canal from Nile to Red Sea
			Mathematics and astronomy flourish in Babylon under
			  Hammurabi
			Hittites employ iron tools and weapons
			Hyksos bring horses and wheeled vehicles to Egypt
			  (c. 1725)

1600	Minoan civilization flourishes (1600–1400) following
	  devastation of palaces
	Hittites conquer Babylonian kingdom; Tlabarna,
	  Hittite king, extends kingdom to the sea
	Southern Mesopotamia falls under rule of Kassites
	New Kingdom, Egypt: Dynasties XVIII-XX
	  (1554–1080); rebirth of Thebes and expulsion of
	  Hyksos; reunification and extension of kingdom		

1500	Shang dynasty, China (c. 1500–1100)
	XVIII Dynasty, Egypt (1554–1305): Amenhotep I
	  (r. 1529–1508), regency of Queen Hatshepsut
	  (r. 1488–1470), Amenhotep III (1403–1365)
	Mycenae flourishes; Crete destroyed
		Oldest Sanskrit literature (*Vedas*) in India
		  (c. 1500–1000)
			China develops silk production (c. 1500)

1400	Amenhotep IV/Akhenaten (r. 1403–1365) removes
	  capital to Tel el Amarna from Thebes
	Tutankhamen restores old religion and transfers capital
	  back to Thebes
	Horemheb (r. 1332–1305)
	XIX Dynasty, Egypt (c. 1319–1200): Seti I
	  (r. 1303–1290), Ramses II (r. 1290–1224)
		Monotheism of Akhenaten; worship of the disk of the
		  Sun, the Aten; temples of Amen-Ra closed
		  (c. 1360)	

1300	Assyrian invasions and conquest (1300–1000)		
1200	Dorians invade Greece; Ionian tribes resettle in Asia Minor; Mycenae destroyed Chou dynasty, China (1027–256)		

1000	Assyrian Empire (1000–612)
	Jerusalem capital of Palestine; David
	  (r. 1000–961); Solomon (r. 961–926)
		Phoenicians develop alphabetic writing (c. 1000);
		  Greeks adopt it (c. 750)
		Hebrews accept monotheism
		Ideographic writing in China
			Earliest iron tools and weapons in China

800	First Greek colonies established in southern Italy and
	  Sicily (Cumae, 754; Syracuse, 735; Taranto, 708)
	Founding of Rome (753)
	Sargon II, Assyr. king (r. 721–705)
		Sacred Hindu writings (c. 800–600)
		First Olympic games (776); Coroebus victor;
		  beginning of time-reckoning by Olympiads
		Great epic poem of Homer (fl.c. 750–700) collected
		  to form the *Iliad* and the *Odyssey* (750–650)	

700	Assyrian conquest of Lower Egypt and destruction of
	  Memphis
	Draconian laws, Athens
	Medes and Scythians storm Nineveh; collapse of
	  Assyria
	Nebuchadnezzar II, Babyl. king (r. 605–562), restores
	  order: Neo-Babylonian period (612–539)
		Zoroaster (born c. 660)	Coinage invented in Lydia (Asia Minor) (c. 700–650);
			  soon adopted by Greeks

600	Reforms of Solon as archon of Athens (594)
	Rome under Etruscan domination
	King Nebuchadnezzar II destroys Jerusalem (586);
	  carries Jews into exile: Babylonian Captivity
	Pisistratus, tyrant of Athens (r. 560–28); succeeded by
	  his sons, Hipparchus and Hippias
	Cyrus II the Great, Per. king (r. 559–529) conquers
	  Babylonia; Mesopotamia becomes province of
	  Persian Empire (539–331)
	Persia conquers Egypt; Egypt becomes satrapy of
	  Persian Empire (524–404)
	Athenians expel Hippias (510) and establish
	  democracy
	Kleisthenes promulgates his laws, a democratic
	  extension of the Solonic institution (509)
	Romans revolt against Etruscans, establish
	  republic (509)
		Guatama Buddha (563–483)
		Confucius (551–479)
		First tragedy performed at Athens by Thespis (534)
		Aeschylus (525–456)
			Thales of Miletos calculates solar eclipse (585);
			  Anaximander of Miletos designs geographic map
			  and celestial globe (c. 560)
			Pythagoras (fl. c. 520)

PAINTING	SCULPTURE	ARCHITECTURE	
	Painted beaker from Susa (117)		5000 B.C.
Tomb painting from Hierakonpolis (45)	Sculptured vase from Uruk (91) *Female Head* from Uruk (92) Palette of King Narmer (47, 48)	Ziggurat and the White Temple, Uruk (88, 89)	4000
Geese of Medum (colorplate 4) Preparatory drawing for scene from Tomb of Neferirkara (69)	Cosmetic palette from Abydos (46) *King Zoser* from Saqqara (55) *Hesira* from Saqqara (57) Statues from the Abu Temple at Tell Asmar (93) Royal harp from the Tomb of Queen Puabi at Ur (94, colorplate 11) *Prince Rahotep and His Wife Nofret* (64) He-Goat from Ur (95) *King Mycerinus Between Two Goddesses* (63) *Stele of King Eannatum (Stele of the Vultures)* from Lagash (96) *Bust of Prince Ankhhaf* from Giza (65) Great Sphinx at Giza (62) *King Chephren* from Giza (colorplate 4) Cycladic idol from Amorgos (118) *Kaaper* from Saqqara (66) *Seated Scribe* from Saqqara (67) Reliefs from the Tomb of Ti, Saqqara (68, colorplate 5) Relief of sculptors at work from Saqqara (56) *Head of an Akkadian Ruler* from Nineveh (97) *Stele of King Naram Sin* from Susa (98) Statues of Gudea from Lagash (99, 100)	Mastabas (49) Step pyramid and funerary complex of King Zoser by Imhotep, Saqqara (50–54) Pyramids and valley temples of Mycerinus, Chephren, and Cheops, Giza (58–61) Ziggurat, Ur (90)	3000
Mural decorations, Queen's Megaron, palace at Knossos (124)	*The Goddess Lilith* (101) *Lyre Player* from Keros (Cyclades) (119) Model of a troop of Nubian mercenaries from a tomb at Assiut (70) Beaked Kamares jug from Phaistos (120) *King Sesostris III* from Medamud (72) *Prince Sennuwy* from Kerma, Sudan (73) *Stele with the Code of Hammurabi* (102)	Hanging Gardens, Babylon Funerary temple of Mentuhotep III, Deir el Bahari (71)	2000
	Snake Goddess from the palace at Knossos (128) Dagger from the citadel of Mycenae (135) *Blind Harper*, relief from the Tomb of Patenemhab at Saqqara (81) *Harvester Vase* from Crete (129) Rhyton from the palace at Knossos (130)	Palace, Knossos (122, 123)	1600
Bull Dance and *Bird in a Landscape* from palace at Knossos (125, 126) Minoan frescoes from Thera (127, colorplate 12) Egyptian Books of the Dead, found at the Theban necropolis (87)	Octopus vase from Palaikastro, Crete (121) Masks from the royal tombs at Mycenae (134) *Three Deities* from Mycenae (137) *Vaphio Cups* from Laconia (136)	Funerary temple of Queen Hatshepsut by Senmut, Deir el Bahari (74, 75)	1500
Banquet scene and *Nebamun Hunting Birds* from the Tomb of Nebamun at Thebes (80, colorplate 8)	*Nefertiti* (colorplate 9) Pillar statue and relief of Akhenaten from the temple of Aten at Karnak (83, 84) Tomb of Tuthankhamen (85, colorplate 10) Reliefs from the Tomb of Horemheb, Saqqara (colorplate 7)	Hittite Lion Gate, Bogazköy, Turkey (103) Temple of Amen-Mut-Khonsu, Luxor (77, 78)	1400
Female head from Mycenae (138)	*Ramses II* from temple at Luxor (86)	Temple of Aten, Karnak (79) Citadel, Tiryns (131) Treasury of Atreus and the Lion Gate, citadel of Mycenae (132, 133)	1300
Tomb of Sen-nedjem at Deir el Medineh (82)			1200
	Alabaster reliefs from the palace of King Ashurnasirpal II, Nimrud (108, 109)		1000
Dipylon Amphora (140)	*Deer Nursing a Fawn* from Thebes (141) Colossal Olmec head from San Lorenzo, Tenochtitlán (309) Portrait of King Sargon II from Dur Sharrukin (107)	Citadel of King Sargon II, Dur Sharrukin (104–106) Heraion temple, near Argos (139)	800
Amphora from Eleusis (142) *Chigi Vase* by the Macmillan Painter (143)	Cinerary urn from Chiusi (239) Alabaster reliefs from the palace of King Ashurbanipal, Nineveh (110, 111) *Lady of Auxerre* (144)		700
François Vase (164) Kylix by Exekias (166) *Oriental Between Two Horses* on amphora by Psiax (165) Calyx-krater by Euphronios (colorplate 14)	*Kouros of Sounion* (145) *Medusa* from the Temple of Artemis, Corfu (156) *Calf Bearer* from the Acropolis, Athens (147) *Hera* from Samos (149) Peplos Kore from Athens (150) *Battle of Gods and Giants* from the Treasury of the Siphnians, Delphi (158) Stele of Aristion by Aristokles (148) *Anavyssos Kouros* (146) *La Delicata* from the Acropolis, Athens (colorplate 13) Sarcophagus from Cerveteri (240) *Apollo of Veii* (colorplate 24)	Temple of Artemis, Corfu (155) Ziggurat of Nebuchadnezzar (Tower of Babel), Babylon Ishtar Gate from Babylon (112) "Basilica" (Temple of Hera), Paestum (154) Treasury of the Siphnians, Delphi (157)	600

TIME LINE

The numbers in italics refer to illustrations in the text.

	POLITICAL HISTORY	RELIGION, LITERATURE	SCIENCE, TECHNOLOGY
500	Persian Wars (499–478); Miletos destroyed by Persians (494); Battle of Marathon (490) Persians destroy much of Athens (480); Battle of Salamis (480); Battle of Plataea (479) Alliance of the Delian League (479–461) Periclean Age in Athens (c. 460–429)	Sophocles (496–406) Euripides (d. 406) Performance of *The Persians* by Aeschylus Socrates (469–399) *Oresteia* by Aeschylus (458)	Hippocrates (b.469) Travels of Herodotos (c. 460–440)
450	Pericles concludes Thirty Year Peace with Sparta (446) Peloponnesian War (431–404) Plague in Athens (430–28); death of Pericles (429) Oligarchic revolution in Athens (411) Defeat of Athens by Sparta; tyranny of the Thirty in Athens (404–403)	The "Sophist" Protagoras of Abdera in Athens for the first time (444) *Antigone* by Sophocles (440) Plato (427–347); founds Academy (386)	
400	Trial and death of Socrates (399) Gauls sack Rome (387) Athenian League (378–77) Rome wars with neighboring peoples (362–345); First Samnite War (343–341)	Aristotle (384–322)	
350	Philip II, Macedon king (r. 359–336), defeats allied Greeks at the Battle of Chaeronea (338) Panhellenic League of Corinth (337) Alexander the Great, Macedon king (r. 336–23), occupies Egypt (333) and founds Alexandria; Battle of Issus (333); Battle of Arbela (331); fall of Persian Empire Second Samnite War (326–304) Death of Alexander the Great (323); five monarchies develop out of his empire: Macedonia (Antigonids), Egypt (Ptolemies), Syria (Selucids), Bithynia, and Pergamon (Attalids)	Epicurus (341–270) Zeno (336–264) Lycurgus has the statues of the three great tragic poets set up in the newly erected theater of Dionysos at Athens (330)	
300	Roman colony founded at Ostia (c. 300) Third Samnite War (298–291) Roman colonies founded at Cosa and Paestum (273) Asoka, Indian king (r. 272–232) Rome defeats Carthage in First Punic War (264–241); Sicily becomes Roman province (241) Attalus I, Pergamon king (r. 241–197) Occupation and colonization of Sardinia and Corsica begins (238); made provinces (227) Great Wall of China built (221–210) Second Punic War (218–202); Hannibal invades Italy, later retreats to Africa (c. 205) Scipio Africanus expels the Carthaginians from Spain, invades Africa; wins the Battle of Zama (c. 202); Rome acquires Spain (201) Han dynasty, China (202 B.C.–A.D. 220)	Manetho, Egyptian priest (c. 280), writes history of Egypt	Theophrastos of Athens, botanist (fl. c. 300) Euclid (fl. c. 300–280) Archimedes (287–212) Eratosthenes of Cyrene measures the globe (c. 240)
200	Roman victory over Perseus of Macedonia at Pydna (168); vast quantities of Greek sculpture brought to Rome in triumph	Carneades of Cyrene, head of Academy, visits Rome with a delegation of Greek philosophers (156)	Invention of paper, China
150	Third Punic War (149–146) ends in the destruction of Carthage Rome destroys Corinth; more Greek art treasures brought to Rome; Rome extends rule over the Diodachi kingdoms: Macedonia (148), Pergamon (133), Bithynia (74), Syria (63), and Egypt (30)		
100	Civil war between Sulla and Marius (88–82) Sack of Athens by Rome (86) Sulla becomes dictator (82–79) Cicero is consul (63) Pompey victorious in Asia (61) First Triumvirate (Pompey, Caesar, Crassus) (60) Caesar is consul (59) Caesar's command in Gaul (58–57)	Golden Age of Roman literature: Cicero (106–43), Catullus (84?–54), Virgil (70–19), Horace (65–8), Ovid (43 B.C.–A.D. 17?) Seneca (54 B.C.?–A.D. 39)	Earliest water mills
50	Caesar crosses the Rubicon and marches on Rome (49); named dictator for ten years (46); triumph of Caesar (45); assassinated March 15 (44) Second Triumvirate (Mark Antony, Lepidus, Octavius) (43) Pact of Brindisi (40): Mark Antony receives command of Orient, Octavius of Occident Battle of Actium (31); death of Mark Antony and Cleopatra Octavius continues as consul (31–27); becomes Roman Emperor as Augustus Caesar (27 B.C.–A.D. 14)	Vitruvius completes his ten books on architecture, *De Architectura*	
A.D.1	Death of Augustus (14) Claudius, RE (r. 41–54)	Crucifixion of Jesus Christ (c. 30)	Pliny the Elder, *Natural History* Invention of glassblowing

TIME LINE

The numbers in italics refer to illustrations in the text.

	POLITICAL HISTORY	RELIGION, LITERATURE	SCIENCE, TECHNOLOGY

A.D. 50	Nero, RE (r. 54–68)
	Flavian dynasty (69–96): Vespasian, RE (r. 69–79);
	  Titus, RE (r. 79–81); Domitian RE (r. 81–96)
	Nerva, RE (r. 96–98)
	Trajan, RE (r. 98–117); dies in Sicily (117)
		Paul (died c. 65) spreads Christianity to Asia Minor
		  and Greece
		Tacitus (55?–after A.D. 117)	

100	Hadrian, RE (r. 117–138) Antoninus Pius, RE (r. 138–161)		
150	Marcus Aurelius, RE (r. 161–180) Lucius Verus, Roman coemperor (r. 161–169) Commodus, son of M. Aurelius, RE (r. 180–192) Septimius Severus, RE (r. 193–211); born in Leptis Magna		Ptolemy, astronomer (d. 160)
200	Caracalla, RE (r. 211–217) Heliogabalus, RE (r. 218–222) Alexander Severus, RE (r. 222–235) Gordianus III, RE (r. 238–244) Philip the Arab, RE (r. 244–249) Diocletian, RE (r. 284–305) The Tetrarchy: fourfold division of power in Roman Empire (293)		Galen, physician and anatomist (d. 201)

TIME LINE

The numbers in italics refer to illustrations in the text.

	PAINTING	SCULPTURE	ARCHITECTURE

A.D. 50	Wall paintings in the house of M. Lucretius Fronto,
	  Pompeii *(272)*
	Architectural and landscape wall paintings from
	  Herculaneum *(colorplate 31)*
	Sacred Landscape from Pompeii *(273)*
	Portrait of Menander from the House of Menander,
	  Pompeii *(374)*
	Landscape with Figures from an Augustan house,
	  Rome *(274)*
		Portrait of Vespasian (270)
		Portrait of a Lady (271)
		Triumph of Titus and *Spoils from the Temple at
		  Jerusalem* from the Arch of Titus, Rome *(268, 269,
		  colorplate 30)*
			Golden House of Nero, Rome
			Porta Maggiore, Rome *(265)*
			Insulae, Ostia *(263)*
			Colosseum, Rome *(266, 267)*
			Flavian Palace, Rome
			Arch of Titus, Rome *(colorplate 30)*

100	Portrait of a Greco-Roman Egyptian from El Faiyûm
	  (colorplate 32)
		Reliefs on Column of Trajan, Rome *(277, 278)*
		Medallions for Hadrianic monument from the Arch of
		  Constantine *(281)*
		Portrait of Antinoüs (Antinoüs of Delphi) (282)
			Basilica Ulpia, Rome *(276)*
			Market of Trajan, Rome *(279)*
			Forum of Trajan by Apollodorus, Rome *(275)*
			Arch of Trajan, Benevento *(280)*
			Pantheon, Rome *(283–285)*
			Hadrian's Villa, Tivoli *(286, 287)*

150		Relief from the Column of Antoninus Pius, Rome *(288)* *Equestrian Statue of Marcus Aurelius,* Rome *(289)* *Commodus as Hercules (292)*	Arch of Trajan and colonnaded street, Timgad *(290)* Theater, Sabratha *(291)*
200	*Family of Vunnerius Keramus (297)*	Portrait of Caracalla *(293)* *The Genius of the Senate Pointing to Gordianus III* from a sarcophagus from Acilia *(294)* *Philip the Arab (295)* *Ludovisi Battle Sarcophagus (296)*	Baths of Caracalla, Rome *(298, 299)* Temple of Venus, Baalbek *(300)* Palace of Diocletian, Split, Yugoslavia *(303–305)*

300	*Exploits of Hercules,* mosaics in imperial villa at
	  Piazza Armerina, Sicily *(colorplate 34)*
		The Tetrarchs (colorplate 33)
		Constantine the Great (302)
			Basilica of Maxentius and Constantine,
			  Rome *(306, 307)*
			Arch of Constantine, Rome *(301)*

500		*Raimondi Monolith* from Chavín de Huántar,
		  Peru *(314)*
		Laughing Man, Mochica vessel from northern
		  Peru *(315)*
			Avenue of temples, Teotihuacán *(308)*
			Mayan ball court, Copán *(310)*

700		Lintel relief from a Mayan house at Yaxchilán *(313)*	
900			
1000			Nunnery, Uxmal, Yucatan *(311)*
1500			Caracol, Chichén Itzá, Yucatan *(312)* Machu Picchu, Peru *(316)*

PART THREE

The Middle Ages

Two overriding circumstances separated the Middle Ages from the ancient world. The first was the gradual dissolution of the Roman Empire into a wide variety of successor states. Some of these retained or revived imperial pretensions, while others frankly proclaimed their ethnic basis; however, all achieved only limited territorial jurisdiction, thus preparing the way for the modern nation-state. The second was the dominance of two religions with universal claims, first Christianity and then, in competition with it, Islam. Each religion demanded total allegiance on the part of the worshiper, sometimes to the point of active judicial and military hostility to other faiths—as exemplified in religious executions and holy wars. Each ordered the worshiper's ethical standards and daily life. In ultimate decisions each valued revelation above unaided reason, that supreme goal of ancient thinkers. Each prepared the worshiper in detail for an afterlife.

Both circumstances were to have profound consequences for art. The first resulted in a far greater repertory of artistic forms, corresponding to the necessities of individual states and regions, than was possible even under the large tolerance of the Roman Empire. The second demanded a religious architecture that could handle ceremonially vast masses of people, and whose interior spaces, therefore, tended to determine the character and appearance of their external forms. Equally important, the emphasis of religion on an otherworldly goal tended to weaken interest in naturalistic representation of the spaces and objects of this world, and it prohibited outright the depiction of the nude human body save when required by a specific religious or historical subject. As an inevitable corollary, schemata inherited from one generation to the next were inexorably substituted for the active pursuit of visual reality which, in one form or another, had occupied the attention of Mediterranean artists for more than three millennia.

At the same time the emphasis on faith and the consequent transcendence accorded to the inner life opened up for artistic exploration rich areas of human experience hitherto peripheral to the visually oriented art of the Helleno-Roman tradition. Formalized shapes, patterns, and color relationships, whether based on nature or wholly abstract, had been permitted only an ornamental role in ancient art. In the Middle Ages such elements took on extreme importance as vehicles for feeling and imagination. In certain aspects of Celtic and Islamic art, in fact (see figs. 349, 353), abstraction entirely replaces elements derived from observation. Paradoxically enough, in the service of otherworldly religions, engineering science took enormous strides in the Middle Ages. Such brilliant achievements as the lofty domes on pendentives, which are the crowning feature of Byzantine churches (see figs. 340, 434); the interlacing arches, which opened up new possibilities for mosques (see colorplate 46); and the soaring ribbed vaults sustained by external buttressing, which roof Gothic cathedrals (see figs. 459, 470), were feats beyond the imaginings of Roman architects.

The dividing line for both the political and the religious determinants fell within the reign of the emperor Constantine. The breakup of the Empire was heralded by his removal of the capital from Italy (where Milan had for decades replaced Rome as the chief administrative center) to Byzantium on the shores of the Bosporus, which he rebuilt and renamed Constantinople. The direct result of this move was a new and eventually permanent division of the Empire under Constantine's successors along more or less the same lines as the tetrarchy. The Eastern Roman (or Byzantine) Empire survived for more than a thousand years, although constantly diminished by foreign inroads, until Constantinople was conquered by the Turks in 1453. The Western Roman Empire was repeatedly invaded during the fifth century by Germanic tribes, who twice succeeded in sacking Rome. These tribes had already eaten away at the outlying provinces, and had infiltrated the very administration of the Empire; many had become Christianized. The deposition in 476 of the last Western Roman emperor, Romulus Augustulus, by the Gothic king Odoacer merely gave formal expression to what had long been a fact, the takeover by Germanic tribes of the whole of the Western Empire as a series of separate kingdoms.

Possibly the religious policy of Constantine, beginning with his promulgation of the Edict of Milan in 313 along with his coemperor Licinius, would have been inevitable no matter who sat on the throne. The number of Christians in all parts of the Empire, even in the imperial administration and in the imperial family, had become too great either to persecute or to ignore. Constantine's later activities as sole emperor—for example, his presiding role at the Council of Nicaea in 325—reinforced the new importance of the Christian religion. His transfer of the capital to the most heavily Christianized region of the Empire made the supremacy of Christianity all but inevitable.

It is sometimes maintained that Early Christian art and Byzantine art are in reality continuations of tendencies that had begun under the later pagan emperors and that they should be treated, therefore, as a final phase of ancient art. In a sense, of course, any new development can be interpreted as an outgrowth of what went before it. But there is a fundamental change between the conceptions of the human figure and surrounding space—and indeed the very nature and purpose of architecture, sculpture, and painting—prevalent in Greek and Roman art and those strongly evident in the new art of Christianity. This change was felt by the early Christians themselves, who used pagan buildings as quarries for materials and architectural elements, and destroyed pagan statues and paintings as idolatrous, without regard for their artistic value. The attitude of the early Christians toward the past contrasts strongly with that of the Romans, who protected their own earlier buildings wherever possible and cherished the statues and paintings of the Greeks.

The break between ancient and Byzantine art was felt by the Italians of the Renaissance; an anonymous Italian writer of the sixteenth century, whose ideas on the subject were repeated by Vasari, the eminent painter, architect, and writer on art (see pages 368, 406), spoke of the "rude manner of the Greeks" (meaning the Byzantines) as something against which the Italians, beginning with Giotto, had to rebel in order to recreate a Classical style based directly on ancient art. The characterization of most medieval art as "Gothic," meaning that it was fit only for barbarians, reached its height in the seventeenth and eighteenth centuries when the current of Neoclassicism was extremely strong. Early Christian art and Byzantine art, viewed as "decadent," shared in the general condemnation.

Rather than forcing Early Christian art and Byzantine art into the ancient period, it would be more significant for us to look at the surprising developments of third-century pagan art as already partly medieval. In any event the new appreciation of both the antinaturalistic art of the late Empire and that of the Middle Ages is an intellectual reconquest, dating from the Romantic period of the later eighteenth century and strongly reinforced in modern times. Twentieth-century artistic developments, in particular Expressionism and the various abstract tendencies (see Vol. 2, Part Six, Chapters 6 and 10), have encouraged a basic reevaluation of Early Christian art and Byzantine art—for that matter, medieval art in general—with whose principles of form and expression many contemporary artists and critics feel a real kinship.

1

Early Christian and Early Byzantine Art

The earliest Christians had no need for art of any sort. Jesus himself, and after him the Apostles, preached and taught in houses, on hillsides, from ships, in streets and squares, and even in the Temple. Persecutions of Christians were by no means as continuous and thorough as is popularly supposed. Between persecutions Christianity flourished and spread in its own quiet way. The new religion had its competitors, of course, among the mystery cults which had abounded even in the days of the Roman Republic—the religions of Dionysos, Isis, Cybele, Attis, and Mithras were the most important. But it would be a mistake to regard early Christianity as in any way comparable to these cults. True, they all promised salvation in an afterlife through the intervention of a particular divinity. But, unlike Christianity, they either culminated in orgiastic rites or included sanguinary ceremonies. For example, votaries of Mithras, the god of the favorite mystery cult of the Roman soldiery, lay on couches surrounding an altar before which a live bull was sacrificed, and then drank his warm blood.

Christianity was nonviolent in essence. Alone save Judaism among the religions of the Roman Empire, it professed a system of ethics that governed the entire behavior of the worshiper in all aspects of daily life, and alone save Judaism it possessed written authority embodied in a rich library of Scriptures, whose authenticity was generally accepted despite disagreement on specific elements and interpretations. And even Judaism, always an ethnic religion, could not vie with the universal claims of Christianity. Thus, Christianity held not only a promise of individual salvation, but it also rapidly became a corporate religion, which created a counter-culture inside the Roman state. Enthusiasts of the mystery cults had no objection to participating in the largely perfunctory aspects of Roman state religion, which included burning incense before the statue of the divine emperor. To the Christian such rites were

anathema, and thus the very strength and pervasiveness of the Christian faith were interpreted as threats to the stability of the Empire. A tribute to the extraordinary success of early Christianity is that the two most systematic persecutions, those of Decius in 249–51 and Diocletian in 303–5, came so shortly before the Edict of Milan in 313, which marked, if not the final triumph of the new religion, at least its liberation from fear.

During the later first and second centuries, Christian communities remained small, and believers worshiped in private houses. The basic ceremony, doubtless simple, was the communal meal, celebrating the Last Supper, which began with the breaking of bread and concluded with the drinking of wine, in ritual perpetuation of Christ's sacrifice. The ceremony included prayers, the reading of passages from the Gospels and the Epistles, discourses on the part of successors to the Apostles, and sometimes "speaking with tongues," which is today so mysterious an aspect of early Christianity. A dining room was essential, and the early Christians used the Roman triclinium (a dining room with a three-part couch extending around three sides of a table). In the crowded cities of the Eastern Empire, the triclinium was often located on an upper floor—the "upper room" mentioned in the Gospels and in Acts. Christianity was at first a religion chiefly for the lower classes, whom it sought to wean from the bloody spectacles of the arenas. Often, therefore, religious meetings took place in humble apartments in tenements, such as the insulae of Rome and Ostia (see fig. 263). By the third century the structure of the Mass had become clear; it was presided over by *episkopoi* (bishops; literally, overseers), whose qualifications are listed in 1 Tim. 3. A clear distinction was maintained between the Liturgy of the Catechumens, consisting of the reading of Epistles, Gospels, prayers, and hymns (today the Ordinary and Proper of the Mass), which those under instruction could attend, and the

Liturgy of the Faithful, the actual Eucharist or sacrifice of bread and wine (today the Canon of the Mass), to which only baptized Christians were admitted. The catechumens were required to leave before the Eucharist, and could only hear but not see the Liturgy from an adjoining room. No altar was used, only a table brought in for the Eucharist and another table to receive offerings, usually in kind.

A special sort of house devoted exclusively to the observance of the Eucharist—a *domus ecclesiae* (house of the church, from which the Italian *duomo* and the German *Dom*, both words for cathedral, were derived) —became the first type of church building. The earliest known, dating from just before 231, was found at Dura-Europos in Syria. It is an ordinary Greek peristyle house, somewhat remodeled for Christian use, with a separate room for the catechumens, a library, and a vestry. It could not have accommodated a congregation of more than sixty, and can scarcely be said to have had any pronounced architectural character; if it contained works of art, they have perished. This building had a dais for a bishop's chair (*cathedra* in Greek), and thus it can be regarded as a cathedral. The baptistery at Dura-Europos, however, did contain very modest wall paintings. The earliest Christian churches, like early synagogues, generally were inconspicuous; their sites were selected in popular quarters near the city walls. There is, however, evidence for the erection of one substantial Christian meeting hall in Rome just before the issuance of the Edict of Milan. The existence of many others, in cities throughout the Empire before the persecution of Diocletian, is mentioned by Eusebius of Caesarea, fourth-century bishop and historian.

A second kind of structure, the martyrium, was built over a martyr's grave or employed as a cenotaph to commemorate a martyr whose body was interred elsewhere. The earliest such structure known, dating from around A.D. 200, is a simple aedicula recently excavated under Saint Peter's in Rome. Inscriptions make it clear that at that time the Christians believed it was the tomb of Peter.

The early Christians also dug catacombs. Since Christian belief in the resurrection of the body prohibited cremation, the Christians could not use the *columbaria* (dovecotes) cemeteries of lower-class Roman burial societies, where urns were kept in little niches, many tiers high. Also the Christians felt the necessity of segregation from pagan burials. Like other Roman citizens, they could and did acquire property—as, for instance, their church buildings—and they bought land outside many cities, choosing sites where it was possible to excavate passages in the rock. Often these catacombs took advantage of local quarries as starting points. From these, tunnels were dug systematically according to plans; to conserve space, the catacombs were sometimes excavated four or five levels deep. Superimposed niches for sarcophagi were hollowed out, and from time to time small chapels for funeral feasts and for commemorative services.

The earliest known works of Christian figurative art have been found in these chapels. These simple paintings on plaster, spread over the rock surface, were executed by modest artisans working by lamplight in the dark, dank, and probably odoriferous surroundings. Most of these paintings were on ceilings, a position that required the painter to work with his head tilted. One of the earliest, on the underside of an arch in the Catacomb of Saint Priscilla, Rome (fig. 317), dates from the time of the Antonine emperors in the late second century. Four men and

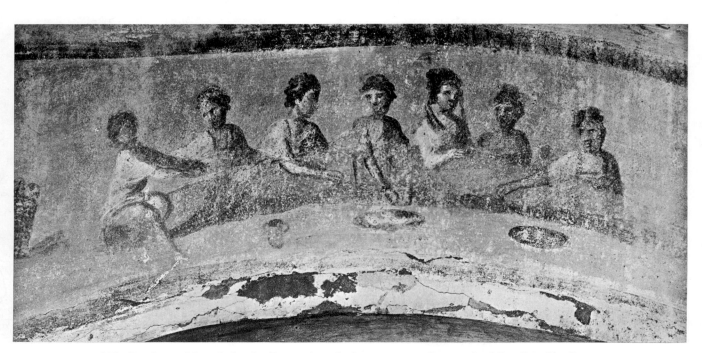

317. *Breaking of Bread* (detail). Fresco. Late 2nd century A.D. Catacomb of Sta. Priscilla, Rome

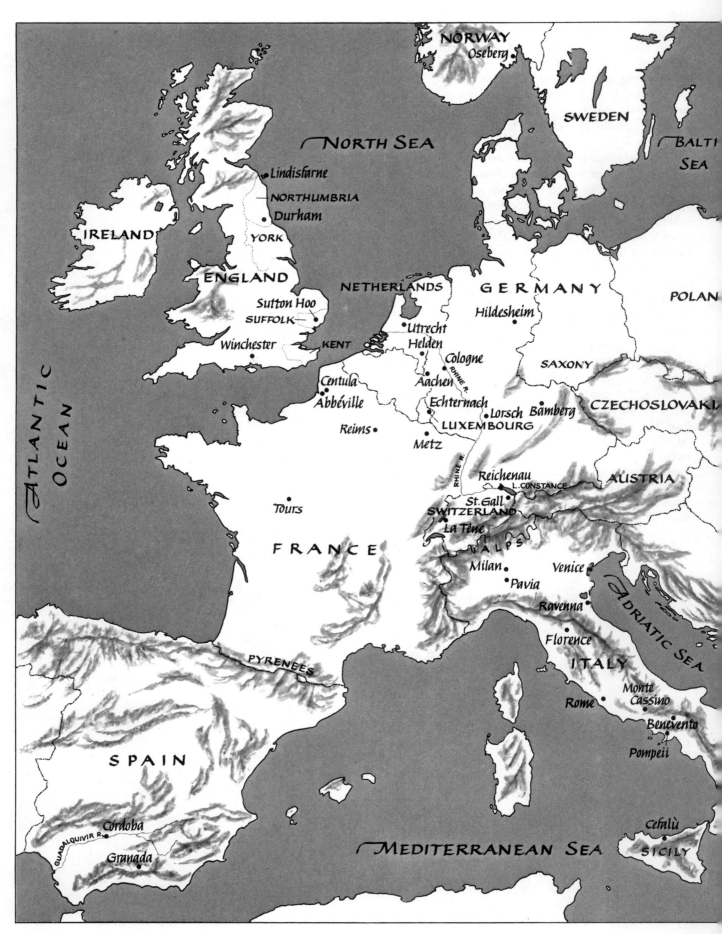

NORWAY

Oseberg

SWEDEN

BALTIC
SEA

NORTH SEA

POLAND

Lindisfarne

NORTHUMBRIA

Durham

YORK

IRELAND

ENGLAND

NETHERLANDS

GERMANY

Hildesheim

Sutton Hoo

SUFFOLK

Utrecht

Helden

Cologne

SAXONY

Winchester

KENT

Aachen

Echternach

Bamberg

CZECHOSLOVAKIA

Centula

Lorsch

Abbéville

LUXEMBOURG

Metz

Reims

RHINE R.

Reichenau

AUSTRIA

L. CONSTANCE

St. Gall

SWITZERLAND

RHINE R.

Tours

La Tène

ALPS

FRANCE

Milan

Venice

Pavia

ADRIATIC SEA

Ravenna

ATLANTIC OCEAN

Florence

ITALY

PYRENEES

Monte
Cassino

Rome

Benevento

SPAIN

Pompeii

Córdoba

Cefalù

GUADALQUIVIR R.

SICILY

Granada

MEDITERRANEAN SEA

MAP 12. *Europe*

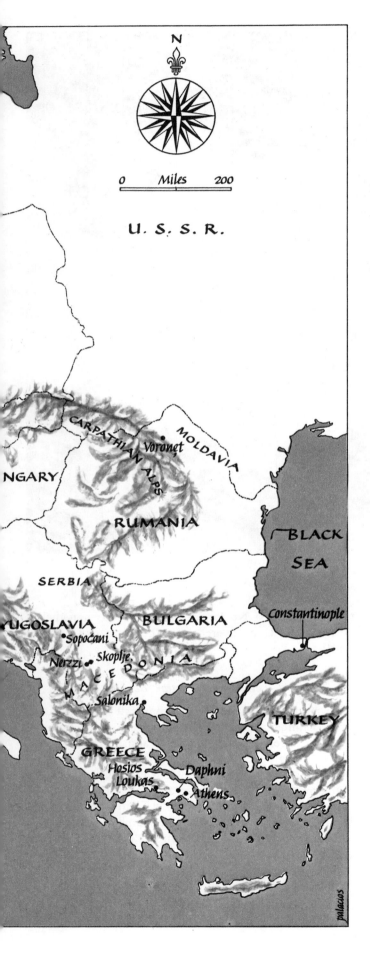

three women are seated—they no longer recline—around a table on which only plates of bread and a small pitcher are visible. The central figure is shown in the act of breaking the bread, which represents the culminating moment of the Eucharistic sacrifice. The style is a sketchy version of Roman illusionism, but it is adequate to convey deep excitement, transmitted from face to face by earnest glances that reveal the exaltation of the participants.

A somewhat less intense ceiling fresco (fig. 318), probably painted in the early fourth century, in the Catacomb of Saints Peter and Marcellinus, Rome, is interesting chiefly from the symbolic standpoint. The circular design, like a miniature Pantheon dome, was doubtless intended to suggest the Dome of Heaven. Four semicircles are arranged about the central circle, and are united by bands forming a Cross to show that this universal Christian symbol both embraces and reveals Heaven itself. In the central medallion, flanked by resting sheep, is the figure repeated countless times in Early Christian paintings and sarcophagus sculpture, the Good Shepherd. These are the earliest images of Christ and, of course, were not intended to inform us about his actual appearance (about which we know nothing). The youthful, beardless shepherd, with a lamb over his shoulder, is a *symbol* of Christ, who said, "I am the good shepherd: the good shepherd giveth his life for the sheep" (John 10:11). One semicircle is lost, but the remaining three tell in simple imagery the story of Jonah, tossed from his ship at the left, swallowed by the whale at the right, and at the bottom reclining below the gourd vine. Here again we are instructed by Christ's own words, "and there shall no sign be given to it, but the sign of the prophet Jonas: For as Jonas was three days and three nights in the whale's belly; so shall the Son of man be three days and three nights in the heart of the earth" (Matt. 12: 39–40). Thus, as always in Christian thought, the Old Testament is interpreted in the light of the New; in the apparent death and miraculous deliverance of Jonah are prefigured the Crucifixion and Resurrection of Christ, and through faith in him, the salvation of the true believer. The "sign of the prophet Jonas" is the Cross, between whose bars stand figures in what is known as the orant pose, the ordinary arms-wide gesture of prayer in early Christian times, still used by the celebrant at many moments in the Mass.

The only biblical wall paintings of truly monumental character that have come down to us from this early period are, however, not Christian but Jewish; they form a remarkable series and originally decorated the entire interior of a synagogue at Dura-Europos. However provincial in execution, these paintings are impressive in the solemn directness with which they set forth the biblical narratives. In *Haman and Mordecai* (fig. 319) these two figures move against a flat background with no indication of groundline, reminding us of the floating figures on the base of the Column of Antoninus Pius (see fig. 288). Mordecai stands in a Roman speaking pose, his

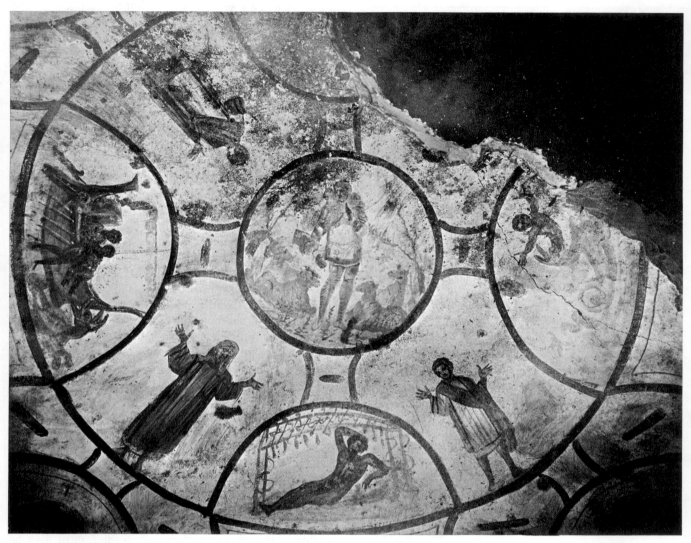

318. *The Good Shepherd.* Ceiling fresco. Early 4th century A.D. Catacomb of SS. Pietro e Marcellino. Rome

right arm outstretched and his body enveloped in the folds of a cloak that strongly recall those of a toga. We can only surmise that Christian counterparts to this large-scale Jewish painting existed; none have yet been found.

THE AGE OF CONSTANTINE

The Edict of Milan brought about immediate and far-reaching transformations in the life of the Church through the new relationship between church and state it established. Given the strong interest and active role of Constantine, Christianity became to all intents and purposes an official religion, inheriting the splendors of the dethroned Roman gods. Although no complete colossal statue of the emperor is still preserved, the solemn *Colossus of Barletta* (fig. 320), a bronze statue probably representing one of his successors in the fifth or sixth century, clearly indicates the majestic and superhuman authority accorded to the person of the emperor in early

Christian times. No longer divine, he was nonetheless sacred—the Unconquered Sun, the Vicar of Christ on earth.

The Early Christian Basilica

The newly official religion, encouraged as an effective arm of imperial administration, soon took on imperial magnificence. It could no longer aim at small and intimate congregations bound together by no other ties than those of Christian love. Huge crowds of worshipers had now to be accommodated and given access to sacred places and to the sacraments of the Church. Enclosed and roofed spaces were needed in great numbers. Constantine donated, probably in 313, the imperial Lateran Palace to the bishop of Rome, and built next to it, construction probably beginning the same year, the Cathedral of Rome, San Giovanni in Laterano. In rapid succession and under direct imperial patronage, scores of churches rose throughout Rome and other great cities of the Empire, especially Milan and Constantinople, and at sacred sites in the Holy Land.

A model for these new buildings was needed. Although the Christians had no compunction about utilizing architectural elements taken from pagan structures, the temples themselves, even when not too small for the crowds of worshipers, were manifestly unsuitable; their very sites were regarded with abhorrence. The obvious solution was the Roman basilica, or meeting hall, which existed in every inhabited Roman center. There was no strict uniformity of plan for these meeting halls. It can only be said that the Basilica of Maxentius and Constantine (see fig. 306), with its groin-vaulted nave and adjacent exedrae, was wholly unique, and that the Basilica Ulpia (see fig. 276) was a superbasilica, unmatched in size and splendor by any other. Many Roman basilicas, some quite large ones, were simple halls with no side aisles; most were entered along one side, and had apses at either end. The apse soon proved convenient for the installation of the clergy and the enthronement of the bishop. The early portable communion table was replaced by a fixed altar, which had to be visible from a considerable distance and accessible to all worshipers at Communion. The long row of columns on either side of the nave played a double role in dramatizing the approach of the faithful to the altar and in segregating, by means of curtains hung between the columns, the catechumens from those who could witness the Mass of the Faithful.

The colonnades characteristically supported a lofty wall pierced by a clerestory. The roof was usually of an open timber construction, as was the case in so many ancient buildings. The large number of churches begun in the reign of Constantine required columns in great numbers and at great speed. It may be fairly doubted whether, in Constantinian Rome, it was possible either to produce so many or to order them from other regions. However, temples and other monuments of the Roman past offered an inexhaustible supply. Borrowed columns were thus uncritically installed in the new basilicas, with little or no regard for consistency of style, color, or size. Granite and marble columns, Corinthian and Ionic capitals were placed side by side; capitals were sometimes set on columns they did not fit.

Saint Peter's was the largest and grandest of the Constantinian basilicas, in fact the largest church building in all Christendom (fig. 321). It differed from most other basilicas not only in its stupendous size—an inner length of 368 feet—but also in its very nature as a combined basilica and martyrium. The apse enshrined the tomb of Peter under a marble canopy supported by

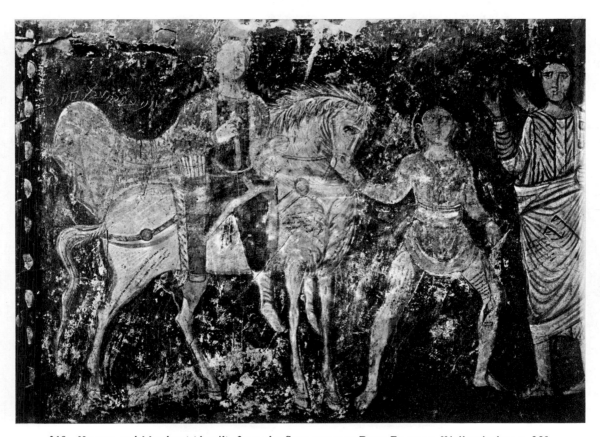

319. *Haman and Mordecai* (detail), from the Synagogue at Dura-Europos. Wall painting. c. 250 A.D. National Museum, Damascus, Syria

four spiral columns (later used by Bernini as a model for his colossal construction in the seventeenth century; see Vol. 2, fig. 238). In order to accommodate the crowds of visitors to the tomb, a large hall—the transept—was erected at right angles to the nave between the nave and the apse (fig. 322). Before the transept came the so-called triumphal arch, a common feature of Early Christian basilicas. The altar, at the head of the nave, was probably movable. The columns of the basilica were either Corinthian or Composite, and of many different materials including green marble, yellow marble, red granite, and gray granite. They were closely spaced, and supported a continuous, straight entablature. As in the Basilica Ulpia, Saint Peter's had double side aisles; the colonnade separating them supported arches. The building was not completed when Constantine died in 337 nor for some time thereafter. It is not known what wall

decorations were originally planned; the frescoes covering the nave walls between the colonnade and the clerestory were painted in the fifth century.

Initially, there was certainly no suggestion that the transept plan symbolized the Cross, as it did in later times. The plan of Santa Sabina, erected in Rome from 422–32 (fig. 323), is more typical of Early Christian churches. It was built without a transept so that the triumphal arch embraced the apse directly. Throughout the early Christian period, the apse was used only by the clergy, and often it contained a throne for the bishop. Arches were substituted for straight entablatures, as at Santa Sabina, in the course of the fifth century. None of the Constantinian basilicas survive in their original state. Saint Peter's, in fact, was demolished section by section in the Renaissance, to be replaced by a new building (see Vol. 2, figs. 234, 235). The beautifully restored interior of

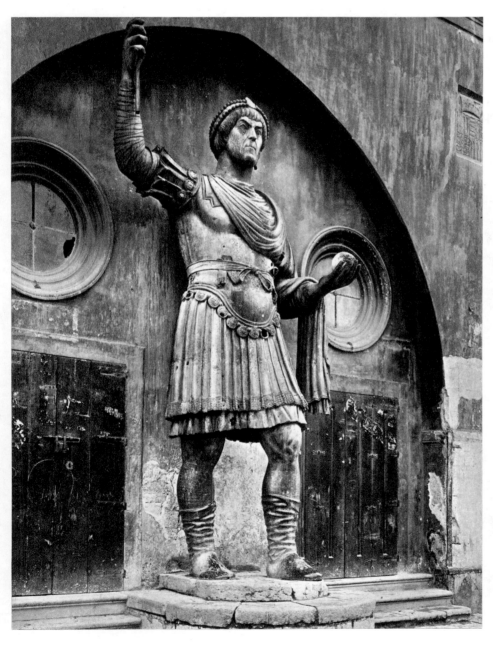

320. *Colossus of Barletta.* c. 5th or 6th century A.D. Bronze, height of original part (head to knee) 11'7¾". Barletta. Italy

Santa Sabina is almost the only one that still conveys the appearance of an Early Christian basilica in Rome, but it is unusual in having carefully matched Corinthian columns—purloined as usual.

All Early Christian buildings were devoid of external decoration, presenting unrelieved brick walls of the utmost simplicity (see figs. 328, 333). The pilgrim to Saint Peter's, for example, arrived at the blank, outer wall of an atrium—in reality a large peristyle court—then proceeded to the narthex or vestibule, and finally emerged into the richly colored nave with its splendid columns and bright frescoes, scores of hanging lamps, jeweled altar cloth, gold and silver vessels of the Mass, and clergy in gorgeous vestments—a far cry from the simplicity of the first centuries of Christianity. The processional principle on which the church was laid out has often been compared with the basic plan of the Egyptian temple, but it should be remembered that a similar processional principle governed the alignment of spaces and structures in the Roman forum as well, especially that of Trajan (see fig. 275).

The Central Plan

A considerable number of variations could occur in the basilican plan, depending on the purpose of the building and on local traditions and requirements. An entirely different arrangement, the circular plan, was also widely used (fig. 324). A handsome early example is the Church of Santa Costanza, built in Rome about 350 to flank the now-destroyed Basilica of Sant'Agnese (fig. 325). Circular churches, manifestly unsuitable for the celebration of Mass before large congregations, were almost always erected as martyria; this one was destined to contain the tomb of Princess Constantia, daughter of Constantine.

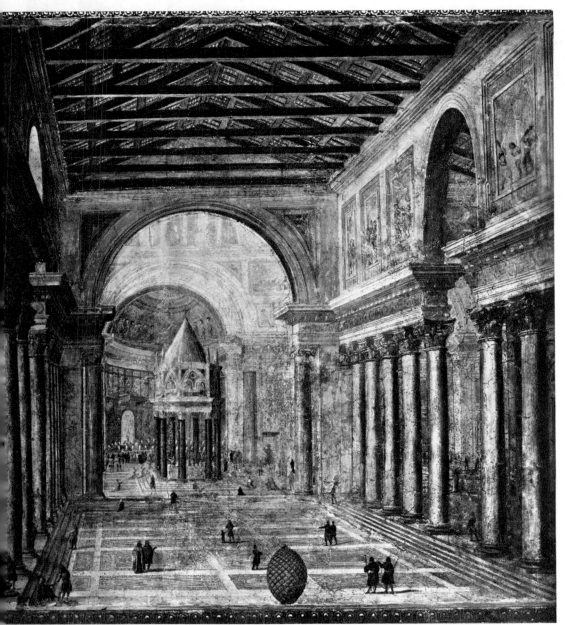

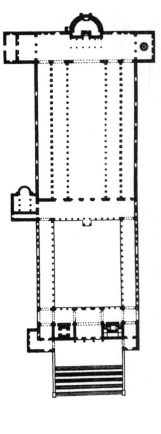

321. *Old St. Peter's, Rome.* Fresco. 16th century. S. Martino ai Monti, Rome

322. Plan of Old St. Peter's. First half 4th century A.D.

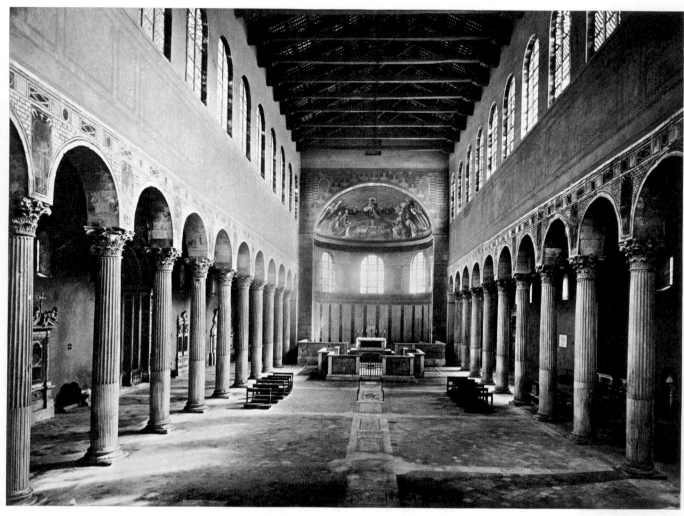

323. Interior, Sta. Sabina. 422–32 A.D. Rome

Basically, of course, the circular plan is that of the Greek tholos type (see fig. 133) and of its lineal descendant, the Pantheon (see fig. 283), but the Early Christian circular church was usually enveloped by a circular side aisle, known as the ambulatory, which was intended for pilgrimages and for ceremonial processions. In cross section such a church, with its elevated clerestory, would suggest a basilica, save only for the central dome. In Santa Costanza the rich mosaic decoration is still preserved in the barrel vault of the ambulatory, although that of the central portion of the church has disappeared. The coupled Composite columns in granite create an impression of outward radiation from the central space, which is enhanced by the swelling, convex frieze of the entablatures.

Any number of variations were, of course, possible in the circular plan, such as its expansion into radiating apses and chapels in the sixth century (see fig. 334). A circular martyrium could also be combined with a basilica, as in the great church commissioned by Constantine for the Holy Sepulcher in Jerusalem. Perhaps the most spectacular fusion of a central martyrium with the basilican plan was the Church of Saint Simeon Stylites at Qal'at Saman in Syria (fig. 326), built about 470. This consists of four distinct basilicas, three with splendid entrances and the fourth with three apses, radiating outward from a central octagon, which enshrined under an octagonal timber roof the pillar on the top of which Saint Simeon spent the last three and a half decades of his life. Syrian architecture is far richer in carved elements than its Early Christian counterparts in the West. The buildings were constructed in the old Hellenic tradition of large, rectangular blocks of stone. The corners of the octagon are supported by piers, flanked by sixteen freestanding, monolithic, and rather stumpy columns of granite, with acanthus capitals derived from Corinthian models; the richly molded entablature sweeps up to form arches, which lead into the four basilicas and into four small chapels fitted into the reentrant angles. The general appearance of Syrian churches is squat and massive as compared with the lofty, brick-walled basilicas of the West; the treatment of moldings and other architectural members is extremely free and imaginative.

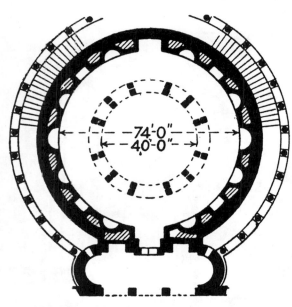

324. Plan of Sta. Costanza. c. 350 A.D. Rome

Mosaics

The new churches completely renounced the screen architecture so dear to the Romans, and had little use for monumental sculpture. A series of lifesize, silver statues of Christ and the Apostles, long since disappeared, once stood below a colonnade across the apse of San Giovanni in Laterano, but they were an exception. These churches possessed no pediments or acroteria for statues, no metopes for reliefs, and when friezes existed, they contained no sculpture. This art, so crucial to the Greeks and Romans, was continued in early Christian times on a grand scale only in the imperial portraits, arches, and columns erected by the emperors in Constantinople. The Christians, on the other hand, relegated sculpture almost entirely to the more modest position of sarcophagi and ivory carvings (see below, pages 259–60). The wall surfaces of Early Christian churches may have been deliberately kept flat so that they might be adorned in brilliant colors with complete narrative illustrations of the new religion for the instruction of the faithful.

Where these wall decorations consisted of frescoes, as, for example, the narrative cycles at Saint Peter's and at San Paolo fuori le Mura, also at Rome, they have per-

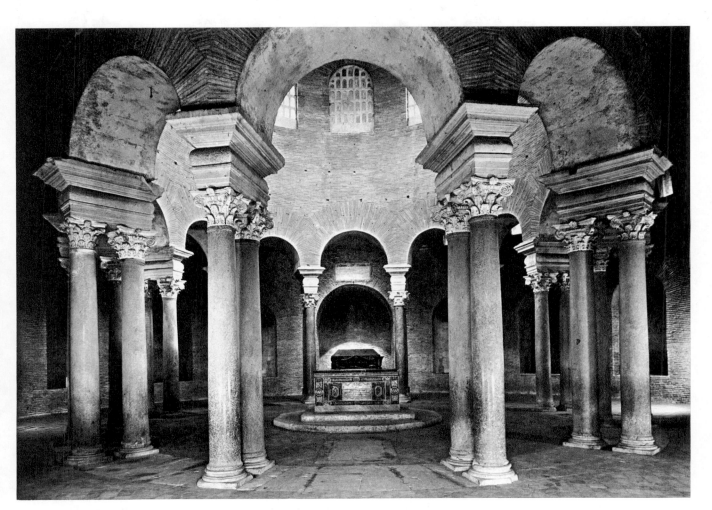

325. Interior, Sta. Costanza

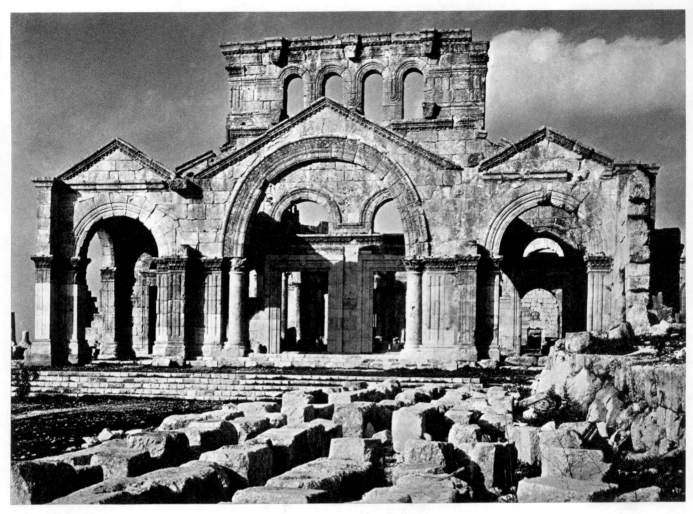

326. St. Simeon Stylites. c. 470 A.D. Qal'at Saman, Syria

ished, with few and fragmentary exceptions. Luckily for posterity, however, Early Christian artists had another and more durable alternative, the medium of mosaic, which the Romans had habitually used where wear or water required it, that is, for floors and for fountains and pools. The Romans had generally employed colored stones for their mosaics, which certainly made for a resistant floor covering but presented severe limitations in the range of available colors. The early Christians used glass, which instantly opened up a whole new world of glowing colors. Moreover, they exploited gold lavishly, not only for the representation of golden objects but also for that of light and even of illuminated surfaces, and with splendid effect. Entire backgrounds came to be made of gold, on a grand scale, particularly in the Eastern Empire, a practice perpetuated for the next millennium and longer in the gold leaf backgrounds characteristic of Byzantine icons and of early Italian painting. Little cubes of glass, known as tesserae, were pressed into soft plaster, laid a section at a time over minutely planned preparatory drawings on the wall surfaces. The tesserae were never exactly leveled off, so that each one presented a slightly varied surface to the light; thus, the observer, as he moves, beholds a constantly changing sparkle across the surface. The technique of gold glass—the baking of gold

leaf inside glass cubes—was not exact, so that the gold mosaic backgrounds have a shimmering appearance rather than the hard uniformity of more precise modern imitations.

One of the earliest series of Early Christian mosaics (colorplate 35 shows one section) ornaments the dome of Hagios Georgios (originally a mausoleum, later transformed into a palace chapel) in Salonika in northeastern Greece. In direct imitation of the towering, fantastic architecture of late Roman stages and other ornamental façades (see colorplate 31), a visionary architecture rises before us in illusionistic space whose two stories are composed of richly interlocking columns, arches, broken pediments, niches, and coffered groin vaults. The architecture, like the background, is entirely of gold glass, but brown tesserae were used to indicate shadows; these shadows have been so subtly deployed as to convey an illusion of light reflected from below into the coffered groin vaults at either side. Shades of brilliant blue were used for curtains and to pick out such details as arches, shell niches, and the crosses at either side, the latter each adored by three blue-green peacocks, symbols of eternal life. Some columns are spirally fluted, others embraced here and there by collars studded with jewels. Under the dome of the tiny central tholos can just be seen an altar bearing a book with a jeweled cover. Before the structure stand Saints Cosmas and Damian, the two physicians, in orant poses, dressed in white chasubles whose soft shadows repeat the palest blues of the architecture.

A series of mosaics radiating imperial grandeur survives in the Roman Basilica of Santa Maria Maggiore, dating from about 432–40. Instead of the architectural framework, which in Roman wall painting tied the images to the structure of the room, the triumphal arch is sheathed in mosaic. As so many Early Christian and Early Byzantine interiors show, this practice has the effect of dissolving the underlying architecture so that it is superseded by a new world of pictorial imagination. The entire left side of the arch is occupied by the first subjects drawn from Gospel narrative to be used in art, the *Annunciation* and the *Adoration of the Magi* (fig. 327). According to Christian doctrine, the Annunciation—the announcement to the Virgin Mary that she is to become the Mother of Christ—is the moment of the conception of his human body, brought about by the Divine Word (the Logos, or Second Person of the Trinity), conveyed by the Archangel Gabriel. Mary is seated upon a throne, robed and crowned exactly as an Augusta (empress) of the fifth century, in all the splendor her due since the Council of Ephesos in 431 had officially proclaimed her the Mother of God. She is regally attended by four white-robed angels, not mentioned in the biblical text (Luke 1: 26–36). She listens with one hand lifted in surprise, while Gabriel flies above her like a Roman Victory, and the white dove, which in Christian art symbolizes the Holy Spirit, descends upon her according to Gabriel's words: "The Holy Ghost shall come upon thee, and the power of the Highest shall overshadow thee." What we witness, therefore, is the moment of the Incarnation, one of the most sacred in Christian belief. At the left appears a closed gate, symbol of Mary's virginity; at the right, by a little aedicula whose hanging lamp indicates night, a majestic angel announces the momentous tidings to Joseph (Matt. 1: 20). The background behind both scenes is a wide plain whose horizon fades off into the sky and strips of cloud.

In the lower register the Christ Child, later usually shown on Mary's lap since he was, at the time of the Three Magi's visit, only twelve days old, appears as a boy of six or seven years seated on an imperial throne, and attended by four angels while the star of Bethlehem shines over his head. Mary is barely visible, standing to Christ's right; the woman to his left may be a personification of Holy Wisdom. Christ and the angels, but oddly enough not Mary in either scene, are endowed with the golden halos used henceforward in Christian art to distinguish sacred figures. The Three Kings from the East, two standing on one side of Christ, one on the other, dressed in that fantastic Oriental garment, trousers, pre-

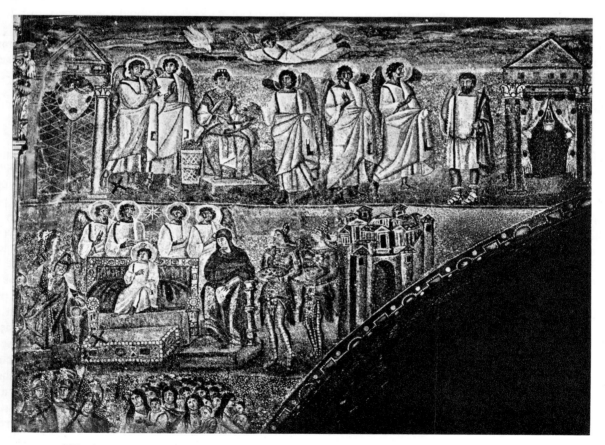

327. *Annunciation*, and *Adoration of the Magi*. Mosaics. c. 432–40 A.D. Sta. Maria Maggiore, Rome. See Colorplate 36

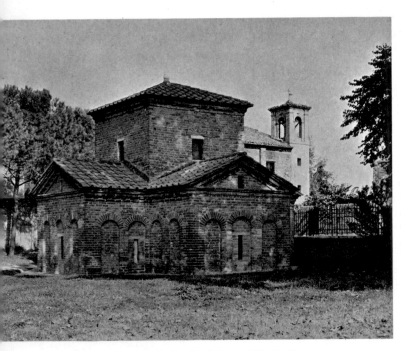

328. Mausoleum of Galla Placidia. c. 425–26. Ravenna.
See Colorplate 37

na from Milan in 402 by Galla Placidia's half-brother, the emperor Honorius. In the following century the Empire reached its height under the Gothic kings and the Byzantine emperors. The simple brick exterior of the mausoleum, ornamented only by a blind arcade and an entablature, gives no hint of the splendors within (fig. 328). The walls are sheathed in smooth slabs of soft gray veined marble. The barrel vaults, the lunettes, and the walls and vault of the central lantern almost disappear under their continuous covering of mosaic. In spite of the alabaster slabs in the windows that now yellow the light, the interior is one of the most beautiful in the history of art, its effect impossible even to suggest in photographs. The dominant color in all the mosaics is a deep sky-blue, which in the barrel vault of the nave is studded with white, blue, and gold floral patterns in medallions that float like magic constellations in some perfect heaven.

The lunette above the portal (colorplate 37), framed by a delicate wave pattern in blue and gold, shows the Good Shepherd seated among six of his sheep in a rocky landscape, which derives from those of Roman painting. His graceful pose becomes almost a spiral, as he holds the cross-staff with his left hand and with his right reaches to feed a sheep. Conventionalization of the rocks has begun, but each one contains a gamut of colors, ranging from gold in the lights to violet and gray in the shadows. The gold of Christ's tunic and the violet of his mantle are echoed in the distant rocks, but in softer and paler values. Rocks of about the shape shown here, but always more and more stylized, remained in the standard repertory of landscape settings throughout the millennial history of Byzantine art, after which they were taken over by Giotto and other early fourteenth-century painters in Italy (see figs. 515, 517, 519).

The Illuminated Manuscript

In addition to mural decoration, a second extremely important field for paintings was the "illumination" (illustration) of manuscripts, which were the only form of books made in Europe until the importation of printing from China in the fifteenth century. Egyptian manuscripts had been written on long rolls of papyrus (see above, page 74; see fig. 87), and such rolls, known as rotuli, were adopted from the Egyptians first by the Greeks and then by the Romans. The rotulus was wound between two spindles, and only two or three vertical columns of text were visible at any one moment. Greek and Roman rotuli were illustrated only when necessity demanded, as, for example, diagrams to explain scientific matters; to avoid flaking, these illustrations were usually drawn in line and colored, if at all, with thin washes. The Hebrew Bible was written on rotuli; the scroll-form of the Torah, although it is no longer written on papyrus, furnishes a modern example. But the Christians were above all the People of the Book; they needed to be able to refer immediately to any verse in the Bible for authority, and

sent gifts. Bethlehem is represented in the manner of one of the cities on the Column of Trajan as a little nugget of walls, temples, and roofs.

Twenty-seven smaller mosaics, immediately under the clerestory windows of the nave, tell stories from the Old Testament. Colorplate 36 shows two rows of two superimposed scenes from the Book of Joshua. Above, to the left, Joshua commands the priests to bear the Ark of the Covenant across the Jordan River, which is shown piling itself "upon an heap" as the text states; the twelve men commanded by Joshua to bear stones from the Jordan to their lodging place have been reduced to four for the purposes of the scene. Below, to the left, Joshua sends out two spies to Jericho, this town also represented like those on the Column of Trajan. In both scenes Joshua is dressed as a Roman general, and the parallels with the Column of Trajan in poses, attitudes, and groupings are compelling. Distant space is suggested by hills of several colors, and the sky is striped with gold clouds against the blue and white tesserae. The construction of the almost cylindrical figures suggests the *Tetrarchs* (see colorplate 33), but the use of color to build up these and the masses of the landscape is prophetic of the devices employed by Cézanne in the later nineteenth century (see Vol. 2, figs. 433, 436, colorplate 58) rather than of the Impressionists of whom illusionistic Roman paintings reminded us.

The finest and best preserved ensemble of fifth-century mosaics is that which decorates the interior of the tiny mausoleum built at Ravenna, on the Adriatic Coast of northern Italy, by the empress Galla Placidia about 425–26 for members of her family. The administrative capital of the Western Empire had been moved to Raven-

from one book to another to verify prophetical relationships and Gospel correspondences. They also required books for their increasingly formalized, complex, and uniform Liturgy.

An individual rotulus could only be unwound to about thirty feet in length before becoming unmanageable; thus, each Greek or Roman literary work had to be divided into a number of rotuli, or "books"; the Bible required scores of them. Even in antiquity the difficulty of using rotuli for ready reference gave rise to the copying of key passages on thin wooden tablets, hinged together at the back. These were the ancestors of the familiar codex (paged volume), which became a practical reality only when parchment came into general use. This material, whose name is a corruption of *Pergamon*, where it was invented in the second century B.C., consisted of the carefully scraped, washed, dried, and stretched skins of young animals, especially lambs, kids, and calves. It could be dried to extreme whiteness, provided a smooth surface for writing and painting, and was durable enough to stand up under constant usage in the Liturgy.

We do not have enough early examples to be sure just when the parchment codex began to replace the rotulus, but recent investigations indicate that the change began during the first century A.D. and was complete by the fourth century. Paradoxically enough, the finest early illuminated codex we know is a pagan work, the *Vatican Virgil*, dating from the fourth or perhaps the early fifth century. It should be remembered, however, that Virgil was considered by Christians throughout the Middle Ages as a prophet of the universality of Christianity, and his works were greatly respected. The *Vatican Virgil* is in fragmentary condition, and the paintings were executed by several hands of widely varying style and quality. One illuminator set forth his portion of the narrative with great vivacity, even if he lacked the refinement of the best Pompeiian painting. His *Miracle of Ascanius* (fig. 329; *Aeneid* II: l. 680ff.) shows the cap of Ascanius, Aeneas' small son, catching fire mysteriously in the midst of the siege of Troy, the holy flames resisting all efforts to douse them. The aged Anchises, Aeneas' father, raises his hands to the gods, and is informed that this miracle is a sign that Aeneas should leave doomed Troy to found Rome. The wildly dramatic poses, especially that of Creusa throwing herself before the departing Aeneas, recall a long tradition of Helleno-Roman sculpture (and possibly painting as well). The expression of the alarmed Ascanius may appear comic, but the coarse, rapid style with its strong contrasts of light and dark is very effective—on a level with catacomb painting; it is just this vivid, cursive method of narration that later formed a basis for the first Christian manuscript illuminations we know from the following century.

Sculpture

As we have seen (see page 255), little monumental sculpture was produced in the early Christian period, and very few works survive. But marble sarcophagi were carved in great quantities. The *Sarcophagus of Junius Bassus*, made for a man who died in 359 (fig. 330), while hardly comparable in quality with the best of Helleno-Roman sculpture, is far more accomplished than the rude fourth-century reliefs on the Arch of Constantine (see fig. 281). Its two stories are divided into ten compartments by stumpy, spirally fluted or vine-encrusted Corinthian columns, supporting niches, entablatures, and pediments drawn from the repertory of Roman stage architecture. From upper left to lower right, the scenes read as follows: the Sacrifice of Isaac, Peter Taken Prisoner, Christ Enthroned Between Peter and Paul, Christ Before Pilate (occupying two compartments), Job on the Dunghill, the Temptation of Adam and Eve, Christ's Entry into Jerusalem, Daniel in the Lions' Den, and Paul Led to Martyrdom. In contrast to the dramatic style of the *Vatican Virgil*, the little figures stand or sit quietly no matter how intense the biblical narrative being enacted; they remind us, in fact, of the stately calm of the scenes on the Arch of Trajan at Benevento (see fig. 280). This is probably because they serve a similar purpose as the

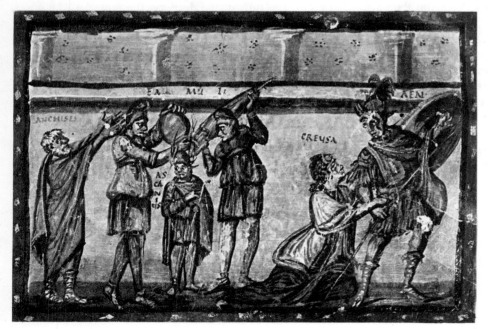

329. *Miracle of Ascanius*, from the *Vatican Virgil*. Illumination. 4th or early 5th century A.D. Biblioteca Apostolica Vaticana, Rome

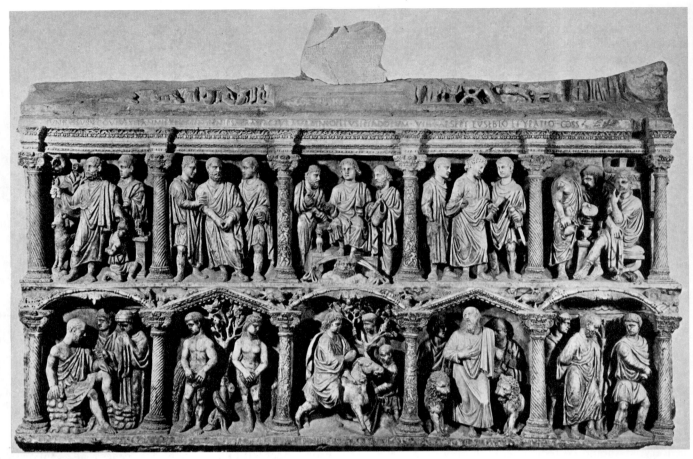

330. *Sarcophagus of Junius Bassus.* c. 359 A.D. Marble, 46½ x 96″. Vatican Grottoes, Rome

coherent exposition of a single symbolic theme, in this case Christian victory over suffering and death. In the upper central compartment Christ appears in triumph both on earth below and in Heaven above. Under his feet is a bearded personification of Heaven, like the personification of the Danube on the Column of Trajan (see fig. 278), holding a scarf over his head like those held by the personifications of Water and Air in the Ara Pacis (see fig. 259). In other compartments Peter and Paul are shown fearless before their captors, as Christ was before Pilate. Adam and Eve represent the origins of death through their sin. The extreme trials of Job, Isaac, and Daniel were declared by early Christian theologians to be "types" (foreshadowings) of the Passion (suffering) and death of Christ. A properly instructed Christian could read the scenes in any order and derive the same meaning: Christ's conquest over death was predicted in the Old Testament; through Christ man will triumph over death; like Peter and Paul man should not fear death.

When necessary, the Early Christian sculptor could handle dramatic situations with simplicity and beauty, as in the numerous ivory plaques on which he carved scenes from the Old and New Testaments. One of the finest panels (fig. 331), dating from the late fourth or early fifth

century, shows at the bottom right the Three Marys coming to the Sepulcher on Easter morning; the authoritative figure of the angel who tells them that the Lord is risen has been likened visually to Christ himself. At the upper right is an early form of the Ascension; Christ strides vigorously up a mountain, assisted by the Hand of God the Father extended from the clouds, while two of the Apostles cower in terror. The fullness and beauty of the figures, the flow of the drapery, the power of the poses, and the intensity of the dramatic realization reveal that the most accomplished Early Christian artists remained in touch with the great Helleno-Roman repertory of form and content.

THE AGE OF JUSTINIAN

For the Western Roman Empire the fifth century was a period of almost unmitigated disaster. Rome was sacked in 410 by the Visigoths, a Germanic people led by Alaric, and threatened in 452 by the Huns, a ruthless Mongol nation, under their king Attila, who died suddenly in 453. Another Germanic group, the Vandals, sacked Rome a second time, very methodically, in 455. Largely in ruins, the city was reduced to the status of a provincial town, with a greatly decreased population. By the time of the deposition of Romulus Augustulus, the last Roman emperor of the West, in 476, Italy lay devastated from constant warfare, and large areas of farmland had returned to wilderness. In 493 the Ostrogothic chieftain Theodoric captured Ravenna from Odoacer, leader of the Visigoths, and attempted to bring order out of the chaos. He made Ravenna the capital of his new and short-lived kingdom of Italy, and established a splendid court there.

Soon after Theodoric's death in 526 his kingdom fell apart. A powerful new figure, Justinian I (reigned 527–65), ascended the throne of the Eastern Roman Empire—which from now on we may as well call by the name it has acquired in history, the Byzantine Empire. Although they spoke Greek and were in many respects the custodians of Greek culture, the Byzantine rulers maintained to the end their position as legal heirs to the Roman Empire and always referred to themselves as Romans. Justinian dedicated his reign to restoring the stability of the Empire against the Huns, the Slavs, and the Parthians in the East and to reconquering the West, especially Italy, from the Vandals and the Ostrogoths. In 540 the imperial forces captured Ravenna and afterward maintained it as their center of power; by 555 Justinian's armies had reestablished Byzantine rule throughout Italy, driving the Ostrogoths across the Alps to a still unknown fate. The Byzantines were not able to hold all of Northern Italy, but before the end of the sixth century they had established the Exarchate of Ravenna, which kept Adriatic Italy and much of Southern Italy in the Byzantine fold for the next two centuries.

Like Constantine, Justinian maintained firm imperial control over the affairs of the church in the East, especially in regard to the establishment of dogma and the extirpation of heresies, the latter of which flourished like weeds in the early centuries of Christianity. During the interregnum of Visigothic and Ostrogothic overlordship of Italy, the bishops of Rome (whom we shall henceforward call by their traditional title of pope) had acquired a certain independence from the constantly changing and always insecure secular control. This freedom encouraged papal claims of supremacy over the other patriarchs of Christendom, who by no means agreed. Pope Gelasius I (492–96) went so far as to proclaim ecclesiastical superiority to imperial power, a claim renewed countless times by his successors for more than a millennium. Meantime, the chaotic conditions prevailing throughout the West strongly favored the establishment of monastic communities, which had long flourished in the East, as a refuge from secular disorder. In 529 Saint Benedict of Nursia founded the great order that bears his name and that spread throughout Western Christendom. Ruled from the Abbey of Monte Cassino in Southern Italy, the Benedictine order, in fact, not only became the greatest single force directed toward the reform and discipline of monasticism, but also assumed responsibility for the transmission of the heritage of Classical learning to the early Middle Ages through the preservation and

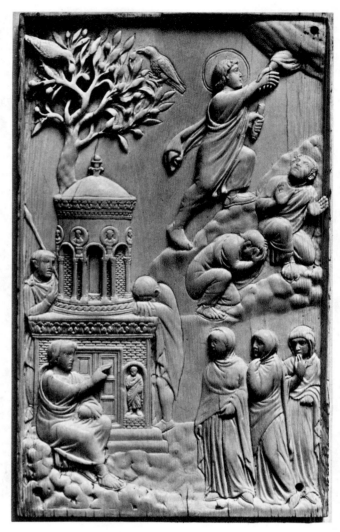

331. *Three Marys at the Sepulcher*, and *The Ascension*. Late 4th or early 5th century A.D. Ivory panel. Bayerisches Nationalmuseum, Munich

copying of manuscripts—a responsibility discharged in the East by Byzantium.

Remarkably enough, considering that Rome had by then been reduced to a town of about fifty thousand inhabitants living under conditions of great economic and political disorder, Roman pictorial tradition was by no means dead. About 530 Pope Felix III commissioned the creation of one of the finest mosaics of the entire Middle Ages to celebrate the remodeling of a Roman temple into the Church of Saints Cosmas and Damian. The mosaic, later reduced in size and disfigured by the addition of a plaster arch, fills the entire triumphal arch and apse (fig. 332). On either side the white-robed figures of Peter and Paul turn to look toward the spectator as they present Saints Cosmas and Damian, who in turn offer their crowns of golden oak leaves. At the extreme left, hardly visible in the photograph, Pope Felix holds forth a little model of the temple that he caused to be transformed

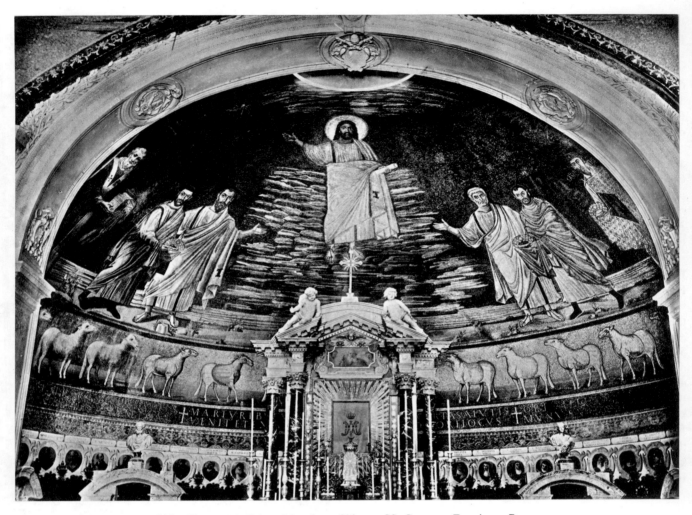

332. *Christ with Saints.* Mosaic. c. 530 A.D. SS. Cosma e Damiano, Rome

into the church. In the center of the triumphal arch, the Lamb of God is shown upon his throne, which stands among the seven candlesticks of Revelation (Rev. 1: 12–20); on the footstool lies a rotulus sealed with seven seals. Four angels appear, two on either side, and at the extreme right and left another angel and an eagle, holding codices, are visible. The angel and the eagle are the symbols of the evangelists Matthew and John (the winged lion of Mark and the winged bull of Luke have disappeared), and they are among the earliest monumental examples of a theme that reappears throughout Christian art.

The center is filled with a vision of overpowering splendor to which the entire composition is directed: on a pathway of sunset clouds, gold, yellow, orange, and red, against a sky of dazzling blue, the gold-robed Christ walks to us from beyond the stars, his left hand holding a scroll, his right extended in the familiar oratorical gesture of Roman tradition (see colorplate 26, fig. 255). This figure is, incidentally, one of the earliest representations of the bearded Christ in contrast to the boyish figure in images of the Good Shepherd and on sarcophagi

(see colorplate 37, fig. 330). In the apse mosaic of the Church of Saints Cosmas and Damian, the real world is restricted to a narrow band of green plain traversed by the shadows of the standing figures; we look above and beyond it into a heavenly realm, which replaces the time and space of our experience, just as all worldly phenomena yield to the coming of the Son of Man "in the clouds of heaven with power and great glory" (Matt. 24: 30). This revelation of ultimate spiritual power may well have been a source of consolation to the shattered Rome of the sixth century. The composition was extremely influential, being copied again and again in Rome throughout the early Middle Ages, and it deeply impressed the Italian artists of the Renaissance.

Ravenna

During the last years of the Ostrogothic kings and the first decades of Byzantine rule in Ravenna, the city was enriched by a series of new ecclesiastical monuments; even the most complex were built of local brick, adorned by columns and incrustations in colored marbles. It is not hard to account for the construction of Early Christian

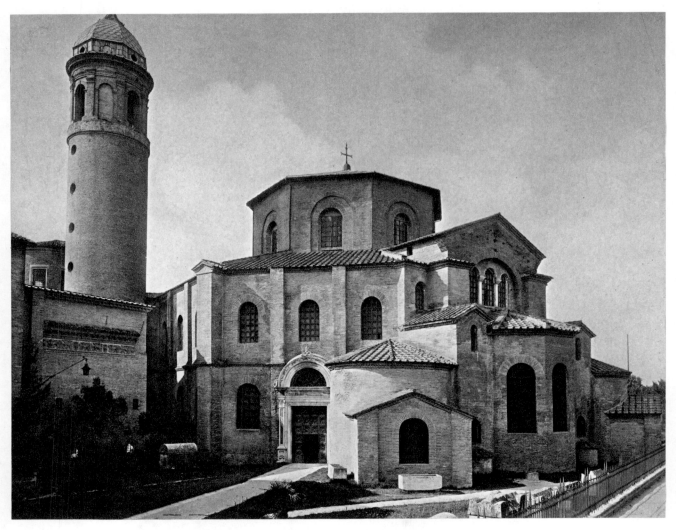

333. S. Vitale. c. 525–47 A.D. Ravenna. See Colorplate 38

basilicas in Rome of brick rather than concrete, since their flat walls posed few masonry problems. San Vitale at Ravenna, however (figs. 333, 334), was built about 525–47 on a subtle and intricate plan deriving from such Roman ancestors as the concave-and-convex structures in Hadrian's Villa at Tivoli. Concrete would seem to be called for; its absence may be explained by the difficulty of obtaining the great quantities of timber required for molds and centering during the chaotic economic and political conditions of the early Middle Ages.

San Vitale is an octagon which, from the outside, looks simple enough. Its bare, brick walls, rising to the height of the second story, are broken only by arched windows and buttresses. The central octagonal lantern is equally simple. The plan and exterior view, however, show that only the outer walls are truly octagonal. The central space is enveloped on the ground story by an ambulatory and on the second by a gallery. At the eight inner corners of the ambulatory stand large piers, sustaining eight great arches, which embrace the smaller arcades of ambulatory and gallery. Instead of being flat, as we would expect, these arcades are concave with respect to the central space, expanding from it to form, as it were, seven

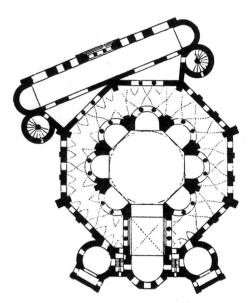

334. Plan of S. Vitale

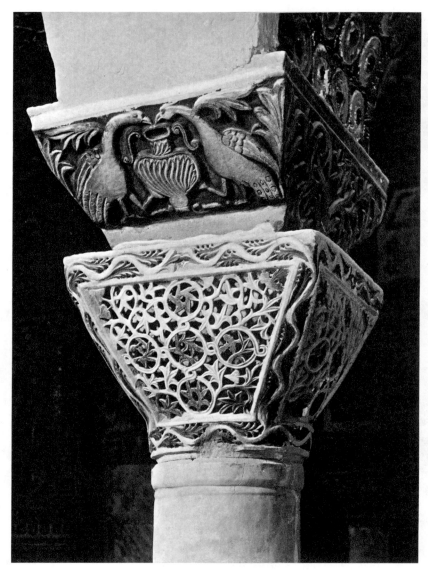

335. Capital, with vinescroll interlace. Marble. S. Vitale

transparent apses; the eighth is replaced by the chancel with its central altar. Even the crowning lantern is not octagonal; its corners are rounded off by tiny arches, called *squinches*, between the windows, which cut the drum in the interior into sixteen sides. The squinches are difficult to make out through the later decoration.

Entering the church through the narthex, whose odd angle deflects the presbytery and apse from the east-west axis and is as yet unexplained, the worshiper proceeds through the ambulatory and then into the central octagon, with its expanding spaces, filled with light from the eight arched windows of the lantern. The impression of dizzying spatial complexity is enhanced by the colorism of the interior. The columns are of veined marble, and richly colored marble sheathes each pier up to the springing point of the smaller arches. The very capitals have been transformed (fig. 335); no longer is there the

slightest reference to any of the Classical orders with their elegant articulation of parts. These capitals resemble baskets, and their smooth sides mask a subtle transition of shape from a square at the top to a circle at the bottom; instead of acanthus leaves, sculptured in depth, they are covered with a continuous interlace of vinescrolls drawn on the surface, incised, and then painted to make them appear even richer and more intricate. All the marble work was imported from the East, where Theodoric, who died in 526, had spent ten years as a hostage.

The entire chancel—apse, side walls, lunettes, jambs, arches, and crowning groin vault—is clothed with a continuous garment of mosaics in gold and other bright colors. Most of the subjects were drawn from the Old Testament, and chosen so as to prefigure the Eucharistic sacrifice. Christ appears in the half dome of the apse, youthful and beardless, robed in imperial purple and gold, and enthroned upon the orb of the heavens (colorplate 38). From the rocky ledges below him gush the four rivers of Paradise. On either side stands a white-robed angel; one presents Saint Vitalis, to whom the church is dedicated and who holds forth hands veiled by his gold-embroidered cloak to receive from Christ a jeweled crown; the other angel introduces Bishop Ecclesius, who commenced the construction of the church, of which he holds a charming if inaccurate model. Rocks, flowers, rivers, even the figures are strongly conventionalized; no hint of bodily structure underlies the thick, tubular folds of their drapery; their feet seem hardly to rest upon the ground. In ostensible conversation with each other, these solemn figures exchange not a glance; they gaze outward, above and past us. But none of the conditions of the real world apply any longer to this symbolic and timeless realm. Christ does not really sit upon his orb, but floats in front of it; nor does the orb rest upon the ground, but is divided from it by a strip of gold.

On the side walls of the chancel are two imperial mosaics. To the left of the altar, the emperor Justinian, flanked by high officials. soldiers, and priests (fig. 336), and, to the right, the empress Theodora among the ladies of her court, stare calmly out at the observer while, without looking, they present with veiled hands gifts to Christ in the half dome above. If anything, these figures are more completely rigid and immobile than those of the apse mosaics. Even more startling, Justinian wears a halo like that of Saint Vitalis; in this ceremonial representation we see a solemn attempt to show the sacred position accorded the emperor as Vicar of Christ on earth. Yet these mosaics contain recognizable portraits of the imperial couple, as well as one of Bishop Maximianus, during whose episcopate the church was consecrated, which depicts even the gray stubble on his cheeks and chin. What we witness in these mosaics is the transformation of a highly developed, naturalistic art into a transcendental and symbolic one, which still retains traces of the old Helleno-Roman illusionism in the treatment of light and surface.

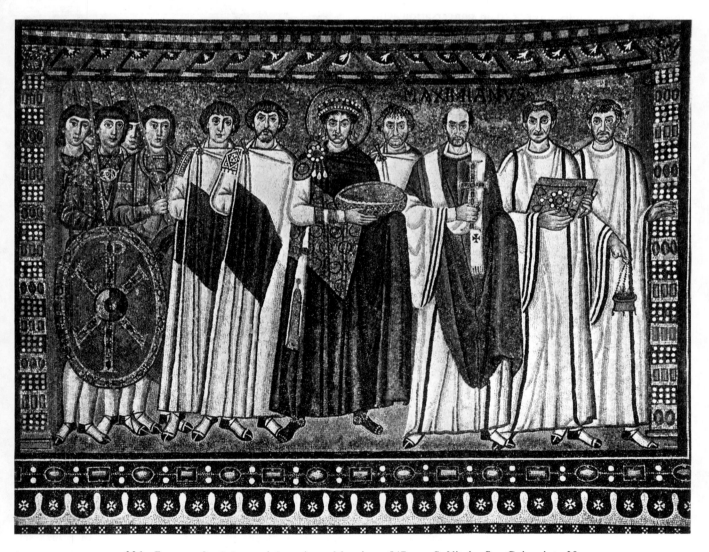

336. *Emperor Justinian and Attendants.* Mosaic. c. 547 A.D. S. Vitale. See Colorplate 38

A wholly symbolic representation, executed in mosaic between 533 and 549, fills the apse of Sant'Apollinare in Classe (fig. 337), located at the site of the old Roman port of Classis a few miles outside Ravenna. Curtains part in the little aediculae between the windows to reveal deceased bishops of Ravenna in orant postures (several are buried in the church). The half dome is partly filled with a green pasture, at the bottom of which twelve identical sheep, symbolizing the Twelve Apostles, march in single file on either side of the orant Saint Apollinaris. Above him, against the gold background, a circle of jewels encloses a disk of blue sown with gold stars, on which floats a golden cross studded with gems, as if appearing to the saint in a vision. On either side of the disk Moses and Elijah, depicted to the waist only, are surrounded by clouds to show that they are visionary apparitions, while below them among the trees three lambs look upward. These figures in the upper part of the apse symbolize the Transfiguration and portray that moment when Christ, who had climbed to a mountaintop with Peter, James, and John, was suddenly transfigured in raiment "white and glistering" (Luke 9:29) and Moses and Elijah were miraculously revealed in conversation with him. Christianity, no longer a new religion, has created its own language of symbols in which it can address the faithful with complete confidence that it will be understood. The mosaics of the triumphal arch, which show sheep emerging from Bethlehem on one side and from Jerusalem on the other before Christ flanked by the symbols of the Four Evangelists, were added in the seventh or eighth century.

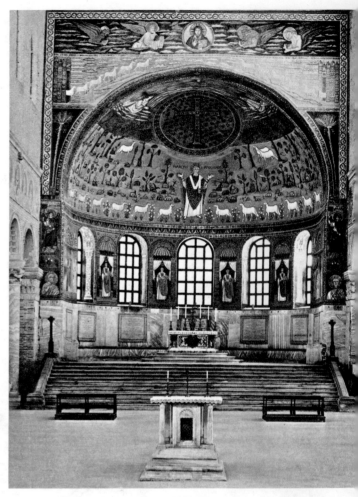

337. Apse mosaic. c. 533–49 A.D. Sant'Apollinare in Classe, Ravenna

Constantinople

After a catastrophic revolt in 532, in which Justinian nearly lost both his crown and his life, he embarked on an ambitious program of rebuilding the churches of his devastated capital, including the Constantinian Basilica of Hagia Sophia (Holy Wisdom), which had burned to the ground. The emperor dreamed of an entirely new kind of church bearing slight relation to the accepted basilican form. Instead of entrusting his bold idea to an experienced architect, he called in two noted mathematicians, Anthemius of Tralles and Isidorus of Miletos. They carried out the emperor's bidding faithfully; despite its many later vicissitudes, Hagia Sophia is an utterly original and successful structure, which makes surprising departures from the Roman tradition of building and—save for the imitations built by the Turks a thousand years later—remains unique.

Its plan (fig. 338) combines the longitudinal axis typical of a basilica with a centralized arrangement of elements. At the corners of an area one hundred Byzantine feet square rise four piers, each seventy feet high, upholding four great arches (fig. 339). These arches are connected by pendentives, which may best be described as triangles with concave sides drawn upon the inner surface of a sphere. The upper edges of the pendentives join to form a continuous circle on which a dome may be erected. Not only do pendentives provide a more graceful transition from a square or polygonal base to a round dome than is possible with the use of squinches, but also they permit the covering of a far greater area of floor space than is allowed by a circular base. The origin of pendentives remains unknown, but they were used for the first time on a large scale in Hagia Sophia. Henceforward, they were employed exclusively to support large domes in Byzantine architecture, and later in the Renaissance, the Baroque period, and modern times. The dome of Hagia Sophia is somewhat less than a hemisphere, and is composed of forty ribs meeting at the center. The web of masonry connecting the ribs is slightly concave, so that the shape has been compared to that of a scallop shell. On the east and west sides the central square is prolonged by half circles, culminating in semidomes, each of which embraces three smaller semidomes, crowning three apses. Such a structure would probably have been impossible to build employing the concrete construction techniques of the Romans. Anthemius and Isidorus achieved their domes and semidomes by means of masonry constructed of bricks set edge-to-edge and only one brick deep—forming a mere shell.

The building is entered from a groin-vaulted narthex, twice the length of the central square, through a portal directly opposite the eastern apse, which sheltered the altar. The arcaded side aisles and the arcaded galleries above them are roofed by groin vaults. The cornice of the galleries marks the springing point of the pendentives and of the four arches. The enclosing membrane of masonry is pierced by arched windows and by arcades in careful numerical arrangements—seven arches in the galleries above five in the side aisles, five windows above seven in the lunettes, and forty windows in the dome above five in each semidome. Since the side walls are nearly flush with their enclosing arches, the piers are hardly visible; the whole immense structure with all its shining windows and dark arches, with great domes embracing smaller ones, seems to be floating, an impression that must surely have been even stronger when the original decoration of gold mosaic, covered over later, delicately harmonized with the richly colored marble and porphyry of the columns and piers, and when the windows, originally more numerous than now, retained their colored glass. In fact, the chronicler Procopius wrote that the dome "seems not to rest upon solid masonry, but to cover the space with its golden dome suspended from Heaven."

Great efforts were made to support the dome. To absorb the thrust of its immense weight, and to keep it from pushing the corner arches out, huge buttresses (masses of solid masonry) were erected, clearly visible on the exterior (fig. 340). Beautiful as they are, the four minarets, built when the church was transformed into a mosque by the Turks after the capture of Constantinople in 1453, change considerably the appearance of the building. The reader should cover them up in the photograph in order to gain an idea of how this enormous pile of semidomes and buttresses culminating in the great central dome, towering 184 feet above the city, originally looked.

The glorious spatial impression we receive in the interior today should be supplemented in imagination by visualizing the majestic processions of the Byzantine emperor and his court to the imperial enclosure at the right of the sanctuary in the south side aisle, the gorgeous vestments of the patriarch and the clergy, and the incense and chanting that accompanied many of the rites. The congregation, of course, could witness only a small portion of the Liturgy, which took place, as it does to this day in Orthodox churches, behind an enclosure, partially hidden save when the clergy emerge, for example, for the reading of the Epistle and the Gospel and for the rite of Communion. Women and catechumens, confined to the galleries, could obtain only a fragmentary view of the vast interior (fig. 341), but it was a wonderful one, with the forms of the arches—curved in plan—playing against the half-seen, half-imagined spaces of the colorful nave. They could also delight in a closeup view of the new and special beauty of the Byzantine capitals, far more delicately designed and carved than those of Ravenna, out of whose undulating ornamented surfaces remnants of Classical shapes protrude like half-sunken ships.

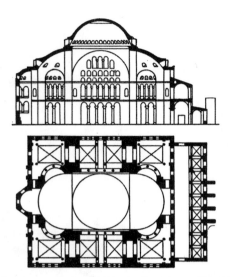

338. Section and plan of Hagia Sophia. c. 532–37 A.D. Istanbul. (Section after Gurlitt; plan after v. Sybel)

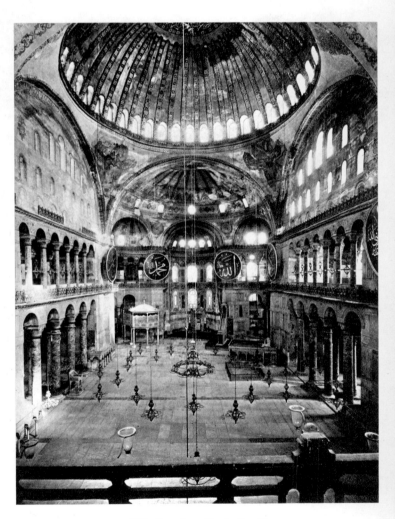

339. Interior, Hagia Sophia

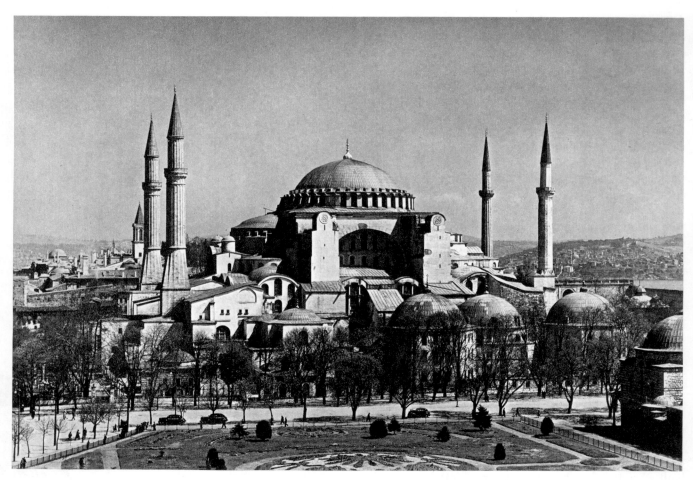

340. Anthemius of Tralles and Isidorus of Miletos. Exterior. Hagia Sophia

The colossal structure, by far the largest of the several major central-plan churches with which Justinian embellished his rebuilt capital, was finished in 537, after only five years' work (and a huge expenditure of money and effort). One can hardly blame Justinian for his supposed boast: "Solomon, I have vanquished thee!" However much Anthemius and Isidorus knew about conic sections, they were certainly less familiar with coefficients of safety, since their dome soon started to push its pendentives out of line and indeed collapsed in 558. The original dome was certainly lower than its replacement, completed in 563, and it perhaps continued the shape of the pendentives, forming a giant sail. The present dome has also had its mishaps, but it has been repaired, and Justinian's church has taken its place as one of the most imaginative architectural visions in the entire history of mankind.

Sinai

The sole surviving mosaic composition commissioned by Justinian outside of Ravenna has come to general attention only very recently because of the almost inaccessible position of the church in which it is located. The fortified

Monastery of Saint Catherine lies more than five thousand feet above sea level on the desert slopes of Mount Sinai, where Moses saw the Lord in the Burning Bush. This mosaic, done after 548 and probably before 565, and recently cleaned, restored, and photographed, fills the apse of the monastery church with a representation of the Transfiguration stated in terms of unearthly abstraction and heavenly radiance (colorplate 39). The Transfiguration (known as the Metamorphosis, or Transformation, in Greek) is depicted as at once sudden and eternal. The real world has shrunk to a mere strip of green at the bottom; all the rest of the surrounding space is gold. Blessing with his right hand, and staring over and beyond us, Christ stands at the center in an almond-shaped glory, an early appearance of the *mandorla* (almond-shaped aureole) that surrounds him in countless representations in the later Middle Ages. Seven rays of light stream from his raiment. The Apostles appear locked in the kneeling or prone positions into which the force of the miracle has thrown them, yet turn to look backward at the wondrous light with open eyes. James and John float against the gold, while Moses and Elijah, who in the biblical text are apparitions, stand with their toes touching the green.

Faces, bodies, and drapery are reduced to hard, clear,

almost geometric shapes. But if the great artist who designed the mosaic treated earthly forms as unreal, he rendered with minute precision the effects of the heavenly light, which reveals Christ's divinity to the apostles in the same manner the Lord had revealed himself to Moses on that very spot. Against the four shades of sky-blue into which the mandorla is gradated, Christ's "glistering" raiment stands forth in a pearly hue over which play magical tones of velvety white. As they cross the zones of the blue mandorla, the seven rays turn a shade lighter in each zone; they become stripes of white and cream as they traverse the gold; the rich mauves, tans, lavenders, and grays of the garments of the Apostles and Prophets are bleached out as the rays pass over them. No more compelling vision of the actual effects and spiritual meaning of light survives from the early Middle Ages.

A similar contrast between abstraction in the statement of form and naturalism in the rendition of light appears in a picture in encaustic, which is at once one of the oldest-known Christian panel paintings and one of the earliest surviving examples of that favorite among all themes in the late Middle Ages and in the Renaissance, the Virgin and Child (colorplate 40). This *icon* (image), also in the Monastery of Saint Catherine at Sinai, probably dates from the sixth century. Throughout human history, as we have seen, many peoples have tended to consider images to be in some way magical (the tomb statues of the Egyptians, the images of deities of the Greeks, the emperor portrait of the Romans) and to venerate them, usually on account of the subject. However, in Christian art icons began rapidly to be endowed with miraculous powers in themselves; innum-

erable stories have been told throughout Christian history of the wonders performed by sacred images, and many are firmly believed to this day. As early as the sixth century, chroniclers reported accounts of suppliants kneeling before images, and the icon preserved at Saint Catherine's may well have been intended to inspire such reverence. The Virgin and Child are shown royally enthroned between the warrior saints Theodore (bearded) and George, dressed as officers of the imperial guard. Behind the throne two angels look up to an arc of blue, representing the heavens, in which appears the Hand of God (the typical method of showing God the Father in Early Christian art), from which a band of white light descends toward the figures on the throne. The Virgin appears in an almost exactly frontal pose, and the Christ Child extends his right hand in teaching while his left holds a scroll, very nearly as in the work of the Italian painter Cimabue, who was brought up in the Byzantine tradition, some seven centuries later (see fig. 513). The saints stand as rigidly and frontally as the imperial attendants at Ravenna (see fig. 336), and the four gold halos are so aligned that they can be read, together with the Hand of God, as a cross. Even though the principal figures are so locked within this pattern that they can move only their eyes, the play of light is unexpectedly rich and the brushwork free. Variations in flesh tones, the dark circles under Mary's eyes, and the shimmer of the damasks are beautifully represented. Illusionist vision and technique, then, survive in the rendering of the play of light, while the grouping of the figures has been subjected to new laws of symbolic rather than naturalistic arrangement.

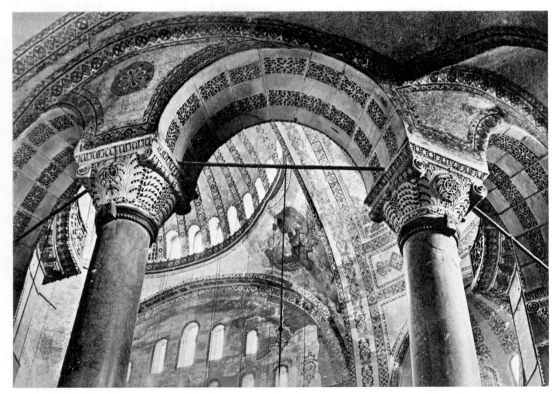

341. Hagia Sophia
(view from
the galleries)

Manuscripts and Ivories

The earliest preserved Christian manuscripts seem to have been made for the imperial court. In contrast to the utilitarian character of Classical books, this group of codices is written in letters of gold or silver on parchment dyed imperial purple. The finest of them is a sixth-century fragment of the Book of Genesis, now in Vienna (colorplate 41); in reality it is a picture book, for the illustrations appear at the bottom of each leaf with just enough text to explain them written above. These little narratives move along at a lively pace on the foreground plane, like scenes on an imperial column (see fig. 278) without any enclosing frame or any divisions between the separate incidents, on a continuous strip of ground. No more background is represented than exactly what the story requires. For example, when Jacob tells Joseph to join his brothers where they feed the flock in Shechem (Gen. 37: 13–17), there is no setting except a wayside pillar to indicate the journey and a hillside when Joseph actually finds his brothers and the flock in Dothan. Otherwise, we see only the little figures themselves, shimmering in fresh and lovely colors against the parch-

ment, which becomes by suggestion a kind of purple air. Doubtless by direction, the artist has added an element here and there. These include a touching farewell between Joseph and Benjamin, which is not in the text any more than is the angel shown accompanying Joseph on his journey.

Somewhat less luxurious is a Gospel book whose text was copied by the monk Rabula in a monastery in Syria in 586. The codex contains several full-page illustrations of great dramatic power. One of the earliest representations of the *Crucifixion* (fig. 342) shows Christ crucified between the two thieves; he wears a long garment—a survival of the Near Eastern tradition that nakedness was shameful (even Ionian kouroi in Archaic times were clothed). We can distinguish a Roman soldier with a sponge filled with vinegar on the end of a reed and another with the lance that pierced Christ's side, the repentant thief turning his head in a beautiful motion toward the dying Saviour, Mary and John at the left, the other Marys at the right, and in the center below the Cross the soldiers playing dice for the seamless robe. Above, over the blue hills, hang the sun and moon, which were darkened at the Crucifixion. Below, in another

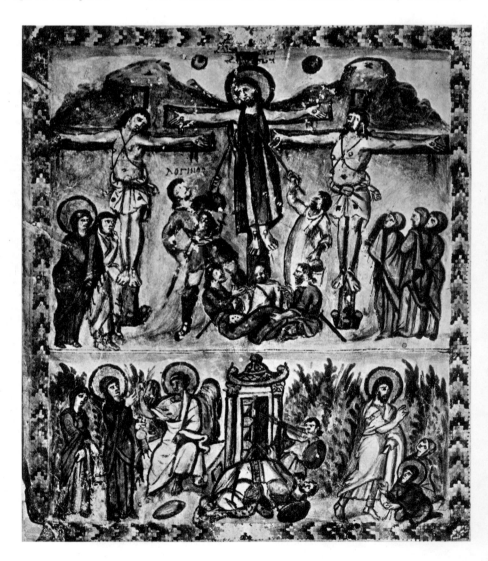

342. *The Crucifixion*, and *The Women at the Tomb*, from the *Rabula Gospel*, Zagba on the Euphrates, Syria. Illumination. c. 586 A.D. Biblioteca Laurenziana, Florence

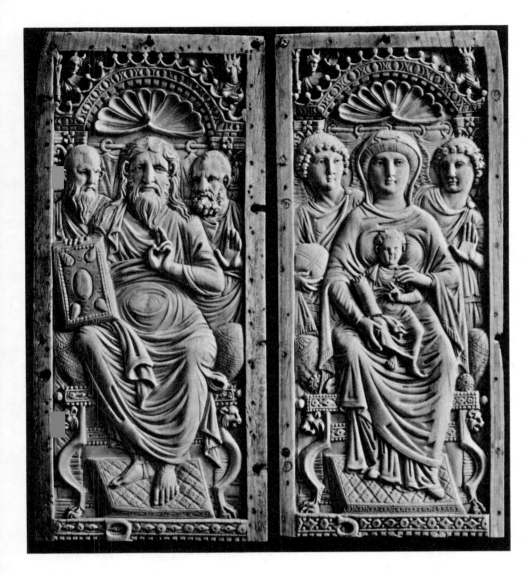

343. *Christ Enthroned Between
Saint Peter and Saint Paul*, and
*The Virgin Enthroned Between
Angels*. Ivory diptych. Middle 6th
century A.D. Staatliche Museen,
Berlin

register, can be seen the empty tomb, with the guards
sleeping before it; on the left the angel tells the two
Marys that Christ is risen; on the right Christ himself
appears in the garden to the Marys, prostrate before him.
Even the zigzag chevrons of the border play their part in
heightening the excitement of the narrative. The bold
sketchy style recalls in some respects the handling of the
Miracle of Ascanius in the *Vatican Virgil* (see fig. 329).
The emotional impact of the scenes foreshadows the
work of Georges Rouault, one of the few great religious
artists of the twentieth century (see Vol. 2, colorplate 65).

A considerable number of ivory panels survive from
Justinian's time, notably *diptychs* (two panels hinged
together), made to be coated with wax on one side for
writing and to be carved into representations on the
other. A splendid example (fig. 343) shows on one leaf
the Virgin and Child enthroned between two angels, and
on the other Christ enthroned between Peter and Paul; in
the first the Christ Child carries a scroll to indicate his
Nativity as the fulfillment of Old Testament prophecies,
and in the second the adult Christ displays the codex of
the New Testament. In the background of both, architectural space survives only as remembered fragments,
beautifully carved, yet without any real suggestion of
depth. The majestic figures seem to float before their
thrones rather than to sit upon them. Mary is a full-
featured young matron; the angels who turn their heads
with such grace still retain the beauty of the Hellenic
tradition. In the strange representation of the adult
Christ, shown with an unusually long beard, he seems to
have assumed the dignity we associate with God the
Father. The drapery folds, as often in Justinianian art, no
longer describe the behavior of actual cloth, but begin to
develop an intense existence of their own as abstract
patterns.

Justinian had overextended himself; the Byzantine
forces could not continue to hold all the territory he had
reconquered. But in sections of Italy and in Asia Minor
the Empire continued (it held sway in the Balkans for
nearly nine hundred years longer), a treasure-house of
Classical Christian culture and a fortress against the
onslaughts of Islam from the east and the Slavs and
Bulgars from the north. The story of its later vicissitudes
and triumphs, especially the unexpected Byzantine cultural expansion into Slavic territory, belongs to another
chapter.

2

The Art of the Migrations

We have already seen how profoundly the history of the ancient world was affected by the migration of peoples of Asiatic origin, notably the Dorians and the Etruscans, into the Mediterranean basin in the centuries just preceding 1000 B.C., where they eventually produced great and stable cultures in partial amalgamation with their predecessors in the area. A second tide of migrations seems to have begun in the fourth century B.C., when the Gauls, a Celtic people, invaded Italy, sacking Rome, and settled permanently in Northern Italy and France, there to become Romanized and Christianized. By the fifth century A.D. a third major wave of migrations had brought Germanic peoples, notably the Ostrogoths and the Visigoths, to Mediterranean lands. The Ostrogoths settled in Italy, and the Visigoths in France and Spain. They in turn became Romanized and Christianized, and soon took over the reins of regional control from the dissolving Roman Empire. But almost immediately these now-settled Germanic nations were threatened, not only by the Byzantines trying to recover former imperial lands, but also by other Germanic tribes. In the late fifth century A.D. the Franks took over the region that comprises modern France (and gave it their name). After the departure of the Romans from Britain in the early fifth century A.D., the Jutes, Angles, and Saxons began their slow conquest of that land, driving the indigenous (Celtic) Britons into Wales. The Lombards entered Italy after the expulsion of the Ostrogoths in the sixth century A.D., and divided it irregularly and unstably with the Byzantines, who retained most of the ports, and the popes, who had assumed temporal as well as spiritual control over Rome and a considerable surrounding area. Both the Lombards and the Franks were soon Christianized and so, in the late sixth century A.D., were the Anglo-Saxons.

Many of the new arrivals had been pushed along in their westward and southward migrations by the fierce Huns, and some had even been pressed into service by Attila, the Hunnish leader, to further his short-lived program of imperial domination. More important than the disappearance of the Roman imperial title in the west was the virtual collapse of Roman administration, economy, manufacture, agriculture, transportation, education, and art and the depopulation of the cities. Only in the Church—especially the monasteries—did learning remain alive. The destruction in the West in two centuries of much of what the ancient world had built up throughout three millennia was by no means compensated for by the Christianization of the invaders. The ensuing era, generally known as the Dark Ages, was nonetheless not as protracted as historians formerly believed, as we shall see when we come to the extraordinary figure of the emperor Charlemagne at the end of the eighth century.

But the few surviving buildings and images created by the invaders once they had settled (with the exceptions of the partially Byzantinized Theodoric and the Visigoths in Spain) are for the most part small, rough, and unpretentious, giving little indication that the Germanic tribes had learned much from the culture they destroyed. Astonishingly enough, few of these examples are comparable in quality to the products of the ancient and highly refined art of metalwork that the tribes brought with them and presumably continued to practice.

This art was totally foreign to Mediterranean culture, but was especially relevant to the needs of nomadic peoples; its practice was restricted to the manufacture of objects of daily life that the migrants could carry on their wanderings—weapons, personal adornments, and horse gear for the most part, often made of precious metals and studded with precious or semiprecious stones. These artifacts might well have been discussed in Part One, Chapter 3, but their consideration is crucial at this juncture because they indicate the source of much of the orna-

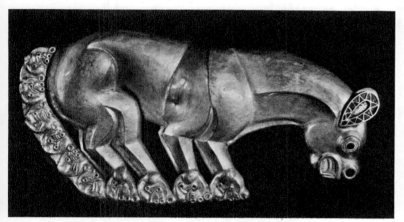

344. Scythian Panther, from Kelermes. c. 6th century B.C. Gold, length 11⅜″. The Hermitage, Leningrad

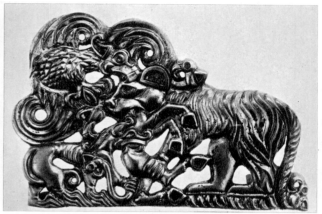

345. Scythian plaque with animal interlace, from the Altai Mountains, Siberia. Gold, 5⅛ x 7¾″. The Hermitage, Leningrad

ment that constitutes a vital aspect of European art in the early Middle Ages. The special patterns and motives carried by the peoples of the Germanic tribes in their metalwork for distances of thousands of miles were retained in the imagination of their descendants, and the Celts, whom they drove out, even amalgamated these patterns with others of La Tène origin.

The chief subject of this nomadic art was animals; for this reason the term Animal Style is often applied to it. Since man is seldom represented, this Germanic art cannot be connected with any of the Germanic or Norse sagas, such as the legends of Beowulf or Siegfried. To find its origin we have to go back to the Scythians, a people who spoke an Indo-Iranian tongue and lived in what is today Southern Russia in the valley of the Don River and along the coasts of the Black Sea. They were regarded by the Greeks as archbarbarians, but before they were Hellenized they produced gold objects of great beauty and frightening intensity, such as the crouching panther (fig. 344) of the sixth century B.C., found in a burial mound at Kelermes. No work of twentieth-century sculpture has surpassed the power of the harsh masses and rhythms into which this animal is divided, nor the sheer ferocity of its snarling expression. The paws and the tail of the beast are beaten into the shapes of panthers, and the ears are executed in cloisonné. This technique consists of soldering small strips of metal to the underlying surface so that the small compartments they form may be filled with enamel, glass, or inlaid stones.

Another Scythian gold plaque apparently came from the Altai Mountains far to the east in southern Siberia, just above the border of Mongolia (fig. 345). After a moment's gaze this seething caldron of destruction resolves itself into a wolf and a tiger that are tearing a colt apart, while an eagle in turn attacks the tiger with beak and wings. The fighting animals have begun to form an interlace, of bewilderingly fluid and complex shapes, whose parallel striations are derived from the stripes of the tiger, the feathers of the eagle, and apparently the shapes of grasses below. An indication of the immense

geographic spread of this style may be seen in the discovery of an obviously related gilded silver disk, possibly a shield ornament, at Helden, the Netherlands (fig. 346). It may have been made at any time between the first century B.C. and the third A.D., either by Scythians or under Scythian influence, and was quite possibly carried for thousands of miles. The disk shows at least seven animals, including wolves and lions—not common in the Netherlands—in conflict over a cow, tearing at each other in the form of a spiral.

What eventually happened to this interlace of fighting beasts may be seen in a purse lid from an Anglo-Saxon royal ship burial at Sutton Hoo in Suffolk, England, dated A.D. 655–56 (fig. 347). The lid, originally ivory or bone, is set with cloisonné plaques, of which those at up-

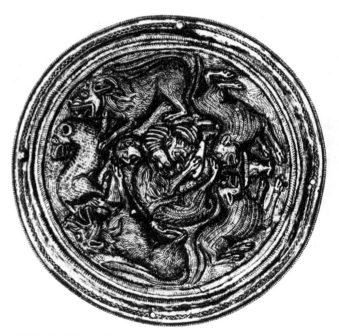

346. Scythian(?) shield ornament, found at Helden, The Netherlands. c. 1st century B.C.–3rd century A.D. Gilded silver, diameter 8⅝″. Rijksmuseum van Oudheden, Leiden, The Netherlands

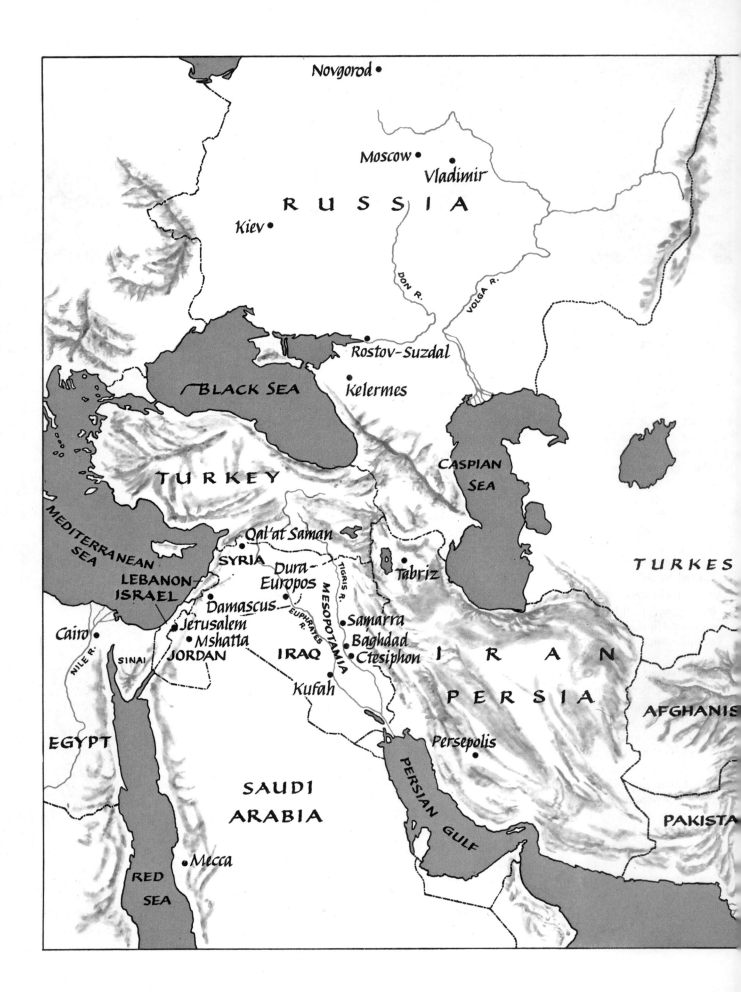

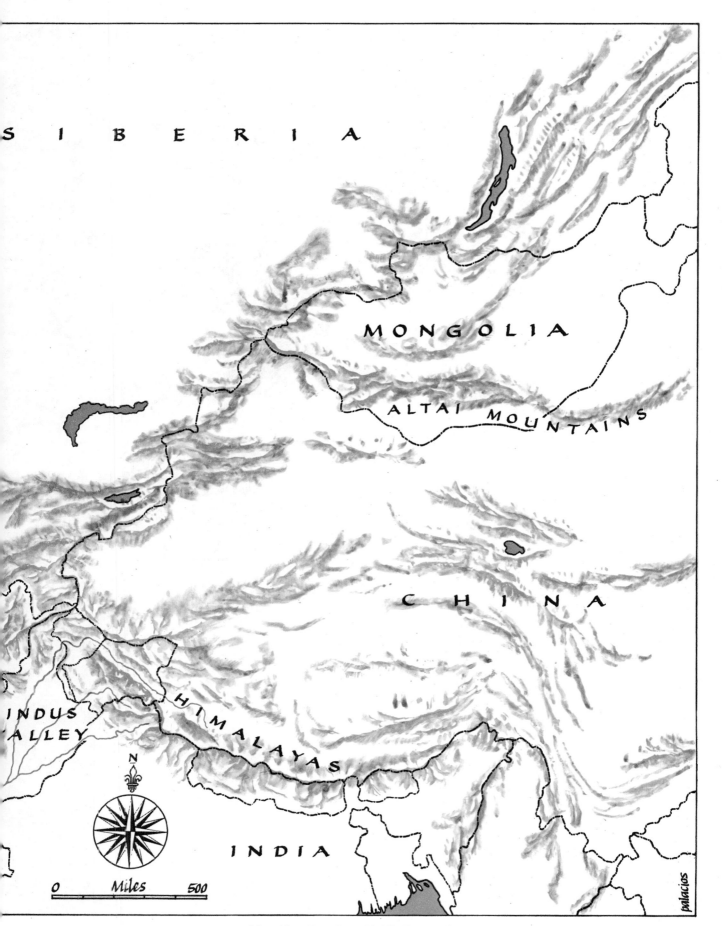

MAP 13.   *Near East, Middle East, and Asia*

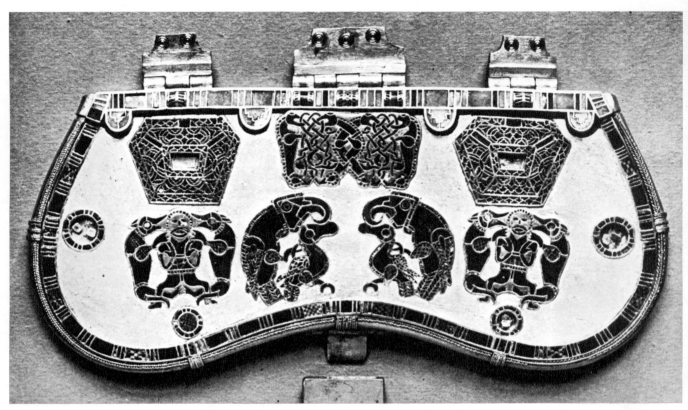

347. Animal interlace, from a ship burial at Sutton Hoo, Suffolk, England. Purse lid. c. 655–56 A.D. Originally ivory or bone, set with cloisonné plaques. British Museum, London

348. Animal head, from a ship burial at Oseberg, Norway. c. 825 A.D. Wood, height of head 5″. University Museum of Antiquities, Oslo

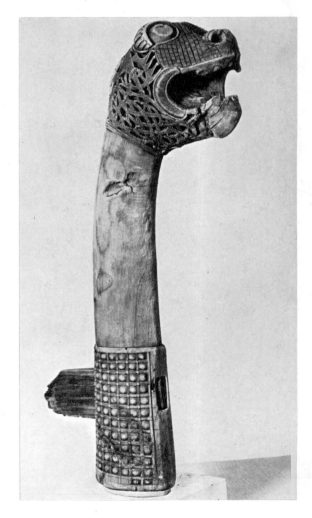

per right and left are ornamented with purely geometric patterns. The central panel is composed of fighting animals whose jaws are prolonged to form interlaced ribbons. Below are two plaques, each composed of an eagle capturing a duck, while at either side appears that rarest of animals in migrations art, man, standing between two hostile wolves in a configuration that recalls the far-off days of the ancient Sumerians (see fig. 94); in fact, the motive may have been derived from heraldic groupings in Mesopotamian art. Surprisingly—and very important—this polyglot Sutton Hoo ship burial included a beautiful Celtic bronze mirror, with whorls and spirals in pure La Tène style (see Part One, Chapter 3). A final stage in the development of the animal interlace is seen in a fierce animal head in carved wood, from a ship burial of Viking seafarers at Oseberg, Norway, datable about A.D. 825 (fig. 348). The animal itself is frightening enough, with open mouth and glaring eyes, reminding one of its ancestry in the panther of Kelermes (see fig. 344), but the wood-carver has embellished its head with a rich interlace of crisscrossing and entwined ribbonlike shapes that one would have difficulty tracing back to their probable origins in animal combat.

3

Hiberno-Saxon Art

The Anglo-Saxon pagan conquest of Britain in the fifth and sixth centuries A.D. left Christianized Ireland cut off from easy access to continental Europe. Under such circumstances it is not surprising that a highly individual form of monasticism flourished in Ireland, a form adapted to the needs of an isolated country without urban centers. What was less to be expected was the rise of an intense Irish missionary activity, directed toward the Continent and toward England. From the sixth through the ninth centuries, Irish monks traveled through Northern and Central Europe, founding monasteries as far south as Switzerland and Italy. In 633, at the invitation of the king of Northumbria, the ruler of one of the seven Anglo-Saxon kingdoms, an Irish monastery was established on the island of Lindisfarne, off the northeast coast of England. Quite independently, however, the Roman missionary Augustine arrived in Kent in 597 to commence the conversion of the southern Anglo-Saxons to the Roman form of Christianity, from which the Irish by that time had deviated in a number of respects. At the Synod of Whitby in 664 the two missions met head on, not without fireworks. Eventually, the Irish submitted to Rome but continued to maintain a certain independence.

An activity essential to the Irish missions was the copying of religious books, especially the Gospels. For the enrichment of their manuscripts, the Irish drew on established traditions, both Germanic and Celtic, as well as on examples of Early Christian illumination. The resultant art, carried out in all probability by Anglo-Saxon artists (although this is by no means certain) under Irish inspiration, is best known as Hiberno-Saxon. The transformations of Early Christian originals produced by these artists are interesting, but these pale in comparison with the marvels they turned out in a tradition they knew and understood. For example, one of the earliest of the Hiberno-Saxon manuscripts, the *Book of Durrow*, done in Northumbria in the second half of the seventh century,

contains a brilliant decorative page (fig. 349) whose ornamentation can be traced directly to three of the four types seen in the purse lid from Sutton Hoo (see fig. 347), the animal interlace, the abstract interlace, and the pure geometric. All of it is carried out in a style based on clear contours bounding flat areas of color obviously derived from the cloisonné technique. But a momentous change has taken place. Instead of being freely scattered across the area as in the purse lid, the three types of ornamentation are combined into a unified whole by powerful embracing shapes and movements. Two horizontal panels of animal interlace at the top and two at the bottom are united by smaller vertical panels to bound a square, in which floats a circle containing abstract interlace. Within this interlace are embedded three smaller circles of geometric ornament, arranged in an equilateral triangle. In the center a smaller circle surrounds a cross, composed of four equal triangular elements. This form combines within itself the numbers of the Gospels and the Trinity, and by means of these numbers—the three outer circles, the four corners of the square, and the four horizontal bands, whose widths and lengths are related to each other as one to four—imposes its own proportional unity on the pagan magnificence of the ornament. The animals-biting-animals pattern now proceeds in a beautiful rhythmic motion, which also obeys distinct laws of repetition, alternation, and reversal as well as laws of color and shape, all of which may be deduced if one is willing to look long enough.

An even more splendid book, the Gospels illuminated at Lindisfarne from 698–721, shows a more highly developed form of this harmony between Christian symbolism and pagan ornamental tradition in a symbolic structure of dizzying complexity and cosmic grandeur (colorplate 42). Cross, circle, and square, extended at top and bottom to fit the oblong format, embrace the entire page in a manner recalling the heavenly Cross of the

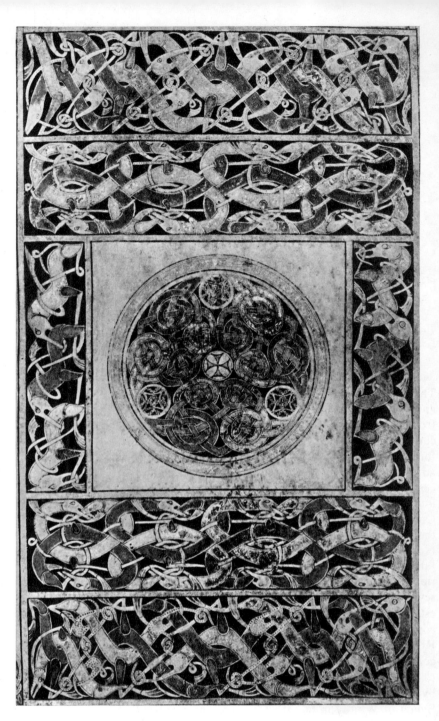

349. Decorative page of the *Book of Durrow*, from Northumbria. Illumination. 2nd half 7th century A.D. Paint on vellum, c. 9¾ x 6". Trinity College, Dublin

catacomb frescoes (see fig. 318). All three symbols are filled with abstract interlace, so divided into different color zones that at the ends of the crossbars four smaller crosses emerge. Between the crossbars the fields are filled with animal interlace of violent activity. The comparatively serene ornament in the central circle discloses one large and four smaller crosses. Animal ornament forms tabs projecting from the four outer corners; on the center of each side is another tab composed of facing birds whose beaks show sharp teeth. Most surprisingly, pure La Tène ornament fills the corners of the extensions with active whorls.

If the Hiberno-Saxon artists had a continental model before them, they translated its imagery recognizably enough into a geometrized equivalent, but when they in-

vented their own figures, the result can be startling. The *imago hominis* (image of man) page from the Gospels illuminated in the first half of the eighth century by a Northumbrian artist at Echternach in Luxembourg (fig. 350) is conveniently labeled, for otherwise we might not know a human being was intended. The little head, with its endearing cross-eyes, appears caught in the mechanism of the cruciform interlace that proceeds from all four sides of the border seemingly to form a vise. The artist, asked to paint the winged man symbolizing Matthew, treated him as a six-winged seraph. Locked in place by the four bars, he completes the form of the Cross.

The freest compositions of the Hiberno-Saxon manuscripts are those that display enormous letters engulfing the entire page. No pagan scribe would have thought of

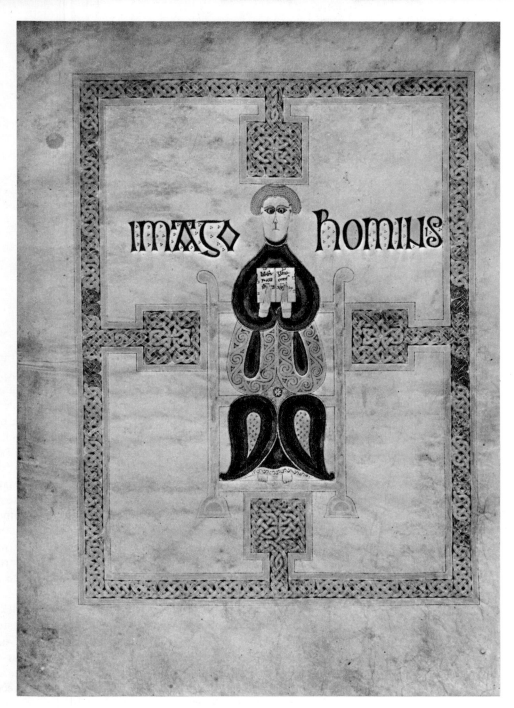

350. *Imago Hominis (Image of Man)* page of the *Echternach Gospels*, from Luxembourg. c. 1st half 8th century A.D. Illumination, c. 10¼ x 7⅝". Bibliothèque Nationale, Paris

endowing initial letters with exceptional importance. But since the Bible was divinely inspired and therefore sacred, its very letters were regarded as exerting magical potency, most of all the initials. What we might call the baroque phase of the Hiberno-Saxon development is exemplified by the *Book of Kells* (colorplate 43), illuminated in southeastern Ireland between 760 and 820. The words *Christi liber generationis* (*the book of the generation of Christ*; Matt. 1: 1) fill the entire page. The name of Christ, reduced to its Greek contraction XPI, becomes like the Cross an immense celestial apparition (divided neatly, of course, into successive areas of animal interlace, abstract interlace, and geometric ornament).

The powerful diminishing curves, like comets, involve whole galaxies of La Tène circles-within-circles, large and small, filled with vibrant whorls—all going at once. After contemplating this revelation for a while, we are astonished to see emerging from its intricacies the faces and upper torsos of three unhappy little people, trapped among feathers and teeth along the clean outer edge of the mighty X. Stranger yet, in the second spiral from the bottom of the page, at the tail of the same shape, two naturalistic mice appear in a heraldic grouping on either side of a small round object (a piece of cheese?), contemplated by two sleepy cats, each with a mouse on its back.

4

Islamic Art

The most unexpected event of medieval history was the lightning expansion of Islam, which combined a speed approaching that of Alexander's conquests with a political tenacity rivaling that of Rome and with at least as much religious unity as Christianity. At the death of Mohammed, its founder, in 632 Islam ruled Arabia, though few in the Christian world were then aware of the existence of so dangerous a rival. Thirty years later Egypt, Syria, Palestine (including the Hebrew and Christian holy places), Mesopotamia, and Persia had fallen into Muslim hands. By 732 Islam had reached into Turkestan, Afghanistan, and the Indus Valley to the east, and its domains to the west, including Spain, Portugal, and southwestern France, stretched to the Atlantic Ocean. In southwestern France the Muslims were stopped—and eventually expelled—by the Franks. The Byzantines and Sassanian Persians crumbled before Islam; Constantinople soon controlled only Asia Minor and the Balkans. All the Asiatic and African regions conquered by Islam in its first century of life, with the sole exception of modern Israel, remain predominantly Islamic today.

The rapid spread of Islam was due to the military genius of the Arabs and to their intense religious fervor. In contrast to the spontaneous diffusion of the initially gentle Christianity in spite of the official opposition of the Roman Empire, not a single country or region has ever willingly adopted Islam. Mohammed himself spread his doctrines with the sword, and he directed and personally participated in the mass slaughter of inconvenient resisters. Throughout the history of Islam determined pockets of Christianity remained—relatively unmolested, to be sure, but nonetheless unyielding—in Egypt, where the Coptic Church survives, and in Syria, Lebanon, and Palestine. In assessing the expansion of Islam, its attractions as a religion should be weighed against the great material advantages attending submission to a militarily dominant Arabic culture. But it would be a mistake to assume that this culture, at least in its developed stages,

was inferior to those it conquered, particularly in France and in Spain. One of the most surprising aspects of Muslim growth is the rapidity with which Islam assumed the role of conservator and continuator of the Helleno-Roman philosophical and scientific heritages. We owe much of our knowledge of Classical science, especially botany and medicine, and the invention of algebra (and of the very numbers used in this book) to the Arabs. However, Mohammed's prohibition of graven images destroyed sculpture, and his disapproval of representation put painting into an ambiguous position. But under Islam architecture made gigantic progress, and the natural mathematical bent of the Arabs, coupled with their highly developed aesthetic sense, produced an art of abstract architectural decoration that is one of the artistic triumphs of mankind.

Compared with the increasing theological complexity of organized Christianity, in either its Roman or Eastern Orthodox form, Islam (the word means *submission*—i.e., to the will of Allah) is a remarkably simple and clear-cut religion. It dispensed with priesthood, sacraments, and liturgy from its very start; every Muslim has direct access to Allah in prayers. But its caliphs, at first deriving authority from their degree of family relationship to Mohammed, exercised supreme political power in a theocratic state. Islam's one sacred book, the Koran, embodies the divinely revealed teachings of Mohammed as set down by himself on either palm leaves or camel bones, or as recalled by his companions and edited by his early followers. These teachings include the doctrine of one indivisible God, who has many Prophets (including those of the Old Testament and Jesus), of which the greatest was Mohammed. Islam posits a Last Judgment, a Heaven, and a Hell, but it makes no clear division between the demands of the body and those of the soul. The good life on earth and the afterlife of Paradise can include many forms of self-indulgence, including a host of delicious concubines. In contrast to the celibacy imposed upon Catholic clergy of all ranks, and upon Orthodox bishops, no such sacrifice was required of the caliphs or the imams (teachers). The duties of a Muslim include circumcision, daily prayer at five stated hours, abstention from certain foods and from alcohol, fasting during the month of Ramadan, charity, and a pilgrimage to Mecca.

Mohammed had no greater need of architecture than had Christ; he could and did teach anywhere, but much of his discourse was carried on in his own house, which served as the model for building the first mosques. His followers required only a simple enclosure, one wall of which, known as the qibla, at first faced Jerusalem, later Mecca. A portico on the qibla side was a practical necessity as a protection from the sun. The sacred well near the Ka'bah in Mecca suggested a pool for ritual ablutions, and every mosque has one in the center of its courtyard, which is known as the sahn. Soon the qibla was given a sacred niche, called the mihrab (see fig. 361), which pointed in the direction of Mecca. To the right of the mihrab stood the minbar (see fig. 361), a lofty pulpit from which the imams read the Koran to the assembled faithful and preached the Friday sermons. These simple early mosques always contained the qibla, the sahn, the mihrab, and the minbar, but unfortunately, none of the first mosques have been preserved. As in the case of Christianity, and indeed following its example, the taste for splendor soon accompanied success.

As early as 670 the mosque at Kufah in Mesopotamia (located in present-day Iraq) was rebuilt with a roof forty-nine feet high, supported by a colonnade in apparent imitation of the Hall of a Hundred Columns at Persepolis (see fig. 115). When Caliph Omar I captured Jerusalem in 638 he left the Christian sanctuaries undisturbed, and built on the ruins of the last Temple, which Titus had totally destroyed in A.D. 70, a square shrine of bricks and wood to enclose the rock on which Abraham had attempted to sacrifice Isaac and from which Mohammed had made an ascent to Heaven on a human-headed horse. But toward the end of the seventh century, the caliph 'Abd al-Malik, as a chronicler tells us, "noting the greatness of the Church of the Holy Sepulcher and its magnificence, was moved lest it should dazzle the minds of the Muslims, and hence erected above the Rock the dome which is now to be seen there." 'Abd al-Malik's new building, the earliest preserved Muslim structure, was magnificent from the start (colorplate 44). The rich fabric of blue, white, yellow, and green tiles which now clothes the upper portion was added only in the sixteenth century, but it replaces decorative glass mosaics that emulated those in Christian churches and were in fact executed by Byzantine artists. The lower portions are still sheathed in their original slabs of veined marble, in which one may note the modest beginnings of the abstract, geometric ornament that became so dazzling in later Muslim architecture. The wooden dome (regilded in 1960 in anodized aluminum) was covered originally with gold leaf.

The plan is not that of the typical mosque, but derives from the central-plan Christian martyrium because pilgrims were required to walk in procession around the sacred Rock just as the Christians did around a martyr's tomb. A simple octagon is surmounted by a graceful, slightly pointed dome, the idea for which may have been suggested by the almost pointed barrel vault of the palace of the Sassanian monarch Shapur I at Ctesiphon in Mesopotamia (fig. 351), near the later site of Baghdad. The shape is repeated in the delicately pointed arches used throughout the building, in the surrounding courtyard, in the blind arcade and windows of the exterior, and in the two concentric ambulatories around the Rock. The pointed arch offers great advantages over its round counterpart, since it can be designed in almost any proportion, thus freeing the architect from the tyranny of that inconvenient quantity *pi* (π) in working out his calculations. As we shall see, the pointed arch is only one of the many flexible features introduced by Muslim architects in the course of time. The pointed arch later found its way to the West where it was employed in the late eleventh century in Romanesque architecture, as at Cluny (see fig. 392), and where it became the standard shape for arches in the Gothic period. As in most mosques, the windows of the Dome of the Rock are filled with a delicate grille of stone in order to temper the harsh rays of the sun. The Muslims, like the early Christians, pressed into service columns and capitals from Roman buildings, but their sensibility admitted none of the gross discrepancies—between juxtaposed Ionic and Corinthian capitals, let us say—which did not seem to bother the early Christians. The exterior capitals of the Dome came from Roman monuments of the fourth century. The interior, with two concentric arcades around the Rock, is sheathed with veined marble and decorated with glass mosaics.

The earliest Muslim building on a gigantic scale is the Great Mosque at Damascus (fig. 352), built by Caliph al-Walid from 705–11, constructed inside the fortified outer enclosure of a Roman sanctuary, measuring 517 by 325 feet, originally containing the temple of a local Syrian deity Latinized as Jupiter Damascenus. The Christians had converted the temple into a church dedicated to Saint John the Baptist, and for decades after their conquest the Muslims left the Christians undisturbed. Then al-Walid demolished everything inside the enclosure, utilizing the salvaged masonry blocks, columns, and capitals for a grand arcade, supported by columns on the short sides and piers on the long; across the south arcade he ran a lofty transept leading to the mihrab. The square corner towers, built for defense, were utilized as minarets, and they are the earliest known. Minarets, still in use today for the muezzin's call to prayer, were not strictly necessary; a rooftop or a lofty terrace could serve the same purpose. But henceforward they became a common if not indispensable feature of the mosque. The present minaret crowning the Roman tower of the Great Mosque is a much later addition. The building has been repeated-

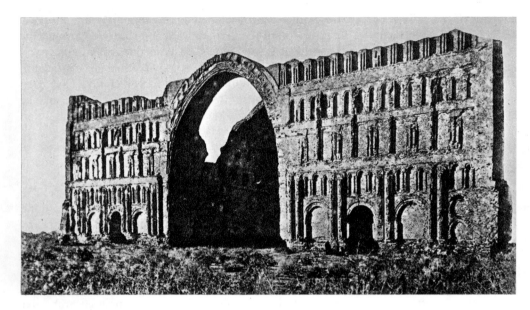

351. Palace of Shapur I.
c. 3rd–6th century
A.D. Ctesiphon,
Mesopotamia (near
present-day Baghdad)

ly burned and rebuilt; originally, its dome was slightly pointed like the dome of the Dome of the Rock. Some of the interior mosaic decoration still survives (colorplate 45), consisting of dreamlike architectural fantasies in the tradition of Roman screen architecture as we have seen it in early Byzantine mosaics at Salonika (see colorplate 35), interspersed with city views like those of the mosaics at Santa Maria Maggiore in Rome (see fig. 327). These mosaics look like a richly designed Islamic textile. The artists who made them were probably Syrian Greeks.

Much of the ornamentation of early Islamic palace architecture gives a similar effect of textile design. For example, the façade of the palace built about 743 in the desert at Mshatta, in what is now Jordan, had a lower zone of almost incredible richness (fig. 353). Here rosette

forms and floral interlace derived from later Roman and early Byzantine traditions mingle with confronted winged griffins of Mesopotamian derivation to clothe considerable areas of masonry with a flickering tissue of light and dark. The resultant pattern, known as arabesque, is quite as bewildering in its complexity as that of Germanic ornament and Hiberno-Saxon manuscripts, but it is equally disciplined and organized into zones by broad zigzags. The ornamentation at Damascus and Mshatta foreshadowed the Islamic intoxication with the mysteries of pure geometric interlace. This interlace dominates Islamic interiors instead of wall paintings (see figs. 359, 364), and in its infinity of activity exercises an effect analogous to that of the abstract paintings of Jackson Pollock in the twentieth century (see Vol. 2, colorplate 78).

The original Umayyad dynasty of caliphs was succeeded by the 'Abbasids, whose great caliph al-Mansur (reigned 754–75) removed his capital from Damascus to Baghdad on the upper Tigris in Mesopotamia. Here he built a round city, considered unique by Arab historians, but actually derived from the circular camps of the Assyrians and from later Mesopotamian models. It had two concentric circles of walls, four gateways, streets radiating outward from the center like the spokes of a wheel, and in the central area stood a great mosque and the caliph's palace. Alas, al-Mansur's wonderful round city, immortalized by the stories of his great successor Harun ar-Rashid, who developed an unlikely friendship with the Frankish emperor Charlemagne, must remain a dream. Like most Mesopotamian monuments, it was made of mud brick, and when the Mongols swept down in the thirteenth century, they destroyed everything.

Caliph al-Mu'tasim built the city of Samarra upstream from Baghdad after 836. It was twenty miles in length and counted a population of about a million; Caliph al-Mutawakkil built between 848 and 852 a mosque that could accommodate at any one moment a considerable

MAP 14. *Mesopotamia*

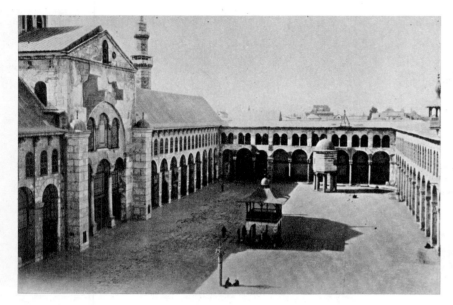

352. Courtyard and façade. Sanctuary of the Great Mosque. c. 705–11 A.D. Damascus. Syria. See Colorplate 45

proportion of the city's inhabitants. The external rectangle, measuring 784 by 512 feet (fig. 354), forms the largest of all mosques and greatly exceeds the dimensions of any Christian house of worship. The fired-brick exterior walls still stand, but little is left of the 464 mud-brick piers that supported the wooden roof, and nothing remains of the mosaics that once ornamented the interior. The stupendous spiral minaret, of fired brick (fig. 355), towers to a height of 176 feet; it forcefully recalls the principle of the Mesopotamian ziggurat, and may well have been suggested by the Tower of Babel, then standing.

Something of the grandeur of the Great Mosque at Samarra, and much of its original character can be seen in the well-preserved mosque built at Cairo by a former inhabitant of Samarra, Ibn Tulun, from 877–79. This new Muslim city rose near the vanished Memphis of the pharaohs, and its surviving Islamic buildings rank second

in quality only to the great monuments of ancient Egypt. Many of these buildings were of great importance to the medieval architecture of Europe. The Mosque of Ibn Tulun is the earliest (fig. 356). The rectangular structure, measuring 460 by 401 feet, was built on a slight eminence and enclosed by a crenellated outer wall. A double arcade lines the wall on three sides (fig. 357), and a five-aisled portico on the fourth contains the mihrab. As at Samarra the piers are of brick, but here they were protected with a thick coating of fine, hard stucco, which has survived almost intact and which makes the building appear monolithic. The sharply pointed arches, of noble simplicity, are supported by massive rectangular piers of brick, into whose corners colonnettes (little columns) are set, an early example of a device used extensively in Christian architecture of the Middle Ages. The ceiling was originally coffered below the wooden beams; little of the coffering is intact, but the rich floral ornament, carved into the plaster of the arches as if into stone, has survived in splendid condition. Especially remarkable are the smaller arches that pierce the spandrels of the larger ones to no apparent purpose; they produce an impression of lightness and variety, treating the arch—as often in Islamic architecture—as something that can be freely played with.

One of the most brilliant achievements of Islamic architecture, the Great Mosque (now the Cathedral) of Córdoba (fig. 358), was built in Spain, very nearly the westernmost outpost of Muslim domination. The original mosque, erected by 'Abd ar-Rahman I in 786, had all its aisles on the qibla side of the sahn. As necessity required, these aisles were repeatedly lengthened in the late eighth century and again in the tenth; eventually, the

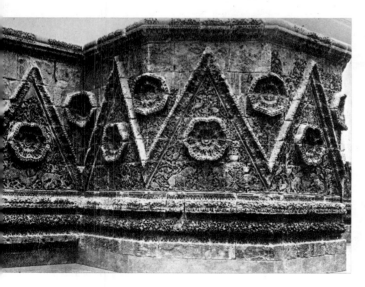

353. Façade. Palace at Mshatta, Jordan (portion). c. 743 A.D. Limestone, height of triangles 9′6″. Staatliche Museen, Berlin

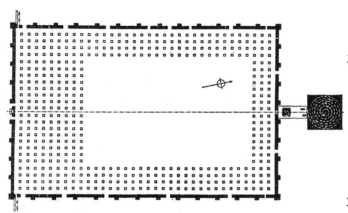

354. Great Mosque of al-Mutawakkil. c. 848–52 A.D. Samarra, Iraq. (Plan after Creswell)

355. Spiral minaret, Great Mosque of al-Mutawakkil. Fired brick, height 176'

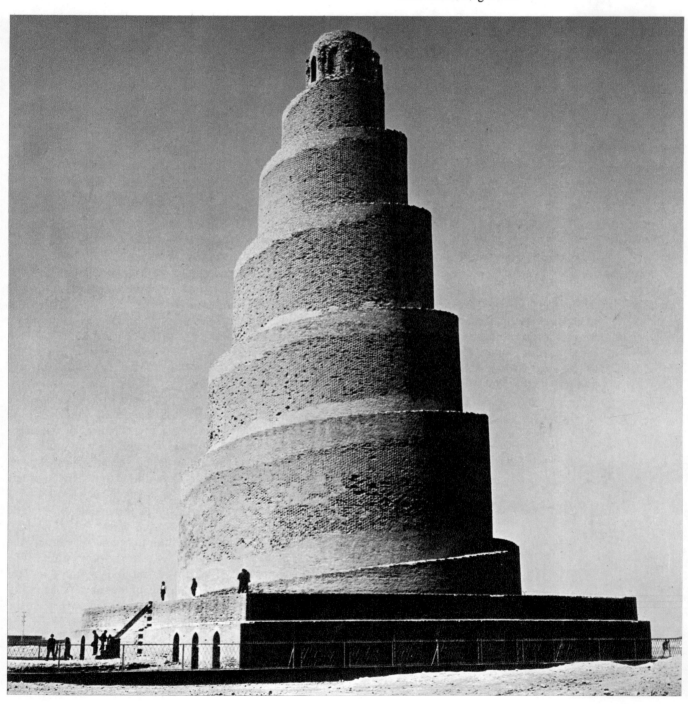

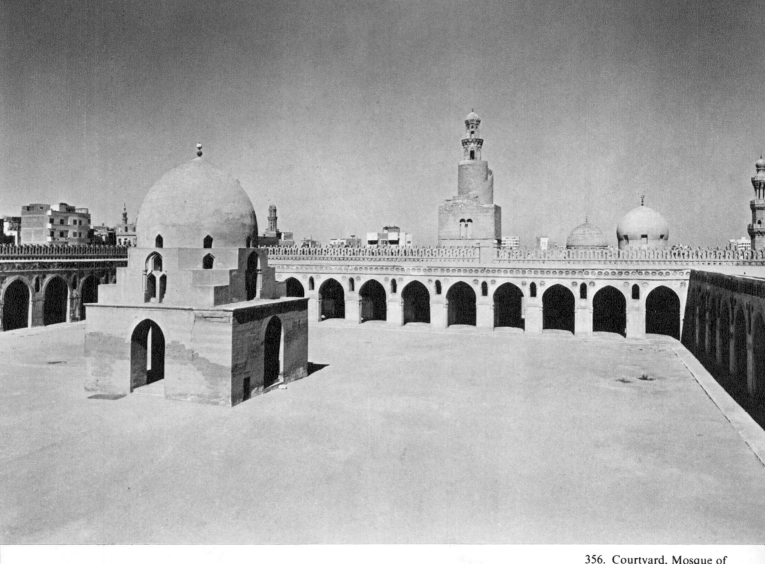

356. Courtyard, Mosque of
Ibn Tulun. c. 877–79
A.D. Cairo

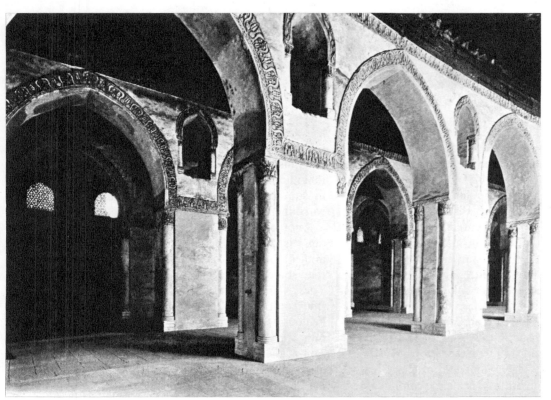

357. Arcades, Mosque of
Ibn Tulun

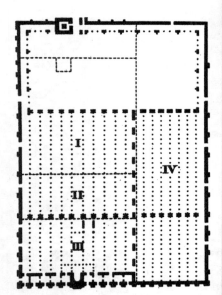

358. Great Mosque, Córdoba, showing successive enlargements. c. 786–987 A.D. Spain. (Plan after Marçais)

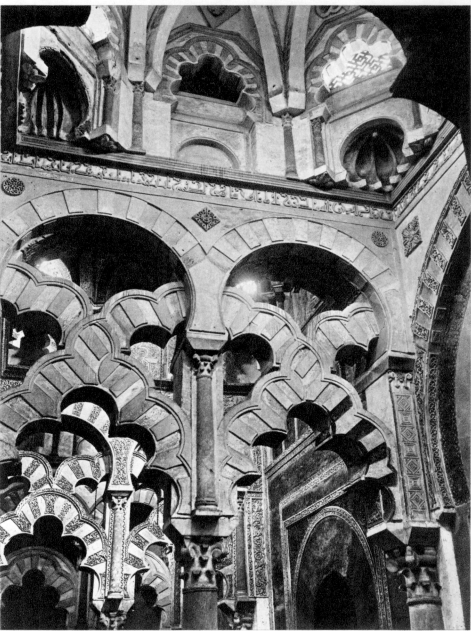

359. Vestibule of the mihrab, Great Mosque, Córdoba. c. 10th century A.D. See Colorplate 46

location of the Guadalquivir River forbade further lengthening in that direction so the structure was extended on the east. Unfortunately, in the sixteenth century the canons of the Cathedral (the mosque had been converted into a Christian place of worship long since) built a chancel inside it, greatly to the displeasure of the emperor Charles V, who rightly accused them of having ruined a monument unique in the world. But from most viewpoints the interior still presents an enthralling spectacle of seemingly infinite extent in any direction (colorplate 46)—an endless forest of columns and arches without an axis. The hundreds of marble or granite columns were, of course, cribbed from Roman and Early Christian buildings, but visually they play second to the striped arches, unknown in architecture before Muslim builders employed them. The uniqueness of the Great Mosque of Córdoba demonstrates a principle common to many mosques—that Islamic space, originally at least,

was not determined by the requirements of a set ritual as was that of Christian interiors. In the basilica the columns, like the worshipers, unite in obedience to the longitudinal vista extending toward the altar; in the mosque the columns are endless and uniform like the worshipers, who are united only in common prayer.

Another striking feature of the Great Mosque of Córdoba is the introduction of a second set of freestanding arches above the first. These spring from square piers that stand on the Roman columns as though on stilts. These flying arches, intended to uphold a wooden roof (the vaulting was added in the sixteenth century), ingenious as they are, are outdone by the inventions in the mihrab, which was built during the last southward extension of the mosque in the tenth century. The arches here are scalloped, and intertwine freely in open space (fig. 359). Other arches soar from the upper corners to cross as ribs for the vault. Here and there, in the archivolts, in the inner surfaces of the arches, and in the vertical panels, appear passages of pure arabesque; the area that in Classical architecture would constitute the frieze is decorated with passages from the Koran in fluid, richly ornamental Arabic writing.

Among the host of splendid religious structures that rose throughout the Islamic world, we must present a completely new type, the madrasah, a building intended for religious and legal instruction (because the two were fused in the Islamic theocracy). The first such combined theological seminary and law school seems to have been built in Persia about A.D 1000. The architectural requirements were a customary central sahn and separate quarters for each of four schools, each school to be administered by one of the four orthodox Muslim sects. The solution was a series of cells for each school at one of the four corners of the sahn; in the center of each face of the sahn a spacious prayer hall separated one school from its neighbor. These halls, with one side entirely open to the court, were known as iwans; the iwan on the Mecca side, of course, contained the mihrab and the minbar. Apparently, the shape of the iwan was suggested by the giant, almost pointed barrel vault of the open audience hall in the third-century palace of Shapur I at Ctesiphon (see fig. 351), a building that could be easily visited from Baghdad. The arches of the iwans, however, were always sharply pointed, in more or less the shape of the pointed arches of the Mosque of Ibn Tulun (see fig. 356), and their majestic open spaces dominate the sahn. Once established, the madrasah became the model for all large mosques in Persia.

In the fourteenth century the Mamluk sultans of Egypt (descendants of Turkish slaves who had seized power) built a number of madrasahs in Cairo. Their size was limited, however, by the existing buildings of the metropolis. The grandest example is the madrasah constructed by Sultan Hasan in 1356–63 (fig. 360), whose towering iwans leave little room for windows in the four stories of student cells at the corners of the restricted sahn. With their pointed barrel vaults, the iwans give an overpowering impression of mass and space, increased by the chains of the seventy bronze lamps that still hang in the sanctuary (as once in Early Christian basilicas). The east iwan, richly paneled in veined marble, contains the usual mihrab and minbar (fig. 361), surmounted by a superb arabesque frieze. Behind the gate to the minbar can be seen the bronze grille that gives access to the domed interior of the sultan's tomb, a new type of structure which the Muslims appear to have emulated from Western examples. From the exterior (fig. 362) the two buildings seem almost separated, both blocklike, their walls pierced with pointed windows, some single, others paired with a round window above, in a grouping that may reflect the tracery of French Gothic cathedrals (see Chapter 9, and fig. 457). The tomb is crowned with a handsome pointed dome; the adjacent minaret, square in plan with several superimposed octagonal stories, rises to a height of nearly three hundred feet.

The achievements of Islamic religious architects, like those of Roman imperial builders, stand throughout North Africa, Spain, the Balkans, and the Near East—and also in northern India and Pakistan. We must limit ourselves here to an epilogue, the architecture of the Ottoman Turks who, in 1453, conquered Constantinople

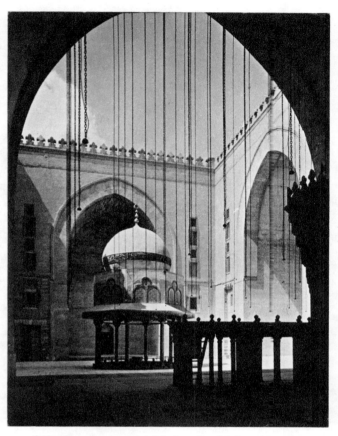

360. Courtyard of the Madrasah of Sultan Hasan. c. 1356–63. Cairo

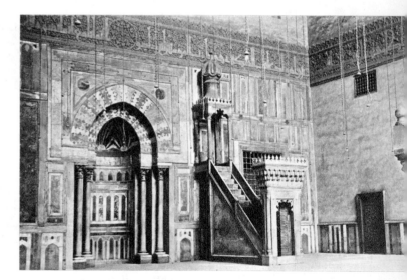

361. The East Iwan containing the mihrab and minbar, Madrasah of Sultan Hasan

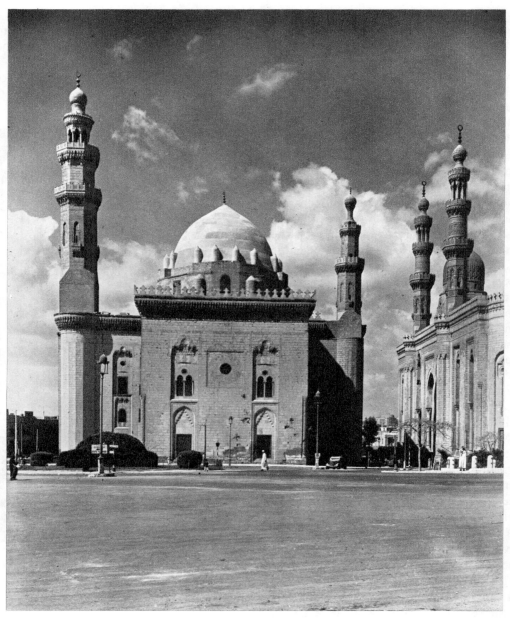

362. Madrasah and Mausoleum of Sultan Hasan

and put an end to the Byzantine Empire. They were by no means as inventive as their Arab predecessors, and the renamed Byzantine capital Istanbul does not offer the infinite surprises that delight the visitor bold enough to brave the dusty and tumultuous alleys of Cairo. Hugely impressed by Hagia Sophia, which along with the other churches of the capital the Turks turned into mosques, the Ottomans confined themselves to producing innumerable replicas of Justinian's masterpiece in large, medium, and small sizes. It is thus extremely difficult to pick out from a distance Hagia Sophia itself in Istanbul's romantic skyline of domes and minarets. Although the interiors of the Ottoman central-plan mosques seem heavy when compared with the seraphic lightness of

Hagia Sophia, their exteriors, such as that of the Mosque of Ahmed I, built from 1609 to 1617 (fig. 363), often resulted in a considerable refinement and systematization of the free arrangements of domes and semidomes designed by Anthemius of Tralles and Isidorus of Miletos eleven hundred years earlier.

To many the supremely original creation of Islamic architecture will always be the Alhambra, the palace built by the Nasrid kings on a lofty rock above Granada in southern Spain in the fourteenth century, only a century and a half before the Moors were expelled from this last European fortress by Queen Isabella and King Ferdinand. The rich valleys and fertile slopes that surround Granada made the final Moorish kingdom in Spain a paradise during the fourteenth and fifteenth centuries, darkened only by the internal strife that eventually laid the kingdom open to Spanish conquest. The extreme refinement of the scholarly and art-loving court of the kingdom of Granada finds its embodiment in the beauty of the Alhambra. Surrounded on its hilltop by towered fortifications, against a backdrop of snow-covered mountains, the palace seems from the outside to be colossal; on entering, the visitor is all the more surprised at the intimacy, human scale, and jewel-like refinement of the porticoes, vaulted chambers, courts, gardens, pools, and fountains. A view across the Court of the Lions (fig. 364) suggests the disembodied fragility of this architecture, cloudlike in its lightness, flowerlike in its delicacy, but pervaded even in its last refinements by a rigorous sense of logic.

The colonnettes we first saw tucked into the corners of massive piers in the Mosque of Ibn Tulun (see fig. 357) reappear here freed from brute substance, standing singly in twos or threes, upholding vaults whose underlying bricks are covered with hard stucco carved into fantastic shapes—a honeycomb of microvaults, or airy structures made up entirely of arabesque interlace, or arches from which hang stalactites of pure ornament. While the individual elements can all be found in structures in Egypt and throughout North Africa, and especially in Persian buildings of the fourteenth century, nothing like this brilliant combination of them had ever been executed before or ever would be again.

Caught in their last redoubt between the Mediterranean Sea and the Spanish sword, the Nasrid kings lived an existence in which luxury was refined to its ultimate

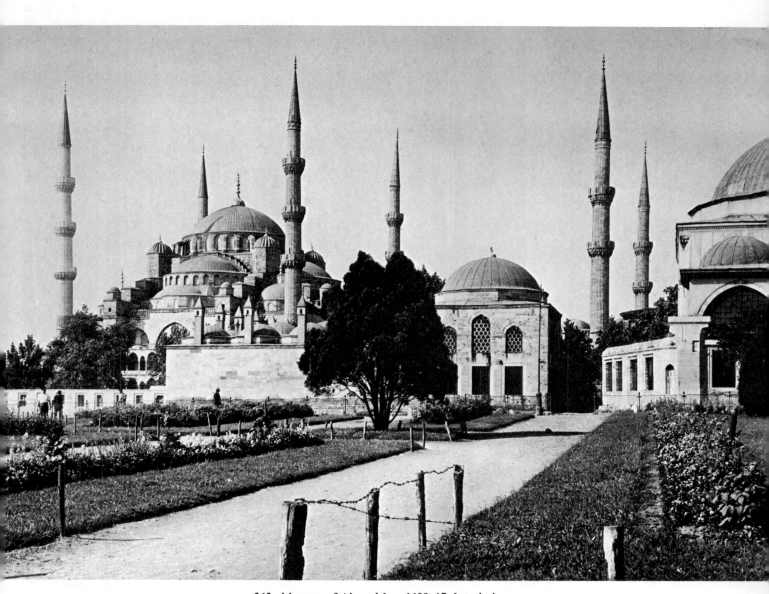

363. Mosque of Ahmed I. c. 1609–17. Istanbul

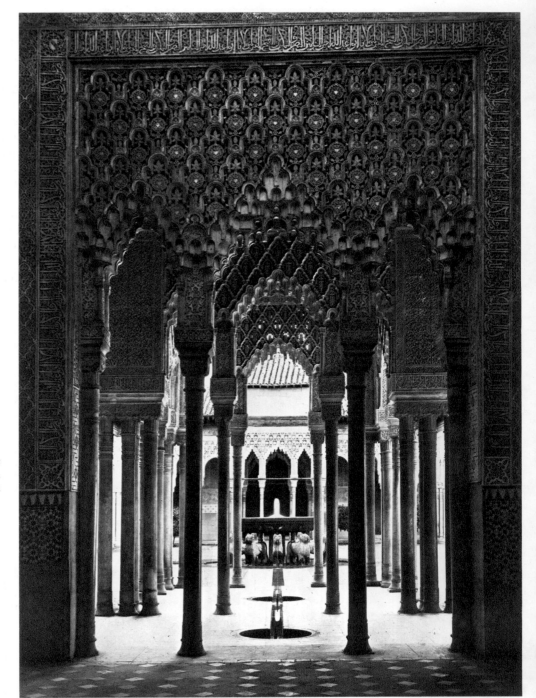

364. Court of the Lions, The
Alhambra. c. 1354–91.
Granada, Spain

distillation. One could contemplate the arabesques at the Alhambra for days on end, and only begin to sample their delights (fig. 365). Such contemplation induces a passivity akin to transcendental meditation, freeing the intellect for the pursuit of the endless ramifications of pure logic. At first it may seem difficult to tarry over such complexities; the Western mind used to literal representation and clear-cut definition turns away frustrated, just as ears accustomed only to melody supported by underlying harmony may be baffled by the endless polyphonic structure of Bach's music. The defeat here is like that which the mind suffers after hearing a Bach fugue—one has not quite been able to experience it

all. But like contrapuntal music, or like the carvings at Mshatta or at Córdoba (or for that matter like the interlace of Hiberno-Saxon manuscripts; see fig. 349, colorplate 42), these arabesques of Granada are severely separated into parts and regions, each assigned its own duty in the final intellectual structure.

To Mohammed sculpture was idolatrous by its very nature, and the device of Satan himself; he cleared all of it out of the Ka'bah, and all the paintings, too, for that matter, save one—strangely enough—of the Virgin and Child. Occasionally, sculpture sneaked back into Islamic art, but usually in the forms of decorative animals, like the richly carved lions that support the Alhambra foun-

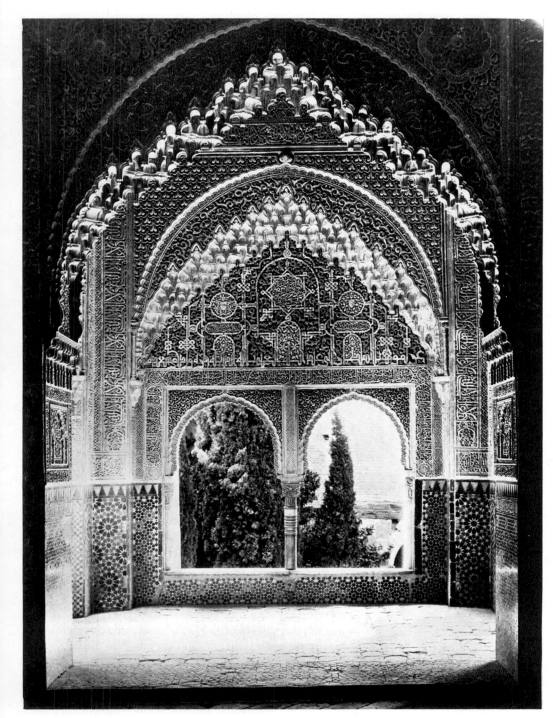

365. The Queen's Chamber,
The Alhambra

tain. Painting, while not permitted on a monumental scale, was useful enough for manuscripts—though always secondary to the art of calligraphy. Islam was blessed with a singularly graceful form of writing. The earliest script, a massive style called Kufic, was especially appropriate to carving in stone. A page from a Koran written in the ninth century in either Syria or Iraq (fig. 366) shows how bold and harmonious this writing can be in manuscripts as well, with its noble black characters punctuated by red dots and adorned with a broad band of gold leaf used to emphasize an especially important passage. But there is more than at first meets the eye. One watches for a moment, and then the written char-

acters come to life, transforming themselves into Muslims with red turbans, seated, prostrate, or kneeling in prayer, or lifting up their hands to Allah. This form of double imagery was not achieved in Western art until the sixteenth century in the so-called Mannerist period, and was exploited systematically only by some of the Surrealists, notably Salvador Dali, in the twentieth century (see Vol. 2, fig. 506).

By the thirteenth century lively explanatory or narrative illustrations were common in Islamic manuscripts, usually with the parchment as the sole background and sometimes without borders. Only a summary indication of setting is given, such as curtains or a plant here and

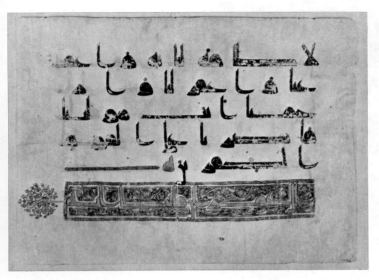

366. Koran page written in Kufic script, from Syria or Iraq. Illumination. c. 9th century A.D. Parchment. The Metropolitan Museum of Art, New York

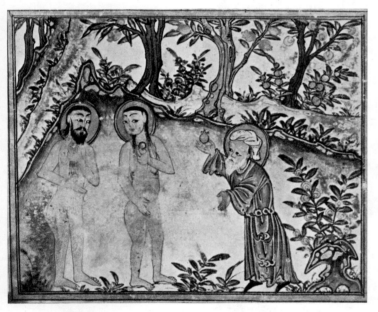

367. *Temptation of Adam and Eve*, from the *Chronology of Ancient Peoples* manuscript of al-Biruni, painted in Tabriz, Iran. 1307. Illumination, 7½ x 12½". Edinburgh University Library

there. Under the Mongol conquerors considerable changes appeared later in the century, partly due to Oriental influence—Chinese artists had been imported into Persia. An example of this hybrid art is the disarming *Temptation of Adam and Eve* (fig. 367) from a manuscript of the *Chronology of Ancient Peoples* of al-Biruni, painted at Tabriz in Persia in 1307. The Garden of Eden is represented by fruit trees, rocks, and flowers, all ornamentalized in a style derived from Chinese painting. A very Oriental-looking Adam and Eve appear naked (almost unparalleled in Islamic art) save for ineffectual bits of transparent drapery, and with halos which to Christian eyes are undeserved. In fact, even Satan, garbed in a robe shaded in a very Chinese style and shown importuning a coy Eve with a golden fruit, has been provided with a halo. The real explosion of pictorial art in Persia occurred under the Mongol conqueror Tamerlane and his successors toward the end of the fourteenth century. Although converted to Islam, the Mongols paid slight attention to its prohibitions and restrictions against representation, and they covered their palace interiors with figurative mural paintings, of which we possess only mouth-watering descriptions by contemporary writers.

But the manuscripts remain, and they are dazzling. An especially beautiful example is the manuscript of the poems of Khwaju Kirmani by Junaid, one of the leading Persian painters, illuminated in 1396. In *Bihzad in the Garden* (colorplate 47), a considerable expanse of landscape has been indicated by means of a division of the page into areas—the smallest being left for the text. The ground in this painting seems to rise like a hillside, although horizontal extent was clearly intended. At the back a wall encloses the garden from the outside world, and above it one sees only the blue sky dotted with gold stars and a gold crescent moon. Even with the exquisite grace of his representation of foliage, flowers, figures, and drapery in a style that seems utterly relaxed, Junaid was never unaware of the inner rhythmic relationships of motives apparently strewn at random. Nor did he neglect the harmonies of rose, soft green, soft red, pale blue, and gold that make his picture sing. It is this enchanting combination of expressive freedom and ornamental unity that so attracted Matisse to Persian manuscripts in the 1920s (see Vol. 2, fig. 449, colorplate 64). Junaid's joyous rediscovery of the visual world came, significantly enough, in the same century as the rebirth of naturalism in the work of the European masters of the Late Gothic period.

5

Carolingian Art

The victorious advance of the Muslims in Europe was stopped in 732 at Tours, two-thirds of the way from the Pyrenees to the English Channel, by Frankish forces under Charles Martel. It is sobering to contemplate how different European history, and consequently European art, might have been had Charles Martel lost this battle. Charles Martel (the word *martel* means *hammer*) was a high official under the weak Merovingian kings, and he gave his name to the Carolingian dynasty that, under his son Pepin the Short, replaced them. Pepin entered Italy, in answer to the pope's appeal, to defend the papacy against the Lombards; in 756 he gave Ravenna and the surrounding territory, which rightly belonged to the Byzantine Empire, to the pope, thereby at once strengthening the ties between Rome and the Frankish kingdom and weakening those between the Eastern and the Western Church.

Pepin's son, known to history as Charlemagne (Charles the Great), ruled as Frankish king from 768 to 814, a reign of forty-six years that transformed the cultural history of northern and central Europe. On Christmas Day in A.D. 800 he was crowned Roman emperor in Saint Peter's by Pope Leo III, an event that did nothing to endear the Carolingian dynasty to the Byzantine emperors, legal holders of the Roman title. In appearance Charlemagne revived the fifth-century division between East and West, but in fact he ruled a region which, counting his personal conquests, included modern France, the Low Countries, Germany, much of Central Europe, a small slice of northern Spain, and Italy down to a border line not far south of Rome. He governed this territory not from Italy but from his court in the German city of Aachen, situated near the modern border of Germany with Belgium and the Netherlands. Charlemagne actually founded a wholly new institution, a northern dominion known after the thirteenth century as the Holy Roman Empire. For more than a thousand years the successors of Charlemagne exercised an often disputed

and never clearly defined authority over much of Europe, until Napoleon dissolved the Holy Roman Empire in 1806. Usually, the emperor ruled directly as German king, but he claimed suzerainty over the rest of western Europe as well, and at times he was in a position to enforce this claim. In the imagination of the Middle Ages, the emperor exercised in temporal affairs the sovereignty that in spiritual matters belonged to the pope. Since the latter was by now a temporal monarch as well, largely by courtesy of the Carolingian rulers, Pepin the Short had opened a Pandora's box, which none of his successors ever quite succeeded in closing.

Abbot Einhard, Charlemagne's biographer, said of him that "he made his kingdom which was dark and almost blind when God committed it to him . . . radiant with the blaze of fresh learning hitherto altogether unknown to our barbarism." If we discount courtly hyperbole, Einhard's claim still contains much truth. We must imagine the Roman cities of Charlemagne's realm as largely in ruins and very nearly depopulated, and there is no indication that he tried to rebuild them. To his court at Aachen, however, he brought Greek and Latin manuscripts, and foreign scholars, especially Alcuin of York, who supervised imperial campaigns aimed at the revival of Greek and Roman learning, and the establishment of the correct text of the Bible, which, through constant recopying, had grown corrupt. Such concerns are remarkable in an emperor who retained Frankish dress and who, although he understood spoken Greek and could converse in Latin, never succeeded in learning to write. The emperor's architectural ambitions seem to have been limited to the embellishment of the imperial court and of the monasteries that, under the Benedictines based at Monte Cassino in southern Italy and under the Irish monks who had founded monasteries in much of the territory to which Charlemagne fell heir, had established themselves as Western guardians of Classical Christian culture.

ARCHITECTURE

Little of what Charlemagne built is still standing in anything like its original condition; luckily, the chapel of his palace at Aachen is preserved, although extended by a Gothic choir in the late Middle Ages and stripped of its splendid decorations. The architect, Odo of Metz, is the first builder known to us by name north of the Mediterranean. The Palatine Chapel of Aachen is an octagon (figs. 368, 369), and a first glance will show that Odo modeled it on San Vitale at Ravenna, a church that Charlemagne must have greatly admired. The next look, however, discloses crucial differences. The flexible, expanding plan of San Vitale (see figs. 333, 334) has been abandoned, possibly because it was unbuildable in stone, possibly because no one knew enough about architectural draftsmanship in 792 to reproduce it; Odo may never have visited Ravenna. Each of the seven transparent apses of San Vitale has been replaced by two superimposed round arches. The upper arch embraces two levels, the lower of which is a straight arcade formed by three round arches, and the upper of which is sheer fantasy—two columns that support the crowning arch at just the point on either side of the keystone where it needs no support, as these lateral archivolts tend to be pushed up, not down, by the pressure of the central keystone. Such a use of Early Christian—in fact, Roman—motives, shorn of their original function and deprived of their true spatial extension, was significant for Carolingian figurative art as well. Needless to say, many if not all of the colored marble and granite columns and white Corinthian capitals were imported from Roman buildings in Italy. The heavy masonry is built of massive blocks of stone, but the cores of the piers are rubble. Originally, the dome was resplendent with a mosaic representing Christ enthroned in Heaven among the four and twenty elders rising from their thrones to cast their crowns before his throne, according to the vision of John (Rev. 4: 1–10), an appropriate subject for a patron who claimed divine authority for his own imperial rule. (Recently, it has been suggested that the enthroned Christ is a later interpolation, and that the original mosaic showed the Lamb upon the throne.)

Interestingly enough, the customary narthex, set at an angle at San Vitale, is replaced here by a central portal flanked by two circular towers and entered from the main court of the palace. The emperor could thus attend Mass in the gallery as though in a box at the theater, and he could appear at an opening above the portal to the populace in the court outside. Here Charlemagne had set up a bronze equestrian statue of Theodoric (a worthy model, as a Romanized Germanic chieftain), which he had brought across the Alps from Ravenna. The court could hold about seven thousand persons. The design of the Palatine Chapel was so successful that it was repeated several times in different parts of Germany.

In the still largely agricultural and patriarchal society of the Franks and their Germanic and Gallic subjects,

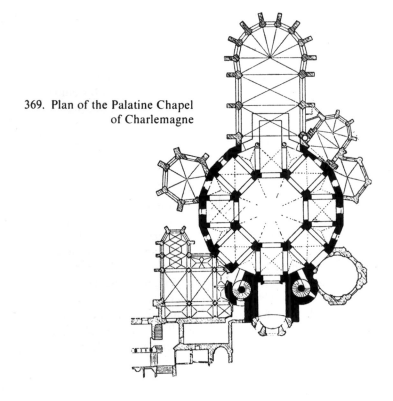

368. ODO OF METZ. Palatine Chapel of Charlemagne. 792–805 A.D. Aachen, Germany

369. Plan of the Palatine Chapel of Charlemagne

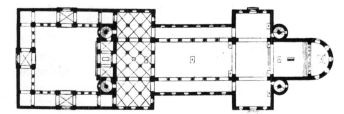

370. Plan of the Abbey Church of St.-Riquier. Late 8th century A.D. Centula, France (after Wilhelm Effmann)

there was no need for new urban churches, but monasteries were essential to Charlemagne's program, and he rebuilt them and founded new ones in great numbers. Only a few remain, largely remodeled, but plans exist that show how crucial these monasteries were for the late Middle Ages. The plan of the now totally vanished Abbey Church of Saint-Riquier at Centula (fig. 370), near Abbéville in northern France, is basically that of a Constantinian basilica with a nave and two side aisles for the congregation, the whole structure roofed with timber. The extensive transept was necessary for processions from the sacristies, where the vestments and vessels for the Mass were kept, to the altar. The apse is separated from the transept by a rectangular space called the choir, intended for the use of the monastic community; the choir became a fixture in monastic and cathedral churches from then on. The church plan has thus assumed a distinctly cruciform character.

At the west end (churches customarily faced east toward Jerusalem) is an important addition—a narthex running at right angles to the nave and projecting beyond it, forming in effect a second transept. This addition is known in German churches as the *westwork* (fine later examples are shown in figs. 378, 413). The westwork was divided into two or even three groin-vaulted stories; the upper levels could be used as chapels for smaller services. Before the westwork is a large atrium, as at Saint Peter's. In the corners of the atrium, on either side of the westwork, are two cylindrical staircase towers, and two more are visible flanking the choir in the angles of the transept. These towers apparently rose to a considerable height. It may fairly be asked what their use could have been. We do not know whether bells were employed in European churches at this time, but if they were a single tower would have sufficed for this purpose. Four clearly represent an attempt to assert the existence of the church and to render it visible from afar. To make its appearance still grander, Saint-Riquier also sported massive round towers above the crossing points of the nave with the westwork and with the transept. These towers culminated in round lanterns; both corner towers and lanterns had conical roofs. All at once the lofty skyline of the medieval cathedral appears in germ, replacing the low profile of the Early Christian basilica.

In 816–17 a council at Aachen devised an ideal plan for a monastery, which was sent to the abbot of Saint Gall in Switzerland (fig. 371); although he did not follow it exactly, the plan is revealing in that it shows all the major features of a later Western medieval monastery. The plan is dominated by the church, whose semicircular westwork is flanked by two cylindrical towers. The customary nave and side aisles of the interior lead as usual to transept, choir, and apse. The buildings to the left of the church include a guest house, a school, and the abbot's house. Behind the apse and to the right is a building for novices. Adjacent to the novitiate and to its right lie the cemetery (frugally used also as an orchard), the vegetable gardens, and the poultry pens. In the position that became customary in all oriented churches, in the southwest corner of the transept—the warmest spot in the monastery—is the cloister, a courtyard surrounded by arcades, under which the monks could walk, write, and converse. Storerooms flank the cloister to the west,

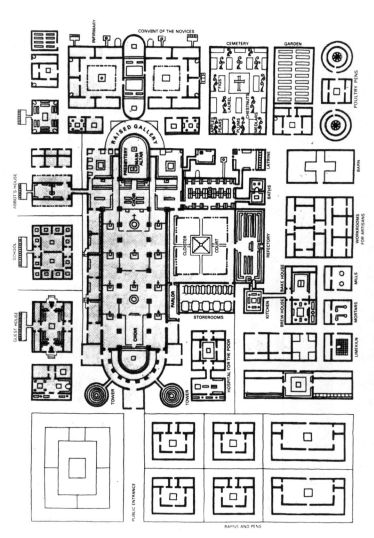

371. Schematic plan for a monastery at St. Gall. Switzerland. c. 819 A.D. (Drawing after a 9th century manuscript)

the monks' dormitory with connecting bath and latrine lies to the east, and a refectory for meals with a nearby kitchen is to the south. To the right of the refectory are workshops, brewhouse, bakehouse, and other work buildings. A hospital for the poor is adjacent to the southwest tower. The whole was laid out with the same sense of system and order that prevailed in a Hellenistic or Roman civic center, for the monastery was indeed a town in itself.

The Carolingian period is often characterized as a renaissance, since Charlemagne made a deliberate effort to revive Classical antiquity. But each renaissance (that of Augustus or of Hadrian, for example) picks and chooses among the treasures of the past only those it feels it needs. Charlemagne did not revive temples or nude statues; he was interested in establishing in the North a durable Christian society after an interregnum of tribal chaos. He went to considerable trouble to work out an administrative system for his empire, and widespread knowledge was necessary for the fulfillment of his purpose. For the acquisition and diffusion of knowledge, the monasteries, with their libraries and busy scriptoria (rooms for copying manuscripts), staffed by disciplined and devoted monks, were essential. It is noteworthy that the earliest extant copies of many ancient, even pagan, authors were made in these very scriptoria.

It is interesting, therefore, to see what dignity could be given to the gateway leading to the imperial Abbey of Lorsch, in the central Rhineland (fig. 372). This little building was imitated from the now vanished triple

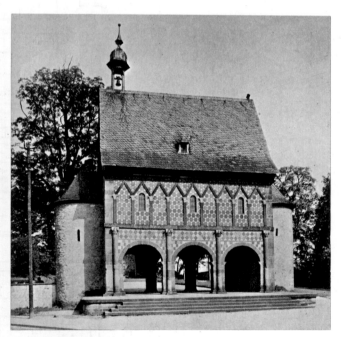

372. Gateway of the Abbey of Lorsch. 768–74 A.D. Hesse, Germany

gateway that gave access to the atrium before Saint Peter's (see fig. 322). Charlemagne has let his gateway stand free like a triple arch of triumph. Undoubtedly, the columns and capitals were culled from a Roman building. But the pilasters above the columns support colored marble zigzags that savor more of Germanic metalwork than of ancient Rome, and the overall effect of the monument, agreeable as it is, is anything but Classical with its flickering background of inlaid colored marble lozenges on the first story and octagons on the second, not to speak of its steep, northern roof.

PAINTING AND MINOR ARTS

From contemporary accounts we know that Charlemagne heard evidence on both sides of the iconoclastic controversy then raging in the East (see Chapter 8); he rejected the views of those who would destroy religious images and would forbid the creation of new ones, yet even more firmly he opposed the worship of images. The emperor was deeply interested in the instructional value and the quality of the mural paintings and mosaics throughout his realm; he commissioned an inventory of their subjects (which still survives) and expected periodic reports on their condition. He ordered that paintings done during his reign were to depict Christ and the Apostles, narratives from the New Testament and to a lesser extent from the Old, and the lives of the saints. Military leaders from ancient history could be shown if paralleled with their Christian counterparts (for example, Alexander/Constantine), but Classical deities and Classical personifications were to be avoided in paintings visible to the public. Alas, little but the written accounts remains of the presumably splendid Carolingian art of mural painting, and what does survive is either so provincial or so fragmentary that we can gain no clear idea of how the murals once looked. But illuminated manuscripts from the period are preserved by the score, often in well-nigh perfect condition. They glow with color and gold and are so beautiful that we mourn the loss of the wall paintings all the more.

The manuscripts illuminated for the emperor himself were often written, like those commissioned by Justinian, in letters of gold on purple parchment. Although he could not write, Charlemagne laid great stress on legibility. He caused the often indecipherable script of Merovingian times to be replaced by a new form of letters, more useful than the capitals that the Romans employed exclusively. (In fact, the capitals used on this page are based on those in inscriptions dating from the reign of Trajan, while the small letters descend from the script invented for Charlemagne and taught throughout his dominions.) Schools of illumination were set up at various centers, including the court at Aachen and the bishoprics of Reims, Metz, and Tours. Although the large initial letters often proudly display the complex interlaces of Hiberno-Saxon

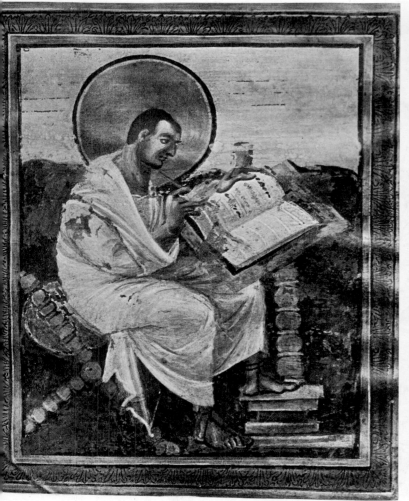

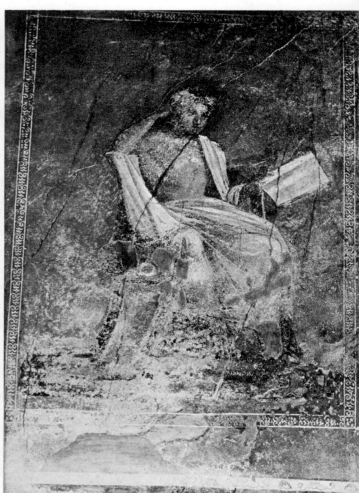

373. *St. Matthew*, from the *Coronation Gospels*.
c. 795–810 A.D. Illumination, c. 6¾ x 9″.
Weltliche Schatzkammer, Hofburg, Vienna

374. *Portrait of Menander*, from the House of
Menander. Wall painting. c. 70 A.D.
Pompeii, Italy

tradition, the illustrations are figurative, either copied from Early Christian originals (this is a hypothesis, since no such originals are known) or invented anew. Christ and the Evangelists were often given full-page illustrations—Christ as King, the Evangelists as authors. King David, naturally enough, was another favorite of the emperor and was often prominently depicted. Pages were also filled with the canon tables (which show the correspondence of passages in the four Gospels), written in under illusionistic arcades.

One of the finest Carolingian manuscripts is the *Coronation Gospels*, which is said to have been found on Charlemagne's knees when his tomb was opened in A.D. 1000. Like most manuscripts of the Palace School, the *Coronation Gospels* are illuminated only with canon tables and with full-page portraits of the Evangelists. The Evangelist Matthew (fig. 373) is painted in a manner so Classical that it is hard to realize we are looking at a work done between 795 and 810, rather than five hundred years earlier. The Evangelist is seated on a folding stool, robed in snowy white, holding his inkhorn above the page with his left hand while his right, grasping a reed

pen, is poised as if he were awaiting inspiration. The background landscape, with its rich blue-greens and with rose and white clouds streaking the sky, not to speak of the lights and shadows and the soft brushwork of the mantle, comes straight from the Helleno-Roman illusionistic tradition. This beautiful illustration has often been compared with Roman author representations, especially the *Portrait of Menander*, of the Fourth Style, dating from about A.D. 70, from the House of Menander at Pompeii (fig. 374). But as Meyer Schapiro has pointed out, there is a fundamental difference, which tells us much about the essential character of illuminated manuscripts. Like all authors in Classical art, Menander is shown reading from a rotulus, in a relaxed and patrician manner. Matthew is pictured *writing*, in a codex, of course. To the Greeks and Romans writing was a manual activity they relegated to slaves, and books were copied quasi-mechanically in shops, which were the ancestors of modern publishing houses.

Christians believe that "In the beginning was the Word, and the Word was with God, and the Word was God" (John 1: 1). Thus, copying the Word was a sacred

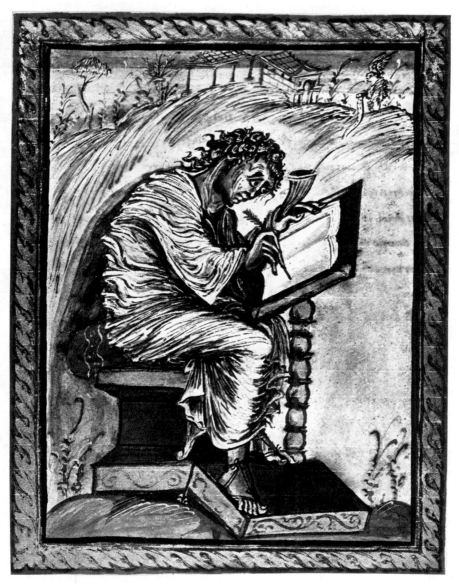

375. *St. Matthew*, from the *Ebbo Gospels* of Reims, France. 816–41 A.D. Illumination, c. 10 x 8″. Bibliothèque Nationale, Paris

duty; how much more elevated then the activity of writing under direct divine inspiration! It is to this solemn moment that the Carolingian painter admits us. And, like all medieval artists, he was not really interested in an exact representation of earthly relationships. We look at the portrait through a Classical acanthus frame as though through a window, but one leg of the stool is clearly outside the frame, the other rests on its edge, and the Evangelist's right foot is placed somewhere near the base of the writing desk, not really on it. The question of the homeland of the artist who illuminated the *Coronation Gospels*, at once so serenely Classical and so profoundly Christian, has often been asked but never answered. He may have been an Italian trained in the Byzantine tradition, but in the absence of any paintings of this style in Italy itself, we cannot say.

A startling transformation of the calm, Classical image takes place in the manuscripts of the Reims School, of which the outstanding example is the *Ebbo Gospels*, illuminated for Ebbo, archbishop of Reims between 816 and 841. The same Matthew (fig. 375), seen through the same acanthus frame, has suddenly been seized as if by the *furor divinus*. He bends over as he writes, clutching his quill pen, his eyes almost starting from their sockets with excitement, his drapery dashing madly about his form, the very locks of his hair on end and writhing like serpents. Not only the figure but also the quivering landscape have been so rapidly set down in quick, nervous strokes of the brush that they seem to participate in his emotion, recalling the words: "The mountains skipped like rams, and the little hills like lambs" (Ps. 114: 4). The tiny structures in the background seem seriously endangered in this cosmic dance, and even the acanthus leaves of the frame run like flames about the edges—left and upper borders together, right and lower borders meeting. The angel, Matthew's symbol, is sketchily brushed in on the right horizon; he brandishes a scroll, the source of the Evangelist's inspiration. We are here confronted with a form of ecstatic mysticism that we shall seldom see again so eloquently expressed before El Greco in the sixteenth century (see Vol. 2, colorplate 35). Free brushwork, till now the recorder of vision, has been transformed into a vehicle for inspiration.

One of the masterpieces of Carolingian art is the *Utrecht Psalter*, a book of psalms written and illustrated in the Reims School (which comprised several monasteries) at about the same moment the *Ebbo Gospels* was being illuminated and in a similar passionate style. This psalter was illustrated entirely with quill pen, and in the course of time the ink has turned a rich brown, running from quite dark brown to soft golden tones. The little drawings are frameless, scattered freely about the page between the psalms, some invading the Latin text (still written, by the way, in traditional Roman capitals, without spaces between the words). The compositions may derive from earlier models, and the sprightly drawings in the psalter are the work of several different hands of varying degrees of quality. However, the style is so consistent that one major master must have inspired the unflagging freshness of the scenes and their rapidly moving and gesticulating figures. The illustrations are quite literal. Figure 376 illustrates both Psalm 82 in the King James Version (81 in the Douay Version), which is written in the central register, and Psalm 83 (82 in the Douay Version), whose text appears on the following page of the psalter. Psalm 82 is pictured in the top register. The illustrations can best be read juxtaposed with the appropriate verses.

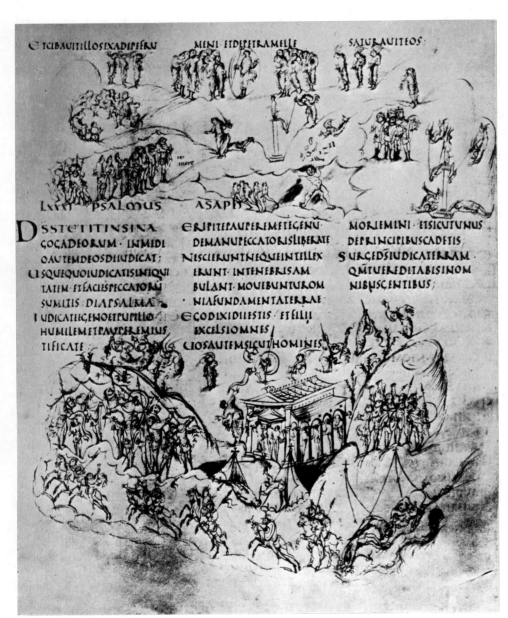

376. *The Last Judgment* (above), and *Angels of the Lord Smiting the Enemies of the Israelites*, (below), from the *Utrecht Psalter*. Illumination. c. 820–32 A.D. University Library, Utrecht, The Netherlands

Verse 1	God standeth in the congregation of the mighty; he judgeth among the gods.	In the center the Lord, in a mandorla and holding a cross-staff, addresses crowds on either side of him; farther out three angels on each side keep a respectful distance.
Verse 4	Deliver the poor and needy: rid them out of the hand of the wicked.	At the lower left an angel with a sword welcomes the poor, while their tormentors slink away.
Verse 5	...all the foundations of the earth are out of course.	At the lower right a giant (Tellus, the Roman god of the earth, shown nude in this manuscript intended for the elite) shakes the earth gleefully, and things fall to bits.
Verse 7	But ye shall die like men, and fall like one of the princes.	Crowned figures watch while an angel sets fire to a statue on a column; two other angels knock a statue down, and two men die at the base of its column.

Psalm 83 (82 in the Douay Version) is illustrated in the bottom register.

Verse 2	For, lo, thine enemies make a tumult: and they that hate thee have lifted up the head.	At the left a confused crowd of armed men lift up their heads.
Verse 12	...Let us take to ourselves the houses of God in possession.	In the center people fill the arches of a pedimented house; one defies the Lord, who bears shield and spear.
Verse 14	...as the flame setteth the mountains on fire;...	Right and left, on either side of the Lord, angels set fire to the mountains with torches.
Verse 17	Let them be confounded and troubled for ever...	At the bottom an army on horseback retreats rapidly; three of the horsemen are trapped in rope snares.

The artist never loses either the compositional coherence of the entire image, made up of several moments in time with the Lord always pictured in the center, or the speed of a sprightly pen style, which fairly dashes across the page.

After Charlemagne's death his descendants partitioned his domains and proved incapable of continuing his great dream of a newly revived Roman Empire. Nonetheless, the lively narrative and expressive style of the Reims School continued to influence the development of manuscript painting under Charlemagne's grandson, Charles the Bald, who ruled over a region corresponding more or less to modern France and whose people spoke a Latin tongue that is the ancestor of French. Charles briefly wore the imperial crown (875–77). The splendid *Bible of Charles the Bald*, now in Rome, contains a rich series of succinct visual narrations, in brilliant colors, picturing scenes from both Old and New Testaments. One full-page illustration (colorplate 48) gives incidents from the ninth chapter of Acts in three registers. At the left of the upper register Saul (not yet Paul) receives a scroll from the high priest on which are written letters for Damascus. At the right, on the way to Damascus, he falls to the ground before the Lord, who appears as the conventional Hand of God, to the astonishment of his companions, who hear a voice but see no one. At the left of the central register Saul is led blind into Damascus. At the right the aged Ananias, asleep on his bed, lifts his hand to the Lord, from whom he receives the command to restore Saul's sight. The miracle, in which Ananias places his hand on Saul's eyes, has been moved out of order to the center of the register and also occupies the center of the page. At the lower left Saul confounds the incredulous Jews; at the right he is let down over the walls of Damascus in a basket.

The scenes unfold according to the continuous method we have seen in all manuscript narrations so far, a scheme derived ultimately from Roman historical reliefs. But the naturalistic concepts of support and of enclosure have been dismissed. Green earth runs under most of the scenes, with blue sky and white clouds above, but often the feet of the figures in one scene project beyond the ground strip into the clouds of the scene below. Likewise, the simple baldachin on four columns, which does triple duty for the Temple in the first scene, for the house of Judas in which Saul receives his sight in the fifth, and for the locale where Saul confounds the Jews in the sixth, does not enclose the figures, who stand or walk in front of columns they should be behind. The little cities of late Roman and Early Christian art are now toylike. The broad strips of energetic figures and ornamental architecture have been worked into a consistent pattern uniting the whole page, enlivened and reinforced by the systematic distribution of blues, greens, red-browns, rose tones, and lavenders.

How precious the illuminated Christian codex, the work of many months and even years, had become as compared with the utilitarian rotulus of antiquity may be seen in the magnificent covers that protected the painted pages. The back cover of the *Lorsch Gospels* (fig. 377), probably carved at the court of Aachen in the early ninth century, is made of ivory, like Early Christian and Byzantine diptychs. In the central relief a beardless Christ stands under an acanthus arch supported by modified Corinthian columns, as mentioned in Psalm 91 (90 in the Douay Version), Verse 13: "Thou shalt tread upon the lion and the adder: the young lion and the dragon shalt thou trample under feet." A rabbit appears at the right, a very wavy adder at the left, and under Christ's feet the lion and the dragon are being firmly trampled. The arches of the side panels shelter the angels who, in Verse 11, are given "charge over thee, to keep thee in all thy ways." In the upper strip two angels uphold a medallion containing the Cross; in the lower left the three Magi come before Herod and on the right they present their gifts to the Virgin and Child. Clearly, the style is directly imitated from Early Christian or Byzantine originals (see fig. 331, for example); the beardless Christ suggests a source in Ravenna. However, as in the manuscripts, the drapery patterns, still fluttering freely at the edges, are beginning to crystallize into ornamental motives that do not derive from the actual performance of cloth over bodies.

Most dazzling of all the covers are, of course, the ones made of gold and studded with precious and semiprecious stones, whose craftsmanship shows that the Germanic tradition of metalwork was by no means extinct. The front cover of the *Lindau Gospels* (colorplate 49), made apparently in the third quarter of the ninth century for a Carolingian monarch, is almost unbelievable in its splendor. Not only the massive acanthus frame but also the interlaced border of the Cross are set with gems, not faceted as is customary today, but smooth and lifted above the gold to receive light from all sides. Christ is represented calmly alive (a type known as the *Christus triumphans*), seeming to stand on the footrest and to extend his arms voluntarily. He is shown as one who has conquered death. Above his head little half figures representing the sun and the moon hide themselves, and in the upper panels four angels float in beautiful poses of grief. In the panels beneath the Cross, in the style of the flying angels, crouch the figures of Mary, John, and the other Marys. The still Hellenic delicacy of the floating drapery contrasts strongly with the barbaric richness of the jeweled setting.

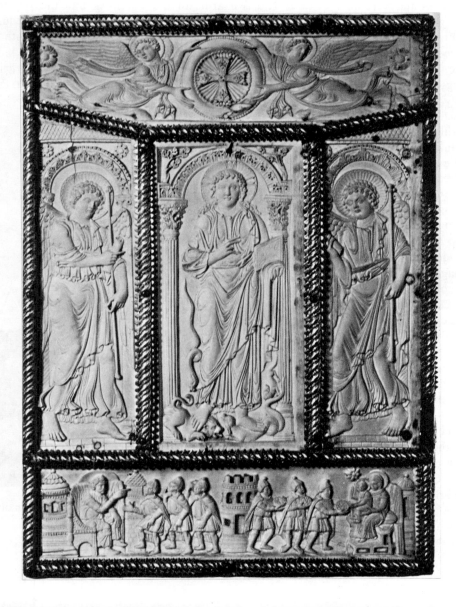

377. Back cover of the *Lorsch Gospels*. Early 9th century A.D. Ivory, 14¾ x 10¾". Vatican Museums, Rome

6
Ottonian Art

Under the uncertain conditions prevailing in northern Europe in the ninth century, the continued maintenance of imperial administration throughout so great an area would have required a dynasty of rulers of Charlemagne's exceptional ability. Unfortunately, his successors divided his empire among themselves and were unequal to the task of repelling renewed waves of invasion. The Vikings made inroads into· France, established themselves in Normandy as semi-independent dukes, and became Christianized. In the east the Carolingian kings were menaced by incursions from Magyars and Slavs. As the dynasty disintegrated, the Holy Roman Empire lapsed. Royal power in France passed to Hugh Capet, whose fourteen dynastic successors ruled without interruption until 1328. In Germany the duke of Saxony was elected king as Henry I, but avoided ecclesiastical coronation. His extraordinary son, Otto I (reigned 936–73), was determined to revive imperial power on a Roman scale, but he succeeded only in reestablishing direct rule over Germany and Italy, often by installing members of his family in crucial positions. He set up relatives as dukes throughout Germany; married the widow of Lothair II, king of Italy; and arranged the marriage of his son, later Otto II, to Theophano, daughter of the Byzantine emperor Romanus II, thereby laying claim to Byzantine southern Italy. Otto I also made three expeditions to Italy, had himself crowned king at Pavia, deposed two popes and nominated their successors, and reinforced the imperial claim to the right to approve papal elections. Before Saxon hegemony came to an end in the eleventh century, two descendants of Otto I had occupied the throne of Peter.

The five Ottonian rulers (919–1024) brought Germany to the artistic leadership of Europe in the construction of monastic buildings, in painting, and in the revived art of monumental sculpture. Only a few Ottonian church buildings remain, including the westwork of the Benedictine Abbey Church of Saint Pantaleon at Cologne, con-

secrated in 980 (fig. 378); the church was especially favored by Archbishop Bruno of Cologne, the brother of Otto I. Although most of the church was transformed in the late Middle Ages, the surviving original fragment shows us something of the grandeur of Ottonian architecture. The two arms of the westwork and the western porch (the latter a modern addition) are of almost equal length, radiating from a square crossing tower with a pyramidal roof. In the angles stand tall towers, which begin square, continue octagonal, and end cylindrical. We are at once aware of two new traits of style. First, the

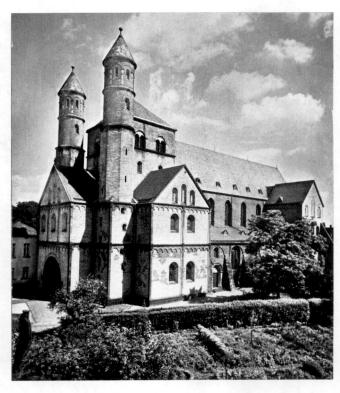

378. Westwork, St. Pantaleon. c. 980 A.D. Cologne, Germany

powerful impression exerted by the exterior is achieved by block masses of heavy masonry rather than by the thin, flat walls used by Early Christian architects to enclose interior spaces. The splaying of the windows, to admit more light, increases the apparent thickness of the walls. Second, the stories are separated by corbel tables (tiny blind arches without supports, upholding a continuous cornice). The establishment of a strong exterior view of the church building, begun in Carolingian architecture, thus culminates in a dramatic massing of clearly demarcated cubes, pyramids, octagons, and cylinders.

One of the most active patrons of the arts during the Ottonian period was Bishop Bernward of Hildesheim, who had been a tutor of Otto III and who had traveled to Rome. The great Church of Saint Michael at Hildesheim, which Bernward rebuilt from 1001–33, was considerably altered in later times and largely destroyed in World War II (fig. 379). It has since been reconstructed so as to reproduce as far as possible its eleventh-century appearance. The exterior view (fig. 380) shows the westwork to the right, the choir and apse to the left, and identical square towers over the two crossings. The side-aisle windows are later Gothic additions. The transept towers have been moved from the inner corners to the ends. In the interior the westwork is raised above the level of the rest of the church in order to provide an entrance to a crypt with an ambulatory (fig. 381 was photographed from the level of the westwork). Especially original is the way in which the sometimes monotonous impression of the customary basilican interior is broken up. The massive masonry construction permitted a high clerestory, separated from the nave arcades by an expanse of unbroken wall surface, doubtless intended for frescoes. The nave arcade itself, as in some Eastern basilicas, is broken by a pier after every second column into three groups of three arches on each side, there being twelve columns and four piers in all. It can scarcely have escaped Bernward's attention that he was founding this numerical arrangement on the number of persons in the Trinity, the number of the Twelve Apostles, and the number of the Four Evangelists.

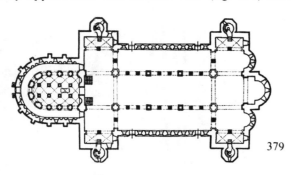

379

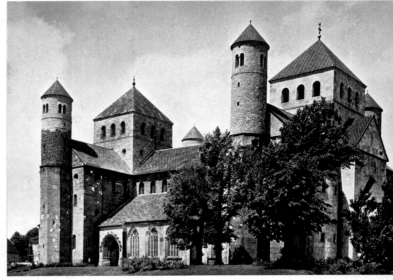

380

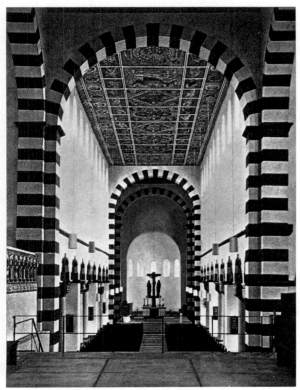

381

379. Plan of St. Michael's, Hildesheim, Germany. 1001–33. (Architectural reconstruction after Beseler)

380. Exterior, St. Michael's (reconstructed after World War II to resemble its 11th century appearance)

381. Interior, St. Michael's (view from the westwork)

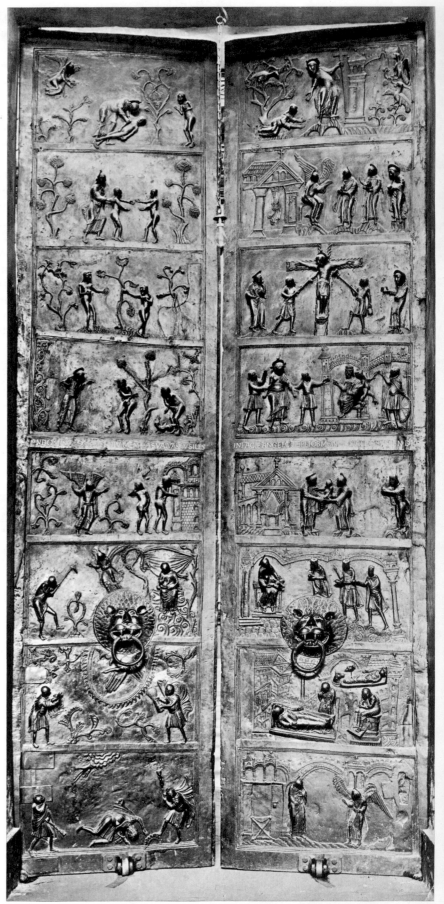

382. Bronze doors with scenes from the Old and New
Testaments. c. 1015. Height c. 15'. Cathedral of
Hildesheim. Germany

383. *Adam and Eve Reproached by the Lord* (detail of the
doors of the Cathedral of Hildesheim). Bronze, 23 x 43"

384. Column of Bishop Bernward. Early 11th century.
Bronze, height c. 12'. Cathedral of Hildesheim

382

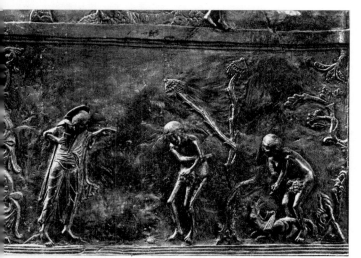

383

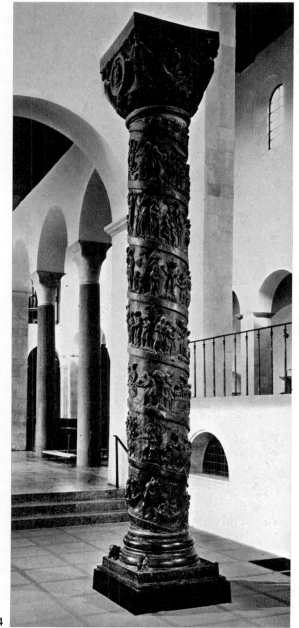

384

Bernward commissioned for the south portal of Saint Michael's a pair of bronze doors (fig. 382), completed by 1015 and probably before 1035 installed in Hildesheim Cathedral. Bronze doors were traditional in ancient times (the Pantheon had a splendid set), and plain bronze doors without sculpture had been made for the Palace Chapel at Aachen. Bernward is recorded to have been an amateur artist, and is generally believed to have supervised not only the iconographic program but also the actual execution of the doors. These massive plates of bronze, about fifteen feet in height, appear each to have been cast in one piece. They begin a long procession of splendid bronze doors created throughout the Middle Ages and the Renaissance in Germany, Italy, and Russia, culminating in Ghiberti's masterpieces for the Baptistery in Florence (see Vol. 2, figs. 47, 48). In sixteen scenes (the number of the Gospels multiplied by itself), the story of man's Fall down through Cain's murder of Abel is told on the left door, reading from top to bottom, and that of man's Redemption through Christ is narrated, reading upward, on the right, a sort of *Paradise Lost* and *Paradise Regained*. Each of the eight scenes on either door is so matched with its counterpart on the other that they complement each other precisely. For instance, in the third pair from the top, the *Temptation of Adam and Eve* (man falls through eating the forbidden fruit of the Tree of the Knowledge of Good and Evil) is opposite the *Crucifixion* (man is redeemed through Christ's sacrifice on the Tree of the Cross). There is little indication of ground, and broad areas of background appear between the figures, so that each scene conveys a strong impression of enveloping space.

The individual narratives are intensely and spontaneously dramatic, and most of them give every sign of having been inspired by a direct reading of the text rather than drawn from iconographic tradition. The fourth scene from the top of the left door, *Adam and Eve Reproached by the Lord* (fig. 383), could hardly be more effective in its staging. An angry God (note that the triune God appears, as often in Creation scenes, in the form of Christ, with a cruciform halo) in a gesture of anger and dismay expostulates with the cowering Adam and Eve, who hide their nakedness with fig leaves. Adam blames Eve, Eve points to the serpent—a dragonlike creature, which in turn snarls back at her. The freely arranged little figures, with their heads almost in the round, contrast strongly with the ornamentalized vegetation, including the fateful tree. Below the scene is a Latin inscription in inlaid silver, added shortly after Bernward's death, which translates: "In the year of Our Lord 1015 Bernward the bishop of blessed memory cast these doors."

A less influential but equally original creation of Bernward's workshop is a bronze column, more than twelve feet in height, which he also gave to Saint Michael's (fig. 384). The crucifix it originally supported is now lost, and the present capital is a nineteenth-century reconstruction. The column itself, obviously derived from the imperial columns of Rome and Constantinople, shows the triumphant deeds of no earthly emperor but of the King of Kings—Christ's earthly ministry in twenty-four scenes, beginning at the bottom with the Baptism in the River Jordan and ending with the Entry into Jerusalem. Like each door, the hollow column was cast in one piece, a remarkable technical achievement. The scenes are more densely spaced than on the doors, but quite as dramatic, and may have been the work of the same team of sculptors. The column gains considerable architectural strength from the broad spiral bands that separate the levels.

An unexpectedly powerful example of the new Ottonian art of monumental sculpture is the lifesize wooden *Crucifix* (fig. 385), given to the Cathedral of Cologne by Archbishop Gero between 969 and 976. This is the oldest surviving large-scale crucifix. The Ottonian sculptor, doubtless under ecclesiastical direction, has represented a type not yet seen in the West and apparently adopted from Byzantine art—where, in fact, Christ was never depicted with such intense emotion or such emphasis on physical torment. Instead of the *Christus triumphans* of the *Lindau Gospels* (see colorplate 49), the *Christus patiens* (*suffering Christ*) is shown, and the viewer is

spared little. The eyes are closed, the face is tense with pain, the body hangs from the crossbar, and the lines of tension in arms and legs are strongly indicated; the belly is swollen as if with gas. Christ's hair seems to writhe upon his shoulders. This kind of expressiveness, which achieves its end even by showing the most repulsive physical conditions, is characteristic of German art throughout its long history, and reappears again and again at different moments (see Vol. 2, figs. 203, 453).

A small ivory plaque representing *Doubting Thomas*, made about the year 1000 (fig. 386), raises Ottonian expressionism to the level of spiritual exaltation. The artist has made the relief look higher than it is through the illusion of a niche that encloses and compresses the two figures. In the spandrels appear Christ's words to Thomas, "Reach hither thy finger. . . ." in Latin (John 20: 27). Christ lifts his right arm, draws aside his mantle, and bends his head with a look of deep compassion, while Thomas inserts his finger into the wound. Every line of Christ's body and drapery is receptive, and every line of Thomas' pose and garments ascends; Thomas' head is turned backward so that we can see his expression. Master and disciple are bound together in a mystic union of faith and love, in which even the ascending shapes of the framing acanthus leaves seem to participate.

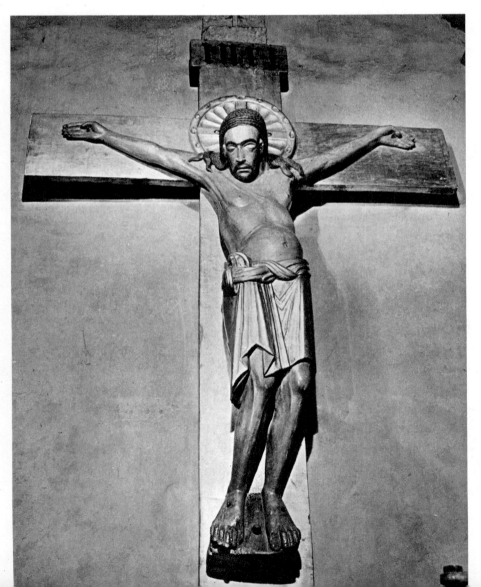

385. *Crucifix* of Archbishop Gero. c. 969–76 A.D. Wood, height 74″. Cathedral of Cologne, Germany

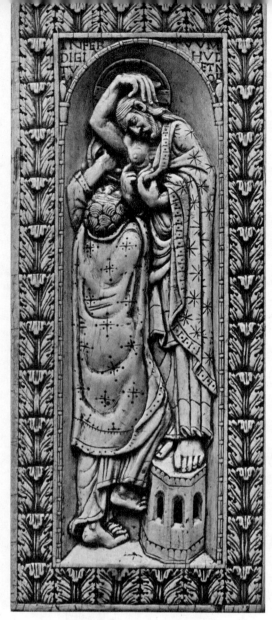

386. *Doubting Thomas.* c. 1000. Ivory plaque, 9½ x 4". Staatliche Museen, Berlin

PAINTING

As so often in the fragmented history of painting from antiquity through the early Middle Ages, we are left with nothing but tantalizing descriptions of the cycles of wall paintings that once brightened the interiors of Ottonian churches. Only in the Church of Saint George on the island of Reichenau in Lake Constance is a fairly complete cycle preserved, and that, like the fragmentary frescoes that survive elsewhere, is too badly faded for reproduction here. Again we must turn to manuscripts to assuage our loss, and again the consolation is great. The expressive and visionary qualities so evident in Ottonian architecture and sculpture are concentrated in Ottonian manuscripts. In a detached leaf from an unknown volume, we behold a youthful crowned emperor (colorplate 50), labeled *Otto Imperator Augustus,*

probably Otto II, majestically enthroned under a baldachin. He holds his staff of office with his right hand and his golden orb of power in his left, while crowned women representing subject countries, optimistically entitled *Germania, Francia, Italia,* and *Alamannia* since he ruled only Germany, present him their orbs as well. In the awesome detachment of Ottonian art, naturalism of expression is unaccompanied by concern with real space. Any attempt to deduce the spatial relationships of the columns upholding the baldachin will leave the observer in a quandary. In order not to cut up the noble Latin inscription, the artist represented only three columns; the throne levitates partly within and partly forward of the front columns, being even higher than their bases. But these unreal spatial relationships are part of the magic of Ottonian manuscripts, and if anything enhance their expressive and spiritual depth. Contours are smooth and unbroken, colors richly and subtly contrasted, surfaces strongly modeled, but the Helleno-Roman careful observation of light has now turned into a conventional pattern of strokes of graduated value.

The half-real, half-unreal Ottonian style is very grand when turned to narrative purposes, as in the *Annunciation to the Shepherds* (fig. 387) from a Gospel lectionary (the Gospel texts arranged in the order in which they are read at Mass) given to the Cathedral of Bamberg by Henry II (reigned 1002–24). The background, partly gold and partly blue, is abstract. On a mountain formed of conventionalized rocks stands a colossal angel, his mantle floating against the gold, ready to announce to the awestruck shepherds the "good tidings of great joy." Yet all seem more overcome with the mystery of the message than by its gladness. The last traces of illusionism have given way to strongly ornamental and unbroken contours; only a few parallel stripes remain to suggest the origin of such strokes in reflections of light.

The highest attainment of Ottonian art is the series of visions from both Old and New Testaments, represented with an explosive power never seen before in figurative art. As if pervaded by something of the ornamental splendor that had flowered in Hiberno-Saxon art, these illuminations yet overflow with the expressiveness of Ottonian religiosity. The *Vision of Isaiah* (colorplate 51), from a commentary illuminated in the late tenth or early eleventh century, should be contemplated along with the text it illustrates, Isa. 6: 1–4:

1 . . . I saw also the Lord sitting upon a throne, high and lifted up, and his train filled the temple.
2 Above it stood the seraphims; each one had six wings; with twain he covered his face, and with twain he covered his feet and with twain he did fly.
3 And one cried unto another, and said, Holy, holy, holy, is the Lord of hosts: the whole earth is full of his glory.
4 And the posts of the door moved at the voice of him that cried, and the house was filled with smoke.

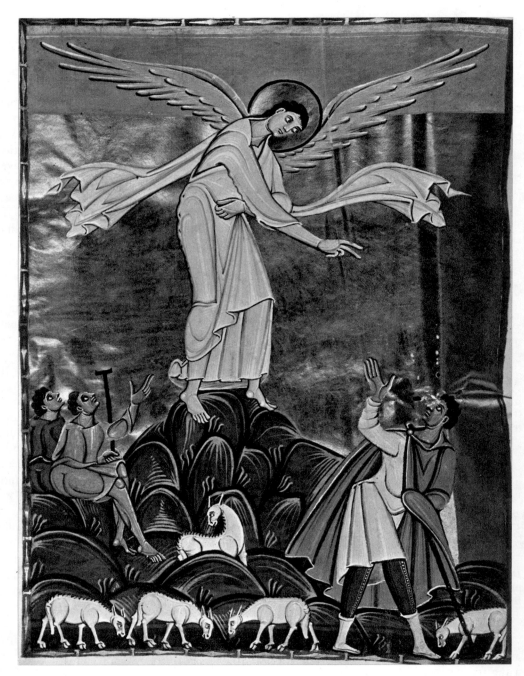

387. *Annunciation to the Shepherds*, from the Gospel lectionary of Henry II.
c. 1002–24. Illumination, 13 x 9⅜″. Bayerische Staatsbibliothek, Munich

The Ottonian artist was less literal and more imaginative than the masters who illustrated the *Utrecht
Psalter* (see fig. 376). He has shown the beardless Lord
sitting upon and within a fantastic shape composed of an
overlapping golden disk and a golden mandorla, both
with rainbow borders, with his arms outstretched and
eyes gazing forward as if he were in a trance. Nine
threefold tongues of gold flame spurt from the mandorla.
The smoke, which the text tells us filled the house, is
shown as concentric bursts of blue and violet with white
edges, like the petals of a gigantic flower. In reciprocal

and often double curves, the six-winged seraphim float
about his throne, making wonderful patterns of feathers.
Below the throne is an altar from which, as related in
verses 6 and 7, an angel takes with tongs the live coal he
will place upon Isaiah's tongue. And yet with the same
surprising disregard for the theme of the principal illustration we found in the XPI page of the *Book of Kells*
(see colorplate 43), two unconcerned rabbits in the lower
corners gnaw on pieces of fruit. Perhaps a contrast between their blind greed and the beauty of revelation was
intended.

7

Romanesque Art

The name *Romanesque* was a catchall term coined in the nineteenth century to designate a style that, while no longer Roman, was not yet Gothic. But *Gothic* itself, as we shall see in Chapter 9, was a misnomer from the start. The word *Romanesque* has other shortcomings as well; originally, it had to cover both Carolingian and Ottonian art, which have assumed distinct identities only in the last hundred years or so; some scholars still so use it. Even worse, it is a term implying transition, inappropriate for a period that has strong positive qualities of its own. Today, the name is so deeply rooted in common usage that it cannot be eradicated. For want of a better term, then, *Romanesque* is now applied to the art of the eleventh and twelfth centuries in western Europe (in France, for special reasons, it is applied to the arts only up to the middle of the twelfth century).

For a rarity in this book since the chapter dealing with the Roman Republic, neither headings nor subheadings in the discussion of Romanesque art will contain the name of a single monarch or dynasty. After the year 1000, there were many competing monarchies, and the very institution of kingship had acquired a powerful competitor—a rising commercial and industrial class. No monarchy could any longer enforce claims to universal rule. In the eleventh and twelfth centuries the emperors were, in effect, kings of Germany only. The kings of France ruled as feudal lords a region in north-central France centering on Paris, and had next to no control over the rest of the area that makes up modern France. Much of southern France was governed by the kings of Arles, and much of the west by the dukes of Normandy, who in 1066 conquered England from the Saxons. Norman dukes wrested Sicily from the Arabs in 1105 and set themselves up as kings, controlling most of formerly Byzantine southern Italy as well. In addition to the Muslims in the south, at least four Christian kingdoms divided Spain. Under the kings and dukes were feudal lords, ruling from their castles and acknowledging often conflicting feudal allegiances. The system was chaotic in the extreme and constantly shifting; the general disorder often involved the papacy, which found itself at times the football of rival monarchs.

But the towns were growing at a pace that exceeded even that of the monarchies. Cities were still small—medieval Rome and Renaissance Rome, for example, each occupied only a fraction of the center of the ancient city, and up until the middle of the nineteenth century, most of the originally urban Roman basilicas were in the country. Yet in France, England, Germany, and the Low Countries, cities devoted to manufacture, trade, and banking demanded and received clear-cut legal rights and charters as corporate persons equal to the feudal lords and sheltered by dukes and kings who depended on them in many respects. In Italy, with the collapse of the remnants of Lombard power in the eighth century and the infrequent visitations of the emperors, the cities became independent communes. At first they were ruled by their bishops, but soon developed republican forms of government with administrations, often chosen by lot among the leading commercial families, succeeding each other for very brief terms. Venice (long a republic), Genoa, Naples, and Amalfi built merchant marines for trade throughout the Mediterranean and navies to protect their commerce from Arab pirates. Venice, in fact, established a commercial empire, with bases in islands and seaports throughout the eastern Mediterranean and a fixed extraterritorial seat in Constantinople, the capital of the Byzantine Empire. The capture of Sicily and the mass movements of the first three Crusades, the latter culminating in the institution of a Western kingdom of Jerusalem (1099–1187), also assisted in opening Western eyes to the worlds of Byzantine and Islamic cultures.

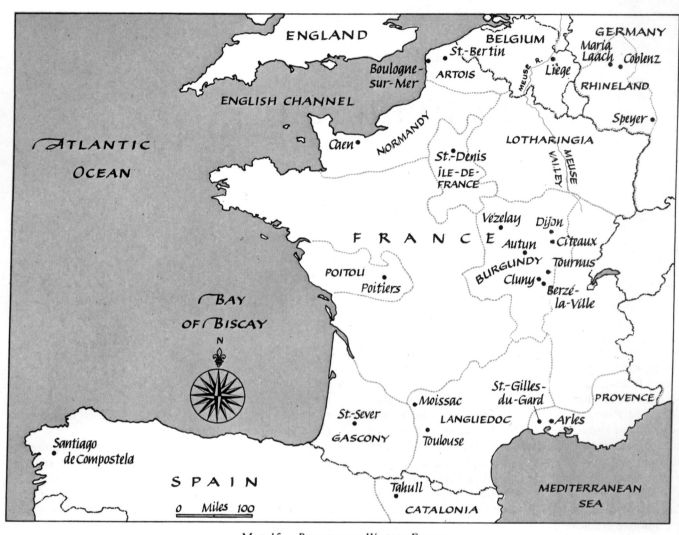

MAP 15.   *Romanesque Western Europe*

ARCHITECTURE AND SCULPTURE IN FRANCE

The few surviving Carolingian and Ottonian churches present difficulties in finding sufficient buildings to illustrate the architectural styles of those periods; in contrast, so many hundreds of Romanesque churches, large and small, still stand in Europe, most in excellent condition, that even a general treatment of Romanesque architecture would require a book as thick as this one. Even more Romanesque churches would have been preserved if in the Gothic period many had not been replaced by more sumptuous edifices. An oft-quoted and invariably misinterpreted passage, written in 1003 by the monk Raoul Glaber at Dijon in Burgundy, tells us about the beginning, at least, of the new wave of church construction after the year 1000:

> Therefore, after the above-mentioned year of the millennium, which is now about three years past, there occurred, throughout the world, especially in Italy and Gaul, a rebuilding of church basilicas.

Notwithstanding the greater number were already well established and not in the least in need, nevertheless each Christian people strove against the others to erect nobler ones. It was as if the whole earth, having cast off the old by shaking itself, were clothing itself everywhere in the white mantle of churches. Then, at last, all the faithful altered completely most of the episcopal seats for the better, and likewise the monasteries of the various saints as well as the lesser places of prayer in the towns. . . .

Considering how many years it took to build a Romanesque church, and how few can be dated between 1000 and 1003, Raoul Glaber's account might be more believable if it had been written in 1103. Perhaps it should be read as a prophecy of what was soon to come to pass.

But the passing of the millennium and the new growth of cities were not the only factors that spurred the building of churches; the requirements of pilgrimages also had to be considered. Populations in the Middle Ages were surprisingly mobile, in part because the old Roman roads were still in fair condition. Pilgrimages, a feature of many religions, were ostensibly undertaken for religious reasons, but the wise Geoffrey Chaucer hinted at other motives as well, once April stirs the blood:

Than longen folk to goon on pilgrimages
(And palmers for to seken straunge strondes)
To ferne halwes, couthe in sondry londes; . . . .

Palmers, of course, were those who had been to the Holy Land and were entitled to wear palms on their garments (the travel stickers of the Middle Ages). Among the "ferne halwes" was that of James, whose shrine at Santiago de Compostela in the far northwestern corner of Spain attracted pilgrims by the thousands, who had to be cared for along the way, thus encouraging the development of churches along the main routes.

In any event, throughout the old Roman cities of northern Europe and of central and northern Italy (with the exception of Rome, whose basilicas were pilgrimage goals in themselves), many Early Christian, Carolingian, and Ottonian churches gave way to larger Romanesque ones. A prime requirement, based on bitter and oft-repeated experience, especially in France where cathedrals were in urban centers constantly subject to conflagrations, was that the new structures be as fire-resistant as possible, therefore vaulted. For some as yet unknown reason, the Roman technique of vaulting with concrete seems never to have been considered by Romanesque builders, although a manuscript of Vitruvius, in which he explained the technique, was in the monastic library at Cluny. The new vaults of brick or stone masonry required massive systems of support. As long as the static problems were imperfectly understood—medieval engineering was unequal to the task of calculating stress scientifically—the massive supports for the vaulting could block out the light. A three-way balance between great church size, stable vaulting, and adequate illumination had somehow to be struck, and the dramatic changes in the form and appearance of church buildings in the Romanesque and Gothic periods are bound up with many trial-and-error attempts to refine this balance.

But there was a fourth factor, seldom taken into consideration in modern studies of medieval architecture and yet doubtless the final determinant: the result had to be aesthetically satisfying. One striking instance should be considered, the Benedictine Abbey Church of Saint-Philibert at Tournus in central France. The church was rebuilt after a fire in the early eleventh century. In the course of the eleventh or in the early twelfth century (the date is still in question), the building was vaulted. The impressive interior (fig. 388) would seem to fulfill all practical requirements for a Romanesque church: it is capacious, stone vaulted, and well lighted due to an ingenious system of vaulting. The nave arcades are sustained by

powerful cylindrical columns, without capitals. Engaged half columns are visible in the side aisles. The columns and the half columns provide excellent support for the groin vaults that cover the side aisles. In the nave above each column rises a shorter, engaged column, sustaining a massive arch that bridges the nave. These arches, in turn, support a series of small barrel vaults, which unexpectedly cross the nave at right angles. The weight of the transverse barrel vaults is adequately borne by the arches. But barrel vaults also thrust outward, and this thrust must be abutted. At Tournus this problem was settled by having the transverse vaults abut each other. The outer walls, relieved of all weight, were pierced by clerestory windows admitting ample light. Why, then, was this practical system never again adopted in any other church? The answer seems to be that the effect of the heavy arches, cutting up the ceiling into a succession of separately barrel-vaulted compartments, was unacceptable aesthetically; architects and patrons wanted a more unified look. It is also possible that such a ceiling had a bad acoustical effect, perhaps creating echoes that blurred the chanting of the services.

The solution utilized on a grand scale for pilgrimage churches erected in the late eleventh and early twelfth centuries may be seen in the Church of Saint-Sernin at Toulouse, the capital of the southern French region of Languedoc (fig. 389). Built about 1080–1120, this structure repeats in many respects the plan and disposition of elements at Santiago de Compostela, the goal of the

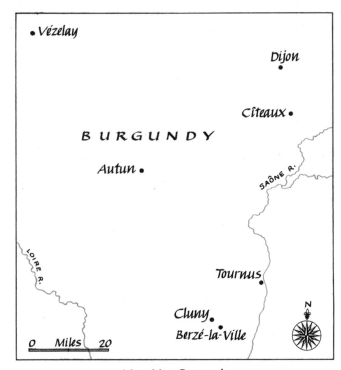

MAP 16. *Burgundy*

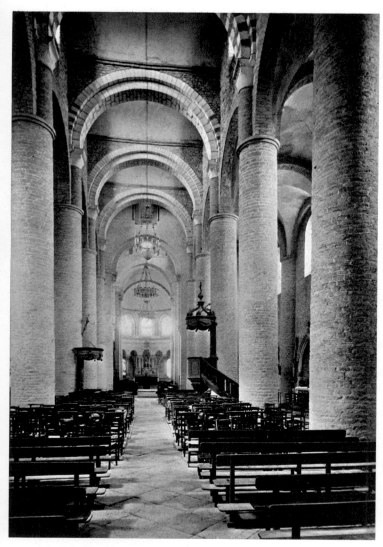

388. Interior, Abbey Church of St.-Philibert. 11th or early 12th century. Tournus, France

barrel vaulted (fig. 391); the triumphal arch has vanished, and the apse (now partly obscured by a much later altar) is a half dome at the same height as nave and choir. The downward pressure of this barrel vault, but not its outward thrust, could have been supported by the arches of the usual clerestory; without abutment, the vault would have collapsed. At Saint-Sernin a gallery (which doubtless also accommodated crowds of pilgrims) runs around the building above the side aisles. stopping only at the apse. This gallery is roofed by a half-barrel vault, which rests against the piers of the nave at the springing point of the nave vault, and abuts the thrust, directing it back inside the piers to the ground. Unfortunately, the gallery windows light only the galleries; little light filters into the nave. Churches roofed by barrel vaults are inevitably dark. The Abbey Church at Cluny, as we shall see, was an exception.

The continuous barrel vault, however, does have a grand effect. Like a great tunnel, it draws attention rapidly down the nave toward the altar. The barrel vault is crossed at every bay by transverse arches, which have an aesthetic rather than a functional purpose; they *seem* to support the barrel vault, and may have helped in its construction, but it would stand quite well without them. The arches spring from capitals, which belong to slender colonnettes of entirely unclassical nature, although their capitals preserve Classical elements, looking like those in the Great Mosque of Ibn Tulun (see fig. 357). These colonnettes run two stories in height, from floor level, where they are engaged to the piers that support the nave arcades, up to the transverse arches and down the other side. At Saint-Sernin, therefore, we encounter a basic feature of Romanesque architecture, the compound pier, which replaces the Early Christian column and the square pier of Ottonian buildings (see fig. 323). As in the Great Mosque of Ibn Tulun, which to be sure utilizes compound piers for a very different purpose and effect, each pier is made up of several elements, each with its own function in the general scheme.

The plan shows that the side aisles, which are relatively low, are groin vaulted (see fig. 390; a groin vault is indicated on a plan by a dotted X). The outward thrust of the groin vaults was met by external buttresses. Each bay of the side aisles is square; the width of the nave corresponds to the width of two of the side-aisle bays, so that each nave bay is an oblong of one to two. This proportion between nave and side-aisle bays was generally maintained in later churches.

From the east end the exterior (the west façade was never completed) shows a superb massing of clearly distinct elements, resembling that we saw in Ottonian churches but far richer and more complex. The transept chapels, radiating chapels, ambulatory roof, semidome over the apse, gallery windows in the transept, gallery roof, transept roof—all culminate in a grand octagonal crossing tower. This tower is Romanesque only in its first three stories; the last two were added in the Gothic

pilgrimages, whose construction began in the 1070s. In contradistinction to Early Christian basilicas, the plan (fig. 390) is unmistakably a cross. The immense nave (eleven bays) is flanked by double side aisles. The inner aisle is continuous, stretching around both ends of the transept and the apse—like the ambulatory in a martyrium—so that crowds of pilgrims could move along constantly and easily. (Medieval sources tell us about the difficulty and danger of handling large crowds in the old basilicas.) Along their way the pilgrims could stop and pray at small chapels, each containing the relics of a saint. The cult of relics was intense in the Romanesque period, and the need for relics to venerate was often satisfied by worse than dubious means. Two chapels open off the east side aisle of each arm of the transept, and five more radiate outward from the ambulatory around the apse. Ambulatory and radiating chapels became an indispensable feature of pilgrimage churches, and were uniformly adopted for cathedral churches in the Gothic period, save only in England and Italy.

The nave, transept, and choir of Saint-Sernin are

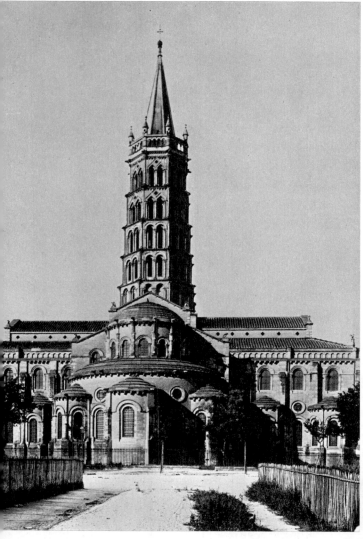

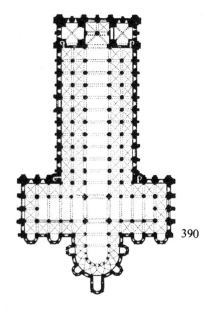

389. St.-Sernin. c. 1080–1120. Toulouse, France

390. Plan of St.-Sernin (after Kenneth John Conant)

391. Nave and choir, St.-Sernin

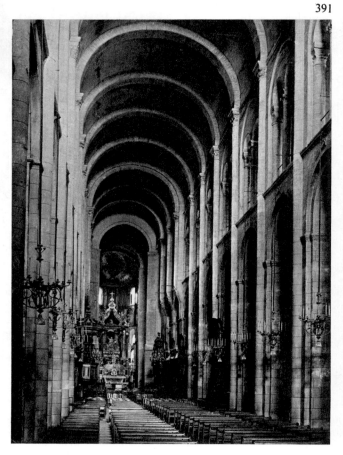

period. The clear, rational articulation of the building is carried into smaller elements as well: each bay of the transept is demarcated by a buttress countering the thrust of the vaults within; below each roof runs a sculptured corbel table; each arched window is framed by a larger blind arch, supported in the gallery windows by engaged colonnettes.

The grandest of all Romanesque buildings was the third Abbey Church of Saint-Pierre at Cluny in Burgundy, in eastern France; it was the mother church of the Cluniac Order, which, in the eleventh and twelfth centuries, comprised hundreds of monasteries scattered throughout western Europe. Its greatest abbot, Saint Hugh, entrusted the building to an ecclesiastical architect, a retired abbot named Gunzo, known also as a musician. Until the rebuilding of Saint Peter's in Rome in the sixteenth and seventeenth centuries, Cluny was the largest church in Christendom. Construction began in 1085 or 1086 and was virtually completed by 1130. Its dimensions were staggering; the total length was 531 feet, the height of the nave vaults above the floor more than

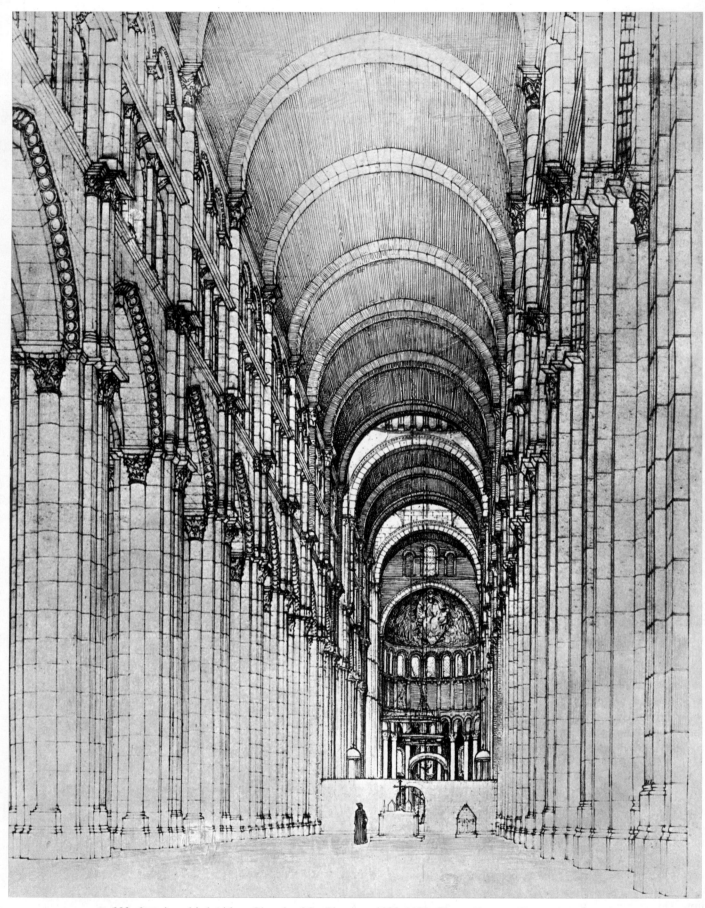

392. Interior, third Abbey Church of St.-Pierre. c. 1085–1130. Cluny, France. (Reconstruction drawing by Kenneth John Conant and Turpin Chambers Bannister)

100 feet, and the richly sculptured central portal was 62 feet high. The nave of eleven bays was preceded by a five-bay narthex; there were four side aisles, double transepts, and five large and two small towers. Only portions of one transept remain. The rest of the vast fabric was demolished by a group of real-estate speculators in the years following the French Revolution, and the stone and other materials sold for profit; it took twenty-five years to blow the church up, section by section.

From the remaining fragment it is possible to gain a clear idea of what the church was once like (fig. 392). The barrel vault was slightly pointed to reduce the outward thrust so that the supporting gallery could be eliminated. Unfortunately, this device proved insufficient, and external supports (flying buttresses, which will be discussed in Chapter 9) had to be added later, although no one knows exactly when. Unexpectedly, the church's architectural details were derived partly from Roman, partly from Islamic sources. The compound piers were cruciform in plan. Engaged colonnettes supported the nave arcade and the transverse arches of the double side aisles, which were groin vaulted, but fluted pilasters were attached to the inner faces of the piers, their long, parallel lines increasing the effect of height. All the capitals were imitated directly from Corinthian models. The arches, however, were strongly pointed, somewhat like those of the Great Mosque of Ibn Tulun.

Above the arcades, in a space measured by the height of the sloping side-aisle roof, was the triforium (so called because it generally has three openings in each bay). The triforium arches, barely visible in the reconstruction, were ornamented all round with little horseshoe-shaped lobes, patterned after Islamic examples. The arches were separated by fluted Corinthian pilasters. Above the triforium was the clerestory, with three windows to each bay, each window framed by a round arch connecting engaged columns. The apse was slightly lower than the three-bay section between the two transepts; its semidome was filled with a gigantic fresco of Christ enthroned in glory. Gunzo's colossal interior was proportioned throughout according to the intervals in medieval music, and contemporary accounts tell us that the barrel vaults carried the chanting beautifully throughout the entire length of the church.

Just as dramatic as the great new wave of church building in the Romanesque period was the revival of architectural sculpture. Save for a few scattered examples, monumental sculpture in stone very nearly died out in Europe after the collapse of the Roman Empire. Contemporary accounts relate that some Carolingian and Ottonian church façades were ornamented with sculptures, but no examples have survived; as far as we now know, sculpture connected with church buildings was mostly limited to doors, pulpits, baptismal fonts, and other interior features. But the new Romanesque churches demanded architectural sculpture just as the Greek temples had—not as additions to fill predetermined spaces, however, but as integral parts of the

architecture. Romanesque church portals, especially, were enlivened with sculptures so as to present in vivid form essential elements of Christian doctrine in order to excite not only the piety but also the imagination of the worshiper at the moment of his entry into the church. The typical Romanesque portal composition, which often included a number of reliefs and statues attached to supporting elements, was centered on a large-scale relief that filled the tympanum (the semicircular space bounded by the arch and the lintel); the tympanum played in Romanesque churches a role somewhat similar to that of the pediment in Greek temples. The destroyed tympanum of Cluny was the largest of all, about twenty feet in width.

Luckily, the ten beautifully carved capitals of the tall, round columns that once stood in the apse of Cluny are preserved. They are among the earliest examples of a new type of capital, which appeared at the end of the eleventh century, showing human figures and sometimes narrative scenes. Figured capitals were relatively rare in Roman art, and were seldom used before the third century; Romanesque artists, however, produced them in enormous numbers before the taste for them died out in the Gothic period. The Cluny capitals are in most architectural details quite correctly Corinthian. In one of them (fig. 393), against the acanthus leaves, as if suspended, is a beautifully shaped mandorla, hollowed out to contain a

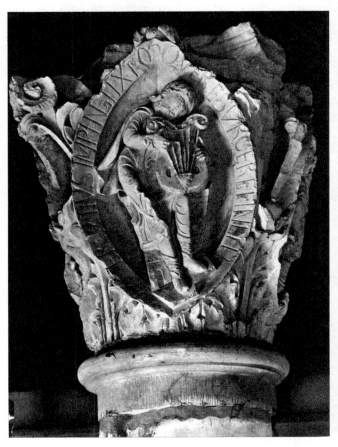

393. Capital, with relief representing the Third Tone of Plain Song, from the Choir, Abbey Church of St.-Pierre, Cluny. Musée Lapidaire du Farinier, Cluny

figure playing a lyre, the relief representing the Third Tone of Plain Song. The energetic pose recalls the tradition of Carolingian manuscripts, as does the floating cloak, but the sculpture already shows a complete mastery of high relief, being strongly undercut, in fact almost in the round. The drapery lines were treated like overlapping layers rather than folds of cloth and executed with crisp, clean curves.

A highly original plan and vaulting solution is seen in another Burgundian church, Sainte-Madeleine at Vézelay, constructed between about 1104 and 1132 (fig. 394); this represents one of the earliest French attempts to roof an entire nave with groin vaults (the choir was rebuilt in the Gothic period). The church has the expected compound piers, almost all of which are enriched with figured capitals; the bays are separated by heavy transverse arches. The eye is immediately struck by a color contrast new to the North, and surely borrowed from such Islamic buildings as the Great Mosque at Córdoba (see colorplate 46). The soft golden limestone of which most of the church is built alternates in the arches with blocks of pale pink granite, achieving a brilliant effect further enhanced by the white limestone used for the capitals. The unknown architect did not dare to carry his edifice to the height of Cluny, nor did he quite understand how to support his massive groin vaults. The illustration shows that they have pushed the walls slightly outward, and the vaults would have fallen if in the Gothic period the walls had not been strengthened by external flying buttresses.

The glory of Vézelay is its set of three sculptured portals, opening from the narthex into the nave and side aisles, carved between about 1120 and 1132; the sculpture of these portals is in such high relief that many of the figures are almost entirely in the round. The central portal represents the *Mission of the Apostles* (fig. 395). Romanesque artists reverted to the archaic system of scale, according to which the size of a figure indicates its importance. A gigantic Christ is enthroned in the center in a mandorla, his knees turned in a zigzag position, his arms outstretched. From his hands (the left one is missing) stream rays of light to the Apostles, who start from their seats to go forth and evangelize the world. On the archivolts, divided into separate compartments, and on the lintel are represented the peoples of many lands, as described in medieval travelers' tales. All of these people—some with heads of jackals, some with pig snouts, some covered with hair and shading themselves with enormous ears, some so small that one must mount a horse with a ladder—await Christian enlightenment. In spite of the heavy damage suffered by projecting portions, the entire scene radiates intense excitement. Partly this is due to the composition, in which each of the central figures breaks through into the area above it, partly to the use of wavy or swirling lines for the drapery, the clouds on either side of Christ, and the trembling floor below the Apostles' feet. The fantastic whorls of drapery

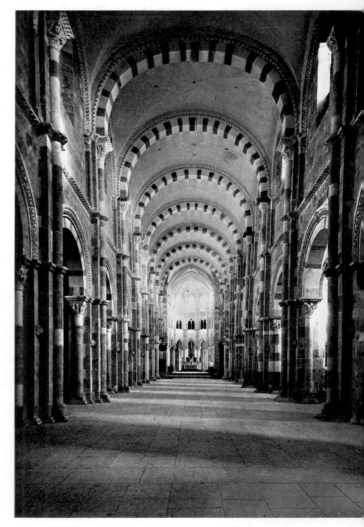

394. Interior, Ste.-Madeleine. c. 1104–32. Vézelay, France

on the right hip and knee of Christ take us back through Hiberno-Saxon manuscripts to La Tène (see fig. 27). When the original brilliant colors and gold were intact, the effect of the portal must have been electric. Scholars have shown that the meaning of this Vézelay portal was closely related to the Crusades, which were intended not only to redeem the holy places but also to carry the Gospel to the infidels, in effect a new Mission of the Apostles; the First Crusade was to have been preached from Vézelay in 1095, the Second actually was (by Saint Bernard) in 1146, and the Third Crusade started from Vézelay in 1190.

An equally awesome, if somewhat less energetic, Burgundian tympanum is that of the Cathedral of Autun (fig. 396), probably dating from about 1130 and representing the *Last Judgment*. This work is an early example among the many representations of the Last Judgment that later appeared in the portal sculptures of almost every Gothic cathedral. Their purpose was to remind each Christian of his final destination before the throne of Christ. Again in a mandorla, the huge, impersonal figure of the Judge stares forward, his hands extended equally on either side. In the lintel the naked dead rise from their graves; on the left souls grasp the arms of a friendly angel; in the center the Archangel Michael, wielding a sword, sends the damned to their fate, and their little bodies quiver with terror. In the tympanum fantastically tall and slender Apostles, on Christ's right, superintend the process of salvation, and angels lift the blessed into Heaven, represented as a house with arched windows. On Christ's left a soul's sins are weighed against its virtues, as in the Egyptian *Book of the Dead* more than two thousand years earlier (see fig. 87). Monstrous demons grasp the damned, and thrust them into the open mouth of Hell. The sculptor of this amazing work signed his name, Gislebertus; along with Renier de Huy (see fig. 403), he is one of the first figurative artists of the Middle Ages whose name can be connected with a surviving work.

An extraordinary complex of Romanesque sculpture enriches the cloister and the portal of the Abbey Church of Saint-Pierre at Moissac in Languedoc, not far from Toulouse. The corner piers of the cloister were sculptured with reliefs showing standing saints about 1100. In this relatively early phase of Romanesque sculptural style, the tradition of Byzantine, Carolingian, and Ottonian ivory carving is still evident. An arch supported by slender colonnettes frames a flattened niche, on whose sharply rising floor stands Peter, to whom the church is dedicated (fig. 397). Save only for the head, turned sharply to the right, the figure is frontal; under the garment the legs appear cylindrical, and although the drapery lines are raised in welts from the surface and given an ornamental linear coherence, they flow about the figure sufficiently to suggest its existence in depth. The figure generally appears stable enough, but the right hand is not; in fact, it is turned violently against the forearm, and displays the Keys to Heaven, as though they were weightless, by merely touching them with thumb and forefinger. The columns of the cloister, alternately single and double, are crowned with capitals of a radically new design, which taper sharply toward a small band above the column; each is a unique and brilliant work, some ornamented but the majority carved with scenes from Scripture.

The sculptural activity of Moissac flowered between about 1120 and 1125 to produce another masterpiece of portal sculpture. A deep porch with a pointed barrel vault, whose supporting walls are enlivened by splendid high reliefs, leads to the pointed tympanum in which the Heavens open to reveal the Lord upon his throne—the *Vision of Saint John* (fig. 398), the same scene that had been represented in the mosaic, now lost, of the Palace Chapel at Aachen (see above, page 294). A colossal crowned Christ is flanked by the symbols of the Evangelists, twisting and turning in complex poses, and by tall and slender angels waving scrolls. The rest of the tympanum is filled by the four and twenty elders in three registers, all of whom turn to gaze at the majestic vision. The relative stability of the cloister relief has now given way to an excitement as intense as that of the later central portal at Vézelay, although produced by subtler, linear means. Wavy lines representing clouds separate the registers; the border is formed by a Greek fret motive treated as if it were an infinitely folded ribbon. Three successive layers of rich foliate ornament of Classical derivation, separated by the slenderest of colonnettes and pointed arches, frame the portal; this is the first example we have seen of splayed enframement, which became a constant feature of church architecture in the Gothic period.

The lintel is ornamented with recessed rosettes, strangely enough cut at each end by the colonnettes as if disappearing behind them. To our surprise the jambs are scalloped (an Islamic element), and so, as a close look shows, are the colonnettes that border them, as if they were collapsing with the earthquake effect of the vision. The trumeau (central support) is even more startling; it consists of lions and lionesses crossed so that the forepaws of each rest on the haunches of the other—an obvious reminiscence of the old tradition of the animal interlace. On the right side of the trumeau (fig. 399), wedged in against the quivering colonnette and the inner scalloped shape, is one of the strangest figures in the whole of Western art, a prophet (possibly Jeremiah) whose painfully slender legs are crossed as if in a ritual dance, which lifts the folds of his tunic and his cloak in complex linear patterns. He clutches nervously at his scroll of prophecy; his head turns languidly as the long locks of his hair and beard stream over his chest and shoulders, and his long mustaches flow across his cheeks.

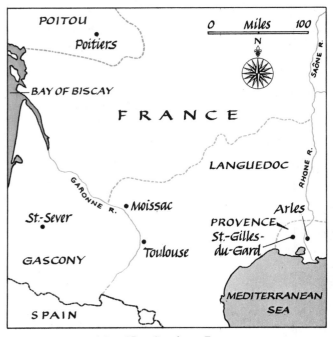

MAP 17. *Southern France*

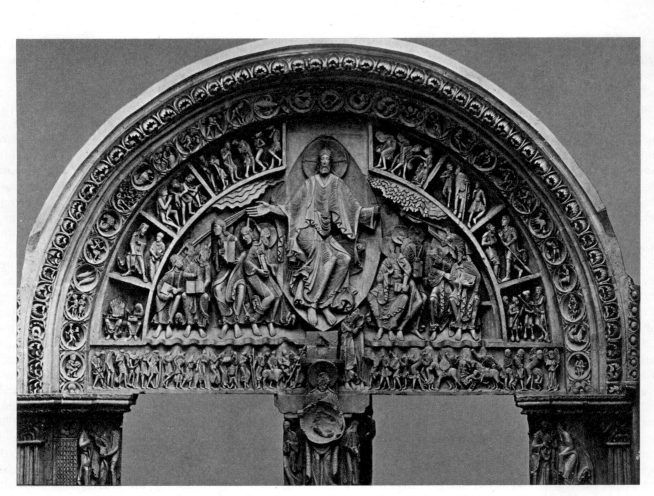

395. *Mission of the Apostles.* Tympanum of the central portal. c. 1120–32. Ste.-Madeleine

For all the fervor of his inspiration, the unknown prophet (doubtless his scroll once bore a painted inscription that identified him) seems trapped in the mechanism of this fantastic portal, a situation that would be completely baffling to us if we did not recall its forebears in Hiberno-Saxon illuminations (see fig. 350, colorplate 43).

The mystical style of Languedoc was strongly related to an earlier work in northern Spain, the cloister reliefs of the Monastery of San Domingo de Silos, near Burgos, probably dating from about 1085–1100. Under the characteristic arch appears the *Descent from the Cross* (fig. 400), a subject that became popular during the Romanesque period on account of its direct appeal to the sympathies of the spectator. The expressions of the figures are quiet; the carrier of intense emotion is, as would be expected in this mystical style, the line itself—the sad tilt of Christ's head, the stiff line of his right arm liberated from the Cross, the gentle line of Mary's head pressed to his right hand, the delicate lines of the drapery, and the looping folds of Christ's garments upheld by two angels. Three more angels emerge from swirling clouds to swing censers above the Cross.

A more Classical manner characterizes the sculpture of the region of Provence in southeastern France, rich in monuments of Roman architecture and sculpture. The triple portal of the Priory Church of Saint-Gilles-du-Gard, whose dating has varied enormously but should probably be set about 1130–40 (fig. 401), has often been compared to the triumphal arches of the late Empire. The general arrangement, superficially at least, looks Roman, and the details of vinescroll ornament, Corinthian capitals, fluted pilasters, and cascading drapery folds are often directly imitated from Roman originals. More important, when compared with the nervous undercutting of Burgundy and the linear style of Languedoc, the figures at Saint-Gilles do not look as if they had been first drawn on the surface and then cut in to a certain degree, but as if they had been fully three-dimensional in the artist's mind from the start. They show the gravity, weight, and richness of form and surface, and the constant play of light and dark that betoken either a continuing Classical tradition or an interest in Roman art or perhaps both.

But the relationship between the various elements is unclassical in the extreme. Two small central columns shorter than those at the sides and jutting out from the jambs in tandem, eagles doing duty for capitals, fierce lions capturing men or sheep, figures moving freely around column bases—all these are unthinkable in a Roman monument. Characteristically Romanesque are

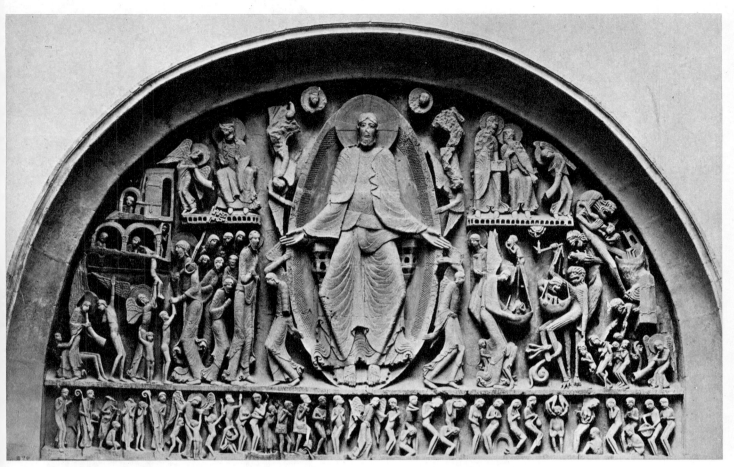

396. GISLEBERTUS. *Last Judgment.* Tympanum. c. 1130. Cathedral of Autun, France

the entwined circles on the high socles; these circles, with their enclosed animals, like the lintel rosettes at Moissac (see fig. 398), are not complete within their spaces. The frieze tells the story of the Passion of Christ (the incidents of the last week in his life, beginning with the Entry into Jerusalem) in great detail. Over the central lintel can be seen the richly draped table of the Last Supper, although the figures of the Apostles are badly damaged. Better preserved is the Betrayal, the dramatic scene in which Judas indicates to the Roman soldiers the identity of Christ by an embrace, in low relief to the right of the central lintel.

In western France the tide of sculpture and sculptural ornament broke loose about 1150 and inundated portals, apses, and entire façades, mingling with and almost submerging the architecture, as in the mid-twelfth-century façade of the Church of Notre-Dame-la-Grande at Poitiers (fig. 402). The clustered columns of the lower story of each corner turret appear to—but do not—carry the arcaded second story, whose paired columns, oddly enough, are arranged side by side on the left, tandem on the right. Even more irresponsible are the conical caps, covered with scales imitating Roman tiles, which pointed downward to shed rainwater; these point up but are said to do the job just as well. In the central portion of the

façade no register corresponds numerically to that below it, and the arch of the central window even moves upward into the irregularly shaped gable. Time has treated the porous stone unkindly, but the light-and-dark effect of the deeply cut ornament remains dazzling.

We conclude this brief survey with the consideration of a work in a totally opposite style—one of the most classical works of sculpture made in Europe during the Romanesque period, the bronze baptismal font now in the Church of Saint-Barthélémy at Liège in modern Belgium, done between 1107 and 1118 and attributed in a fifteenth-century document to the master Renier de Huy. The Meuse Valley, in which Liège is situated, was known in the Middle Ages as Lotharingia, after Lothair II, one of Charlemagne's grandsons, and was now under the rule of French-speaking monarchs, now of German. The entire region preserved from the Carolingian period a strong classical tradition derived from the Palace School and the Reims School, and Renier's font is probably the most strongly classical work of Romanesque sculpture made outside Italy. The idea for the font (fig. 403), which appears to be supported on twelve half-length bronze oxen in the round (only ten survive), was drawn from the Old Testament account of Solomon's bronze basin in the forecourt of the Temple. The Baptism of Christ takes

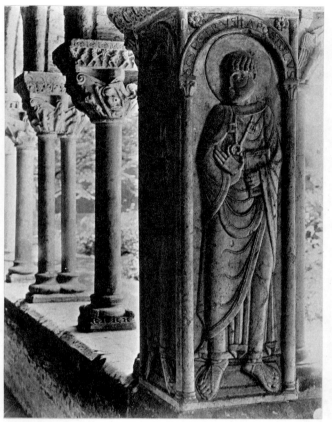

397

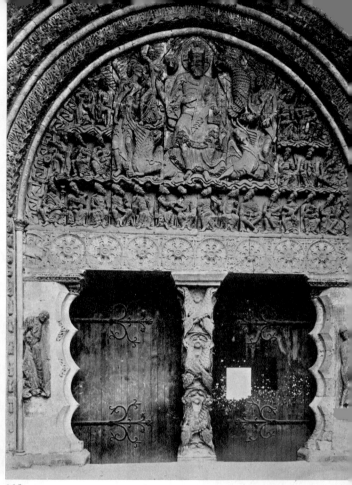

398

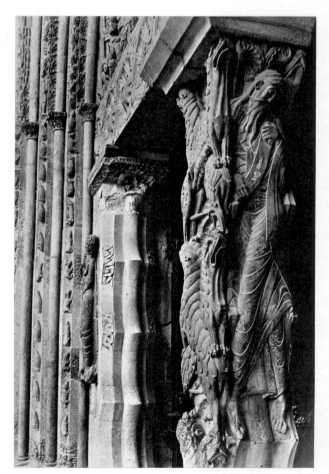

399

397. Corner pier, with relief of Saint Peter. c. 1100.
Cloister, Abbey Church of St.-Pierre, Moissac,
France

398. *Vision of Saint John.* Tympanum. c. 1120–25. Abbey
Church of St.-Pierre, Moissac

399. Prophet, from the south portal, Abbey Church of
St.-Pierre, Moissac

place against an impenetrable cylinder of bronze, quite the reverse of the almost atmospheric backgrounds of Bernward's doors (see fig. 382). The figures are modeled almost in the round, with no hint of the fantastic, visionary styles of Burgundy and Languedoc. The fullness and grace of the figures, their harmonious balance and spacing, and the sculptor's sensitive understanding of the play of drapery over bodies and limbs are unequaled in any French stone sculpture of the time. The lovely classical figure seen from the back at the left may well have derived from an ancient model; one very like it appears in Ghiberti's famous Gates of Paradise of the Early Italian Renaissance (see Vol 2, fig. 48). Renier's figures actually seem to move forward into our space; the head of God the Father (instead of the Hand of God we have seen up until now) leans downward from the arc of Heaven so strongly as to appear foreshortened from above.

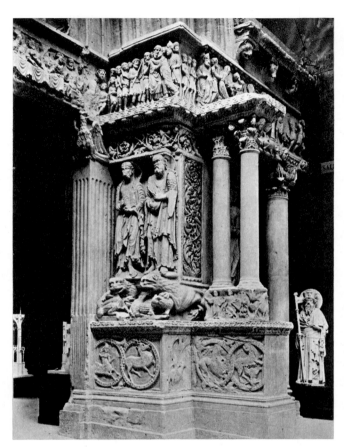

401. Triple portal of the Priory Church (detail). c. 1130–40. St.-Gilles-du-Gard, France

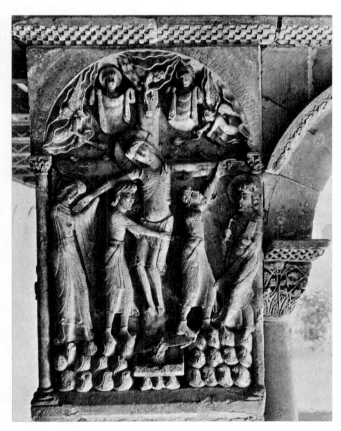

400. *Descent from the Cross*, from the cloister, Monastery of S. Domingo de Silos. Relief. c. 1085–1100. Near Burgos, Spain

402. Façade, Notre-Dame-la-Grande. Middle 12th century. Poitiers, France

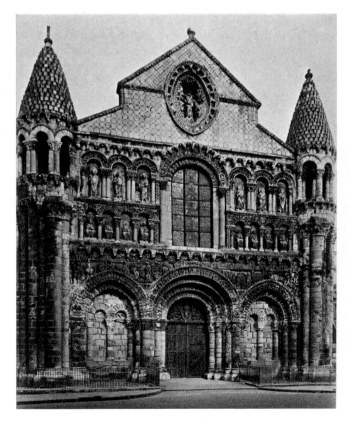

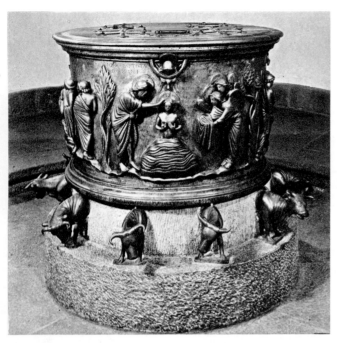

403. RENIER DE HUY. Baptismal font. 1107–18. Bronze, height 25″. St.-Barthélémy, Liège, Belgium

ARCHITECTURE AND SCULPTURE IN ITALY

Throughout the eleventh and twelfth centuries, the prosperous communes of central and northern Italy and the cities of the kingdom of Naples and Sicily built Romanesque churches on a grand scale. The tradition of basilican architecture had never quite died out in Italy; in fact, many Roman basilicas formerly believed to have been built in Early Christian times have recently been proved to date from the ninth or tenth centuries. In addition to the persistence of classical tradition and the presence of many Roman monuments—far more than are standing today—central Italy possessed an unlimited source of beautiful white marble in the mountains of Carrara, to the north of Pisa, as well as green marble from quarries near Prato, just to the west of Florence. While the use and emulation of classical elements and classical details in the Romanesque architecture of Tuscany (a region corresponding roughly to ancient Etruria) is so striking as to have caused art historians to speak of a Romanesque renaissance (like the Carolingian renaissance), these classical elements were generally played against an accompaniment of strongly unclassical Romanesque green-and-white marble paneling, in some cases very sprightly and witty.

The most remarkable Tuscan Romanesque building is certainly the octagonal Baptistery of San Giovanni in Florence (colorplate 52). In many communes in central and northern Italy, all children born in each commune were baptized in a centrally located building, which was separate from the cathedral and took on considerable civic importance. The Florentine Baptistery was consecrated in 1059, but it is so classical, in so many ways, that the controversy over the original date of its construction has never been entirely settled. The Florentines of a later era believed that the building had once been a Roman temple dedicated to the god Mars; the foundations of the present edifice are certainly of Roman origin, but the weight of evidence indicates that the building itself dates from the eleventh century. The external decorative work on the Baptistery went on through the twelfth century, and the corners were not paneled in their zebra-striped marbles until after 1293. The interior is crowned by a pointed dome, masked on the outside by an octagonal pyramid of plain white marble.

The classical aspect of the exterior is limited to the blind arcades and pilasters, whose Corinthian capitals are carved with a precise understanding of Roman architectural detail. But nowhere in Roman architecture can one find anything like the vertically striped green-and-white engaged columns or the striped arches. The most vividly anticlassical feature is the succession of tiny paneled arch shapes in the second story, too small to connect with the pilaster strips that should support them. Such effects are in the tradition of irresponsible linear activity, which was strong in Romanesque ornament throughout Europe.

Somewhat more accurately classical at first sight is the twelfth-century façade of the Abbey Church of San Miniato al Monte (fig. 404). The church was built 1018–62 high on a hill and commands a superb view of Florence. This building represents a quite successful attempt to integrate the inconvenient shape of a Christian basilica, with high nave and low side aisles, into a harmonious architectural façade by the ingenious device of setting a pedimented, pilastered temple front on a graceful arcade of Corinthian columns. But the triangles formed by the low roofs of the side aisles are paneled in a diagonal crisscross that again recalls the tradition of the interlace. Both the Baptistery and San Miniato were, as we shall see in Vol. 2, Part Four, Chapter 1, influential in establishing the style of Early Renaissance architecture in Florence, particularly in the work of the great innovators, Brunelleschi and Alberti. But it is instructive to note how these Renaissance masters always strove to regularize the capricious shapes of the Romanesque marble paneling they imitated.

The grandest of the Tuscan Romanesque architectural complexes is that at Pisa (fig. 405). The Cathedral (begun in 1063), the Baptistery (begun in 1153), whose upper stories and dome were completed in the Gothic period, the Campanile or bell tower (begun in 1174), and the Campo Santo or cemetery (dating from 1278–83) form a snowy marble group set apart from the buildings of the town on a broad, green lawn. The Campanile—the famous Leaning Tower—started to lean before construction was far advanced; the builder's efforts to straighten

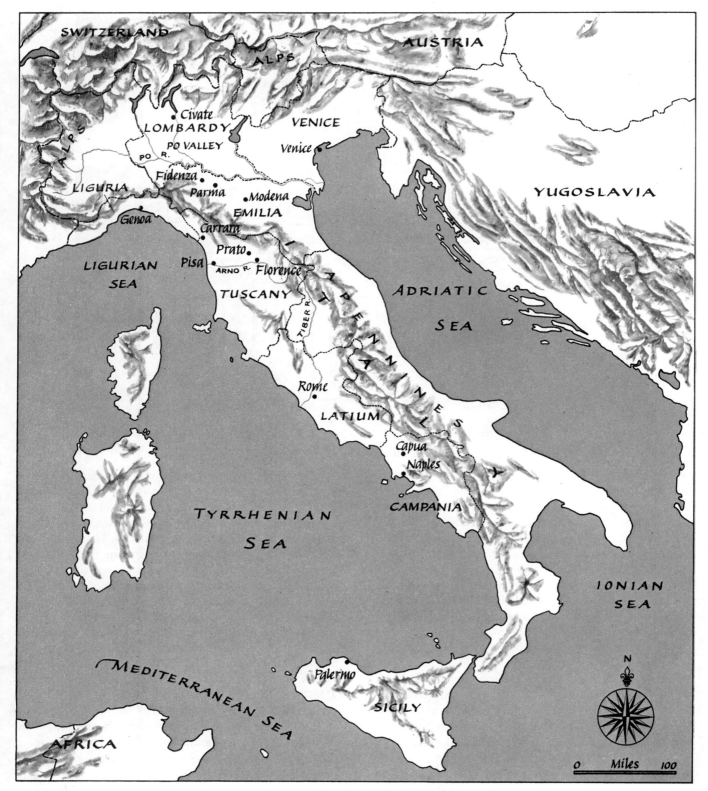

MAP 18. *Italy*

the tower by loading the upper stories and bending its shaft resulted in a noticeable curve. The earth beneath has continued to settle, and all efforts to stop the tower's increasing tilt have proved futile. The Cathedral was designed by a Greek architect named Busketus on the plan of Hagios Demetrios at Salonika. As in all the Romanesque churches of Pisa and nearby Lucca, superimposed arcades divide the façade, and are continued in blind arcades that run around the entire building. Each arm of the transept ends in a small apse,

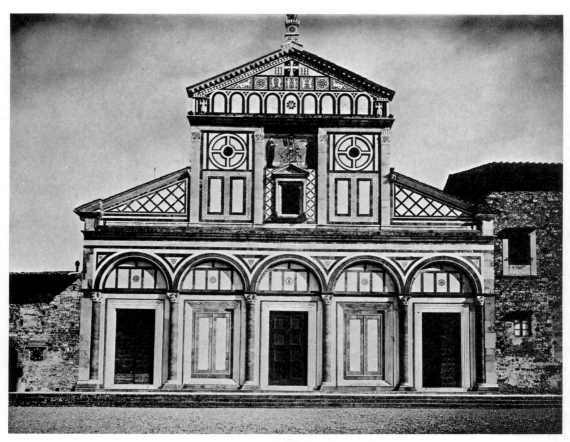

404. Façade, Abbey Church of S. Miniato al Monte. 1018–62. Florence

and a pointed dome crowns the crossing. The total effect is serene and harmonious; so indeed is the grand interior of the Cathedral (fig. 406). The pointed arch at the crossing is Gothic, and the timber roof was masked by a flat, coffered ceiling during the Renaissance, but the rest of the interior is original. The steady march of freestanding columns upholding an arcade is familiar from Early Christian basilicas as is the use of Roman gray granite columns. It is often difficult to tell at first glance which of the capitals are Roman and which are Romanesque imitations. The widely separated, narrow strips of black marble on the exterior have become an insistent zebra striping in the triforium.

The Pisan style strongly influenced church building in southern Italy, but Sicily in the eleventh and twelfth centuries was a special case. The local population was part Greek, the descendants of settlers in ancient times, and part Muslim; the conquerors were French-speaking Normans. In this polyglot land a remarkable ethnic harmony prevailed, resulting in unexpected architectural juxtapositions. One might have encountered in Palermo during this era Norman architects, sculptors from the Île-de-France (the territory ruled directly by the French kings), a bronze caster from Pisa and another from southern Italy, Muslim craftsmen, and Byzantine mosaicists directing artisans of all these races.

The Cathedral of Monreale, founded in 1174 by King William II of Sicily on a mountainous slope above Paler-

mo (fig. 407), is a spacious, three-aisled basilica, whose Roman gray granite columns support pointed Islamic arches. The floors and lower wall surfaces are paneled in Byzantine style in white and gray marbles, every inch of the timber roof is brilliantly painted in Islamic designs, and all the rest of the interior, including the arches and the impost blocks above the Roman capitals, is covered with a continuous fabric of Byzantine mosaics—the most extensive still in existence. Despite misguided restorations, the total effect of the interior is overwhelming in its coloristic richness, in the completeness of its narrative sequences, and in the rhythmic movement of its elements, which reach a climax in the gigantic mosaic of the *Pantocrator* (*Christ as the All-Ruler*; see Chapter 8, page 358) that fills the pointed semidome of the apse (for an earlier Pantocrator, see fig. 432).

The exterior of the Cathedral is even more fantastic (fig. 408). Its three apses are clothed with blind arcades in the Pisan manner, but the imaginative Muslim craftsmen interlaced them (Norman architects had done this in England) as in the flying arches of the Great Mosque at Córdoba and enlivened both the arches and the intervening spaces with sparkling patterns in inlaid marbles that seem more appropriate to the decoration of a mihrab or a minbar.

The most pronounced individual personalities among Italian Romanesque sculptors were two gifted masters both of whom we know by name. Both worked in a

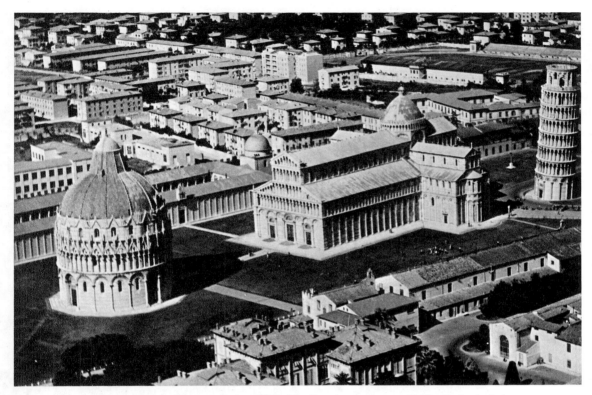

405. Aerial view of the Campo Santo (1278–83), Baptistery (begun 1153), Cathedral (begun 1063), and Campanile (begun 1174). Pisa

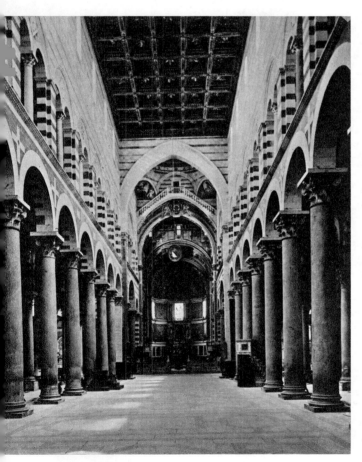

406. Interior. Cathedral of Pisa

region of north-central Italy known today as Emilia-Romagna, at the southern edge of the Po Valley. The earlier of these was Wiligelmo da Modena, whose principal work is a signed series of reliefs, executed about 1100–10, on the façade of the Cathedral of Modena. In one relief strip (fig. 409), the Lord is first shown half length at the left in a mandorla upheld by two angels, then placing one hand on the head of the still strengthless Adam to "make him a living soul," then creating Eve from the rib of the sleeping Adam; finally, at the right, Adam is shown holding the apple with one hand as he eats it and keeping his fig leaf in place with the other while Eve places her left hand in the serpent's mouth. Wiligelmo treated the enframing architecture with complete irreverence. Rarely do the figures correspond to the corbeled arches above; more often they move in front of the corbels, and their feet overlap the edge of the groundline. At the extreme right a column has been transformed into the trunk of the Tree of Knowledge of Good and Evil, around which is wound the hissing serpent. These strange figures, with their heavy heads, hands, and feet, give the impression of clumsiness, but the block masses have great power, and the moments chosen for illustration bring out intense human feeling.

A more accomplished phase of northern Italian Romanesque style is seen in the work of Benedetto Antelami (c. 1150 – c. 1230), an architect as well as a sculptor. His earliest known work is a *Descent from the Cross* (fig. 410) in the Cathedral of Parma, signed and

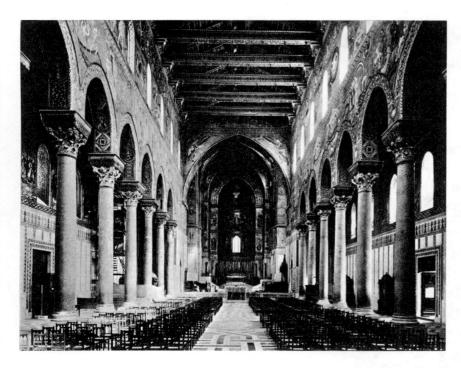

407. Interior, Cathedral of
Monreale. 1174. Monreale,
Sicily

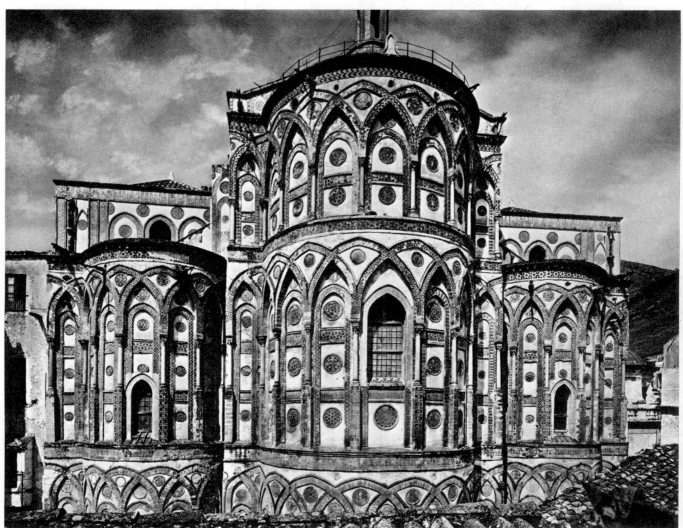

408. Exterior, Cathedral of Monreale (view of the apses)

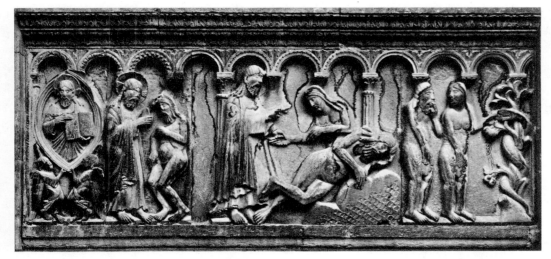

409. WILIGELMO DA MODENA. Old Testament scenes and reliefs, Cathedral of Modena. c. 1100–10. Italy

dated 1178 in an inscription in the background; the artist's name appears above the left arm of the Cross. Perhaps under the influence of such Provençal sculpture as that at Saint-Gilles-du-Gard (see fig. 401), certainly through study of Roman reliefs, but above all through his native genius, Antelami composed a beautiful melodic flow from one figure to the next, so that the lifting of Christ's right hand from the Cross becomes an act of ritual grace accomplished with the aid of an angel. Accents of grief ebb and rise, suggesting and then avoiding symmetry; the solemn chord progression of the figures at the left, with their clustered drapery folds, is contrasted with the huddle of oblivious soldiers at the right around the flowing seamless robe. The background is enriched with a delicate web of melodic lines in the vinescroll ornament and in the inscription, which forms an accompaniment to the foreground scene.

Probably during the following decade Antelami contributed some sculptures to the façade of the Cathedral of Fidenza; the town was then called Borgo San Donnino. His statues of *King David* (fig. 411) and *Ezekiel*, in which each Old Testament figure has been treated as if he were having a vision, appear in niches under scenes from the

New Testament. The *Presentation of the Christ Child in the Temple* hovers over David's crowned head. He turns to look over his shoulder as if inspired, holding his long scroll of prophecy. The cadences of his flowing beard and of the folds of his garments are recognizable as permanent elements of Antelami's style. Although not entirely in the round, the figure—pedestal and all—seems to issue from its niche when compared with its direct ancestor, the low-relief *Peter* at Moissac (see fig. 397). Antelami's *King David*, in turn, is a worthy precursor of such great niche statues of the Early Renaissance as those created by Donatello (see Vol. 2, figs. 38, 39, 41) and Nanni di Banco (see Vol. 2, fig. 49).

VAULTING IN THE RHINELAND, LOMBARDY, NORTHUMBRIA, AND NORMANDY

Many more solutions to the insistent problem that concerned twelfth-century builders—how to construct a lofty, safe, well-lighted, yet aesthetically unified interior—were advanced than can possibly be treated here. It is a significant fact that the regions that produced the most elaborate sculpture and the richest decoration did not contribute notably toward solving the vaulting

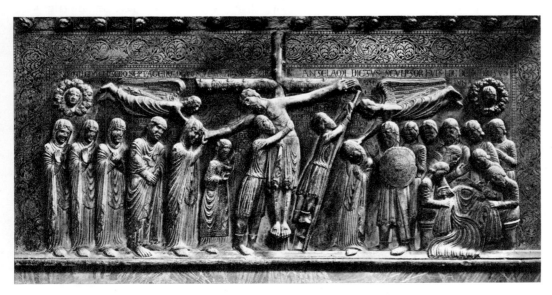

410. BENEDETTO ANTELAMI. *Descent from the Cross.* Relief. 1178. Cathedral of Parma, Italy

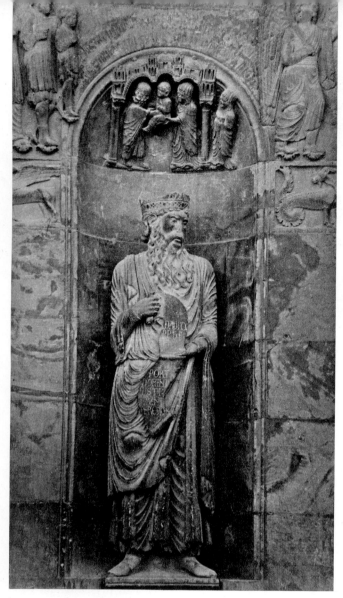

411. BENEDETTO ANTELAMI. *King David.* c. 1180–90. Façade, Cathedral of Fidenza, Italy

by a window, thus forming a second series of small clerestory windows. Over each double bay bounded by transverse and longitudinal arches groin vaults were constructed. The method of building, starting from masonry arches supported on temporary wooden centering, was strikingly different from the Roman technique employing formed concrete, which resulted in groin vaults with horizontal crown lines (see figs. 267, 279). At Speyer each double bay was treated almost like a separate dome, with its crown several feet above the keystones of the arches.

The heavy outward thrust of this construction was supposed to be absorbed by the thick walls and reinforced piers, but although the supports were better calculated than the somewhat later ones at Vézelay (see fig. 394), they tended to push the walls out, as can clearly be seen in the illustration. At a later period the springing points of the vaults had to be joined together by iron tie rods in order to prevent collapse. The Cathedral, though provided with a western entrance, preserved the westwork of Carolingian and Ottonian churches. Later rebuilding has severely altered the west end; the church's original appearance, with octagonal crossing lantern, central western tower, and a smaller tower on each arm of the transept and of the westwork, can be imagined from a somewhat smaller version of this type, the Abbey Church of Maria Laach near Coblenz (fig. 413), consecrated in 1156. The double-ended shape appears in several of the massive Romanesque cathedrals that dominate Rhenish cities (fig. 414).

An important innovation was made in the Church of Sant'Ambrogio at Milan (fig. 415), the principal city of Lombardy, whose nominal subjection to the Holy Roman Empire kept it in relatively close touch with events in Germany. A glance at the plan (fig. 416) shows that vaulting must have been planned for the nave from the very start. Each double bay of the nave is square, exactly twice as long as one of the side-aisle bays. The alternating system was also built in from the beginning. Stone piers support brick arches and vaults; in the angle between each heavy pier and the nave arcade (fig. 417) was set an additional colonnette, which supports an entirely new feature—a diagonal arch intersecting its counterpart from the other side in the center of the bay. In other words the groin vault has now been provided with ribs *along the groins*, on the principle of the ribs of an umbrella. The account by Abbot Suger of the rebuilding of Saint-Denis in France in 1140 (see below, Chapter 9) makes clear that the three pairs of arches, longitudinal, transverse, and diagonal, were customarily built first, the centering was then removed, and when the mortar was thoroughly dry, the intervening compartments were filled with a web of masonry.

This use in Sant'Ambrogio is possibly the earliest example of what has come to be known as the ribbed vault. As we shall see, this invention was the absolute essential for the creation of Gothic architecture in northern

problem. This solution was brought close to its final form in several widely scattered churches that are notable rather for their austerity—in fact, for their virtual elimination of sculptural enrichment. One of these is the immense Cathedral of Speyer, originally built in the early eleventh century as a timber-roofed basilica, in the Rhineland. Between 1082 and 1106 the interior was considerably remodeled in order to receive groin vaults, towering about 107 feet at the crown line, the highest of all Romanesque vaults (fig. 412).

A firm supporting structure was essential; to that end, every second pier of the nave arcade was reinforced by the addition of a massive colonnette sustaining a transverse arch. This example is the earliest datable one of the alternating system of large and small piers, or piers and columns, which became a standard feature of vaulted churches by about the middle of the twelfth century. Longitudinal arches were built, each uniting two bays of the clerestory, and each intervening lunette was pierced

Europe. Unfortunately, we do not know the date of the vaulting at Sant'Ambrogio, but it is generally agreed that this pioneer attempt must have been started about 1080 and that the church may not have been vaulted until after the earthquake of 1117. The outward thrust of the vault at Sant'Ambrogio was intended to be contained by a vaulted gallery, which not only darkens the interior badly but also appears not to have done its job. The ominous tie rods have had to be installed.

Norman architects built at Durham in Northumbria one of the most forceful interiors of the Middle Ages, a massive cathedral which was clearly intended for ribbed vaulting from the start (fig. 418). Construction began in 1093, and the choir had been vaulted by 1104 (the rose window is a Gothic addition). The building was completed about 1130. As may be seen in the plan (fig. 419), the double bays are oblong rather than square, and the diagonal ribs cross only a single bay. As a result each double bay is cut into seven vaulting compartments. This device may have been used in order to flatten out the crown line, which was also partly accomplished by pointing the very heavy transverse arches. The most dramatic feature of the interior is the use of powerful cylindrical pillars in alternation with compound piers; the pillars are boldly ornamented with enormous incised chevrons, lozenge patterns, and other designs in a style that recalls

the geometric ornament of Hiberno-Saxon art. Originally, the whole interior was even painted in bright colors. The capitals are plain blocks, each trimmed to a circle at the bottom, and are without ornament.

The alternating diagonal ribs rest only on small corbels above the capitals of the triforium, which looks like a constructional gallery intended to abut the thrust of the vaulting but is actually covered only by the side-aisle roofs, which do, however, hide relieving arches. The architects seem to have relied on the immense mass of the piers, pillars, and walls to contain the thrust of the vaults, and their confidence was well placed. Tie rods have never been required. A small, columned clerestory is let into the thickness of the walls at the level of the vaulting, and a catwalk runs behind the conoids of the vaults.

The most influential building for early Gothic architecture, however, was the Abbey Church of Saint-Étienne at Caen, in Normandy, started in 1067 by William the Conqueror and completed by the time of his interment there in 1087 (fig. 420). The nave does not seem to have been planned for vaulting, but the square double bays (as at Sant'Ambrogio) easily accommodated a daring and very refined system of ribbed vaulting built over the nave about 1115–20 (or perhaps later; the vaults were rebuilt in the seventeenth century). Its thrust is strongly abutted by the vaults of the gallery, which act as a gigantic girdle.

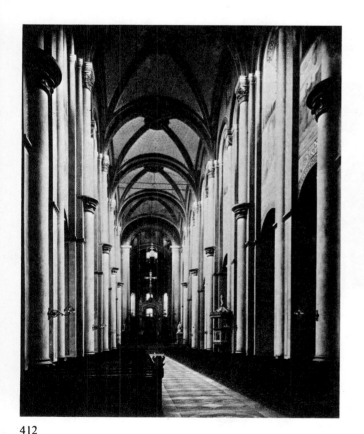

412

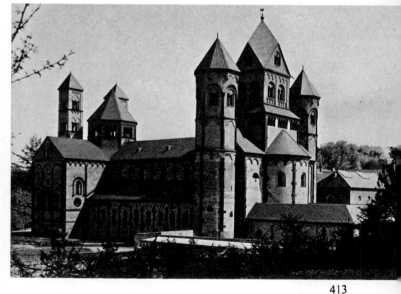

413

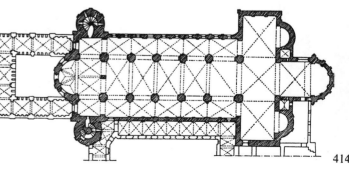

414

412 Interior. Cathedral of Speyer. c. 1082–1106. Germany

413. Abbey Church of Maria Laach. c. 1156. Near Coblenz, Germany

414. Plan of the Abbey Church of Maria Laach

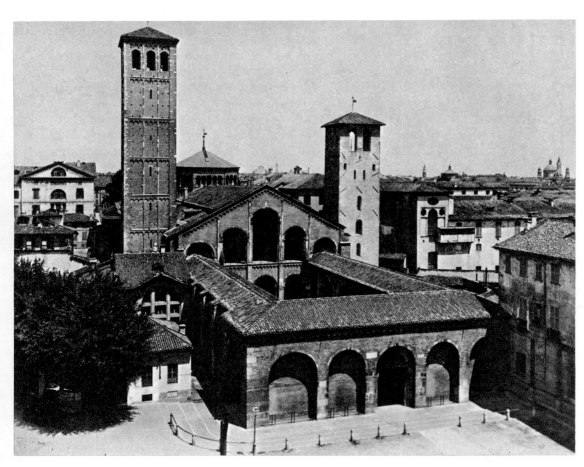

415. Exterior, Sant'Ambrogio. Late 11th–early 12th century. Milan

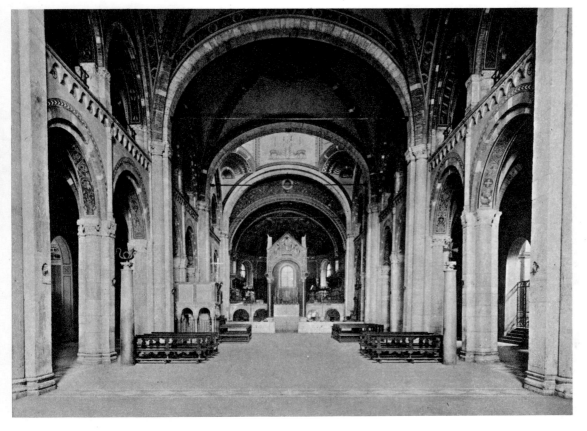

416. Plan of Sant'Ambrogio

417. Interior, Sant'Ambrogio

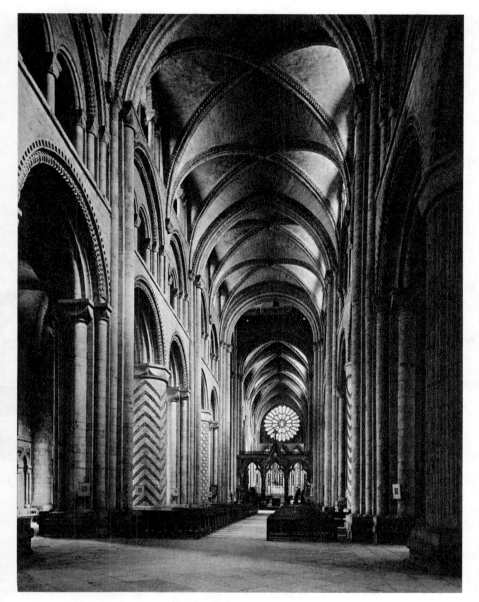

418. Nave, Cathedral of Durham. c. 1093–1130. England

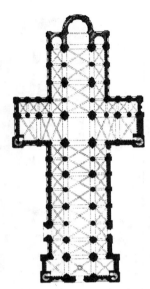

419. Plan of the Cathedral of Durham (after Kenneth John Conant)

As at Durham a small clerestory was built at the level of the vaulting with a catwalk running behind the conoids (fig. 421). The alternating system was preserved only through the addition of two oblique colonnettes, much slenderer than their counterparts at Sant'Ambrogio, to every second compound pier. The striking innovation at Saint-Étienne was the introduction of a second transverse rib, cutting across the vault from side to side and splitting it into six compartments. The six-part vault may have been thought necessary to sustain the slender diagonal ribs before they could be anchored together by the masonry webs of the vault compartments; in any event, it was adopted in the first cathedrals of the Gothic style. The six-part vaults succeeded, at long last, in creating a far more unified interior appearance than had any earlier technique.

Another decisive feature of Saint-Étienne is the three-part, two-tower façade, which later became standard for all French Gothic cathedrals (fig. 422). The elaborate—and indeed very beautiful—spires were added in the Gothic period; they must be thought away in order to recreate the effect of austere simplicity intended by the original builders. Of crucial importance to our understanding of the symbolic basis of medieval architecture is the division of the façade of Saint-Etienne so as to embody in almost every reading the number of the Trinity. For example, the façade has three stories, each of which is divided into three parts; the church possesses three portals (those at the sides enter the towers); the second and third stories of the central part are each lighted by three windows; finally, the towers themselves are each divided into three stories.

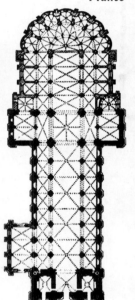

420. Plan of the Abbey Church of St.-Étienne. 1067–87. Caen. France

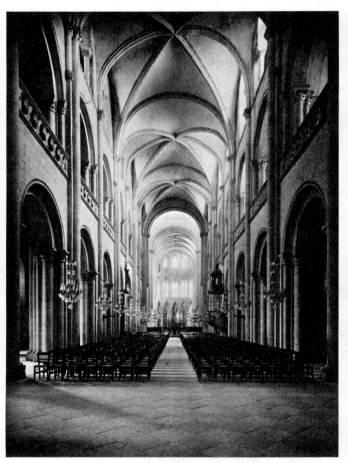

421. Interior, Abbey Church of St.-Étienne

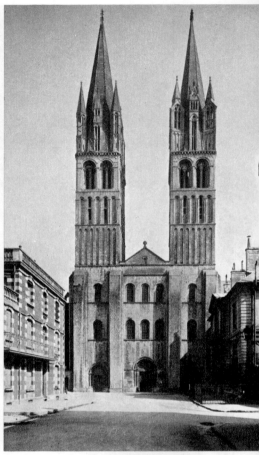

422. Façade, Abbey Church of St.-Étienne. (Gothic spires added later)

MURAL PAINTING

In contrast to Carolingian and Ottonian mural painting, a great deal of Romanesque painting survives, some in fairly legible condition, including complete cycles of high quality. We may, however, mourn the loss of the mosaics done by Greek artists, who were brought to Monte Cassino by Abbot Desiderius in the eleventh century to reform painting, which—in contrast to its achievements in Carolingian France and Ottonian Germany—had sunk to a low ebb in Italy. Desiderius, according to a delightful contemporary account by his archivist and biographer Leo of Ostia, made provision for the Greek artists to train Italian monks and craftsmen in the techniques of religious art. The most impressive example of the Monte Cassino style is the almost complete cycle of frescoes commissioned by Desiderius before 1087 for the interior of the Church of Sant'Angelo in Formis on a mountainside above Capua, north of Naples. As in all such cycles, the cumulative effect of the whole is far greater than the sum of its parts. Although the frescoes have faded sadly in recent years, the succession of biblical narratives and the great *Last Judgment* on the entrance wall still exert a profound emotional effect on the visitor. In spite of the teaching of Byzantine masters, the style of

the Sant'Angelo frescoes seems somewhat rough in comparison with the extraordinary stage of refinement achieved by the art of Constantinople, which we shall study in the following chapter. Yet their dramatic and decorative power depends in no small measure on their naïveté.

Especially beautiful among the Sant'Angelo frescoes is the *Crucifixion*, which fills most of the space above two arches of the nave (fig. 423). Christ is represented as alive, triumphant over suffering as in the *Lindau Gospels* (see colorplate 49), his perfect serenity in sharp contrast to the grief of the Virgin and John and to the two mourning angels in midair. The forces of the architecture have been allowed to determine the disposition of the elements; the Cross is planted over one of the columns of the nave arcade; on the arch to the left stand weeping women and Apostles; on that to the right the Roman centurion detaches himself from the soldier's dice game for the seamless robe, having been moved by the revelation of Christ's divinity. The coloring of the frescoes is limited to gray-blue for the background and to terra-cotta red, tan, oranges, greens, and grays. As in Romanesque sculpture, the drapery is strongly compartmentalized. The simplified faces, with enormous eyes, exhibit startling disks of red on each cheek.

A very nearly contemporary cycle of Italian Romanesque painting, dating from the late eleventh or early twelfth century, adorns the simple Romanesque church of San Pietro al Monte in Civate, a remote spot in the foothills of the Alps. The lunette above the triple arcade at the west end of the nave, framed by crisp acanthus ornament in stucco, is filled by the celestial drama related in Rev. 12 (colorplate 53). Christ is enthroned in a mandorla (unfortunately, his head is lost), and all about him angels led by the Archangel Michael spear a magnificent dragon, who unfolds his scaly coils below the throne. On the left a woman "clothed with the sun" reclines upon a couch, while her newborn child is saved from the dragon. "And there was war in heaven: Michael and his angels fought against the dragon . . . " (Rev. 12: 7). The scene floats toward the top of the arch in a mighty involvement of linear curves and stabbing spears, forming one of the most powerful pictorial compositions of the Middle Ages.

A number of Romanesque fresco cycles survive in France in varying stages of preservation; most are very difficult to reproduce adequately. The small former Cluniac Priory of Berzé-la-Ville in Burgundy, whose apse shows a colossal *Christ in Majesty* imitated from the larger one at Cluny, has well-preserved wall frescoes that

include the *Martyrdom of Saint Lawrence* (colorplate 54), a work of immense power. From its coloring we may gain an idea of how the tympanum at Vézelay (see fig. 395) must have looked when its original painted surface was intact. Saint Lawrence lies upon the gridiron, which is arranged schematically parallel to the picture surface, and stylized flames rise from below it. The rest of the arched space is completely filled by the two executioners and the gigantic judge. The diagonal thrust of the two long rods ending in iron forks, which hold the victim on the gridiron, crosses the compartmentalized drapery masses, whose striations show the influence of Byzantine drapery conventions but whose folds move with a fierce energy totally alien to the elegant art of Constantinople. Note also that the French-limestone columns flanking the fresco have been painted to resemble the veined marble ones of Byzantine architecture.

The Romanesque frescoes that once decorated the great metropolitan churches of Europe have for the most part been replaced by later and more fashionable works of art; the best-preserved group of Romanesque frescoes originally adorned the mountain churches of Catalonia in the picturesque and productive northeast corner of Spain. Almost all of these have been detached from their original walls, and are today in museums. A powerful ex-

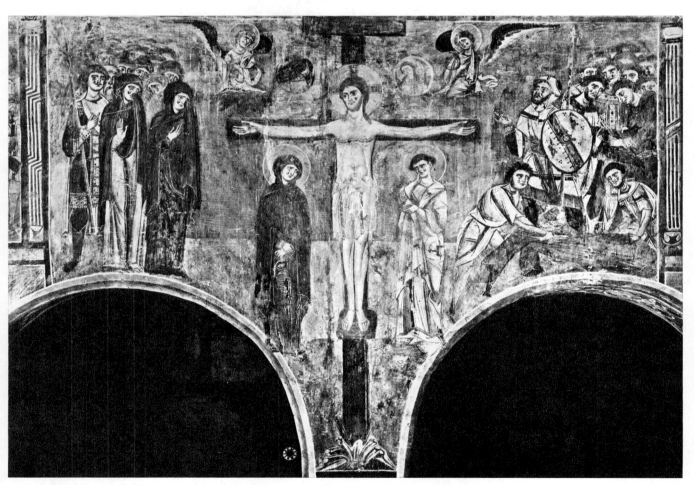

423. *Crucifixion.* Nave fresco. Before 1087. Sant'Angelo in Formis, near Capua, Italy

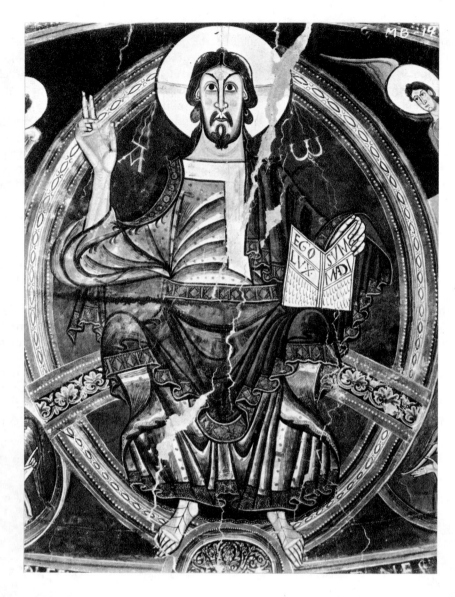

424 *Christ in Majesty,* from S. Clemente de Tahull, Spain. Fresco. c. 1123. Museo de Bellas Artes de Cataluña, Barcelona

ample is the *Christ in Majesty,* painted about 1123 in the Church of San Clemente de Tahull (fig. 424). The style is somewhat less accomplished than that of the Burgundian masterpiece we have just seen, but it is by no means less expressive. Christ's mandorla is signed with the Alpha and Omega (the first and last letters of the Greek alphabet), and he holds a book inscribed (in Latin): "I am the light of the world" (John 8: 12). The drapery is rendered in broad, parallel folds, shaded arbitrarily with little elegance and much force. The delicacy of Christ's hands and feet and the portrait quality of his face are therefore the more surprising.

MANUSCRIPTS

Romanesque manuscript illumination shows as rich a profusion of regional styles as do the churches, the sculptures, and the murals. England in the late tenth century produced a strongly independent style characterized by a freedom recalling that of the Reims School. This energetic art, which flourished especially at Winchester in southern England, was carried across the Channel to

France. An English painter was surely responsible for the illustrations in the *Gospel Book* illuminated at Saint-Bertin, near Boulogne-sur-Mer on the Channel coast, at the end of the tenth century. The first page of the *Gospel of Matthew* (colorplate 55) is divided in two vertically; on the right a large initial *L* (for *Liber generationis*) preserves echoes of the old Hiberno-Saxon interlace, but carried out with little interest and already invaded by acanthus ornament. What really fascinated the artist was the figurative side of the page. On a little plot of ground at the top a benign angel gives the glad tidings to two shepherds (the scene is very different from the solemn apparition in the Gospel lectionary of Henry II; see fig. 387). Directly below, Mary is stretched out on a couch, apparently already lonely for her Child, after whom she reaches out her hands. A midwife bends over to comfort her, while Joseph admonishes her vehemently from his seat at the right. At the bottom of the page Joseph bends affectionately over the Christ Child, wrapped in swaddling clothes and lying in a manger, as the ox and ass look on astonished. Above the initial letter the arc of

Heaven discloses five delighted angels. The human, narrative style is matched by the sprightly drawing and the delicate and transparent colors.

The strongest contrast to this charming illustration is offered by the mid-eleventh-century *Apocalypse* illustrated at Saint-Sever in Gascony in southern France. This book is actually a commentary on the Apocalypse written by a Spanish monk of the eighth century, Beatus of Liébana, which had been frequently illustrated in Spain. The illuminator of the Saint-Sever manuscript, who was called Garsia, may well have been Spanish. An especially powerful illustration (colorplate 56) shows the plague of locusts loosened upon the earth to strike men with their scorpions' tails so that they "seek death and shall not find it." So vividly is the passage [Rev. 9: 7–12 (Apoc. 9: 7–12 in the Douay Version)] illustrated that it demands quotation:

> And the shapes of the locusts were like unto horses prepared unto battle; and on their heads were as it were crowns like gold, and their faces were as the faces of men.
>
> And they had hair as the hair of women, and their teeth were as the teeth of lions.
>
> And they had breastplates, as it were breastplates of iron; and the sound of their wings was as the sound of chariots of many horses running to battle.
>
> And they had tails like unto scorpions, and there were stings in their tails: and their power was to hurt men five months.
>
> And they had a king over them, which is the angel of the bottomless pit, whose name in the Hebrew tongue is Abaddon, but in the Greek tongue hath his name Apollyon.

The ferocity of the linear style in which these terrible beasts are drawn is intensified by the harsh coloring of the background rectangles: red ocher, brown, green, yellow, and blue.

Still another possibility for the Romanesque manuscript style is seen in a highly imaginative illumination from the *Moralia in Job* of Saint Gregory (colorplate 57), painted at the very beginning of the twelfth century, under strong English influence, at the monastery of Cîteaux in Burgundy (ruled by an English abbot, Stephen Harding, from 1109–33), the mother church of the reforming Cistercian Order. A border of floral ornament at the sides and of zigzag at top and bottom, in delicate tones of orange, lavender, green, and blue, surrounds the initial letters of Gregory's dedication of the book to Bishop Leander. The *R* (for *Reverentissimo*) is partly formed by a standing knight, possibly Saint George, whose left leg in blue hose emerges elegantly from his orange tunic. He holds a green shield and brandishes a blue sword high above a delightful dragon, which makes up the rest of the *R* and which has two heads and green, blue, orange, and gold wings—an unnecessary ritual, really, because the hapless squire on whose back the knight stands has already taken the precaution of running the dragon through with a spear. Here again is the linear energy and brilliance of design we have seen in Burgundian architecture, sculpture, and painting, accompanied by a wit that could be given free rein only in manuscripts intended for the few. At this point it is interesting to quote from Saint Bernard's famous letter of 1127 on the subject of the impieties of Romanesque art:

> . . . what profit is there in those ridiculous monsters, in that marvelous and deformed comeliness, that comely deformity? To what purpose are those unclean apes, those fierce lions, those monstrous centaurs, those half men, those striped tigers, those fighting knights, those hunters winding their horns? Many bodies are there seen under one head, or again, many heads to a single body. . . .

In fact, Saint Bernard, who clearly enjoyed and understood what he was condemning, put an end to all figurative art not only at Cîteaux but also throughout the Cistercian Order—luckily not before the illumination of this and other beautiful manuscripts.

A final glimpse into the inexhaustible world of Romanesque illumination is afforded by the lavishly illustrated *Bible of Bury St. Edmunds*, illuminated in England probably just before the middle of the twelfth century. At the top of an illustration to Deuteronomy (colorplate 58), Moses and Aaron reveal the Law to the assembled Hebrews, delightfully individualized in their faces and in their reactions. Moses is pictured with the horns he was given in art according to Saint Jerome's translation of the Hebrew word that also means *rays*, but which, it has been shown recently, is also connected with a long tradition of horned deities and even with the shape of the Christian miter. In the lower illustration Moses points out the clean and the unclean beasts; two defiant red pigs rejoice in their uncleanness. This style is a very elegant and accomplished one, with its enamel-like depth and brilliance of color and high degree of technical finish. The sparkling perfection of the ornament, the smooth linear flow of poses and draperies, and the minute gradations of value have brought the art of painting about as far as it could go within the conventions of Romanesque style. In the words of Marion Roberts Sargent, referring to this illustration, "The real achievement of Romanesque illumination is the complete domination of two-dimensional space. Figures, border, ornament, architecture, and landscape, even the text, are treated equally in brilliant color, resulting in total mastery of surface design."

One of the astonishing things about the Romanesque period is its brevity. The great creative moment began at the end of the eleventh century. By 1140 the Gothic style had already replaced the Romanesque in the Île-de-France, and long before the twelfth century was over, the onrush of the Gothic, which was to rule in northern Europe at least for more than three hundred years, had banished the Romanesque to remote provincial centers.

8

Middle and Later Byzantine Art

In 1944 a stroller in a dense forest just west of the heavily traveled road connecting Milan with the Lake of Como came upon a small, rudely built, and totally unknown church near the village of Castelseprio; this church contained a series of small-scale frescoes of scenes from the Infancy of Christ, freely painted in an extraordinarily fresh and spontaneous style, reminiscent in some respects of the Hellenistic qualities of Pompeiian painting. In the *Appearance of the Angel to Joseph*, for example (fig. 425), one of the frescoes in this church, the figures, the draperies, the foliage, the rocks, and even the wayside pillar with its votive scarf must have been set down with great freedom, though on closer examination the schematic patterns in the brushwork betray that the style was not derived from observation of nature but from repeated, learned methods of rendering the effects of light. It is worthwhile noting, in this connection, that as recently as the early nineteenth century a visitor to a Greek monastery on Mount Athos watched a Byzantine master sketch an entire scene, full-scale, on a wall prepared for fresco in one hour without the aid of any drawing or model whatsoever. This combination of inherited compositions and techniques with great manual freedom runs through the entire course of Byzantine painting.

A controversy over the date of the Castelseprio frescoes arose soon after they became generally known at the close of World War II. Although their date remains uncertain, one early in the eighth century now seems probable. Apparently, a Greek painter was traveling through northern Italy, then controlled by the Lombards, painting wherever he could find work. Isolated though this single incident may seem, it is symptomatic of a Western need that later became endemic; when Western patrons wanted paintings or mosaics of a high quality, they often sent to Constantinople for competent artists brought up in a pictorial tradition that, from Archaic

Greek times through the successors of Justinian, had remained virtually unbroken.

It is all the more tragic, therefore, that the Byzantine pictorial tradition, which for centuries constantly recharged the depleted batteries of the West, was itself menaced and for a while almost extinguished by a violent internal controversy that broke out about 726 during the reign of the emperor Leo III the Isaurian. A strong party at the court, led by the emperor himself, deeply disapproved of the increasing attribution of miraculous powers to icons as a form of idolatry. Their opposition was also bound up with their distrust of monks, who had achieved a dominant position in the Empire, and of monasteries, whose immense possessions were exempt from taxation. Leo objected chiefly to portable icons, but a fierce persecution broke out during the reign of Constantine V in 765 in which the possessors of images were tortured, blinded, mutilated, even executed, and representations of all sorts, including the figured mosaics that once adorned the interior of Hagia Sophia, were systematically destroyed. All the great pictorial art of the age of Justinian perished in this campaign, save only that in Byzantine Italy and in such remote fastnesses as Sinai (see Chapter 1 and colorplates 39, 40). For more than a century the controversy raged between the Iconoclasts (image breakers) who would permit only the Cross and ornament based on animal and plant forms in church decoration, and the Iconodules (image venerators), who hid their icons at great personal risk.

Although the triumph of Orthodoxy and the Iconodules was celebrated in 843, it was not until 867 that the patriarch Photios could preach a sermon in Hagia Sophia, in the presence of the coemperors Michael III and Basil I the Macedonian, mourning the loss of the mosaics that had been scraped off the church's walls and rejoicing that the image of the Theotokos (*Mother of God*) could now be restored to its former glory and that

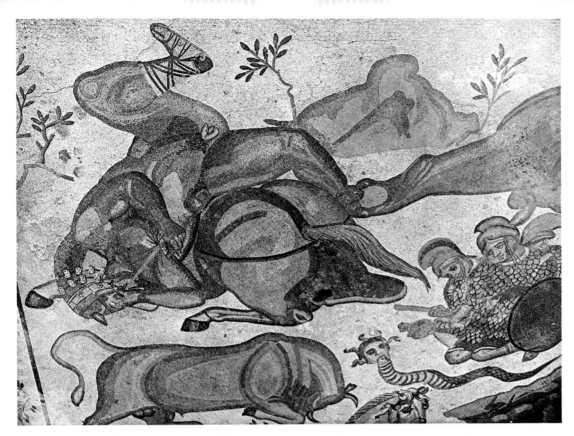

COLORPLATE 34.   Roman. *Exploits of Hercules* (portion of a floor mosaic at the imperial villa). Early 4th century A.D. Piazza Armerina, Sicily

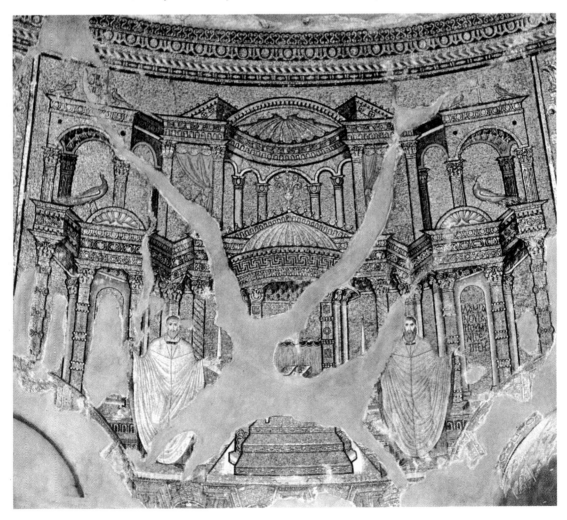

COLORPLATE 35.   Early Christian. Dome mosaic, with Saints Cosmas and Damian. c. 400 A.D. Hagios Georgios, Salonika, Greece

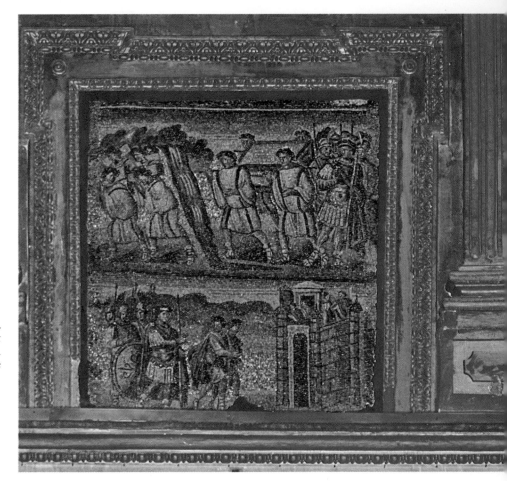

COLORPLATE 36.
Early Christian. Scenes from the *Book of Joshua.* Mosaic. c. 432–40 A.D.
Sta. Maria Maggiore, Rome

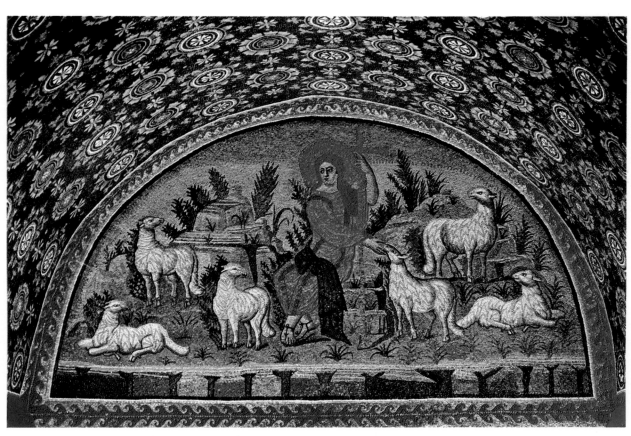

COLORPLATE 37.   Early Byzantine. *The Good Shepherd.* Mosaic. c. 425–26 A.D. Mausoleum of Galla Placidia, Ravenna

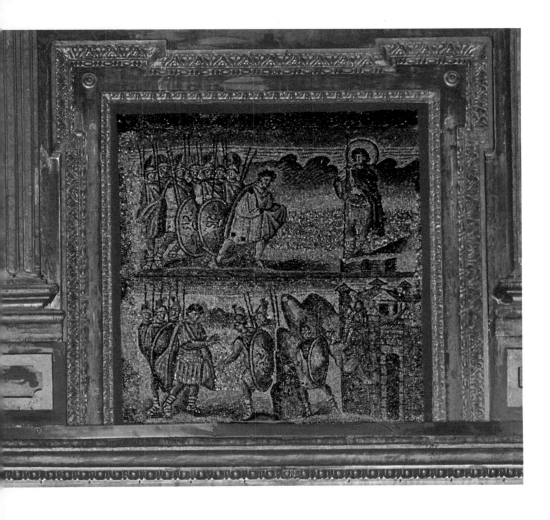

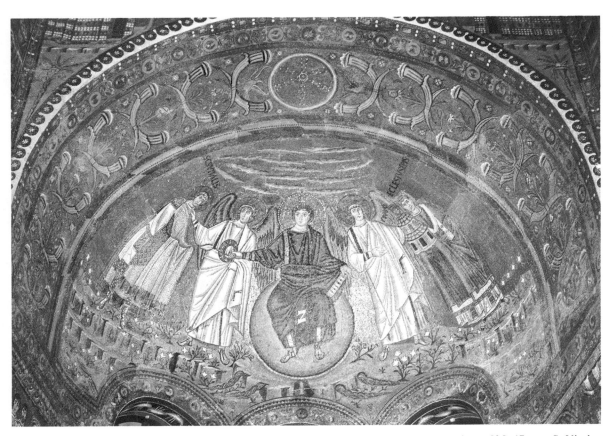

COLORPLATE 38.   Early Byzantine. *Christ Enthroned Between Angels and Saints.* Mosaic. c. 525–47 A.D. S. Vitale, Ravenna

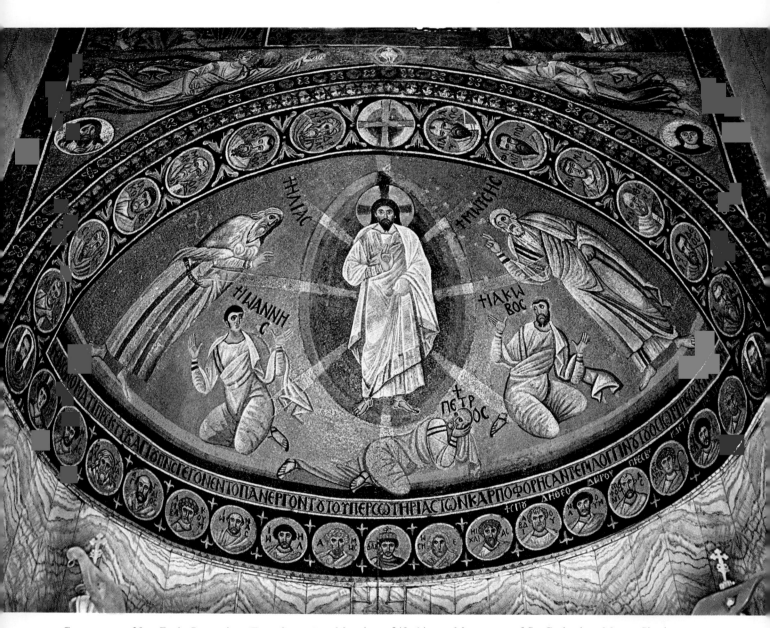

COLORPLATE 39.   Early Byzantine. *Transfiguration.* Mosaic. c. 549–64 A.D. Monastery of St. Catherine, Mount Sinai

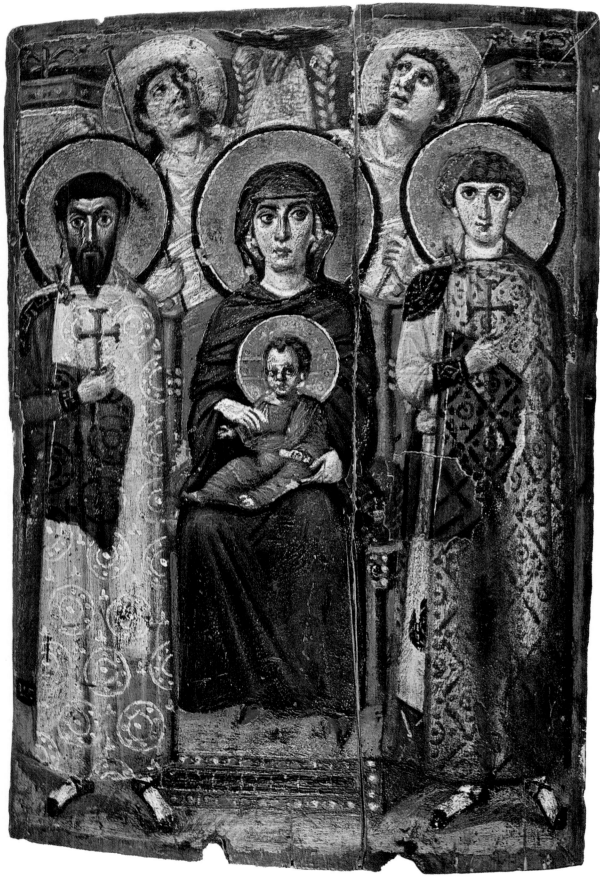

COLORPLATE 40.   Early Byzantine. *The Virgin and Child Enthroned Between St. Theodore and St. George.* c. 6th
century A.D. Panel painting. 27 x 18⅞″. Monastery of St. Catherine, Mount Sinai

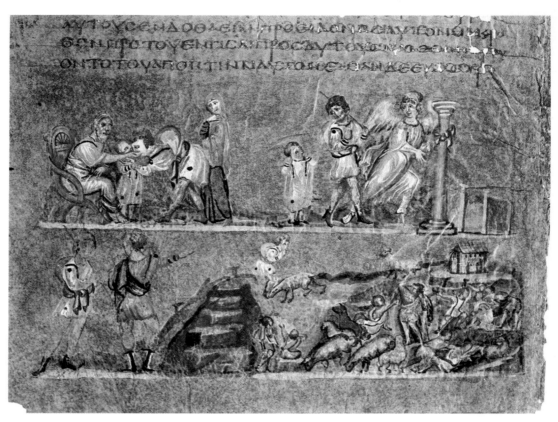

COLORPLATE 41.
Early Christian. *Joseph and His Brethren*, from the *Vienna Book of Genesis*. Illumination. Early 6th century A.D. Osterreichische Nationalbibliothek, Vienna

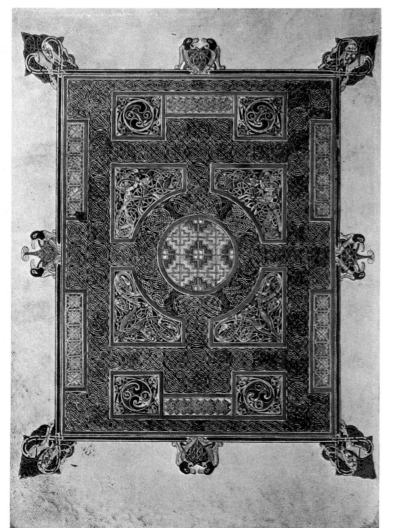

COLORPLATE 42.
Hiberno-Saxon. Cruciform page, from the *Lindisfarne Gospels*. Illumination. c. 698–721 A.D. British Museum. London

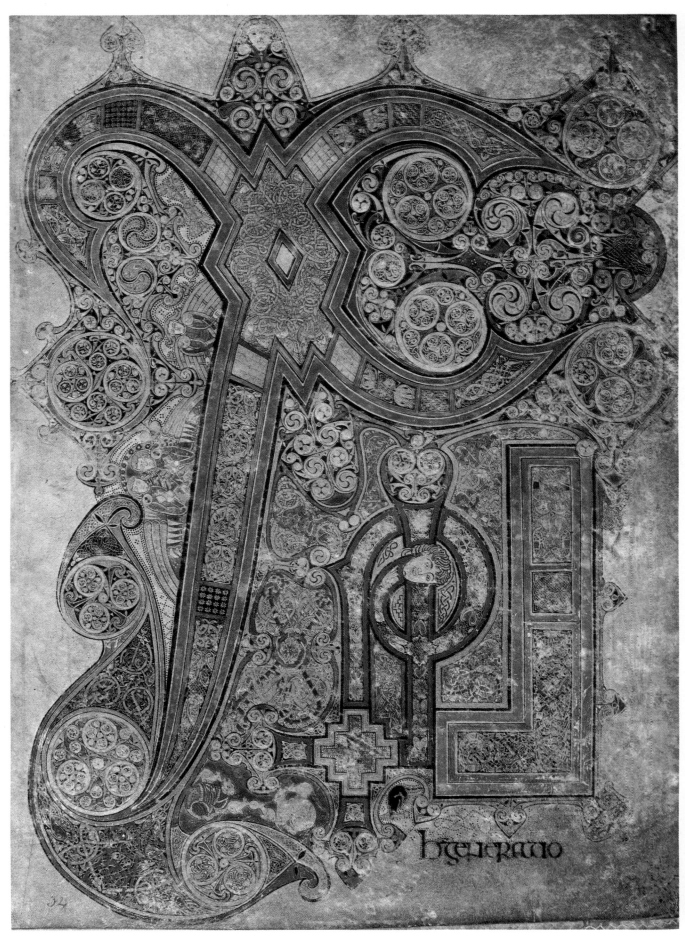

COLORPLATE 43.   Hiberno-Saxon. *XPI* page, from the *Book of Kells*. c. 760–820 A.D. Illumination, c. 13 x 9½".
Trinity College, Dublin

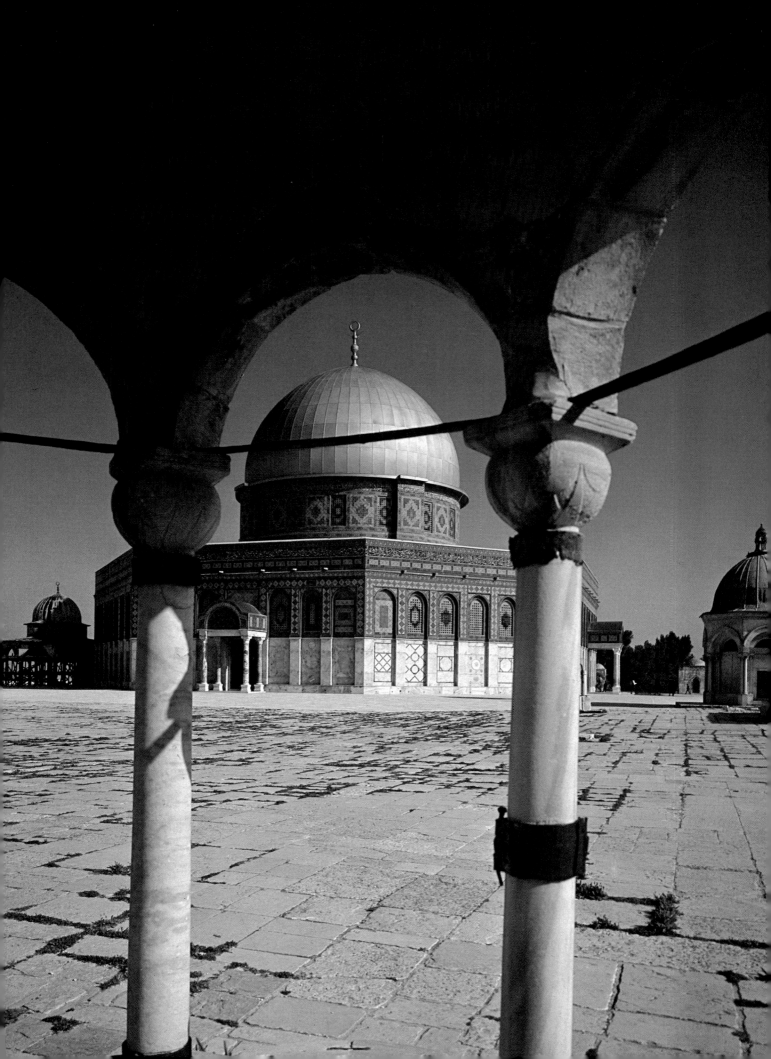

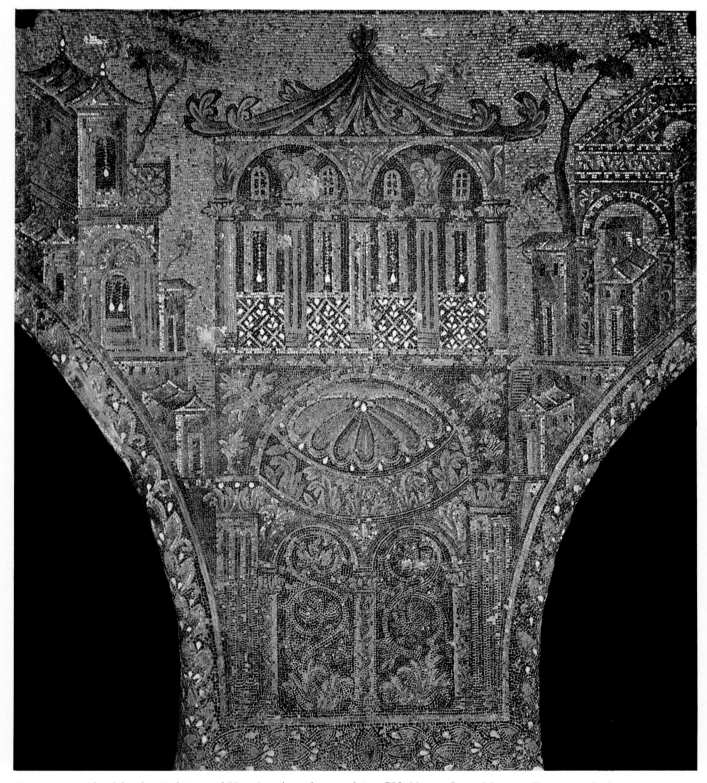

COLORPLATE 45.   Islamic. *Architectural View* (portion of a mosaic). c. 705–11 A.D. Great Mosque. Damascus, Syria

◀ COLORPLATE 44.   Islamic. Dome of the Rock. Late 7th century A.D. Jerusalem

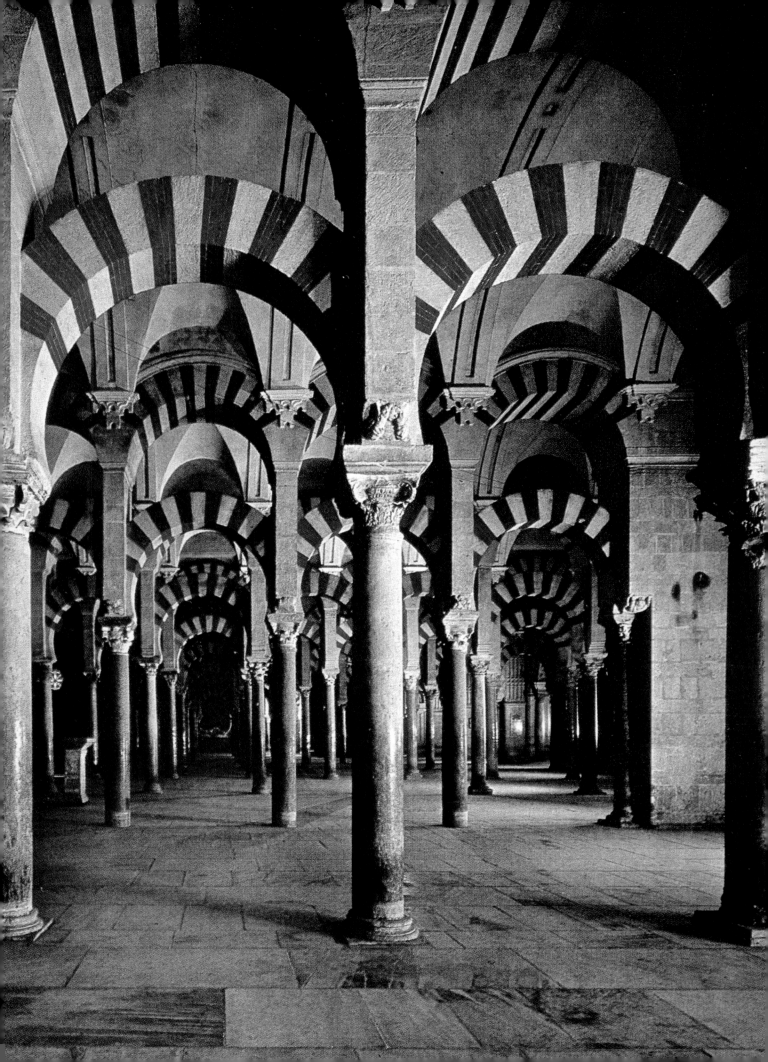

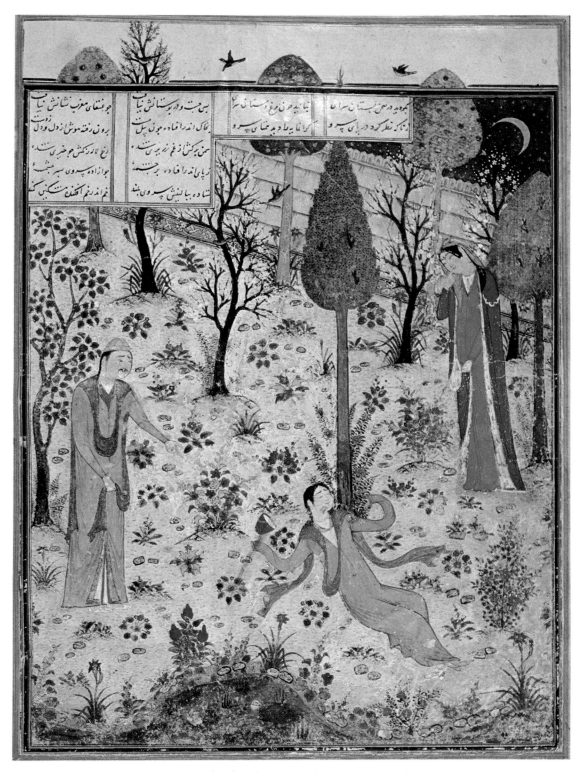

COLORPLATE 47.   Islamic. JUNAID. *Bihzad in the Garden,* from the manuscript of the poems of
Khwaju Kirmani. Illumination. 1396 A.D. British Museum, London

◀ COLORPLATE 46.   Islamic. Interior, Great Mosque (Arcades of 'Abd ar-Rahman I).
c. 786 A.D. Córdoba, Spain

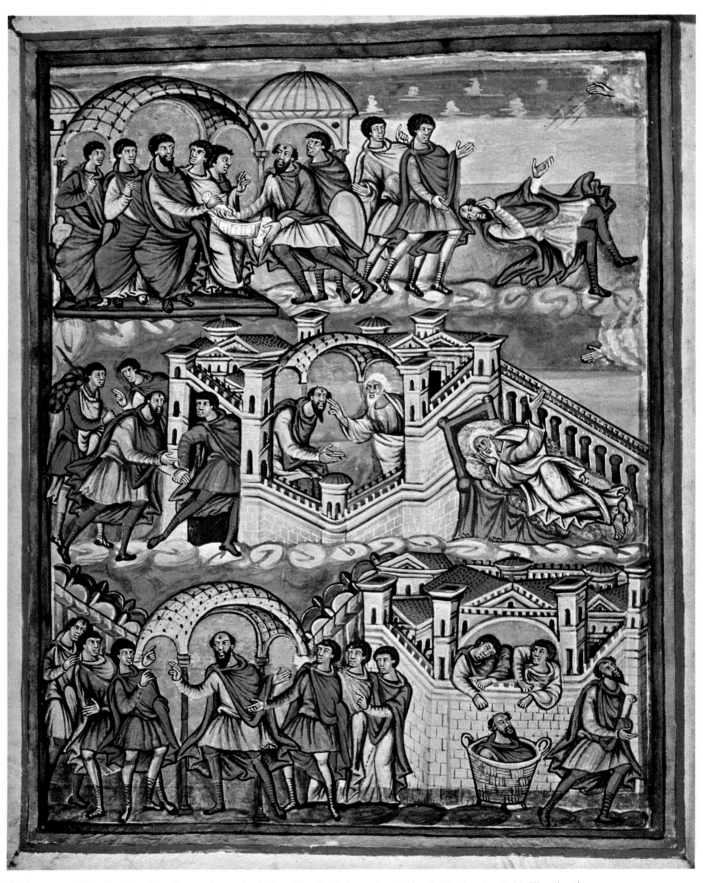

COLORPLATE 48. Carolingian. Scenes from the Life of St. Paul, from the *Bible of Charles the Bald*. Illumination. c. 875–77 A.D. S. Paolo fuori le Mura, Rome

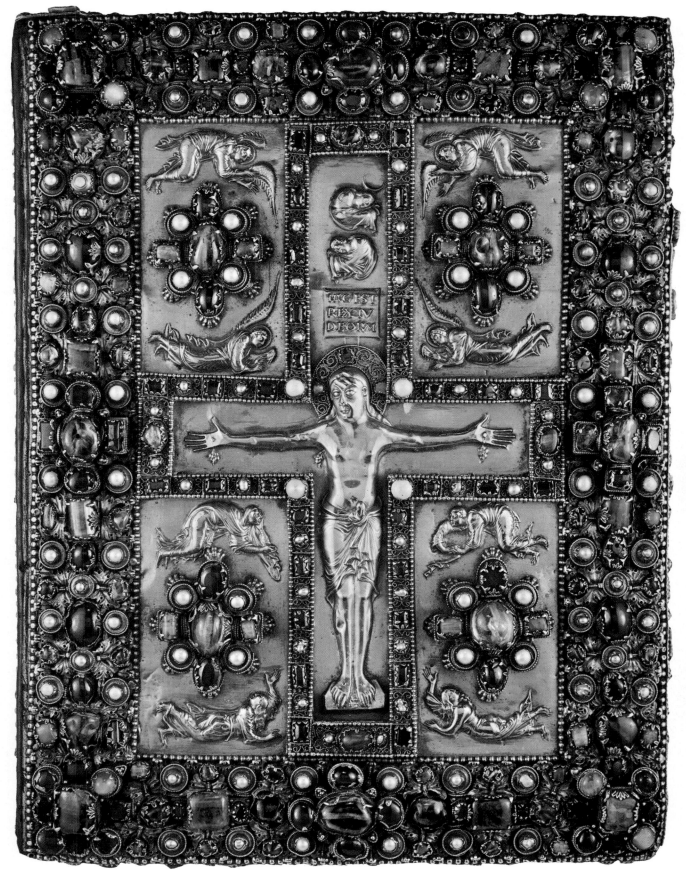

COLORPLATE 49.   Carolingian. Front cover of the *Lindau Gospels*. c. 870 A.D. Gold with precious and semiprecious
stones. 13¾ x 10½". Pierpont Morgan Library, New York

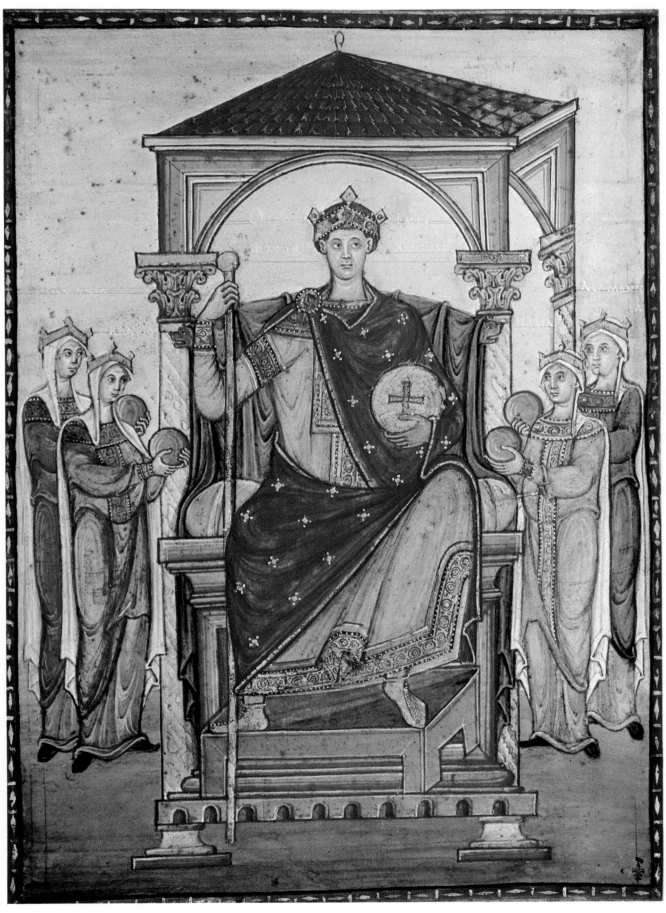

COLORPLATE 50.   Ottonian. *Otto Imperator Augustus* (detached page from an unknown illuminated manuscript).
c. 985 A.D. Musée Condé, Chantilly, France

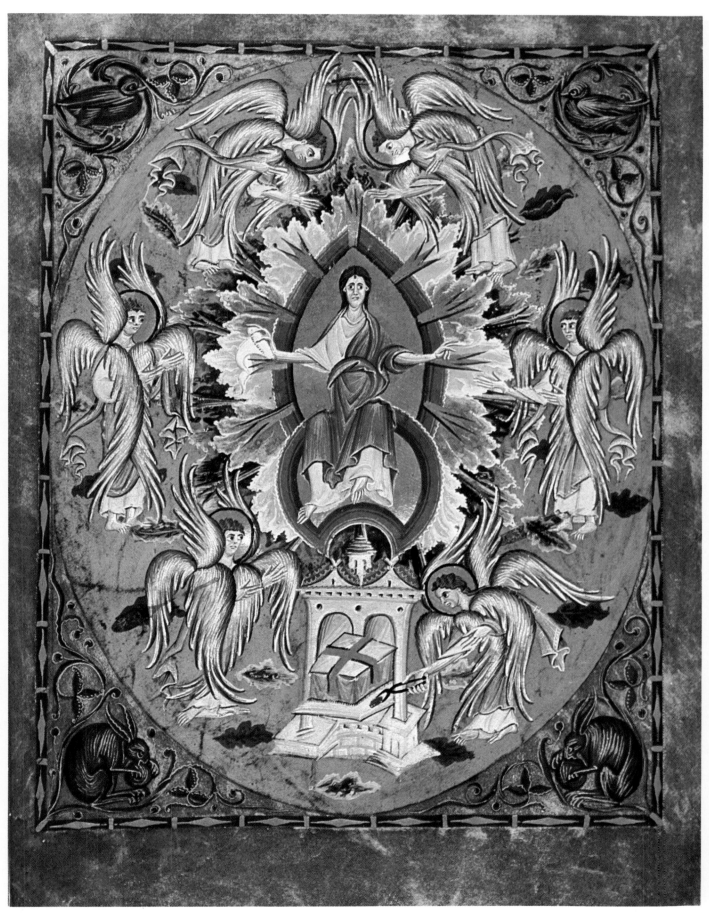

COLORPLATE 51.   Ottonian. *Vision of Isaiah*, from a Commentary. Illumination. Late 10th or early 11th century.
Staatsbibliothek, Bamberg, Germany

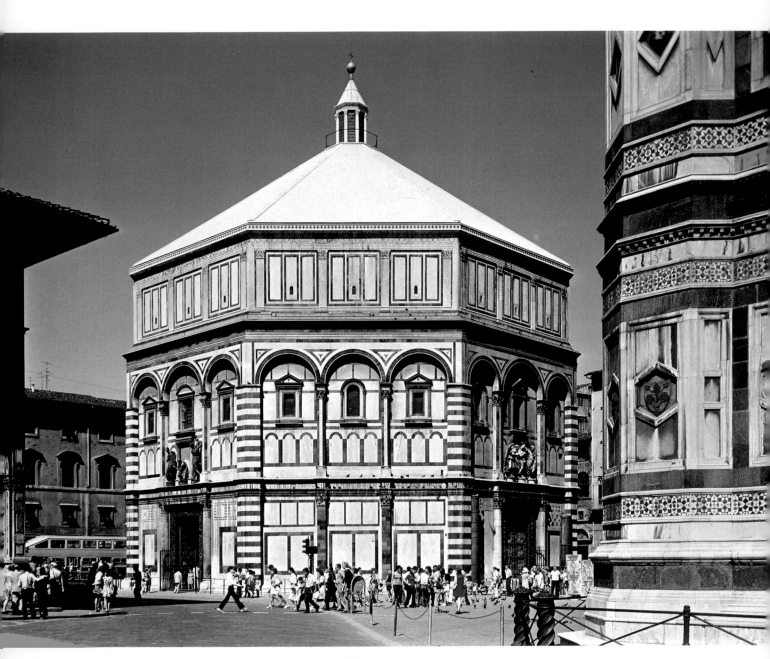

COLORPLATE 52.   Romanesque. Baptistery of S. Giovanni. 11th century. Florence

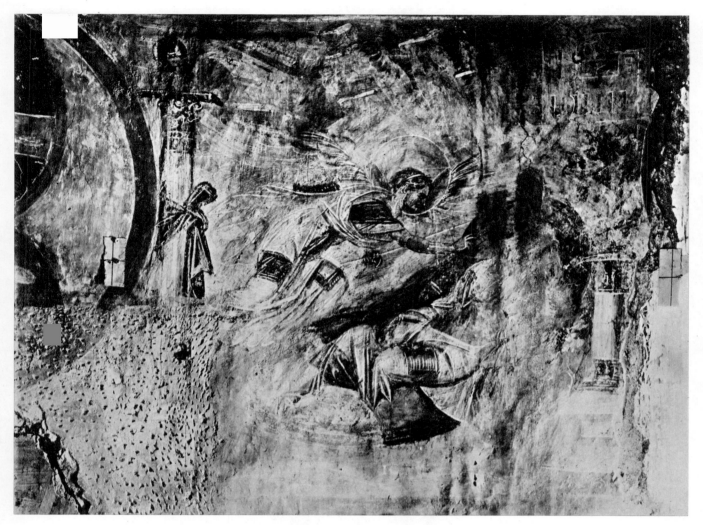

425. *Appearance of the Angel to Joseph*. Fresco. Sta. Maria Foris Portas, Castelseprio, Italy

the restoration of the images of the saints would soon follow. Photios was doubtless referring to the mosaic of the *Virgin and Child Enthroned* (fig. 426), which still appears in the apse of Hagia Sophia, although today in somewhat damaged condition because of the Turkish whitewash that covered it for centuries. The figures are three times lifesize, but the dimensions of Hagia Sophia are so vast that the image is best appreciated through binoculars. It is tempting to see in the grave beauty of the Virgin's oval face and in the depth of her great eyes traces of sadness occasioned by the terrible period her devotees lived through before Photios' sermon. We can certainly discern in the grace of her delicate hands, in the precision with which the drapery folds are shown as they appear along the contour, and above all in the clear definition of the masses of the body and limbs under the shimmering blue garments a new artistic ideal of refinement and definition very different from the light-mysticism of the Sinai mosaic (see colorplate 39) or the entranced solemnity of the Sinai icon (see colorplate 40). The Virgin is remote, almost lost in the immensity of the golden semidome. Within a few years, however, during the latter

quarter of the ninth century, many other mosaics were added to Hagia Sophia, the greatest of which was a Pantocrator in the center of the dome with angels in the pendentives. The entire ninth-century cycle has perished either in structural collapses or at the hands of the Ottoman Turks.

The last six centuries in the life of the Byzantine Empire were only intermittently peaceful. The emperors had to wage almost continuous defensive war against invasions of the Arabs and Seljuk Turks in Asia Minor, the Slavs in Macedonia and Greece, and the Bulgars, the Avars, and the Russians, directly to the north. Time and again invaders appeared under the very walls of Constantinople, and sieges of the capital, frequently imminent from one direction or another, were often protracted and severe. By one means or another, including the highly effective Greek fire (an incendiary mixture), the Byzantines always repelled the invaders, and from time to time they regained portions of Justinian's former empire. Unexpectedly, their pagan enemies (but not the Muslims) were converted to Christianity; after some oscillation most accepted the Eastern Orthodox form. Quite as

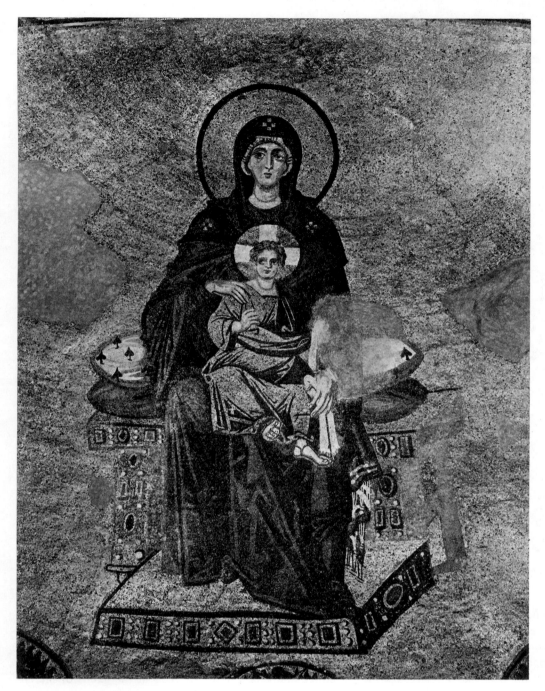

426. *Virgin and Child
Enthroned* (portion).
Apse mosaic.
Before 867 A.D.
Hagia Sophia,
Istanbul

dangerous as invaders were internal dissensions, which could break out at any moment in the form of palace revolutions, often engineered by members of the emperor's family or entourage. Nonetheless, the person of the emperor was still regarded as sacred, and palace ritual was controlled by an elaborate scenario. For example, the emperor received ambassadors while seated on the Throne of Solomon, which was flanked by bronze lions and gilded trees bearing gilded birds. As the ambassadors prostrated themselves, the lions put out their tongues and roared, the birds sang (each its own tune), and the throne bearing the emperor rose nearly to the ceiling; when it descended, he was wearing a different costume. The number and riches of the palace halls, adorned with marble columns and gold mosaics, were legendary in the West. The Great Palace must have been

laid out in informal groupings of chambers and buildings, somewhat on the order of Hadrian's Villa (see fig. 286). Possibly the Alhambra (see fig. 364) reflects some of the character of the Byzantine imperial palaces, whose chambers were interspersed with courtyards, fountains, and pools. When Constantinople was captured by the Crusaders in 1204, the Great Palace, like the rest of the city, was sacked and left a burned-out ruin. Little trace of its splendor now remains.

THE MACEDONIAN RENAISSANCE

The Macedonian dynasty founded by Basil I ushered in a period of intense cultural activity, especially under Constantine VII (Porphyrogenitos), a scholar and amateur painter who reigned from 913 to 959. Although their dating is still by no means certain, a group of illuminated manuscripts, whose classicism is even more impressive than that of the works of the Palace School in the Carolingian period (see fig. 373), is now attributed by most scholars to the tenth century and to the personal influence of Constantine VII. A wholly unique work is the *Joshua Roll* (fig. 427), the kind of continuously illustrated rotulus mentioned in the discussion of the Column of Trajan (see Part Two, Chapter 6; see fig. 277). Undoubtedly, however, the *Joshua Roll* was influenced by Roman imperial columns, two of which stood in Constantinople. The commissioning of a rotulus to depict the military campaigns of a great biblical hero may well have been prompted by a desire to commemorate allegorically the victories of the Macedonian emperors against the Muslims. In the section illustrated, two Israelite spies are sent out toward distant Jericho, then ride in search of Joshua, and finally Joshua, dressed as a Byzantine general and provided with a halo, leads the army of the Israelites toward the Jordan River.

Landscape elements are depicted much as they were in the Vienna Genesis (see colorplate 41) and in the Castelseprio frescoes, but are not restricted to the foreground plane. The illuminator has worked out an extremely effective technique for rendering foliage, rocky hillsides, and distant cities in a soft, golden-brown wash, which suggests great distances and atmospheric haze. Certain details (in one instance Joshua prostrates himself before the angel in the posture dictated by tenth-century court ritual) indicate that the work may not be a copy. But in all certainty the artist studied paintings of the Helleno-Roman tradition with great care. The complex and vivid action poses and the movement of the horses show a firm control of the basic principles of Classical art, and the rhythmic movement of the figures through landscape space is totally unexpected.

The brilliant work of this group is the *Paris Psalter*, which contains several full-page illustrations in color, richly painted in a style so close to that of Pompeiian art (see figs. 253, 272) that it is hard to convince ourselves that we are not looking at a Classical original. *David the Psalmist* (colorplate 59) has all the appearance of an Orpheus charming the animals with his music (they are, of course, David's goats, sheep, and dog). As he plays, he is attended by a lovely Greek female figure labeled Melody; a nymph peeps shyly from behind the usual wayside column; and in the lower right-hand corner a muscular, deeply tanned, superbly painted male figure, clinging to the stump of a tree, is—of all things—the divinity of Bethlehem! Classicism could hardly have been carried further. The scene is painted with such grace and luminosity that it is a shock to be called back to chronological reality by the stiffness and mannered quality of the drapery folds and by the parallel striations used to render light. These medieval artists could emulate Classical models, possibly at the behest of the scholar-emperor, and even feel the beauty of the Hellenic style they were learning without clearly understanding the analysis of space and light that had originally given rise to it.

MONASTIC CHURCHES AND MOSAICS

When the Macedonian renaissance began, Hagia Sophia and other grand-scale churches already existed in the capital, and the other large cities of the Empire were also graced with elaborate churches. These buildings were well maintained, and there was no need for more of their kind. Eleventh- and twelfth-century builders could devote their efforts to the construction of monastic buildings, intended for communities numbering a few monks, and a profusion of such churches was erected. Despite all their richness of marble paneling and mosaic decoration,

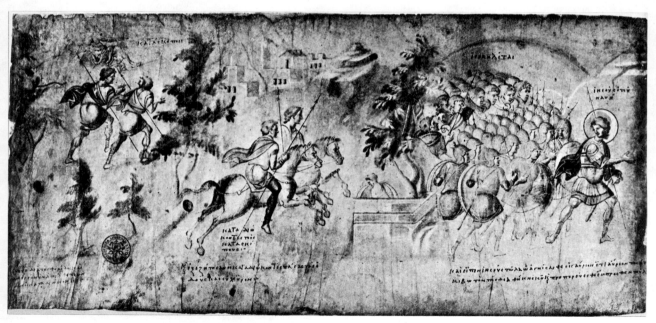

427. *Joshua Leading the Israelites Toward the Jordan River* (portion), from the *Joshua Roll.*
Constantinople. Illumination. 10th century. Biblioteca Apostolica Vaticana, Rome

therefore, these churches are surprisingly intimate in scale. The basic plan, which had countless individual variations, was the so-called Greek cross with four equal arms inscribed within a square and crowned by a dome. This plan maintained a central axis in that the church was prolonged on the west by a narthex and in that the east wall was broken by one or more apses. The interior was quite small and designed chiefly for the celebration of the Liturgy by monks. At the Monastery of Hosios Loukas in Phocis, between Athens and Delphi in west-central Greece, two connected monastic churches were built early in the eleventh century. Both the Katholikon and the Theotokos (fig. 428) were laid out on Greek-cross plans; the Katholikon was provided with galleries girdling its interior. In both churches the central dome was lifted on a high drum, pierced by windows. Compared with the austerity of Early Christian exteriors, the churches at Hosios Loukas seem ornate indeed, yet the richness is one of construction, not mere decoration. Courses of stone alternate with courses of brick, set at an angle to provide even greater variety of texture. This kind of construction was used throughout Greece and the Balkans from the eleventh through the fifteenth century.

When compared with the apparently measureless space of Hagia Sophia (see fig. 339), the interior of the Katholikon seems at first cramped (fig. 429); the movement is, however, entirely vertical, and carries the eye aloft into the dome, which is the only part of the central space lighted directly by its own windows. The light in the church is subdued, originating from windows in the galleries, in the corner spaces flanking the sanctuary, in the prothesis and the diakonikon (areas intended respectively for the preparation of the sacred elements of the Eucharist, and for the storage of vessels and vestments, much like the sacristy of a Roman Catholic church), and in the arms of the transept. The dome, interestingly enough, does not spring from pendentives as at Hagia Sophia but rests on squinches as at San Vitale. In all Byzantine churches the bema (sanctuary) is closed off by means of an iconostasis, a screen bearing icons whose subjects and order are largely predetermined by tradition. Tradition also determined the order of the mosaics in a church interior. The Theotokos, invariably enthroned or standing, adorned the semidome of the apse; and the Pantocrator looked down from the center of the dome, surrounded by the heavenly hierarchy between the windows, and scenes from the life of Christ pictured in the squinches, vaults, and upper wall surfaces. Figures of standing saints decorated the lower wall surfaces. These soaring interiors, with their rich and subtle variations of spaces and lights, must always be imagined not only with their marble and mosaic decorations but also with their Liturgy, accompanied by clouds of incense and by chanted music whose deep sonorities bear little relation to the sound of Western plainchant.

The finest remaining mosaics of the Middle Byzantine period are those in the Church of the Dormition at Daphni, not far from Athens, dating from about 1100. The *Annunciation* (fig. 430), unfortunately damaged at the right, fills one of the four squinches. The artist has

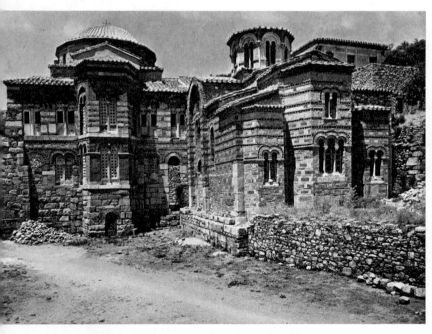

428. The Katholikon and Theotokos (churches), Monastery of Hosios Loukas. Early 11th century. Phocis, Greece

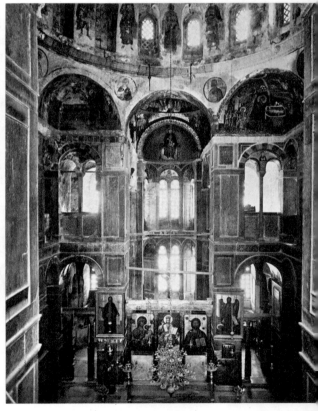

429. Interior, Katholikon, Hosios Loukas

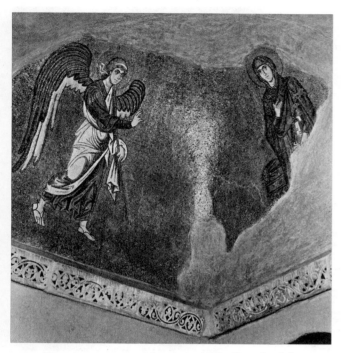

430. *Annunciation.* Mosaic. c. 1100. Church of the
Dormition, Daphni, Greece

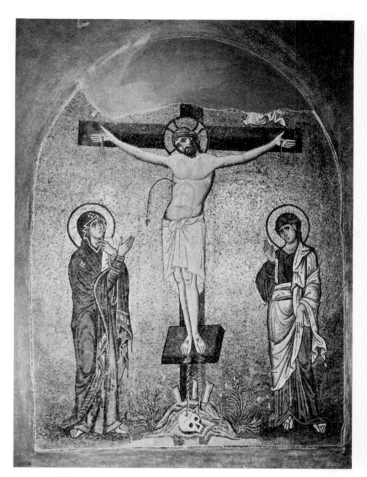

431. *Crucifixion.* Mosaic. c. 1100. Church of the
Dormition, Daphni, Greece

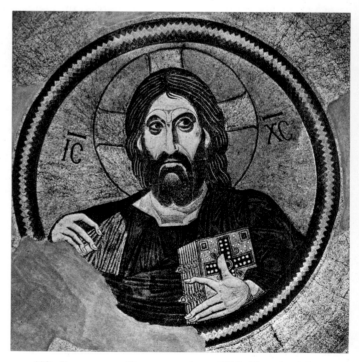

432. *Pantocrator.* Dome mosaic. c. 1100. Church of the
Dormition, Daphni, Greece

utilized this space so that the angel Gabriel makes his
salutation to Mary across the corner; as there is no indication of groundline, the figures seem to float in glittering golden air. Mary is represented in the state of mind
indicated by Luke 1: 29: "And when she saw him, she was
troubled at his saying, and cast in her mind what manner
of salutation this should be." The subtlety of the psychological characterization is in keeping with the refinement of the style. Especially beautiful is the harmony
between the convex curvature of the angel's wings and the
concave line of his arm, and the integration of these
curves with those of his himation and tunic. As in Ottonian and Romanesque painting, the light is generalized
and the drapery formalized, but at Daphni this formality
is always under careful control, so that one is constantly
aware of subtle balances and counterbalances of movement.

Although the *Christus patiens* type was chosen for the
Crucifixion at Daphni (fig. 431), the representation is
timeless and symbolic; there are no soldiers, no Apostles,
no thieves, only the grieving Mary and the suffering John
on either side of the Cross, and originally mourning
angels above the Cross on either side. The emotion is intense, but it is held in check by a reserve comparable to
that of the Classical period in Greek sculpture; in fact,
the three figures have been disposed with the grand
simplicity of those on a metope. Christ hangs upon the
Cross, his arms describing a shallow curve, his hips
toward his right in a pose repeated in most Crucifixions
under Byzantine influence. His head is gently inclined
toward Mary as she gazes up at him with one hand slightly extended; John, on the other hand, turns toward us.
Formalized though the broad flow of the drapery masses
may be in detail, it remains sculptural in feeling. As is
characteristic of much Middle and Late Byzantine pic-

torial art, the modulations of tone are delicate in the extreme. Christ's side has been pierced, and blood accompanied by water spurts from it in a bright arc (John 19: 34), symbolizing the sacraments of the Eucharist and Baptism. The streams of blood that flow from Christ's feet strike the skull at the foot of the Cross. Golgotha means *the place of a skull* in Hebrew (John 19:17). Theologians have always interpreted the skull as that of Adam. Paul had said (I Cor. 15: 22): "For as in Adam all die, even so in Christ shall all be made alive." As if in fulfillment of Paul's promise, flowers grow from the rocks below the Cross.

From the lyrical *Annunciation* and the elegiac *Crucifixion*, we turn with amazement to the revelation of the *Pantocrator* (fig. 432) at the summit of the dome. We may possibly gain from this image some idea of the vanished mosaic that in the Macedonian renaissance adorned the center of the dome at Hagia Sophia. The light from the windows of the drum illuminates the rainbow circle in which the colossal Christ appears, his face worn by suffering ("Surely he hath borne our griefs, and carried our sorrows," Isa. 53: 4). The extraordinary human sensitivity of the great mosaicist at Daphni appears in the drawing of the long, aquiline nose, the flow of brows and cheekbones, the light on the half-open mouth, the streaming lines of the hair, and above all in the incomparable depth and power of the eyes.

THE EXPANSION OF BYZANTINE STYLE

In the Middle and Late Byzantine periods, the artistic achievements of Greek masters were carried throughout the territory stretching from Russia to Sicily. In 989 Vladimir, grand prince of Kiev (who ruled most of the territory now comprising European Russia), married Princess Anna, sister of the Byzantine emperor Basil II, and brought Byzantine craftsmen back with him from Constantinople to build and decorate churches in his newly converted principality as well as to instruct local artisans. His son Yaroslav commenced in 1037 the construction of the magnificent Cathedral of Hagia Sophia at Kiev. This church, in Byzantine style, with five aisles surrounded on three sides by an open arcade, has thirteen domes, representing the number of Christ and the Apostles. Its mosaics date from 1043 to 1046. The apse mosaics have miraculously survived the abandonment and partial ruin of the cathedral in the sixteenth century, its rebuilding in the seventeenth century, and its partial destruction in World War II. A monumental *Theotokos* (fig. 433) in orant position adorns the semidome; her powerful drapery folds recall those at Hosios Loukas. She appears to stand in a golden niche, supporting its arch like one of the maidens of the Erechtheion (see fig. 201). Below her unfolds an extraordinary scene, seldom represented in Western art—the *Communion of the Apostles*. Christ officiates as priest at the central altar, distributing bread on the left and wine on the right.

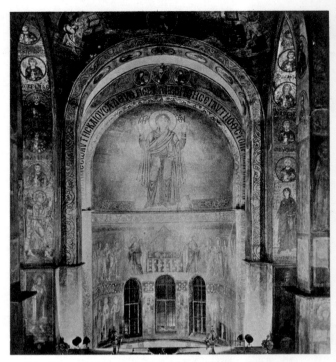

433. *Theotokos*, and *Communion of the Apostles.* Apse mosaics. 1043–46. Cathedral of Hagia Sophia, Kiev, Russia

The most ambitious of all Byzantine monuments built outside the Empire is San Marco in Venice (fig. 434); this state enjoyed strong if not always cordial commercial relationships with Constantinople. The church, now the Cathedral of Venice, was commenced in 1063 as a ducal basilica connected directly with the Doges' Palace. Its plan (fig. 435) was imitated from that of the destroyed sixth-century Church of the Holy Apostles at Constantinople, built by Justinian. It is basically a Greek cross, designed on five squares, each surmounted by a dome on a high drum, now crowned by a helmet-like structure of wood and copper, which imparts a verticality unknown to Early Byzantine domes. The exterior was greatly modified in the Gothic period by the addition of elaborate pinnacles and foliate ornament along the skyline, but the original Byzantine arches and unusual clustered columns are still visible (see fig. 434). The vast interior spaces of the basilica have much more to do with the spatial fluidity of Hagia Sophia than with the compressed feeling of the usual Middle Byzantine interiors (fig. 436). The domes, set on pendentives rather than on the insistent squinches of the era's monastic churches, seem to float above their arches.

Powerful barrel vaults separate the bays and abut the thrust of the pendentives; the vaults in turn are supported on massive cubic piers, pierced by arches connecting with the galleries, which are entirely open in contrast to the arcaded galleries of Eastern churches. The nave galleries are sustained by triple arcades supported by modified Corinthian columns. The veined marble columns and the gray marble paneling of walls and piers were, of course, imported from the Byzantine East. Dim at all times, the interior shines with a soft, golden radiance shed by the continuous mosaics that line the domes, barrel vaults, and lunettes and softly veil all architectural demarcations. Mosaic artists were brought from Constantinople, but how much they accomplished is not known; presumably much of their work was destroyed in a disastrous fire in 1106. Many of the present mosaics, in Byzantine style but with Romanesque influence here and there, were done by Venetian artisans during the twelfth and thirteenth centuries; several, however, were completely replaced in the late Renaissance or in the Baroque period. Those that remain are especially important as witnesses to the beginning of the Venetian school of painting, which in the Renaissance became one of the two leading Italian schools.

In the earliest of the five dome mosaics, executed about 1150 in the dome above the nave, the *Pentecost* (fig. 437) is represented. The Descent of the Holy Spirit upon the Apostles is described in Acts as "a sound from heaven as of a rushing mighty wind." As the Apostles met "there appeared unto them cloven tongues like as of fire, and it sat upon each of them"; they then began to speak in many tongues, which were understood by people from all nations, who were in the streets outside. The event is reorganized in conformity with the architecture of the dome. In the center is a throne, on which is the dove of the Holy Spirit; from the throne rays extend to the Apostles, enthroned in a circle above the windows. Between the windows stand pairs of people from all nations. The design is like a vast wheel, but it contains a startling discrepancy: there are Twelve Apostles over sixteen windows, as if three-four time in music were being played over four-four, each measure being marked by an archangel in one of the spandrels.

At the other extreme of Italy, Roger II ruled as the first Norman king of Sicily from 1130 to 1154. Like other monarchs in southern and eastern Europe, he called Byzantine artists to his court to decorate a series of religious buildings and the salon of his palace. The church at Cefalù was raised to cathedral status at the request of Roger II, who intended it as his tomb-church. The team of Greek artists, who finished the mosaic decoration of the apse in 1148 (the later mosaics in the choir are by local masters) had to adapt Byzantine iconographic systems to the architectural requirements of a Western basilica and the desires of a royal patron (fig. 438). In the two lowest registers stand the Twelve Apostles. In the next register the beautiful Theotokos, robed in white with soft blue shadows, extends her delicate hands in orant position between four magnificent archangels, bending their heads as they hold forth

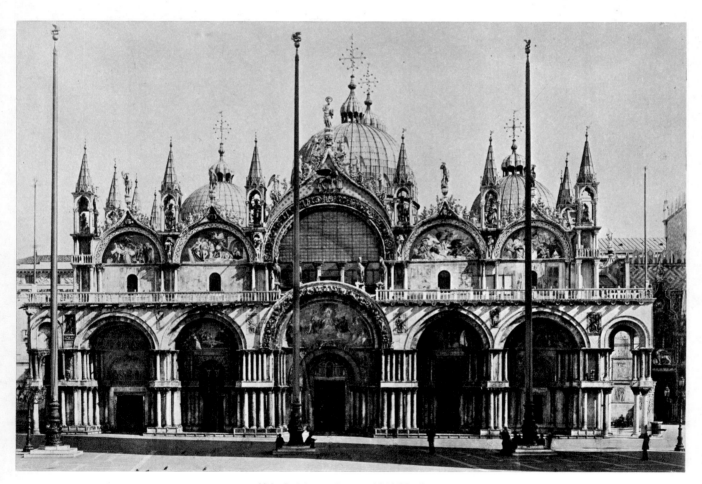

434. S. Marco. Begun 1063. Venice

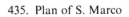

435. Plan of S. Marco

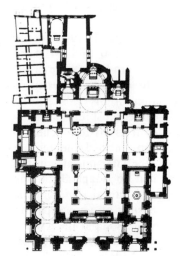

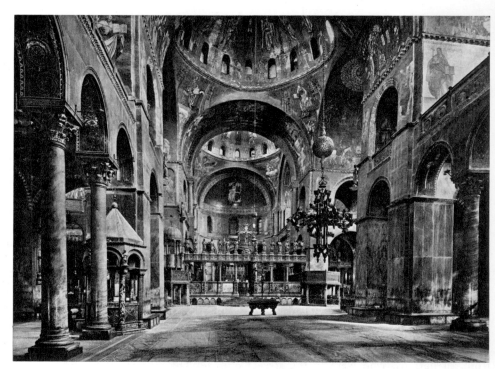

436. Interior, S. Marco

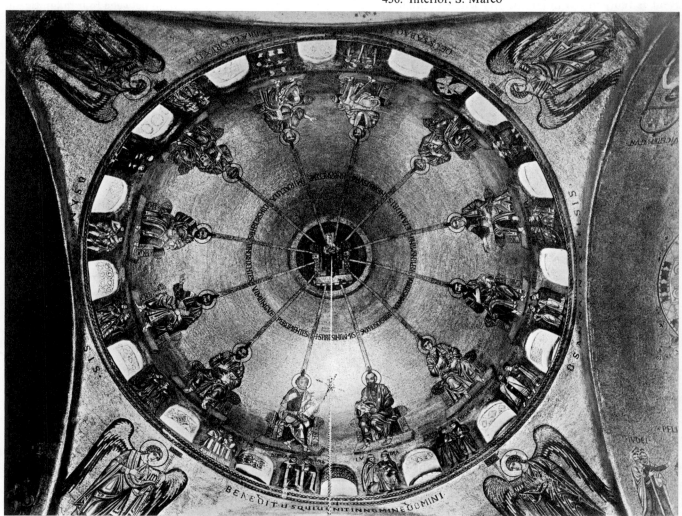

437. *Pentecost.* Dome mosaic. c. 1150. S. Marco, Venice

scepters and orbs. Above this heavenly court, in the semidome (the church has no dome), appears the Pantocrator, as he does later at Monreale. In contrast to the austere Saviour at Daphni, the Cefalù Christ seems a poet and a dreamer, sensitive and merciful. His right hand is outstretched in blessing; in his left, instead of a closed book as at Daphni, he upholds the Gospel of John, written in Greek and Latin, open at Chapter 8, Verse 12,

for all of King Roger's Christian subjects to read: "I am the light of the world: he that followeth me shall not walk in darkness, but shall have the light of life." Light shimmers through the Cefalù mosaics with a delicacy that proclaims them one of the finest achievements of Byzantine art—not the radiance of revelation we saw represented at Sinai (see colorplate 39), but the light of Paradise, a soft, uniform radiance resulting in the sub-

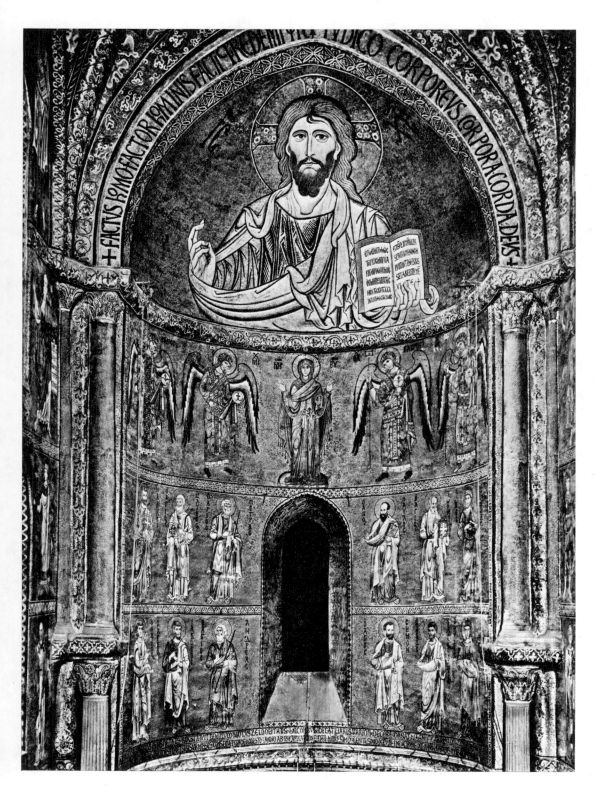

438. Apse mosaics. Cathedral of Cefalù. Completed 1148. Sicily

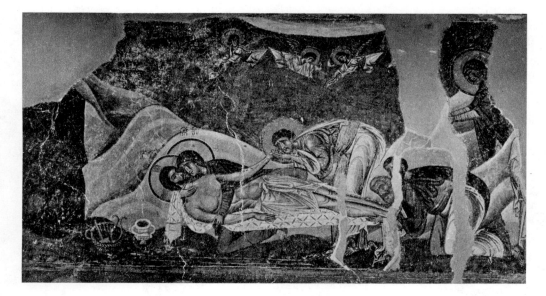

439. *Lamentation*. Fresco. c. 1164. St. Pantaleimon, Nerezi, Yugoslavia

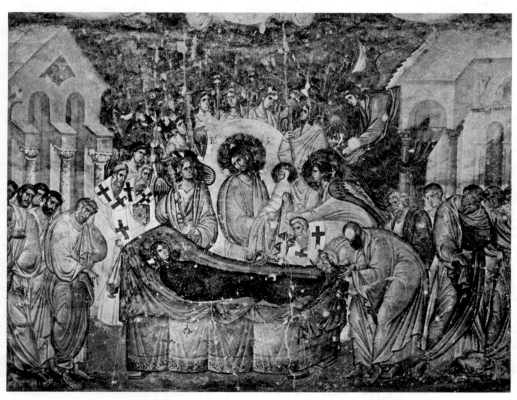

440. *Dormition of the Virgin* (central section). Fresco. 1258–64. Church of the Trinity, Sopoćani, Serbia, Yugoslavia

tlest refinement of gradations in hue and value throughout the drapery masses, the feathers of the angels' wings, and above all in the modeling of faces and hands. Even the ornament sparkles with a new and special brilliance—the decoration above and below the arch, the jewels that stud the Cross of Christ's halo, and an entrancing bit of illusionism, the mosaic acanthus capitals crowning the real colonnettes that uphold the arch. Along with the light at Cefalù line proliferates in amazing multiplicity through the countless strands of Christ's hair and beard and the crinkled folds of the drapery. On the brown tunic appear for the first time sun-

bursts of gold rays, fusing light and line, soon to be adopted by such Italo-Byzantine painters as Cimabue (see fig. 513).

An extraordinary series of frescoes (certainly less expensive to produce than mosaics) is still preserved in churches, cathedrals, and monasteries throughout Macedonia and Serbia, in what is today Yugoslavia. At least fifteen major cycles remain, executed from the eleventh well into the fifteenth century, the last of them done barely ahead of the invading Turks. These cycles form the richest and most consistent body of mural painting left from Middle and Late Byzantine art. The finest paintings in each series were almost invariably done by artists from Constantinople or from other Greek centers; some were painted by refugees after the conquest of the capital by the Crusaders in 1204. Many of the signatures on these works are Greek, and some painters can be traced from one cycle to the next. Local, presumably monastic, artists often completed a cycle begun by an artist from Constantinople or elsewhere with frescoes of considerably less interest (usually those farthest from the eye).

An especially impressive cycle covers all of the interior walls of the beautiful little domed church of Saint Pantaleimon at Nerezi, high on a mountainside overlooking the Macedonian city of Skoplje; the church was completed in 1164 by a grandson of the emperor Alexius I Comnenus. The styles of several painters can be distinguished in the cycle, which is held together by an overall unity of color—especially the intense blue of the backgrounds—and by its intimacy of scale. The painter who set down the scenes of the Passion with a directness and intensity of emotion not seen in Eastern art since the days of the *Rabula Gospels* (see fig. 342) was undeniably a master. The *Lamentation* (fig. 439) shows Christ laid out for burial, his body turned toward us, his eyes closed in death. John holds His left hand to his face, and the Virgin enfolds her dead son in her arms; both faces are contorted with grief. The scene must have been painted at dizzying speed; the authority of the brushstrokes and the brilliant handling of light on the drapery show that Greek painters had lost nothing of their mastery since the far-off days of Castelseprio (see fig. 425). The expressive power shown in this Nerezi fresco leads us far in the direction of early Italian art; if he could speak today, Giotto might tell us that it was this "rude manner of the Greeks," as Vasari mistakenly called it, that opened his eyes to ways of embodying human thought and feeling in works of visual art.

The greatness of the Italian debt to Byzantine art is again indicated by the large-scale fresco cycle in the long-abandoned, recently restored Church of the Trinity at Sopoćani in Serbia. This church was one of a series of monasteries built by the Serbian kings (who wore Byzantine dress and imitated Byzantine court ritual) so that monks could celebrate the Liturgy before the royal tombs. In all of these Serbian churches the entire west wall of the interior above the doorway was given over to a vast fresco representing the Dormition of the Virgin, a nonscriptural scene in which the grieving Apostles, who surround the bier of the Virgin Mary, are astonished by the appearance of Christ from Heaven, attended by angels, who takes her soul in his arms in the form of a tiny child. The Sopoćani frescoes must have been done between 1258 and 1264, and although the artist did not go to the same expressionistic lengths as the twelfth-century master at Nerezi, he had quite as much understanding of drama and deployed both figures and architecture with authority. Movement and emotion sweep through the scene with tremendous effect. The

coloring is unexpectedly delicate; Christ and Peter, for example, are wrapped in lemon-yellow mantles, and Mary's bier is draped in alternating passages of blue and rose. The illustration (fig. 440) shows only the central section of the fresco, which stretches out at the sides to involve both additional grieving figures and more architecture. The new sense of drama and of scale in the Sopoćani frescoes was accompanied by increasing powers of observation; throughout this scene faces are strongly individualized. Most powerful of all is the new sense of unified modeling in light and shade, of both features and draped figures, as compared to the divided drapery shapes of Middle Byzantine art. The creation of volumes in light has always been credited to Giotto and his immediate predecessors, especially Pietro Cavallini (see colorplate 69), but it is clear from the Sopoćani frescoes that Greek painters shortly after the middle of the thirteenth century already knew how to bring out a volume in depth by the action of light, even though that light has as yet no single, identifiable source.

LATER BYZANTINE MOSAICS AND PAINTING IN CONSTANTINOPLE

In 1261 the emperor Michael VIII (Palaeologus), who had been governing in exile from Nicaea as coemperor, returned to Constantinople and started cleaning up the devastation left by the Crusaders. To the Palaeologan period is generally attributed a very large, fragmentary, but beautiful mosaic representing the *Deësis* (*Christ Between the Virgin and Saint John the Baptist*; for its later reappearance in the *Ghent Altarpiece* by Jan van Eyck, see Vol. 2, fig. 98) in the south gallery of Hagia Sophia (fig. 441). The tenderness of the expressions, the grace of the poses and the linear movement, and the extraordinary sensitivity to light in the rendering of faces, hands, and hair mark a master very different from the bold dramatist at Sopoćani, but, nonetheless, one who had a similar understanding of the role of light in creating volume. In the *Deësis* mosaic the diffused light, apparently from an external source, is also very different from the allover glow of the Cefalù mosaics.

During the reign of Michael's son and successor Andronicus II, the Monastery and Church of Christ in Chora, adjacent to the imperial palace in Constantinople and now known under the Turkish name of Kariye Djami, were rebuilt, the church and its narthex decorated with mosaics, and the parecclesion (an adjacent funerary chapel) painted in fresco. This extensive cycle, which has been dated between 1315 and 1321, was carried out after the creation of Giotto's revolutionary works, and it is just possible that the cubic rocks and massive figures in the *Nativity* mosaic (fig. 442) were influenced by Giotto's new ideas (cf. colorplate 70). The scene is represented according to Eastern tradition, derived partly from the account in Luke, and partly from the apocryphal stories of the fifth and sixth centuries, which were widely accepted in the East. For example, the cave in the background does not derive from the Gospels, but from one of these later accounts, and is represented throughout Byzantine art (the Church of the Nativity in Bethlehem was later erected over the cave where Christ is believed to have been born). The first bath of the Christ Child, also apocryphal, is depicted at the lower left.

In the startling frescoes of the parecclesion, Late Byzantine style is exemplified in its most vigorous and imaginative phase. The technique of these frescoes has recently been analyzed; they were executed in the method Italian artists call *secco su fresco* (*dry on fresh*). The color was suspended in a vehicle containing an organic binding material (such as oil, egg, or wax) and laid on over the still-damp plaster. Paint thus applied forms a continuous and very hard skin. This method also allows free and rapid painting over large areas. This technique differs sharply from the "true fresco" method generally used by Italian artists during the Gothic period and the Renaissance (see Chapter 9, page 407). Probably, the *secco su fresco* technique was also used in the Macedonian and Serbian frescoes, but this has not been proved.

The fresco filling the semidome of the apse (colorplate 60) represents what the Greeks call the *Anastasis* (*Resurrection*). Although the Gospel accounts do not describe this scene, both the Apostles' Creed and the Nicene Creed declare that during the three days when Christ's body lay in the tomb he descended into Hell. Apocryphal accounts, widely believed throughout the Christian world, tell how Christ caused the gates of Hell to burst open before him, filled its darkness with light, commanded that Satan be bound until the Second Coming,

and lifted Adam and Eve, followed by all the patriarchs and prophets, from the unhappy realm to which they had been doomed by Original Sin. This theme, known in Western art as the Harrowing of Hell or the Descent into Limbo, is highly appropriate for a funerary chapel, as it sets forth vividly the realization of the hope all men have for resurrection. The composition is unusual in that in order to centralize the scene in the apse the artist has shown Christ lifting Adam with one hand and Eve with the other. The unknown painter represented the subject in a style strongly related to that of the vivid frescoes of Sopoćani in freedom of movement, in brilliance of color, in naturalism of facial expressions, and in the effect of light in modeling volumes. As in the mosaics of Sinai (see colorplate 39), Christ is clothed in pearly garments whose white highlights create the impression of blinding radiance. Shadow fills the tombs from which Adam and Eve are drawn up, and the side of Eve's sarcophagus opposite to the source of light in Christ remains deep in shadow. As we shall find when we examine the contemporary frescoes of Giotto and his followers in Italy (Chapter 9), this apparently naturalistic observation of the effects of light proceeding from a single source is in reality bound up entirely with its religious meaning. The Old Testament kings and patriarchs to the left are led by Saint John the Baptist, who accompanied Christ into Hell, and to the right the prophets are grouped behind Abel. The brilliant colors of the drapery and the creamy, off-white of the rocks shine against the intense blue of the background. Satan, bound, prone, partly across the shattered gates of Hell, is surrounded by a veritable shower of locks, hasps, and bolts.

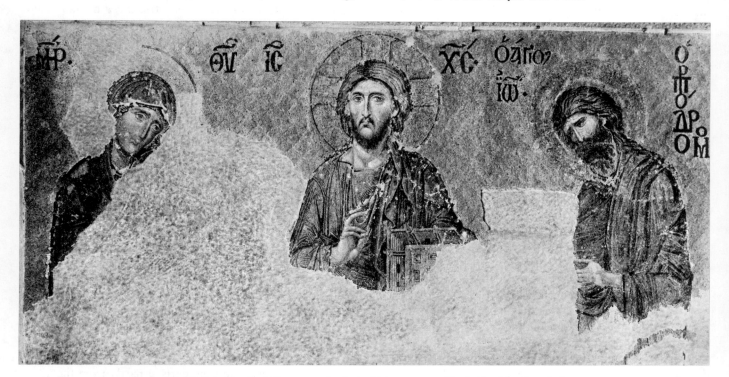

441. *Deësis*. South gallery mosaic. Late 13th century. Hagia Sophia, Istanbul

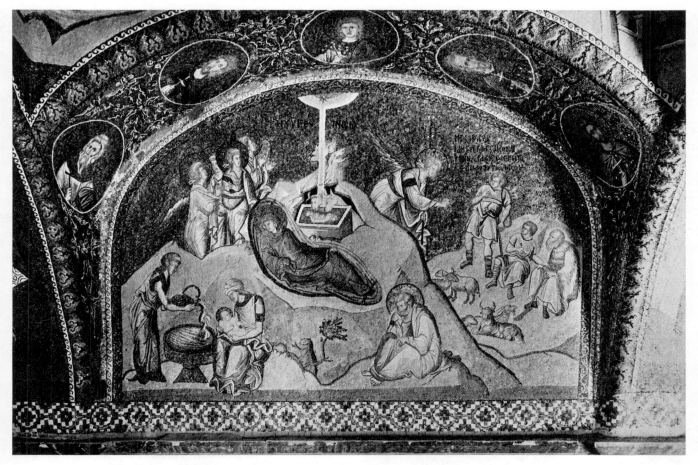

442. *Nativity*. Narthex mosaic. 1315–21. Church of Christ in Chora (Kariye Djami), Istanbul

RUSSIA AND RUMANIA

Russian religious architecture owes its origins to Byzantine models, and throughout its long and rich development, it has retained the central plan for churches because of this arrangement's suitability to Orthodox liturgical requirements. Soon, however, local tastes began to modify the Byzantine heritage; artisans imported from Western countries to carry out Russian projects added their own traditions to the amalgam. An early example of Russian hybrid style is the Cathedral of Saint Demetrius (fig. 443), built about 1193–97 at Vladimir in the principality of Rostov-Suzdal, far to the northeast of Kiev and beyond the sway of its metropolitan (archbishop). The square block of Saint Demetrius, showing traces of the inner Greek-cross plan into whose arms the corner blocks housing prothesis, diakonikon, and galleries are fitted, and the central dome on its high drum pierced by round-arched windows are immediately recognizable as Byzantine. The screen architecture, consisting of two-story blind arcades whose arches appear along the roof line and are supported by lofty colonnettes, is also derived from Byzantine churches of the tenth and eleventh centuries. But the elaborate fabric of stone sculpture that fills the arches of the upper story and the walls of the drum with figural and ornamental

reliefs of great decorative effect are derived from such Western Romanesque models as Notre-Dame-la-Grande at Poitiers (see fig. 402) and are wholly alien to Byzantine tradition.

The domes of many Russian churches built in the following centuries are lifted on drums so high that they look like towers; the need to protect these domes against snow and ice led to the erection of bulbous external shells, generally onion-shaped. The Kremlin at Moscow contains several such churches, some designed by Italian architects in a style combining Renaissance details with Russian architectural tradition. A final expression of pure Russian architectural fantasy, in which Byzantine elements, detached from their original meaning, were multiplied in unbelievable extravagance, is the Cathedral of Saint Basil the Blessed in Moscow (fig. 444), built for Czar Ivan IV the Terrible from 1554–60 by the architects Barma and Postnik in what is today called Red Square, adjacent to the Moscow Kremlin. The plan is more rational than the startling appearance of the exterior might lead one to believe. A tentlike octagonal central church (a favorite shape in the sixteenth century in the region of Moscow) is surrounded by eight smaller but lofty separate churches arranged in a lozenge pattern. Each of the corner churches is octagonal and supports a tower-

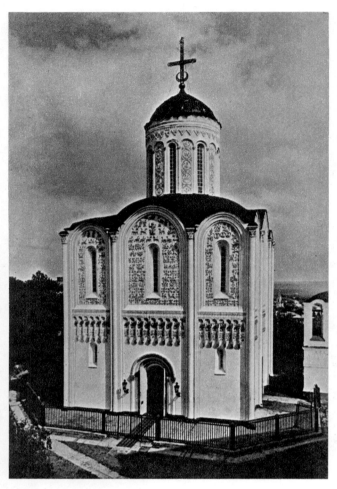

443. Cathedral of St. Demetrius. c. 1193–97. Vladimir, Russia

at work in Novgorod, and at the turn of the century in Moscow, then the center of a powerful principality. Theophanes is known to have been able to paint from memory with great rapidity and sureness, and his technique can be appreciated in his few surviving works, such as the wonderful fresco of a stylite (pillar sitter) in the Church of Our Saviour of the Transfiguration at Novgorod (fig. 445). The free, brilliant pictorial style of Castelseprio, with all its echoes of Helleno-Roman illusionism, still continues in the work of Theophanes seven centuries later. However, his brush dashes along at such speed carrying such a message of religious mysticism that we are reminded of the last of the great Greek painters, El Greco, who worked in Spain in the sixteenth century (see Vol. 2, colorplate 35, fig. 223). The zigzag, lightning strokes of Theophanes show a personal variant of the Byzantine tradition and vibrate at an intensity that could not be transmitted to a pupil.

In Moscow Theophanes worked in association with a younger and native Russian artist, the monk Andrei Rublev, who painted a fine series of frescoes that still survives at Vladimir but who is best known for his icons. In the fourteenth and fifteenth centuries, the iconostases in Russian churches had been heightened with the addition of upper rows of images, and thus the demand for icons was very great. The style of Russian icons is usually distinguished by flat masses of only slightly modulated color, often of great brilliance, and by a keen sense of the importance of contour. Rublev was content to work within the limitations of this style, but he certainly raised it to its highest level of aesthetic and spiritual achievement. His best-known work is the *Old Testament Trinity* (colorplate 61), an icon painted in memory of the Abbot Sergius, who died in 1411. The painting is heavily damaged; almost all of the background is lost and much of the drapery gone, but even in its present state, it is a picture of haunting beauty. The scene is a traditional one in Russian icons, but Rublev did not handle it in the traditional manner. The meeting of Abraham and Sarah with the three angels, who sat down to supper under a tree in the plains of Mamre (Gen. 18: 1–15), was interpreted in Christian thought as a revelation of the Trinity. In Russian icons Abraham and Sarah had always been represented, and a lamb's head, symbolic of the sacrifice of Christ, substituted for the textual calf. Rublev goes to the heart of the mystery, showing us only the three angels as if we were Abraham and Sarah experiencing the vision. The relationships among the three angels are treated with the greatest poetic intensity and linear grace; the contours flow from body to body as the glances move from face to face. In Western art such attenuated figures, sloping shoulders, long waists and arms, and pensive expressions can only be compared with the art of another great fifteenth-century painter—Botticelli (see Vol. 2, fig. 76, colorplate 12), who doubtless knew nothing about Rublev but shows a real affinity of feeling and taste.

Throughout the area that now comprises Russia and

ing onion dome. The architects inserted four even smaller churches, two of which are square and two heart-shaped, all four crowned by onion domes, between the corner churches. The connecting gallery and the conical bell tower, however, are seventeenth-century additions. The drums of all eight domes are ornamented with innumerable arch-shapes derived from the Byzantine blind arcade but reduced to ornaments, and with gables that become zigzags. The onion domes are fluted, twisted, or reticulated (so that they remind us of pineapples) and painted green and white in stripes that make a vivid contrast to the orange-red of the brick.

The rich tradition of church murals and icon painting in Russia, which began perhaps as early as the tenth century with the importation of Byzantine icons, continued unabated into the nineteenth. Many of the innumerable examples are of extremely high quality, and at least two of the painters are major figures, known to us by name. Theophanes the Greek, born between 1330 and 1340, had worked in Constantinople and in other Byzantine centers and brought to Russia the dramatic Palaeologan style we have seen at the Kariye Djami. In 1378 Theophanes was

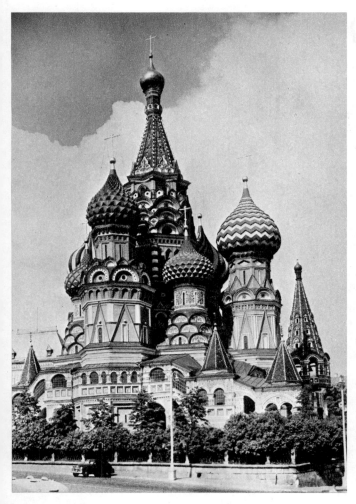

444. BARMA and POSTNIK. Cathedral of St. Basil the Blessed. 1554–60. Moscow

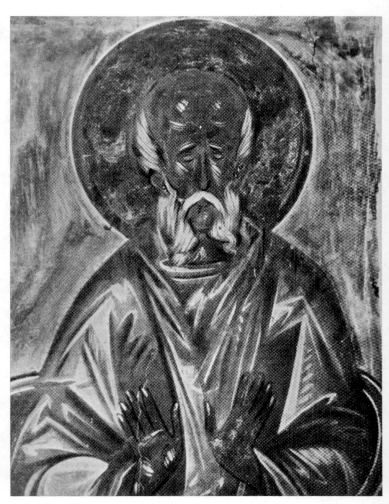

445. THEOPHANES THE GREEK. *Stylite* (detail). Fresco. 1378. Church of Our Saviour of the Transfiguration, Novgorod, Russia

the Balkan states, icons were produced in great numbers long after the fall of Constantinople to the Turks in 1453. The region of Moldavia, the eastern portion of Rumania, preserves a handsome group of monastic churches erected in the late fifteenth and early sixteenth centuries and frescoed not only in the interior but also over all the outside walls, where the frescoes are protected only by wide, overhanging eaves. Unlikely though it may seem in view of the severe winters of this region in the foothills of the Carpathian Alps, the exterior frescoes on all but the north walls are better preserved than those in the interiors; apparently, rain, sun, and wind are not as injurious to paintings as are candle smoke and incense.

One of the best of the Moldavian fresco cycles is that of the *Last Judgment*, which adorns the west front of the former Voroneţ monastery church. The *Last Judgment* (colorplate 62), dating from about 1550, covers the entire west wall of the narthex above the entrance. At the top angels roll up the heavens as a scroll (Isa. 34: 4; Rev. 6: 14). In a circle in the center is God the Father; below him

is the Deësis with six Apostles enthroned on each side and angels behind them. In the next tier below choirs of ecclesiastical saints are grouped on either side of the throne prepared for Christ's Second Coming. A river of fire pours from the throne of Christ and falls upon the damned in Hell to Christ's left, penetrating earth and sea, which give up their dead. On his right Heaven opens up in two tiers of the blessed, whose halos blend into an almost continuous surface of gold. It is instructive that at the time when this, one of the last great Byzantine murals, was painted, carrying into the sixteenth century an unbroken tradition of Greek painting, Michelangelo, one of the greatest artists of the Italian Renaissance, had already gone back to the source of the ancient conception of the beauty and dignity of the human body, long forsworn by Byzantine art, and had painted the selfsame scene of the *Last Judgment* (see Vol. 2, fig. 181) on the wall of the Sistine Chapel in Rome, almost entirely populated with heroic nude figures corresponding to his revived Classical ideal and his study of the *Laocoön*.

9

Gothic Art

The term *Gothic* is used today to designate the style of art that began in northern France about the middle of the twelfth century and in the rest of western Europe anywhere from a generation to a century later. We now know that the name is a misnomer for Gothic art has nothing whatever to do with the Goths, who swept down on Roman Italy in the fifth century (see Chapter 2). But the Italians of the Renaissance thought that it had. The style of the medieval buildings surrounding them seemed so barbaric in comparison with the beauty of Roman architecture that they believed this style could have been imported into Classical Italy only by the Vandals, the Goths, the Lombards, and the Huns, according to an anonymous biographer of the pioneer architect of the Renaissance, Filippo Brunelleschi (see Vol. 2, Part Four, Chapter 1). Giorgio Vasari, the Renaissance artist and writer who characterized Byzantine pictorial style as "the rude manner of the Greeks," was even more caustic about medieval architecture, which he claimed "was invented by the Goths." The disparaging term *Gothic* took root; by the seventeenth century the great French dramatist Molière was referring to the "torrent of odious Gothic monsters" that had been unleashed on France. Not until the beginnings of Romanticism in the late eighteenth century did the taste for Gothic art begin to catch hold of the imaginations of a cultivated elite as a welcome escape from the rules of Classical art into a past that seemed both natural and intriguingly remote. And only with the historical studies of the early nineteenth century did it become clear that so-called Gothic art was really a phenomenon separated from the Gothic invasions by at least seven centuries. Soon Gothic art became recognized as the refined intellectual and aesthetic achievement of a highly developed society, but there was no longer any possibility of changing the name.

Non-French European regions in the late twelfth and early thirteenth centuries, however, were well aware of the origin of the Gothic style. They referred to it as *opus francigenum* (*French work*), and they were right—in the narrow and restricted sense denoted by the term *French* at the time. The Gothic style was born in that region of north-central France centering around Paris, known as the Île-de-France, which as we have seen (see page 309) was the personal domain of the French kings. Today art historians are in a position to add the birthdate of the Gothic style: shortly before the year 1140. From the Île-de-France the style radiated outward, winning acceptance in region after region, first throughout northern France, then almost immediately in England, then in Germany, the Low Countries, central Europe, and Spain, and finally in a reluctant Italy—which never fully understood or accepted it and was, as we have noted, the first to brand it barbarous and to rebel against it.

In contrast to the individuality of the local Romanesque schools, their wide diversity of styles and technical methods, and the extreme brevity of their period of full bloom, five outstanding phenomena characterize the Gothic. First, the Gothic is remarkably consistent throughout wide areas of central and northern France; it was carried almost unaltered into Germany, the Low Countries, and Spain; and it was only somewhat modified by local requirements in England. Second, it developed a competitive momentum; architects, sculptors, and painters were well aware of what was being done elsewhere and were constantly trying to beat their rivals at their own game. Third, the Gothic lasted, although transformed by regional tastes and requirements, well into the sixteenth century (everywhere except Italy, of course). Fourth, the Gothic created structures completely without precedent in the history of art, surpassing in technical daring anything man had ever before imagined. Finally, after the long interregnum of the early Middle Ages, the Gothic was the first Western art to present a believable image of man as the complete human being.

We tend to think of Romanesque as the architecture of the monasteries, and to a great extent this is true, but largely because in most Western cities, even some very

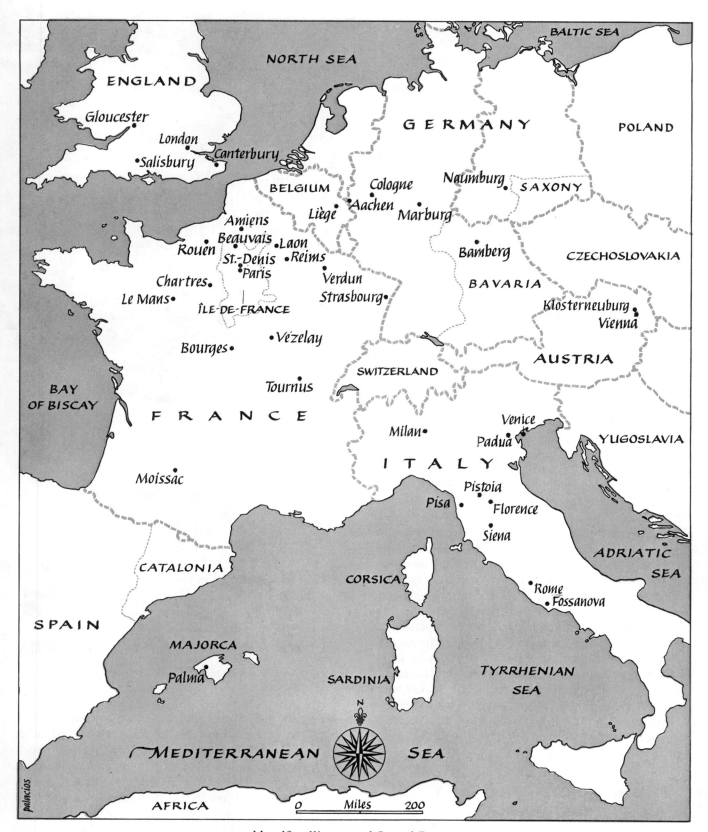

MAP 19. *Western and Central Europe*

small ones, the Romanesque cathedrals of the eleventh and twelfth centuries were replaced in the late twelfth or thirteenth by Gothic ones. But the distinction is valid in a general sense because, with the exception of Saint-Denis, which as we shall see proves the rule, it was cathedrals, not monasteries, that required rebuilding. By the beginning of the Gothic period, the great cultural and economic mission of the monasteries had largely come to an end. Their role as conservators of learning was being assumed by the universities, and their economic importance had been superseded by that of the towns. It has long been pointed out by Meyer Schapiro that the Gothic cathedrals were the largest economic enterprises of the Middle Ages. The cathedrals absorbed the activities of architects, builders, masons, sculptors, stonecutters, painters, stained-glass makers, carpenters, metalworkers, jewelers—utilizing materials brought sometimes from great distances—and gave back nothing in a material sense.

Monasteries were generally located in the country; a cathedral, by definition the seat of a bishop, was in a town, and it became a symbol of the town's corporate existence. To a great extent this is still true. A contemporary Florentine will boast of being *fiorentino di cupolone* (*Florentine from the great dome* [of the Cathedral]); during the air attacks of World War II, Londoners kept watch nightly, risking their lives, on the roofs and towers of Saint Paul's Cathedral in order to extinguish fire bombs as they fell. In the Gothic period communal devotion to the construction of the cathedrals was so great that, according to contemporary chroniclers, not only did the rich contribute financially to the limit of their ability to the building and decoration of the cathedrals but also rich and poor alike joined with laborers and oxen to pull the carts laden with building materials.

With their soaring height, their immense interiors, their pinnacles, towers, and spires, their innumerable images and narratives in stone, paint, and glass, the cathedrals summed up the knowledge and experience of man's brief earthly tenancy in artistic forms and iconographic cycles of astonishing completeness, united in a structure that constituted a comprehensive medieval picture of the universe from the heights of Heaven to the depths of Hell. But we have not said what the Gothic style is, and that will not be an easy task. It is best to illustrate its nature and the main lines of its development with a few selected works.

THE BEGINNINGS OF GOTHIC STYLE

On June 9, 1140, Abbot Suger consecrated a new façade, with a triple, sculptured portal and two square towers (of which only one was ever completed) on the Carolingian church of the Abbey of Saint-Denis, just north of Paris; on June 11, 1144, the same abbot brought to completion a new choir with ambulatory and radiating chapels that replaced the Carolingian apse. Both additions were

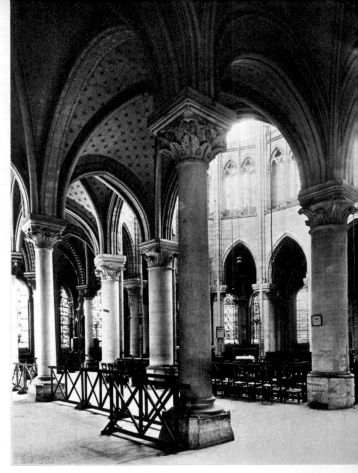

446. Ambulatory, Abbey Church of St.-Denis. 1140–44. Paris

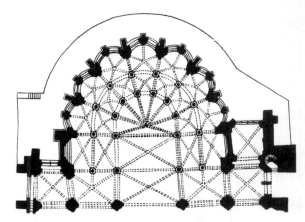

447. Ambulatory, Abbey Church of St.-Denis. (Plan after Sumner Crosby)

necessary to accommodate the crowds of pilgrims who came to venerate the relics of Saint Denis and other saints preserved in the apse. Saint-Denis was not only a pilgrimage monastery but also a royal foundation in which Charles Martel, Pepin the Short, and Charles the Bald were buried. As its abbot, Suger was a person of great political importance, the power behind the thrones of Louis VI (ruled 1108–37) and Louis VII (ruled 1137–80) and regent of France (1147–49) during the latter's absence on the Second Crusade.

Suger intended eventually to replace the Carolingian nave of his church as well. Ironically, when this nave was replaced in the thirteenth century by a Gothic one,

Suger's choir was also demolished, except for the ambulatory. The portal was so badly damaged during the French Revolution and so thoroughly recarved in the nineteenth century that it is no longer a medieval work. But the surviving ambulatory is an extraordinary achievement (figs. 446, 447). At first sight the ambulatory with its radiating chapels recalls Saint-Sernin at Toulouse (see fig. 389), but the ambulatory of Saint-Denis is doubled at the expense of the chapels, which are reduced to hardly more than bay windows, expanding and contracting at regular intervals so as to carry the crowds easily around the high altar with its reliquary shrine.

Suger left a written account, unique in the annals of patronage, explaining his feelings about the work and his reasons for doing as he did, recounting its history (not without miracles), and preserving valuable information about architectural practices in the twelfth century. According to a famous study by Erwin Panofsky (see Bibliography), Suger believed that the writings of an obscure fifth-century Syrian mystic, known as Dionysius the Pseudo-Areopagite, preserved at Saint-Denis, were in fact those of Saint Denis, the patron saint of France and of the abbey (*Denis* is French for *Dionysius*). The complex Neoplatonic system according to which Dionysius identified light with divinity was seen by Panofsky as the justification for Suger's enthusiasm for the light from the "circular string of chapels, by virtue of which the whole [church] would shine with the wonderful and uninterrupted light of most luminous windows. . . ."

One is tempted to ask why such a theological explanation of light would not be equally applicable to other ways of admitting it—as at Hagia Sophia, for example, with its rows on rows of windows under and around the floating dome. One notices also that Suger reserved his special raptures for the beauty of the gold used to cover the new doors and for the gold and jewels of the reliquary shrine, without mentioning the design of either. He was so unresponsive, in fact, to the style of his time that he caused a gold mosaic instead of sculpture to be set up in the tympanum of the left portal, although he admitted it was contrary to "modern" practice. One is almost more impressed by what Suger omitted from his account, such as the name of the architect, than by what he mentioned. Suger was also silent about the master's technical and stylistic innovations, but he recounted with admiration the architect's ability to measure the Gothic choir so accurately that when the Carolingian apse left standing inside it was finally taken down, the new choir was found to be in perfect alignment with the old nave. About the columns Suger said no more than that their number corresponds to the numbers of the Apostles and the minor prophets.

So far from being in any way responsible for the new style evolving around him, Suger in his account reveals himself to have been unaware that it was new. Modern studies of the development of ribbed vaults have shown that for a decade or so before the rebuilding of Saint-Denis, architects—under probable Norman influence—had been experimenting with ribbed vaults in the parish churches of the Île-de-France. Whoever he was, the architect of Saint-Denis was probably of local origin (only the stained-glass makers, Suger tells us, were brought from throughout France). A glance at the illustration (see fig. 446) makes clear what is really new: for the first time we have an architecture not of walls but of supports. Columns or compound piers including colonnettes support the ribs, between which the concave vault surfaces are constructed. Walls tend to be replaced by windows. From this moment walls in French cathedral architecture are residual, and architects will vie with one another to reduce them to a minimum, while at the same time they refine the connection between the supports and slim down the supports to the ultimate. In each of the trapezoidal bays and pentagonal chapels of the ambulatory at Saint-Denis, the transverse ribs are pointed so as to lift the sides of the bays as high as possible, thereby concentrating the outward thrust of the vaults on the columns and piers. The plan shows that this thrust is carried to the exterior of the church where it is met by the buttresses, which appear as black, rectangular projections between the windows.

Architecture at Saint-Denis has become an organic system of interacting supports (columns, colonnettes, ribs, buttresses), both inside the church and outside, enclosing vaulting surfaces above and windows on the sides. Four thousand years of post-and-lintel construction and at least a thousand years of massive vault design have suddenly become obsolete. The only derivation of early Gothic architecture from the past can be found in the ribbed domes of Byzantine architecture, such as that of Hagia Sophia (see fig. 339), but even Byzantine ribs stop at the pendentives and walls remained necessary. Suger recorded his gratitude for divine intervention when the bare ribs of the incomplete choir vaults of Saint-Denis, protected by the outer roof but still without the stabilizing factor of the inner triangles of the vaulting, were shaken by a terrible storm; they vibrated visibly, but remained standing. It would have been more to the point for Suger to congratulate his architect on his extraordinary knowledge and skill.

Like many medieval patrons before him, Suger thought of plundering Rome for marble columns and even worked out the route by which they could be transported. Luckily (again, according to Suger, by miracle) he found an inexhaustible quarry of local limestone. But it was not by accident that in this new organic architecture not only Roman columns but also Roman, Byzantine, and Romanesque capitals have been abandoned. The new capital shapes are based, however schematically, on the growth of actual foliage that the architects had seen rather than on Greek acanthus leaves that they had not. It is worth remembering that several Renaissance writers felt that Gothic architecture had

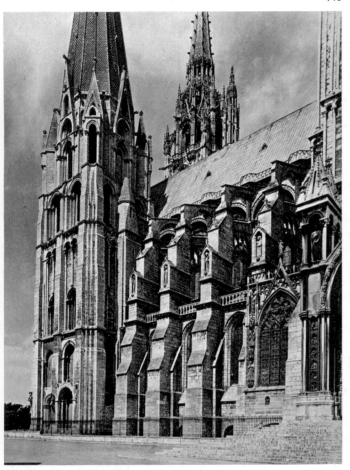

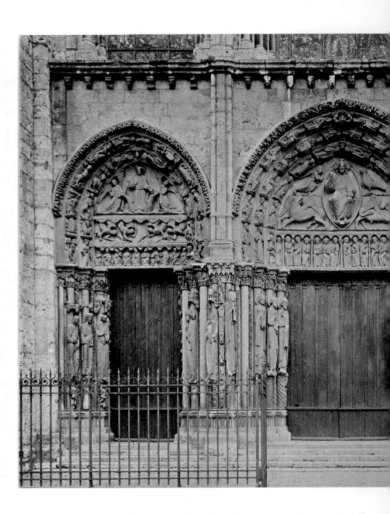

originally been suggested by primitive shelters formed by tying trees together.

One masterpiece of transitional Gothic architecture, sculpture, and stained glass survives intact: the façade of the Cathedral of Chartres, to the southwest of Paris. In 1134 the façade of the eleventh-century cathedral was damaged by fire, necessitating its replacement. The north tower was built first without a spire. Then about 1142 the south tower (fig. 448) was erected to its full height, culminating in one of the most beautiful spires of the Gothic period. The simple addition of one element to the next, visible throughout Romanesque structures (see fig. 390), has here given way to a delicately adjusted inter-connection. The transition from the square to the oc-tagon, for instance, is prepared as early as the second story by placing the colonnettes of the blind arcade directly on the keystones of the arched windows and by the splaying of the corner buttresses. By the time the eye rises to the fourth story, which is clearly octagonal, the transition has been accomplished almost unnoticeably. The tower rose high above the roof of the Romanesque cathedral at the beginning of the third story; its effect was somewhat diminished by the taller Gothic structure com-menced in 1194 (see page 376).

The façade was built to connect the towers at their eastern flanks, so that they would project on either side and appear partly to enclose it. At some undetermined time these plans were changed, and the Royal Portal dating from about 1140–50 (fig. 449) was set up in its present position flush with the towers. The splayed triple portal is completely sculptured, and devoted to a unified theme: the Nativity and scenes from the Infancy of Christ on the right, the Ascension on the left, scenes from Christ's life in the capitals of the colonnettes, and in the center his heavenly apparition according to the Vision of John, as at Moissac, but including the Twelve Apostles (see fig. 398). The freedom of Romanesque sculpture has been abandoned here in favor of a disciplined structure that embraces every element in the portal, and of which Christ himself is the center. In contrast to the rich confu-sion of the Moissac tympanum, the central lunette at Chartres is immediately legible. Each of the symbols of the Evangelists occupies its predetermined position. Each of the four-and-twenty elders of the Apocalypse in the outer archivolts and the twelve angels in the inner archivolts moves in conformity with the motion of the arch, even though that involves tilting over, till they con-verge at the keystone, where two other angels uphold a royal crown.

The tall, infinitely slender figures on the jambs of the doors (fig. 450) represent in all probability kings, queens, and prophets from the Old Testament. They, too, obey

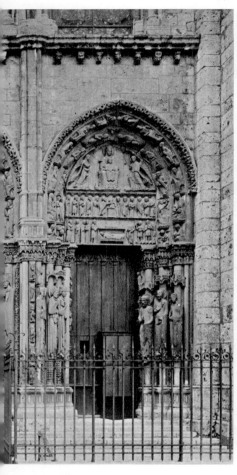

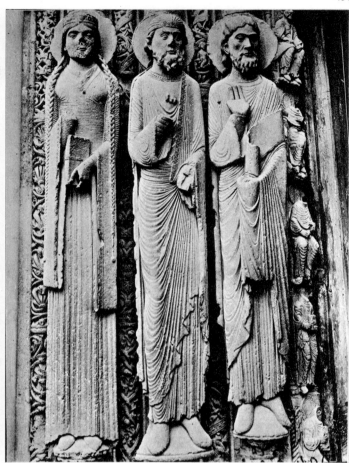

448. Exterior,
Cathedral of Chartres.
South Tower.
c. 1142. France

449. Royal Portal.
Cathedral of
Chartres.
c. 1140–50

450. Jamb statues.
Royal Portal,
Cathedral of
Chartres

the forces of the architecture to the extent of assuming the shapes of the colonnettes of which they form a part. They stand upon firm pedestals, and the long, taut drapery lines contrast in their severity with the luxuriance of the interlaced ornament between the colonnettes. Paradoxically, the columnar figures support nothing; each usurps the shape of a column, but not its function, in contrast to the maidens of the Erechtheion, for example (see fig. 201), who took over the function of columns without relinquishing their own shapes. Calm has settled over the scene after the wildness of Vézelay and Moissac only twenty years or so before. The figures seem to enjoy their role in a perfect system, which, incidentally, includes among its minor sculptures the seven liberal arts, the signs of the zodiac, and the labors of the months. The figures assume a cylindrical existence in depth, which in Romanesque sculpture had been seen only in Provence (see fig. 401). The delicacy of the parallel drapery lines, recalling those of Archaic kore figures (see fig. 149, colorplate 13), is surpassed only by the sensitive delineation of the quiet faces. The serenity of this royal allegory was never again achieved, but the decisive step in the creation of a new architectural sculpture had been taken. Henceforward, the figure could assert its individual existence in harmony with the forces of an all-embracing architecture.

THE FRENCH CATHEDRAL

The story of French cathedral building in the late twelfth and thirteenth centuries is made more exciting by the element of intense competition. No sooner was a new form or a new device established in one cathedral than it was outdone in another. One architect and sculptor, Villard de Honnecourt, went from cathedral to cathedral drawing the latest architectural and sculptural achievements (fig. 451). The earliest major Gothic cathedral is that at Laon, to the northeast of Paris. The situation is spectacular because Laon itself is a hill town lifted high above an almost flat plain; the cathedral with all its towers may thus be seen for many miles (fig. 452). It was to have had seven towers, but only four (two on the west facade and one on each arm of the transept) were ever carried to their full height. The number seven had mystical significance, since it was the sum of the Trinity and the Gospels, the number of the Virtues (and the Vices), the number of the gifts of the Holy Spirit, the number of the liberal arts, and the number of the candlesticks in Heaven. No Gothic cathedral ever boasted all seven towers, but many were planned for that number (Chartres was to have had eight). Whether the towers at Laon were also intended to receive spires is uncertain, but unlikely; the tiny steeple on one of the transept towers is a much later addition.

Gothic Art / 373

The façade, begun about 1190, is unexpectedly dramatic. The triple portal is protected by three porches; above the central porch is an early example of a rose window, a circular window filled with elaborate stone tracery radiating from the center. Stone grilles had been used in Byzantine and Islamic windows, and the Gothic rose window derives from this tradition. However, the tracery, intended to hold stained glass, obeys precise geometrical laws. Above the rose and its flanking arched windows runs an open arcade, broken to indicate on the exterior the relation of the clerestory and side aisles within. The façade towers are flanked by superimposed aediculae with pointed arches, square on the first two stories and octagonal on the third. In contrast to the lofty pointed central windows these aediculae create a broken and irregular silhouette. The towers are transparent, skeletal structures, through which the wind blows easily. From the uppermost aediculae protrude statues of oxen, popularly believed to be those who dragged the stones for the cathedral up the steep hill of Laon. For some as-yet-unexplained reason, the round apse at Laon, begun about 1160, was replaced only a few years after its completion by a square east end on the English model (fig. 453). The present great length of the noble interior (fig. 454)—eleven bays for the nave and ten for the choir—is as dramatic as the towers. The interior is four stories high. The nave arcade, supported by heavy cylindrical piers instead of compound square ones, is surmounted first by a gallery with coupled arches under an embracing arch, then by a small triforium, and finally by a clerestory tucked into the vaults. As at Caen, the vaults are six-part, but somewhat less domical. There is an even more significant difference, in which resides the secret of Gothic as opposed to Romanesque vaulting: the conoids

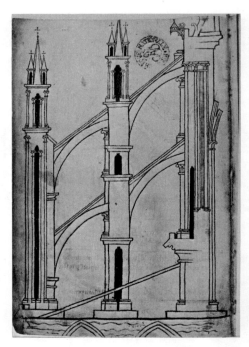

451. VILLARD DE HONNECOURT. Flying buttresses. c. 1230–35. Pen and ink. Bibliothèque Nationale, Paris

(the conelike shapes formed by the convergence of ribs and vault surfaces on the capitals of the colonnettes) are sharply pinched together on the side next to the clerestory. This pinching of the conoids frees the diagonal ribs from the clerestory, allowing them to establish their own positions in space. The thrust of the vaults seems to have been contained by the girdle of the gallery, but in the thirteenth century cautious architects added flying buttresses on the exterior (for an explanation of and a look at flying buttresses, see page 376, figs. 451, 464).

The façade of Notre-Dame at Paris was planned about 1200 (fig. 455) and completed about 1250. The dramatic effects of Laon are avoided; the elements are brought under the control of a majestic rectilinear design, which has won universal admiration. The porches are retracted into the mass of the building, and the towers rise only a single story above the nave roof, which can be seen through the screen of tracery. The coupled windows of the towers were widely imitated. The plan of the church (fig. 456), laid out about 1163, is much more regular than that of Laon (see fig. 453). The nave is ten bays long, the choir before the apse exactly half that; the apse vault is divided into five compartments. Instead of the wide transepts of Laon, those of Notre-Dame are retracted like the porches so that they hardly project beyond the church. Intended for a larger city, Notre-Dame has four side aisles rather than the customary two (the outer line of chapels was added between the buttresses in the thirteenth century, thereby darkening the interior).

But the interior design of Notre-Dame (fig. 457) proved obsolete within sixty years. Only the last bay on the right, next to the crossing, shows the original four-story design of the nave, with a triorium made up of tiny rose win-

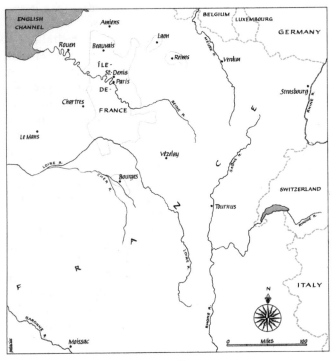

MAP 20. *France*

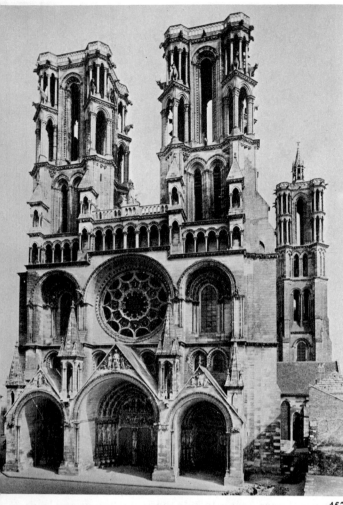

452

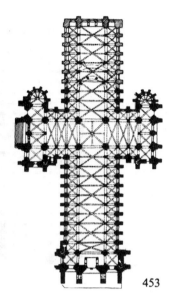

452. Façade. Cathedral of Laon.
c. 1190. France

453. Cathedral of Laon.
Begun c. 1160.
(Plan after E. Gall)

454. Nave. Cathedral of Laon

453

dows (the remaining one has been much restored) and a small clerestory. About the middle of the thirteenth century, the original row of flying buttresses in the nave (required to supplement the containing action of the gallery) was replaced by the present ones, and the clerestory was greatly enlarged into tall windows filled with tracery extending well below the springing points of the vaults, influenced by developments at Chartres, Reims, and Amiens. The photograph renders it clear that the pinching of the conoids by the original architect made this "modernization" possible, as it allowed the diagonal ribs to pass freely across the edge of the clerestory windows. Each rib, incidentally, is channeled so that the appearance of a cluster is maintained at all points from the capitals to the vault. The vaults are still slightly domical, but have been carried to a height of 107 feet, 27 feet higher than those at Laon and higher than any Romanesque vaults except those of Speyer Cathedral.

The fire of 1194, which consumed the town and the Romanesque Cathedral of Chartres, except for the two towers and the Royal Portal, gave Gothic architects the opportunity to take the next and definitive step, which ushered in the phase known as High Gothic. After the conflagration at Chartres, almost every old cathedral in northern France and some in Germany caught fire when it seemed most opportune to replace them with Gothic ones. The Cathedral of Chartres is the most nearly complete of all in architecture, sculpture, and stained glass, and it demands study as an integrated whole. Smaller than Paris, the town of Chartres needed a cathedral with a nave of only seven bays and a choir of four, and two side aisles (fig. 458). Nonetheless, the vaults rise to a height of 118 feet in one unbroken ascent.

The architect eliminated the gallery since flying buttresses were, for the first time, planned from the start

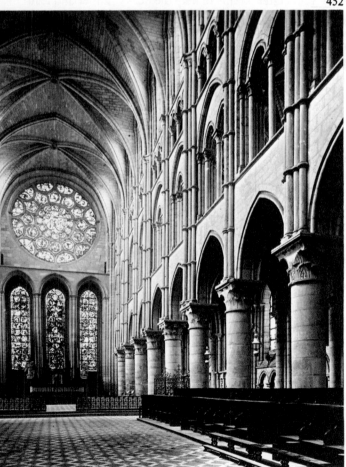

454

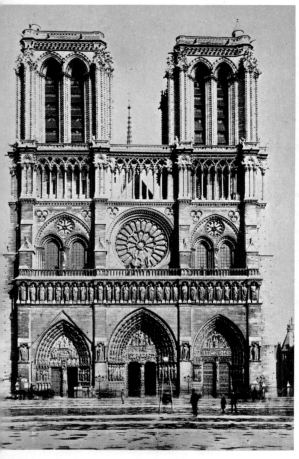

455. Façade, Notre-Dame. c. 1200–50. Paris

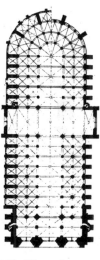

456. Plan of
Notre-Dame.
1163–c. 1250

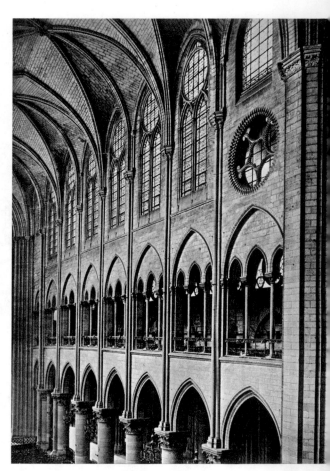

457. Nave, Notre-Dame

(fig. 459). Only a small triforium separates the clerestory from the nave arcade. Liberated from the vaults, the clerestory has become almost equal in height to the nave arcade, and now dominates the interior. The cylindrical piers, still inviolate at Laon and at Notre-Dame in Paris, have now been absorbed into the skeletal system; the colonnettes supporting the transverse ribs are coupled to the piers and run straight to the floor. The resulting new type of compound pier became universal. The six-part vault is given up as unwieldy, and the interior thus presents a more unified appearance. In the choir the enlarged clerestory is composed of simple lancet (single pointed-arch) windows, but in the nave the windows are filled with tracery, achieved by piercing the wall of each bay with two lancets under a small rose; this form is known as plate tracery. At the crossing the four supporting piers have been enriched with colonnettes, in the manner of clustered organ pipes, to great effect.

The massive buttresses (see fig. 448) rise in steps to a height far above the sloping roof of the side aisle, to be connected with the clerestory by means of two slanting, superimposed arches joined together by a tiny arcade. These are flying buttresses, which "fly" from the buttresses to make contact with the clerestory at the two points where, so the architects believed, pressure was necessary to counteract the outward thrust of the nave vaults. A third flying buttress, above the other two, added

a few years later, seems to help the heavy timber and lead roof over the vaults resist the action of the wind. With the adoption of flying buttresses the concept of skeletal architecture began to determine the exterior as well as the interior appearance of a building; every exterior member corresponds to a necessity created by an interior pressure. The resultant Gothic structural system has been aptly termed an exoskeleton.

Chartres was planned for two western façade towers, two flanking each arm of the transept, and one flanking each side of the choir, or a total of eight; all but the western towers were left unfinished at the height of the vaults. The south transept façade (fig. 460), built about 1215–20, shows a richness of articulation far beyond that of the main façade of Notre-Dame, designed only a few years earlier; slender colonnettes, like those at the crossing, screen the buttresses. The projecting triple porch was an afterthought, added to the portal when the sculpture was already in place.

The three portal statues of standing saints to the right (fig. 461) are still columnar, but when compared with those of the Royal Portal, they are partially liberated from the architecture and stand on pedestals more nearly suited to their function; on these pedestals are figures or images alluding to the legend of each saint. The wealth of tiny sculptures above the statues of the Royal Portal has been replaced here by naturalistic foliate capitals,

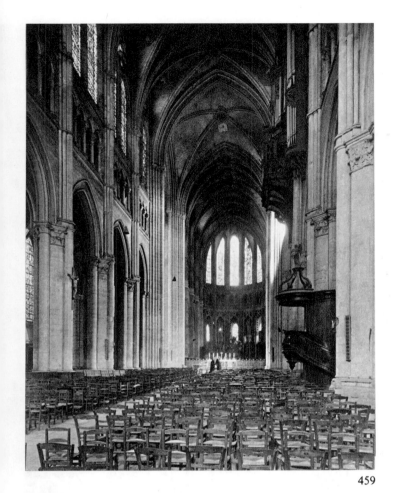

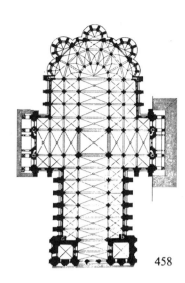

458

458. Cathedral of Chartres. 1194–1220. (Plan after Dehio)

459. Nave. Cathedral of Chartres. See Colorplate 63

460. Façade, south transept. Cathedral of Chartres.
c. 1215–20

461. Jamb statues. South transept portal. Cathedral of
Chartres. c. 1215–20

459

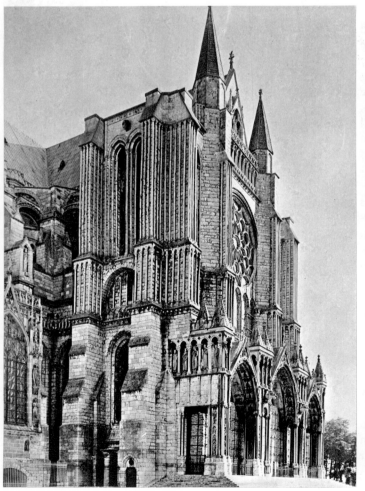

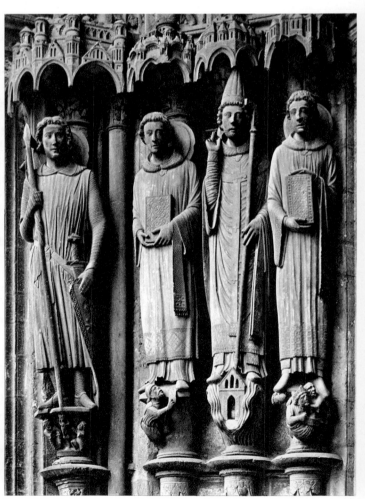

460   461

enshadowed by greatly enlarged canopies, which resemble little city views with arches, windows, pinnacles, and towers. The portrait-like heads are thrown into stronger light against the shadow, and the figures, wrapped in complete cylindrical envelopes of drapery, are far more strongly projected than those of the Royal Portal.

The statue at the left, probably representing *Saint Theodore*, was added at the same time as the porch, and shows an increased freedom of style. For the first time since Roman art a figure is balanced with the weight largely on the right foot and the left leg at least partially free. Gothic sculpture seems in a way to recapitulate the development of sculpture in Greece from the late Archaic to the Severe Style (see figs. 163, 172), with the crucial difference that in Christian art the movement of the figure must be carried out under voluminous clothing. Once established in the portal figures of Chartres, the freedom of the figure from the architecture increased, along with the freedom of the architectural members themselves from the obsolete concept of the wall. With his knightly attitude, his spear at the ready, and his calm and handsome face, Saint Theodore seems the very ideal of the Christian warrior fostered by the Crusades.

The lightening and heightening of Gothic cathedrals cannot be adequately explained by the desire for illumination—that, as we have seen, could have been handled by a system along the lines of Saint-Philibert at Tournus (see fig. 388). The entire cathedral in the twelfth and thirteenth centuries became a framework to hold stained glass. Stained glass inevitably darkened the interior but had its own indescribable beauty of color and pattern. Much Gothic stained glass has perished, some deliberately destroyed in later times either by Protestant reformers or simply in order to lighten cathedral interiors. Chartres contains the most nearly complete cycle of medieval stained glass, much of it in good condition, from the twelfth-century lancets above the Royal Portal to the thirteenth-century windows girdling the rest of the church. Between the windows, some of which have scores of separate, carefully organized subjects, and the innumerable sculptures on the three triple portals, it takes a studious visitor several days, guidebook in hand, just to identify all the images. One comes away from such an experience with a deep respect for the Middle Ages, because the representations encompass the entire range of medieval knowledge—Old and New Testaments, lives of the saints, fundamentals of Christian doctrine, labors of the months, signs of the zodiac, Virtues and Vices, and the activities of the guilds that contributed to the building of the cathedral.

The gigantic window of the north arm of the transept (colorplate 63) is a rose, still in the form of plate tracery, above five lancets. In the central lancet, Saint Anne, mother of the Virgin, holds her child; she is flanked by two kings, to the left David and Solomon to the right. Two high priests, Melchizedek to the left and Aaron to the right, flank the kings. The rose above, more than forty-two feet in diameter, shows Mary in the center

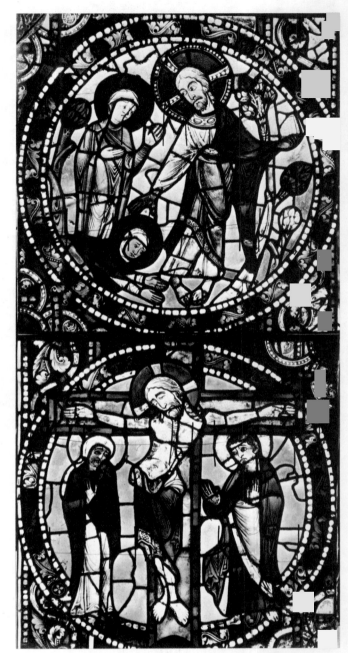

462. *Noli me tangere*, and *Crucifixion* (details). Stained-glass window. 12th century. Cathedral of Chartres

enthroned as Queen of Heaven holding the Christ Child. With the growth of the cult of the Virgin, under the direct influence of Saint Bernard, Mary has now displaced the Romanesque Christ in Majesty and the Byzantine Pantocrator. In the next circle four doves indicating the Gospels proceed toward Mary, and below them eight angels kneel or stand in adoration. Twelve kings from the Old Testament, clearly labeled, all ancestors of Christ, sit in the next circle of twelve lozenges. Finally, in the twelve semicircles around the rim stand prophets. Significantly enough, the twelve quatrefoil (four-leaf) shapes between the kings and the prophets are filled with the golden lilies of the kings of France on a blue field.

Stained glass achieves its effect by the passage of

sunlight through it rather than by the reflection of light from it, as in mosaics. Stained glass is, therefore, the most brilliant coloristic medium invented by man before the twentieth century. It is best to experience the stained-glass windows of Chartres (or any other Gothic church) in the gray weather all too common in northern France, for which this glass was planned; otherwise, the glitter from the south windows not only destroys their unity but also cancels out the glow from the north. In the early morning or in the late afternoon the colored windows float like immense jewels in the dim interior. Medieval theologians saw in the beauty of stained glass a symbol of the sacred mystery of the Incarnation, for as Divine Light, which is Christ (see pages 268, 269, colorplate 39), entered the mortal body of Mary without violating her virginity and took on mortal flesh, so the light of the sun passes through colored glass without breaking it and assumes its color.

In thirteenth-century glass the predominant colors are red and blue; white, yellow, and green appear, but the red and blue contrast is what one remembers. Unlike mosaics, which are made up of uniform tesserae, stained glass is fabricated from pieces shaped as closely as possible to the contour of a section of face, figure, drapery, or background. First, a full-scale model is made, drawn on wood or later on paper, and the pieces of colored glass are cut to fit. The lines are then painted on the glass with a dark pigment. After this paint dries, a coating of pigment is sometimes applied and scraped away with a stiff brush while still wet, so that what remains in the hollows will increase the sparkle of the underlying color. The pieces are then fired (baked) in a kiln, so that the pigment will harden and at least partially amalgamate with the glass. Finally, the pieces are arranged on the model and joined together by lead soldering strips. Each scene is then enclosed in an iron frame, and the frames are bolted together within the tracery so that they can easily be taken down for repairs.

In two panels from a twelfth-century window in the façade at Chartres (fig. 462), a *Noli me tangere* and a *Crucifixion*, the technique can be clearly seen. The lines of the pigment are close to those of the drapery and hair of the sculpture in the Royal Portal below. The lead contours, a bit disturbing in black-and-white reproductions, serve in the colored original to reinforce by contrast the glowing splendor of the glass. The iron frames were often set into an elaborate master design built up of lozenges and circles. Panels of colored glass were known from early Christian times and were certainly used in Constantinian basilicas, as well as later in Hagia Sophia and in other Byzantine churches. They also appeared commonly in mosques. But glass treated in this manner does not seem to have been known before Carolingian times, and only a few fragments that date before the Romanesque period remain. Only in Gothic architecture does such stained glass become universal.

The general architectural arrangement established at Chartres became the model for most High Gothic cathedrals, but there is a beautiful variant at Bourges in central France, where the Cathedral has four side aisles (fig. 463) as at Notre-Dame in Paris. So that the inner side aisles would not be dark, the architect raised them above the outer side aisles, giving them triforia and clerestories of their own and thereby making them look like complete three-story naves. The nave arcade in turn rises above the inner side aisles, supporting still another triforium and another clerestory. The spatial effect is very open, with views out on every side. The absence of a transept at Bourges affords the eye a clean sweep of arches from façade to apse.

This brilliant device was seldom repeated in France. In the artistic vocabulary of the High Gothic, the façade with its two towers soon came to compete in interest with the chevet—the apse, with its radiating chapels and flying buttresses, crowned by a conical roof. Le Mans Cathedral has the most spectacular chevet in France (fig. 464), in compensation, perhaps, for its low and unobtrusive late Romanesque nave, contrasting with the High Gothic choir, built between 1217 and 1254. As at Bourges, the inner ambulatory has its own clerestory above the radiating chapels, and the windows pile up in three stories. Two flights of flying buttresses carry the thrust of the choir vaults across the intervening ambulatory, and to abut the thrust of the ambulatory vaults

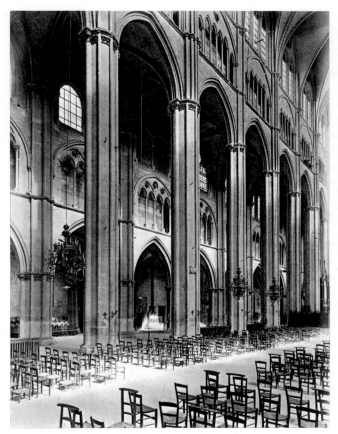

463. Nave and aisles, Cathedral of Bourges.
12–13th century. France

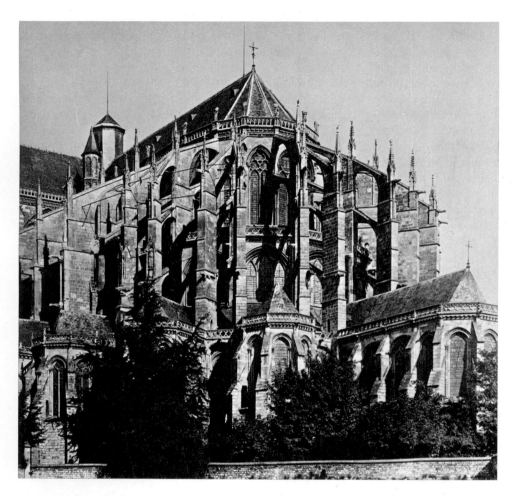

464. Exterior of chevet, Cathedral of Le Mans. 1217–54. France

they divide in a Y-shape. The lines have been kept as clean and orderly as those of a flight of wild geese, massing in perfect harmony buttresses, flying buttresses, pinnacles, windows, and conical roof.

The Cathedral of Reims, in Champagne in northeastern France, was traditionally the coronation church of the French kings. Designed in 1210 (after a fire), probably by Jean d'Orbais, Reims was intended for six towers and a central spire; only the façade towers rise above the roof. At first sight the interior (fig. 465) resembles that of Chartres, with four-part vaults, cylindrical compound piers, three stories, lofty clerestory, and colonnettes rising from floor to vault interrupted only by capitals and rings to mark the stories. The height of the vault has risen to 127 feet, and three additional differences are visible in the illustration. First, the arches are more sharply pointed than those at Chartres, which increases the feeling of verticality. Second, the richly sculptured capitals are composed of naturalistic foliage that seems to follow no predetermined scheme but to grow in place. Finally, a new kind of tracery appears —bar tracery, erected as a linear fabric of slender pieces of stone inside the window opening, preserving only in line the arrangement of two lancets and rose as a framework for the glass.

It will be noticed that in the apse the ribs move so freely and in so sharply pointed an arch that they actually pass in front of the clerestory windows. During World War I some of the ribs fell while under bombardment, but the vaults stood, a tribute to the craft of the medieval masons. One almost never finds tie rods in French Gothic cathedrals! Villard de Honnecourt, as we have seen, made a careful drawing of the flying buttresses at Reims (see fig. 451), in two flights over the ambulatory as at Le Mans, and indicated the points at which they sustain the vaults. The pinnacles are not merely ornamental, but act as counterweights, helping to send the thrust of the vaults harmlessly downward to the ground.

The façade of Reims Cathedral (fig. 466) may have been started as early as 1225 but was under construction until late in the thirteenth century. The general arrangement repeats that of Notre-Dame in Paris, but the differences disclose both the rapid growth of the Gothic style and its organic character. Solid matter has been dissolved into lines moving through air, with the sole exception of the gallery in the third story, which had to be solid in order to hold statues of the French kings (added in the fourteenth century). The very tympana of the portals have given way to windows filled with bar tracery. The porches culminate in gables that move into the second story. The second story is transparent, and one looks through the open tracery of the lancet windows (they have no glass) to see the flying buttresses of the nave. The nave roof appears as a gable above the gallery. Finally, the towers, among the most beautiful creations of Gothic architecture, are entirely made of tracery with no wall surface whatever. The corner turrets, constructed entirely of tracery, were intended to support corner pinnacles, whose octagonal bases can just be distinguished, just as each central section, with its window of bar tracery and its pointed gable, was designed to support an octagonal spire.

The façade sculpture at Reims, dating from about 1225–45, continues the tendency toward freedom from architecture that had begun in the transept sculpture of Chartres, and the humanism of the figures is even more pronounced. Two groups side by side were obviously made by two sculptors working in strongly individual styles and probably at slightly different times (fig. 467). The sculptor of the *Visitation* (the group to the right), done about 1225–30 (the visit of Mary to the house of her cousin Elizabeth, when the two women rejoiced in each other's pregnancy), while strongly aware of the call of visual reality, responds to it in a classical style. He must have seen and studied Roman sculpture during his travels. The mantles of Mary and Elizabeth sweep about their bodies and over their heads like Roman togas. Mary stands with the grace of a young Roman woman, Elizabeth with the dignity of a Roman matron. But there are differences; these poses do not entirely achieve the balance between the reciprocally tilted masses of the body that was instinctive for all ancient sculptors after about 480 B.C. The faces are only superficially classical. The folds break into more tiny facets than can be explained by the fall of the cloth. Nonetheless, we are clearly confronted with evidence of yet another renaissance of interest in ancient art, of which this is by no means the only Northern example in the thirteenth century (see page 391).

In the *Annunciation*, dating from the 1230s or 1240s, a very different style appears, made more apparent by the unfortunate inclusion, in a seventeenth-century restoration, of the wrong angel; he smiles a bit too broadly—though for the first time since Classical antiquity—for his religious function. His figure bends and sways in an accentuated S-curve, and his cloak is a complete and continuous fabric, which can move about his body as cloth will, responding to pressures and tugs and breaking into real folds. In the figure of Mary, shyly waiting, the change in style is even more surprising, because for the first time since antiquity (again) a body really shows through drapery—not just a volume of some undetermined substance, but a warm, human body. Mary's bosom can be clearly seen swelling through the soft garment that enfolds her, much as the bosom of Athena is visible through her peplos in the metope from Olympia (see fig. 182).

Another significant step was taken at Reims by the sculptor who carved, after 1251, the statues in the niches that fill the inside of the west façade. In spite of the fact that the two figures inhabit separate niches, the *Priest and the Knight* (fig. 468; long misnamed *Melchizedek and Abraham*) forms a unified psychological and compositional group. The knight looks from his niche, hands folded in prayer, to the priest robed in a billowing chasuble (a vestment worn by the celebrant at Mass in commemoration of the seamless robe of Christ), whose folds obscure his body. However, the artist was well aware of the proportions and movements of the masses of the body, as can be seen in the way he has handled the figure of the knight, in spite of chain mail and tunic. We have reached a Classical moment in Gothic sculpture, in which figures, fully in the round, are endowed with the capability of movement in space. The sculptor has set forth eloquently the contrast between the earnest, slightly frowning glance of the priest, with his richly curling beard, and the expectant look of the knight preparing to receive Communion before battle.

The climax of the High Gothic architectural style was achieved at the Cathedral of Amiens, in Picardy, due north of Paris, begun in 1220 by the architect Robert de Luzarches (fig. 469). The soaring effect of the Amiens interior surpasses that of any other Gothic cathedral (fig. 470); the vaults leap to a height of 144 feet. The proportions of all the elements are even more slender than at Reims. The last trace of doming is gone from the vaults, whose crown line is level. The triforium openings are filled with bar tracery rather than the continuous arcade of Reims. In the clerestory a momentous step has been taken: the same molding serves as wall rib and window frame, thus canceling out the wall. The nave of Amiens was built first; the two upper stories of the choir show still another step in the direction of dematerialization, probably taken by Robert de Luzarches' successor, Thomas de Cormont, after 1258. The roof covering the ambulatory vaults is no longer sloping, but converted into a succession of pyramidal caps, one over each bay. This change permitted the architect to turn the triforium into a second row of windows, greatly lightening the interior, which now looks bare without its stained glass. As the photograph of the choir vaults from below clearly shows (fig. 471), the entire cathedral has become a cage of delicate stone members—colonnettes, ribs, tracery—to hold the vault surfaces above and the stained glass on the sides. Mass has been almost totally replaced by linear fabric. This ultimate phase of the High Gothic style in France is called the Rayonnant on account of the tracery patterns that in the rose windows expand like rays.

The flying buttresses of the nave at Amiens resemble those at Reims, but those of the choir show a transformation, again probably due to Thomas de Cormont, and teach a striking lesson in the combined imaginative daring and structural logic of Gothic building. The architect has largely dematerialized the very device on which he depends for the support of the building: the flying buttress itself (fig. 472) is composed of bar tracery, connecting an upper strut and a lower arch, which were clearly

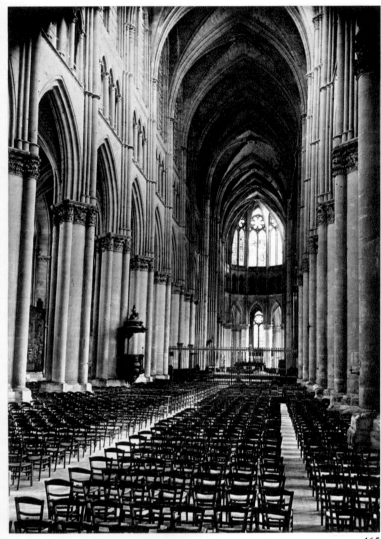

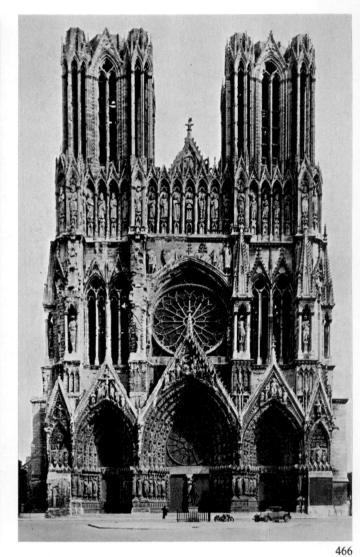

465

466

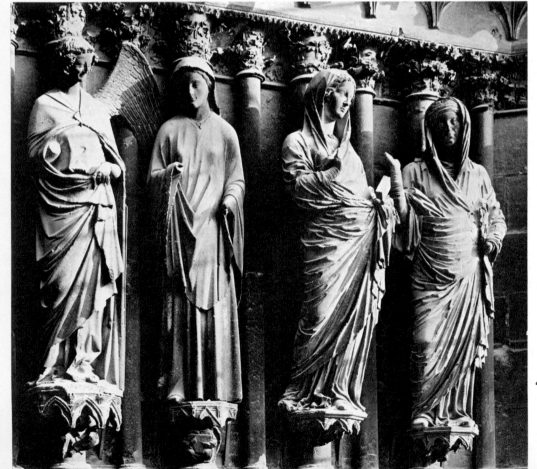

465. Nave, Cathedral of Reims.
     Begun 1210. France

466. West façade, Cathedral of
     Reims. c. 1225-99

467. *Annunciation*, and *Visitation*.
     c. 1225-45. Jamb statues, west
     portal, Cathedral of Reims

467

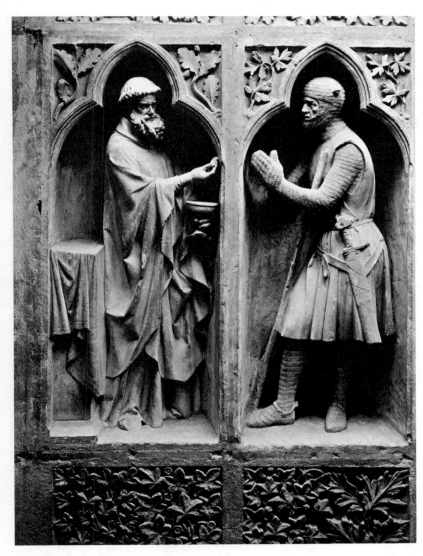

468. *Priest and the Knight.* After 1251. West interior wall, Cathedral of Reims

sufficient to sustain the thrust of the slender vaults. Even the buttresses and their pinnacles have been decorated by a fabric of applied colonnettes and arches, which have no structural function but make the solid masses appear lighter and more vertical. As a final touch the choir windows, one of which is to be seen at the right of the illustration, are surmounted by false gables made of tracery in order to dissolve the last remaining strip of wall above the window and to break the horizontal line of the cornice molding.

As compared with those of Laon, Paris, and Reims, the façade of Amiens, probably begun in 1220 (fig. 473), is not a complete success. The center pinnacle marks the height of the nave roof, almost level with the south tower. From the side view the height of the church is so great as to render towers superfluous. The unity of the façade at Amiens is also disturbed by the much later—and in themselves very fine—rose window and details crowning the towers and the screen, belonging to the Flamboyant phase (see page 387). However, the Amiens portals contain sculpture of great dignity, especially the statue of *Christ Treading on the Lion and the Basilisk* (fig. 474; compare with the earlier version of the same theme in fig. 377), which stands against the trumeau of the central portal. Stylistically, the figure, with its firm stance and flow-

ing but controlled drapery folds, represents a stage between that of the transept sculpture at Chartres and the highly developed naturalistic and classicistic statues at Reims. Nicknamed locally "le beau Dieu," the image is that of a man in early maturity, with straight nose, broad brow, calm expression, short beard, and flowing hair. With a few striking exceptions, this is the Christ-type that has replaced in Western imagination both the Apollonian youth of the Ravenna mosaics and the awesome Pantocrator of Byzantine art. It is a remarkable paradox that Gothic artists should have populated their dematerialized, linear cathedrals with believable, many-faceted, and very solid images of complete human beings, even when it was necessary to portray the second person of the Trinity. The canopy over Christ's head, instead of showing the usual generalized array of domes and towers, is a tiny model of a Gothic chevet, with radiating chapels, possibly a reminder that the apse of a cathedral encloses the Eucharistic Christ of the Mass. The nobility of the Amiens statues contrasts with the vivid naturalism of the little scenes from the Old and New Testaments, and from such allegorical cycles as the Virtues and Vices, the signs of the zodiac, and the labors of the months, which appear in low relief in the quatrefoils on the bases of the portal jambs (fig. 475).

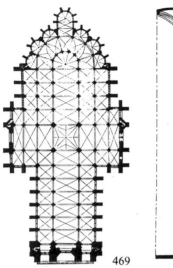
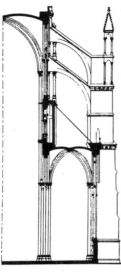

469

469. ROBERT DE LUZARCHES. Plan and transverse section of the Cathedral of Amiens. Begun 1220. France

470. Nave, Cathedral of Amiens

471. Choir vaults (from below), Cathedral of Amiens

472. Exterior of choir and south transept, showing flying buttresses. Cathedral of Amiens

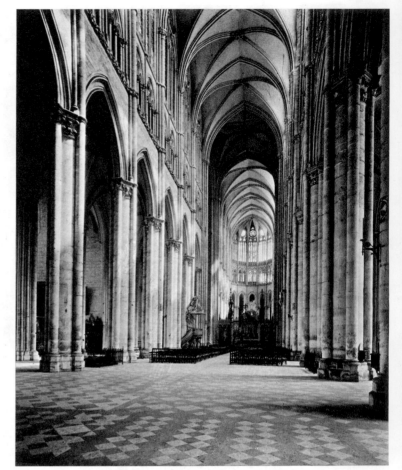

470

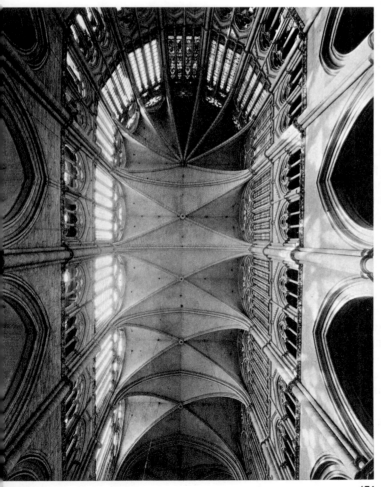

471

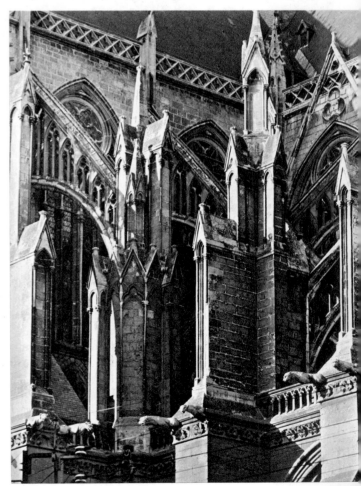

472

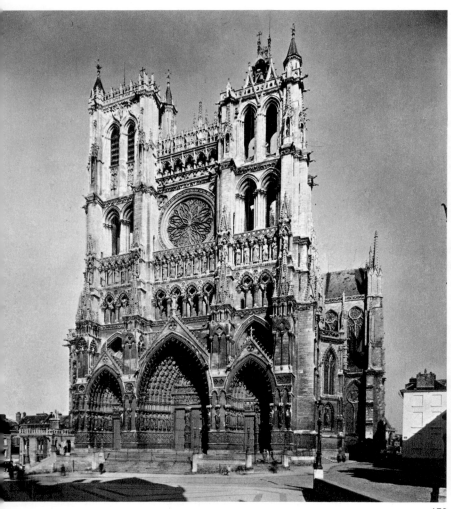

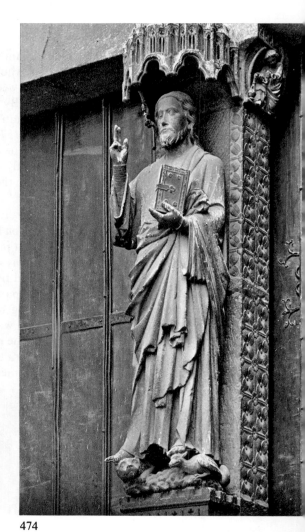

473   474

473. Façade, Cathedral of
     Amiens. Begun c. 1220

474. *Christ Treading on the
     Lion and the Basilisk.*
     Central portal, Cathedral
     of Amiens

475. *Signs of the Zodiac,* and
     Labors of the Months
     (portion). Relief. c. 1220–30.
     West façade portal jamb,
     Cathedral of Amiens

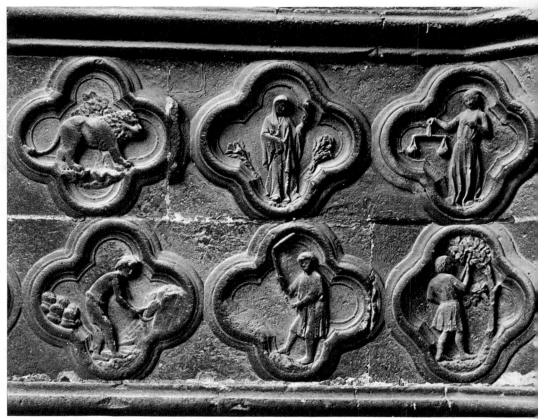

475

The practical limit of the Gothic dream was reached at Amiens. About 1225 the architect who designed the Cathedral of Beauvais, located between Paris and Amiens, tried to surpass it (fig. 476). By 1272 the lofty skeleton of stone, with a glazed triforium as at Amiens, had reached the unbelievable height of 157 feet above the floor. Then in 1284, before the transept could be completed, the choir vault fell, leaving only the apse vault standing. Collapses like this, frequent in the Romanesque period, were rare in the thirteenth century, when architects had, through trial and error, arrived at a system that generally worked. The reason for the disaster at Beauvais is not entirely understood; it may have been a matter of inadequate foundations. In any event the choir was rebuilt, the number of supports and flying buttresses being doubled and old-fashioned six-part vaults being revived for the last time. The building of the transept lagged on into the fourteenth century, with yet another calamity, the fall of a tower, and then the money ran out. From the outside the truncated choir, towering sadly above the Carolingian nave, is a monument to the unat-

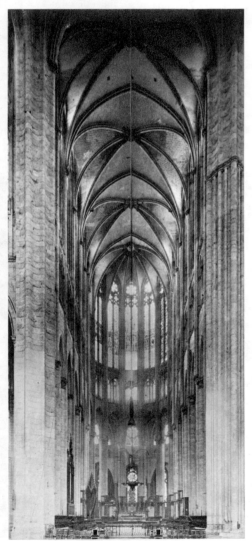

476. Interior, Cathedral of Beauvais. c. 1225. France

tainable, but the effect of the interior, catapulting in one leap from floor to lofty vault, is exhilarating.

In contrast to the Beauvais catastrophe, the small-scale Sainte-Chapelle in Paris is a brilliant achievement of the Rayonnant style. The chapel was built from 1243 to 1248 by Louis IX of France, later canonized as Saint Louis, to enshrine relics of the Crucifixion. Louis met these relics, which were brought to France from Syria and Constantinople, at the gates of Paris and walked barefoot behind them in solemn procession. Although deprived of its surrounding buildings, and badly repainted in the nineteenth century, the chapel is structurally intact. It consists of a lower and rather modest story supporting an upper chapel that represents the utter perfection of the High Gothic (colorplate 64), a delicate framework of slender stone elements enclosing stained-glass windows. As there are no side aisles, flying buttresses were not required. Only a small strip of wall remains below the windows, broken at the right by a simple niche. Behind and above the usual location of the altar stands a Gothic shrine in which the relics were kept and in which they could be displayed. For completeness and for quality the stained-glass windows of the Sainte-Chapelle compete only with those at Chartres. Their innumerable scenes organized as parallels between Old and New Testaments are small, and the upper ones are not easy to read from the floor—a problem we have encountered before in the sculpture of the Column of Trajan (see fig. 277). From a slight distance the windows fuse into an indescribable radiance of red and blue.

FRENCH GOTHIC MANUSCRIPTS

Never before or again in the history of art was architecture so completely dominant as in the Gothic period. Pictorial imagination was directed toward stained glass rather than mural painting, for which few wall surfaces remained in Gothic churches. Even illuminated manuscripts, which survive in great numbers from this period, are dominated on every page by architectural concepts. One of the finest is a *Bible Moralisée* (moralized Bible—a collection of biblical passages and illustrations arranged as parallels between Old and New Testaments, as, for example, in the manner of the windows of the Sainte-Chapelle), probably written and illustrated in the mid-thirteenth century at Reims for Thibaut V, count of Champagne and king of Navarre, and his wife Isabelle, daughter of Louis IX. On one magnificent page God himself is shown as an architect, using that indispensable tool of architectural draftsmanship, the compass, to create heaven and earth, which "was without form, and void" (colorplate 65). The artist has imagined the Deity on such a cosmic scale that the universe is literally in his hand. The border, brilliant in its flashing alternation of patterned red and blue, is insufficient to contain him as he strides through space. The folds of his blue tunic and rose mantle, lined respectively with orange and yellow, are depicted in a free pictorial approximation of the parallel folds of the classicistic sculpture of Reims Cathedral. The artist has imagined the Creation as a moment of intense artistic inspiration; the Lord's eyes are dilated, his mouth slightly open, as he measures the circle containing green and blue waters, dark blue sky with stars, sun, and moon, and a still formless earth, giving it form by a supreme act of creative will. This unforgettable image should be compared with the totally different view of Creation in the Renaissance (see Vol. 2, colorplate 23).

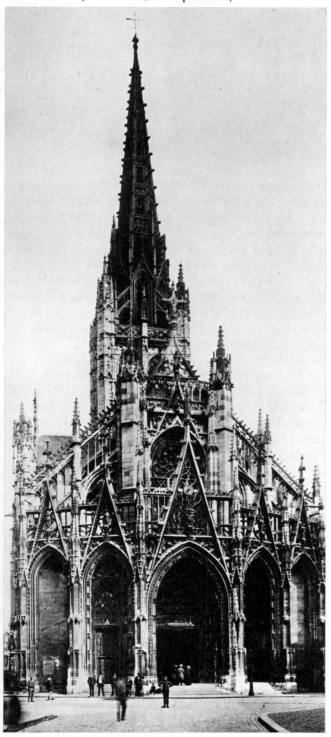

A dazzling page in the *Psalter of Saint Louis*, made for Louis IX and datable between 1253 and 1270 (colorplate 66), represents the appearance of the three angels to Abraham and the supper served them by Abraham and Sarah, the two incidents separated by the beautifully ornamentalized oak at Mamre. The excitement of the painting, which vibrates with brilliant color and tense, incisive line, could hardly be more different from the serene icon by Andrei Rublev dedicated to a synthesis of the same subject (see colorplate 61). The elegant, swaying figures with tiny hands and feet are embraced, as often in Gothic illumination, by shapes derived from cathedral architecture. The gables and tracery are recognizable as belonging to the period of the choir of Amiens (see fig. 472), and a clerestory can be seen, too. As in stained glass, red and blue, white and green predominate. The border, which Saint Bernard would have hated, repeats the age-old theme of animal interlace.

THE LATER GOTHIC IN FRANCE

After the thirteenth century, the pace of church-building slowed in the domain of the French kings; almost every town that could afford a Gothic cathedral had built one. But in spite of constant warfare with the English, who controlled Normandy and much of western France, the elaborate and expensive process of finishing towers, façades, and gables continued in an always more imaginative style. The latest phase, beginning in the middle of the fourteenth century, is known as the Flamboyant because of the characteristic flamelike shapes of the tracery, based on double curvature rather than on the logical mullions, pointed arches, and circles of the High Gothic. A striking example is the rose window of Amiens Cathedral, done about 1500 (see fig. 473). The climax of the Flamboyant style is represented by the façade of the Church of Saint-Maclou at Rouen, the capital of Normandy (figs. 477, 478), built in the early sixteenth century, the moment of the High Renaissance in Florence and Rome (see Vol. 2, Part Four, Chapter 3). The lower portion of the façade bays sharply outward. Of the five

477. Façade. St.-Maclou.
Early 16th century.
Rouen, France

478. Plan of St.-Maclou

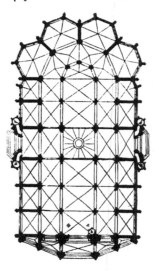

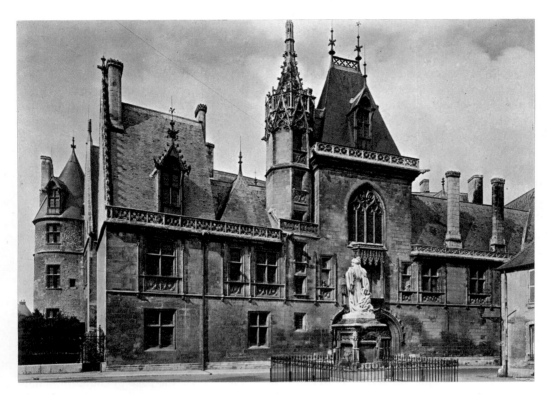

479. Palais Jacques Coeur. 1443–51. Bourges, France

apparent portals, two are blind. No inert surfaces remain; transparent, linear shapes of stone merge with each other as they flicker upward, the transparent central gable even passing in front of the rose window. Only the main contours of the flying buttresses, gables, and arches are still apparent, drawn in thin air with lines of stone; the rest is sheer fantasy.

The finest surviving monument of late Gothic domestic architecture (fig. 479) is the mansion built at Bourges from 1443 to 1451 by the wealthy merchant, Jacques Cœur, Treasurer to Charles VIII of France during and after the unhappy period when this weak monarch, driven out of Paris by the English, was known disparagingly as the king of Bourges. The house is a freely arranged succession of blocks, with steeply pitched roofs of different heights, the highest being reserved for the owner's private chapel with a Flamboyant window located over the main entrance. Flamboyant ornament is restricted to the balustrades at the eaves, to the panels under the windows, and to the rich staircase tower, ending in an openwork octagonal cap. This delightful, asymmetrical structure, with its inviting appearance of improvisation, should be compared with the rigidly symmetrical palaces being built by the same merchant class in Italy at the same moment (see Vol. 2, fig. 28). Alas, Jacques Cœur had only two years to enjoy his house before he was falsely accused of attempting to poison the king's mistress and had to flee France.

The sculptural style of the fourteenth century does not continue either the classicistic or the naturalistic tendencies we have seen in the sculpture of the great cathedrals. A typical early fourteenth-century example, the *Virgin of Paris* (fig. 480; originally from the Church of Saint-Aignan), moves with an elegant lassitude that embodies the ultimate in courtly insouciance. The face looks

almost Far Eastern in its soft contours and slightly slanting eyes. The folds, despite the sculptor's exact observation of the behavior of cloth, are nonetheless so voluminous that they give little hint of the Virgin's body beneath them. She wears her heavy crown with languid grace, but her pose, one hip sharply moved to the left to support the Child, shows a distinct element of exaggeration. Nonetheless, the sculptor has observed a delicate and affectionate byplay between mother and Child as the babe holds the orb of power in his left hand and toys with a fold of her mantle with his right.

Fourteenth-century painting in France, luxurious and worldly, may be represented by a delightful page from the *Belleville Breviary* (fig. 481), illuminated at Paris c. 1323–26 and attributed to Jean Pucelle, a still undefined artistic personality. The architectural frame of the thirteenth century has been replaced by a delicate border of gold and blue; at the upper left a painting of *David Before Saul* was either executed under direct Italian influence or painted by an Italian artist (cf. the modeled architecture in fig. 519). At the bottom of the page the French style reappears, in the tiny strip representing at the left Cain killing Abel, in the center the Eucharist offered by a priest to the dove of the Holy Spirit, and on the right Charity as a queen, assisted in her almsgiving by the Hand of God. A breviary is a book containing the readings for the Divine Offices—the prayers recited at the seven canonical hours. The patron who ordered the manuscript and the artists who illuminated it had other concerns as well as the strictly religious, as a glance at the border will reveal. The animal interlace has disappeared, but animals, birds, and insects have been revived in very lifelike terms—a beautifully painted pheasant, a dragonfly, a butterfly, a monkey, a snail, a dragon, among which three musicians play a lute, a bagpipe, and a flute.

What we witness in these caprices of sculpture and painting, which lingered into the fifteenth century, is the first glimmer of a new and exciting naturalistic style (which will be considered in Vol. 2, Part Four, Chapter 2).

GOTHIC ART IN GERMANY, SPAIN, AND ENGLAND

At first French Gothic was imported directly into the Rhineland, which was already amply provided with massive, apparently fireproof Romanesque double-ended cathedrals. When the Carolingian Cathedral of Cologne burned down in 1248, Bishop Gerhard was ready with complete plans for a Gothic replacement; work started within three and a half months. Building continued into the fourteenth century, then languished, and the choir remained incomplete as we see it in the faithfully painted background of Hans Memlinc's *Martyrdom of Saint Ursula* (see Vol. 2, fig. 107C). Only the lower story of the south tower had been built; unexpectedly, in the nineteenth century a large and detailed drawing for the

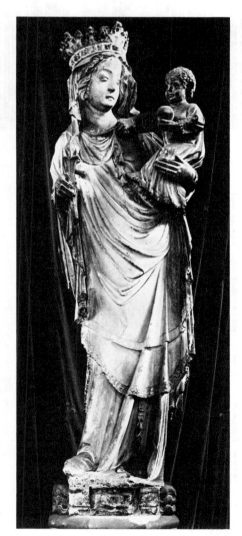

480. *Virgin of Paris*, from St.-Aignan. Early 14th century. Stone. Notre-Dame, Paris

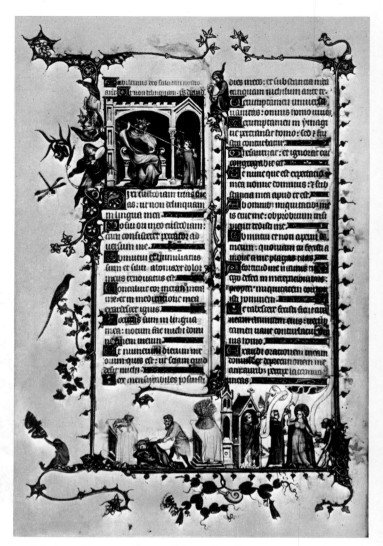

481. JEAN PUCELLE. Page of the *Belleville Breviary*, from Paris. c. 1323–26. Illumination. c. 9½ x 6¾". Bibliothèque Nationale, Paris

façade and the towers, dating from about 1320, came to light, and the rest of the cathedral was then completed.

While the details of the nave and façade betray nineteenth-century handling, the general appearance of the Cathedral is correct, and overwhelming (fig. 482). The interior is only slightly less daring in its verticality and slenderness than Beauvais, and the glazed triforium may even have been designed earlier than that by Thomas de Cormont at Amiens. The French would probably never have countenanced the efflorescence of heavy foliate ornament around the arches of the arcade, but otherwise the interior is French (fig. 483). So indeed are the tracery flying buttresses and the pinnacles veiled in tracery, as well as the gables over the clerestory windows. But French architects had never solved the problem posed by the effect of a lofty church on the design of the towers. The fourteenth-century architect at Cologne made a fresh start, treating the second stories of his towers as extensions of the clerestory, imposing majestic third and fourth stories, and bringing the towers to a brilliant climax in two pointed tracery spires.

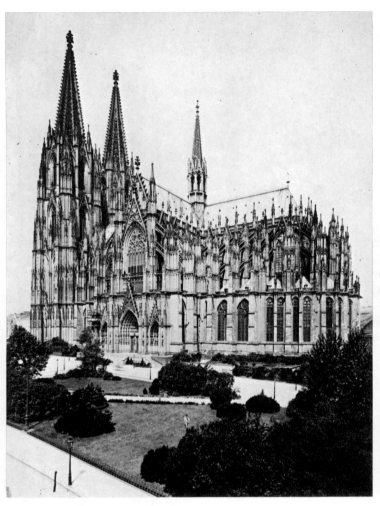

482. Cathedral of Cologne. 1248–1322. Germany

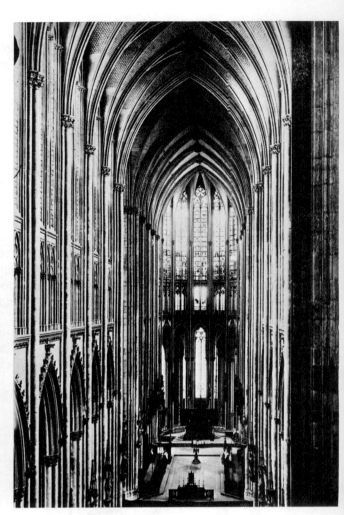

483. Choir, Cathedral of Cologne

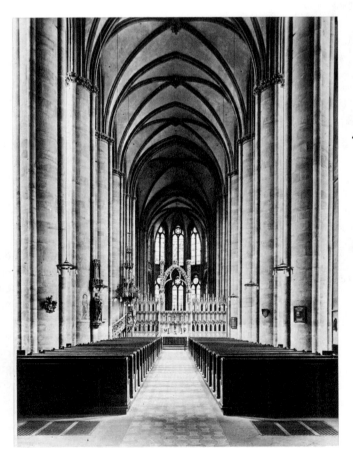

484. Interior, St. Elizabeth. 1235–83.
Marburg, Germany

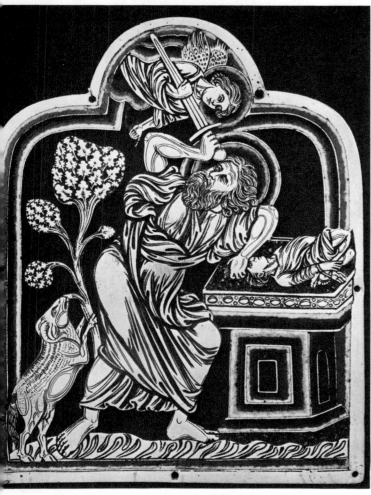

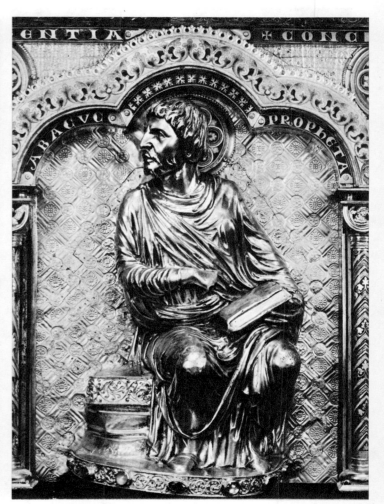

485. NICHOLAS OF VERDUN. *Sacrifice of Isaac*. 1181.
Gold and enamel plaque, height 5½". Abbey
of Klosterneuburg, Austria

486. NICHOLAS OF VERDUN. *Prophet Habakkuk*, from the
Shrine of the Three Kings. c. 1182–90. Gold, enamel,
and precious stones. Cathedral of Cologne. Germany

The basically French plan at Cologne was not popular in Germany; almost contemporary with it appeared a more influential design, the *Hallenkirche* (hall-church), of which an early example is the Church of Saint Elizabeth at Marburg (fig. 484), dating from 1235 to 1283. In this type, widely followed throughout Central Europe (and, oddly enough, also southern France), the nave and side aisles are the same height, eliminating the necessity for flying buttresses. Although exterior forms and interior spaces are inevitably less dramatic in the Hallenkirche type, space does flow more freely throughout the church, rendering it especially suitable for preaching.

German thirteenth-century sculpture can scarcely be understood without a consideration of the art of metalwork, highly regarded in the Middle Ages, and without a return to the valley of the Meuse, where in the twelfth century the classicism of Renier de Huy (see fig. 403) held sway at Liège. Another master from the same region, Nicholas of Verdun, had great success in Germany. In 1181 he completed an extensive cycle of gold and enamel scenes for a pulpit at the Abbey of Klosterneuburg, not far from Vienna; these were later remounted to form an altarpiece. The persistent debate

as to whether Nicholas' style should be considered Romanesque or Early Gothic should be settled by the characteristically Gothic trefoil (three-lobed) arches of the borders. Nicholas' strong classicism is also Gothic in the sense that all his figures stand or move firmly on the ground, and though the drapery lines still retain some Romanesque ornamental character, the convincing action poses and the thoroughly consistent drapery folds are Gothic. The *Sacrifice of Isaac* (fig. 485) is presented in terms of physical action; the angel swoops down to withhold Abraham's sword, as he holds Isaac bound upon the altar. The stormy movement brings back memories of Hellenistic sculpture, and perhaps more relevant echoes of Nerezi (see fig. 439). This scene should be compared with Lorenzo Ghiberti's rendering of the same incident at the beginning of the Italian Renaissance (see Vol. 2, fig. 45).

The Klosterneuburg plaques were followed by the gold figures of the rich Shrine of the Three Kings, made by Nicholas about 1182–90 for the Cathedral of Cologne. The *Prophet Habakkuk* is surely one of the most classicistic figures of the entire Middle Ages—even more so than the *Visitation* group at Reims (fig. 486). The prophet is seated in a strongly Hellenistic pose, his man-

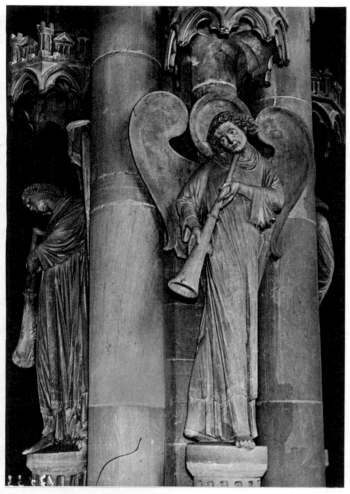

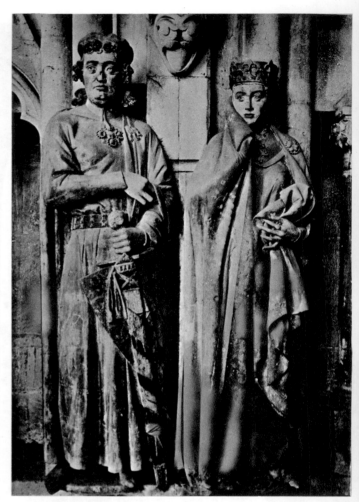

487. Angels. c. 1220–25. Stone. Choir pillar, south transept, Cathedral of Strasbourg, France

488. *Ekkehard and Uta.* c. 1250–60. Cathedral of Naumburg, Germany

tle sweeping around him in folds that recall fifth-century Greek sculpture (see fig. 170) as much as they do the togas of Roman sculpture (see fig. 245). His head is turned in an attitude of tense alertness, as if he were listening to divine inspiration. The movement of surfaces has surpassed even that of the work of Renier de Huy, with which it appears in a continuous tradition.

German Gothic sculpture reflects also at the start the classicism of Nicholas of Verdun. Especially impressive is the *Death of the Virgin* tympanum (colorplate 67), of about 1220, in the Cathedral of Strasbourg; today in France, Strasbourg has been throughout most of its history a German city. The ornament of the preexistent arch is Romanesque, and the heads of the Apostles radiate outward from the center as at Vézelay, but the sweep and flow of the drapery are strongly Gothic, as are the delicacy of psychological observation and the intensity of the emotion displayed by the grieving Apostles.

At the same moment a different and vividly original style was developing elsewhere in Strasbourg Cathedral. The trumpet-blowing angels attached to a choir pillar (fig. 487) only vaguely suggest French prototypes, but the

leg-crossed pose, reminiscent of the *Prophet* at Moissac (see fig. 399), had long been renounced by French Gothic sculpture. Nonetheless, the forthright realism of these Strasbourg angels has no more to do with the visionary quality of the Romanesque than it has with the elegance of French Gothic. The fall of the tunic is easy and natural, the face homely and everyday. The wings, with their vigorous abstract curvature, would have been unacceptable in France. But these are the very qualities that make German Gothic sculpture individual.

Massive sculptural cycles like those of the French cathedral portals were apparently not needed in Germany. German thirteenth-century masters, with less compulsion to conform to a corporate style, are impressive in their directness. The best of these is an anonymous artist known for his work in the Gothic Cathedral of Naumburg in Saxony (today in East Germany). This powerful sculptor carved a series of statues of nobles from local history who were believed to have been founders of the Cathedral and brought these subjects—about whose actual appearance he knew nothing—to convincing life. The heavyset, pouting Ekkehard (fig. 488), with his hand resting from habit on his sword hilt, is contrasted with the aloof beauty of his wife Uta, who gathers up her cloak with her left hand while with her right she draws it closer about her neck.

Perhaps the most memorable achievement of German Gothic sculpture is the mid-thirteenth-century *Rider* (fig. 489), who stands against one of the Romanesque piers of Bamberg Cathedral in Bavaria, under a French-style canopy that seems both inappropriate to Germany and inadequate for a man on horseback. The earliest monumental equestrian group we know since the days of *Marcus Aurelius* (see fig. 289), this work may preserve some memory of the vanished bronze *Theodoric* that once stood in front of Charlemagne's Palace Chapel at Aachen, but it is in every way unclassical. The horse is hardly to be compared with the fiery steed of Marcus Aurelius; his forefeet are planted side by side, his left hind hoof is lifted to paw the ground. He looks nervous and tense. In contrast to Classical equestrian figures, it should be noted, the Bamberg rider is represented to the same scale as his mount. We do not know the identity of the subject—he may be the emperor Conrad III—but in its calm, dignity, and apparent courage, the statue sums up as nobly as does the *Saint Theodore* at Chartres the qualities essential to the knightly idea.

French Gothic architecture was also imported into Spain, and there are three major Spanish cathedrals that, save for the absence of a high-pitched roof, can hardly be told from their French models. Nonetheless, French motives were brilliantly reinterpreted in Catalonia and in Majorca, especially in the fourteenth-century Cathedral of Palma (fig. 490), whose plan with four side aisles is related to that of Bourges in that the inner aisle on each side has a clerestory. But at Palma the slender supports have been simplified into octagons, eliminating the whole French machinery of ribs and colonnettes that makes up a compound pier. Also, the choir rises only to the height of the inner aisle, which leaves above the apse a wall surface resembling the Early Christian triumphal arch; this surface is pierced by a huge oculus (circular window) without tracery, to grand effect.

Gothic architectural principles were adopted immediately and enthusiastically in England, already prepared to a certain extent by the structural innovations of the Norman Romanesque. It has been claimed—and quite correctly—that in no century since the eleventh has Gothic architecture *not* been built in England (for eighteenth- and nineteenth-century buildings in Gothic style, see Vol. 2, figs. 349, 396). In the last quarter of the twelfth century, the French Gothic architect William of Sens brought the latest French techniques to Canterbury. But the minute French ideas crossed the English Channel they became distinctly English. First of all, the English neither shared the French enthusiasm for height nor renounced their preference for the extreme length of Romanesque churches. The plan of Salisbury Cathedral, begun in 1220 and consecrated in 1258 (fig. 491), with its double transept, recalls in that respect the arrangement

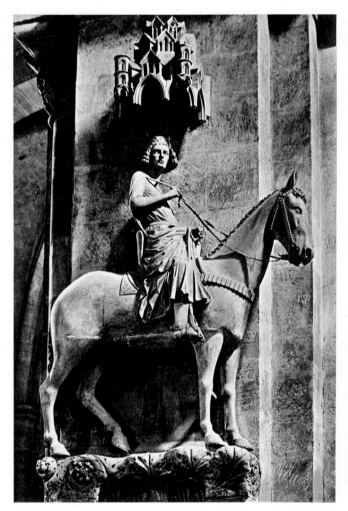

489. *Rider*. Middle 13th century. Cathedral of Bamberg, Germany

at Cluny and resembles the layout of no French Gothic building, save that its characteristic square east end recalls that at Laon (see fig. 453). The square east end and lengthy choir of English cathedrals probably correspond to the need to accommodate a larger number of clergy than was customary in France; English cathedrals also have cloisters like those of monasteries (many, in fact, were served by Benedictine monks). Second, the majority of English cathedrals are situated not in the centers of towns but in the midst of broad lawns (originally graveyards) and massive shade trees.

In the interior of Salisbury Cathedral (fig. 492) every effort was made to increase the appearance of length and to diminish what to the French would seem a very modest height. No colonnettes rise from floor to ceiling; those attached to the compound pillars support only the ribs that make up the arches of the nave arcade. The triforium is large, and the clerestory is small—tucked away under the vaults as in French Early Gothic cathedrals. Characteristically English is the use of dark Purbeck marble for the colonnettes and capitals, establishing a color contrast similar to that of Romanesque interiors. In this chaste, unpretentious thirteenth-century style known as Early

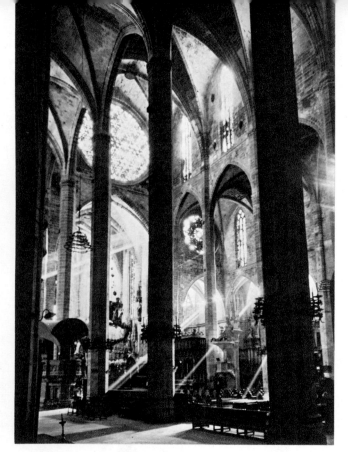

490. Interior, Cathedral of Palma. Begun 1306. Majorca, Spain

English, there is no tracery; lancet windows are grouped in threes and fives. The appearance of the interior was doubtless far richer when the stained glass (partly destroyed during the Reformation and partly removed in the eighteenth century) was intact.

Compared with the soaring lines of French or German cathedrals, the exterior of Salisbury looks earthbound (fig. 493). There is no true façade with flanking towers (although these are present in a number of English cathedrals), but a mere screen that extends without supports to mask the angle of the side-aisle roof. In few English cathedrals are there massive sculptural programs in the French manner; statues and reliefs were scattered over the screen façades, but few have escaped the axes of the reformers. Flying buttresses, in so low a building, did not seem necessary; nonetheless, some had to be added here and there. There is no dramatic chevet; the effects at Salisbury are obtained by the sensitive balancing of elements kept deliberately simple. The square east end is prolonged by the Lady Chapel (a chapel dedicated to the Virgin). The glorious distinguishing feature of Salisbury is the spire over the crossing, a fourteenth-century addition in the second phase of English Gothic, known as Decorated. Although the building was not originally intended for so tall a central tower, the spire, rising to a height of 404 feet, was designed so as to complete the diagonal massing of the exterior composition, and its ornamentation is restrained in order not to conflict with the purity of the Early English building. The effect of this im-

mense weight on the interior was less happy; it required elaborate new supports.

The most original invention in English architectural history is the style appropriately known as the Perpendicular, which began to appear in the fourteenth century. The choir of the massive Romanesque Cathedral of Gloucester (fig. 494) was remodeled from 1332–57 and is a pioneer example of the new style; the Romanesque nave was left intact. The original round arches of the arcade and the gallery may still be made out under the covering screen of Perpendicular tracery. If the English were slow in adopting the idea of tracery, they soon went at it with a will; in this respect the Perpendicular may be considered the English answer to the Flamboyant, whose caprices are countered with brilliant logic. The entire interior of the choir is transformed into a basketwork of tracery, with predominantly vertical members, which form the windows and dissolve into the vault. In this refined stage the ribs have lost any constructional function they may once have had. The triangular compartments are subdivided by additional diagonal ribs, and all the ribs are connected by an intricate system of crisscrossing diagonals. The original Romanesque apse is replaced by an east window 72 feet in height, which not only extends from wall to wall but also even bows slightly outward, doubtless to increase resistance to wind.

The final development of Perpendicular flowered in the fan vaults of the late fifteenth and early sixteenth centuries, the richest of which are those in King Henry VII's Chapel in Westminster Abbey in London (fig. 495), dating from the first quarter of the sixteenth century, nearly contemporary with Saint-Maclou at Rouen (see fig. 477). The complex shapes are as bewildering at first sight as those of Hiberno-Saxon interlace (see fig. 349) and as open to logical analysis. The vault is made up of tangent cones of tracery, each composed of tiny coupled trefoil arches, surmounted by quatrefoils and enclosed by gables—the standard repertory of High Gothic tracery,

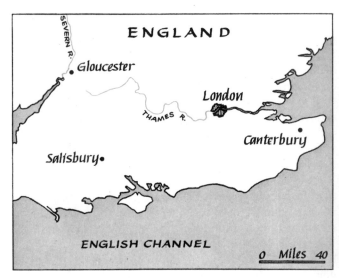

MAP 21. *Southern England*

as compared to the flickering shapes of the Flamboyant. The cones radiate from central pendants; in the interstices between the cones are smaller ones, also culminating in pendants. The larger cones are held in position by cusped tracery arches, springing from between the windows. Tie rods added later indicate that on this occasion the imagination of the Perpendicular architects may have been carried too far.

Among the rare panel paintings surviving from the Gothic period in England one masterpiece stands out, the *Wilton Diptych* (colorplate 68), a small work painted in the tempera technique we shall presently encounter in Italy (see below, page 405). On rocky ground to the left kneels Richard II, represented as a youth and accompanied by his patron saints, John the Baptist and Kings Edward the Confessor and Edmund. Most of the background is gold, tooled in a neat, regular pattern to increase its sparkle, but beside the figure of John the Baptist we look into a deep wilderness. The young king's hands are extended less in prayer than in astonishment at the apparition in the facing panel of the Virgin Mary, holding the Christ Child and attended by eleven rose-crowned blond angels, each displaying on his left shoulder the same badge of the white hart as the king wears (he was eleven years old at the time of his coronation in 1377). The sacred figures stand or kneel on a carpet of rich foliage, on which plucked roses and irises are strewn. The rich crimsons of Richard's damasks and the white of the ermines contrast with the sky-blues that dominate the right panel, ranging from the deep tones of the tunics in the upper row of angels through the medium value of Mary's mantle and tunic to the pale blues in the foreground; even the angels' wings are white, tipped with blues.

The faces, hands, arms, and feet show an unprecedented delicacy of drawing and shading, and accuracy of anatomical observation, held in check by an extreme refinement of taste. This exquisite style is the more

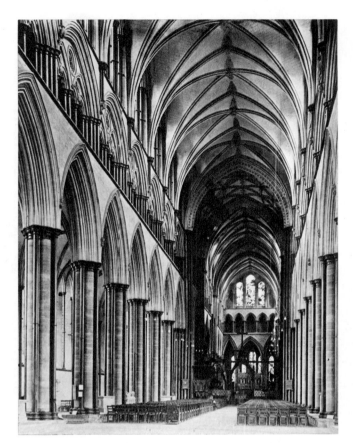

492. Nave and choir. Salisbury Cathedral

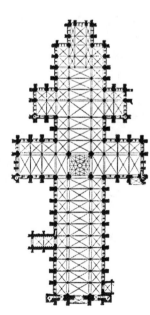

491. Plan of Salisbury Cathedral. Begun 1220. England

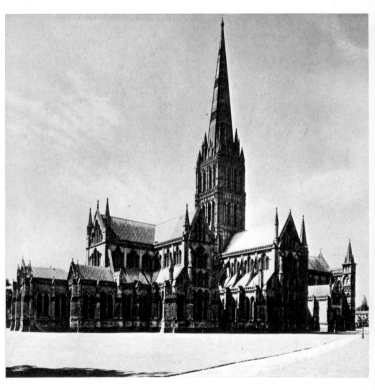

493. Exterior, Salisbury Cathedral (view from the northeast)

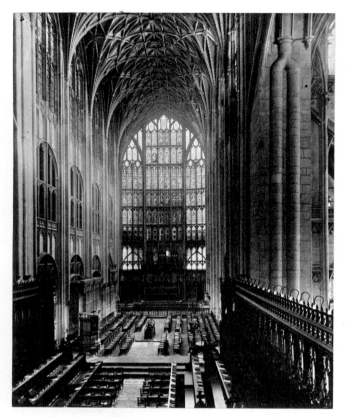

494. Choir, Cathedral of Gloucester. Remodeled 1332–37. England

mysterious since so little panel painting of the period survives in England. There are many theories regarding the diptych's date (anywhere from 1377 to 1413) and authorship, but no sure conclusions. The painter was certainly trained in the Italian tradition, and knew Sienese art, especially the work of Duccio and Simone Martini (see pages 410, 412, figs. 518, 521) and even more intimately that of Giovanni da Milano (see fig. 526). He was also one of the most accomplished painters of the fourteenth century in Europe. But we have no clear indication whether he was from England or the Continent; something in the poetry of the picture suggests England. The least that can be said on this subject is that the painting corresponds to the rarefied taste of the court of Richard II; since his reign was destined for an unhappy end, it is comforting to hope that the unknown master of the *Wilton Diptych* gave it a beautiful beginning.

GOTHIC ARCHITECTURE IN ITALY

France's neighbors, in general, welcomed the new Gothic style, and imported French architects and architecture, subject only to modifications in accordance with local taste and customs. In the kingdom of Naples, ruled by French descendants of Louis IX, the existence of French Gothic churches is not surprising. Elsewhere in Italy the

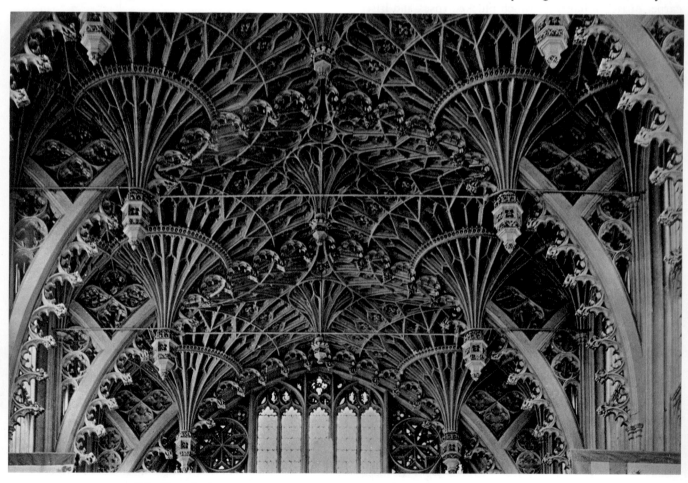

495. Chapel of Henry VII, Westminster Abbey (detail of vault). 1503–19. London

only French-style churches are those of the Cistercian Order, itself French and governed from Citeaux in Burgundy. The austerity decreed by Saint Bernard forbade anything like the splendors of the cathedrals. The essentials of the Cistercian Abbey of Fossanova, south of Rome (fig. 496), commenced in 1187 and consecrated in 1208, might as easily be found in Cistercian buildings in France or in England and clearly reflect the bleakness of Saint Bernard's tradition. The east end is square. Massive compound piers support pointed transverse arches and groin vaults over nave and choir. Only the crossing is rib-vaulted. The capitals are French transplants, close to those at Laon and Paris. As there was to be no stained glass, there was no need for the refinements of the Early Gothic.

In the independent republics of central and northern Italy, the Romanesque often continued into the thirteenth century, although many Gothic details were adopted. The major influence on church building emanated from two remarkably different religious figures, Saint Francis of Assisi (1182–1226) and Saint Dominic (1170–1221), both of whom founded orders with innumerable branches, devoted not to a life of work and study apart from the people but to direct preaching before urban masses and to missionary endeavors. The preaching orders revolutionized traditional Italian basilican architecture. Simple but very large interiors were required, usually timber-roofed both for economy and for speed in construction. Santa Croce in Florence, started in 1294 (fig. 497), is one of the most imposing. Its octagonal columns, pointed arches, and foliate capitals, and its impression of lightness and openness mark the church as Gothic, although at first sight it resembles nothing we have seen elsewhere. As the church was not planned for vaulting, there was no need for the usual French system of colonnettes rising two or more stories. The light and heat of Italian summers would have made large French windows intolerable. The windows at Santa Croce were, however, designed for stained glass, much of which is still in place, although it is very different from French stained glass.

When we look at the choir of Santa Croce, beyond the triumphal arch, we see that the unknown architect (perhaps Arnolfo di Cambio, c. 1245–before 1310) did indeed understand French Gothic principles and adapted them intelligently to Italian requirements. The choir and the five chapels on either side of it, entered from the west side of the transept (two may be seen in the illustration), show a familiarity with the refinements of ribbed vaulting. The tall windows with their bar tracery resemble those inserted into the clerestory of Notre-Dame in Paris in the thirteenth century (see fig. 457). Large wall surfaces were needed in Italy, especially in Tuscany, for the highly respected art of fresco painting, and the two chapels to the right of the choir were frescoed entirely by Giotto and two others by his pupils while the nave was under construction. The timber roof, recalling that at

Monreale (see fig. 407), retains its original Gothic painted decoration.

An entirely different problem was presented by the Cathedral of Florence (fig. 498), which has so long and so complex a building history that its final appearance can be attributed to no single architect. A fairly large structure was planned by the architect Arnolfo di Cambio in 1296, with choir and apse-shaped transept arms radiating outward from a central octagonal dome. In the main Arnolfo's plan was followed but much expanded by the architects who, under close supervision of a commission, commenced building from the final design in 1368 (fig. 499). The colossal interior is only four bays long, and the impression so simple and bare in comparison with the complexity and mystery of French interiors that it is a surprise to discover that the height of the vaults is approximately the same as at Amiens. The compound piers are cubic rather than cylindrical as in France, and their foliate capitals are treated as cubes of ornament. Pilasters continue above the giant arches to the catwalk supported on brackets required by the commission of 1368, which also insisted that the vaults spring directly from the level of the catwalk, thus canceling out any considerable clerestory. The interior, therefore, appears as one enormous story, lighted by oculi in the lunettes under the vaults. Walking through the building, one experiences immense cubes of space, which, as soon as their size becomes apparent, are dwarfed by the grandeur of the octagonal central space under the dome, from which the three half-octagonal apses radiate. The vaults are strongly domic and exert strong outward thrust. In the absence of flying buttresses, tie rods had to be installed.

The simple, cubic exterior masses of the nave (fig. 500) and the more complex forms of the semidomes surrounding the central octagon were paneled in white, green, and rose marbles to harmonize with the Baptistery. The separate campanile, also paneled in marbles, was commenced by Giotto, who designed only the lower two stories; the much richer upper five stories are the work of Francesco Talenti in the middle of the fourteenth century. At the opening of the fifteenth century (so uncertain was the art of building), no one in Florence had the faintest idea how the octagonal central space could be covered. How *that* problem was solved is one of the dramas of the Early Renaissance (See Vol. 2, Part Four, Chapter 1).

Perhaps because of the long tradition of Early Christian basilicas in Italy, the two-tower façade, universal in France and common throughout England, Spain, and Germany, was almost never adopted in Italy. In fact, the building of any sort of façade often lagged behind the construction of the rest of the church. Not one of the major churches of Florence received its façade during the period of its original construction; those of the Cathedral and Santa Croce were added only in the nineteenth century. But the Cathedral of Siena, the independent merchant republic forty miles to the south of Florence,

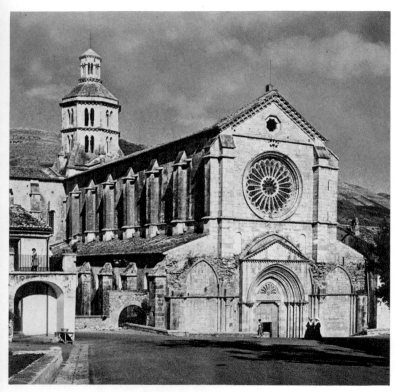

496. Abbey Church of Fossanova. Begun 1187. Italy

was given a dazzling marble façade in Gothic style that shows certain standard features of Gothic facades in other Italian cities, and gives some notion of what that of the Cathedral of Florence might have looked like had it been completed in the Gothic period. The lower half of the Siena façade (fig. 501) was designed—probably in the late 1280s—by Giovanni Pisano, whom we shall encounter later as one of the two leading masters of Italian Gothic sculpture (see pages 403, 405).

Giovanni flanked his three gabled portals with rich, tracery turrets, whose black and white marble bases incorporate the striping of the body of the cathedral. The splayed jambs, with their alternating white and rose colonnettes, lack the statues one would have expected by French standards. Giovanni has transferred his figures to more independent positions on the turrets, where they appear to issue from shallow niches, in lively attitudes and even in conversation. This new freedom of the human figure from its architectural bonds is not only symptomatic of the role of the individual in the Italian city-republics but also indicative of the emergence of independent personalities among the artists themselves. From time to time we have encountered artists whose names we know and can associate with specific works outside Italy, and a few (such as Renier de Huy and Nicholas of Verdun) have even assumed a certain individuality in our minds, but they are exceptions. In Italy such instances become the rule. In fact, no decisive figure in painting or sculpture from the fourteenth century—or in any of the three leading arts in succeeding centuries—is unknown to us by name.

In northern Italy the severe architecture of the Lombard Romanesque was replaced in the later fourteenth century by an especially florid phase of Gothic under the domination of the Visconti family, who had made themselves dukes of Milan and had absorbed into a powerful monarchy most of the independent north Italian communes, with the notable exception of the Venetian Republic. The construction of the Cathedral of Milan, one of the largest of all Christian churches, was subject to the committee procedure we have already seen in Florence, carried on, however, not only by north Italian masters but also by builders imported from France and Germany, each of whom brought to bear arguments based on his own national architectural tradition and theory. As in Florence, the colossal project had been commenced (probably in 1386) and the columns partly erected before anyone was certain how high they were going to go or what shape of arches and vaults they would support. The often acrimonious discussions continued, off and on, from 1392 to 1401. An Italian mathematician, Gabriele Stornaloco, subjected the fabric to the governance of an abstract system of expanding equilateral triangles, and one of the French architects, Jean Mignot, summarized his bitter denunciation of Italian methods with the oft-quoted remark, "*Ars sine scientia nihil est.*" This should not be taken to mean literally that art is nothing without science, but rather that practice is meaningless without theory. But that Mignot's theory should include appeals to God on his

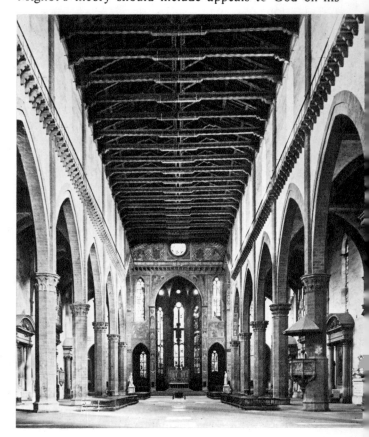

497. Nave and choir, Sta. Croce. Begun c. 1294. Florence

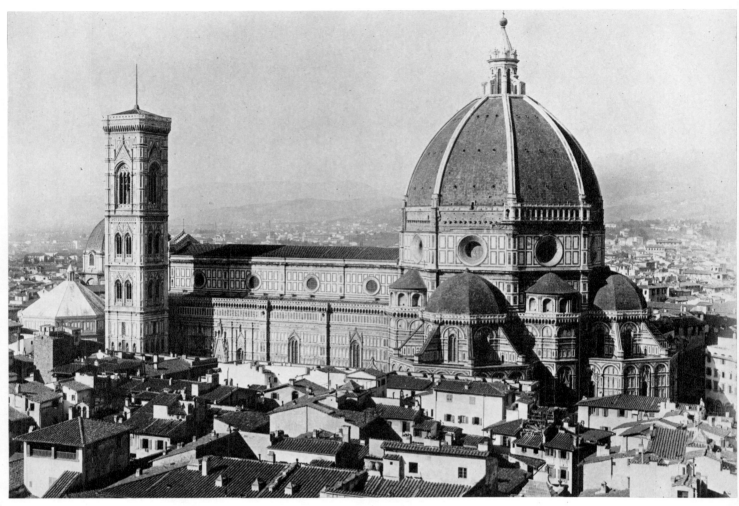

498. Cathedral of Florence. Begun 1368

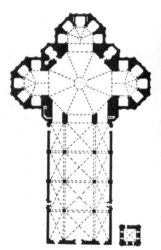

499. Cathedral of Florence.
(Plan after Arnolfo di
Cambio, 1296)

500. Interior, Cathedral
of Florence

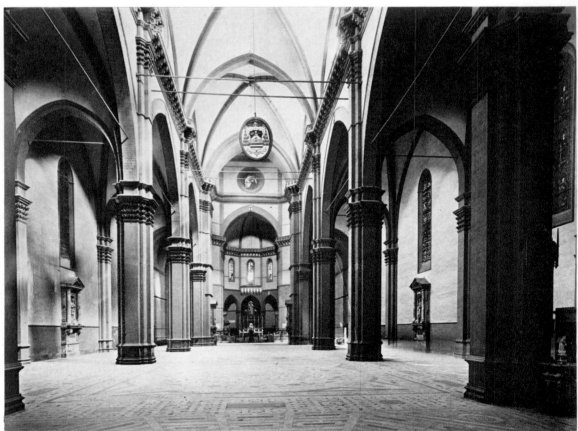

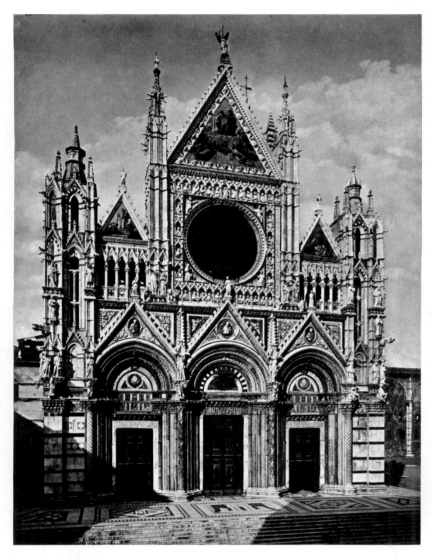

501. Giovanni Pisano.
Façade. Cathedral of
Siena. Begun late 1230s

throne surrounded by the Evangelists demonstrates how far medieval builders were from being able to calculate static problems by what we would recognize as engineering science. The resultant interior (figs. 502, 503) resembles partly the arrangement at Bourges (see fig. 463) with its four side aisles of diminishing heights and partly that at Florence (see fig. 500) with its single colossal story dwarfing a tiny clerestory under the vaults. The clustered columns are surmounted by outsize capitals intended for a host of statues—eight to a column—in the gathering gloom of the arches. The four-part vaulting is based on French High Gothic examples. The exterior (fig. 504) shows the characteristic Italian desire to keep the whole structure within the limits of a block, so that the flying buttresses are invisible from street level. That they were also insufficient is betrayed by the telltale tie rods in the interior. The forest of pinnacles was added in the eighteenth and nineteenth centuries. The Flamboyant windows, on a gigantic scale, would have been totally unacceptable to severe Florentine taste.

Italian communes demanded impressive civic centers, fortified against the chronic disorders of the period. The grandest example is the Palazzo Vecchio at Florence, built in an astonishingly short time, from 1299 to 1310; the Priori (council or cabinet) was actually installed in the building as early as 1302. Its castle-like appearance (fig. 505) carries into large-scale civic architecture the roughly trimmed stone used for town houses in medieval Florence. This technique had a Classical precedent in the rustication of such Roman civic buildings as the Porta Maggiore (see fig. 265). The impression of block mass, relieved only by relatively small Gothic windows, was intended not only for defense but also for psychological effect. The asymmetrical placing of the mighty bell tower was due to the requirements of the site, and not followed elsewhere; yet to modern eyes the result is extremely powerful.

One could hardly imagine a greater difference in appearance than that which distinguishes this mountainous structure from the elegant and largely open Palazzo Ducale (Doges' Palace) in Venice, built for a similar purpose, as the official residence of the doge (the chief magistrate of the Venetian Republic) and the grand council. In spite of the fact that construction continued from 1340 until after 1424, the appearance of the

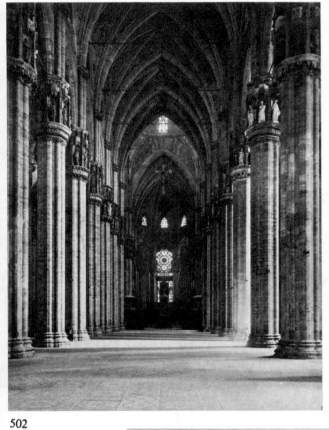

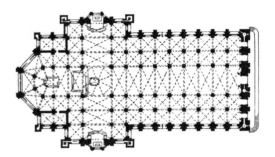

502. Interior, Cathedral of Milan. Begun 1386

503. Plan of the Cathedral of Milan

504. Exterior of choir, Cathedral of Milan

502

504

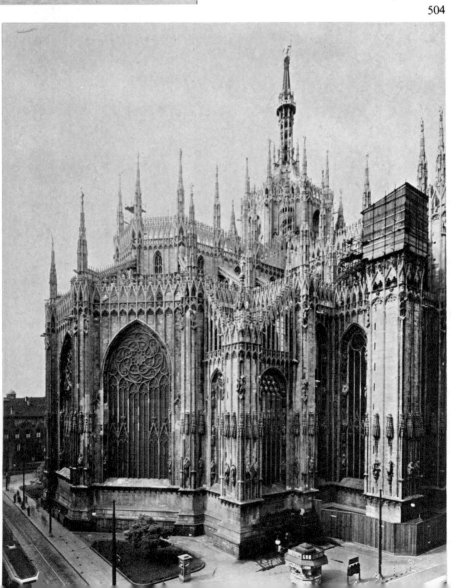

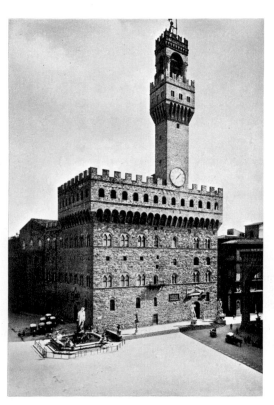

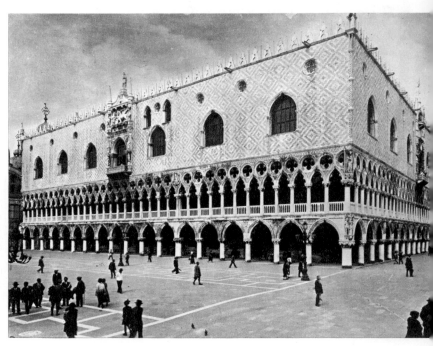

505. Palazzo Vecchio. 1299–1310. Florence

506. Palazzo Ducale (Doges' Palace). 1340–after 1424. Venice

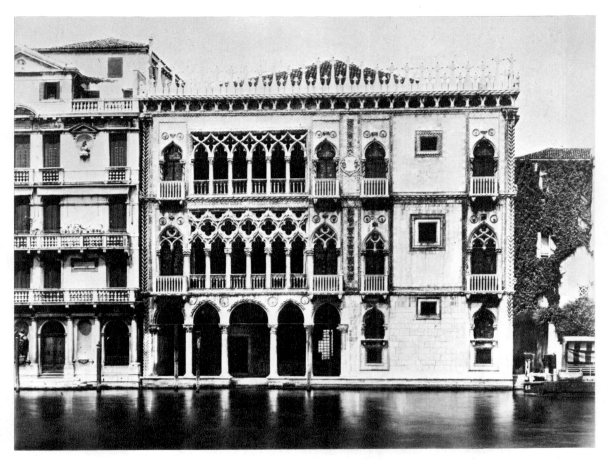

507. Ca' d'Oro. 1422–c. 1440. Venice

building is remarkably unified (fig. 506). A simple arcade of pointed arches on low columns supports a more elaborate loggia (open gallery) on the second story, with twice as many columns under trefoil arches and quatrefoil tracery drawn from the standard High Gothic repertory. The massiveness of the upper story, broken only by pointed-arch windows, is relieved by an allover lozenge pattern of white and rose marble facing. The distinction between Florentine mass on the one hand and Venetian interest in color, texture, and light effects on the other is one we shall see maintained throughout the long history of these two leading Italian schools, especially in painting.

Through the first half of the fifteenth century (the Early Renaissance in Florence), Venetian architecture remained Gothic. The most sumptuous dwelling from this period is the Ca' d'Oro (Golden House) on the Grand Canal (fig. 507), built between 1422 and about 1440. The façade was designed for the effect of glittering white arcades and interlaced arches against dark openings and of walls paneled in softly veined marbles in the Byzantine manner, rather than the hard contrast of white and green used in Tuscany; probably neither the architect nor the patron was oblivious to the beauty of the reflections of all this light and color in the blue-green water below, and the very existence of the open loggias reveals the Venetian

delight in observing from such vantage points the passing spectacle of traffic on the Grand Canal. Insubstantial as such architecture may seem in comparison with the severity of the Florentine palaces built at the same time for the same class of wealthy merchants (see Vol. 2, figs. 28, 31), it looks compact and unified in contrast to the free improvisation of shapes in the almost contemporary house of Jacques Coeur at Bourges (see fig. 479).

GOTHIC SCULPTURE AND PAINTING IN ITALY

NICOLA AND GIOVANNI PISANO. Two extremely original sculptors, Nicola Pisano (active 1258–78) and his son Giovanni (c. 1250–c. 1314) (whom we have already encountered as the principal architect of the façade of Siena Cathedral), embody sharply different phases of the rather tardy change from Romanesque to Gothic style in Italian sculpture. Although Nicola's name indicates his Pisan citizenship, he came to Tuscany from southern Italy, where since the days of Frederick II (reigned 1215–50), more Italian king than German emperor, there had flourished a strong current of interest in ancient art. Nicola's first great work was the hexagonal marble pulpit in the Baptistery at Pisa (fig. 508),

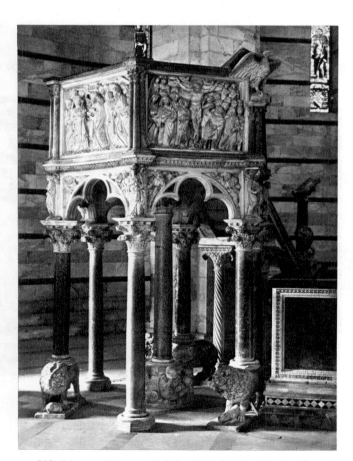

508. NICOLA PISANO. Pulpit. 1259–60. Marble, height c. 15'. Baptistery, Pisa

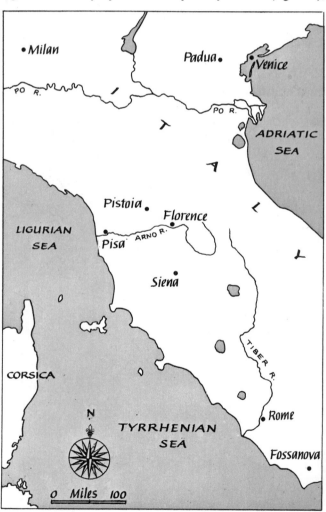

MAP 22. *Romanesque and Gothic Italy*

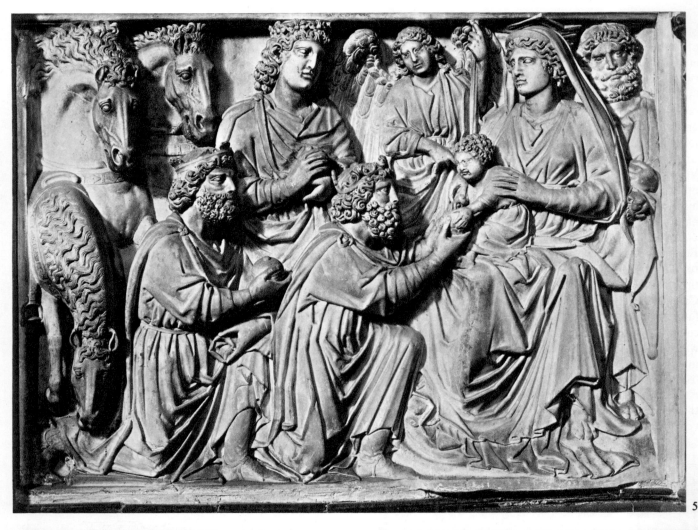

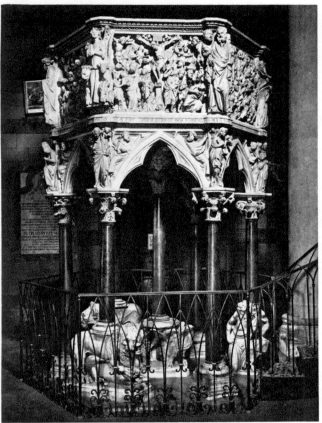

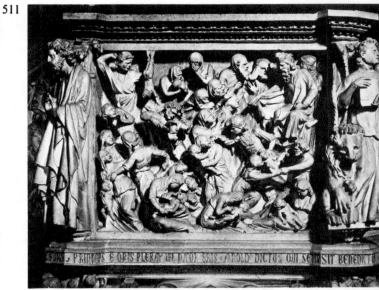

509. NICOLA PISANO. *Adoration of the Magi* (detail of the pulpit at Pisa). Marble relief

510. GIOVANNI PISANO. Pulpit. 1298–1301. Marble. Sant'Andrea, Pistoia, Italy

511. GIOVANNI PISANO. *Slaughter of the Innocents* (detail of the pulpit at Pistoia). Marble relief, 33 x 40″

signed with a long, self-laudatory inscription in 1260. Sculptured pulpits were traditional in Italy; that one could be needed in a baptistery may indicate the special importance of the sacrament of Baptism in the Italian republics as the moment in which a child took his place in the Christian community. Nicola's handsome creation combines elements already familiar from central Italian medieval art, such as columns of red porphyry, red and gray granite, and richly veined brown marble with Gothic trefoil arches. The capitals, partly Corinthian, partly Gothic, seem to partake of both styles. Like his earlier namesake Nicholas of Verdun and like the Visitation Master at Reims, Nicola had a strong interest in ancient art. Luckily, he had no dearth of models in Pisa. The close packing of forms filling the entire frame of the *Adoration of the Magi* (fig. 509) recalls the density of Roman sarcophagus relief, and in fact Nicola repeated almost exactly the pose of a seated figure in a sarcophagus still in the Campo Santo in Pisa for his Virgin, who has become a Roman Juno, impassive and grand. The carving of the beards of the Magi and the parallel drapery folds of all the figures also recall Roman examples (see figs. 256, 294), but the angular breaking of the folds betrays Nicola's familiarity with Byzantine mosaic art (see colorplate 38).

Giovanni, who claims in inscriptions to have outdone his father, was responsible for a sharply different octagonal pulpit at Pistoia (fig. 510), dated 1298–1301, distinguished by its greater Gothicism in the sharp pointing of the arches as well as in the freer shapes of the foliate capitals, which only here and there disclose Classical derivations. As we would expect from his unconventional shapes and animated statuary for the Siena façade, Giovanni's sculptural style is far more dramatic than his father's serene manner, and shows almost no interest in Classical art. Instead, the relaxed poses and free, full drapery folds of the corner statues suggest a familiarity with the portal sculptures of Amiens and Reims; Giovanni's inscriptions proclaim him as a traveler, and in all probability he visited the great French cathedrals. In the *Slaughter of the Innocents* (fig. 511), a panel of the Pistoia pulpit, he shows himself the master of a free narrative style, depending for its effect on rapid, even violent movement of ferocious soldiers and screaming mothers, and considerable undercutting, which produces sharp contrasts of light and dark. The expressive power of Giovanni's style is brought under firm control, possibly in emulation of the great painter Giotto, in the marble statue of the *Virgin and Child* (fig. 512), which Giovanni carved about 1305 for the altar of the Arena Chapel in Padua, whose walls and ceiling were being frescoed by Giotto (see figs. 515, 516, colorplate 70). The boldness of the masses, the clarity of the contours, and the firmness of the pose of Giovanni's *Madonna* should be compared with the elegance and lassitude of the almost contemporary *Virgin of Paris* (see fig. 480).

Changes in thirteenth-century religious ritual gave rise to the demand for a new kind of image—of immense importance for the development of art, especially painting—the altarpiece. Until now the Mass had been celebrated, as again in the Roman Catholic Church since Vatican II, behind the altar, with the priest facing the congregation, which precluded the placing of anything more than the required crucifix, candlesticks, and sacred vessels upon the altar. In the course of the century, the celebrant's position was moved to the front of the altar, thus freeing the back of the altar for the development of imagery, both sculptural and pictorial. Although the icon, that all-important focus of Byzantine devotion, had been imported into the West in the early Middle Ages, it had not taken root. But in the thirteenth century, large-scale painted crucifixes, which had already been used in other positions in Italian churches, began to appear on altars. Soon the Madonna and Child competed for this prominent place, and eventually won. The altarpieces, which rapidly grew to considerable size so as to be visible to the congregation, were painted in a technique known as tempera, with egg yolk used as the vehicle. The procedure was slow and exacting. A wooden panel had to be carefully prepared and coated with gesso (fine plaster mixed with glue) as a ground for the underdrawing. Gold leaf was applied to the entire background, and then the figures and accessories were painted with a fine brush. As egg dries fast and does not permit corrections, the painter's craft called for accurate and final decisions at every stage. Under the impulse of this new demand, and

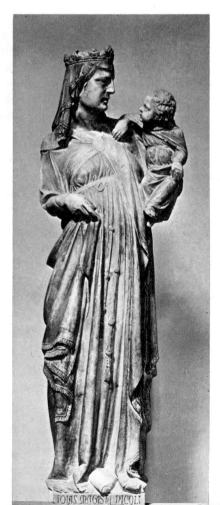

512. GIOVANNI PISANO. *Virgin and Child.* c. 1305. Marble. Altar, Arena Chapel, Padua

spurred by the intense political and economic life of the Tuscan republics, painting rapidly developed in a direction that had no Northern counterparts until the *Wilton Diptych* (see colorplate 68).

CIMABUE. Although at least two generations of Tuscan painters had preceded him in the thirteenth century, the first Italian painter known to Vasari was the Florentine Cenni di Pepi, called Cimabue (active c. 1272–1302). About 1280 Cimabue painted the *Madonna Enthroned* (fig. 513), an altarpiece more than eleven feet high, which in Vasari's day stood on the altar of Santa Trinita in Florence. The derivation of Cimabue's style from that of the Greek painters with whom Vasari said he worked is clear enough in the poses of the Virgin and the Child (cf. fig. 426) and also in the gold-striated patterns of their drapery folds, which resemble those of the *Pantocrator* at Cefalù (see fig. 438). But in the delicate modeling of the faces and drapery of the angels, Cimabue also shows his familiarity with the refined Constantinopolitan style of his own time (see fig. 442). Clearly, Cimabue was trying to rival in paint the monumental effects of Byzantine mosaics, but the gabled shape of his huge altarpiece is unknown in the East, as is the complex construction of the carved and inlaid throne; the effect is that of strong verticality, increased by the constant flicker of color in the angels' rainbow wings.

CAVALLINI. A Roman contemporary of Cimabue, Pietro Cavallini (active 1273–after 1308), was certainly familiar with such advanced Byzantine works as the frescoes at Sopočani (see fig. 440), which show an extraordinary advance in the interrelationship of light and form. Cavallini's fragmentary fresco of the *Last Judgment* of about 1290 in Santa Cecilia in Trastevere in Rome (colorplate 69), impossible to photograph as a whole because of a gallery later built in front of it, carries the knowledge of the effects of light to a point inaccessible to Cimabue. Light and light alone brings out the fullness and sweep of the mantles that envelop these majestic figures. Their heads, however, especially those of the beardless Apostle in the center and the bearded James (?) on the right, show a familiarity with French Gothic sculpture, such as the *Saint Theodore* at Chartres (see fig. 461) and the *Beau Dieu* at Amiens (see fig. 474).

GIOTTO. The final break with Byzantine tradition was accomplished by Giotto di Bondone (c. 1267–1337), the first giant in the long history of Italian painting. Even in his own day Giotto's greatness was recognized by his contemporaries. Dante puts in the mouth of a painter in *Purgatory* (XI, 94–96) his famous remark:

Cimabue believed that he held the field
In painting, and now Giotto has the cry,
So that the fame of the former is obscure.

The *Chronicles* of the historian Giovanni Villani (d. 1348) list Giotto as one of the great men of the Florentine

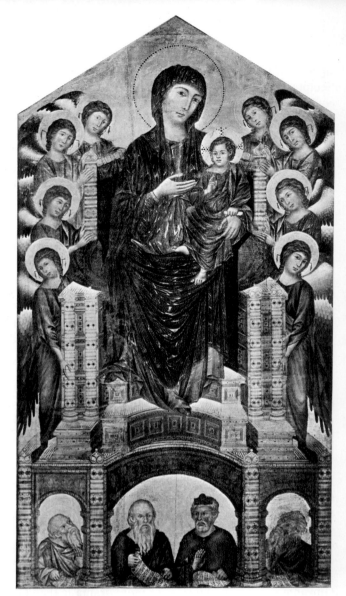

513. CIMABUE. *Madonna Enthroned*, from Sta. Trinita, Florence. c. 1280. Tempera on panel, 12'7½" x 7'4". Galleria degli Uffizi, Florence

Republic, a position such as had been accorded to no other artist since the days of ancient Greece. The sources also indicate wherein Giotto's greatness was thought to lie. Vasari summed up Italian estimates when he said that Giotto revived the art of painting, which had declined in Italy because of many invasions, and that since Giotto continued to "derive from Nature, he deserves to be called the pupil of Nature and no other." Cennino Cennini, a third-generation follower of Giotto, wrote in his *Book on Art*, a manual on technical methods, that Giotto had translated painting from Greek into Latin.

A comparison of Giotto's *Madonna and Child Enthroned* (fig. 514) of about 1310 with its counterpart by Cimabue will test these traditional observations. Nature, in the modern sense of the word, would hardly enter our minds in connection with Giotto's picture any more than with Cimabue's. Both are ceremonial representations of the Virgin as Queen of Heaven, remote from ordinary experience, and both rule out distant space by the use of a

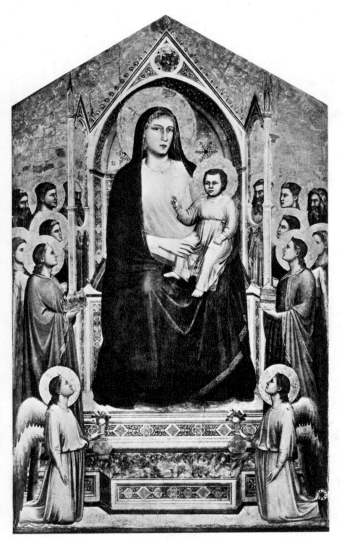

514. GIOTTO. *Madonna and Child Enthroned*, from
the Church of the Ognissanti, Florence. c. 1310.
Tempera on panel, 10'8" x 6'8¼". Galleria
degli Uffizi, Florence

traditional gold background. But in contemporary
Italian eyes the step from Cimabue to Giotto was immense in that weight and mass, light and inward extension were suddenly introduced in a direct and convincing
manner. In contrast to Cimabue's fantastic throne, which
needs a steadying hand from the attendant angels, Giotto's structure is firmly placed above a marble step, which
can be climbed, and the Virgin sits firmly within it. The
poses of the angels kneeling in the foreground are so
solid, in comparison to the uncertain placing of
Cimabue's angels, that we are willing to believe that the
angels and saints behind them, on either side of the
throne, stand just as securely. Light, still diffused and
without indication of source, models the forms so strongly that they resemble sculptural masses. By translating
painting from Greek into Latin, Cennini meant that
Giotto had abandoned Byzantine models in favor of
Western ones, and in the early fourteenth century those
could only have been French cathedral statues. Not only

do Giotto's facial types and drapery motives recall the
sculptures at Chartres, Reims, and Amiens, but also the
Virgin's throne is set in an aedicula whose pointed central
arch, trefoil side arches, and culminating pinnacles are
taken directly from the French architectural repertory.
Giotto's miracle lay in being able to produce for the first
time on a flat surface three-dimensional forms, which the
French could achieve only in sculpture. Effects of
shoulders and knees showing through drapery masses, of
the Child's body and legs, and of the Virgin's hand
holding his thigh are at every point convincing. For the
first time since antiquity a painter has truly conquered
solid form. Giotto did not, however, adopt as yet a
naturalistic scale. The Virgin and Child are represented
as almost twice the size of the attendant figures.

Cennini tells us that the painting of frescoes was the
most agreeable of all pictorial activities. The technique
he describes was probably based on that of Roman
painting as handed down through the ages. The painter
first prepared the wall with a layer of rough plaster, on
which he proceeded to draw with the brush (probably on
the basis of preliminary sketches) the figures and background in a mixture of red earth and water known as
sinopia (see fig. 525). Over this preparatory drawing he
laid on as much smooth plaster as he could paint in a day,
and painted it while wet so that the color in its water vehicle would amalgamate with the plaster. The following
day he added another section, covering up the sinopia as
he went. This procedure meant that the fresco was literally built section by section, and acquired a solidity of composition and surface handling that would preclude such
spontaneous painting technique as that of Castelseprio
(see fig. 425) or Nerezi (see fig. 439) or even the broad,
fluid manner of the Kariye Djami (see colorplate 60).

Giotto's masterpiece is the cycle of frescoes illustrating
the life of the Virgin and the life of Christ, dating from
1305–6, which lines the entire interior of the Arena
Chapel in Padua in northern Italy, not far from Venice.
Here he shows the full range of his naturalism in a new
kind of pictorial drama for which nothing we have seen in
the history of art could prepare us. In one of the early
scenes, Joachim, father of the Virgin, takes refuge with
shepherds in the wilderness after his expulsion from the
Temple because of his childlessness (colorplate 70).
Humiliated, his head bowed, he stands before two
shepherds, one of whom scans his companion's face to
see whether they dare receive the outcast. The subtlety of
the psychological interplay is enriched by Giotto's
delicate observation of the sheep crowding out of the
sheepfold and of the dog, symbol of fidelity in the Middle
Ages as today, who leaps in joyful greeting.

As in the *Madonna*, Giotto recognizes one scale for the
figures, another for the surroundings, including the
animals and the sheepfold. Cennini recounts that to paint
a mountainous landscape one need only bring a rock into
the studio, and that a branch could do duty for a tree.
The results of this principle show that Giotto, for all his

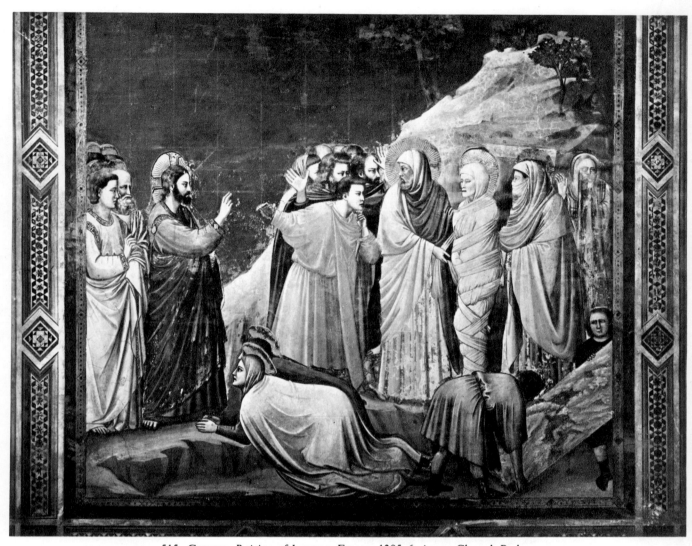

515. GIOTTO. *Raising of Lazarus.* Fresco. 1305-6. Arena Chapel, Padua

ability to project three-dimensional form, is far from accepting the notion of visual unity. His landscape, however, has an expressive purpose; the rock behind Joachim bends along with his head, and the jagged edges toward the center underscore the division between him and the shepherds. The cubic rocks form a definite stage in space, limited by the blue background, which, like that at the Kariye Djami (see colorplate 60), does not represent the sky—there are no clouds—but is an ideal, heavenly color continuing behind all the scenes and covering the barrel vault above. In order to emphasize the three-dimensionality of the columnar figure of Joachim, Giotto has designed his halo foreshortened in perspective.

In the *Raising of Lazarus* (fig. 515) the composition divides into two groups: one centered around Lazarus, who has just risen from the tomb, still wrapped in graveclothes, is read together with the rock; the other, beginning with the prostrate Mary and Martha, culminates in Christ, who calls the dead man forth by a single gesture of his right hand against the blue. Giotto's Christ strongly resembles the *Beau Dieu* of Amiens (see

fig. 474) even to the pose and the gesture. His calm authority is contrasted with the astonishment of the surrounding figures. But the Byzantine tradition is by no means forgotten; the arrangement of figures in the *Lamentation* (fig. 516) owes a debt to the tradition exemplified at Nerezi (see fig. 439). But Giotto has enriched the dialogue between life and death with all the subtlety of his psychological observation. Instead of an explosion of grief, he has staged a flawlessly organized tragedy, the equal of Sophocles or Shakespeare in its many-faceted analysis of a human situation. Each figure grieves in the manner possible to his individual personality—John, the beloved disciple, most deeply of all. Giotto has added to the scene anonymous mourners who turn their eloquent backs to us; one upholds Christ's head, the other his right hand. Instead of pressing her face impulsively to that of her son as at Nerezi, Mary, with one arm around Christ's shoulder, searches his countenance, conscious of the widening gulf of death. Only the angels are released to cry in pure grief, each half-hidden in clouds—the only ones that appear in the Chapel—to show that they are supernatural.

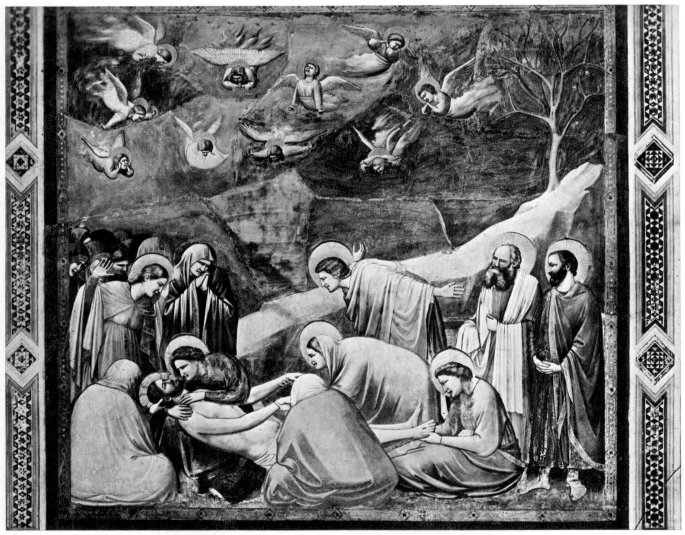

516. GIOTTO. *Lamentation.* Fresco. 1305–6. Arena Chapel, Padua

Giotto's brushwork remains as calm in this scene as in any other. He achieved his effect not only by the grouping of the figures but also by the inexorable diagonal line of the rocks, descending toward the faces of Mary and Christ, its course weighted by the downward tug of the drapery folds. At the upper right, as if to typify the desolation of the scene, a leafless tree stands against the blue. Giotto surely expected his audience to remember that, according to medieval legend, the Tree of Knowledge was withered after the sin of Adam and Eve and made fruitful again after the sacrifice of Christ, and that Christ himself was believed to have alluded to this doctrine on his way to Calvary: "For if they do these things in a green tree, what shall be done in the dry?" (Luke 23: 31).

GADDI. Giotto indeed had the cry; within a decade after his great works made their appearance, the style of Cimabue had been relegated to country churches, and Giotto, his many pupils, and still more numerous

followers dominated the Florentine scene. One of the closest of his pupils, Taddeo Gaddi (active c. 1330–c 1366), although he could never approach the heights of Giotto's achievements, continued some aspects of his style, especially in the representation of light, perhaps under the master's personal direction, in his frescoes in the Baroncelli Chapel of Santa Croce in Florence, probably dating from 1332–38. In the fourteenth century natural light was always diffused and generalized, without indication of a specific source. But Taddeo has shown the traditional scene of the *Annunciation to the Shepherds* (fig. 517; for earlier medieval representations, see colorplate 55, fig. 387) as a revelation of light, which in a long Christian tradition symbolizes the second person of the Trinity (see the discussion of the Cefalù mosaics, pages 359–362). After all, every Christian knew the sublime words of John 1: 4–5:

In him was life; and the life was the light of men.
And the light shineth in darkness; and the darkness comprehended it not.

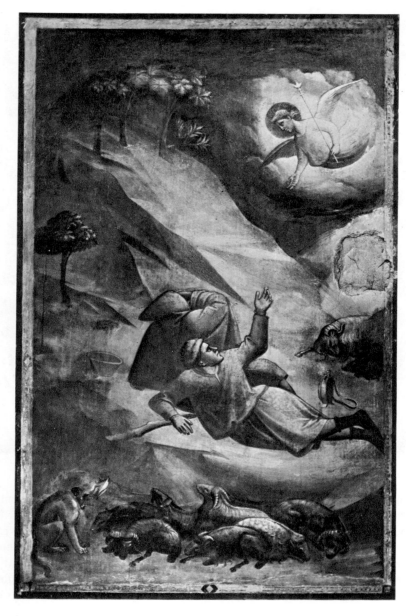

517. TADDEO GADDI.
Annunciation to the Shepherds.
Fresco. c. 1332-38.
Baroncelli Chapel,
Sta. Croce, Florence

As a devoted Giotto follower, Taddeo never represents natural light, but he presents the announcing angel in the midst of a wonderful display of light, which descends upon the shepherds who have fallen to the ground in amazement and lights the whole dark landscape with its radiance. We are here experiencing the reversal of the process by which, at the beginning of the Middle Ages, the illusionistic art of the Helleno-Roman tradition was transformed into the otherworldly art of Byzantium. Techniques derived from naturalistic painting were used at Sinai to represent supernatural light (see colorplate 39 and pages 268, 269). Now, at the end of the Middle Ages, that same spiritual light is used to aid the artist in the rediscovery of material reality.

DUCCIO. In Siena the Byzantine tradition continued into the fourteenth century and was refined to the ultimate in the work of Duccio di Buoninsegna (active 1278–1318). His great altarpiece, the *Maestà* (*Madonna in Majesty*), more than thirteen feet in length, was started in 1308 for the high altar of the Cathedral of Siena. It was considered such a triumph for the artist and such an important contribution to the welfare of the Sienese Republic (whose patron saint was the Virgin) that on its completion in 1311 it was carried at the head of a procession of dignitaries and townspeople from Duccio's studio to the Cathedral, to the ringing of church bells and the sound of trumpets. The high altar was freestanding, so that the back of the altarpiece and even its pinnacles were covered

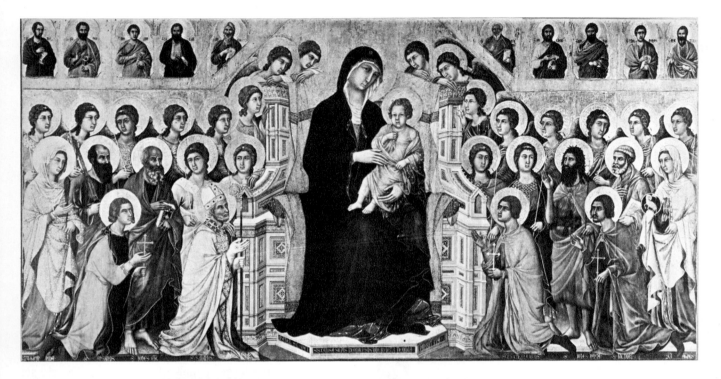

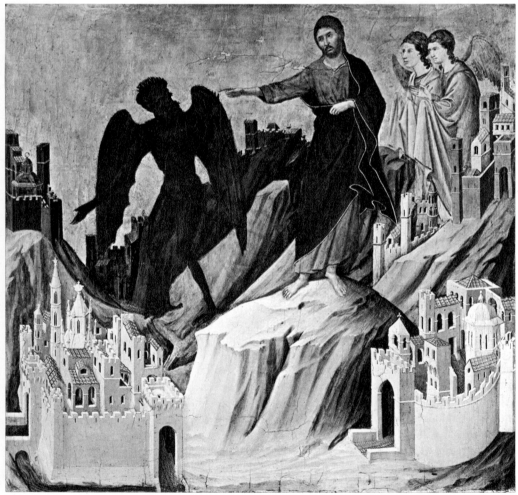

518. DUCCIO.
*Virgin as Queen
of Heaven*,
center panel of
the *Maestà* altarpiece.
from the Cathedral
of Siena. 1308-11.
Panel painting, 7 x 13'.
Museo dell'Opera
del Duomo. Siena

519. DUCCIO.
*Temptation of
Christ* (detail of the
back predella of
the *Maestà* altarpiece).
from the Cathedral
of Siena. 1308-11.
Panel painting, 17 x
18⅛". © The Frick
Collection, New York

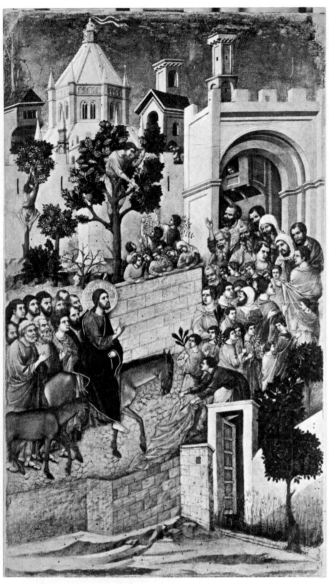

520. DUCCIO. *Entry into Jerusalem* (detail of the back predella of the *Maestà* altarpiece), from the Cathedral of Siena. 1308–11. Panel painting. 40 x 21″. Museo dell'Opera del Duomo, Siena

faces are Byzantine, their small almond eyes bear no relation to the lustrous orbs of the saints in most Byzantine mosaics, frescoes, and icons.

Although Duccio accepted neither Giotto's cubic rocks nor his columnar figures, and although he could not achieve Giotto's subtlety of psychological observation, he was an artist of great individuality, especially in the handling of landscape elements, as can be seen in the *Temptation of Christ* (fig. 519), once a part of the *Maestà*. The kingdoms of the world, shown to Christ by Satan, were depicted by Duccio, a good republican Sienese, as seven little city-states crowded into a panel not quite eighteen inches square. Obviously, they derive from the late Roman and Early Christian tradition of little nugget-cities, but each one is different, with its own houses, public buildings, city gates, and towers, all modeled in a consistent light. If we are willing to accept the medieval convention of the double scale for figures and setting, we must admit that within it Duccio was very successful in indicating the scope and sweep of landscape, which soon became Siena's great contribution to the history of art.

In one of the larger panels of the *Maestà*, Duccio set the stage, as it were, for the *Entry into Jerusalem* (fig. 520) in the suburban orchards outside the walls of Siena. We look over trees, garden walls, and a gate in the foreground to the road moving uphill, more garden walls on the other side, the city gates, and houses fronting a street. The towering octagonal building is the Temple, combining travelers' tales of the Dome of the Rock (see colorplate 44), built on the site of the Temple, with the familiar outlines of the Baptistery of Florence (see colorplate 52). This setting, of unexampled spatial complexity, Duccio filled with more than fifty people, all sharply individualized (within the range of Byzantine-Sienese facial types), from the solemn Christ mounted on an ass to the excited populace and children climbing trees, including some inhabitants looking out of windows and over the city wall.

SIMONE MARTINI. Duccio's pupil, Simone Martini (active 1315–44), while fully abreast of all his master could achieve in the realm of landscape and urban settings, finally broke with the Byzantine tradition in favor of the more fashionable courtly French Gothic style of the early fourteenth century. He worked for the French king Robert of Anjou at Naples and brought back to Siena the latest French imports. Even more than the *Maestà* of Duccio, Simone's *Annunciation* (fig. 521) is a condensed cathedral façade, Gothic this time, with all the richness of Flamboyant double curvature, which had not as yet made its appearance in the architecture of Giovanni Pisano. The angel Gabriel is dressed magnificently in white and gold brocade with a floating, plaid-lined mantle, and the Virgin's blue mantle is edged with a deep gold border. The swirling drapery rhythms recall the curvilinear exaggerations of the *Virgin of Paris* (see fig. 480)

with a cycle of scenes from the life of Christ even more complete than that Giotto had just painted for the Arena Chapel. In the sixteenth century the altarpiece was taken down and partially dismembered; panels are scattered throughout the world, but most remain in Siena. The central panel shows the Virgin as Queen of Heaven (fig. 518), adored by her court of kneeling and standing saints and angels and half-length prophets in the arches above—a sort of cathedral façade in paint. And though the pose of the Virgin and Child shows that Duccio is still working in the Byzantine tradition, nonetheless, he has learned from the works of Giovanni Pisano new and Gothic ways to handle flowing masses of drapery and dense crowds of figures. While the oval shapes of the

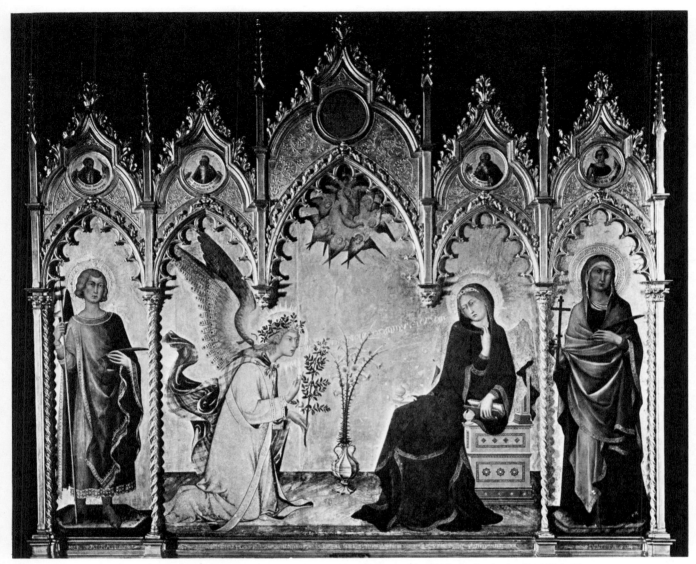

521. SIMONE MARTINI. *Annunciation.* 1333. Panel painting, 10' x 8'9". Galleria degli Uffizi, Florence

rather than the controlled shapes of cathedral statues. The angel's message, *Ave gratia plena dominus tecum* ("Hail, thou that art highly favored, the Lord is with thee"; Luke 1: 28) is embossed on the gold background. Mary, "troubled at his saying," recoils elegantly, her face clouded with apprehension. This is an extraordinary and unexpected style, but graceful in the extreme, with all the characteristic Sienese fluency of line translated from Byzantine Greek into Flamboyant French.

THE LORENZETTI. Giotto's new devices reached Sienese painting in the work of two brothers, Pietro (c. 1280–1348?) and Ambrogio (c. 1285–1348?) Lorenzetti, who, nonetheless, continued independently the Sienese tradition of the exploration of landscape and architectural settings, and brought Sienese painting to a position of absolute leadership in Europe during the decade following Giotto's death. In Pietro's *Birth of the Virgin* of 1342, for

the Cathedral of Siena, we are aware of Giotto's cubic space and columnar figures (fig. 522), but Pietro has taken a significant step in the direction of illusionism. The gold background is eliminated save where it peeks through a tiny window at the left. The architectural setting has been identified with the actual carved shape of the frame, which it was customary for the artist himself to design and which was usually built and attached to the panel before the process of painting was begun. The picture thus becomes a little stage into which we can look, so that we cannot help wondering from the illustration what is carved and what is painted. Pietro's altarpiece is a pioneer attempt to build up the consistent interior space that never seems to have occurred to the Romans. His perspective is not entirely consistent, but the upper and lower portions of the interior are drawn so that the parallel lines in each converge to a single separate vanishing point. An enormous step has been taken in the

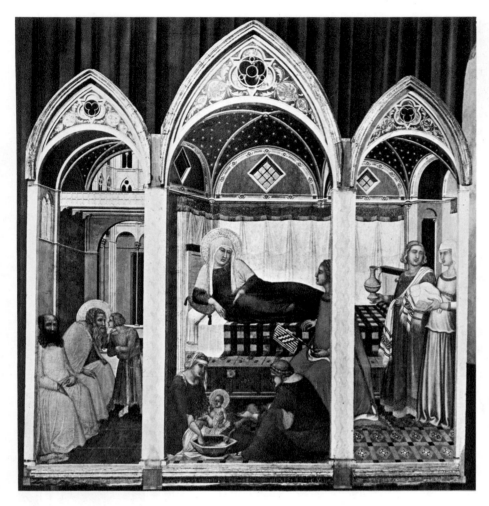

522. PIETRO LORENZETTI.
Birth of the Virgin.
1342. Panel painting,
73½ x 72½". Museo
dell'Opera del
Duomo, Siena

direction of the unified perspective space of the Renaissance (see Vol. 2, Masaccio, fig. 57; Donatello, fig. 42).

Not even Pietro's formulation of interior space is quite as startling as what Ambrogio had already achieved in the fresco representing the effects of Good Government in city and country (colorplate 71, fig. 523), a panorama that fills one entire wall of a council chamber in the Palazzo Pubblico (the Sienese counterpart of the Florentine Palazzo Vecchio), so extensive in fact that it cannot be shown in one photograph. Ambrogio has assumed the high point of view taken by Duccio for his exterior scenes, but he has immensely expanded it. On the right we look over the zigzag line of the city wall into open squares and streets lined with houses, palaces, and towers, some still under construction (note the masons at work under the center beam). At the upper left can barely be made out the campanile and dome of the Cathedral. Richly dressed Sienese burghers and their wives ride by on horseback; one horse has already half-disappeared down a street in the center. The three arches of the building in the foreground contain (from left to right) a shoe shop, a school with a teacher at a desk on a platform and a row of pupils, and a wineshop with a little bar in front. Groups of happy citizens dance in the street.

To the right, under a friendly floating near-nude labeled *Securitas*, who brandishes a scroll with one hand and a loaded gallows with the other, the city people ride downhill into the country and the country people walk uphill into the city. The view of the countryside is amazing: roads, hills, farms and orchards with peasants hard at work, a lake, a country chapel, villas and castles, hills beyond hills, stretching to the horizon. But just where we would expect a blue sky with clouds, Ambrogio drops the Iron Curtain and reminds us that we are still in the Middle Ages. The background is a uniform gray black. This encyclopedic view of the Sienese world and everything in it is an exciting preview of the Renaissance, but there it stops. The Black Death, an epidemic of the bubonic plague that swept Europe in 1348, killed from half to two-thirds of the populations of Florence and Siena, probably including Ambrogio and Pietro Lorenzetti, and put an end to such explorations.

TRAINI. The frescoes representing the *Triumph of Death* in the Campo Santo at Pisa, probably the work of a local master named Francesco Traini (active c. 1321–63), are doubtless a reflection of the universal gloom following the Black Death. In this panorama (fig. 524), very different from the carefree world of Ambrogio Lorenzet-

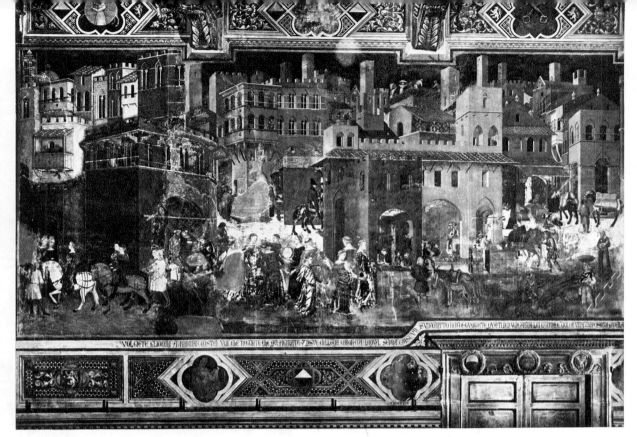

523. AMBROGIO LORENZETTI. *Allegory of Good Government: the Effects of Good Government in the City and the Country* (portion of fresco). 1338–39. Sala della Pace, Palazzo Pubblico, Siena

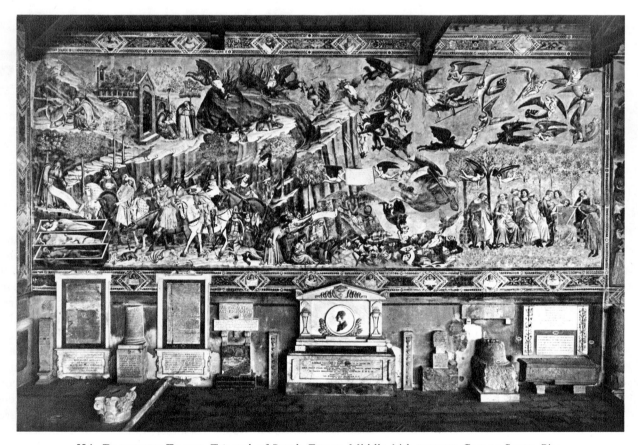

524. FRANCESCO TRAINI. *Triumph of Death*. Fresco. Middle 14th century. Campo Santo, Pisa

ti, no one escapes. At the left three richly dressed couples on horseback, out a-hunting, come upon three open coffins containing corpses in varying stages of putrefaction, a common enough sight in 1348; they draw back in consternation, one rider holding his nose. At the right in a grove of orange trees sits a happy group of gentlemen and ladies, engaged in music and conversation, reminding us of Boccaccio's *Decameron*, written at the time of the Black Death. They seem not to see Death, a winged, white-haired hag, sweeping down on them with a scythe. In the air above angels and demons are in conflict over human souls, and the rocky path to the upper left leads to hermits' cells, as if to demonstrate that the only road to salvation is retreat from the world. The severe damage suffered by these frescoes in World War II necessitated the detachment from the wall of all those that still adhered; underneath was found the most extensive series of sinopias then known (fig. 525), which shows the boldness and freedom of brushwork, recalling Byzantine painting, that underlie the meticulous finish of four-teenth-century frescoes.

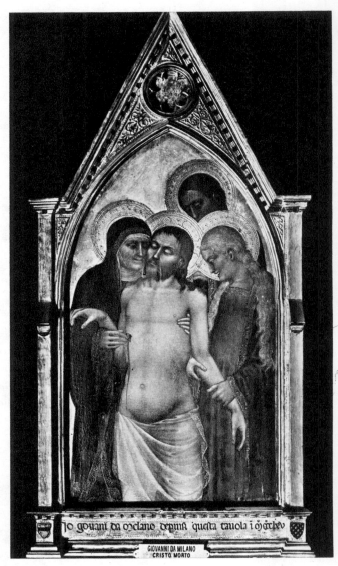

526. GIOVANNI DA MILANO. *Pietà*. 1365. Panel painting, 48 x 22¾". Galleria dell'Accademia, Florence

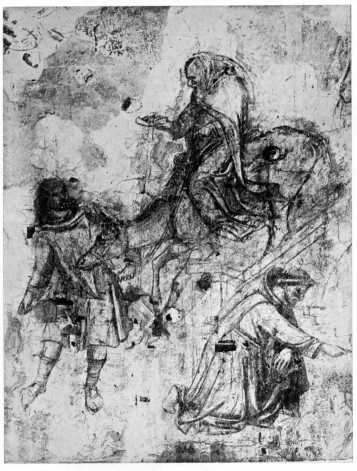

525. FRANCESCO TRAINI. *Triumph of Death* (detail of sinopia)

GIOVANNI DA MILANO. In the wake of the Black Death, no new figures emerged of anything near the stature of the great masters of the early fourteenth century, but some painters showed new observations and insights. One of the most gifted was Giovanni da Milano (active 1346–66), a Lombard working in Florence, where in 1365 he signed a new kind of image, a *Pietà* (fig. 526), from the Italian word for both *pity* and *piety*, both of which it was intended to excite. The intensified religious life of Italy after the catastrophe required new images, which would draw from biblical sources figures, situations, and emotions rather than narrative incidents and recombine them in timeless configurations designed to strengthen the reciprocal emotional bond between sacred figures and the individual worshiper. In an attempt at once to arouse the sympathies of the observer and to demonstrate to him

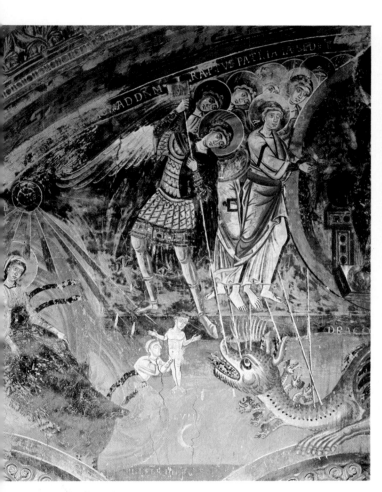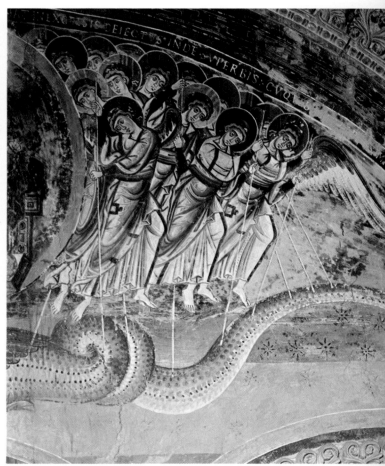

COLORPLATE 53.   Romanesque. *Christ Enthroned with the Archangel Michael Battling a Dragon*. Wall painting. Late 11th–early 12th century. S. Pietro al Monte, Civate, Italy

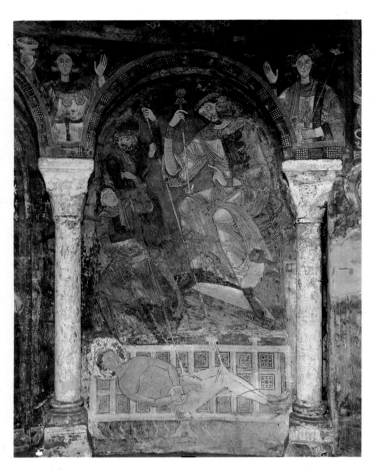

COLORPLATE 54.
Romanesque. *Martyrdom of Saint Lawrence.* Wall painting. Early 12th century. Cluniac Priory Church, Berzé-la-Ville, France

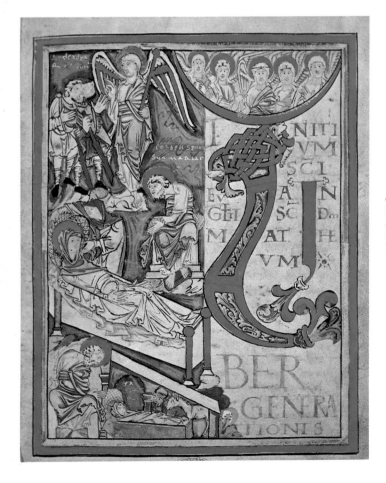

COLORPLATE 55.
Romanesque. Initial *L* and scenes of the Nativity, from the *Gospel Book*, St.-Bertin, France. Illumination. Late 10th century. Bibliothèque Municipale, Boulogne-sur-Mer, France

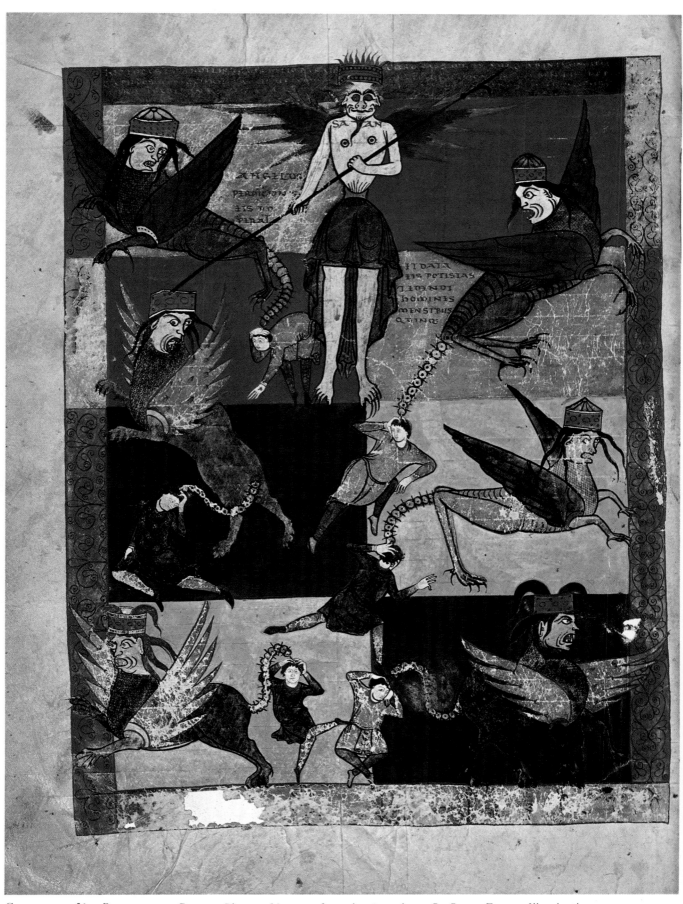

COLORPLATE 56.   Romanesque. GARSIA. *Plague of Locusts*, from the *Apocalypse*, St.-Sever. France. Illumination. Middle 11th century. Bibliothèque Nationale. Paris

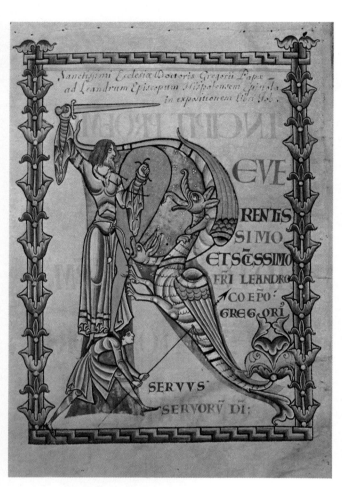

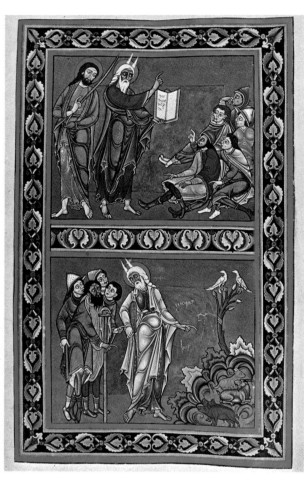

COLORPLATE 57.
Romanesque. Initial *R* with Saint
George and the Dragon, from the
Moralia in Job, Cîteaux, France.
Illumination. Early 12th century.
Bibliothèque Municipale, Dijon

COLORPLATE 58.
Romanesque. Frontispiece of the Book
of Deuteronomy, from the *Bible of
Bury St. Edmunds*, Abbey of Bury St.
Edmunds, England. Illumination. 1st
half 12th century. Corpus Christi
College, Cambridge, England

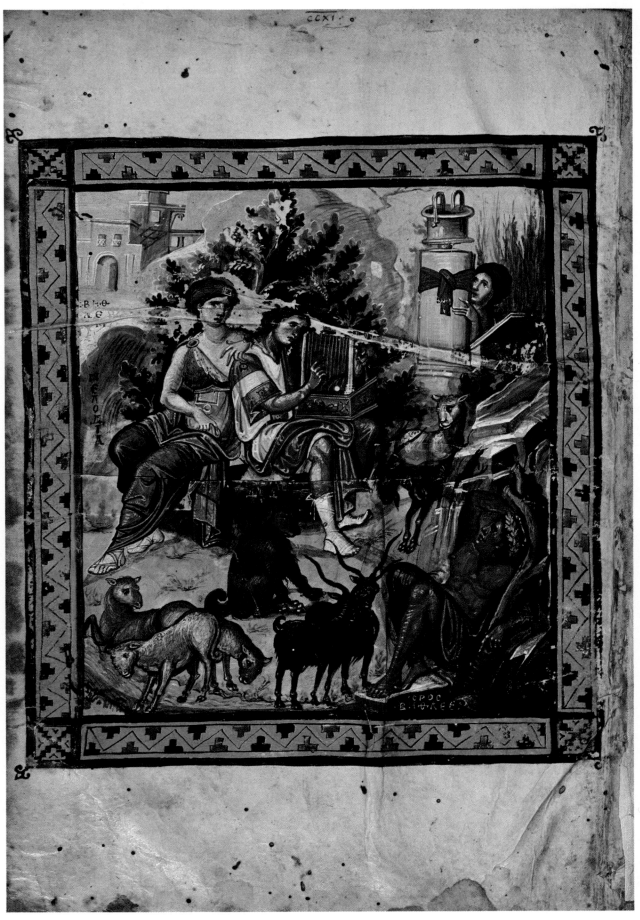

COLORPLATE 59.   Byzantine. *David the Psalmist*, from the *Paris Psalter*. c. 900 A.D. Illumination, 14⅛ x 10¼".
Bibliothèque Nationale, Paris

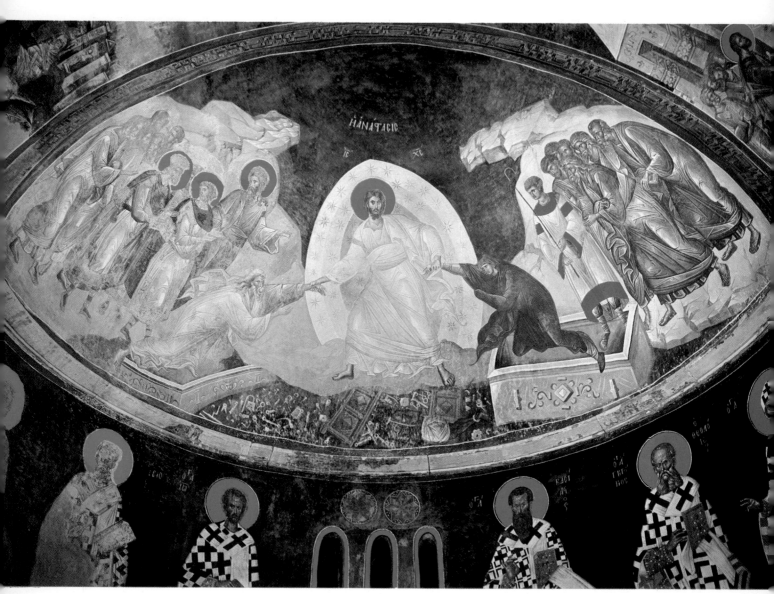

COLORPLATE 60.   Byzantine. *Anastasis (Resurrection).* Apse fresco. 1315–21. Kariye Djami (Church of Christ in Chora), Istanbul

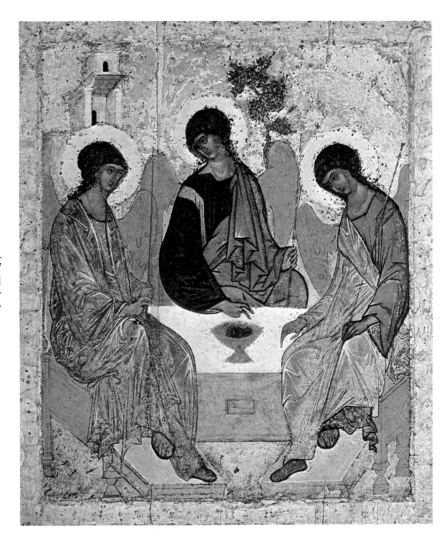

COLORPLATE 61.
Byzantine. ANDREI RUBLEV. *Old Testament Trinity*. c. 1410–20. Panel painting, 55½ x 44½″. Tretyakov Gallery, Moscow

COLORPLATE 62.
Byzantine. *Last Judgment*. Fresco. c. 1550. West wall of narthex, Church of St. George, Voronet, Rumania

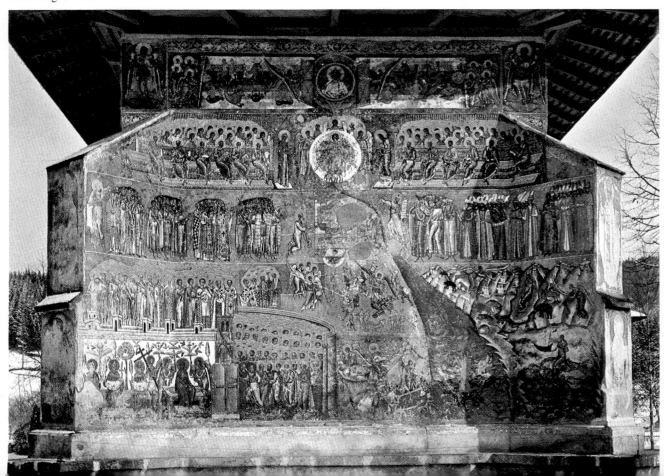

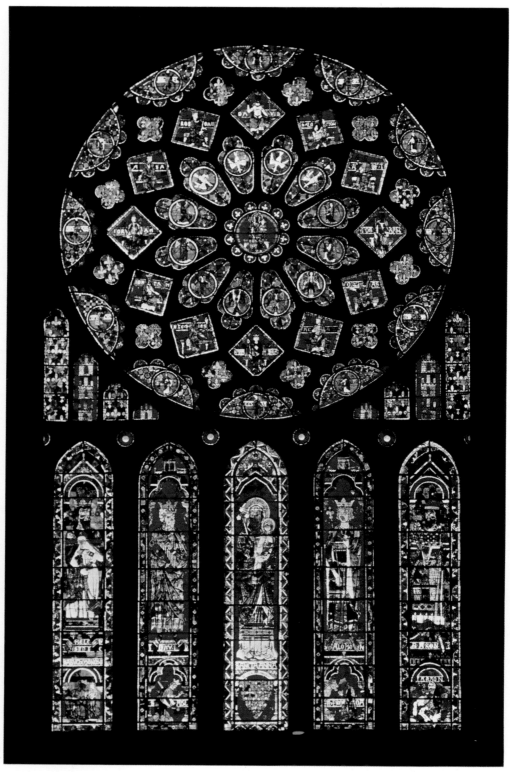

COLORPLATE 63.   Gothic. Rose windows and lancets. 13th century. Stained glass, diameter of
rose 42'8". North transept, Cathedral of Chartres, France

COLORPLATE 64.   Gothic. Interior, Ste.-Chapelle. 1243–48. Paris ▶

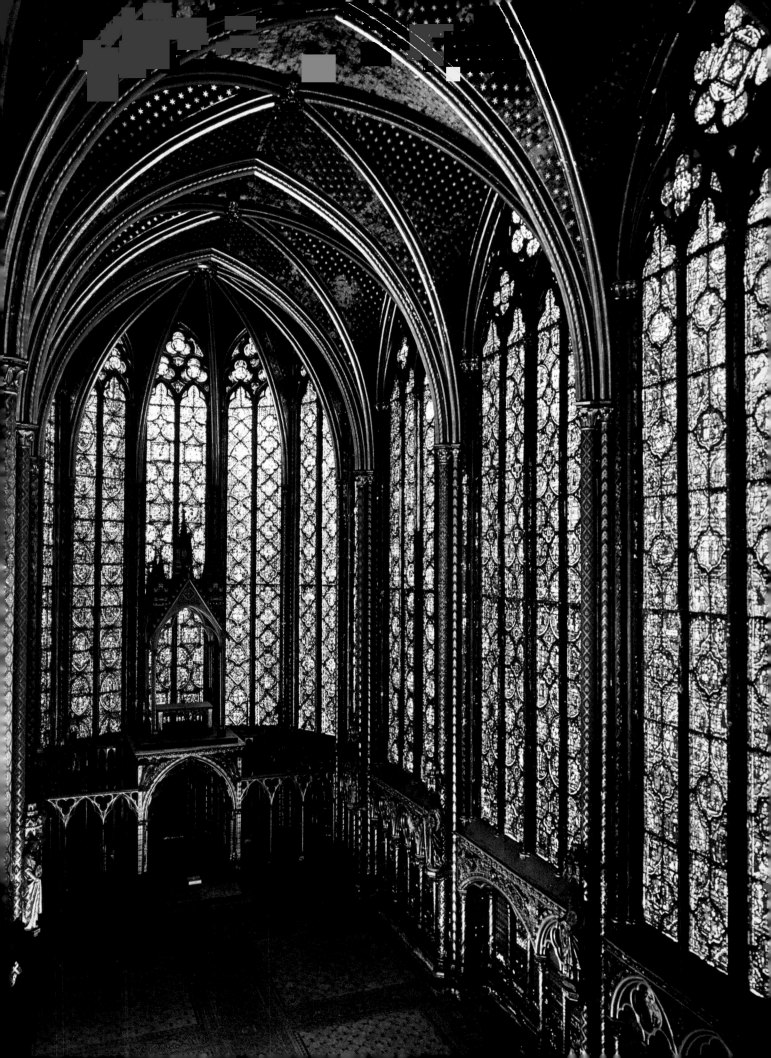

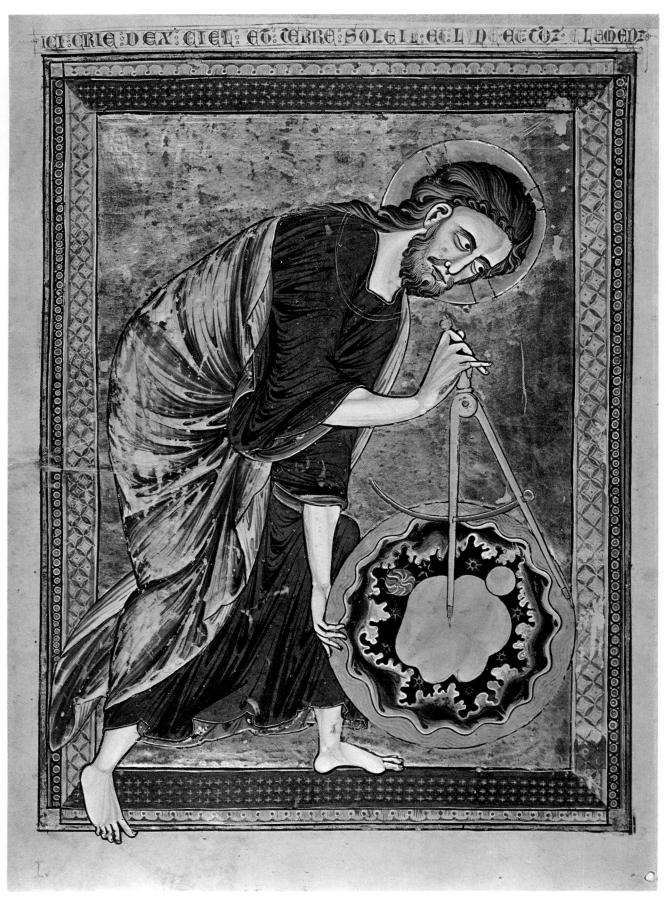

COLORPLATE 65.   Gothic. *God the Father as Architect*, from the *Bible Moralisée.* Illumination. Middle 13th century.
Österreichische Nationalbibliothek, Vienna

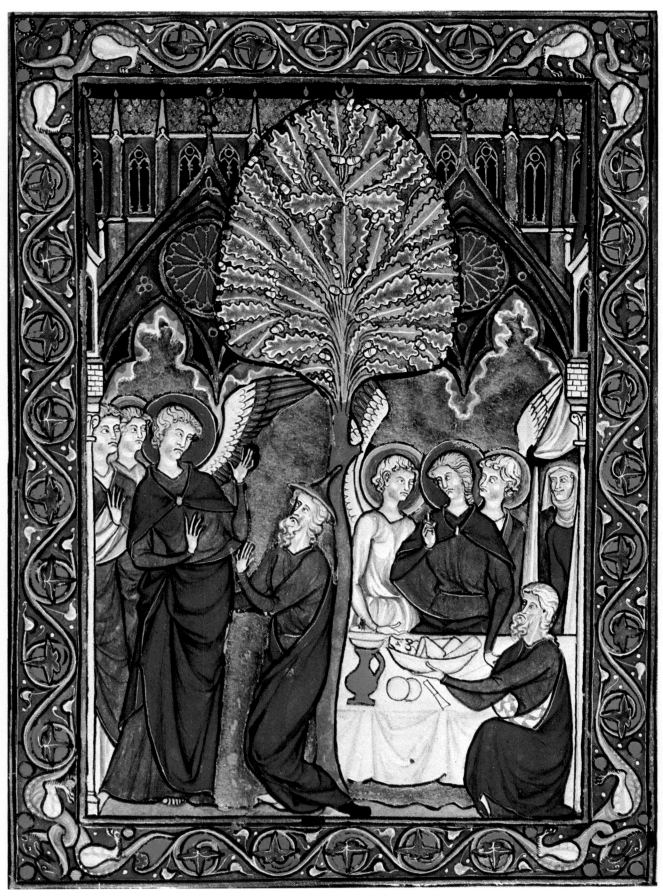

COLORPLATE 66. Gothic. *Abraham and the Three Angels*, from the *Psalter of Saint Louis*. Illumination. 1253–70. Bibliothèque Nationale, Paris

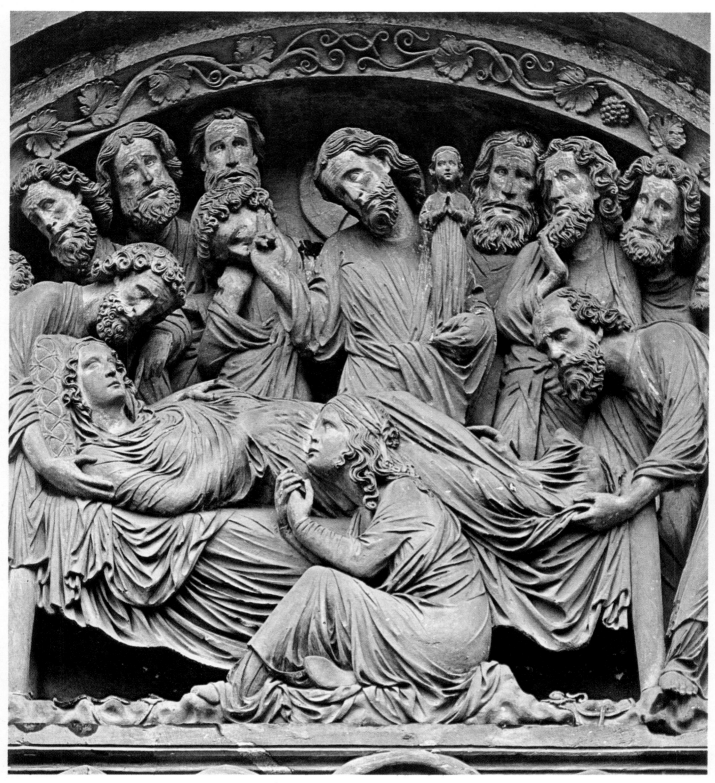

COLORPLATE 67. Gothic. *Death of the Virgin.* c. 1220. Tympanum of the south transept portal, Cathedral of Strasbourg, France

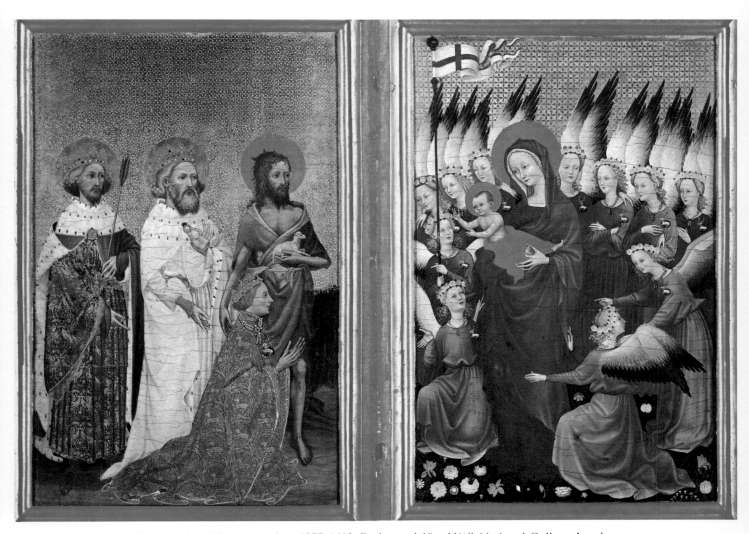

COLORPLATE 68.   Gothic. *Wilton Diptych.* c. 1377–1413. Each panel 18 x 11½″. National Gallery, London

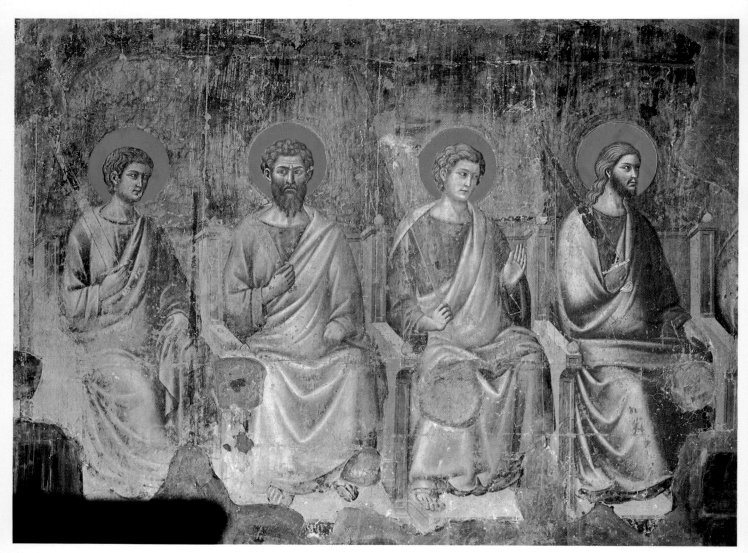

COLORPLATE 69.   Gothic. PIETRO CAVALLINI. *Last Judgment* (portion of fresco). c. 1290. Sta. Cecilia in Trastevere,
Rome

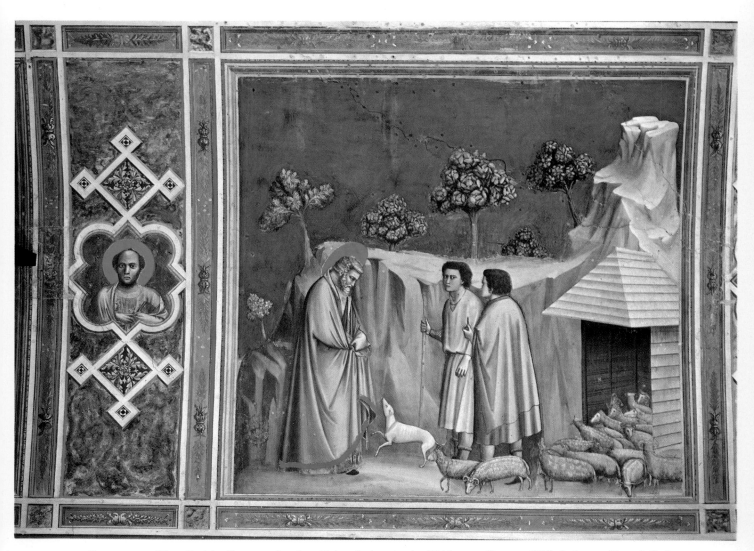

COLORPLATE 70.   Gothic. GIOTTO. *Joachim Takes Refuge in the Wilderness.* Fresco. 1305–6. Arena Chapel, Padua

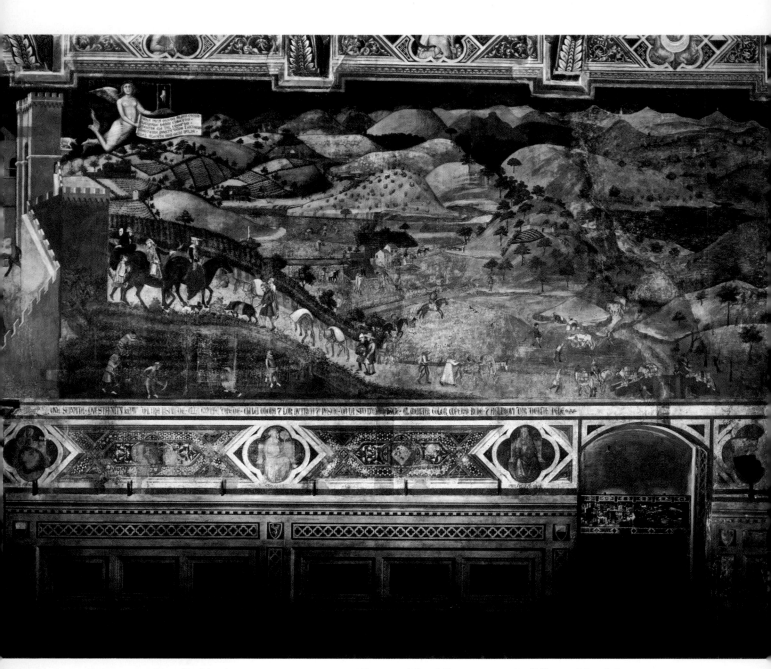

COLORPLATE 71.   Gothic. AMBROGIO LORENZETTI. *Allegory of Good Government: the Effects of Good Government in the City and the Country* (portion of fresco). 1338–39. Salla della Pace, Palazzo Pubblico, Siena

that Christ had shared the sufferings of all mankind, he is depicted after death in Giovanni's picture, lifted in the arms of Mary, Mary Magdalene, and John. The emotional intensity of the painting has reached fever pitch, but it is no longer expressed in outbursts; it is felt within, rather, like a self-inflicted wound. As impressive as the content of Giovanni's painting is his new attention to muscles, bones, and tendons not only where they affect the texture of an anatomical surface but also where they appear along the sensitive contour. His art illuminates to some degree the origin of the mysterious painter of the *Wilton Diptych* (see colorplate 68) and also prepared the way for the great discoveries of the approaching Renaissance, in both Italy and the North.

TIME LINE

The numbers in italics refer to illustrations in the text.

	POLITICAL HISTORY	RELIGION, LITERATURE	SCIENCE, TECHNOLOGY
600 B.C.			
100			
A.D 150			
200	Shapur I, Sassanian king of Persia (r. 242–272)		
250	Emperor Diocletian, RE (r. 284–305), restores Britain to the empire (296)	Christian persecutions in Roman Empire (250) Gallienus, RE (r. 253–268), issues Edict of Toleration granting Christians the right to possess their own churches (260) Mithraism spreads in Roman Empire Plotinus (d. 270)	
300	Constantine defeats Maxentius, RE (r. 306–12), at the Battle of the Milvian Bridge (312) Constantine the Great, RE (r. 324–337) Constantinople (formerly Byzantium) made new Imperial city (330) and entire administrative apparatus reorganized Constantine baptized on his deathbed (337); first division of Roman Empire	Great persecution (303–305) Edict of Milan: Constantine proclaims religious toleration (313)	
350	Theodosius I becomes ruler of Eastern Roman Empire (r. 379–395); permits Ostrogoths to settle in Pannonia (Hungary); issues an edict (380) condemning Arianism and making belief in the Trinity the test of orthodoxy Theodosius in effect divides Empire, East (Arcadius) and West (Honorius) (395) Alaric I, Visig. king (r. 370–410) invades Macedonia	First Council of Nicaea convened to solve problems raised by Arianism (325); established model for later ecumenical councils Constantina (Sta. Costanza), Constantine's daughter (?–d. 354) Valens and Valentinian divide East and West into Arians and Orthodox (364) Milan becomes religious center of N. Italy under St. Ambrose, bp. of Milan (r. 373–97) Council of Constantinople outlaws Arianism (381) St. Jerome translates Bible into Latin (Vulgate) (382)	
400	Alaric I invades Italy (400) Honorius makes Ravenna capital of West (402) Alaric I sacks Rome (410); after his death, Visigoths leave Italy and begin conquest of S. Gaul and N. Spain from Vandals Galla Placidia, regent of the West (r. 423–25) Merovingian dynasty rules Frankish kingdom (428–751) Vandals invade N. Africa (429) Attila, king of the Huns (r. 433–53)	St. Augustine, bp. of Hippo (r. 395–430), writes *City of God* (412) Council of Ephesos: Virgin Mary proclaimed *Theotokos*, "Mother of God" (431)	Invention of the stirrup in China Silk cultivation brought to eastern Mediterranean from China
450	Huns destroy Milan (450) Pope Leo persuades Attila to spare Rome (452) Odoacer takes Empire of West, Ravenna (476); Western Roman Empire comes to an end Alaric II, Visig. king (r. 484–507), in Spain Theodoric the Great founds Ostrogothic kingdom in Italy (488–526); kills Odoacer and his son	St. Patrick (d. 461) said to have founded Celtic Church in Ireland	
500	Clovis defeats Alaric II (507) Justinian becomes emperor of Byzantium, initiates "Golden Age" (527–565); codifies Roman law Riots in Constantinople; Hagia Sophia burns (532) Peace (532) between Rome and Chosroes I, king of Persia (r. 531–79) Byzantine army recaptures Ravenna (540) Persian Wars (541–72)	St. Benedict (c. 480–c. 547) founds Benedictine Order at Monte Cassino (c. 529)	
550	Lombards take N. Italy, establish kingdom; Pavia made capital (568); destroy abbey buildings at Monte Cassino (581)	Muhammed, Prophet of Islam (c. 570–632) St. Gregory of Tours writes *History of the Franks* (c. 575) Pope St. Gregory I the Great (r. 590–604) greatly increases papal authority	
600	Heraclius I, BE (r. 610–41) repulses Avar and Persian attacks on Constantinople T'ang dynasty, China (623–906) Byzantium loses Near Eastern and African provinces to Muslims (637–640)	Pope St. Gregory I sends St. Augustine (d. 604) to England (596); St. Augustine becomes first archbp. of Canterbury (r. 601–604) Hegira: Muhammed flees to Medina (622) True Cross brought back to Constantinople (630) St. Isidore of Seville (d. 636)	Earliest cast iron, in China
650	Omayyad caliphate, Damascus (661–750) Bulgarians settle in Balkans (680)	Scotland accepts Christianity (650) Text of Koran established (651) Synod of Whitby: England accepts Roman liturgy (664) Caedmon, first Eng. poet (fl. 670) Venerable Bede (673–735)	
700	Muslims take Visigothic Spain (711) Battle of Poitiers: Charles Martel defeats Muslims (732)	Iconoclastic Controversy (726–843)	Porcelain invented in China (c. 700) Papermaking introduced into Near East from China Stirrup introduced into western Europe
750	Abbasid caliphate, Baghdad (750–1256) Pepin crowned Frank. king in St.-Denis (754) Pepin drives Lombards from Ravenna, gives it to pope (756); the Donation of Pepin establishes pope as a temporal ruler Independent Muslim state established in Spain (756) Charlemagne (Charles the Great), Carol. king (r. 768–814)	Rhabanus Maurus (784–856) Council of Nicaea: rejects Iconoclasm (787) *Beowulf* epic Alcuin (735–804) begins revision of Vulgate (796)	
800	Charlemagne crowned emp. of the West at Rome (r. 800–814) "Macedonian Renaissance" (829–976) marks return to Hellenistic ideals; Photius (820?–91) is outstanding advocate Arabs capture Palermo (831) Vikings begin raids on England (835)	Earliest version of *1001 Nights* (c. 800) Ebbo, archbp. of Reims (r. 816–35) Carolingian revival of Latin classics Einhard, Carol. historian (c. 770–840) writes *Life of Charlemagne* (821) Drogo, archbp. of Metz (r. 823–55)	Earliest documented church organ, Aachen (822) Earliest printed book, China (868) Adoption of horse collar in western Europe makes horse efficient draft animal

PAINTING	SCULPTURE	ARCHITECTURE	
	Scythian panther from Kelermes (344)		600 B.C.
	Scythian gold plaque from the Altai Mountains, Siberia (345)		
	Scythian (?) shield ornament from Helden, The Netherlands (346)		100
Ceiling fresco, Catacomb of Sta. Priscilla, Rome (317)			A.D. 150
			200
		Earliest known martyrium, St. Peter's, Rome	
		"Domus ecclesiae" at Dura-Europos, Syria	
Haman and Mordecai from the Synagogue at Dura-Europos (319)		Palace of Shapur I, Ctesiphon, Mesopotamia (351)	250
Ceiling fresco, Catacomb of SS. Pietro e Marcellino, Rome (318)		Basilica of Maxentius and Constantine, Rome (306, 307)	300
		S. Giovanni in Laterano, Rome	
		Old St. Peter's, Rome (321, 322)	
	Sarcophagus of Junius Bassus (330)	Sta. Costanza, Rome (324, 325)	350
	Early Christian ivory plaque with Three Marys at the Sepulcher and The Ascension (331)	Hagios Georgios, Salonika	
Dome mosaics, Hagios Georgios, Salonika, Greece (colorplate 35)		Sta. Sabina, Rome (323)	400
Vatican Virgil (329)		Mausoleum of Galla Placidia, Ravenna (328, colorplate 37)	
Mosaics, Mausoleum of Galla Placidia, Ravenna (328, colorplate 37)		Sta. Maria Maggiore, Rome	
Mosaics, Sta. Maria Maggiore, Rome (327, colorplate 36)			
	Colossus of Barletta (320)	St. Simeon Stylites, Qal'at Saman, Syria (326)	450
Mosaics, SS. Cosma e Damiano, Rome (332)		S. Vitale, Ravenna (333, 334, colorplate 38)	500
Vienna Book of Genesis (colorplate 41)		Hagia Sophia by Anthemius of Tralles and Isidorus of Miletos, Constantinople (338–341)	
Apse mosaics, Sant'Apollinare in Classe, Ravenna (337)		Sant'Apollinare in Classe, Ravenna	
Mosaics, S. Vitale, Ravenna (336, colorplate 38)			
Mosaic and icon, Monastery of St. Catherine, Mount Sinai (colorplates 39, 40)	Justinianian ivory diptych (343)		550
Rabula Gospels from Syria (342)			
			600
Book of Durrow from Northumbria (349)	Purse lid from ship burial at Sutton Hoo, England (347)	Mosque, Kufah, Mesopotamia	650
		Dome of the Rock, Jerusalem (colorplate 44)	
Lindisfarne Gospels (colorplate 42)		Great Mosque, Damascus, Syria (352, colorplate 45)	700
Mosaics, Great Mosque, Damascus, Syria (colorplate 45)		Desert palace at Mshatta, Jordan (353)	
Echternach Gospels from Luxembourg (350)			
Appearance of the Angel to Joseph, fresco, Sta. Maria Foris Portas, Castelseprio (425)			
Book of Kells from Iona (colorplate 43)		Round city of al-Mansur, Baghdad	750
		Great Mosque, Córdoba (358, 359, colorplate 46)	
		Abbey Church of St.-Riquier, Centula, France (370)	
		Abbey of Lorsch and gatehouse, Hesse, Germany (372)	
Coronation Gospels (373)	Animal head from ship burial at Oseberg, Norway (348)	Palatine Chapel by Odo of Metz, Aachen (368, 369)	800
Lorsch Gospels (377)		Plan for monastery, St. Gall, Switzerland (371)	
Ebbo Gospels from Reims, France (375)		City of Samarra, built by al-Mu'tasim	
Koran page in Kufic script from Syria or Iraq (366)			
Utrecht Psalter (376)			

TIME LINE

The numbers in italics refer to illustrations in the text.

	POLITICAL HISTORY	RELIGION, LITERATURE	SCIENCE, TECHNOLOGY
840	Charles II the Bald, Carol. king (r. 840–77) Treaty of Verdun (843); Carol. empire divided among sons of Louis the Pious: Louis the German (E. Franks), Lothair I (Lotharingia), Charles II the Bald (W. Franks) Arabs from Sicily pillage Rome (846) Lothair II, Carol. king (r. 855–69) Louis II, Ital. king and emp. (r. 855–75) Byzantines convert Bulgaria (864) Lotharingia split between Charles the Bald and Louis the German (870) Hungarians invade Lombardy (899)		
900	Vikings raid France; Charles III the Simple, Carol. king (r. 898–923) cedes Normandy to Viking leader, Rollo (911) Constantine VII Porphyrogenitos, BE (r. 912-59) Al-Manzor, Sp. Arab regent (914–1002), invades Christian Spain (10th c.) Henry I, Ger. king and uncrowned emp. (r. 919–36)	Cluniac Order founded (910)	Earliest documented use of windmills, in Near East Earliest application of water power to industry Vikings discover Iceland (860)
950	Otto the Great, Ger. king (r. 936–72), crowned HRE (r. 962–72); renews Carolingian traditions Sung dynasty, China (960–1279) St. Vladimir I, duke of Kiev (r. 980–1015) Hugh Capet, Fr. king (r. 987–96), founds Capetian dynasty in France	Gero, archbp. of Cologne (r. 969–76) Conversion of Russia to Orthodox Church (c. 990) St. Bernward, archbp. of Hildesheim (r. 993–1033)	Vikings discover Greenland (c. 980)
1000	William the Conqueror, Norm. duke (r. 1035–87) Normans begin conquest of Sicily (1043)	St. Dominic of Silos (d. 1037)	Leif Ericson sails to North America (1002) Avicenna (980–1037), chief medical authority of Middle Ages
1050	Final schism between Rome and Constantinople (1054) Henry IV, HRE (r. 1056–1106) Normans sack Rome (1064) Battle of Hastings (1066): William the Conqueror defeats Harold, conquers England Emperor Henry IV humiliated by pope at Canossa (1077) Spanish *reconquista* begins (1085–1492)	Hariri, Arab scholar and poet (1054–1121) College of Cardinals formed to elect popes (1059) Order of Knights Hospitalers founded in Jerusalem (c. 1070) Pope Gregory VII (r. 1073–83) First Cluniac priory in England (c. 1075) Investiture Contest: papacy vs. Empire concerning right to select bishops (1075–1122) Peter Abelard (1079–1142) St. Bruno founds Carthusian Order at La Grande Chartreuse (1084) First Crusade to Holy Land (1095–99); crusaders found Latin kingdom of Jerusalem (1099) Cistercian Order founded at Cîteaux (1098) Hildegard of Bingen (1098–1179) *Song of Roland* composed (c. 1098)	Lateen sail first used in Italy
1100	Louis VI the Fat of France (r. 1108–37) strengthens monarchy Henry the Lion, Sax. duke (r. 1129–95) Roger II, Sic. king (r. 1130–54) Eleanor of Aquitaine, Fr. queen (r. 1137–52), Eng. queen (r. 1154–89) Portugal becomes independent (1143)	Omar Khayyam (fl. c. 1100) Monk Theophilus writes *De diversis artibus* (c. 1100) St. Stephen Harding, abt. of Cîteaux (r. 1109–34) St. Bernard, abt. of Clairvaux (r. 1115–53) Roger, abt. of Moissac (r. 1115–31) Order of Knights Templars founded in Jerusalem (1119) Suger, abt. of St.-Denis (r. 1122–51) Treaty of Worms settles Investiture Contest (1122) Aymery Picard writes *Pilgrim's Guide* (1138) Second Crusade, to Acre and Damascus, initiated by St. Bernard of Clairvaux (1147)	Earliest manufacture of paper in Europe, by Muslims in Spain Invention of soap Use of the crossbow against Christians forbidden by the Church (1123) Mined coal supplements use of charcoal as fuel
1150	Lombard League, aided by Sic. kings, defeats Frederick I Barbarossa, HRE (r. 1152–90), at Legnano (1176) Saladin captures Jerusalem (1187) Pope Innocent III recognizes Frederick Hohenstaufen as king of Sicily (1198); later Frederick II, HRE (r. 1215–50)	Rise of universities based on faculties of law, medicine, theology; Bologna founded before end of twelfth century; Paris, c. 1150–60; Oxford, 1167. Geoffrey of Monmouth (d. 1154) First flowering of vernacular literature (epics, fables, *chansons de geste*); age of the troubadours Order of Teutonic Knights founded at Acre (1189) Third Crusade (1189–92), to rescue Jerusalem, succeeds Chartres Cathedral burns (1194)	Earliest use of magnetic compass for navigation Earliest documented windmill in Europe (1180)
1200	Magna Carta, limiting powers of kings, signed in England (1215) St. Louis IX, Fr. king (r. 1226–70) Mongols conquer China (1234–79), invade Russia (1237) Mongols conquer much of Russia (1240)	Fourth Crusade (1202–1204) sails from Venice; Crusaders sack Constantinople and found Latin Empire of the East (1204–61) Nibelung epic (1205); age of minnesingers in Germany St. Dominic (1170–1221) founds Dominican Order at Toulouse (1206) Inquisition established to combat heresy Albigensian Crusade (1208) against heretics in southern France St. Francis (1182–1226) founds Franciscan Order at Assisi (1209) Reims Cathedral burns (1210) Roger Bacon (1214–92) Lateran Council: redefines spiritual requirements of Church (1215) Sixth Crusade (1228–29), to Holy Land, led by Frederick II Seventh Crusade (1248–54), to Egypt, departs from Aigues-Mortes, led by Louis IX	Albertus Magnus (1193–1280)
1250	Greeks retake Constantinople from Latins (1261) Philip III the Bold, Fr. king (r. 1270–85) Marco Polo returns from court of Kublai Khan (1285) Turks take Acre, last Christian holding in the Holy Land (1291)	Dante Alighieri (1265–1321) *Golden Legend* by Jacobus de Voragine (1266–83) Master Eckhart, German theologian and mystic (d. 1327) St. Thomas Aquinas (1225–75) writes *Summa Theologica* (1266–73) Eighth Crusade (1270), to Jaffa and Antioch, led by Louis IX, who dies in Tunis (1270)	Marco Polo travels to China and India (c. 1275–93) Arabic (actually Indian) numerals introduced in Europe Spectacles invented (c. 1286) First documented use of spinning wheel in Europe (1298)

436

TIME LINE

The numbers in italics refer to illustrations in the text.

	POLITICAL HISTORY	RELIGION, LITERATURE	SCIENCE, TECHNOLOGY
1300	Philip IV the Fair, Fr. king (r. 1285–1314), humiliates Pope Boniface VIII (1303) Hundred Years' War begins between France and England (1337–1453) Black Death—epidemic throughout Europe (1347–50)	William of Occam (c. 1300–49) St. Bridget of Sweden (1303–73) Papacy moves from Rome to Avignon (1309)	First large-scale production of paper in Italy and Germany First large-scale production of gunpowder; earliest known use of cannon (1326) Earliest cast iron in Europe
1350	John II the Good, Fr. king (r. 1350–64) Jacquerie revolt in France (1358) Philip the Bold, Burg. duke (r. 1363–1404) Ming dynasty, China (1368–1644) Giangaleazzo Visconti, Milanese duke (r. 1378–1402) Russia begins expulsion of Mongols (1380)	Boccaccio (1313–75) writes the *Decameron* (1353) Papacy returns to Rome (1378); Great Schism begins John Wycliffe (d. 1384) *Canterbury Tales* by Chaucer (c. 1387)	
1400	Ottoman Turks conquer Constantinople (1453) Isabella I of Castile, Ferdinand II of Aragon, Sp. queen and king (r. 1479–1504) Spain takes Granada, Moorish capital (1492)	Council of Constance (1414–18): ends Great Schism Jan Hus burned at stake for heresy (1415) Moscow becomes center of Orthodox Church (1453)	Gutenberg invents printing with movable type (1446–50) Earliest account of the sea-quadrant (1456) Columbus discovers America (1492)

TIME LINE

The numbers in italics refer to illustrations in the text.

	PAINTING	SCULPTURE	ARCHITECTURE
1300	*Raising of Lazarus, Lamentation,* and *Joachim Takes Refuge in the Wilderness* by Giotto, Arena Chapel, Padua (515, 516, colorplate 70) *Chronology of Ancient Peoples* of al-Biruni, Tabriz, Iran (367) *Maestà* altarpiece by Duccio, Cathedral of Siena (518–520) *Madonna and Child Enthroned* by Giotto from the Church of the Ognissanti, Florence (514) *Nativity* (mosaic) and *Anastasis* (fresco), Church of Christ in Chora (Kariye Djami), Istanbul (442, colorplate 60) *Belleville Breviary* by Jean Pucelle from Paris (481) *Annunciation* by Simone Martini (521) *Annunciation to the Shepherds* by Taddeo Gaddi, Baroncelli Chapel, Sta. Croce, Florence (517) Frescoes by Ambrogio Lorenzetti, Palazzo Pubblico, Siena (523, colorplate 71) *Birth of the Virgin* by Pietro Lorenzetti (522)	Pulpit by Giovanni Pisano, Sant'Andrea, Pistoia (510, 511) *Virgin and Child* by Giovanni Pisano, Arena Chapel, Padua (512) *Virgin of Paris* from St.-Aignan (480)	Palazzo Vecchio, Florence (505) Cathedral of Palma, Majorca, Spain (490) Choir, Cathedral of Gloucester (494) Palazzo Ducale (Doge's Palace), Venice (506)
1350	*Triumph of Death* by Francesco Traini, Campo Santo, Pisa (524, 525) *Pietà* by Giovanni da Milano (526) Fresco by Theophanes the Greek, Church of Our Saviour of the Transfiguration, Novgorod, Russia (445) *Wilton Diptych* (colorplate 68)		The Alhambra, Granada (364, 365) Madrasah of Sultan Hasan, Cairo (360–362) Cathedral, Florence (498–500) Cathedral, Milan (502–504)
1400	*Bihzad in the Garden* by Junaid from manuscript of poems of Khwaju Kirmani (colorplate 47) *Old Testament Trinity* by Andrei Rublev (colorplate 61)		Ca' d'Oro, Venice (507) Palais Jacques Coeur, Bourges (479)
1500		Rose window, Cathedral of Amiens (473)	Chapel of Henry VII, Westminster Abbey, London (495) St.-Maclou, Rouen (477, 478)
1550	*Last Judgment*, fresco, Church of St. George, Voronet, Rumania (colorplate 62)		Cathedral of St. Basil the Blessed by Barma and Postnik, Moscow (444)
1600			Mosque of Ahmed I, Istanbul (363)

Glossary

ABACUS (pl. ABACI). In architecture, the slab that forms the uppermost member of a CAPITAL and supports the ARCHITRAVE.

ABBEY. The religious body governed by an abbot or an abbess, or the monastic buildings themselves. The abbey church frequently has special features such as a particularly large CHOIR to accommodate the monks or nuns.

ACANTHUS. A plant having large toothed and scalloped leaves whose forms were imitated on CAPITALS and used to ornament MOLDINGS, BRACKETS, and FRIEZES.

ACROTERIUM (pl. ACROTERIA). A sculpture or other ornament placed at the lower angles and the apex of a PEDIMENT, or the PEDESTAL, often without a BASE, on which it stands.

ADOBE. A sun-dried brick used by the Indians of the western United States and Central America. A structure made of the same.

AEDICULA (pl. AEDICULAE). Latin word for *niche* or *small shrine.*

AGORA. Greek word for *assembly,* thus denoting the square or marketplace that was the center of public life in every Greek city.

AISLE. See SIDE AISLE.

ALABASTER. A fine-grained gypsum or calcite, often white and translucent, though sometimes delicately tinted.

ALTARPIECE. A painted and/or sculptured work of art that stands as a religious image upon and at the back of an altar, either representing in visual symbols the underlying doctrine of the MASS, or depicting the saint to whom a particular church or chapel is dedicated, together with scenes from his life. Examples from certain periods include decorated GABLES and PINNACLES, as well as a PREDELLA. See MAESTÀ.

AMBULATORY. A place for walking, usually covered, as in an ARCADE around a cloister, or a semicircular passageway around the APSE behind the main altar. In a church or mosque with a centralized PLAN, the passageway around the central space that corresponds to a SIDE AISLE and that is used for ceremonial processions.

AMPHIPROSTYLE. Having a PORTICO in the rear as well as in the front, but not on the sides.

AMPHITHEATER. A double THEATER. A building of elliptical shape with tiers of seats rising one behind another about a central open space or arena.

AMPHORA (pl. AMPHORAE). A storage jar used in ancient Greece having an egg-shaped body, a foot, and two handles, each attached at the neck and shoulder of the jar.

APOCALYPSE. The Book of Revelation, the last book of the New Testament, in which are narrated the visions of the future experienced by Saint John the Evangelist on the island of Patmos.

APOCRYPHA. A group of books included at one time in authorized Christian versions of the BIBLE (now generally omitted from Protestant versions).

APOSTLES. In Christian usage the word commonly denotes the twelve followers or disciples chosen by Christ to preach his GOSPEL, though the term is sometimes used loosely. Those listed in the Gospels are: Andrew; James, the son of Zebedee, called James the Major; James, the son of Alphaeus, called James the Minor; Bartholomew; John; Judas Iscariot; Matthew; Philip; Peter; Simon the Canaanite; Thaddeus; and Thomas (Matt. 10:1–4; Mark 3:13–19).

APSE. A large semicircular or polygonal niche. In a Roman BASILICA it was frequently found at both ends of the NAVE; in a Christian church it is usually placed at one end of the nave after the CHOIR; it may also appear at the ends of the TRANSEPT and at the ends of chapels.

AQUEDUCT. From the Latin for *duct of water.* An artificial channel for conducting water from a distance, which, in Roman times, was usually built overground and supported on ARCHES.

ARCADE. A series of ARCHES and their supports. Called a *blind arcade* when placed against a wall and used primarily as surface decoration.

ARCH. An architectural construction, often semicircular, built of wedge-shaped blocks (called VOUSSOIRS) to span an opening. The center stone is called the KEYSTONE. The weight of this structure requires support from walls, PIERS, or COLUMNS, and the THRUST requires BUTTRESSING at the sides. When an arch is made of overlapping courses of stone, each block projecting slightly farther over the opening than the block beneath it, it is called a CORBELED ARCH.

ARCHBISHOP. The chief BISHOP of an ecclesiastical province or archbishopric.

ARCHITRAVE. The main horizontal beam and the lowest member of an ENTABLATURE; it may be a series of LINTELS, each spanning the space from the top of one support to the next.

ARCHIVOLT. The molding or moldings above an arched opening; in Romanesque and Gothic churches, frequently decorated with sculpture.

ARK OF THE COVENANT. The wooden chest containing a handwritten scroll of the TORAH. It is kept in the holiest place in the TABERNACLE, which, in Western countries, is usually against the east wall, the direction of the Holy Land.

ARRICCIO, ARRICCIATO. The rough coat of coarse plaster that is the first layer to be spread on a wall when making a FRESCO.

A SECCO. See FRESCO.

ATRIUM. The open entrance hall or central hall of an ancient Roman house. A court in front of the principal doors of a church.

ATTIC. The upper story, usually low in height, placed above an ENTABLATURE or main CORNICE of a building, and frequently decorated with PILASTERS.

BACCHANTE. See MAENAD.

BALDACHIN. From Italian *baldacchino,* a rich silk fabric from Baghdad. A canopy of such material, or of wood, stone, etc., either permanently installed over an altar, throne, or doorway, or constructed in portable form to be carried in religious processions.

BALUSTRADE. A row of short pillars, called *balusters,* surmounted by a railing.

BAPTISTERY. Either a separate building or a part of a church in which the SACRAMENT of Baptism is administered.

BARREL VAULT. A semicylindrical VAULT that normally requires continuous support and BUTTRESSING.

BAR TRACERY. See TRACERY.

BASALT. A fine-grained volcanic rock of high density and dark color.

BASE. The lowest element of a COLUMN, temple, wall, or DOME, occasionally of a statue.

BASILICA. In ancient Roman architecture, a rectangular building whose ground PLAN was generally divided into NAVE, SIDE AISLES, and one or more APSES, and whose elevation sometimes included a CLERESTORY and GALLERIES, though there was no strict uniformity. It was used as a hall of justice and as a public meeting place. In Christian architecture, the term applied to any church that has a longitudinal nave terminated by an apse and flanked by lower side aisles.

BAY. A compartment into which a building may be subdivided, usually formed by the space bounded by consecutive architectural supports.

BEMA. The SANCTUARY of an Early Christian or modern Eastern Orthodox church.

BENEDICTINE ORDER. Founded in 529 by Saint Benedict of Nursus (c. 480–543), at Subiaco, near Rome, the Benedictine ORDER spread to England and much of western Europe in the next two centuries. Less austere than other early orders, the Benedictines divided their time into periods of religious worship, reading, and work, the last generally either educational or agricultural.

BIBLE. The collection of sacred writings of the Christian religion that includes the Old and the New Testaments, or that of the Jewish religion, which includes the Old Testament only. The versions commonly used in the Roman Catholic Church are based on the Vulgate, a Latin translation made by Saint Jerome in the fourth century A.D. An English translation, made by members of the English College at Douai, France, between 1582 and 1610, is called the Douay. Widely used Protestant translations include Martin Luther's German translation from the first half of the sixteenth century, and the English King James Version, first published in 1611.

BISHOP. A spiritual overseer of a number of churches or a DIOCESE; in the Greek, Roman Catholic, Anglican, and other churches, a member of the highest order in the ministry. See CATHEDRAL.

BLIND ARCADE. See ARCADE.

BRACKET. A piece of stone, wood, or metal projecting from a wall and having a flat upper surface that serves to support a statue, beam, or other weight.

BREVIARY. A book containing the daily offices or prayers and the necessary psalms and hymns for daily devotions. Frequently illustrated and generally intended for use by the clergy.

BROKEN PEDIMENT. See PEDIMENT.

BRONZE and IRON AGES. The period from approximately 3000 B.C. to the first century B.C., characterized in general by the use of metal and the smelting of metal. Farming communities were settled, and the making and use of pottery became widespread.

BUTTRESS. A masonry support that counteracts the lateral pressure, or THRUST, exerted by an ARCH or VAULT. See FLYING BUTTRESS and PIER BUTTRESS.

CALIPH. A leader of Muslims in both a spiritual and political sense; in theory, there should be only one, but in fact, after the loss of power by the Abbasid caliph in the tenth century, a Sunni caliphate was established at Córdoba (925–1030) and a Shia caliphate was established by the Fatimids (915–1171). With the murder of the last Abbasid caliph at Baghdad in 1258, a shadow caliphate survived in Egypt until the Turkish conquest of 1517. The claim of the later Turkish sultans to the caliphate was not legitimate.

CALLIGRAPHY. In a loose sense, handwriting, but usually refers to beautiful handwriting or fine penmanship.

CALVARY. See GOLGOTHA.

CAMEO. A carving in RELIEF upon a gem, stone, or shell, especially when differently colored layers of the material are revealed to produce a design of lighter color against a darker background. A gem, stone, or shell so carved.

CAMPANILE. From the Italian word for *bell (campana).* A bell tower, either attached to a church or freestanding nearby.

CAMPO. Italian word for *field;* used in Siena, Venice, and other Italian cities to denote certain public squares. See PIAZZA.

CAMPO SANTO. Italian phrase for *holy field;* thus, a cemetery.

CANON. A clergyman who serves in a CATHEDRAL or a collegiate church.

CANON OF THE MASS. The part of the Christian MASS between the Sanctus, a hymn, and the Lord's Prayer; the actual EUCHARIST, or sacrifice of bread and wine, to which only the baptized were admitted.

CANOPY. An ornamental rooflike projection or covering placed over a niche, statue, tomb, altar, or the like.

CAPITAL. The crowning member of a COLUMN, PIER, or PILASTER on which rests the lowest element of the ENTABLATURE. See ORDER.

CARDINAL VIRTUES. See VIRTUES.

CARTOUCHE. An ornamental SCROLL-shaped tablet with an inscription or decoration, either sculptured or drawn.

CARVING. The shaping of an image by cutting or chiseling it out from a hard substance, such as stone or wood, in contrast to the additive process of MODELING.

CARYATID. A figure, generally female, used as a COLUMN.

CASTING. A method of reproducing a three-dimensional object or RELIEF by pouring a hardening liquid or molten metal into a mold bearing its impression.

CATACOMBS. Subterranean burial places consisting of GALLERIES with niches for SARCOPHAGI and small chapels for funeral feasts and commemorative services.

CATECHUMEN. One under instruction in the rudiments of Christian doctrine, usually a new convert.

CATHEDRAL. The principal church of a DIOCESE, containing the bishop's throne, or cathedra.

CATWALK. A narrow footway at the side of a bridge or near the ceiling of a building.

CELLA. The body of a temple as distinct from the PORTICO and other external elements, or an interior structure built to house an image.

CENOTAPH. An empty tomb; a commemorative sepulchral monument not intended for burial.

CENTAUR. In Greek mythology, a creature with the head and torso of a man and the body and legs of a horse.

CENTERING. A wooden framework used as support during the construction of a stone ARCH or VAULT.

CHANCEL. In a church, the space reserved for the clergy and the CHOIR, between the APSE and the NAVE and TRANSEPT, usually separated from the latter two by steps and a railing or a screen.

CHASUBLE. A long, oval, sleeveless mantle with an opening for the head; it is worn over all other vestments by a priest when celebrating MASS, and it is used in commemoration of Christ's seamless robe.

CHERUB (pl. CHERUBIM). One of an order of angelic beings

ranking second to the SERAPH in the celestial hierarchy, often represented as a winged child or as the winged head of a child.

CHEVET. The eastern end of a church or CATHEDRAL, consisting of the AMBULATORY and a main APSE with secondary apses or chapels radiating from it.

CHEVRON. A zigzag or V-shaped pattern used decoratively, especially in Romanesque architecture.

CHITON. A sleeveless Greek TUNIC, the basic garment worn by both men and women in ancient times.

CHOIR. A body of trained singers, or that part of a church occupied by them. See CHANCEL.

CHOIR SCREEN. A partition of wood or stone, often elaborately carved, that separates the CHOIR from the NAVE and TRANSEPT of a church. In Byzantine churches, the choir screen, decorated with ICONS, is called an ICONOSTASIS.

CHRISTUS MORTUUS. Latin phrase for *dead Christ.*

CHRISTUS PATIENS. Latin phrase for *suffering Christ.* A cross with a representation of the dead Christ, which in general superseded representations of the CHRISTUS TRIUMPHANS type.

CHRISTUS TRIUMPHANS. Latin phrase for *triumphant Christ.* A cross with a representation of the living Christ, eyes open and triumphant over death. Scenes of the PASSION are usually depicted at the sides of the cross, below the crossarms.

CISTERCIAN ORDER. A reform movement in the BENEDICTINE ORDER started in France in 1098 by Saint Robert of Molesme for the purpose of reasserting the original BENEDICTINE ideals of field work and a life of severe simplicity.

CLAUSURA. Latin word for *closure.* In the Roman Catholic Church the word is used to signify the restriction of certain classes of nuns and monks prohibited from communication with outsiders to sections of their convents or monasteries. Those living within these restrictions are said to be *in clausura* or CLOISTERED.

CLERESTORY. The section of an interior wall that rises above adjacent rooftops, having a row of windows that admit daylight. Used in Roman BASILICAS and Christian basilican churches; in Christian churches, the wall that rises above the nave ARCADE or the TRIFORIUM to the vaulting or roof.

CLOISTER. Generally, a place of religious seclusion; a monastery, nunnery, or convent. Specifically, a covered walk or AMBULATORY around an open court having a plain wall on one side and an open ARCADE or COLONNADE on the other. It is commonly connected with a church, monastery, or other building, and is used for exercise and study. See CLAUSURA.

CLOSED DOOR or CLOSED GATE. Ezekiel's vision of the door or gate of the SANCTUARY in the temple that was closed because only the Lord could enter it (Ezekiel 44:1–4). Interpreted as a prophecy and used as a symbol of Mary's virginity.

CLOSED GARDEN. "A garden enclosed is my sister, my spouse; a spring shut up, a fountain sealed" (Song of Solomon 4:12). Used like CLOSED DOOR as a symbol of Mary's virginity.

CLUNIAC ORDER. A reformed ORDER of BENEDICTINE monks founded in 910 by William I the Pious at the monastery of Cluny in eastern France. For about 250 years it was headed by a succession of remarkable abbots who extended its rule over hundreds of monasteries in western Europe and exerted great influence in ecclesiastical and temporal affairs. With the rise of the CISTERCIAN and the mendicant ORDERS, its strength declined, and it became merely a group of French houses. The order was dissolved in 1790.

CODEX (pl. CODICES). A manuscript in book form as distinguished from a SCROLL. From the first to the fourth century A.D., the codex gradually replaced the scroll.

COFFER. A casket or box. In architecture, a recessed panel in a ceiling.

COLONNADE. A series of COLUMNS spanned by LINTELS.

COLONNETTE. A small COLUMN.

COLOR. See HUE, SATURATION, and VALUE.

COLUMN. A vertical architectural support, usually consisting of a BASE, a rounded SHAFT, and a CAPITAL. When half or more of it is attached to a wall, it is called an *engaged column.* Columns are occasionally used singly for a decorative or commemorative reason. See also ORDER.

COMPOUND PIER. A PIER with COLUMNS, PILASTERS, or SHAFTS attached to it, which members usually support or respond to ARCHES or RIBS above them.

CORBEL. An overlapping arrangement of stones, each course projecting beyond the one below, used in the construction of an ARCH or VAULT, or as a support projecting from the face of a wall.

CORBEL TABLE. A horizontal piece of masonry used as a CORNICE or part of a wall and supported by CORBELS.

CORNICE. The crowning, projecting architectural feature, especially the uppermost part of an ENTABLATURE. It is frequently decorated. When it is not horizontal, as above a PEDIMENT, it is called a *raking cornice.*

COURSED MASONRY. Masonry in which stones or bricks of equal height are placed in continuous horizontal layers.

CRENELLATED. Fortified or decorated with battlements (notched or indented parapets).

CRO-MAGNON. A species of PALEOLITHIC man, the ancestor of modern European man, whose remains were discovered in the Cro-Magnon cave in the Dordogne region of France.

CROMLECH. A circle of standing unhewn stones; the term is sometimes used interchangeably with DOLMEN.

CROSSING. That part of a church where the TRANSEPT crosses the NAVE; it is sometimes emphasized by a DOME or by a tower over the crossing.

CROSS SECTION. See SECTION.

CRUCIFIX. From the Latin word *crucifixus.* A representation of a cross with the figure of Christ crucified on it. See CHRISTUS MORTUUS, CHRISTUS PATIENS, and CHRISTUS TRIUMPHANS.

CRYPT. A VAULTED chamber, usually beneath the raised CHOIR of a church, housing a tomb and/or a chapel. Also, a vaulted underground chamber used for burial as in the catacombs.

CUFIC. See KUFIC.

CUNEIFORM. From the Latin for *wedge-shaped.* Used to describe Mesopotamian scripts, which were written in soft clay with the wedge-shaped end of a reed.

CUPOLA. A rounded, convex roof or VAULTED ceiling, usually hemispherical, on a circular BASE and requiring BUTTRESSING. See DOME.

CUSP. The pointed projection where two curves meet.

CYCLOPEAN MASONRY. Walls constructed with massive stones more or less irregular in shape, once thought to be the work of the mythical race of giants called CYCLOPES.

CYCLOPS. A member of a mythical race of giants with one round eye in the center of the forehead. The Cyclopes were believed to have forged Zeus' thunderbolts and to have built massive prehistoric walls.

DEËSIS. The Greek word for *supplication.* A representation of Christ Enthroned between the Virgin Mary and Saint John the Baptist, who act as intercessors for mankind, which appears frequently in Byzantine MOSAICS and in later depictions of the Last Judgment.

DENTILS. A series of small, ornamental, projecting, teethlike blocks found on Ionic and Corinthian CORNICES.

DIAKONICON. See VESTRY.

DIOCESE. The district, or see, in which a BISHOP has authority.

DIPTERAL. Having a double COLONNADE or PERISTYLE.

DIPTYCH. A pair of wood, ivory, or metal plaques usually hinged together, with the interior surfaces either painted or CARVED with a religious or memorial subject, or covered with wax for writing.

DOGE. Italian word for the *chief magistrate* in the former republics of Venice and Genoa.

DOLMEN. A structure of large unhewn stones set on end and covered with a single stone or several stones.

DOME. A large CUPOLA supported by a circular wall or DRUM, or, over a noncircular space, by corner structures. See PENDENTIVE and SQUINCH.

DOMINICAN ORDER. A preaching ORDER of the Roman Catholic Church founded by Saint Dominic in 1216 in Toulouse. The Dominicans live austerely, believe in having no possessions, and subsist on charity. It is the second great mendicant order, after the FRANCISCAN.

DOUAY VERSION. See BIBLE.

DRUM. One of several sections composing the SHAFT of a COLUMN. Also, a cylindrical wall supporting a DOME.

ECHINUS. In architecture, the rounded cushion-shaped molding below the ABACUS of a Doric CAPITAL.

ELEVATION. One side of a building or a drawing of the same.

ENAMEL. Powdered colored glass thermally fused to a metal ground. *Champlevé* is a method by which the areas to be filled with enamel are dug out of the ground with a cutting tool. *Cloisonné* is a method in which the surface to be decorated is divided into compartments or *cloisons* by strips of metal attached to the ground. The compartments are filled with enamel powder and the piece is fused.

ENCAUSTIC. A method of painting on wood panels and walls with colors dissolved in hot wax.

ENGAGED COLUMN. See COLUMN.

ENTABLATURE. The upper part of an architectural ORDER, usually divided into three major parts: ARCHITRAVE, FRIEZE, and CORNICE.

ENTASIS. The subtle convex curvature swelling along the line of taper of classical COLUMNS.

EPISTLE. In Christian usage, one of the apostolic letters that constitute twenty-one books of the New Testament. See also MASS.

EUCHARIST. From the Greek word for *thanksgiving*. The SACRAMENT of the Lord's Supper; the consecrated bread and wine used in the rite of Communion, or the rite itself.

EVANGELISTS, FOUR. Matthew, Mark, Luke, and John, generally assumed to be the authors of the GOSPELS in the New Testament. They are usually represented with their symbols, which are derived either from the four mysterious creatures in the vision of Ezekiel (1:5) or from the four beasts surrounding the throne of the Lamb in Revelation (4:7). Frequently, they are referred to by the symbols alone: an angel for Matthew, a lion for Mark, a bull for Luke, and an eagle for John, or by a representation of the four rivers of Paradise.

EXARCHATE. A province of the Byzantine Empire ruled by a provincial governor called an *exarch*.

EXEDRA (pl. EXEDRAE). A semicircular PORCH, chapel, or recess in a wall.

EXOSKELETON. By extension from zoology, the system of supports in a French Gothic church, including the RIBBED VAULTS, FLYING BUTTRESSES, and PIER BUTTRESSES.

FAÇADE. The front or principal face of a building; sometimes loosely used to indicate the entire outer surface of any side.

FAIENCE. Glazed earthenware or pottery used for sculpture, tiles, and decorative objects.

FAN VAULT. A complex VAULT, characteristic of late English Gothic architecture, in which radiating RIBS form a fanlike pattern.

FASCIA (pl. FASCIAE). Any long flat surface of wood or stone. In the Ionic and Corinthian ORDERS, the three surfaces, the top two of which project slightly over the one below, that make up the ARCHITRAVE.

FLUTING. The shallow vertical grooves in the SHAFT of a COLUMN that either meet in a sharp edge as in Doric columns or are separated by a narrow strip as in Ionic columns.

FLYING BUTTRESS. An ARCH that springs from the upper part of the PIER BUTTRESS of a Gothic church, spans the AISLE roof, and abuts the upper NAVE wall to receive the THRUST from the nave VAULTS; it transmits this thrust to the solid pier buttress.

FONT. A receptacle in a BAPTISTERY or church for the water used in Baptism; it is usually of stone and frequently decorated with sculpture.

FORESHORTENING. In drawing, painting, etc., a method of reproducing the forms of an object not parallel to the PICTURE PLANE so that the object seems to recede in space and to convey the illusion of three dimensions as perceived by the human eye.

FORUM (pl. FORA). In ancient Rome, the center of assembly for judicial and other public business, and a gathering place for the people.

FOUR RIVERS OF PARADISE. See EVANGELISTS

FRANCISCAN ORDER. The first great mendicant ORDER. Founded by Saint Francis of Assisi (Giovanni de Bernardone, 1182?–1226) for the purpose of ministering to the spiritual needs of the poor and imitating as closely as possible the life of Christ, especially in its poverty; the monks depended only on alms for subsistence.

FRESCO. Italian word for *fresh*. A painting executed on wet plaster with pigments suspended in water so that the plaster absorbs the colors and the painting becomes part of the wall. *Fresco a secco,* or painting on dry plaster (*secco* is the Italian word for *dry*), is a much less durable technique; the paint tends to flake off with time. The *secco su fresco* method involves the application of color in a vehicle containing some organic binding material (such as oil, egg, or wax) over the still damp plaster.

FRIEZE. The architectural element that rests upon the ARCHITRAVE and is immediately below the CORNICE; also, any horizontal band decorated with MOLDINGS, RELIEF sculpture, or painting.

GABLE. The vertical, triangular piece of wall at the end of a ridged roof, from the level of the eaves or CORNICE to the summit; called a PEDIMENT in Classical architecture. It is sometimes used with no roof, as over the PORTALS of Gothic cathedrals, and as a decorative element on ALTARPIECES.

GALLERY. An elevated floor projecting from the interior wall of a building. In a BASILICAN church it is placed over the SIDE AISLES and supported by the COLUMNS or PIERS that separate the NAVE and the side aisles; in a church with a central PLAN, it is placed over the AMBULATORY; in an ancient Roman basilica, it was generally built over each end as well as over the side aisles.

GESSO. A mixture of finely ground plaster and glue spread on wooden panels in preparation for TEMPERA painting.

GILDING. Coating paintings, sculptures, and architectural ornament with gold, gold leaf, or some gold-colored substance, either by mechanical or chemical means. In panel painting and wood sculpture, the gold leaf is attached with a glue sizing that is usually a dull red in color.

GLAZE. In pottery, a superficial layer of molten material used to coat a finished piece before it is fired in a kiln.

GLORY. The circle of light represented around the head or figure of the Savior, the Virgin Mary, or a saint. When it surrounds the head only, it is called a *halo*. See MANDORLA.

GOLGOTHA. From the Aramaic word for *skull;* thus, *the Place of the Skull.* The name of the place outside Jerusalem where Christ was crucified (Matthew 27:33). *Calvary,* from *calvaria* meaning *skull* (Luke 23:33), is the Latin translation of the Aramaic word.

GORGON. In ancient Greece, one of three mythological sisters, having snakes for hair, whose hideous appearance turned every beholder to stone. Of the three, Medusa is represented most frequently.

GOSPEL. In Christian usage, the story of Christ's life and teaching, as related in the first four books of the New Testament, traditionally ascribed to the Evangelists Matthew, Mark, Luke, and John. Also used to designate an ILLUMINATED copy of the same; sometimes called a Gospel LECTIONARY. See MASS.

GREEK CROSS. A cross with four equal arms.

GRIFFIN. A fabulous animal usually having the head and wings of an eagle and the body of a lion.

GROIN. The sharp edge formed by two intersecting VAULTS.

GROIN VAULT. A VAULT formed by the intersection at right angles of two BARREL VAULTS of equal height and diameter so that the GROINS form a diagonal cross.

GROUND PLAN. See PLAN.

GUILDS. *Arti* (sing. *Arte*) in Italian. Independent associations of bankers and of artisan-manufacturers. The seven major guilds in Florence were: *Arte della Calimala*—refiners of imported wool; *Arte della Lana*—wool merchants who manufactured their own cloth; *Arte dei Giudici e Notai*—judges and notaries; *Arte del Cambio*—bankers and money changers; *Arte della Seta*—silk weavers, to which sculptors in metal belonged; *Arte dei Medici e Speziali*—doctors and pharmacists, to which painters belonged; *Arte dei Vaiai e Pellicciai*—furriers. Other important guilds were *Arte di Pietra e Legname*—workers in stone and wood; *Arte dei Corazzai e Spadai*—armorers and sword makers; *Arte dei Linaioli e Rigattieri*—linen drapers and peddlers.

HALLENKIRCHE. German word for *hall church.* A church in which the AISLES are as high, or almost as high, as the NAVE; especially popular in the German Gothic style.

HALO. See GLORY.

HIEROGLYPHS. Characters (pictures or symbols representing or standing for sounds, words, ideas, etc.) in the picture-writing system of the ancient Egyptians.

HIMATION. A mantle worn in ancient times by Greek men and women and draped in a variety of styles over the CHITON.

HOST. From the Latin word for *sacrificial victim (hostia).* In the Roman Catholic Church it is used to designate the bread or wafer, regarded as the body of Christ, consecrated in the EUCHARIST.

HUE. The name of a color. The spectrum is usually divided into six basic hues: the three primary colors of red, yellow, and blue, and the secondary colors of green, orange, and violet.

ICON. Literally, any image or likeness, but commonly used to designate a panel representing Christ, the Virgin Mary, or a saint and venerated by Orthodox (Eastern) Catholics.

ICONOCLASM. Breaking or destroying of images, particularly those set up for religious veneration. Many paintings and statues were destroyed in the Eastern church in the eighth and ninth centuries as a result of the Iconoclastic Controversy. In the sixteenth and seventeenth centuries, especially in the Netherlands, the Protestants also destroyed many religious images.

ICONOSTASIS. In Eastern Christian churches, a screen separating the main body of the church from the SANCTUARY; it is usually decorated with ICONS whose subject matter and order were largely predetermined.

ILLUMINATED MANUSCRIPTS. CODICES or SCROLLS decorated with illustrations or designs in gold, silver, and bright colors.

IMAM. Muslim teacher who, serving as a priest in a mosque, recites the prayers and leads the devotions of the faithful.

IMPERATOR. Freely translated from the Latin as *emperor,* but in Roman times it literally meant *army commander.*

IMPOST BLOCK. A block placed between the CAPITAL of a COLUMN and the ARCHES or VAULTS it supports.

INSULA (pl. INSULAE). Latin word for *island.* In Roman antiquity, a mapped-out space or a city block. Also, a group of buildings or a large building similar to a modern apartment house.

IRON AGE. See BRONZE and IRON AGES.

JAMB. The vertical piece or pieces forming the side of a doorway or window. In Romanesque and Gothic churches, these supports were slanted or splayed outward to increase the impression of thickness in the walls and to provide space for sculptural decoration.

KA'BAH. The most sacred shrine of the Muslims. A small cube-shaped building in the great mosque at Mecca toward which Muslims face when praying. It contains a sacred stone said to have been turned black by the tears of repentent pilgrims or, according to another tradition, by the sins of those who have touched it.

KEEP. The innermost central tower of a medieval castle, which served both as a last defense and as a dungeon and which contained living quarters, a prison, and sometimes a chapel; or a tower-like fortress, square, polygonal, or round, generally built on a mound as a military outpost.

KEYSTONE. See ARCH.

KING JAMES VERSION. See BIBLE.

KORAN. The sacred Muslim writings as revealed by Allah to Mohammed and taken down by him or his companions.

KORE (pl. KORAI). Greek for *maiden.* An archaic Greek statue of a standing clothed female.

KOUROS (pl. KOUROI). Greek for *youth.* An archaic Greek statue of a standing nude young man.

KRATER. A Greek or Roman bowl with a wide neck, used for mixing wine and water. The body has two handles projecting vertically from the juncture of the neck and body.

KUFIC or CUFIC. The earliest Arabic script used on CARVINGS and manuscripts, and, in the West, sometimes as pure ornament.

KYLIX. In Greek and Roman antiquity, a drinking vessel shaped like a shallow bowl with two horizontal handles projecting from the sides; often set upon a stem with a foot.

LABORS OF THE MONTHS. Representations of occupations suitable to the twelve months of the year; frequently CARVED around the PORTALS of Romanesque and Gothic churches together with the signs of the ZODIAC, or represented in the calendar scenes of ILLUMINATED MANUSCRIPTS.

LANCET WINDOW. A high, narrow window with a pointed arch at the top.

LANTERN. In architecture, a tall, more or less open structure crowning a roof, DOME, tower, etc., and admitting light to an enclosed area below.

LAPIS LAZULI. A deep blue stone or complex mixture of minerals used for ornamentation and in the making of pigments.

LA TÈNE. An IRON AGE culture named after its site on Lake Neuchâtel in Switzerland.

LECTIONARY. A book containing portions of the Scriptures arranged in the order in which they are read at Christian services.

LEKYTHOS. In ancient Greece, a tall vase with an ellipsoidal body, a narrow neck, and a flanged mouth. The curved handle extends from below the lip to the shoulder, and the narrow base ends in a foot. It was used to contain oil or perfumes.

LIBERAL ARTS, SEVEN. Derived from the standard medieval prephilosophical education, they consisted of the trivium of Grammar, Rhetoric, and Logic, and the quadrivium of Arithmetic, Music, Geometry, and Astronomy. During the Middle Ages and the Renaissance, they were frequently represented allegorically.

LINTEL. See POST AND LINTEL.

LITURGY. A collection of prescribed prayers and ceremonies for public worship; specifically, in the Roman Catholic, Orthodox, and Anglican churches, those used in the celebration of the MASS.

LOGGIA (pl. LOGGIE). A GALLERY or ARCADE open on at least one side.

LUNETTE. A semicircular opening or surface, as on the wall of a VAULTED room or over a door, niche, or window. When it is over the PORTAL of a church, it is called a TYMPANUM.

LUTHER, MARTIN. See BIBLE.

MADRASAH. Arabic word meaning *place of study.* An Islamic theological college providing student lodgings, a prayer hall, lecture halls, and a library. Perhaps first established in the tenth century by the Ghaznavids to combat the influence of dissenting sects, such as the Shi'ites; by the fourteenth century madrasahs were located in all great cities of the Muslim world. Usually consists of an open quadrangle bordered by VAULTED CLOISTERS called *iwans.*

MAENAD. An ecstatic female follower of the wine god Dionysos (Greek) or Bacchus (Roman); hence, also called a *bacchante* (pl. *bacchae*).

MAESTÀ. Italian word for *majesty,* and in religion signifying the Virgin in Majesty. A large ALTARPIECE with a central panel representing the Virgin Enthroned, adored by saints and angels.

MAGUS (pl. MAGI). A member of the priestly caste in ancient Media and Persia traditionally reputed to have practiced supernatural arts. In Christian art, the Three Wise Men who came from the East to pay homage to the Infant Jesus are called the *Magi.*

MANDORLA. The Italian word for *almond.* A large oval surrounding the figure of God, Christ, the Virgin Mary, or occasionally a saint, indicating divinity or holiness.

MARTYRIUM. A shrine or chapel erected in honor of or over the grave of a martyr.

MASS. The celebration of the EUCHARIST to perpetuate the sacrifice of Christ upon the Cross, plus readings from one of the GOSPELS and an EPISTLE; also, the form of LITURGY used in this celebration. See CANON OF THE MASS and ORDINARY AND PROPER OF THE MASS.

MASTABA. Arabic for *bench.* In Egyptian times, a tomb constructed of masonry and mud brick, rectangular in plan, with sloping sides and a flat roof. It covered a burial chamber and a chapel for offerings.

MAUSOLEUM. The magnificent tomb of Mausolus, erected by his wife at Halikarnassos in the middle of the fourth century B.C. Hence, any stately building erected as a burial place.

MAZZOCCHIO. A wire or wicker frame around which a hood or *cappuccio* was wrapped to form the turban-like headdress commonly worn by Florentine men in the fifteenth century.

MEANDER. From the name of a winding river in Asia Minor. In Greek decoration, an ornamental pattern of lines that wind in and out or cross one another.

MEGARON. Principal hall in a Mycenaean palace or house.

MENDICANT ORDERS. See DOMINICAN and FRANCISCAN.

MENHIR. A prehistoric monument consisting of an upright monumental stone, left rough or sometimes partly shaped, and either standing alone or grouped with others.

MESOLITHIC ERA. Middle Stone Age, approximately 19,000–18,000 to 9000–8000 B.C. An intermediate period charac-

terized by food-gathering activities and the beginnings of agriculture.

METOPE. A square slab, sometimes decorated, between the TRIGLYPHS in the FRIEZE of the ENTABLATURE of the Doric ORDER. Originally, the openings left by Greek builders between the ends of ceiling beams.

MIHRAB. Arabic word for a niche in the QIBLA wall of a mosque, pointing in the direction of Mecca. Perhaps of Egypto-Christian origin, it was first installed in the early eighth-century rebuilding of the mosque at Medina.

MINARET. A tall slender tower attached to a mosque and surrounded by one or more balconies from which the MUEZZIN calls the people to prayer.

MINBAR. Arabic word initially referring to the pulpit used in Medina by Mohammed, and later referring to the pulpit installed in each mosque to the right of the MIHRAB for the reading of the KORAN and prayers by the IMAM.

MINOTAUR. In Greek mythology, a monster with the body of a man and the head of a bull, who, confined in the labyrinth built for Minos, king of Crete, in his palace at Knossos, fed on human flesh and who was killed by the Athenian hero Theseus.

MITER. A tall cap terminating in two peaks, one in front and one in back, that is the distinctive headdress of BISHOPS (including the pope as bishop of Rome) and abbots of the Western Church.

MOAT. A deep defensive ditch that surrounds the wall of a fortified town or castle and is usually filled with water.

MODELING. The building up of three-dimensional form in a soft substance, such as clay or wax; the CARVING of surfaces into proper RELIEF; the rendering of the appearance of three-dimensional form in painting.

MOLDING. An ornamental strip, either depressed or projecting, that gives variety to the surface of a building by creating contrasts of light and shadow.

MOSAIC. A type of surface decoration (used on pavements, walls, and VAULTS) in which bits of colored stone or glass (*tesserae*) are laid in cement in a figurative design or decorative pattern. In Roman examples, colored stones, set regularly, are most frequently used; in Byzantine work bits of glass, many with gold baked into them, are set irregularly.

MUEZZIN. In Muslim countries, a crier who calls the people to prayer at stated hours, either from a MINARET or from another part of a mosque or high building.

MULLION. A vertical element that divides a window or a screen into partitions.

MURAL. A painting executed directly on a wall or done separately for a specific wall and attached to it.

MUSES. The nine sister goddesses of Classical mythology who presided over learning and the arts. They came to be known as Calliope, muse of epic poetry; Clio, muse of history; Erato, muse of love poetry; Euterpe, muse of music; Melpomene, muse of tragedy; Polyhymnia, muse of sacred song; Terpsichore, muse of dancing; Thalia, muse of comedy; and Urania, muse of astronomy.

NARTHEX. A PORCH or vestibule, sometimes enclosed, preceding the main entrance of a church; frequently, in churches preceded by an ATRIUM, the narthex is one side of the open AMBULATORY.

NAVE. From the Latin word for *ship.* The central aisle of an ancient Roman BASILICA or a Christian basilican church, as distinguished from the SIDE AISLES; the part of a church, between the main entrance and the CHANCEL, used by the congregation.

NEANDERTHAL MAN. A species of Middle Paleolithic man.

NEOLITHIC ERA. New Stone Age, approximately 9000–8000 to 3000 B.C. Characterized by fixed settlements and farming, and the beginnings of architecture and religion.

NIKE. See VICTORY.

OCULUS (pl. OCULI). Latin word for *eye*. A circular opening in a wall or at the apex of a DOME.

OINOCHOE. A Greek pitcher with a three-lobed rim for dipping wine from a bowl and pouring it into wine cups.

ORANT. From the Latin word for *praying*. Used to describe figures standing with arms outstretched in an attitude of prayer.

ORDER (architectural). An architectural system based on the COLUMN (including BASE, SHAFT, and CAPITAL) and its ENTABLATURE (including ARCHITRAVE, FRIEZE, and CORNICE). The five classical orders are the Doric, Ionic, Corinthian, Tuscan, and Composite.

ORDER (monastic). A religious society or confraternity whose members live under a strict set of rules and regulations, such as the BENEDICTINE, CISTERCIAN, DOMINICAN, FRANCISCAN, Carthusian, CLUNIAC, Jesuit, and Theatine.

ORDINARY AND PROPER OF THE MASS. The service of the MASS exclusive of the CANON. It includes prayers, hymns, and readings from the EPISTLES and the GOSPELS.

ORTHOGONALS. Lines that are at right angles to the plane of the picture surface, but that, in a representation using one-point PERSPECTIVE, converge toward a common vanishing point in the distance.

PALAZZO (pl. PALAZZI). Italian word for a *large town house*; used freely to refer to large civic or religious buildings as well as to relatively modest town houses.

PALEOLITHIC ERA. Old Stone Age, approximately 30,000 to 19,000 B.C. Populated by a society of nomadic hunters who used stone weapons and implements, and who lived largely in caves that they decorated with paintings.

PALESTRA (pl. PALESTRAE). In Greek antiquity, a public place for training in wrestling or athletics. A gymnasium.

PALETTE. A thin, usually oval or oblong tablet, with a hole for the thumb, upon which painters place and mix their colors.

PANTHEON. From the Greek words meaning *all the gods*; hence, a temple dedicated to all the gods. Specifically, the famous temple built about 25 B.C. in Rome and so dedicated.

PANTOCRATOR. A representation of Christ as the Almighty Ruler of the Universe (from the Greek) in which the attributes of God the Father are combined with those of the Son; an image frequently found in the apse or dome MOSAICS of Byzantine churches.

PAPYRUS. A tall aquatic plant formerly very abundant in Egypt. Also, the material used for writing or painting upon by the ancient Egyptians, Greeks, and Romans. It was made by soaking, pressing, and drying thin strips of the pith of the plant laid together. Also, a manuscript or document of this material.

PARAPET. A low protective wall or barrier at the edge of a balcony, roof, bridge, or the like.

PARCHMENT. A paper-like material made from animal skins that have been carefully scraped, stretched, and dried to whiteness. The name is a corruption of *Pergamon,* the city in Asia Minor where parchment was invented in the second century B.C. Also, a manuscript or document of such material.

PARECCLESION. A funeral chapel.

PASSION. In the Christian Church, used specifically to describe the sufferings of Christ during his last week of earthly life; the representation of his sufferings in narrative or pictorial form.

PEDESTAL. An architectural support for a COLUMN, statue, vase, etc.; also, a foundation or BASE.

PEDIMENT. A low-pitched triangular area, resembling a GABLE, formed by the two slopes of a roof of a building (over a PORTICO, door, niche, or window), framed by a raking CORNICE, and frequently decorated with sculpture. When pieces of the cornice are either omitted or jut out from the main axis, as in some late Roman and Baroque buildings, it is called a *broken pediment*. See TYMPANUM.

PENDENTIVE. An architectural feature, having the shape of a spherical triangle, used as a transition from a square ground PLAN to a circular plan that will support a DOME. The dome may rest directly on the pendentives or on an intermediate DRUM.

PENTATEUCH. See TORAH.

PEPLOS. A simple, loose outer garment worn by women in ancient Greece.

PERICOPE. Extracts or passages from the BIBLE selected for use in public worship.

PERIPTERAL. Having a COLONNADE or PERISTYLE on all four sides.

PERISTYLE. A COLONNADE or ARCADE around a building or open court.

PERSPECTIVE. The representation of three-dimensional objects on a flat surface so as to produce the same impression of distance and relative size as that received by the human eye. In one-point *linear perspective,* developed during the fifteenth century, all parallel lines in a given visual field converge at a single vanishing point on the horizon. In *aerial* or *atmospheric perspective* the relative distance of objects is indicated by gradations of tone and color, and by variations in the clarity of outlines. See ORTHOGONALS and TRANSVERSALS.

PHARAOH. From the Egyptian word meaning *great house*. A title of the sovereigns of ancient Egypt; used in the Old Testament as a proper name.

PIAZZA (pl. PIAZZE). Italian word for *public square*. See also CAMPO.

PICTURE PLANE. The actual surface on which a picture is painted.

PIER. An independent architectural element, usually rectangular in section, used to support a vertical load; if used with an ORDER, it often has a BASE and CAPITAL of the same design. See COMPOUND PIER.

PIER BUTTRESS. An exterior PIER in Romanesque and Gothic architecture, BUTTRESSING the THRUST of the VAULTS within.

PIETÀ. Italian word meaning both *pity* and *piety*. Used to designate a representation of the dead Christ mourned by the Virgin, with or without saints and angels. When the representation is intended to show a specific event prior to Christ's burial, it is usually called a *Lamentation*.

PILASTER. A flat vertical element, having a CAPITAL and BASE, engaged in a wall from which it projects. It has a decorative rather than a structural purpose.

PINNACLE. A small ornamental turret on top of BUTTRESSES, PIERS, or elsewhere; mainly decorative, it may also have a structural purpose, as in Reims Cathedral.

PLAN. The general arrangement of the parts of a building or group of buildings, or a drawing of these as they would appear on a plane cut horizontally above the ground or floor.

PODIUM (pl. PODIA). In architecture, a continuous projecting BASE or PEDESTAL used to support COLUMNS, sculptures, or a wall. Also, the raised platform surrounding the arena of an ancient AMPHITHEATER.

PORCH. An exterior structure forming a covered approach to the entrance of a building.

PORPHYRY. A very hard rock having a dark purplish-red base. The room in the Imperial Palace in Constantinople reserved for the confinement of the reigning empress was decorated with porphyry so that the child would be "born to the purple," or "Porphyrogenitus."

PORTA. Italian word for *gate*.

PORTA CLAUSA. Latin phrase for CLOSED DOOR or CLOSED GATE.

PORTAL. A door or gate, especially one of imposing appearance, as in the entrances and PORCHES of a large church or other building. In Gothic churches the FAÇADES frequently include three large portals with elaborate sculptural decoration.

PORTICO. A structure consisting of a roof, or an ENTABLATURE and PEDIMENT, supported by COLUMNS, sometimes attached to a building as a PORCH.

POST AND LINTEL. The ancient but still widely used system of construction in which the basic unit consists of two or more upright posts supporting a horizontal beam, or lintel, which spans the opening between them.

POTSHERD. A fragment or broken piece of earthenware.

PREDELLA. PEDESTAL of an ALTARPIECE, usually decorated with small narrative scenes that expand the theme of the major work above it.

PRIORI. Italian word for *priors*. The council or principal governing body of a town.

PRIORY. A monastic house presided over by a prior or prioress; a dependency of an ABBEY.

PRONAOS. The vestibule in front of the doorway to the SANCTUARY in a Greek or Roman PERIPTERAL temple.

PROPYLAION (pl. PROPYLAIA). Generally, the entrance to a temple or other sacred enclosure. Specifically, the entrance gate to the Acropolis in Athens.

PROSTYLE. Used to describe a temple having a PORTICO across the entire front.

PROTHESIS. In an Early Christian or modern Eastern Orthodox church, a space or chamber next to the SANCTUARY for the preparation and safekeeping of the EUCHARIST. See BEMA.

PSALTER. The Book of Psalms in the Old Testament, or a copy of it, used for liturgical or devotional purposes; many psalters illuminated in the Middle Ages have survived. See ILLUMINATED MANUSCRIPTS.

PUEBLO. Communal houses or groups of houses built of stone or ADOBE by the Indians of the southwestern United States.

PYLON. Greek word for *gateway*. In Egyptian architecture, the monumental entrance to a temple or other large edifice, consisting of two truncated pyramidal towers flanking a central gateway. Also, applied to either of the flanking towers.

QIBLA. The direction of Mecca, which Muslims face when praying, indicated by the MIHRAB in the qibla wall of a mosque.

QUATREFOIL. A four-lobed form used as ornamentation.

RAKING CORNICE. See CORNICE.

REFECTORY. From the Latin verb meaning to *renew* or *restore*. A room for eating; in particular, the dining hall in a monastery, college, or other institution.

REGISTER. One of a series of horizontal bands used to differentiate areas of decoration when the bands are placed one above the other as in Egyptian tombs, medieval church sculpture, and the pages of a manuscript.

RELIEF. Sculpture that is not freestanding but projects from the background of which it is a part. *High relief* or *low relief* describes the amount of projection; when the background is not cut out, as in some Egyptian sculpture, the work is called *incised relief*.

RELIQUARY. A casket, COFFER, or other small receptacle for a sacred relic, usually made of precious materials and richly decorated.

RHYTON. An ancient Greek drinking vessel having one handle and, frequently, the shape of an animal.

RIB. A slender projecting ARCH used primarily as support in Romanesque and Gothic VAULTS; in late Gothic architecture, the ribs are frequently ornamental as well as structural.

RIBBED VAULT. A compound masonry VAULT, the GROINS of which are marked by projecting stone RIBS.

ROSE WINDOW. A circular window with stone TRACERY radiating from the center; a feature characteristic of Gothic church architecture.

ROSTRUM (pl. ROSTRA). A pulpit or platform for public speakers. In the Roman FORUM, the orator's platform that was decorated with the beaks of warships captured in 338 B.C.

ROTULUS (pl. ROTULI). Latin word for SCROLL.

RUSTICATION. Masonry having indented joinings and, frequently, a roughened surface.

SACRAMENT. A rite regarded as an outward and visible sign of an inward and spiritual grace. Specifically, in the Roman Catholic Church, any one of the seven rites recognized as having been instituted by Christ: Baptism, confirmation, the EUCHARIST, penance, matrimony, holy orders, and extreme unction.

SACRISTY. See VESTRY.

SAHN. Arabic name for the open interior courtyard of a mosque; it usually has a pool in the center.

SANCTUARY. A sacred or holy place. In architecture, the term is generally used to designate the most sacred part of a building.

SARCOPHAGUS. From the Greek words meaning *flesh-eating*. In ancient Greece, a kind of limestone said to reduce flesh to dust; thus the term was used for coffins. A general term for a stone coffin often decorated with sculpture or bearing inscriptions.

SATURATION. The degree of intensity of a HUE and its relative freedom from an admixture with white.

SATYR. One of the woodland creatures thought to be the companions of Dionysos and noted for lasciviousness, represented with the body of a man, pointed ears, two horns, a tail, and the legs of a goat.

SCRIPTURE. See BIBLE and KORAN.

SCROLL. A roll of paper, PARCHMENT, or the like intended for writing upon. In architecture, an ornament resembling a partly unrolled sheet of paper or having a spiral or coiled form, as in the VOLUTES of Ionic and Corinthian COLUMNS.

SECTION. A drawing or diagram of a building showing its various parts as they would appear if the building were cut on a vertical plane.

SERAPH (pl. SERAPHIM). A celestial being or angel of the highest order, usually represented with six wings.

SHAFT. A cylindrical form; in architecture, the part of a COLUMN or PIER between the BASE and the CAPITAL.

SIBYL. Any of various women of Greek and Roman mythology who were reputed to possess powers of prophecy and divination. In time, as many as twelve came to be recognized, some of whom Michelangelo painted in the frescoes adorning the Sistine Chapel ceiling because they were believed to have foretold the first coming of Christ.

SIDE AISLE. One of the corridors parallel to the NAVE of a church or BASILICA, separated from it by an ARCADE or COLONNADE.

SINOPIA (pl. SINOPIE). An Italian term taken from *Sinope*, the name of a city in Asia Minor famous for its red earth. Used to designate the preliminary brush drawing executed in red earth mixed with water, for a painting in FRESCO; usually done on the ARRICCIO of the wall.

SINS, SEVEN DEADLY. See VICES.

SIREN. In Classical mythology, one of several fabulous creatures, half woman and half bird, who were reputed to lure sailors to destruction by their seductive singing.

SLIP. Potter's clay reduced with water to a semiliquid state and used for coating or decorating pottery, cementing handles, etc.

SOCLE. A square block supporting a COLUMN, statue, vase, or other work of art, or a low BASE supporting a wall.

SPANDREL. An area between the exterior curves of two adjoining ARCHES, or, enclosed by the exterior curve of an arch, a perpendicular from its springing and a horizontal through its apex.

SPHINX. In Egyptian mythology, a creature with the body of a lion and the head of a man, a bird, or a beast; the monumental sculpture of the same. In Greek mythology, a monster usually having the winged body of a lion and the head of a woman.

SQUINCH. An architectural device that uses ARCHES, LINTELS, or CORBELS across the corners of a square space to support a DOME and to make the transition from the square space to a polygonal or round one.

STEATITE. A variety of talc or soapstone.

STELE (pl. STELAE). A Greek word meaning *standing block*. An upright slab bearing sculptured or painted designs or inscriptions.

STOA. In Greek architecture, a PORTICO or covered COLON-NADE, usually of considerable length, used as a prome-nade or meeting place.

STONE AGE. See MESOLITHIC, NEOLITHIC, and PALEOLITHIC.

STUCCO. Any of various plasters used for CORNICES, MOLD-INGS, and other wall decorations. A cement or concrete for coating exterior walls in imitation of stone.

STYLOBATE. The top step of a stepped BASE of a Greek temple, on which COLUMNS rest.

STYLUS. A pointed instrument used in ancient times for writing on tablets of a soft material, such as clay.

SUPERIMPOSED ORDERS. One ORDER on top of another on the face of a building of more than one story. The upper order is usually lighter in form than the lower.

TEMPERA. Ground colors mixed with yolk of egg, instead of oil, as a vehicle; a medium widely used for Italian panel painting before the sixteenth century.

TERRA-COTTA. Italian words for *baked earth*. A hard glazed or unglazed earthenware used for sculpture and pottery or as a building material. The word can also mean something made of this material or the color of it, a dull brownish red.

TESSERA (pl. TESSERAE). See MOSAIC.

THEATER. In ancient Greece and Rome, an open-air structure in the form of a segment of a circle, frequently excavated from a hillside, with the seats arranged in tiers behind and above one another.

THEOLOGICAL VIRTUES. See VIRTUES.

THEOTOKOS. The Virgin Mary as the Mother of God.

THOLOS. In Greek and Roman architecture, a circular building derived from early Greek tombs and used for a variety of purposes.

THRUST. The outward force exerted by an ARCH or VAULT that must be counterbalanced by BUTTRESSING.

TIE ROD. An iron rod used as a structural element to keep the lower ends of a roof or ARCH from spreading.

TOGA. A loose outer garment consisting of a single piece of material, without sleeves or armholes, which covered nearly the whole body, worn by the citizens of ancient Rome when appearing in public in times of peace.

TORAH. The Jewish books of the law or the first five books of the Old Testament. Also called the *Pentateuch* in both Jewish and Christian usage.

TOTEM POLE. A wooden post carved and painted with the emblem (totem) of a clan or family, and erected in front of the homes of the Indians of northwestern America.

TRACERY. Ornamental stonework in geometric patterns used primarily in Gothic windows as support and decoration, but also used on panels, screens, etc. When the window

appears to be cut through the solid stone, the style is called *plate tracery;* when slender pieces of stone are erected within the window opening, the style is called *bar tracery.*

TRANSEPT. In a BASILICAN church, the crossarm, placed at right angles to the NAVE, usually separating the latter from the CHANCEL or the APSE.

TRANSVERSALS. Horizontal lines running parallel to the PIC-TURE PLANE and intersecting the ORTHOGONALS.

TRAVERTINE. A tan or light-colored limestone used in Italy, and elsewhere, for building. The surface is characterized by alternating smooth and porous areas.

TREE OF THE KNOWLEDGE OF GOOD AND EVIL. A tree in the Garden of Eden bearing the forbidden fruit, the eating of which destroyed Adam's and Eve's innocence (Gen. 2:9; 3:17).

TREFOIL. A three-lobed form used as ornamentation or as the basis for a ground PLAN.

TRICLINIUM. The dining room in a Roman house.

TRIFORIUM. The section of the wall in the NAVE, CHOIR, and sometimes in the TRANSEPT above the ARCHES and below the CLERESTORY. It usually consists of a blind ARCADE or a GALLERY.

TRIGLYPH. From the Greek for *three grooves*. An ornamental member of a Doric FRIEZE, placed between two METOPES and consisting of a rectangular slab with two complete grooves in the center and a half groove at either side. Originally the end of a ceiling beam.

TRILITHON. Greek for *three stones*. A structure consisting of large unhewn stones, two upright and one resting on them like a LINTEL.

TRIUMPHAL ARCH. In ancient Rome, a freestanding mon-umental ARCH or series of three arches erected to com-memorate a military victory; usually decorated with sculptured scenes of a war and its subsequent triumphal procession. In a Christian church, the transverse wall with a large arched opening that separates the CHANCEL and the APSE from the main body of the church, and that is frequently decorated with religious scenes executed in MOSAIC or FRESCO.

TRUMEAU (pl. TRUMEAUX). A central PIER, dividing a wide doorway, used to support the LINTEL; in medieval churches, trumeaux were frequently decorated with sculpture.

TUFA. Any of various porous rocks composed of calcium deposited by springs or streams; or a volcanic stone.

TUMULUS (pl. TUMULI). An artificially constructed mound of earth raised over a tomb or sepulchral chamber.

TUNIC. In ancient Greece and Rome, a knee-length garment with or without sleeves usually worn without a girdle by both sexes.

TYMPANUM (pl. TYMPANA). In Classical architecture, the verti-cal recessed face of a PEDIMENT; in medieval architecture, the space between an ARCH and the LINTEL over a door or window, which was often decorated with sculpture.

VALUE. The degree of lightness or darkness of a HUE.

VAULT. An ARCHED roof or covering made of brick, stone, or concrete. See BARREL VAULT, GROIN VAULT, RIBBED VAULT, and CORBEL.

VELLUM. A fine kind of PARCHMENT made from calfskin and used for the writing, ILLUMINATING, and binding of medieval manuscripts.

VESTRY. A room in or a building attached to a church where the vestments and sacred vessels are kept; also called a *sacristy.* Used, in some churches, as a chapel or a meeting room.

VICAR. An ecclesiastic of the Roman Catholic Church who represents a pope or BISHOP; the pope himself as the vicar of Christ.

VICES. Coming from the same tradition as the VIRTUES, and

frequently paired with them, they are more variable, but usually include Pride, Avarice, Wrath, Gluttony, and Unchastity. Others such as Folly, Inconstancy, and Injustice may be selected to make a total of seven.

VICTORY. A female deity of the ancient Romans, or the corresponding deity the ancient Greeks called NIKE. The representation of the deity, usually as a winged woman in windblown draperies and holding a laurel wreath, palm branch, or other symbolic object.

VIRTUES. Divided into the three Theological Virtues of Faith, Hope, and Charity, and the four Cardinal Virtues of Prudence, Justice, Fortitude, and Temperance. As with the VICES, the allegorical representation of the Virtues derives from a long medieval tradition in manuscripts and sculpture, and from such literary sources as the *Psychomachia* of Prudentius and the writings of Saint Augustine.

VOLUTE. An ornament resembling a rolled SCROLL. Especially prominent on CAPITALS of the Ionic and Composite ORDERS.

VOUSSOIR. See ARCH.

VULGATE. See BIBLE.

WESTWORK. The multistoried, towered western end of a Carolingian church that usually included a second TRANSEPT below and a chapel and GALLERIES above.

ZIGGURAT. From the Assyrian-Babylonian word *ziqquratu (mountaintop)*. A staged, truncated pyramid of mud brick, built by the Sumerians and later by the Assyrians as a support for a shrine.

ZODIAC. An imaginary belt encircling the heavens within which lie the paths of the sun, moon, and principal planets. It is divided into twelve equal parts called *signs*, which are named after twelve constellations: Aries, the ram; Taurus, the bull; Gemini, the twins; Cancer, the crab; Leo, the lion; Virgo, the virgin; Libra, the balance; Scorpio, the scorpion; Sagittarius, the archer; Capricorn, the goat; Aquarius, the water-bearer; and Pisces, the fishes. Also, a circular or elliptical diagram representing this belt with pictures of the symbols associated with the constellations.

Bibliography

INTRODUCTION

ARNHEIM, RUDOLF, *Art and Visual Perception,* 2d ed., University of California Press, Berkeley, 1974

——————, *Visual Thinking,* University of California Press, Berkeley, 1969

BEAM, PHILIP C., *The Language of Art,* Ronald Press, New York, 1958

BERNHEIMER, RICHARD, *The Nature of Representation,* New York University Press, 1961

BOAS, GEORGE, *The Heaven of Invention,* Johns Hopkins Press, Baltimore, 1962

COLLIER, GRAHAM, *Art and the Creative Consciousness,* Prentice-Hall, Englewood Cliffs, N.J., 1972

COLLINGWOOD, R. C., *Principles of Art,* Clarendon Press, Oxford, 1938

DESSOIR, MAX, *Aesthetics and Theory of Art* (tr. S. A. Emery), Wayne State University Press, Detroit, 1970

DICKIE, GEORGE, *Art and the Aesthetic: An Institutional Analysis,* Cornell University Press, Ithaca, N.Y., 1974

DUCASSE, C. J., *The Philosophy of Art,* 2d ed., Dover, New York, 1966

FEIBLEMAN, JAMES K., *The Quiet Rebellion: The Making and Meaning of the Arts,* Horizon, New York, 1972

FOCILLON, HENRI, *The Life of Forms in Art* (tr. C. B. Hogan and G. Kubler), 2d ed., Wittenborn, New York, 1958

GILSON, ÉTIENNE, *Painting and Reality,* Pantheon, New York, 1957

GOLDWATER, ROBERT, and TREVES, M., *Artists on Art,* Pantheon, New York, 1945

GOMBRICH, ERNST H., *Art and Illusion,* 2d ed., Princeton University Press, 1969

HOLT, ELIZABETH B., *Literary Sources of Art History,* Princeton University Press, 1947

HUYGHE, RENÉ, *Ideas and Images in World Art* (tr. N. Guterman), Abrams, New York, 1959

JENKINS, IREDELL, *Art and Human Enterprise,* Harvard University Press, Cambridge, Mass., 1958

KEPES, GYORGY, ed., *The Man-Made Object,* Braziller, New York, 1966

KRAUSE, JOSEPH H., *The Nature of Art,* Prentice-Hall, Englewood Cliffs, N.J., 1969

KUBLER, GEORGE, *The Shape of Time,* Yale University Press, New Haven, Conn., 1962

LOWRY, BATES, *The Visual Experience,* Abrams, New York, 1967

MALRAUX, ANDRÉ, *The Voices of Silence,* Doubleday, New York, 1953

MUNRO, THOMAS, *The Arts and Their Interrelations,* 2d ed., Press of Western Reserve University, Cleveland, 1967

NAHM, MILTON CHARLES, *The Artist as Creator,* Johns Hopkins Press, Baltimore, 1956

PACH, WALTER, *The Classical Tradition in Modern Art,* Yoseloff, New York, 1959

PANOFSKY, ERWIN, *Meaning in the Visual Arts,* Doubleday, Garden City, N.Y., 1955

PODRO, MICHAEL, *The Manifold in Perception: Theories of Art from Kant to Hildebrand,* Clarendon Press, Oxford, 1972

READ, SIR HERBERT E., *Art and Alienation: The Role of the Artist in Society,* Horizon, New York, 1967

——————, *Art and Society,* Schocken Books, New York, 1966

——————, *Art Now,* 5th ed., Faber & Faber, London, 1968

ROSENBERG, HAROLD, *The Anxious Object: Art Today and Its Audience,* Horizon, New York, 1964

——————, *The De-definition of Art,* Horizon, New York, 1972

SIRCELLO, GUY, *Mind and Art,* Princeton University Press, 1972

PART ONE

ART BEFORE WRITING

PERICOT-GARCIA, LUIS, GALLOWAY, J., and LOMMEL, A., *Prehistoric and Primitive Art,* Abrams, New York, 1967

1. PALEOLITHIC ART

GENERAL

BANDI, HANS GEORG, et al., *The Art of the Stone Age,* Crown, New York, 1961

BOAS, FRANZ, *Primitive Art,* 2d ed., Dover, New York, 1955

BRENTJES, BURCHARD, *African Rock Art* (tr. A. Dent), Dent, London, 1969

BREUIL, HENRI, *Four Hundred Centuries of Cave Art* (tr. M. A. Boyle), Montignac, France, Centre d'études et de documentation préhistorique, 1952

——————, and LANTIER, R., *The Men of the Old Stone Age* (tr. B. B. Rafter), 2d ed., St. Martin's Press, New York, 1965

BURKITT, MILES C., *The Old Stone Age,* 3d ed., New York University Press, 1956

CHILDE, V. GORDON, *The Dawn of European Civilization,* 4th ed., Kegan Paul, Trench, Trubner, 1947

CLARKE, GRAHAME, *The Stone Age Hunters,* McGraw-Hill, New York, 1967

FROBENIUS, LEO, and FOX, D. C., *Prehistoric Rock Pictures in Europe and Africa,* Museum of Modern Art, New York, 1937

GIEDION, SIGFRIED, *The Eternal Present,* 2 vols., Pantheon, New York, 1962–64.

GRAZIOSI, PAOLO, *Paleolithic Art,* McGraw-Hill, New York, 1960

KÜHN, H., *The Rock Pictures of Europe* (tr. A. H. Brodrick), Essential Books, Fair Lawn, N.J., 1957

LEROI-GOURHAN, ANDRÉ, *Treasures of Prehistoric Art* (tr. N. Guterman), Abrams, New York, 1967

LOMMEL, ANDREAS, *Shamanism, The Beginnings of Art,* McGraw-Hill, New York, 1967

MARINGER, JOHANNES, and BANDI, H. G., *Art in the Ice Age, Spanish Levant Art, Arctic Art* (tr. R. Allen), Praeger, New York, 1953

POWELL, T. G., *Prehistoric Art,* Praeger, New York, 1966

SANDARS, NANCY K., *Prehistoric Art in Europe,* Penguin, Baltimore, 1968

UCKO, PETER J., and ROSENFELD, A., *Palaeolithic Cave Art,* Weidenfeld & Nicholson, London, 1967

MONOGRAPHS

BERENGUER ALONSO, MAGÍN, *Prehistoric Man and His Art: The Caves of Ribadesella* (tr. M. Heron), Souvenir Press, London, 1973

BREUIL, HENRI, et al., *The Rock Paintings of Southern Africa,* 4 vols., Trianon Press, London, 1955–66

——————, and BURKETT, M. C., *Rock Paintings of Southern Andalusia,* Clarendon Press, Oxford, 1929

HEIZER, ROBERT F., and BAUMHOFF, M. A., *Prehistoric Rock Art of Nevada and Eastern California,* University of California Press, Berkeley, 1962

LAMING, ANNETTE, *Lascaux: Paintings and Engravings,* Penguin, Baltimore, 1959
LHOTE, HENRI, *The Search for the Tassili Frescoes* (tr. A. H. Brodrick), 2d ed., Hutchinson, London, 1973
RENFREW, COLIN, *Before Civilization: The Radiocarbon Revolution and Prehistoric Europe,* Knopf, New York, 1973
RUDNER, JALMAR and IONE, *The Hunter and His Art: A Survey of Rock Art in Southern Africa,* C. Struik, Cape Town, 1970
WILLCOX, A. R., *The Rock Art of South Africa,* Nelson, Johannesburg, 1963

2. NEOLITHIC ART

GENERAL

ARRIBAS, ANTONIO, *The Iberians,* Praeger, New York, 1963
DANIEL, GLYN E., *The Megalith Builders of Western Europe,* Praeger, New York, 1959
KENYON, KATHLEEN M., *Archaeology in the Holy Land,* Praeger, New York, 1960
PIGGOTT, STUART, *Ancient Europe,* Aldine, Chicago, 1966

MONOGRAPHS

ATKINSON, R. J. C., *Stonehenge,* Macmillan, New York, 1956
DANIEL, GLYN E., *Lascaux and Carnac,* Lutterworth, London, 1955
EVANS, JOHN DAVIES, *The Prehistoric Antiquities of the Maltese Islands,* Athlone, London, 1971
KENYON, KATHLEEN M., *Digging Up Jericho,* Praeger, New York, 1957
MELLAART, JAMES, *Çatal Hüyük: A Neolithic Town in Anatolia,* McGraw-Hill, New York, 1967
THOM, ALEXANDER, *Megalithic Sites in Britain,* Clarendon Press, Oxford, 1967
UCKO, PETER J., *Anthropomorphic Figurines of Predynastic Egypt and Neolithic Crete with Comparative Material from the Prehistoric Near East and Mainland Greece,* A. Szmidla, London, 1968

3. THE BRONZE AND IRON AGES

GENERAL

FOX, SIR CYRIL F., *Life and Death in the Bronze Age,* Routledge & Kegan Paul, London, 1959
GIMBUTAS, MARIJA A., *Bronze Age Cultures in Central and Eastern Europe,* Mouton, The Hague, 1965
MEGAW, J. V. S., *Art of the European Iron Age,* Harper & Row, New York, 1970
MELLAART, JAMES, *The Chalcolithic and Early Bronze Age in the Near East and Anatolia,* Khayats, Beirut, 1966
SANDARS, NANCY K., *Bronze Age Cultures in France,* Cambridge University Press, 1957
VERMEULE, EMILY, *Greece in the Bronze Age,* University of Chicago Press, 1964

MONOGRAPHS

ANATI, EMMANUEL, *Camonica Valley* (tr. L. Asher), Knopf, New York, 1961
KASTELIC, JOŽE, *Situla Art: Ceremonial Bronzes of Ancient Europe,* McGraw-Hill, New York, 1965

4. BLACK AFRICAN ART

GENERAL

BASCOM, WILLIAM R., *African Art in Cultural Perspective: An Introduction,* Norton, New York, 1973
BODROGI, TIBOR, *Art in Africa,* McGraw-Hill, New York, 1968
DAVIES, OLIVER, *West Africa Before the Europeans: Archaeology and Prehistory,* Methuen, London, 1967
ELISOFON, ELIOT, and FAGG, W. B., *The Sculpture of Africa,* Praeger, New York, 1958
FAGG, WILLIAM B., *Tribes and Forms in African Art,* Tudor, New York, 1965
GERBRANDS, A. A., *Art as an Element of Culture, Especially in Negro Africa,* Brill, Leiden, 1957
GUILLAUME, PAUL, and MUNRO, T., *Primitive Negro Sculpture,* 2d ed., Hacker, New York, 1968

LAUDE, JEAN, *The Arts of Black Africa* (tr. J. Décock), University of California Press, Berkeley, 1971
LEIRIS, MICHEL, and DULANGE, J., *African Art* (tr. M. Ross), Thames & Hudson, London, 1968
LEUZINGER, ELSY, *The Art of Black Africa* (tr. R. A. Wilson), New York Graphic Society, Greenwich, Conn., 1972
PAULME, DENISE, *African Sculpture* (tr. M. Ross), Viking, New York, 1962
RACHEWITZ, BORIS DE, *Introduction to African Art* (tr. P. Whigham), Murray, London, 1966
SCHMALENBACH, WERNER, *African Art* (tr. G. T. Hughes), Macmillan, New York, 1954
SEGY, LADISLAS, *African Sculpture Speaks,* 3d ed., Hill & Wang, New York, 1969
TROWELL, KATHLEEN MARGARET, and NEVERMANN, H., *African and Oceanic Art,* Abrams, New York, 1968
————, *African Design,* 3d ed., Praeger, New York, 1971
WASSING, RENÉ S., *African Art: Its Background and Traditions* (tr. D. Imber), Abrams, New York, 1968
WILLETT, FRANK, *African Art: An Introduction,* Praeger, New York, 1971
WINGERT, PAUL S., *The Sculpture of Negro Africa,* Columbia University Press, New York, 1959

MONOGRAPHS

ALLISON, PHILIP, *African Stone Sculpture,* Praeger, New York, 1968
BEIER, ULLI, *African Mud Sculpture,* Cambridge University Press, 1963
DARK, PHILIP J. C., *An Introduction to Benin Art and Technology,* Clarendon Press, Oxford, 1973
FAGG, WILLIAM B., *Miniature Wood Carvings of Africa,* New York Graphic Society, Greenwich, Conn., 1971
KOCHNITZKY, LÉON, *Negro Art in Belgian Congo,* 3d ed., Belgian Government Information Center, New York, 1952
SANNES, G. W., *African "Primitives": Function and Form in African Masks and Figures* (tr. M. King), Africana, New York, 1970
SHAW, THURSTAN, *Igbo-Ukwa: An Account of Archaeological Discoveries in Eastern Nigeria,* 2 vols., Northwestern University Press, Evanston, Ill., 1970
UNDERWOOD, LEON, *Bronzes of West Africa,* 2d ed., Tiranti, London, 1968
————, *Masks of West Africa,* 2d ed., Tiranti, London, 1964
WILLETT, FRANK, *Ife in the History of West African Sculpture,* Thames & Hudson, London, 1967

5. OCEANIC ART

GENERAL

BÜHLER, ALFRED, BARROW, T. and MOUNTFORD, C. T., *The Art of the South Sea Islands,* Crown, New York, 1962
GUIART, JEAN, *The Art of the South Pacific* (tr. A. Christie), Golden Press, New York, 1963
SCHMITZ, CARL A., *Oceanic Art: Myth, Man, and Image in the South Seas,* Abrams, New York, 1971
TROWELL, KATHLEEN MARGARET, and NEVERMANN, H., *African and Oceanic Art,* Abrams, New York, 1968

MONOGRAPHS

NEWTON, DOUGLAS, *Art Styles of the Papuan Gulf,* Museum of Primitive Art, New York, 1961
BARROW, TERRY, *The Decorative Arts of the New Zealand Maori,* H. H. and A. W. Reed, Wellington, New Zealand, 1964

6. NORTH AMERICAN INDIAN ART

GENERAL

CHRISTENSEN, ERWIN O., *Primitive Art,* Crowell, New York, 1955
COVARRUBIAS, MIGUEL, *The Eagle, The Jaguar and the Serpent: Indian Art of the Americas,* Knopf, New York, 1954
DOCKSTADER, FREDERICK J., *Indian Art in America,* New York Graphic Society, Greenwich, Conn., 1961

450 / Bibliography

DOUGLAS, FREDERIC H., and D'HARNONCOURT, R., *Indian Art of the United States,* 2d ed., Museum of Modern Art, New York, 1949

FEDER, NORMAN, *American Indian Art,* Abrams, New York, 1971

GRANT, CAMPBELL, *Rock Art of the American Indian,* Crowell, New York, 1967

HABERLAND, WOLFGANG, *The Art of North America,* Crown, New York, 1968

MARTIN, PAUL SIDNEY, et al., *Indians Before Columbus,* University of Chicago Press, 1947

PATTERSON, NANCY-LOU, *Canadian Native Art,* Collier-Macmillan Canada, Don Mills, Ont., 1973

WHITEFORD, ANDREW H., *North American Indian Arts,* Golden Press, New York, 1970

MONOGRAPHS

AMSDEN, CHARLES A., *Prehistoric Southwesterners from Basket-maker to Pueblo,* Southwest Museum, Los Angeles, 1949

BARBEAU, MARIUS, *Totem Poles,* 2 vols., E. Cloutier, Ottawa, 1950-51

CHAPMAN, K. M., *Pueblo Indian Pottery,* 2 vols., C. Szwedzicki, Nice, France, 1933–36

DEWDNEY, SELWYN H., and KIDD, K. E., *Indian Rock Paintings of the Great Lakes,* 2d ed., University of Toronto Press, 1967

DRUCKER, PHILIP, *Cultures of the North Pacific Coast,* Chandler, San Francisco, 1965

DUNN, DOROTHY, *American Indian Painting of the Southwest and Plains Areas,* University of New Mexico Press, Albuquerque, 1968

GRANT, CAMPBELL, *The Rock Paintings of the Chumash,* University of California Press, Berkeley, 1965

HAWTHORN, AUDREY, *Art of the Kwakiutl Indians and Other Northwest Coast Tribes,* University of Washington Press, Seattle, 1963

HEIZER, ROBERT F., and CLEWLOW, C. W., JR., *Prehistoric Rock Art of California,* 2 vols., Ballena Press, Ramona, Calif., 1973

HOLM, BILL, *Northwest Coast Indian Art: An Analysis of Form,* University of Washington Press, Seattle, 1965

INVERARITY, ROBERT BRUCE, *Art of the Northwest Coast Indians,* University of California Press, Berkeley, 1950

KIRKLAND, FORREST, and NEWCOMB, W. W., JR., *The Rock Art of Texas Indians,* University of Texas Press, Austin, 1967

PETERSEN, KAREN DANIELS, *Plains Indian Art from Fort Marion,* University of Oklahoma Press, Norman, 1971

SCHAEFSMA, POLLY, *Rock Art in the Navajo Reservoir District,* Museum of New Mexico Press, Santa Fe, 1963

TANNER, CLARA LEE, *Southwest Indian Painting,* University of Arizona Press, Tucson, 1973

PART TWO

THE ANCIENT WORLD

DOERINGER, SUZANNAH, et al., *Art and Technology: A Symposium on Classical Bronzes,* MIT Press, Cambridge, Mass., 1970

GROENEWEGEN-FRANKFORT, H. A., and ASHMOLE, B., *Art of the Ancient World,* Prentice-Hall, Englewood Cliffs, N.J., 1971

LLOYD, SETON, et al., *Ancient Architecture,* Abrams, New York, 1974

1. EGYPT

GENERAL

ALDRED, CYRIL, *Middle Kingdom Art in Ancient Egypt, 2300–1590 B.C.,* Tiranti, London, 1950

——————, *New Kingdom Art in Ancient Egypt During the Eighteenth Dynasty, 1570–1320 B.C.,* 2d ed., Tiranti, London, 1961

——————, *Old Kingdom Art in Ancient Egypt,* Tiranti, London, 1949

BADAWY, ALEXANDER, *Architecture in Ancient Egypt and the Near East,* MIT Press, Cambridge, Mass., 1966

——————, *A History of Egyptian Architecture,* 3 vols., Sh. Studio Misr, Giza (I), University of California Press, Berkeley (II, III), 1954–68

BRATTON, FRED G., *A History of Egyptian Archaeology,* Cornell University Press, Ithaca, N.Y., 1968

DAVIES, NINA M., and GARDINER, A. H., *Ancient Egyptian Paintings,* University of Chicago Press, 1936

GROENEWEGEN-FRANKFORT, H. A., *Arrest and Movement,* University of Chicago Press, 1951

HARRIS, J. R., ed., *The Legacy of Egypt,* Clarendon Press, Oxford, 1971

HAYES, WILLIAM C., *The Scepter of Egypt,* 2 vols., Harper, New York, 1953–59

LANGE, KURT, and HIRMER, M., *Egypt: Architecture, Sculpture, Painting in Three Thousand Years* (tr. H. R. Boothroyd), 4th ed., Phaidon, New York, 1968

MEKHITARIAN, ARPAG, *Egyptian Painting* (tr. S. Gilbert), Skira, New York, 1954

MICHALOWSKI, KAZIMIERZ, *Art of Ancient Egypt* (tr. N. Guterman), Abrams, New York, 1969

PORTER, BERTHA, and MOSS, R., *Topographical Bibliography of Ancient Egyptian Hieroglyphic Texts, Reliefs, and Paintings,* 7 vols., Clarendon Press, Oxford, 1927–51 (2d ed., 1964– , in progress)

POULSEN, VAGN, *Egyptian Art* (tr. R. and U. Harrison), New York Graphic Society, Greenwich, Conn., 1968

SMITH, WILLIAM STEVENSON, *The Art and Architecture of Ancient Egypt,* Penguin, Baltimore, 1958

WESTENDORF, WOLFHART, *Painting, Sculpture, and Architecture of Ancient Egypt* (tr. L. Mins), Abrams, New York, 1969

WOLDERING, IRMGARD, *The Art of Egypt* (tr. A. E. Keep), Greystone Press, New York, 1963

MONOGRAPHS

ALDRED, CYRIL, *Akhenaten, Pharaoh of Egypt: A New Study,* McGraw-Hill, New York, 1969

——————, *Akhenaten and Nefertiti,* Brooklyn Museum, New York, 1973

BAUMGARTEL, ELISE J., *The Culture of Prehistoric Egypt,* 2 vols., Oxford University Press, 1955–60

BOTHMER, BERNARD VON, *Egyptian Sculpture of the Late Period: 700 B.C. to A.D. 100,* Brooklyn Museum, New York, 1960

DESROCHES-NOBLECOURT, CHRISTIANE, *Tutankhamen,* New York Graphic Society, Greenwich, Conn., 1964

EDWARDS, I. E. S., *The Pyramids of Egypt,* 2d ed., Viking, New York, 1972

——————, *The Treasures of Tutankhamun,* Viking, New York, 1972

EMERY, WALTER B., *Archaic Egypt,* Penguin, Baltimore, 1962

——————, *Great Tombs of the First Dynasty,* 3 vols., Government Press, Cairo and London, 1949–58

FAKHRY, AHMED, *The Pyramids,* 2d ed., University of Chicago Press, 1969

FRANKFORT, HENRI, ed., *The Mural Painting of El-'Amarneh,* Egyptian Exploration Society, London, 1929

HASSAN, SELIM, *The Great Pyramid at Khufu and Its Mortuary Chapel* (Excavations at Gîza, 10), Cairo, 1960

——————, *The Sphinx: Its History in the Light of Recent Excavations,* Government Press, Cairo, 1949

HAYES, WILLIAM C., *Most Ancient Egypt,* University of Chicago Press, 1965

IVERSEN, ERIK, *Canon and Proportions in Egyptian Art,* Sidgwick & Jackson, London, 1955

NIMS, CHARLES F., *Thebes of the Pharaohs,* Stein & Day, New York, 1965

ZAKI YUSUF SAAD, *The Excavations at Helwan: Art and Civilization in the First and Second Egyptian Dynasties,* University of Oklahoma Press, Norman, 1969

TERRACE, EDWARD L. B., *Egyptian Paintings of the Middle Kingdom: The Tomb of Djehuty-nekht,* Braziller, New York, 1969

2. MESOPOTAMIAN ART

GENERAL

AKURGAL, EKREM, *Art of the Hittites,* Abrams, New York, 1962

EHRICH, ROBERT W., ed., *Chronologies in Old World Archaeology,* University of Chicago Press, 1965
FRANKFORT, HENRI, *The Art and Architecture of the Ancient Orient,* 4th ed., Penguin, Baltimore, 1969
——————,et al., *Before Philosophy,* Penguin, Baltimore, 1971
——————, *The Birth of Civilization in the Near East,* Doubleday, Garden City, N.Y., 1956
GHIRSHMAN, ROMAN, *The Arts of Ancient Iran from Its Origins to the Time of Alexander the Great* (tr. S. Gilbert and J. Emmons), Golden Press, New York, 1964
——————, *Persian Art: The Parthian and Sassanian Dynasties, 249 B.C.–A.D. 651* (tr. S. Gilbert and J. Emmons), Golden Press, New York, 1962
GODARD, ANDRÉ, *The Art of Iran* (tr. M. Heron), Praeger, New York, 1965
KRAMER, SAMUEL N., *The Sumerians: Their History, Culture, and Character,* University of Chicago Press, 1963
LLOYD, SETON, *The Art of the Ancient Near East,* Praeger, New York, 1961
MARGUERON, JEAN CLAUDE, *Mesopotamia* (tr. H. S. O. Harrison), World, Cleveland, 1965
MELLAART, JAMES, *Earliest Civilizations of the Near East,* McGraw-Hill, New York, 1965
MOORTGAT, ANTON, *The Art of Ancient Mesopotamia* (tr. J. Filson), Phaidon, New York, 1969
PARROT, ANDRÉ, *The Arts of Assyria* (tr. S. Gilbert and J. Emmons), Golden Press, New York, 1961
——————, *Nineveh and Babylon,* Thames & Hudson, London, 1960
——————, *Sumer: The Dawn of Art* (tr. S. Gilbert and J. Emmons), Golden Press, New York, 1961
PORADA, EDITH, *The Art of Ancient Iran: Pre-Islamic Cultures,* Crown, New York, 1965
DU RY VAN BEEST HOLLE, CAREL J., *Art of the Ancient Near and Middle East* (tr. A. Brown), Abrams, New York, 1970
SAGGS, H. W. F., *The Greatness That Was Babylon,* Hawthorn, New York, 1962
SMITH, WILLIAM STEVENSON, *Interconnections in the Ancient Near East,* Yale University Press, New Haven, Conn., 1965
STROMMENGER, EVA, and HIRMER, M., *5000 Years of the Art of Mesopotamia* (tr. C. Haglund), Abrams, New York, 1964
WOOLLEY, SIR CHARLES L., *Mesopotamia and the Middle East,* Methuen, London, 1961

MONOGRAPHS

ALBRIGHT, WILLIAM F., *The Archaeology of Palestine,* 2d ed., Penguin, Harmondsworth, England, 1956
MADHLOOM, T. A., *The Chronology of Neo-Assyrian Art,* Athlone Press, London, 1970
MOSCATI, SABATINO, *Historical Art in the Ancient Near East,* Università di Roma, 1963
WOOLLEY, SIR CHARLES L., *Ur of the Chaldees,* rev. ed., Norton, New York, 1965

3. AEGEAN ART

GENERAL

COTTRELL, LEONARD, *Realms of Gold: A Journey in Search of the Mycenaeans,* New York Graphic Society, Greenwich, Conn., 1963
DEMARGNE, PIERRE, *The Birth of Greek Art* (tr. S. Gilbert and J. Emmons), Golden Press, New York, 1964
HIGGINS, REYNOLD, *Minoan and Mycenaean Art,* Praeger, New York, 1967
HOOD, SINCLAIR, *The Minoans: The Story of Bronze Age Crete,* Praeger, New York, 1971
MARINATOS, SPYRIDON, and HIRMER, M., *Crete and Mycenae* (tr. J. Boardman), Abrams, New York, 1960
MATZ, FRIEDRICH, *The Art of Crete and Early Greece* (tr. A. E. Keep), Crown, New York, 1962
NILSSON, MARTIN P., *Minoan-Mycenaean Religion,* 2d ed., Gleerup, Lund, Sweden, 1950
PENDLEBURY, JOHN D. S., *The Archaeology of Crete,* Methuen, London, 1939
RENFREW, COLIN, *The Emergence of Civilisation: The Cyclades and the Aegean in the Third Millennium B.C.,* Methuen, London, 1972

TAYLOUR, LORD WILLIAM, *The Mycenaeans,* Praeger, New York, 1964
VERMEULE, EMILY, *Greece in the Bronze Age,* University of Chicago Press, 1964

MONOGRAPHS

BLEGEN, CARL W., and RAWSON, M., *The Palace of Nestor at Pylos in Western Messenia,* 2 vols., Princeton University Press, 1966.
BRANIGAN, KEITH, *The Foundations of Palatial Crete: A Survey of Crete in the Early Bronze Age,* Praeger, New York, 1970
——————, *The Tombs of Mesara: A Study of Funerary Architecture and Ritual in Southern Crete, 2800–1700 B.C.,* Duckworth, London, 1970
CATLING, H. W., *Cypriot Bronzework in the Mycenaean World,* Clarendon Press, Oxford, 1964
DESBOROUGH, VINCENT R. d'A., *The Last Mycenaeans and Their Survivors: An Archaeological Survey, c. 1200–c. 1000 B.C.,* Clarendon Press, Oxford, 1964
EVANS, SIR ARTHUR JOHN, *The Palace of Minos,* 4 vols., Macmillan, New York, 1921–35
GRAHAM, J. WALTER, *The Palaces of Crete,* Princeton University Press, 1962
HIGGINS, REYNOLD, *The Archaeology of Minoan Crete,* H. Z. Walck, New York, 1973
HUTCHINSON, ROBERT W., *Prehistoric Crete,* Penguin, Baltimore, 1962
MYLONAS, GEORGE E., *Mycenae and the Mycenaean Age,* Princeton University Press, 1966
WACE, ALAN J. B., *Mycenae: An Archaeological History and Guide,* Princeton University Press, 1949

4. GREEK ART

SOURCES

JEX-BLAKE, K., and SELLERS, E., *The Elder Pliny's Chapters on the History of Art,* Argonaut, Chicago, 1968
POLLITT, J. J., *The Art of Greece (1400–31 B.C.): Sources and Documents,* Prentice-Hall, Englewood Cliffs, N.J., 1965

GENERAL

ASHMOLE, BERNARD, *Architect and Sculptor in Classical Greece,* New York University Press, 1972
BEAZLEY, SIR JOHN D., and ASHMOLE, B., *Greek Sculpture and Painting to the End of the Hellenistic Period,* Cambridge University Press, 1966
BECATTI, GIOVANNI, *The Art of Ancient Greece and Rome,* Abrams, New York, 1967
BERVE, HELMUT, GRUBEN, G., and HIRMER, M., *Greek Temples, Theatres, and Shrines,* Abrams, New York, 1963
BOARDMAN, JOHN, et al., *Greek Art and Architecture,* Abrams, New York, 1967
BRILLIANT, RICHARD, *Arts of the Ancient Greeks,* McGraw-Hill, New York, 1973
CARPENTER, RHYS, *Greek Sculpture: A Critical Review,* University of Chicago Press, 1960
CHARBONNEAUX, JEAN, et al., *Archaic Greek Art* (tr. J. Emmons and R. Allen), Braziller, New York, 1971
——————, *Classical Greek Art* (tr. J. Emmons), Braziller, New York, 1972
——————, *Hellenistic Greek Art* (tr. P. Green), Braziller, New York, 1973
COOK, ROBERT M., *Greek Art: Its Development, Character, and Influence,* Farrar, Straus & Giroux, New York, 1973
DINSMOOR, WILLIAM B., *The Architecture of Ancient Greece,* Batsford, New York, 1950
DUNBABIN, THOMAS J., *The Greeks and Their Eastern Neighbours,* Society for the Promotion of Hellenic Studies, London, 1957
FYFE, THEODORE, *Hellenistic Architecture: An Introductory Study,* Cambridge University Press, 1936
HAFNER, GERMAN, *Art of Crete, Mycenae, and Greece,* Abrams, New York, 1969
HAVELOCK, CHRISTINE M., *Hellenistic Art,* New York Graphic Society, Greenwich, Conn., 1970
HOMANN-WEDEKING, ERNST, *The Art of Archaic Greece* (tr. J. R. Foster), Crown, New York, 1968

LANGLOTZ, ERNST, and HIRMER, M., *The Art of Magna Graecia* (tr. A. Hicks), Thames & Hudson, London, 1965

LAWRENCE, ARNOLD W., *Greek and Roman Sculpture,* Harper & Row, New York, 1972

——————, *Greek Architecture,* 2d ed., Penguin, Baltimore, 1967

LULLIES, REINHARD, and HIRMER, M., *Greek Sculpture,* Abrams, New York, 1960

NOSHY, IBRAHIM, *The Arts in Ptolemaic Egypt,* Oxford University Press, London, 1937

PFUHL, ERNST, *Masterpieces of Greek Drawing and Painting* (tr. Sir J. Beazley), 2d ed., Macmillan, New York, 1955

POLLITT, J. J., *The Ancient View of Greek Art,* Yale University Press, New Haven, Conn., 1974

——————, *Art and Experience in Classical Greece,* Cambridge University Press, 1972

RICHTER, GISELA M. A., *A Handbook of Greek Art,* 6th ed., Phaidon, New York, 1969

——————, *The Sculpture and Sculptors of the Greeks,* 4th ed., Yale University Press, New Haven, Conn., 1970

——————, *Three Critical Periods in Greek Sculpture,* Clarendon Press, Oxford, 1951

ROBERTSON, MARTIN, *Greek Painting,* Skira, Geneva, 1959

SCHODER, RAYMOND V., *Masterpieces of Greek Art,* 2d ed., New York Graphic Society, Greenwich, Conn., 1965

SCRANTON, ROBERT L., *Greek Architecture,* Braziller, New York, 1962

SWINDLER, MARY H., *Ancient Painting,* Yale University Press, New Haven, Conn., 1929

WACE, ALAN J. B., *An Approach to Greek Sculpture,* Cambridge University Press, 1935

WEBSTER, THOMAS B. L., *The Art of Greece: The Age of Hellenism,* Crown, New York, 1966

WHITE, JOHN, *The Birth and Rebirth of Pictorial Space,* 2d ed., Faber & Faber, London, 1967

WYCHERLEY, RICHARD E., *How the Greeks Built Cities,* Macmillan, New York, 1949

MONOGRAPHS

ADAM, SHEILA, *The Technique of Greek Sculpture in the Archaic and Classical Periods,* Thames & Hudson, London, 1967

AKURGAL, EKREM, *The Art of Greece: Its Origins in the Mediterranean and Near East,* Crown, New York, 1968

ARIAS, PAOLO E., and HIRMER, M., *A History of 1000 Years of Greek Vase Painting,* Abrams, New York, 1963

ASHMOLE, BERNARD, and YALOURIS, N., *Olympia: The Sculptures of the Temple of Zeus,* Phaidon, London, 1967

BEAZLEY, SIR JOHN D., *Attic Black-Figure Vase-Painters,* Clarendon Press, Oxford, 1956

——————, *Attic Red-Figure Vase-Painters,* 2d ed., 3 vols., Clarendon Press, Oxford, 1963

——————, *The Development of Attic Black-Figure,* University of California Press, Berkeley, 1964

——————, *Paralipomena,* Clarendon Press, Oxford, 1971

BIEBER, MARGARETE, *The History of the Greek and Roman Theater,* 2d ed., Princeton University Press, 1961

——————, *The Sculpture of the Hellenistic Age,* 2d ed., Columbia University Press, New York, 1961

BROWN, BLANCHE R., *Ptolemaic Paintings and Mosaics and the Alexandrian Style,* Archaeological Institute of America, Cambridge, Mass., 1957

BUNDGAARD, J. A., *Mnesicles: A Greek Architect at Work,* Scandinavian University Books, Copenhagen, 1957

CARPENTER, RHYS, *The Esthetic Basis of Greek Art of the Fifth and Fourth Centuries B.C.,* 2d ed., Indiana University Press, Bloomington, 1965

CHARBONNEAUX, JEAN, *Greek Bronzes* (tr. K. Watson), Viking, New York, 1962

COOK, ROBERT M., *Greek Painted Pottery,* 2d ed., Methuen, London, 1966

HIGGINS, REYNOLD A., *Greek and Roman Jewellery,* Methuen, London, 1961

——————, *Greek Terracottas,* Methuen, London, 1967

JENKINS, ROMILLY J. H., *Dedalica: A Study of Dorian Plastic Art in the Seventh Century B.C.,* Cambridge University Press, 1936

KARO, GEORG H., *Greek Personality in Archaic Sculpture,* Harvard University Press, Cambridge, Mass., 1948

KRAAY, COLIN M., and HIRMER, M., *Greek Coins,* Abrams, New York, 1966

LAMB, WINIFRED, *Greek and Roman Bronzes,* 2d ed., Argonaut, Chicago, 1969

MARTIENSSEN, R. D., *The Idea of Space in Greek Architecture,* 2d ed., Witwatersrand University Press, Johannesburg, 1968

NOBLE, J. V., *The Techniques of Painted Attic Pottery,* Watson-Guptill, New York, 1965

PAYNE, HUMFRY, and YOUNG, G. M., *Archaic Marble Sculpture from the Acropolis,* 2d ed., Morrow, New York, 1951

RICHTER, GISELA M. A., *The Portraits of the Greeks,* 3 vols., Phaidon, London, 1965

RIDGWAY, B. S., *The Severe Style in Greek Sculpture,* Princeton University Press, 1970

SCHEFOLD, KARL, *Myth and Legend in Early Greek Art* (tr. A. Hicks), Abrams, New York, 1966

SCHWEITZER, BERNHARD, *Greek Geometric Art* (tr. P. and C. Usborne), Phaidon, New York, 1971

WARD PERKINS, JOHN B., *The Cities of Ancient Greece and Italy: Planning in Classical Antiquity,* Braziller, New York, 1974

WEBSTER, THOMAS B. L., *Art and Literature in Fourth-Century Athens,* Greenwood Press, New York, 1969

——————, *Potter and Painter in Classical Athens,* Methuen, London, 1972

5.   ETRUSCAN ART

GENERAL

BANTI, LUISA, *Etruscan Cities and Their Culture* (tr. E. Bizzarri), University of California Press, Berkeley, 1973

BLOCH, RAYMOND, *The Etruscans* (tr. S. Hood), Praeger, New York, 1958

BOETHIUS, AXEL, et al., *Etruscan Culture: Land and People,* Columbia University Press, New York, 1961

LAWRENCE, D. H., *Etruscan Places,* Viking, New York, 1932

MANSUELLI, G. A., *The Art of Etruria and Early Rome* (tr. C. E. Ellis), Crown, New York, 1965

VON MATT, LEONARD, et al., *The Art of the Etruscans* (tr. P. Martin), Abrams, New York, 1970

PALLOTTINO, MASSIMO, *Etruscan Painting,* Skira, New York, 1953

——————, and HÜRLIMAN, MARTIN, *Art of the Etruscans,* Vanguard, New York, 1955

RICHARDSON, EMELINE, *The Etruscans: Their Art and Civilization,* University of Chicago Press, 1964

RIIS, P. J., *An Introduction to Etruscan Art,* Munksgaard, Copenhagen, 1953

MONOGRAPHS

BEAZLEY, SIR JOHN D., *Etruscan Vase-Painting,* 2d ed., Oxford University Press, New York, 1947

BROWN, WILLIAM L., *The Etruscan Lion,* Clarendon Press, Oxford, 1960

MORETTI, MARIO, *New Monuments of Etruscan Painting* (tr. D. Kiang), Pennsylvania State University Press, University Park, 1968

6.   ROMAN ART

SOURCES

POLLITT, J. J., *The Art of Rome and Late Antiquity: Sources and Documents in the History of Art,* Prentice-Hall, Englewood Cliffs, N.J., 1966

VITRUVIUS POLLIO, *Ten Books on Architecture* (tr. M. H. Morgan), Dover, New York, 1960

GENERAL

BECATTI, GIOVANNI, *The Art of Ancient Greece and Rome,* Abrams, New York, 1967

BIANCHI BANDINELLI, RANUCCIO, *Rome: The Center of Power* (tr. P. Green), Braziller, New York, 1970

——————, *Rome: The Late Empire* (tr. P. Green), Braziller, New York, 1971

BOETHIUS, AXEL, *Roman and Greek Town-Architecture,* Elanders, Göteborg, 1948

_____,and WARD PERKINS, J. B., *Etruscan and Roman Architecture*, Penguin, Baltimore, 1970

BRENDEL, OTTO J., *Prolegomena to a Book on Roman Art* (Memoirs of the American Academy in Rome, XXI), American Academy in Rome, 1953

BRILLIANT, RICHARD, *Roman Art from the Republic to Constantine*, Phaidon, New York, 1974

BROWN, FRANK E., *Roman Architecture*, Braziller, New York, 1961

HAMBERG, PER GUSTAF, *Studies in Roman Imperial Art*, Almqvist, Upsala, 1945

HANFMANN, GEORGE M. A., *Roman Art*, New York Graphic Society, Greenwich, Conn., 1964

KÄHLER, HEINZ, *The Art of Rome and Her Empire* (tr. J. R. Foster), Crown, New York, 1963

MACDONALD, WILLIAM L., *The Architecture of the Roman Empire*, I, Yale University Press, New Haven, 1965

MAIURI, AMEDEO, *Roman Painting* (tr. S. Gilbert), Skira, New York, 1953

MANSUELLI, GUIDO A., *The Art of Etruria and Early Rome* (tr. C. E. Ellis), Crown, New York, 1965

POBÉ, MARCEL, and ROUBIER, J., *The Art of Roman Gaul*, University of Toronto Press, 1961

ROBERTSON, DONALD S., *A Handbook of Greek and Roman Architecture*, 2d ed., Cambridge University Press, 1954

STRONG, DONALD S., *Roman Imperial Sculpture: An Introduction to the Commemorative and Decorative Sculpture of the Roman Empire Down to the Death of Constantine*, Tiranti, London, 1961

TARRADELL I MATEU, MIGUEL, *Roman Art in Spain*, Tudor, New York, 1969

TOYNBEE, JOCELYN M. C., *Art in Britain Under the Romans*, Clarendon Press, Oxford, 1964

_____, *The Art of the Romans*, Praeger, New York, 1965

VERMEULE, CORNELIUS C., *Roman Imperial Art in Greece and Asia Minor*, Belknap Press, Cambridge, Mass., 1968

WHEELER, SIR MORTIMER, *Roman Art and Architecture*, Praeger, New York, 1964

MONOGRAPHS

BIEBER, MARGARETE, *The History of the Greek and Roman Theater*, 2d ed., Princeton University Press, 1961

BOETHIUS, AXEL, *The Golden House of Nero*, University of Michigan Press, Ann Arbor, 1960

BRILLIANT, RICHARD, *Gesture and Rank in Roman Art* (Memoirs of the Connecticut Academy, XIV), The Academy, New Haven, 1963

GRANT, MICHAEL, *Cities of Vesuvius*, Weidenfeld & Nicholson, London, 1971

HANFMANN, GEORGE M. A., *Observations on Roman Portraiture*, Latomus, Brussels, 1953

_____, *The Seasons Sarcophagus in Dumbarton Oaks*, 2 vols., Harvard University Press, Cambridge, Mass., 1952

HANSON, JOHN A., *Roman Theater-Temples*, Princeton University Press, 1955

L'ORANGE, HANS PETER, *Art Forms and Civic Life in the Later Roman Empire* (tr. Dr. & Mrs. K. Berg), Princeton University Press, 1965

_____, *Likeness and Icon*, Odense University Press, Odense, Denmark, 1973

MAU, AUGUST, *Pompeii: Its Life and Art* (tr. F. W. Kelsey), Macmillan, New York, 1904

NASH, ERNEST, *Pictorial Dictionary of Ancient Rome*, 2d ed., 2 vols., Praeger, New York, 1968

ROULLET, ANNE, *The Egyptian and Egyptianizing Monuments of Imperial Rome*, Brill, Leiden, 1972

RYBERG, INEZ S., *The Rites of the State Religion in Roman Art* (Memoirs of the American Academy in Rome, XXII), American Academy in Rome, 1955

TOYNBEE, JOCELYN M. C., *The Hadrianic School*, Cambridge University Press, 1934

7. PRE-COLUMBIAN ART

GENERAL

BUSHNELL, GEOFFREY H. S., *Ancient Arts of the Americas*, Praeger, New York, 1965

DOCKSTADER, FREDERICK J., *Indian Art in Middle America*, New York Graphic Society, Greenwich, Conn., 1964

KELEMEN, PÁL, *Medieval American Art: Masterpieces of the New World Before Columbus*, 3d ed., 2 vols., Dover, New York, 1969

KUBLER, GEORGE, *The Art and Architecture of Ancient America*, Penguin, Baltimore, 1962

LOTHROP, S. K., et al., *Essays in Pre-Columbian Art and Archaeology*, Harvard University Press, Cambridge, Mass., 1961

_____, *Treasures of Ancient America*, Skira, Geneva, 1964

WEAVER, MURIEL P., *The Aztecs, Maya, and Their Predecessors: Archaeology of Mesoamerica*, Seminar Press, New York, 1972

WESTHEIM, PAUL, et al., *Prehispanic Mexican Art*, Putnam, New York, 1972

VON WINNING, HASSO, *Pre-Columbian Art of Mexico and Central America*, Abrams, New York, 1968

MONOGRAPHS

ANTON, FERDINAND, *Ancient Mexican Art* (tr. B. and P. Ross), Putnam, New York, 1969

_____, *The Art of Ancient Peru*, Putnam, New York, 1972

_____, *Art of the Maya* (tr. M. Whittall), Putnam, New York, 1970

BENSON, ELIZABETH P., *The Mochica: A Culture of Peru*, Praeger, New York, 1972

BERNAL, IGNACIO, et al., *The Iconography of Middle American Sculpture*, Metropolitan Museum of Art, New York, 1973

_____, *The Olmec World* (tr. D. Heyden and F. Horcasitas), University of California Press, Berkeley, 1969

BOOS, FRANK H., *The Ceramic Sculptures of Ancient Oaxaca*, A. S. Barnes, South Brunswick, N.J., 1966

COE, MICHAEL D., *The Maya*, Praeger, New York, 1966

EMMERICH, ANDRÉ, *Art Before Columbus: The Art of Ancient Mexico*, Simon & Schuster, New York, 1963

_____, *Sweat of the Sun and Tears of the Moon: Gold and Silver in Pre-Columbian Art*, University of Washington Press, Seattle, 1965

GAY, CARLO T. E., and PRATT, F., *Chalcacingo*, Akadem. Druck- und Verlagsanstalt, Graz, 1971

GREENE, MERLE, et al., *Maya Sculpture from the Southern Lowlands, the Highlands and Pacific Piedmont, Guatemala, Mexico, Honduras*, Lederer, Street & Zeus, Berkeley, Calif., 1972

JORALEMON, PETER D., *A Study of Olmec Iconography*, Dumbarton Oaks, Washington, D.C., 1971

KAMPEN, MICHAEL E., *The Sculptures of El Tajón, Veracruz, Mexico*, University of Florida Press, Gainesville, 1972

LUMBRERAS, LUIS G., *The Peoples and Cultures of Ancient Peru* (tr. B. J. Meggers), Smithsonian Institution Press, Washington, D.C., 1974

MASON, JOHN ALDEN, *The Ancient Civilizations of Peru*, Penguin, Harmondsworth, England, 1957

MONTI, FRANCO, *Precolumbian Terracottas* (tr. M. Crosland), Hamlyn, New York, 1969

MORLEY, SYLVANUS G., *The Ancient Maya*, 3d ed., Stanford University Press, 1956

PROSKURIAKOFF, TATIANA, *A Study of Classic Maya Sculpture*, Carnegie Publications, Washington, D.C., 1950

REICHEL-DOLMATOFF, GERARDO, *Colombia*, Praeger, New York, 1965

_____, *San Agustín: A Culture of Colombia*, Praeger, New York, 1972

THOMPSON, JOHN ERIC S., *The Rise and Fall of Maya Civilization*, 2d ed., University of Oklahoma Press, Norman, 1966

WICKE, CHARLES R., *Olmec: An Early Art Style of Precolumbian Mexico*, University of Arizona Press, Tucson, 1971

VON WUTHENAU, ALEXANDER, *The Art of Terracotta Pottery in Pre-Columbian Central and South America*, Crown, New York, 1970

PART THREE

THE MIDDLE AGES

SOURCES

DAVIS WEYER, CAECILIA, *Early Medieval Art, 300–1150:*

Sources and Documents, Prentice-Hall, Englewood Cliffs, N.J., 1971

GENERAL

HÖLLANDER, HANS, *Early Medieval Art* (tr. C. Hillier), Universe, New York, 1974

KIDSON, PETER, *The Medieval World,* McGraw-Hill, New York, 1967

MOREY, CHARLES R., *Christian Art,* Longmans, New York, 1935

—————, *Mediaeval Art,* Norton, New York, 1942

OAKESHOTT, WALTER F., *Classical Inspiration in Medieval Art,* Chapman & Hall, London, 1959

SAALMAN, HOWARD, *Medieval Architecture,* Braziller, New York, 1962

VERZONE, PAOLO, *The Art of Europe: The Dark Ages from Theodoric to Charlemagne* (tr. P. Waley), Crown, New York, 1965

ZARNECKI, GEORGE, *Art of the Medieval World,* Prentice-Hall, Englewood Cliffs, N.J., 1975

MONOGRAPHS

KLINGENDER, FRANCIS D., *Animals in Art and Thought to the End of the Middle Ages* (eds. E. Antal and J. Harthan), MIT Press, Cambridge, Mass., 1971

LADNER, G. B., *Ad imaginem Dei: The Image of Man in Mediaeval Art,* Archabbey Press, Latrobe, Pa., 1965

L'ORANGE, HANS PETER, *Likeness and Icon,* Odense University Press, Odense, Denmark, 1973

MARTINDALE, ANDREW, *The Rise of the Artist in the Middle Ages and Early Renaissance,* McGraw-Hill, New York, 1972

1. EARLY CHRISTIAN AND EARLY BYZANTINE ART (INCLUDING BYZANTINE ART IN GENERAL)

SOURCES

MANGO, CYRIL A., *The Art of the Byzantine Empire, 312–1453: Sources and Documents,* Prentice-Hall, Englewood Cliffs, N.J., 1972

GENERAL

BECKWITH, JOHN, *The Art of Constantinople: An Introduction to Byzantine Art (330–1453),* Phaidon, New York, 1961

—————, *Early Christian and Byzantine Art,* Penguin, Baltimore, 1970

BON, ANTOINE, *Byzantium* (tr. J. Hogarth), Barrie & Jenkins, London, 1973

DEMUS, OTTO, *Byzantine Art and the West,* New York University Press, New York, 1970

DU BOURGUET, PIERRE, *Early Christian Art* (tr. T. Burton), Reynal, New York, 1971

GRABAR, ANDRÉ, *The Art of the Byzantine Empire: Byzantine Art in the Middle Ages* (tr. B. Forster), Crown, New York, 1966

—————, *Byzantine Painting* (tr. S. Gilbert), Skira, Geneva, 1953

HAMILTON, JOHN A., *Byzantine Architecture and Decoration,* 2d ed., Batsford, London, 1956

HUTTER, IRMGARD, *Early Christian and Byzantine Art,* Universe, New York, 1971

KRAUTHEIMER, RICHARD, *Early Christian and Byzantine Architecture,* Penguin, Baltimore, 1965

MACDONALD, WILLIAM L., *Early Christian and Byzantine Architecture,* Braziller, New York, 1962

MATHEW, GERVASE, *Byzantine Aesthetics,* John Murray, London, 1963

MICHELIS, P. A., *An Aesthetic Approach to Byzantine Art,* Batsford, London, 1955

MOREY, CHARLES R., *Early Christian Art,* 2d ed., Princeton University Press, 1953

RICE, DAVID TALBOT, *The Appreciation of Byzantine Art,* Oxford University Press, London, 1972

—————, *Art of the Byzantine Era,* Praeger, New York, 1963

SCHUG-WILLE, CHRISTA, *Art of the Byzantine World* (tr. E. M. Hatt), Abrams, New York, 1969

VAN DER MEER, F., *Early Christian Art* (tr. P. and F. Brown), London, Faber & Faber, 1967

VOLBACH, WOLFGANG F., and HIRMER, M., *Early Christian Art* (tr. C. Ligota), Abrams, New York, 1962

MONOGRAPHS

AINALOV, DMITRI V., *The Hellenistic Origins of Byzantine Art* (tr. E. and S. Sobolevitch), Rutgers University Press, New Brunswick, N.J., 1961

CREMA DE IONGH, DANIEL, *Byzantine Aspects of Italy,* Norton, New York, 1967

DEMUS, OTTO, *Byzantine Mosaic Decoration,* Routledge & Kegan Paul, London, 1953

FORSYTH, GEORGE H., and WEITZMANN, K., *The Church and Fortress of Justinian,* University of Michigan Press, Ann Arbor, 1973

GOUGH, MICHAEL, *The Origins of Christian Art,* Praeger, New York, 1974

GRABAR, ANDRÉ, *The Beginnings of Christian Art, 200–395* (tr. S. Gilbert and J. Emmons), Thames & Hudson, London, 1967

—————, *The Golden Age of Justinian: From the Death of Theodosius to the Rise of Islam* (tr. S. Gilbert and J. Emmons), Odyssey Press, New York, 1967

INAN, JALE, and ROSENBAUM, E., *Roman and Early Byzantine Portrait Sculpture in Asia Minor,* Oxford University Press, London, 1966

KÄHLER, HEINZ, *Hagia Sophia* (tr. E. Childs), Zwemmer, London, 1967

MATHEWS, THOMAS F., *The Early Churches of Constantinople,* Pennsylvania State University Press, University Park, 1971

OAKESHOTT, WALTER, *The Mosaics of Rome,* New York Graphic Society, Greenwich, Conn., 1967

OVADIAH, ASHER, *Corpus of the Byzantine Churches in the Holy Land,* P. Hanstein, Bonn, 1970

RICE, DAVID TALBOT, *The Beginnings of Christian Art,* Abingdon, Nashville, 1957

ROSTOVTSEV, MIKHAIL I., *Dura-Europos and Its Art,* Clarendon Press, Oxford, 1938

SIMSON, OTTO VON, *Sacred Fortress,* University of Chicago Press, 1948

SMITH, EARL BALDWIN, *Architectural Symbolism of Imperial Rome and the Middle Ages,* Princeton University Press, 1956

SWIFT, EMERSON H., *Hagia Sophia,* Columbia University Press, New York, 1940

—————, *Roman Sources of Christian Art,* Columbia University Press, New York, 1951

WEITZMANN, KURT, *Studies in Classical and Byzantine Manuscript Illumination,* University of Chicago Press, 1971

2. THE ART OF THE MIGRATIONS

CARTER, DAGNY, *The Symbol of the Beast: The Animal-style Art of Eurasia,* Ronald Press, New York, 1957

HUBERT, JEAN, PORCHER, J., and VOLBACH, W. F., *Europe of the Invasions* (tr. S. Gilbert and J. Emmons), Braziller, New York, 1969

JETTMAR, KARL, *Art of the Steppes: The Eurasian Animal Style,* Methuen, London, 1967

KNOBLOCH, EDGAR, *Beyond the Oxus: Archaeology, Art and Architecture of Central Asia,* Benn, London, 1972

ROSS, MARVIN C., *Arts of the Migration Period in the Walters Art Gallery,* Walters Art Gallery, Baltimore, 1961

ROSTOVTSEV, MIKHAIL I., *The Animal Style in South Russia and China,* Princeton University Press, 1929

—————, *Iranians and Greeks in South Russia* (repr.), Russell & Russell, New York, 1969

3. HIBERNO-SAXON ART

GENERAL

DE PAOR, MÁIRE and L., *Early Christian Ireland,* 3d ed., Praeger, New York, 1964

FINLAY, IAN, *Celtic Art: An Introduction,* Faber & Faber, London, 1973

HENRY, FRANÇOISE, *Irish Art in the Early Christian Period, to 800 A.D.,* Cornell University Press, Ithaca, N.Y., 1965

KENDRICK, THOMAS D., *Anglo-Saxon Art to A.D. 900,* Barnes & Noble, New York, 1972

LUCAS, A. T., *Treasures of Ireland,* Gill & Macmillan, Dublin, 1973

MAHR, ADOLF, ed., *Christian Art in Ancient Ireland,* 2 vols., Stationery Office, Dublin, 1932–41

PORTER, ARTHUR KINGSLEY, *The Crosses and Culture of Ireland,* Yale University Press, New Haven, Conn., 1931

RICKERT, MARGARET, *Painting in Britain: The Middle Ages,* Penguin, Baltimore, 1954

STOLL, ROBERT, *Architecture and Sculpture in Early Britain* (tr. J. M. Brownjohn), Thames & Hudson, London, 1967

MONOGRAPHS

ÅBERG, NILS, *The Occident and the Orient in the Art of the Seventh Century,* I, Wahlström & Widstrand, Stockholm, 1943

HENRY, FRANÇOISE, ed., *The Book of Kells,* Knopf, New York, 1974

JACOBSTHAL, PAUL, *Early Celtic Art,* Clarendon Press, Oxford, 1944

4. ISLAMIC ART

GENERAL

ASLANAPA, OKTAY, *Turkish Art and Architecture,* Praeger, New York, 1971

BLOCHET, EDGAR, *Muselman Painting, XII–XVIIth Century* (tr. C. M. Binyon), Methuen, London, 1929

CRESWELL, K. A. C., *Early Muslim Architecture,* 2 vols., Clarendon Press, Oxford, 1932–40

——————, *A Short Account of Early Muslim Architecture,* Penguin, Baltimore, 1960

DIMAND, MAURICE S., *A Handbook of Muhammadan Art,* 3d ed., Metropolitan Museum of Art, New York, 1958

ETTINGHAUSEN, RICHARD, *Arab Painting,* Skira, New York, 1962

GRABAR, OLEG, *The Formation of Islamic Art,* Yale University Press, New Haven, Conn., 1973

GRUBE, ERNST J., *The World of Islam,* McGraw-Hill, New York, 1967

HILL, DEREK, *Islamic Architecture and Its Decoration: A.D. 800–1500,* University of Chicago Press, 1964

HOAG, JOHN D., *Western Islamic Architecture,* Braziller, New York, 1963

İPŞİROĞLU, M. Ş., *Painting and Culture of the Mongols* (tr. E. D. Phillips), Abrams, New York, 1966

KÜHNEL, ERNST, *Islamic Art and Architecture* (tr. K. Watson), Bell, London, 1966

POPE, ARTHUR UPHAM, and ACKERMAN, P., eds., *A Survey of Persian Art from Prehistoric Times to the Present,* 7 vols., Oxford University Press, New York, 1938–39

RICE, DAVID TALBOT, *Islamic Painting: A Survey,* Edinburgh University Press, 1971

DU RY VAN BEEST HOLLE, CAREL J., *Art of Islam* (tr. A. Brown), Abrams, New York, 1970

MONOGRAPHS

BINYON, LAWRENCE, WILKINSON, J. V. S., and GRAY, B., *Persian Miniature Painting,* Oxford University Press, New York, 1933

CHAGHTAI, M. A., *Painting During the Sultanate Period (C.E. 712–1571),* Kitab Khama-i-Nauras, Lahore, 1963

CRESWELL, K. A. C., *The Muslim Architecture of Egypt,* 2 vols., Clarendon Press, Oxford, 1952–59

DAMI, AHMAD HASAN, *Muslim Architecture in Bengal,* Asiatic Society of Pakistan, Dacca, 1961

GARLAKE, PETER S., *The Early Islamic Architecture of the East African Coast,* Oxford University Press, London, 1966

GOODWIN, GODFREY, *A History of Ottoman Architecture,* Johns Hopkins Press, Baltimore, 1971

POPE, ARTHUR UPHAM, *Masterpieces of Persian Art,* Dryden Press, New York, 1945

UNSAL, BEHCET, *Turkish Islamic Architecture in Seljuk and Ottoman Times, 1071–1923,* Tiranti, London, 1970

WILBER, DONALD H., *Architecture of Islamic Iran: The Il Khānid Period,* Princeton University Press, 1955

5/6. CAROLINGIAN AND OTTONIAN ART

BACKES, MAGNUS, and DÖLLING, R., *Art of the Dark Ages* (tr. F. Garvie), Abrams, New York, 1971

BECKWITH, JOHN, *Early Medieval Art,* Praeger, New York, 1964

CONANT, KENNETH J., *Carolingian and Romanesque Architecture, 800–1200,* new ed., Penguin, Norwich, England, 1974

DODWELL, C. R., *Painting in Europe, 800 to 1200,* Penguin, Baltimore, 1971

GRABAR, ANDRÉ, and NORDENFALK, C., *Early Medieval Painting,* Skira, New York, 1957

HENDERSON, GEORGE, *Early Medieval,* Penguin, Baltimore, 1972

HENRY, FRANÇOISE, *Irish Art During the Viking Invasions, 800–1200 A.D.,* Cornell University Press, Ithaca, N.Y., 1967

HINKS, ROGER P., *Carolingian Art,* Sidgwick & Jackson, London, 1935

HUBERT, JEAN, PORCHER, J., and VOLBACH, W. F., *The Carolingian Renaissance,* Braziller, New York, 1970

LASKO, PETER, *Ars Sacra, 800–1200,* Penguin, Baltimore, 1972

7. ROMANESQUE ART

GENERAL

ANTHONY, EDGAR W., *Romanesque Frescoes,* Princeton University Press, 1951

AUBERT, MARCEL, *Romanesque Cathedrals and Abbeys of France* (tr. C. Girdlestone), N. Vane, London, 1966

BOASE, T. S. R., *English Art 1100–1216,* 2d ed., Clarendon Press, Oxford, 1968

BOLOGNA, FERDINANDO, *Early Italian Painting,* Van Nostrand, Princeton, N.J., 1964

CLAPHAM, SIR ALFRED WILLIAM, *English Romanesque Architecture,* 2 vols., Clarendon Press, Oxford, 1964

CONANT, KENNETH J., *Carolingian and Romanesque Architecture, 800–1200,* new ed., Penguin, Norwich, England, 1974

COURTENS, ANDRÉ, *Romanesque Art in Belgium* (tr. J. A. Kennedy), M. Vokaer, Brussels, 1969

CRICHTON, GEORGE H., *Romanesque Sculpture in Italy,* Routledge & Kegan Paul, London, 1954

DECKER, HEINRICH, *Romanesque Art in Italy* (tr. J. Cleugh), Abrams, New York, 1959

FOCILLON, HENRI, *The Art of the West in the Middle Ages* (tr. D. King, ed. J. Bony), I, Phaidon, New York, 1963

GARDNER, ARTHUR, *Medieval Sculpture in France,* Macmillan, New York, 1931 (repr. 1969)

GRABAR, ANDRÉ, and NORDENFALK, C., *Romanesque Painting from the Eleventh to the Thirteenth Century* (tr. S. Gilbert), Skira, New York, 1958

HENRY, FRANÇOISE, *Irish Art in the Romanesque Period, 1020–1170 A.D.,* Cornell University Press, Ithaca, N.Y., 1970

KÜNSTLER, GUSTAV, comp., *Romanesque Art in Europe,* New York Graphic Society, Greenwich, Conn., 1968

MICHEL, PAUL H., *Romanesque Wall Paintings in France,* Éditions du Chêne, Paris, 1949

OURSEL, RAYMOND, *Living Architecture: Romanesque* (tr. K. M. Leake), Grosset & Dunlap, New York, 1967

DE PALOL SALELLAS, PEDRO, and HIRMER, M., *Early Medieval Art in Spain,* Abrams, New York, 1967

PORTER, ARTHUR KINGSLEY, *Lombard Architecture,* 4 vols., Yale University Press, New Haven, Conn., 1915–17

——————, *Romanesque Sculpture of the Pilgrimage Roads,* 10 vols., Marshall Jones, Boston, 1923

RICE, DAVID TALBOT, *English Art 871–1100,* Clarendon Press, Oxford, 1952

SOUCHAL, FRANÇOIS, *Art of the Early Middle Ages* (tr. R. Millen), Abrams, New York, 1968

STODDARD, WHITNEY S., *Art and Architecture in Medieval France,* Harper & Row, New York, 1972

STONE, LAWRENCE, *Sculpture in Britain in the Middle Ages,* Penguin, Baltimore, 1955

SWARZENSKI, HANNS, *Monuments of Romanesque Art: The Church Treasuries in North-Western Europe,* 2d ed., University of Chicago Press, 1967

TIMMERS, J. J. M., *A Handbook of Romanesque Art* (tr. M. Powell), Macmillan, New York, 1969

WEBB, GEOFFREY, *Architecture in Britain: The Middle Ages,* 2d ed., Penguin, Baltimore, 1965

ZARNECKI, GEORGE, *Romanesque Art,* Universe, New York, 1971

MONOGRAPHS

BLINDHEIM, MARTIN, *Norwegian Romanesque Decorative Sculpture, 1090–1210,* Tiranti, London, 1965
BORG, ALAN, *Architectural Sculpture in Romanesque Provence,* Clarendon Press, Oxford, 1972
COLLON-GEVAERT, SUZANNE, et al., *A Treasury of Romanesque Art: Metalwork, Illuminations and Sculpture from the Valley of the Meuse* (tr. S. Waterston), Phaidon, New York, 1972
CROSBY, SUMNER McKNIGHT, *The Apostle Relief at Saint-Denis,* Yale University Press, New Haven, Conn., 1972
EVANS, JOAN, *Cluniac Art of the Romanesque Period,* Cambridge University Press, 1950
——————, *The Romanesque Architecture of the Order of Cluny,* 2d ed., AMS Press, New York, 1972
FORSYTH, GEORGE H., *The Church of St. Martin at Angers,* Princeton University Press, 1953
FORSYTH, ILENE H., *The Throne of Wisdom,* Princeton University Press, 1972
GARRISON, EDWARD B., *Italian Romanesque Panel Painting: An Illustrated Index,* Olschki, Florence, 1949
GRIVOT, DENIS, and ZARNECKI, G., *Gislebertus: Sculpture of Autun,* Orion, New York, 1961
HELL, VERA and HELLMUT, *The Great Pilgrimage of the Middle Ages* (tr. A. Jaffe), Barrie & Rockliff, London, 1966
OAKESHOTT, WALTER, *Sigena: Romanesque Paintings in Spain and the Winchester Bible Artists,* New York Graphic Society, Greenwich, Conn., 1972
SAXL, FRITZ, *English Sculptures of the Twelfth Century* (ed. H. Swarzenski), Faber & Faber, London, 1954
STODDARD, WHITNEY S., *The Façade of Saint-Gilles-du-Gard,* Wesleyan University Press, Middletown, Conn., 1973
WHITEHILL, WALTER MUIR, *Spanish Romanesque Architecture of the Eleventh Century,* Oxford University Press, London, 1968
WORMALD, FRANCIS, *The Winchester Psalter,* Harvey Miller and Medcalf, London, 1973

8. MIDDLE AND LATER BYZANTINE ART (SEE ALSO NO. 1, *SUPRA)*

GENERAL

BEZA, MARCU, *Byzantine Art in Roumania,* Batsford, London, 1940
CHATZIDAKIS, MANOLIS, *Byzantine Monuments in Attica and Boeotia,* Athens Editions, Athens, 1956
GRABAR, ANDRÉ, *The Art of the Byzantine Empire: Byzantine Art in the Middle Ages* (tr. B. Forster), Crown, New York, 1966
PAPAIOANNOU, KOSTAS, *Byzantine and Russian Painting* (tr. J. Sondheimer), Heron, London, 1968

MONOGRAPHS

BIHALJI-MERIN, OTO, *Byzantine Frescoes and Icons in Yugoslavia,* Abrams, New York, 1960
DER NERSESSIAN, SIRARPIE, *Armenia and the Byzantine Empire,* Harvard University Press, Cambridge, Mass., 1945
HAMILTON, GEORGE H., *Art and Architecture of Russia,* Penguin, Baltimore, 1954
HODDINOT, R. F., *Early Byzantine Churches in Macedonia and Southern Serbia: A Study of the Origins and the Initial Development of East Christian Art,* Macmillan, London, 1963
LAZAREV, VIKTOR N., *Old Russian Murals and Mosaics from the Eleventh to the Sixteenth Century* (tr. B. Roniger, ed. N. Dunn), Phaidon, London, 1966
Medieval Bulgarian Culture (tr. M. Alexieva et al.), Foreign Languages Press, Sofia, 1964
MILLET, GABRIEL, and RICE, D. T., *Byzantine Painting at Trebizond,* G. Allen & Unwin, London, 1936
ONASCH, KONRAD, *Icons,* A. S. Barnes, New York, 1963
OUSPENSKY, LEONID, and LOSSKY, V., *The Meaning of Icons* (tr. G. E. H. Palmer and E. Kadloubovsky), Boston Book and Art Shop, Boston, 1969
PAPAGEORGIOU, ATHANASIOS, *Icons of Cyprus* (tr. J. Hogarth), Cowles, New York, 1970

RICE, DAVID TALBOT, and RADOJCIC, S., *Yugoslavia: Mediaeval Frescoes,* New York Graphic Society, Greenwich, Conn., 1955
STYLIANOU, ANDREAS and JUDITH, *The Painted Churches in Cyprus,* Research Center, Cyprus, 1964
UNDERWOOD, PAUL A., *The Kariye Djami,* 3 vols., Pantheon, New York, 1966
VOYCE, ARTHUR, *The Art and Architecture of Medieval Russia,* University of Oklahoma Press, Norman, 1967
——————, *The Moscow Kremlin: Its History, Architecture, and Art Treasures,* University of California Press, Berkeley, 1954
WEITZMANN, KURT, et al., *A Treasury of Icons: Sixth to Seventeenth Centuries* (tr. R. E. Wolf), Abrams, New York, 1967

9. GOTHIC ART

SOURCES

Abbot Suger on the Abbey Church of St.-Denis and Its Art Treasures (tr. E. Panofsky), Princeton University Press, 1946
FRISCH, TERESA GRACE, *Gothic Art 1140–c.1450: Sources and Documents,* Prentice-Hall, Englewood Cliffs, N.J., 1971

GENERAL

ARNOLD, HUGH, *Stained Glass of the Middle Ages in England and France,* 2d ed., Macmillan, New York, 1940
AUBERT, MARCEL, *The Art of the High Gothic Era* (tr. P. George), Crown, New York, 1965
BRIEGER, PETER, *English Art 1216–1307,* Clarendon Press, Oxford, 1957
BUNT, CYRIL G. E., *Gothic Painting,* Avalon Press, London, 1947
BUSCH, HARALD, and LOHSE, B., *Gothic Sculpture* (tr. P. George), Macmillan, New York, 1963
CASTELFRANCHI VEGAS, LIANA, *International Gothic Art in Italy* (tr. B. D. Phillips), Edition Leipzig, 1966
COULTON, GEORGE G., *Art and the Reformation,* 2d ed., Cambridge University Press, 1953
DEUCHLER, FLORENS, *Gothic Art* (tr. V. Menkes), Universe, New York, 1973
DUPONT, J., *Gothic Painting,* Skira, New York, 1954
DVOŘÁKOVÁ, VLASTA, et al., *Gothic Mural Painting in Bohemia and Moravia, 1300–1378,* Oxford University Press, New York, 1964
EVANS, JOAN, *Art in Medieval France,* Oxford University Press, New York, 1948
FOCILLON, HENRI, *The Art of the West in the Middle Ages* (tr. D. King, ed. J. Bony), II, Phaidon, New York, 1963
FRANKL, PAUL, *The Gothic,* Princeton University Press, 1959
——————, *Gothic Architecture* (tr. D. Pevsner), Penguin, Baltimore, 1963
GODFREY, FREDERICK M., *Italian Sculpture 1250–1700,* Tiranti, London, 1967
HARTT, FREDERICK, *History of Italian Renaissance Art,* Abrams, New York, 1969
HARVEY, JOHN H., *Gothic England,* Scribner, New York, 1947
——————, *The Gothic World,* Batsford, London, 1950
HENDERSON, GEORGE, *Gothic,* Penguin, Baltimore, 1966
HOFSTÄTTER, HANS H., *Living Architecture: Gothic* (tr. A. N. Wells), Macdonald, London, 1970
MÂLE, ÉMILE, *The Gothic Image: Religious Art in France of the Thirteenth Century* (tr. D. Nussey), Harper, New York, 1958
MARLE, RAIMOND VAN, *The Development of the Italian Schools of Painting,* I–IX, Nijhoff, The Hague, 1923–38
MARTINDALE, ANDREW, *Gothic Art,* Praeger, New York, 1967
MENCL, VÁCLAV, *Czech Architecture of the Luxemburg Period* (tr. L. Kollmannová), Artia, Prague, 1955
PANOFSKY, ERWIN, *Gothic Architecture and Scholasticism,* Archabbey Press, Latrobe, Pa., 1951
POPE-HENNESSY, SIR JOHN, *Italian Gothic Sculpture,* Phaidon, London, 1955
PORCHER, JEAN, *Medieval French Miniatures* (tr. J. Brown), Abrams, New York, 1960
RADOCSAY, DÉNES, *Gothic Panel Painting in Hungary,* Corvina Press, Budapest, 1963
SAUERLÄNDER, WILLIBALD, and HIRMER, M., *Gothic Sculpture in France 1140–1270* (tr. J. Sondheimer), Abrams, New York, 1973

SIMSON, OTTO G. VON, *The Gothic Cathedral,* 2d ed., Princeton University Press, 1974

STALLEY, R. E., *Architecture and Sculpture in Ireland, 1150–1350,* Gill & Macmillan, Dublin, 1971

STEWART, CECIL, *Gothic Architecture,* Longmans, New York, 1961

SWANN, WIM, *The Gothic Cathedral,* Doubleday, Garden City, N.Y., 1969

VAN DE WALLE, A. J. L., *Gothic Art in Belgium* (tr. J. A. Kennedy), M. Vokaer, Brussels, 1971

WHITE, JOHN, *Art and Architecture in Italy, 1250–1400,* Penguin, Baltimore, 1966

WORRINGER, WILHELM, *Form in Gothic,* Tiranti, London, 1957

MONOGRAPHS

ACLAND, JAMES H., *Medieval Structure: The Gothic Vault,* University of Toronto Press, 1972

ARSLAN, EDOARDO, *Gothic Architecture in Venice* (tr. A. Engel), Phaidon, London, 1971

AYRTON, MICHAEL, *Giovanni Pisano, Sculptor,* Weybright & Talley, New York, 1969

BATTISTI, EUGENIO, *Cimabue* (tr. R. and C. Enggass), Pennsylvania State University Press, University Park, 1967

——————, *Giotto* (tr. J. Emmons), World, Cleveland, 1960

BORSOOK, EVE, *The Mural Painters of Tuscany from Cimabue to Andrea del Sarto,* Phaidon, London, 1960

BRANNER, ROBERT, *Burgundian Gothic Architecture,* Zwemmer, London, 1960

——————, *Chartres Cathedral,* Norton, New York, 1969

——————, *St. Louis and the Court Style in Gothic Architecture,* Zwemmer, London, 1965

CRICHTON, GEORGE H. and SYLVIA R., *Nicola Pisano and the Revival of Sculpture in Italy,* Cambridge University Press, 1938

DEWALD, ERNEST, *Pietro Lorenzetti,* Harvard University Press, Cambridge, Mass., 1930

FITCHEN, JOHN, *The Construction of Gothic Cathedrals,* Clarendon Press, Oxford, 1961

JANTZEN, HANS, *High Gothic: The Classic Cathedrals of Chartres, Reims, Amiens* (tr. J. Palmes), Pantheon, New York, 1962

KATZENELLENBOGEN, ADOLF, *The Sculptural Programs of Chartres Cathedral,* Johns Hopkins Press, Baltimore, 1959

KIDSON, PETER, *Sculpture at Chartres,* Tiranti, London, 1958

MEISS, MILLARD, *Painting in Florence and Siena After the Black Death,* Princeton University Press, 1951

Old Testament Miniatures (intro. S. C. Cockerell, pref. J. Plummer), Braziller, New York, 1969

RANDALL, LILIAN M. C., *Images in the Margins of Gothic Manuscripts,* University of California Press, Berkeley, 1966

ROWLEY, GEORGE, *Ambrogio Lorenzetti,* 2 vols., Princeton University Press, 1958

SANDLER, LUCY FREEMAN, *The Peterborough Psalter in Brussels and Other Fenland Manuscripts,* Harvey Miller and Medcalf, London, 1973

STUBBLEBINE, JAMES, ed., *Giotto: The Arena Chapel Frescoes,* Norton, New York, 1969

TINTORI, LEONETTO, and BORSOOK, E., *Giotto: The Peruzzi Chapel,* Abrams, New York, 1965

Index

Page numbers are in roman type. Figure numbers of black-and-white illustrations are in *italic* type.
Colorplates are specifically so designated. Names of artists and architects are in CAPITALS. Titles of works are in *italic*.

GISLEBERTUS, *Last Judgment*, Cathedral of Autun, 316; *369*
Giza, *Great Sphinx*, 62; *62;* pyramids, 61–62; *58, 59, 60;* Temple of Chephren, 62; *61*
Gloucester, Cathedral, 394; *494*
God the Father as Architect, illumination from the *Bible Moralisée*, 386–87; colorpl. 65
Goddess Giving Birth, from Catal Hüyük, 32; *15*
Goddess Lilith, relief, 81; *101*
Golden House, Rome, 186, 187, 189
Good Shepherd, fresco, Catacomb of SS. Pietro e Marcellino, Rome, 249, 278; *318*
Good Shepherd, mosaic, Mausoleum of Galla Placidia, Ravenna, 258, 262; colorpl. 37
Gordianus I, II, III, 204
Gospel Book, from St.-Bertin, 334–35, 409; colorpl. 55
gospel books, 277
Gospel lectionary of Henry II, 307, 334, 409; *387*
Goths, 368
Granada, Alhambra, 282, 288–90, 291, 354; *364, 365*
grave stelai, 151–52
Great Mosque, Córdoba, 282, 283–87, 316; *358, 359;* colorpl. 46
Great Mosque, Damascus, 281, 282; *352;* colorpl. 45
Great Mosque of al-Mutawakkil, Samarra, 282–83; *354, 355*
Great Sphinx, Giza, 62; *62*
Greece, ancient, 100–104
Greece, city-states, 52, 88, 101, 119, 158
Greek art, Archaic period, 107–19; Classical period: Age of Pericles, 126–53; Classical period: Fourth Century, 154–58; Classical period: Severe style, 119–26; Geometric and Orientalizing styles, 104–6; Hellenistic period, 158–69
Gudea, 81; *Head of Gudea,* from Lagash, *100;* seated statue of, from Lagash, 81, 226; *99*
GUNZO, 313, 315

Hadrian, 162, 176, 197–99
Hadrian's Villa, Tivoli, 199, 227–28, 263, 354; *286;* Canopus of Alexandria, *287*
HAGESANDROS, POLYDOROS, and ATHENODOROS, *Laocoön and His Two Sons,* 102; *234;* Head of Odysseus from *Odysseus Blinding Polyphemos,* 102; *235*
Hagia Sophia, Constantinople, 161, 244, 266–68, 288, 336, 355, 356, 371; *339, 340, 341;* Deësis, mosaic, 363; *441;* section and plan, 266; *338; Virgin and Child Enthroned,* mosaic, 353; *426*
Hagia Sophia, Kiev, 358; *Theotokos* and *Communion of the Apostles,* mosaics, *433*
Hagios Demetrios, Salonika, 323
Hagios Georgios, Salonika, 256, 282; Architectural Illusion with Saints Cosmos and Damian, mosaic, 256, 282; colorpl. 35
Haida Bear Mask, 47, 233; colorpl. 3
Halikarnassos, Mausoleum, 155; *210; Battle of Greeks and Amazons,* frieze, *212*
Hall of Bulls, cave painting, Lascaux, 30; *6*
Hallstatt culture, 37
Haman and Mordecai, wall painting, synagogue, Dura-Europos, 249–50; *319*
Hammurabi, 82; stele with the Code of Hammurabi, *102*
Harding, Stephen, abbot, 335
Harp from the Tomb of Queen Puabi, Ur, 78; *94;* colorpl. 11
Harun ar-Rashid, 282
Hatshepsut, Temple of, Deir el Bahari, 67, 68, 111; *74, 75*
Head of a Girl, from Chios, 164; *230*
Head of an Akkadian Ruler, from Nineveh, 80; *97*

Head of Pompey, Roman, 178; *246*
Helladic art, 90
Hellenistic period, *see* Greek art
Henry I, emperor, 302
Henry II, emperor, 307
Hera, from Samos, 89, 109–10, 373; *149*
Herakles and the Infant Telephos, fresco from Herculaneum, 103, 157, 165–68; colorpl. 21
Herculaneum, 157, 180–81; *Architectural View,* wall painting, 192, 256; colorpl. 31; *Herakles and the Infant Telephos,* 103, 157, 165–68; colorpl. 21
Herd of Fleeing Gazelles, relief, Ashurbanipal's Palace, Nineveh, 87; *111*
Hermes with the Infant Dionysos (PRAXITELES), from Olympia, 155–56; *215*
Herodotus, 170
Hesira, from Saqqara, wood relief, 60; *57*
Hiberno-Saxon art, 277–80, 307, 316, 329; *349, 350;* colorpl. 42, 43
Hierakonpolis, 55; tomb painting, *45*
Hildesheim, Cathedral, Bernward's doors, 37, 305, 321; *382, 383;* Bernward's Column, 305; *384;* St. Michael's, 303–5; *380, 381;* plan, *379*
Hittite Lion Gate, Boğazköy, Turkey, 82; *103*
Hittites, 82
Holy Roman Empire, 293, 302, 328
Holy Sepulcher, Jerusalem, 254
Homer, 90, 91; *Iliad, Odyssey,* 105, 118
Hopewell culture, North American Indian, 47; Hopewell pipe in form of hawk, *42*
Horus, Temple of, Edfu, 69, 73; *76*
Hosios Loukas, Monastery, Phocis, 356; Katholikon and Theotokos churches, *428, 429*
house at Delos, mural decoration, 169; *236*
Huns, 260, 368
Hunting and Fishing, Etruscan tomb painting, Tarquinia, 175; colorpl. 25
Hunting Scene, El Cerro Felío, copy of cave painting, 31; *10*
Hyksos, 68

Ibn Tulun, Mosque of, Cairo, 283, 287, 289, 312; *356, 357*
Iconoclasts, 336
Iconodules, 336
icons, 256, 269, 336, 366–67, 405
Ife civilization, Nigeria, 41; *Head of Queen Olokun,* 41; *30*
IKTINOS, Temple of Apollo, Bassai: 151; *204;* colorpl. 17; *Amazonomachy,* frieze, *205;* Parthenon, 105, 145; *187, 188*
Île-de-France, 368, 371
Iliad, 105, 118; *see also* Homer
Imago Hominis (Image of Man), illumination from *Echternach Gospels,* 278, 318; *350*
IMHOTEP, 69, 110; Funerary Complex of King Zoser, Saqqara, 58–59, 62; *50–54*
Imperial Forums, Rome, plan, 186; *261*
Impressionists, 193
Inca Empire, Incas, 231, 236–37
Indian art, *see* North American Indian art
Initial L and the Nativity, Gospel Book, 334–36, 409; colorpl. 55
Initial R with Saint George and the Dragon, Moralia in Job, 335; colorpl. 57
Insula (Roman apartment house), reconstruction, Ostia, 187; *263*
insulae, Rome, Ostia, 246
Interior of the Pantheon, GIOVANNI PAOLO PANNINI, 161, 198–99; *285*
Ionians, 104
Ionic capital, Greek, 37, 110–11, 178; *153*
Ionic order, in architecture, 93, 110–11, 151; *152*
Iron Age art, *see* Bronze and Iron Ages, art
Ishtar Gate, Babylon, 87; *112*

Isin-Larsa period, 81
Islamic art, 88, 244, 280–92; *351–67;* colorpl. 45, 46, 47
Istanbul, Mosque of Ahmed I, 288; *363; see* Constantinople
Italy, Romanesque architecture and sculpture, 322–27
Ivan IV the Terrible, czar, 365

Jacques Coeur, Palais, Bourges, 388; *479*
JEAN D'ORBAIS, 380
Jericho, 32; fortifications, *12;* Plastered Skull, *13*
Jerusalem, 190, 281; Dome of the Rock, 281, 412; colorpl. 44; Holy Sepulcher, 254; kingdom of, 309
Joachim Takes Refuge in the Wilderness (GIOTTO), Arena Chapel, Padua, 363, 407–8; colorpl. 70
Joseph and His Brethren, from the *Vienna Book of Genesis,* 270; colorpl. 41
Joshua Leading the Israelites Toward the Jordan River, illumination from *Joshua Roll,* 355; *427*
Joshua Roll, manuscript, 355; *427*
Julian the Apostate, emperor, 226
Julius II, pope, 126
Julius Caesar, 181, 183
JUNAID, *Bihzad in the Garden,* illumination, 292; colorpl. 47
Junius Bassus, Sarcophagus of, 259, 262; *330*
Justinian, 266, 268, 271, 336
Justinian, Age of, 260–71
Jutes, 272

ka, 57
Kaaper (Sheik el Beled), from Saqqara, 64; *66*
KALLIKRATES, Temple of Athena Nike, Athens, 149, 178; *198; see also* IKTINOS
KALLIMACHOS, 151
Kariye Djami, *see* Church of Christ in Chora, Istanbul
Karnak, temples, 68, 69, 161; Temple of Aten: 71–72, *83;* Hypostyle Hall of the Temple, 70; *79*
Katholikon, Hosios Loukas, Phocis, 356; *428, 429*
Khorsabad, Palace of Sargon II, 83–84; Citadel, *104;* Gate of the Citadel, *106;* plan of the Citadel, *105*
Khwaju Kirmani, 292
Kiev, Hagia Sophia, 358; *Theotokos* and *Communion of the Apostles,* mosaics, *433*
King David (BENEDETTO ANTELAMI), Fidenza Cathedral, 327; *411*
KLEITIAS and ERGOTIMOS, *François Vase,* 117; *164*
KLEOPHRADES PAINTER, *Dionysos Between Maenads,* 119; *167; Rapt Maenad,* colorpl. 15
Klosterneuburg, Abbey, *Sacrifice of Isaac,* plaque, 391; *485*
Knights of Saint John, 155
Knossos, palace, 92–96; *122, 123; Bird in a Landscape,* fresco, palace, 95; *126; Bull Dance,* fresco, palace, 94; *125;* Queen's Megaron, palace, 94; *124*
Koran, 280; illumination, 291; *366*
kore, 107; at Erechtheion, Athens, 151; *201;* at Treasury of the Siphnians, Delphi, 114; *158; Hera from Samos,* 109–10; *149; La Delicata,* 110, 114, 373; colorpl. 13; *Peplos Kore,* 109; *150*
kouros, 107, 119–20, 122; *Kouros of Sounion,* 107; *145; Anavyssos Kouros,* 107, 120; *146*
Kouros of Sounion, 107; *145*
Kremlin, Moscow, 365
KRITIOS, 119
Kritios Boy, from Acropolis, Athens, 119–20, 122; *171*
Kufic script, 291; *366*

Photographic Credits

The author and publisher wish to thank the libraries, museums, and private collectors for permitting the reproduction of works of art in their collections and for supplying the necessary photographs. Photographs from other sources are gratefully acknowledged below.

A.C.L., Brussels, 403; Alinari, Florence, 67, 174, 176, 181, 232, 239, 241, 243, 248, 251, 252, 253, 256, 263, 265, 268, 269, 272, 277, 280, 281, 282, 286, 289, 292, 296, 297, 298, 303, 320, 321, 323, 327, 332, 333, 335, 336, 342, 404, 406, 408, 409, 410, 415, 417, 423, 434, 436, 437, 438, 497, 498, 500, 501, 502, 504, 505, 506, 507, 508, 509, 510, 511, 512, 513, 514, 515, 516, 517, 521, 523, 524, 526; colorplates 37, 70, 71; Alinari, courtesy Deutsches Archäologisches Institut, 274; American School of Classical Studies, Athens, 185; Anker, Peter, Oslo, 348; Arnold, Dieter, *Der Tempel des Koenigs Mentuhopet von Deir el Bahari*, Band I, Architektur und Deuting, Mainz am Rhein, Verlag Philipp von Zabern, 1974, 71; The Athlone Press, University of London, 19, 20; Audinet, Jack, Boulogne, colorplate 55; Avery Library, Columbia University, New York, 276; Babey, Maurice, Basel, 70, 87; Biblioteca Apostolica Vaticana, Rome, 377; Bibliothèque Nationale, Paris, colorplate 50; Böhm, Erwin, Mainz, 355, 407, 413, colorplate 44; British Library, London, colorplates 42, 47; Bulloz, Paris, 144, 396; Bundesdenkmalamt, Vienna, 485; Caisse Nationale des Monuments Historiques, Paris, 4, 6, 7, 117, 388, 389, 393, 394, 397, 398, 399, 401, 402, 446, 450, 454, 455, 462, 465, 466, 477, 487; Canali, Ludovico, Rome, colorplates 24, 36; Chambi, Victor, Cuzco, Peru, 316; Cine Grassi, Siena, 518; Clements, Geoffrey, New York, from a proof supplied by Kurt Weitzmann, Princeton, colorplate 39; Compania Mexicana Aerofoto, Mexico City, 308; Conant, Kenneth J., Wellesley, 392; Department of the Environment, Edinburgh (British Crown Copyright), 21; Deutsche

Fotothek, Dresden, 443; Deutscher Kunstverlag, Munich, 368, 488 (Walter Hege); Deutsches Archäologisches Institut, Athens, 136, 156, 172; Deutsches Archäologisches Institut, Cairo, 69; Deutsches Archäologisches Institut, Rome, 213, 235, 242, 257, 262, 270, 271, 287, 293, 294, 301; Dieuzaide, Jean, Toulouse (YAN), 8, 9; Dumbarton Oaks Center for Byzantine Studies, Washington, D.C., 426; École Française d'Athènes, 236; Éditions Cercle d'Art, Paris, 433; Éditions d'Art Skira, Geneva, colorplate 45; Sansoni Editore, Florence, 10; Enciclopedica Romana, Bucharest, Courtesy Romanian Library, New York, 26; Rev. Fabbrica di S. Pietro, Rome, 330; Felton, Herbert, London, 495; Fotocielo, Rome, 405; Fototeca Unione, Rome, 234, 238, 247, 249, 250, 258, 259, 264, 266, 267, 275, 279, 283, 291, 299, 300, 306, 374, 496; Frantz, Alison, Athens, 132, 142, 187, 198, 200, 206, 428, 429; Frick Collection, New York, 519; Fürböck, Graz, 25; Gabinetto Fotografico Nazionale, Rome, 240, 425; GAI, Baghdad, 88; Gardner, *Art Through the Ages*, Fifth Edition, Revised by Horst de la Croix and Richard G. Tanney, copyright © 1970 by Harcourt Brace Jovanovich, 371; Giraudon, Paris, 351, 395, 457, colorplates 63, 64; The Green Studio, Ltd., Dublin, 349, colorplate 43; Held, André, Ecublens, colorplates 6, 21, 60; Hell, Dr. Hellmut, Reutlingen, 326; Hinz, Hans, Basel, 35, 36; Hirmer Fotoarchiv, Munich, 47, 53, 55, 57, 58, 61, 62, 63, 64, 68, 74, 75, 76, 78, 81, 83, 85, 86, 90, 91, 96, 98, 108, 120, 121, 123, 124, 125, 128, 129, 137, 139, 140, 143, 146, 147, 148, 149, 150, 154, 158, 159, 164, 166, 167, 168, 169, 170, 171, 173, 177, 178, 179, 182, 183, 189, 190, 191, 192, 194, 196, 197, 199, 201, 202, 203, 211, 212, 215, 222, 225, 227, 228, 231, 302, 328, 337, 339, 341, 441, 442, 474, colorplates 4, 13, 17, 18, 19, 53, 54; Holton, George, New York, 40; Hornung, Professor Erik, Basel, colorplate 7; Hurlimann, Martin, Zurich, 444; Istituto Centrale del Restauro, Rome, 520, 522; Istituto di Etruscologia e Antichità Italiche, Università di Roma, 237; Kersting, A.F., London, 356, 362, 418, 459; Kessel, Dimitri, Paris, 127, colorplate 12; Studio Koppermann, Gauting, Germany, 161, 162, 175; Mannino, Giovanni, Rome, 11; Bildarchiv Foto Marburg, Marburg/Lahn, Germany, 66, 72, 208, 224, 245, 372, 381, 412, 421, 422, 448, 449, 460, 463,

464, 468, 472, 476, 479, 480, 482, 483, 484, 489; Mariani, Enrico, Como, 363; Marzari, P., Milan, 273; MAS, Barcelona, 359, 364, 365, 400, 424, 490; Mellaart, James, London, 14, 15, 16, 17, 18; Metropolitan Museum of Art, New York, Egyptian Expedition, 82; Meyer, Erwin, Vienna, colorplate 29; Mills, Charles, Philadelphia, colorplate 11; Ministry of Public Building and Works, London, 22, 23; Museum of Fine Arts, Boston, Harvard-Boston Expedition, 73; Mylonas, Professor G. E., Athens, 138; National Monuments Record, London, 492, 493, 494; Ohio Historical Society, Columbus, 42; Oriental Institute, University of Chicago, 46, 93, 103, 104, 106, 113, 114; Peabody Museum, Harvard University, Cambridge, Mass., 311; Percheron, René, Puteaux, France, 361; Pericot-Garcia, Galloway and Lommel, *Prehistoric and Primitive Art*, © 1967 by Sansoni Editore, Florence, 5; Pontificia Commissione di Architettura Sacra, Vatican City, 317, 318; Powell, Josephine, Rome, 184, 430, 431, 432, 439, colorplate 16; Proskouriakoff, Tatiana, *An Album of Maya Architecture*, 1946, The Carnegie Institution of Washington, D.C., 310; Rémy, Dijon, colorplate 57; Rheinisches Bildarchiv, Cologne, 378, 385, 486; Roos, George, New York, colorplate 34; Foto Rosso, Turin, 107; Roubier, Jean, Paris, 391, 452, 467, 475; Scala Fine Arts Publishers, Inc., 56, colorplates 31, 38, 52; Schmidt-Glassner, Helga, Stuttgart, 260; Service de Documentation Photographique de la Réunion des Musées Nationaux, Paris, 99; Smith, Edwin, Essex, England, 110; Smith, G. E. Kidder, New York, 79, 278, 290, 340, 360; Soprintendenza alle Antichità, Rome, 229; Sovfoto, New York, colorplate 61; Staatsbibliothek, Preussische Kulturbesitz, Berlin, colorplate 32; Steinkopf, Walter, Berlin, 343; Stierlin, Henri, Geneva, 50, 312 Stoedtner, Dr. Franz, Düsseldorf, 157; T.A.P., Athens, 145; Tasic, D., Belgrade, 440; Taylor & Dull, Inc., New York, 37; Uht, Charles, New York, 33; Photo Vaghi, Parma, 411; Vertut, Jean, Issy-les-Moulineaux, France, colorplate 2, 10; von Matt, Leonard, Buochs, Switzerland, 126, 130; Ward, Clarence, Oberlin, 470, 473; Webb, John, London, colorplate 68; Wehmeyer, Hermann, Hildesheim, 380, 382, 383, 384; Yugoslav State Tourist Office, New York, 305.